AF449138

Trends in
THEORETICAL
COMPUTER SCIENCE

PRINCIPLES OF COMPUTER SCIENCE SERIES

ISSN 0888-2096

Series Editors

Alfred V. Aho, *Bell Telephone Laboratories, Murray Hill, New Jersey*
Jeffrey D. Ullman, *Stanford University, Stanford, California*

1. *Algorithms for Graphics and Image Processing**
   Theo Pavlidis
2. *Algorithmic Studies in Mass Storage Systems**
   C. K. Wong
3. *Theory of Relational Databases**
   Jeffrey D. Ullman
4. *Computational Aspects of VLSI**
   Jeffrey D. Ullman
5. *Advanced C: Food for the Educated Palate**
   Narain Gehani
6. *C: An Advanced Introduction**
   Narain Gehani
7. *C for Personal Computers: IBM PC, AT&T PC 6300, and compatibles**
   Narain Gehani
8. *Principles of Computer Design**
   Leonard R. Marino
9. *The Theory of Database Concurrency Control**
   Christos Papadimitriou
10. *Computer Organization**
    Michael Andrews
11. *Elements of Artificial Intelligence Using LISP*
    Steven Tanimoto
12. *Trends in Theoretical Computer Science*
    Egon Börger, Editor

*These previously-published books are in the *Principles of Computer Science Series* but they are not numbered within the volume itself. All future volumes in the *Principles of Computer Science Series* will be numbered.

OTHER BOOKS OF INTEREST

Jewels of Formal Language Theory
Arto Salomaa

Principles of Database Systems
Jeffrey D. Ullman

Fuzzy Sets, Natural Language Computations, and Risk Analysis
Kurt J. Schumucker

LISP: An Interactive Approach
Stuart C. Shapiro

Trends in THEORETICAL COMPUTER SCIENCE

Editor: EGON BÖRGER

UNIVERSITY OF PISA
PISA, ITALY

COMPUTER SCIENCE PRESS

Computer Science Press
1803 Research Boulevard
Rockville, Maryland 20850

1 2 3 4 5 6   Printing   Year   93 92 91 90 89 88

Library of Congress Cataloging-in-Publication Data

Trends in theoretical computer science.

    Bibliography: p.
    Includes index.
    1. Electric data processing. 2. Computers.
I. Börger, E. (Egon), 1946—
QA76.C88   1988   004   87-21219
ISBN 0-88175-084-0

Contents

INTRODUCTION

This book grew out from a course on computation theory which took place at the International Centre for Mechanical Science (CISM) in Udine, Italy, from September 24 to October 5, 1984. The course gave a systematical and comprehensive overview of main themes in current research in theoretical computer science. It was addressed to graduate students and research assistants. The course was subdivided into the following 10 subcourses of 6–10 lectures each:

K. Ambos-Spies: Polynomial time degrees of NP-sets

K. Apt: Verification of concurrent and distributed programs

E. Börger: Complexity relations between machine and logical decision problems

P. Flajolet: Mathematical analysis of important sorting and searching techniques

Y. Gurevich: Logic and the challenge of computer science

M. Karpinski: Probabilistic algorithms and probabilistic computational complexity

P. Martin-Loef: Unifying intuitionistic type theory and Scott's theory of domains

E. Shamir: Distributed algorithms, coordination, and routing procedures

E. Specker: Application of logic and combinatorics to complexity problems

M. Y. Vardi: Fundamentals of dependency theory

The contributions to this book considerably extend the material presented in those courses. The material is arranged into four main areas: logic and complexity, database theory, analysis of algorithms, concurrency and distributed algorithms. The book's purpose is to serve as high-level introduction to the state-of-the-art of these areas of research in theoretical computer science.

Egon Börger
Pisa, January 1987

Part I
Logic and Complexity

Chapter 1

Logic and the Challenge of Computer Science*

YURI GUREVICH[†]

Abstract—Nowadays computer science is surpassing mathematics as the primary field of logic applications, but logic is not tuned properly to the new role. In particular, classical logic is preoccupied mostly with infinite static structures whereas many objects of interest in computer science are dynamic objects with bounded resources. This chapter consists of two independent parts. The first part is devoted to finite model theory; it is mostly a survey of logics tailored for computational complexity. The second part is devoted to dynamic structures with bounded resources. In particular, we use dynamic structures with bounded resources to model Pascal.

INTRODUCTION

These days computer science is characterized by an explosive growth in activities intimately related to logic. Consider for example formal languages. For years formal languages were in the private domain of logicians. But what formal language is most popular today? Is it a Hilbert type predicate calculus or the Genzen sequent calculus? Neither. The most popular formal languages of today are programming languages. Another kind of popular formal languages are database query languages. Some other formal languages emerge in artificial intelligence like languages for knowledge representation. Old discussions on names, denotations, types, etc. are suddenly revitalized to unprecedented magnitude.

---

*Supported in part by NSF grants MCS 83-01022 and DCR 8503275.

†Electrical Engineering and Computer Science Department, The University of Michigan, Ann Arbor, MI 48109-2122.

The work on axiomatic semantics, logic programming and verification is related to classical proof theory; the work on computational complexity is related to the classical theory of algorithms. Even propositional logic is not left untouched by developments in computer science; for almost any number k between 3 and 20, there is a commercial logic circuit simulator based on k-valued logic (41).

This is altogether good news for logicians. Logic grows more relevant to computer science than any other part of mathematics. But the new applications call, we believe, for new developments in logic proper. First-order predicate calculus and its usual generalizations are not sufficient to support the new applications. On the other hand, the new developments will most probably build on existing achievements of logic. In this connection it is worth trying to understand what made classical mathematical logic so successful.

Even though logic is an ancient subject, the origins of modern mathematical logic are closely related to the discovery of paradoxes and the subsequent crisis in the foundations of mathematics (47). In 1930 came the triumph of Gödel's completeness theorem. The syntax of first-order predicate calculus and its semantics were proven to match perfectly. In addition first-order logic was restrictive enough to avoid paradoxes and expressive enough to provide a basis for Zermelo-Fraenkel set theory and resolve this way, to a large extent, the foundational crisis. This perfect match of syntax and semantics together with a reasonable expressive power made first-order logic an invaluable tool and a source of innumerable generalizations.

Extremely important features of first-order logic are a formal language and a clear notion of models. The models are so-called first-order structures or, simply, structures. (Some people object to the term "first-order structure" on the ground that logic is first-order rather than structures. This is a good point. But some structures are not first-order, topological spaces for example; and we all know exactly what first-order structures are.) This familiar pattern—a formal language with well-defined models—persists through familiar generalizations of first-order logic.

Let us mention another interesting feature of first-order logic. Even though a consistent first-order theory has usually a multitude of models, the theory itself does not refer directly to different models; it "speaks" about "the" model of discourse.

Classical logic facilitated numerous and impressive achievements. Let us mention only the Church-Turing thesis and the Gödel-Cohen resolution of the continuum hypothesis. It seems that we (the logicians) were somewhat hypnotized by the success of classical systems. We used first-order logic where it fits well and where it fits not so well. We went on working on computability without paying adequate attention to feasibility. One seemingly obvious but nevertheless important lesson is that different applications may require formalizations of different kinds. It is necessary to "listen" to the subject in order to come up with the right formalization. (We philosophized on this topic in [30].)

An important feature of many computer science objects is finiteness. Relational databases constitute an especially important example. Finiteness does not seem to be such a great novelty in classical logic. Nevertheless it poses a nontrivial challenge. Being so closely related to foundations of mathematics, classical logic is preoccupied with infinity. Many famous theorems collapse when only finite structures are allowed; among them are Gödel's Completeness Theorem, Craig's Interpolation Theorem, Beth's Definability Theorem and the Substructure Preservation Theorem (29).

Variants of first-order logic serve as standard relational query languages (15, 67), but the expressive power of first-order logic is not sufficient for many purposes (2). On the other hand, second-order logic is overly expressive. It expresses queries that are too hard to compute. Even existential monadic second-order formulas can express NP complete queries. Of course, the notion of what is hard may change from one application to another. One idea is to fix a reasonable complexity class, like polynomial time, and to devise an intermediate logic that "captures" this complexity class i.e. expresses exactly the queries of that complexity. The idea happens to be realizable to an extent. The pioneering papers include those of Aho and Ullman (2), Chandra and Harel (12b), Fagin (20), Immerman (44), and Vardi (68). In particular, Immerman and Vardi proved that, in the presence of linear order, the least-fixed-point extension of first-order logic captures polynomial time. The program of designing logics to capture complexity classes was clearly spelled out in (45) where Immerman captured log-space and a number of other natural complexity classes. We have written on finite model theory and logic tailored for complexity in different places; see in particular (29).

Part 1 (Sections 1–9) of this chapter is devoted to finite model theory; it is mostly a subjective survey of logics tailored for computational complexity. Section 1 contains provisos and definitions that are used throughout Part 1. In particular, the notions of global relations and global functions are introduced; these notions provide convenient semantics for complexity tailored logics. In Sections 2, 3, 4 and 6 we consider different extensions of first-order logic by additional constructs; in the presence of linear order the extended logics capture natural complexity classes. In Section 5 we consider two logics with an emphasis on functions rather than predicates; a linear order is built in, and the logics capture log-space and polynomial time respectively. Section 7 is devoted to those properties of structures which do not depend on presentation. In Section 8, some evidence is given that certain familiar complexity classes cannot be captured by any logic. Circuit definability and topology on finite sets are briefly discussed in Section 9.

REMARK   Several relevant issues are left out in this survey. In particular, we do not discuss derivability in first-order predicate calculus. The questions of expressibility and derivability are quite different. For example, no first-order formula φ expresses on finite graphs that (x, y) belongs to the transitive closure of the edge relation E. This is well known (21, 23, 29) and remains true even if φ is allowed to use additional predicate symbols: just consider the case when all additional relations are trivial. On the other hand, the first-order formula

$$[\forall uv(Euv \rightarrow Tuv) \ \& \ \forall uvw(Euv \ \& \ Tvw \rightarrow Tuw)] \rightarrow T(x, y)$$

is derivable from the diagram of an arbitrary finite graph if and only if (x, y) belongs to the transitive closure of the edge relation E.

Another important feature of many computer science structures, which is harder to swallow, is their dynamic character. Mathematical structures (graphs, groups, topological spaces, etc.) do not change in time whereas computer science objects (databases, machines) often do. Considering time as a new dimension, a mathematician turns a dynamic situation into a static one. Complexity considerations may make such a transformation inadvisable in computer science (see Section 10 in this connection).

In Part 2 of this chapter we generalize the static structures of mathematical logic to dynamic structures. We are especially interested in dynamic structures with bounded resources. In Section 10, among other things, we discuss the adaptation of Turing's thesis to the case of machines with bounded resources. In Section 11, on the example of Pascal, we demonstrate an approach to semantics based on dynamic structures.

There are still mathematicians that consider computer science a lower subject. There are former logicians that work now in computer science or computer applications and consider logic not very relevant to their new occupation. We happen to think that computer science badly needs what logicians are supposed to do best: logic. The situation seems to us reminiscent of that in the beginning of the century. Again we face most basic questions like what is the right logic and even what are the right structures.

Acknowledgements.   This chapter grew out of my part in the Course on Computation Theory in the International Center for Mechanical Sciences, Udine, Italy in September–October 1984. I am happy to thank the organizer—Dr. Egon Börger—and the Center for the invitation, and the listeners for their attention, good will and hard work. Special thanks are due to Dr. Klaus Ambos-Spies who faithfully recorded my lectures. An edited version of the lectures was published as a technical report (32). I am thankful to John Holland for his comments on the report. In Summer and Fall of 1986, the report was updated; in particular, Section 10 was enhanced and Section 11 was added. These two sections carry their own acknowledgements, but I am only too glad to repeat here that I am thankful to Kit Fine, Bernie Galler, David Gries, Albert Meyer, and Jim Morris. Finally, it gives me special pleasure to thank Andreas Blass for his numerous comments and many clarifying enjoyable discussions.

PART 1. FINITE MODEL THEORY

SECTION 1. GLOBAL RELATIONS AND FUNCTIONS

This section is devoted primarily to the notions of global relations and global functions which will be used to provide semantics for numerous logics. The section contains a number of definitions, two principles and one proviso that will be widely used throughout Part 1.

The notions of global relations and global functions were introduced in (28). To motivate the defintion of a global relation, let us consider a formula $\varphi(x, y)$, with two free individual variables, in the first-order language of graphs. What is the meaning of $\varphi(x, y)$? Is it a binary relation? Well, it is and it is not. Given a graph, one can interpret $\varphi(x, y)$ as a binary relation. In general, $\varphi(x, y)$ can be interpreted as a function that assigns a binary relation to each graph. Such functions will be called global relations.

DEFINITION 1.1 Let K be a class of first-order structures of some signature (vocabulary) σ. An *r-ary K-global relation* ρ assigns to each structure S in K an r-ary relation ρ^S on S; the relation ρ^S is the *specialization* of ρ to S. The signature σ is the *signature* of ρ. If K is the class of all permissible σ-structures we say that ρ is σ-*global*.

Right now all structures are permissible. Later we will permit only finite structures satisfying some additional restrictions.

The notion of global relations generalizes Tarski's notion of sentential functions (62). Sentential functions are global relations of arity zero. In a sense, the notion of global relations reduces to the notion of sentential functions: an r-ary global relation of signature σ can be viewed as a sentential function whose signature is an extension of σ by r additional individual constants. But it is more convenient to work directly with global relations.

Tarski's semantics for first-order logic can be conveniently formulated in terms of global relations (disallow function symbols for a moment). The meaning of a first-order formula φ with r free individual variables is a σ-global r-ary relation where σ is the signature (vocabulary) of φ, i.e., the set of predicate symbols in φ. The meaning is defined by an obvious induction.

REMARK There is one relatively minor issue that we are going to ignore. Different orderings of the free individual variables of a first-order formula give different global relations. One way to resolve this difficulty is to stick to the lexicographical ordering of individual variables. Another possibility is to use a more explicit notation like $\{(x_1, \ldots, x_n) : \varphi\}$.

Examples of global relations:

1. Let GRAPH be the class of finite graphs seen as structures with exactly one relation which is binary, irreflexive and symmetric. The following GRAPH-global relations are of arities 0, 1, and 2, respectively:

   The graph is connected,
   Node x has at most $\log n$ neighbors where n is the number of nodes,
   There is a path from node x to node y.

2. Let GROUP be the class of finite groups. The following GROUP-global relations are of arities 0, 1, and 3, respectively:

   The group is abelian,
   The index of the subgroup, generated by element x, is at most $\log n$ where
      n is the number of elements,
   The subgroup generated by elements x and y contains element z.

DEFINITION 1.2   Let K be a class of structures of some signature σ. A K-*global function f of type* (Universe)$^r \to$ Universe assigns to each structure S in K an r-ary function f^S that, given an r-tuple of elements of S, produces an element of S. The signature σ is the *signature* of f.

First-order terms denote global functions. In the obvious way, global relations and global functions of types (Universe)$^r \to$ Universe provide semantics for first-order logic with function symbols. (View individual constants as zero-ary functions.)

We will keep the notion of global functions informal (and very general) and will deal only with global functions of specific types. In particular, an r-ary global relation is a global function of type Universe$^r \to$ Bool where Bool is the set of the two truth values. A K-global function f of type (Universe)$^p \to$ (Universe)^q assigns to each S in K a function f^S that, given a p-tuple of elements of S, produces a q-tuple of elements of S; we say that f, as well as each specialization f^S of f, is p-ary and q-coary. The notion of a K-global partial function f of type (Universe)$^p \to$ (Universe)^q is an obvious generalization; f itself is total (defined on the whole K) but its specializations may be partial. Other possible types of global function include

$$[(\text{Universe})^p \to \text{Bool}] \to [(\text{Universe})^q \to \text{Bool}], \quad \text{and}$$

$$[(\text{Universe})^p \times (\text{Power-Set(Universe)})^q] \to \text{Bool}.$$

The latter is the type of second-order formulas with p free individual variables and q free predicate variables that are all monadic. The meaning of any second-order formula is a global function of an appropriate type.

The Localization Principle. Think about global relations and global functions as relations and functions (of appropriate types) on the structure of discourse.

The localization principle allows us to speak about the negation of a given global relation, about the transitive closure of a given binary global relation, about composition of unary global functions, etc.

Proviso. In Part 1,

1. any structure is a finite first-order structure of finite signature,
2. the universe of any structure is an initial segment of natural numbers,
3. any class of structures consists of structures of the same signature, and
4. the domain of any global relation comprises all structures of some signature that are permitted in the context, unless the contrary is said explicitly.

The proviso allows us to associate a decision problem with each global relation.

DEFINITION 1.3 Let ρ be an r-ary K-global relation. An *instance* of the decision problem for ρ is a pair $\langle S, x \rangle$ where S belongs to K and x is an r-tuple of elements of S; the corresponding *question* is whether $\rho(x)$ holds in S (in other words, whether x belongs to ρ^S).

However, we need to agree on a standard way to represent structures as inputs for computing devices. To simplify the exposition, we choose to represent structures by means of several input tapes. Suppose that S is a structure of cardinality n. One input tape, called the *universe tape*, represents the universe $\{0, 1, \ldots, n-1\}$ of S; it is of length n, its end-cells are specially marked but the intermediate cells are all blank. (Ignore the case of $n = 1$.) If R is a basic r-ary relation of S or the graph of an $(r-1)$-ary basic function of S then R is represented by a special tape of length n^r; for all elements $x_0, \ldots, x_{r-1}$, the cell number $\Sigma x_i \cdot n^i$ contains 1 if $R(x_{r-1}, \ldots, x_0)$ holds, and 0 otherwise.

The Globalization Principle. View relations and functions under discussion as the specializations of global relations and global functions to the structure of discourse.

The globalization principle can be applied only if the context uniquely defines appropriate relations or functions on all relevant structures. For example, suppose that a discussion involves the transitive closure R of a basic relation of the structure of discourse. Then the globalization principle allows us to speak about R being polynomial time recognizable.

Fagin proved (20) that existential second-order logic captures nondeterministic polynomial time.

THEOREM 1.1   A global relation is definable by an existential second-order formula if and only if it is recognizable by a polynomial time bounded nondeterministic Turing machine.   ■

The proof of Theorem 1.1 may be found in the third section of Börger's contribution to this volume (Chapter 2).

It is easy to see that every first-order definable global relation is log-space (and therefore polynomial time) recognizable. The converse is not true. For example, the global relation "The cardinality of the universe is even" is log-space recognizable but not first-order definable. As we will see below, some natural extensions of first-order logic express exactly log-space (respectively polynomial time) recognizable global relations.

DEFINITION 1.4   Let L be first-order logic or an extension of first-order logic by additional logical operators. (A number of such extensions will be defined in subsequent sections.) $L + <$ is the extension of L by means of a logical constant $<$ (just as first-order logic with equality is the extension of first-order logic by means of a logical constant $=$). The logical constant $<$ is interpreted on each structure S as the restriction of the usual order of natural numbers to the universe of S.

SECTION 2.   TRANSITIVE CLOSURES

This section is devoted to transitive closure logics. We start our treatment of different extensions of first-order logic with transitive closure logics because of their relative simplicity. The use of two-way multihead automata will allow us to simplify the proofs related to capturing complexity classes.

The localization principle implicitly introduces the transitive closure of a given binary global relation. The transitive closure of a first-order expressible binary global relation may be not first-order expressible; see (2, 23, 29). In this connection, Aho and Ullman (2) suggested extending the relational calculus, a standard relational query language and a variant of first-order logic, by a powerful least fixed point operator. Immerman (45) turned the transitive closure itself into a logical operator TC. He defined also a deterministic transitive closure operator DTC, and proved that the corresponding extensions FO + TC + $<$ and FO + DTC + $<$ of first-order logic capture natural complexity classes. We prove here some of Immerman's results.

DEFINITION 1.5 If R is a relation of an even arity $2r$ over some universe U then the relation $\{(x,y)$: tuples x,y belong to U^r, and the concatenation $x*y$ belongs to $R\}$ is the *binary companion* $BC(R)$ of R. The *transitive closure* of a $2r$-ary relation relation R is the $2r$-ary relation $TC(R)$ (over the same universe) whose binary companion is the transitive closure of $BC(R)$. With respect to the localization principle, the *transitive closure* of a $2r$-ary global relation ρ is the global relation $TC(\rho)$ such that the domain of $TC(\rho)$ equals that of ρ and for each structure S in the domain of ρ, the specialization of $TC(\rho)$ to S is the transitive closure of ρ^S.

It will be convenient for us in this section to play down the distinction between relations of even arity and their binary companions.

LEMMA 1.1 If a $2r$-ary global relation ρ is nondeterministically log-space recognizable (i.e. if the decision problem for ρ is solvable in nondeterministic logspace) then so is $TC(\rho)$.

Proof Let S be a structure in the domain of ρ, R be the specialization of ρ to S, and a,b be r-tuples of elements of S. The desired algorithm is:

```
begin
   x: = a;
   repeat
      guess y;
      if (x, y) ε R   then   x: = y
   until x = b;
   halt with output YES
end.
```

Notice the use of the globalization principle in the exposition of the proof.

We define a logic FO + TC. The syntax of FO + TC is the extension of the syntax of first-order logic by:

Transitive Closure Formation Rule. Let r be a positive integer and $\varphi(x,y)$ be a well-formed formula where x and y are r-tuples of individual variables such that the $2r$ variables are distinct. Then $TC_{x,y}\varphi(x,y)$ is a well-formed predicate, and if s,t are r-tuples of well-formed terms then $[TC_{x,y}\varphi(x,y)](s,t)$ is a well-formed formula.

$TC_{x,y}$ binds the $2r$ individual variables in the new predicate (but the additional occurrences of these variables in the tail of a formula $[TC_{x,y}\varphi(x,y)](x,y)$ are free). $\varphi(x,y)$ may have additional free individual variables. A more explicit notation for the new predicate is $TC_{x,y}\varphi(w,x,y)$ where w is the list of those additional variables. The new formula $[TC_{x,y}\varphi(w,x,y)](s,t)$ means (on each relevant structure) that (s,t) belongs to the transitive closure of the relation $R_w = \{(x,y): \varphi(w,x,y)\}$. The global function semantics for first-order logic naturally extends to logic FO + TC; again the meaning of a formula with r free individual variables is a global r-ary relation.

The transitive closure formation rule introduces well-formed predicates in addition to well-formed formulas. The only well-formed predicates in first-order logic are predicate symbols. The transitive closure formation rule is essentially a predicate formation rule. The new predicate is then used to form new formulas. But it is possible to deal only with formulas of course.

REMARK   Immerman (45) seems to define directly a new formula $TC[\varphi(x,y)]$ which is a simpler notation for $[TC_{x,y}\varphi(x,y)](x,y)$. Unfortunately, the simpler notation is somewhat deficient. Try to express $[TC_{x,y}P(x,y,x)](x,x)$ or $[TC_{x,y}P(x,y,x)](fx,x)$ in the simplified notation.

Positive and negative occurrences of a predicate in a formula are defined by induction. In particular, every positive (respectively negative) occurrence of a predicate in a formula φ remains so in any formula $[TC_{...}\varphi](.\ .\ .)$. Say that a formula φ is *positive with respect to TC* if every occurrence of every predicate $TC_{...}\psi$ in φ is positive.

In Section 1, we spoke about extensions $L + <$ of logics L by means of the built-in linear order. In particular, we have an extension FO + TC + $<$ of FO + TC. Viewing 0 and 1 as logical constants yields a further extension FO + TC + $<$ + $\{0,1\}$.

THEOREM 1.2   Let ρ be a global relation. The following are equivalent:

1. ρ is nondeterministic log-space recognizable,
2. ρ is definable by an FO + TC + $<$ formula φ which is positive with respect to TC.
3. ρ is definable by a FO + TC + $<$ + $\{0,1\}$ formula $[TC_{x,y}\psi(x,y)](s,t)$ where s,t are sequences of zeros and ones, and ψ is first-order.

Proof   (3) $\rightarrow$ (2).   The constants 0 and 1 are definable in FO + $<$.

(2) $\rightarrow$ (1).   Without loss of generality, one may suppose that only first-order subformulas can be negated in the defining formula φ: use the usual duality laws for first-order logic. Then an easy induction shows that every subformula of the defining formula is nondeterministicly log-space recognizable. The case of TC is taken care of in Lemma 1.1.

To prove the implication (1) $\rightarrow$ (3), suppose that ρ is recognizable in nondeterministic log-space. According to the Appendix, there is a nondeterministic two-way multihead automaton that recognizes ρ. Let formula $\text{Next}(w,x,y)$ and tuples Initial, Final be as in the Appendix. Then the desired FO + TC + < + $\{0,1\}$ formula is

$$[\text{TC}_{x,y}\text{Next}(w,x,y)](\text{Initial}, \text{Final}). \qquad \blacksquare$$

DEFINITION 1.6   The *deterministic version* of a binary relation R is the relation $\{(x,y): (x,y)\varepsilon R \text{ and there is no } z \neq y \text{ with } (x,z)\varepsilon R\}$. The *deterministic version* of a $2r$-ary relation R is the $2r$-ary relation whose binary companion is the deterministic version of $\text{BC}(R)$. The *deterministic transitive closure* $\text{DTC}(R)$ of a $2r$-ary relation R is the transitive closure of the deterministic version of R. With respect to the localization principle, the *deterministic transitive closure* of a $2r$-ary global relation ρ is the global relation $\text{DTC}(\rho)$ such that the domain of $\text{DTC}(\rho)$ equals that of ρ and for each structure S in the domain of ρ, the specialization of $\text{DTC}(\rho)$ to S is the deterministic transitive closure of ρ^S.

LEMMA 1.2   If a $2r$-ary global relation ρ is log-space recognizable then so is $\text{DTC}(\rho)$.

Proof   Let S range over the domain of ρ, U be the universe of the structure S, $R = \rho^S$, and a,b be r-tuples of elements of U. We need an algorithm which, given S and (a,b), will decide whether (a,b) belongs to $\text{DTC}(R)$.

The deterministic version of R is the graph of some partial function f on U^r. Given x in U^r, one can find in log-space whether there is some y with $(x,y)\varepsilon R$ and whether there are different y,z with $(x,y)\varepsilon R$ and $(x,z)\varepsilon R$. This yields a log-space algorithm which, given x, computes fx or UNDEFINED. Given a and b, compute $f^k a$ for $k = 1$, 2, etc. and halt when b comes along or UNDEFINED is returned or k reaches n. If b has come along then return YES, otherwise return NO. $\qquad \blacksquare$

Again, the globalization principle was used to simplify the exposition of the proof.

The definition of an extension FO + DTC of first-order logic is similar to the definition of FO + TC. Just change "TC" to "DTC," and "transitive closure" to "deterministic transitive closure."

THEOREM 1.3   Let ρ be a global relation. The following are equivalent:

1. ρ is log-space recognizable,
2. ρ is definable in FO + DTC + <,

3. ρ is definable by a FO + DTC + < + $\{0,1\}$ formula $[\text{DTC}_{x,y}\psi(x,y)](s,t)$
   where s, t are sequences of zeros and ones, and ψ is first-order.

Proof Similar to that of Theorem 1.2.   ∎

Since the deterministic version of a given relation is first-order definable, FO + DTC can be seen as a sublogic of FO + TC.

SECTION 3.   LEAST FIXED POINTS

In this section we define the extension FO + LFP of first-order logic by the least fixed point operator (2, 12) and prove Immerman and Vardi's theorem that FO + LFP + < captures polynomial time (44, 68). Again, the use of two-way multihead automata will allow certain simplification.

DEFINITION 1.7   Let F be a unary operation on a partially ordered set. If $Fx = x$ then x is a *fixed point* of F. If $Fx = x$ and $\forall y(Fy = y \rightarrow x \leq y)$ then x is the *least fixed point* LFP(F) of F. If $Fx \leq Fy$ for all $x \leq y$ then F is *monotone*.

DEFINITION 1.8   A partially ordered set is *complete* if every subset of it has a least upper bound and a greatest lower bound.

For example, the set of relations of a fixed arity on a fixed nonempty set is a complete partially ordered set with respect to inclusion. The following fact is well-known.

Fact Let D be a finite (or infinite complete) partially ordered set with a least element. A monotone unary operation F on D has a least fixed point.

Proof Let $g0 = \min(D)$ and each $g(\alpha + 1) = F(g\alpha)$. (In the case of infinite D, let additionally $g\alpha = \sup\{g\beta : \beta < \alpha\}$ for limit α.) By monotonicity, the function g is increasing (though not necessarily strictly increasing). Hence, there is α with $g\alpha = g(\alpha + 1)$; let $\gamma = \min\{\alpha : g\alpha = g(\alpha + 1)\}$. Obviously, $g\gamma$ is a fixed point of F. Given a fixed point y of F, prove by induction that each $g\alpha \leq y$. Hence $g\gamma = \text{LFP}(F)$.   ∎

The localization principle gives:

DEFINITION 1.9   Let F be a σ-global function of type

$$[\text{Power-Set(Universe}^r)] \rightarrow [\text{Power-Set(Universe}^r)],$$

so that each specification of F takes an r-ary relation to an r-ary relation. F is *monotone* if every specialization of F is so. If F is monotone then the *least fixed point* LFP(F) of F is the σ-global r-ary relation that assigns to each σ-structure S the least fixed point of F^S. F is *polynomial time computable* if there is a polynomial time algorithm that, given a σ-structure S and an r-ary relation P on S, computes $F^S(P)$.

LEMMA 1.3   Let F be a monotone σ-global function of type

$$[\text{Power-Set}(\text{Universe}^r)] \to [\text{Power-Set}(\text{Universe}^r)].$$

If F is polynomial time computable then LFP(F) is polynomial time recognizable.

Proof   Given a structure S and an r-tuple x of elements of S, compute $P_0 = \emptyset$, $P_1 = F^S(P_0)$, $P_2 = F^S(P_1)$, etc. until you come across $P_{m+1} = P_m$. Then check whether x belongs to P_m. Since $m \leq |S|^r$, this algorithm works in polynomial time.   ∎

The syntax of logic FO + LFP is the result of augmenting the syntax of first-order logic by the following formation rule. (If all predicate symbols of first-order logic are treated as predicate constants then first-order logic should be augmented by predicate variables first.)

Least Fixed Point Formation Rule.   Let r be a positive integer, x be an r-tuple $x_1, \ldots, x_r$ of individual variables, P be an r-ary predicate variable, and $\varphi(P,x)$ be a well-formed formula. If $\varphi(P,x)$ is positive in P (i.e. all free occurrences of P in $\varphi(P,x)$ are positive) then $\text{LFP}_{P;x}\varphi(P,x)$ is a well-formed predicate and, for every r-tuple t of well-formed terms, $[\text{LFP}_{P;x}\varphi(P,x)](t)$ is a well-formed formula.

$\text{LFP}_{P;x}$ binds the predicate variable P and the individual variables $x_1, \ldots, $ x_r (but of course additional occurrences of these individual variables in the tails of formulas $[\text{LFP}_{P;x}\varphi(P,x)](t)$ are free). If Q is a predicate variable different from P then every positive (respectively, negative) occurrence of Q in $\varphi(P,x)$ remains positive (respectively, negative) in the new predicate and the new formulas.

REMARK   A simplified notation $\text{LFP}_P\varphi(P,x)$ for $[\text{LFP}_{P;x}\varphi(P,x)](x)$ is deficient: just try to express $[\text{LFP}_{P;x}\varphi(P,x)](t)$ in the simplified notation.

To be on the safe side, let us emphasize that logic FO + LFP allows interleaving LFP with propositional connectives (including negation) and quantifiers; in particular, one can negate an LFP formula then use the LFP formation rule again, etc.

The formula $\varphi(P,x)$ may have additional free individual variables; let w be the list of the additional individual variables. The meaning of the predicate $\text{LFP}_{P;x}\varphi(P,w,x)$ is the least fixed point of the operator $F_w(P) = \{x: \varphi(P,w,x)\}$ on the set of r-ary relations ordered by inclusion. Since the formula $\varphi(P,w,x)$ is positive in P, the operator F_w is monotone and therefore has a least fixed point. The global function semantics for first-order logic naturally extends to FO + LFP.

THEOREM 1.4   Let ρ be a global relation. The following are equivalent:

1. ρ is polynomial time recognizable,
2. ρ is definable in logic FO + LFP + $<$,
3. ρ is definable by a FO + LFP + $<$ + $\{0,1\}$ formula $[\text{LFP}_{P;x}\psi(P,x)](t)$ where ψ is first-order and t is a sequence of zeros and ones.

Proof   The implications (3)$\mapsto$(2) and (2)$\mapsto$(1) are obvious. To prove the implication (1)$\mapsto$(3), suppose that ρ is polynomial time recognizable. According to the Appendix, there is an alternating two-way multihead finite automaton that recognizes ρ. Let the formula $\text{Next}(w,x,y)$ and the tuples Initial, Final be as in the Appendix. It is easy to write down first-order formulas $\text{Existential}(x)$ and $\text{Universal}(x)$ asserting that the internal state of the automaton in the given configuration x is respectively existential or universal. Let

$$\text{Accepted}(w,\_) = \text{LFP}_{P;x}[x = \text{Final}, \quad \text{or}$$

$$\text{Universal}(x) \ \& \ \forall y(\text{Next}(w,x,y) \rightarrow P(y)), \quad \text{or}$$

$$\text{Existential}(x) \ \& \ \exists y(\text{Next}(w,x,y) \ \& \ P(y))].$$

The desired FO + LFP formula is $\text{Accepted}(w,\text{Initial})$.   ■

SECTION 4.   BRANCHING QUANTIFIERS

We turn now to an extension of first-order logic by branching (or Henkin) quantifiers whose introduction was motivated by considerations quite distant from computer science (42).

Let us start with an example. The expression

$$\begin{bmatrix} \forall u \exists v \\ \forall x \exists y \end{bmatrix} \varphi(u,v,x,y) \tag{1.1}$$

means that for all u and x there are v and y such that v depends only on u, y depends only on x, and $\varphi(u,v,x,y)$ holds. In other words, there are functions $V(u)$ and $Y(x)$ such that $\varphi(u,V(u),x,Y(x))$ holds.

In general, a branching quantifier is a partially ordered set of expressions $\forall x$ and $\exists y$; an existentially quantified variable y depends upon the universally quantified variables x such that $\forall x$ precedes $\exists y$ in the partial order (69).

THEOREM 1.5   For any global relation ρ the following are equivalent:

1. ρ is NP,
2. ρ is expressible by an existential second-order formula,
3. ρ is expressible by a formula $Q\varphi$ where Q is a branching quantifier and φ is a first-order formula.

Proof   The equivalence (1) $\leftrightarrow$ (2) is Theorem 1.1 in §1, the implication (3) $\rightarrow$ (2) is obvious, the implication (2) $\rightarrow$ (3) is proved in (69). ∎

In the rest of the section we describe a few results from (8). The only novelty is the direct proof of Theorem 1.8 below. A branching quantifier Q will be called *mighty* if there is a first-order formula φ such that the global relation $Q\varphi$ is NP-complete under polynomial time reductions.

THEOREM 1.6   The quantifier (1.1) is mighty.

Proof   The idea is to express 3-colorability of a graph with individual constants 0, 1, and 2. The desired φ is the conjunction of the formulas:

$$u = x \rightarrow v = y,$$

$$v = 0 \quad \text{or} \quad v = 1 \quad \text{or} \quad v = 2,$$

$$\text{Edge}(u, x) \rightarrow v \neq y. \qquad \blacksquare$$

Note that, in the proof of Theorem 1.6, the existentially quantified variables range, in effect, over $\{0, 1, 2\}$. Let α, β, γ range over $\{0, 1\}$, and μ range over $\{0, 1, 2\}$.

THEOREM 1.7   The quantifiers

$$\begin{bmatrix} \forall x \; \exists \alpha \\ \forall y \; \exists \beta \\ \forall z \; \exists \gamma \end{bmatrix} \quad \text{and} \quad \begin{bmatrix} \forall x \; \exists \alpha \\ \forall y \; \exists \mu \end{bmatrix} \quad \text{are mighty.}$$

We omit the proof of Theorem 1.7. ∎

In the rest of this section, x and y are tuples of individual variables. The branching quantifier

$$\begin{bmatrix} \forall x \ \exists \alpha \\ \forall y \ \exists \beta \end{bmatrix}$$

will be called the *narrow Henkin quantifiers* and denoted $NH(x, \alpha; y, \beta)$. Without loss of generality, x and y always have the same length: just pad the shorter tuple. Let $ENH(x, \alpha; y, \beta)$ be the equality bound version of $NH(x, \alpha; y, \beta)$:

$$NH(x, \alpha; y, \beta)[(x = y \ \rightarrow \ \alpha = \beta) \ \& \ \varphi(x, y, \alpha, \beta)].$$

$ENH(x, \alpha; y, \beta)$ asserts (in each relevant structure) the existence of a function f from the universe to $\{0, 1\}$ such that for all x and y, $\varphi(x, y, f(x), f(y))$ holds. In the rest of this section, we assume that α and β range over the truth-values rather than over $\{0, 1\}$. Then $ENH(x, \alpha; y, \beta)\varphi(x, y, \alpha, \beta)$ is equivalent to the second-order formula

$$\exists R \, \forall xy \, \varphi(x, y, R(x), R(y)).$$

An arbitrary $NH(x, \alpha; y, \beta)\varphi(x, y, \alpha, \beta)$ is equivalent to

$$ENH(xu, \alpha; yv, \beta)[(u = 0 \ \& \ v = 1) \ \rightarrow \ \varphi(x, y, \alpha, \beta)].$$

Let FO + NH be the extension of first-order logic by narrow Henkin quantifiers. Positive and negative occurrences of a subformula ψ in a formula φ are defined by the obvious induction on φ; in particular, any positive (respectively negative) occurrence of ψ in $\varphi(u, v, \gamma, \delta)$ remains so in $NH(x, \alpha; y, \beta)\varphi(x, y, \alpha, \beta)$. We will say that a formula φ is *positive with respect to* NH if every occurrence of every subformula of the form $NH(x, \alpha; y, \beta)\psi(x, y, \alpha, \beta)$ in φ is positive. Abbreviate ''nondeterministic log-space'' as ''Nlog-space.''

THEOREM 1.8   For a global relation ρ the following are equivalent:

1. ρ is co-Nlog-space recognizable,
2. ρ is expressible by an FO + NH + $<$ formula which is positive with respect to NH,
3. ρ is expressible by an FO + NH + $<$ formula $ENH(x, \alpha; y, \beta)\varphi(x, y, \alpha, \beta)$ with a first-order φ.

Proof (1)$\mapsto$(3).   Suppose that ρ is co-Nlog-space recognizable, and let ρ' be the complement of ρ (so that on each relevant structure, the specification of ρ' is the complement of the specification of ρ). According to the Appendix, there is a two-way multihead nondeterministic finite automaton that recognizes ρ'. Let formula $Next(w, x, y)$ and tuples Initial and Final be as in the Appendix. The desired formula expresses the nonacceptance by the automaton:

$$\mathrm{ENH}(x, \alpha; y, \beta)[(x = \mathrm{Initial} \rightarrow \alpha = 1) \ \&$$
$$((\alpha = 1 \ \& \ \mathrm{Next}(w, x, y)) \rightarrow \beta = 1) \ \&$$
$$(y = \mathrm{Final} \rightarrow \beta = 0)].$$

The implication (3)$\mapsto$(2) is trivial.

(2)$\mapsto$(1). Without loss of generality, we may suppose that only first-order subformulas of the defining formula can be negated: use the usual duality laws of first-order logic. By induction, we will prove that every subformula of the defining formula is co-Nlog-space recognizable. It suffices to prove that if $\varphi(x, y, \alpha, \beta)$ is co-Nlog-space then so is $\psi = \mathrm{ENH}(x, \alpha; y, \beta)\varphi(x, y, \alpha, \beta)$. Thus, suppose that M' is a log-space bounded nondeterministic Turing machine that recognizes the negation $\varphi'(x, y, \alpha, \beta)$ of $\varphi(x, y, \alpha, \beta)$. We have

$$\psi \ \leftrightarrow \ \exists R \ \forall x \forall y \ \varphi(x, y, Rx, Ry) \ \leftrightarrow \ \exists R \ \forall x \forall y \ \mathrm{not} \ \varphi'(x, y, Rx, Ry) \ \leftrightarrow$$

$$\exists R \ \Pi_{x,y} \ \mathrm{not} \ \Sigma_{\varphi'(x,y,\alpha,\beta)}(Rx = \alpha \ \& \ Ry = \beta) \ \leftrightarrow$$

$$\exists R \ \Pi_{\varphi'(x,y,\alpha,\beta)}(Rx \neq \alpha \ \mathrm{or} \ Ry \neq \beta).$$

Here $\Pi_{x,y}$ means (in each relevant structure) the conjunction over all values of x and y. For given values of x and y, $\Sigma_{\varphi'(x,y,\alpha,\beta)}$ means the disjunction over the values of α and β satisfying $\varphi'(x, y, Rx, Ry)$. And $\Pi_{\varphi'(x,y,\alpha,\beta)}$ means the conjuncton over all values of x, y, α and β satisfying $\varphi'(x, y, Rx, Ry)$. For every value a of x, view Ra as a propositional variable. Then ψ asserts satisfiability of the propositional formula $\Pi_{\varphi'(x,y,\alpha,\beta)}(Rx \neq \alpha \ \mathrm{or} \ Ry \neq \beta)$. Recall that a literal is a propostional variable or the negation of such.

Fact (49) A conjunction C of binary disjunctions of literals is unsatisfiable if and only if there are a propostional variable p and a sequence $l_1 \rightarrow l_2 \rightarrow \ldots$ $\rightarrow l_m \rightarrow l_1$ of literals such that each implication $l_i \rightarrow l_{i+1}$ as well as the implication $l_m \rightarrow l_1$ is equivalent to a conjunct of C, and both p and the negation of p appear in the sequence.

Now we are ready to describe a log-space bounded nondeterministic Turing machine N that recognizes the negation of ψ. Let M be a log-space bounded nondeterministic Turing machine that recognizes φ'. Step-by-step N guesses a sequence $l_1 \rightarrow l_2 \rightarrow \ldots \rightarrow l_m \rightarrow l_1$ of literals that witnesses the unsatisfiability of $C = \Pi_{\varphi'(x,y,\alpha,\beta)}(Rx \neq \alpha \ \mathrm{or} \ Ry \neq \beta)$. To check that an implication $l_i \rightarrow l_{i+1}$ (where $i+1 = 1$ if $i = m$) is equivalent to a conjunct of C, N presents l_i in the form $Ra = \alpha$, presents l_{i+1} in the form $Rb \neq \beta$, and uses M to check $\varphi'(a, b, \alpha, \beta)$. ∎

SECTION 5.   FUNCTION LOGICS

First-order logic is essentially a logic of relations. It has one function construct: the composition, and a number of relation constructs: boolean connectives and the two quantifiers. It allows constructing formulas from terms but not the other way round. In Sections 2–4 we studied extensions of first-order logic by means of additional relation constructs. In this section, we turn to logic of functions in the case when only finite structures are permitted.

Consider the classical language of functions primitive recursive relative some given functions (47). Usually, primitive recursive terms are interpreted over the set of natural numbers. But here we interpret primitive recursive terms as functions over a nonempty finite initial segment of natural numbers. View the individual constant 0 as a name of the number zero, view the sign of successor function as a name of the partial successor function on the universe of discourse, and so on. Then every primitive recursive term means a global function. We take the liberty of extending the syntax by a new individual constant End for the last element of the universe of discourse. It turns out then that a global function is primitive recursive if and only if it is log-space computable (28). Similarly, a global function is recursive if and only if it is polynomial time computable (28, 57). This section recapitulates some of the paper (28). It has also a couple of new elements: a remark that primitive recursion can be replaced by a WHILE construct, and a simpler universal recursive schema.

We start with primitive recursive global functions. The language of primitive recursive functions will be reformulated in a form that is convenient for our purposes. In the same time we will extend the language by the individual constant End.

According to the proviso of Section 1, the universe of every structure is an initial segment of natural numbers. In this section, we have three additional provisos:

1. Every structure contains at least two elements. (Alternatively, one may assume existence of an extra universe Bool $= \{$False, True$\}$.)

2. Individual constants 0, End and a unary function symbol Successor are logical constants (as equality is a logical constant in first-order logic with equality). In every structure, 0 denotes the number zero, End denotes the maximal number in the universe, and Successor denotes the partial function $\lambda x(x+1)$. The three logical constants will not be counted as members of any signature.

3. A certain (possibly empty) signature σ is fixed. Every structure is a σ-structure. Every global function is σ-global.

In this section, a function (resp. global function) means a partial function (resp. partial global function) of type Universe$^p \to$ Universe^q for some nonnegative integer p (the arity) and some positive integer q (the coarity). A function of coarity $q > 1$ can be seen as a sequence of q functions of coarity 1, but it will be convenient to deal directly with functions of higher coarity. If $t_1, \ldots,$ t_k are tuples of elements then $(t_1, \ldots, t_k)$ will denote the concatenation of tuples $t_1, \ldots, t_k$ rather than a k-tuple of tuples.

With respect to the localization principle, we view global functions as functions on the structure S of discourse. Let $U = \{0, \ldots, n-1\}$ be the universe of S. The *value* of a nonempty tuple $(x_{k-1}, \ldots, x_1, x_0)$ of elements of U is the number $\Sigma_{i<k} x_i \cdot n^i$. If elements of U are seen as digits over the radix n then any nonempty tuple of elements of U is a positional notation over the radix n for its value.

DEFINITION 1.10   The *initial functions* are:

1. For every nonnegative p, the constant p-ary functions with values 0 or End.

2. For every positive p, the p-ary p-coary successor function. Given a p-tuple of value $V < n^p - 1$, the function produces the p-tuple of value $V+1$; it is not defined on the p-tuple of value $n^p - 1$. We will denote the successor of a tuple t as $t+1$.

3. For all $p \geq q \geq 1$ and every sequence $1 \leq i_1 \leq i_2 \leq \ldots \leq i_q \leq p$, the corresponding p-ary q-coary projecton function. For example, if $p = 4$, $q = 2$ and $i_1 = 2$, $i_2 = 4$ then the projection of $(0,1,2,3)$ is $(1,3)$.

4. The basic σ-functions, and the characteristic functions of basic σ-predicates. (Individual constants are functions of arity 0 and coarity 1.)

The *composition* $g(h_1(x), \ldots, h_k(x))$ of functions g and $h_1, \ldots, h_k$ is defined in the obvious way. It is required that $\mathrm{arity}(h_1) = \ldots = \mathrm{arity}(h_k)$ and $\mathrm{arity}(g) = \mathrm{coarity}(h_1) + \ldots + \mathrm{coarity}(h_k)$.

As usual, the *primitive recursion* schema is the schema

$$f(x, \mathrm{Zero}) = g(x), \quad f(x, t+1) = h(x, t, f(x, t)) \tag{1.2}$$

which defines a new function f by means of given functions g and h of the same coarity. Here Zero is the tuple of zeros of the appropriate length.

DEFINITION 1.11   A global function is *primitive recursive* if it belongs to the closure of initial global functions under compositions and primitive recursions. A global relation is *primitive recursive* if its characteristic function is so.

Example   Let us check that if a 2-coary function $f(x)$ and a 3-coary function $g(x)$ are primitive recursive then the 5-coary function $h(x) = (f(x), g(x))$ is primitive recursive. The 5-ary 5-coary identity function $I(y) = y$ is primitive recursive because it is an initial projection function. But $h(x) = I(f(x), g(x))$.

THEOREM 1.9   A global function f is primitive recursive if and only if it is log-space computable.

We skip the proof of Theorem 1.9, see (28).

The language of primitive recursive functions can be viewed as a programming language such that exactly log-space computable global functions can be programmed. Programming languages of that sort may be useful in applications where the complexity of computations is bounded *a priori*. In this connection, let us mention that the primitive recursion schema can be replaced by more familiar programming constructs. Consider, for example, the construct

$$y := e_0; \quad \text{FOR} \quad s := e_1 \quad \text{TO} \quad e_2 \quad \text{DO} \quad y := e_3 \tag{1.3}$$

where e_0, e_1, e_2, e_3 are expressions (terms) and e_0, e_1, e_2 contain neither s nor y. If the expressions e_i define primitive recursive global functions then (1.3) defines a primitive recursive global function $y = f(. . .)$. The primitive recursion schema (1.2) is expressible by means of (1.3):

$$y := g(x); \quad \text{FOR} \quad s := \text{Zero} \quad \text{TO} \quad t - 1 \quad \text{DO} \quad y := h(x, s, y)].$$

Another possible replacement for (1.2) is the construct

$$y := e_0; \quad \text{WHILE} \quad e_1 R e_2 \quad \text{DO} \quad y := e_3 \tag{1.4}$$

where e_0, e_1, e_2, e_3 are expressions, and e_0, e_1, e_2 do not contain y, and R is a relation $=$, $<$ or $\leq$. (It would be desirable of course to introduce boolean expressions and to allow an arbitrary boolean expression b instead of $e_1 R e_2$.) If the expressions e_i define primitive recursive global functions then (1.4) defines a primitive recursive global function $y = f(. . .)$. (1.2) is expressible by means of (1.4) and a projection:

$$(s, y) := (\text{Zero}, g(x)); \quad \text{WHILE} \quad s < t \quad \text{DO} \quad (s, y) := (s + 1, h(x, s, y)).$$

Consider now the classical Herbrand-Gödel-Kleene equation language of recursive functions (47) extended by the individual constant End. The recursive definitions are naturally adaptable to global functions; it turns out that a global function is recursive iff it is polynomial time computable. Moreover, recursive functions form the closure of primitive recursive functions under a single additional recursion schema. Two schemas are specified for this purpose in (28). Here is a simpler recursion schema for the same purpose:

$$f(x, \text{Zero}) = gx, \quad f(x, t + 1) = h(x, f(\alpha x, t), f(\beta x, t)) \tag{1.5}$$

which defines a new function f by means of given functions g, h, α and β.

THEOREM 1.10   A global function is polynomial time computable if and only if it belongs to the closure of initial primitive recursive global functions by means of composition and recursion schemas (1.2), (1.5).

Proof The "if" implication is clear. To prove the "only if" implication, let RECFUN be the closure of initial primitive recursive global functions by means of composition and recursion schemas (1.2), (1.5), and let RECREL be the class of global relations with characteristic functions in RECFUN. The localization principle allows us to speak about the graph of a global function. It suffices to prove that an arbitrary polynomial time recognizable global relation ρ belongs to RECREL because a polynomial time computable global function can be recovered from its graph by primitive recursive means. According to the Appendix, there is an alternating two-way multihead automaton that recognizes ρ; it accepts a structure S with a tuple w of an appropriate length if and only if $\rho(w)$ holds in S. Let tuples Initial and Final be as in the Appendix.

Without loss of generality, every configuration of the automaton has at most two next configurations. There are primitive recursive functions α and β such that if y codes a configuration then $\alpha(w,y)$ and $\beta(w,y)$ code the next configurations; if there is only one next configuration then $\alpha(x,y) = \beta(w,y)$. Without loss of generality, every internal state of A is either existential or universal; the deterministic states (with only one next configuration) can be counted either way. We say that a configuration is existential (respectively universal) if the corresponding internal state is so. There is a primitive recursive function E such that if y codes an existential (respectively universal) configuration then Ey equals 0 (respectively 1). Schema (1.5) allows us to define an auxiliary function Accept(w,y,t):

$$\text{Accept}(w,y,\text{Zero}) = \text{If } y = \text{Final then 1 else 0},$$

$$\text{Accept}(w,y,t+1) = \text{If } Ey = 0 \text{ then } \max\{\text{Accept}(\alpha(w,y),t),$$
$$\text{Accept}(\beta(w,y),t)\} \text{ else } \min\{\text{Accept}(\alpha(w,y),t),$$
$$\text{Accept}(\beta(w,y),t)\}.$$

Notice that $\rho(w) \leftrightarrow \exists t[\text{Accept}(w,\text{Initial},t) = 1]$.

Here t is a tuple $(t_1, \ldots, t_r)$ of a fixed length r, and $\exists t$ means $\exists t_1 \ldots \exists t_r$. But RECREL is closed under the existential quantification over the elements. Hence ρ is in RECREL. ■

SECTION 6.   INDUCTIVE FIXED POINTS

The LFP formation rule of Section 3 had one *ad hoc* feature. To ensure that the operator $F(P) = \{x: \varphi(P,x)\}$ is monotone, the formula $\varphi(P,x)$ was supposed to be positive in P. The positivity of φ is sufficient but not necessary for the monotonicity of F. Unfortunately, replacing the positivity condition by the monotonicity condition results in an extension FO + LFP$'$ of first-order logic that we would not like to call a logic: the set of FO + LFP$'$ formulas is undecidable (29). Fortunately, there is a better fixed-point extension of first-order logic, called the inductive fixed-point extension FO + IFP, which is even more liberal than FO + LFP'. It was introduced in (29) as a development of an idea of Livchak (52). This section recapitulates the papers (37) and (38) where the inductive fixed-point logic was stuidied.

DEFINITION 1.12   Let F be a unary operation on a (finite) complete partially ordered set D. Let $g0 = \min(D)$ and each $g(i+1) = F(gi)$. F is *inductive* if $gi \le g(i+1)$ for every i. It is easy to see that if F is inductive then it has a unique fixed point of the form gi; this fixed point will be called the *inductive fixed point* IFP(F) of F. F is *inflationary* if $X \le F(X)$ for every $X \varepsilon D$.

LEMMA 1.4   Let F be a unary operation on a complete partially ordered set.

(a) If F is inflationary then it is inductive.
(b) The operation $F'(X) = \sup\{X, F(X)\}$ is inflationary; if F is inductive then
    IFP(F') = IFP(F).
(c) If F is monotone then it is inductive and LFP(F) = IFP(F).

Proof   is clear.   ■

Examples   Consider the power set of U $= \{0,1,2\}$ ordered by inclusion.

1. Define $FX = X \cup \{$the cardinality of $X\}$ if $X \ne$ U, and $FU =$ U. Then F
   is inflationary but not monotone. Moreover, F does not have a least fixed
   point: both $\{1\}$ and $\{0,2\}$ are fixed points of f but $F\emptyset \ne \emptyset$.
2. Define $G = F$ except $G\{1\} = \emptyset$. Then G is inductive but neither inflationary
   nor monotone.
3. The constant operations $HX = \{0\}$ is monotone but not inflationary.

The syntax of logic FO + IFP is the extension of the syntax of first-order logic by:

The Inductive Fixed Point Formation Rule.   Let r be a positive integer, x be an r-tuple $x_1, \ldots, x_r$ of individual variables, P be an r-ary predicate variable, $\varphi(P,x)$ be a well-formed formula, and $\varphi'(P,x) = [P(x)$ or $\varphi(P,x)]$. Then IFP$_{P;x}\varphi'(P,x)$ is a well-formed predicate and [IFP$_{P;x}\varphi'(P,x)](x)$ is a well-formed formula.

The meaning of the predicate IFP$_{P;x}\varphi'(P,x)$ is the inductive fixed point of the inflationary operator $F(P) = \{x: \varphi'(P,x)\}$. The global function semantics for first-order logic naturally extends to FO + IFP.

The statement (c) of Lemma 1.4 implies that FO + IFP is at least as expressive as logic FO + LFP' mentioned above.

THEOREM 1.11   The logics FO + LFP and FO + IFP have the same expressive power.

COROLLARY   A global relation is expressible in FO + IFP + < if and only if it is polynomial time recognizable.

Proof   Use Theorem 1.4 of Section 3.   ∎

Theorem 1.11 is a consequence of a stronger theorem. Let r be an arbitrary positive integer, and let Γ range over monotone global functions of the empty signature and of type

$$\text{Power-set}(\text{Universe}^r) \times \text{Power-set}(\text{Universe}^r) \times \text{Universe}^r \longrightarrow \text{Bool}.$$

The monotonicity of Γ means that (on every finite structure) $\Gamma(P_1, P_2, x)$ implies $\Gamma(P_3, P_4, x)$ if $P_1 \subseteq P_3$ and $P_2 \subseteq P_4$. We are interested in the inflationary operator $G(P) = \{x: P(x) \text{ or } \Gamma(P, \text{not } P, x)\}$.

Define an extension FO + Γ of first-order logic by means of the following formation rule: if x is an r-tuple of individual variables and $\varphi(x)$, $\psi(x)$ are well-formed formulas then so is $\Gamma(\{x: \varphi(x)\}, \{x: \psi(x)\}, x)$. The global function semantics for the extended logic is clear. Treat Γ as a positive operator: every positive (respectively negative) occurrence of a predicate symbol in $\varphi(x)$ or $\psi(x)$ remains so in $\Gamma(\{x: \varphi(x)\}, \{x: \psi(x)\}, x)$. If an FO + Γ formula $\psi(Q, y)$ is positive in a predicate symbol Q then the operator $\hat{\psi}(Q) = \{y: \psi(Q, y)\}$ is monotone; if $\hat{\psi}$ is repetitive (i.e., if the length of the sequence y of individual variables equals the arity of Q) then it has a least fixed point.

We say that a relation A is a *diagonal* of a relation B if A is obtained from B by identifying some arguments. For example, if B is given by some formula $\beta(v_1, v_2, v_3, v_4)$ and A is given by the formula $\alpha(v_1, v_2) = \beta(v_1, v_2, v_1, v_2)$ then A is a diagonal of B.

THEOREM 1.12   There is an FO + Γ formula $\psi(Q, y)$ such that ψ is positive in Q, the operator $\hat{\psi}(Q) = \{y: \psi(Q, y)\}$ is repetitive, and the inductive fixed point of the operator $G(P) = \{x: P(x) \text{ or } \Gamma(P, \text{not } P, x)\}$ is a diagonal of the least fixed point of $\hat{\psi}$.

To deduce Theorem 1.11 from Theorem 1.12, prove by induction on FO + IFP formula φ that φ is equivalent to (i.e., defines the same global relation as) some FO + LFP formula. The only nontrivial case is when $\varphi = [\text{IFP}_{P;x}(P(x) \text{ or } \Phi(P, x))](x)$. Let $\Gamma(P, P', x)$ be the result of replacing all negative occurrences of P in Φ by a new predicate symbol P'. Then Γ is monotone in both relational variables, and $\Phi(P, x)$ is equivalent to $\Gamma(P, \text{not } P, x)$. Now use Theorem 1.12.

THEOREM 1.13　For every FO + IFP definable global relation ρ there is a first-order formula $\varphi(P,x)$ such that the operator $\hat{\varphi}(P) = \{x: P(x)$ or $\varphi(P,x)\}$ is repetitive and

(a) if the arity of ρ is positive then ρ is a diagonal of IFP($\hat{\varphi}$),
(b) if ρ is 0-ary then the unary global relation ρ' such that $\forall v(\rho'(v) \leftrightarrow \rho)$ is a diagonal of IFP($\hat{\varphi}$).

Theorems 1.12 and 1.13 imply the analog of Theorem 1.13 for FO + LFP announced in (44).

Jiazhen Cai, a student of Bob Paige in New York University, questioned the proof of Theorem 1.13 (more exactly, the proof of Lemma 2 in §4 of (38). The following claim removes the difficulty in the proof and is interesting all by itself.

CLAIM　Let $\varphi(P,x,y) = [P(x)$ or $\varphi_0(P,x,y)]$ be an FO + IFP formula where x and y are tuples of individual variables such that the length of x equals the arity of P. Suppose that y-variables do not have bound occurrences in φ. Let Q be a new predicate variable whose arity allows to form a formula $Q(x,y)$, and let $\psi(Q,x,y)$ is the result of replacing each $P(u)$ by $Q(u,y)$ in $\varphi(P,x,y)$. Then

$$[\mathrm{IFP}_{P;x}\varphi(P,x,y)](x) \leftrightarrow [\mathrm{IFP}_{Q;x,y}\psi(Q,x,y)](x,y)$$

Proof　For each y, let

$$P_0(y) = \emptyset, \quad P_1(y) = \{x: \varphi(P_0,x,y)\}, \quad P_2(y) = \{x: \varphi(P_1,x,y)\}, \ldots$$

be the approximations to $\mathrm{IFP}_{P;x}\varphi(P,x,y)$, and let

$$Q_0 = \emptyset, \quad Q_1 = \{(x,y): \varphi(Q_0,x,y)\}, \quad Q_2 = \{(x,y): \varphi(Q_1,x,y)\}, \ldots$$

be the approximations to $\mathrm{IFP}_{Q;x,y}\varphi(Q,x,y)$. (Here (x,y) is the concatenation of tuples rather than a pair of tuples.) It suffices to check that each $P_i(y) = \{x: Q_i(x,y)\}$. The case $i = 0$ is trivial. Further,

x belongs to $P_{i+1}(y) \leftrightarrow \varphi(P_i(y),x,y) \leftrightarrow$ (by the induction hypothesis)

$\varphi(\{x: Q_i(x,y)\},x,y) \leftrightarrow \psi(Q_i,x,y) \leftrightarrow (x,y)$ belongs to Q_{i+1}.　　■

To formulate a similar claim for FO + LFP, replace the assumption that $\varphi(P,x,y) = [P(x)$ or $\varphi_0(P,x,y)]$ by the assumption that $\varphi(P,x,y)$ is positive in P.

REMARK　Theorem 1.13 can be strengthened further: φ can be taken to be a boolean combinaton of existential first-order formulas (11).

REMARK　The well-known zero-one law for first-order logic extends to inductive fixed-point logic (10).

SECTION 7. INVARIANT GLOBAL RELATIONS

We saw above that in the case of structures with built-in linear order there are nice logics which capture polynomial time. In this section we discuss the problem of capturing polynomial time in the general case. The problem was posed (in slightly different terms) in (12b) and discussed in (29).

DEFINITION 1.13   An r-ary global relation ρ of some signature σ is *abstract* if for every isomorphism f from a σ-structure S onto a σ-structure T and all elements $x_1, \ldots, x_r$ of S,

$$\rho^S(x_1, \ldots, x_r) \leftrightarrow \rho^T(fx_1, \ldots, fx_r).$$

A logic capturing polynomial time is supposed to express exactly polynomial time computable abstract global relations.[1]

REMARK   Some polynomial time complete abstract properties are expressible in FO + LFP (45). But the abstract property that the universe is of even cardinality is not expressible in FO + LFP (12b). In virtue of Theorem 1.11 in Section 6, that abstract property is not expressible in FO + IFP.

We do not believe that there is a reasonable logic that captures polynomial time. To express our feeling in the form of a formal conjecture, we adapt the notion of logical systems (18) to our purpose.

DEFINITION 1.14   A *logic L* is a pair (SEN, SAT) satisfying the following requirements. SEN is a function that associates with every finite signature σ a recursive set SEN(σ) whose elements are called *L-sentences* of signature σ. SAT is a function that associates with every finite signature σ a recursive subset SAT(σ) of $\{(S, \varphi): S$ is a finite first-order σ-structure and φ is an L-sentence of signature $\sigma\}$ such that if structures S and S' are isomorphic and (S, φ) belongs to SAT(σ) then (S', φ) belongs to SAT(σ) as well. If (S, φ) belongs to some SAT(σ), we say that S *satisfies* φ.

DEFINITION 1.15   If L is a logic and φ is an L-sentence of some signature σ, then MOD(φ) be the set of σ-structures satisfying φ.

DEFINITION 1.16   A logic L *captures* polynomial time if:

1. For every L-sentence φ, the class MOD(φ) is polynomial time recognizable; moreover, for every σ there is a Turing machine M that, given an L-sentence

---

[1]A logic capturing partial (not necessarily defined on all structures of the appropriate signature) recursive abstract global relations was designed in (12a).

φ of signature σ, produces a polynomial time bounded Turing machine $M(\varphi)$ that recognizes $\text{MOD}(\varphi)$.

2. For every polynomial time recognizable class K of structures of some signature σ, if K is closed under isomorphisms then there is an L-sentence φ of signature σ such that $\text{MOD}(\varphi) = K$.

REMARK   In this section, a polynomial time bounded Turing machine can be viewed as a pair (T,p) where T is a Turing machine and p is a polynomial with integer coefficients; (T,p) accepts an input w of T if T accepts w within $p(|w|)$ steps.

CONJECTURE   There is no logic that captures polynomial time.

Our adaptation of the notion of logics in (18) includes some alterations. In particular, we consider only finite signatures and finite structures, and require the recursivity of sets $\text{SEN}(\sigma)$ and $\text{SAT}(\sigma)$. Let $R1$ and $R2$ be the two recursivity requirements, respectively.

CLAIM 1   Waiving the recursivity requirements in Definition 1.14 falsifies the conjecture.

Proof   Call a Turing machine M σ-appropriate if (a) it is able to take σ-structures as inputs, and (b) the class $\{S: S$ is a σ-structure and M accepts $S\}$ is closed under isomorphisms. Define $L = (\text{SEN}, \text{SAT})$ where each $\text{SEN}(\sigma)$ consists of all σ-appropriate Turing machines, and each $\text{SAT}(\sigma)$ consists of all pairs (S,M) such that S is a σ-structure and M is a σ-appropriate Turing machine that accepts S. It is easy to see that L is a logic in the liberalized sense and L captures polynomial time.   ■

We could omit the second recursivity requirement $R2$ in Definition 1.14 because it follows from the condition of capturing polynomial time, but we consider it necessary in general and it complements $R1$ in the following sense (7). Suppose that $L = (\text{SEN}, \text{SAT})$ satisfies the requirements of Definition 1.14 except for $R1$ and $R2$, and suppose that the sets $\text{SEN}(\sigma)$ are countable. Fix one-to-one mappings f_σ from $\text{SEN}(\sigma)$ onto the set of natural numbers and rename every σ-sentence φ as the number $f_\sigma(\varphi)$. The resulting system is similar to L and satisfies $R1$.

The definition of logics may be justifiably tightened in many ways. One may require that every embedding $f: \sigma \rightarrow \sigma'$, taking any predicate (respectively function) symbol to a predicate (respectively function) symbol of the same or greater arity, gives rise to a recursive embedding of $\text{SEN}(\sigma)$ to $\text{SEN}(\sigma')$; that the functions SEN and SAT themselves are recursive (when signatures are presented by codes if necessary); that the signature of a sentence is computable from the sentence; that all recursivity conditions are replaced by corresponding polynomial time conditions; etc. Similarly, the notion of capturing polynomial time can be justifiably tightened in many ways. For example, one may require that the existence of a polynomial time bounded Turing machines M that, given (the code of) an arbitrary sentence φ, produces a Turing machine recognizing φ. We have chosen our definitions taking into account the negative character of the conjecture. Notice however the necessity of the requirement of the existence of machines M in clause (a) of Definition 1.16.

CLAIM 2 Waiving the requirement of the existence of machines M in Definition 1.16 falsifies the conjecture.

Proof (7) Let SEN(σ) comprise polynomial time bounded Turing machines able to take σ-structures as inputs. Call such a machine M symmetric with respect to n if for every pair $(S1, S2)$ of isomorphic σ-structures of cardinality at most n, M accepts $S1$ if and only if it accepts $S2$. Given a σ-structure S of cardinality n and a machine M in SEN(σ), put (S, M) into SAT(σ) if M is symmetric with respect to n and M accepts S. Notice that each MOD(M) is closed under isomorphisms. The pair (SEN, SAT) is a logic capturing polynomial time in the liberalized sense. ∎

REMARK The conjecture is closely related to an open question of Chandra and Harel [(12b) Section 5]. They ask (in somewhat different words) whether there is a recursive set T of polynomial time bounded Turing machines such that for every σ and every polynomial time recognizable class K of σ-structures, K is closed under isomorphisms if and only if it is the collection of structures accepted by some machine in T. Also, see the paper (5) of Arvind and Biswas in connection with the conjecture.

The conjecture can be slightly simplified by restricting the attention to graphs.

DEFINITION 1.17 A *graph logic L* is a pair (SEN, SAT) satisfying the following requirements. SEN is a recursive set whose elements are called *L-sentences*. SAT is a recursive subset of $\{(S, \varphi): S$ is a finite graph and φ is an L-sentence$\}$ such that if graphs S and S' are isomorphic and (S, φ) belongs to SAT then (S', φ) belongs to SAT as well. If (S, φ) belongs to some SAT, we say that S *satisfies* φ.

DEFINITION 1.18 If L is a graph logic and φ is an L-sentence, then MOD(φ) is the set of σ-structures satisfying φ.

DEFINITION 1.19   A graph logic L *captures* polynomial time if:

1. For every L-sentence φ, the class $\text{MOD}(\varphi)$ is polynomial time recognizable; moreover, there is a Turing machine M that, given an L-sentence φ, produces a polynomial time bounded Turing machine $M(\varphi)$ that recognizes $\text{MOD}(\varphi)$.
2. For every polynomial time recognizable class K of graphs, if K is closed under isomorphisms then there is an L-sentence φ with $\text{MOD}(\varphi) = K$.

THEOREM 1.14   The following statements are equivalent.

1. There is a logic that captures polynomial time.
2. There is a graph logic that captures polynomial time.

Proof   The implication (1) $\rightarrow$ (2) is obvious. To prove the other implication, we use the well-known fact that an arbitrary structure S can be efficiently represented by a graph $G(S)$ in such a way that two structures $S1$ and $S2$ of the same signature are isomorphic if and only if the graphs $G(S1)$ and $G(S2)$ are isomorphic. Moreover, there is a polynomial time Turing machine that, given the standard encoding of an arbitrary structure S, produces the desired graph $G(S)$. If a graph logic $L = (\text{SEN}, \text{SAT})$ captures polynomial time, define $L' = (\text{SEN}', \text{SAT}')$ where for each σ, $\text{SEN}'(\sigma) = \text{SEN}$ and $\text{SAT}'(\sigma) = \{(S, \varphi): S$ is a σ-structure and $G(S)$ satisfies $\varphi\}$. Obviously, L' captures polynomial time. ∎

Let us notice that both the special case, when the presence of linear order is assumed, and the general case, when the presence of linear order is not assumed, are important. As an input for a computing device, a structure should be represented in some way. A representation itself can be viewed as a structure, and in that richer structure a certain ordering of elements is usually definable. On the other hand, one is often interested in properties of structures that are independent of representaton; let us call such properties invariant. To simplify somewhat the situation, let us view ordered versions of a given structure S as representations of S.

One way to ensure the invariance of a property of structures is to express the property in a logic that does not distinguish between different representations. For example, FO + LFP sentences express only invariant properties. There is another approach which is *a priori* more promising: allow linear order and concentrate on those properties that do not depend on order. In the rest of this section, interpretations of the binary predicate symbol $<$ are restricted to linear orders. If the signature of a structure S contains $<$ then S will be called *ordered*, otherwise it will be called *unordered*. If σ is a signature without $<$, S is a structure of signature $\sigma \cup \{<\}$ and S_0 is the reduct of S to σ, we will say that S_0 is the *unordered version* of S, and S is an *ordered version* of S_0, and any ordered version of S_0 is a *reordering* of S.

DEFINITION 1.20   An r-ary global relation ρ of some signature $\sigma \cup \{<\}$ is *invariant on* a structure S of signature $\sigma \cup \{<\}$ if for every reordering T of S, $\rho^S(x) \leftrightarrow \rho^T(x)$. The global relation ρ is *invariant* if it is abstract and invariant on every structure of signature $\sigma \cup \{<\}$.

It is easy to see that ρ is invariant if and only if the boolean value of $\rho^S(x)$ depends only on the isomorphism type of $\langle S_0, x \rangle$ where S_0 is the unordered version of S.

The definition of invariant global relation ρ generalizes in a natural way to the case when ρ is K-global where K is an arbitrary class of ordered structures of some signature $\sigma \cup \{<\}$ closed under isomorphisms and reorderings. Notice that an algorithm computing an invariant K-global relation may use the given ordering.

Example   Given a group with a linear order, the following algorithm computes the center of the group:

```
C := ø;
for x := (the first element) to (the last element) do
begin
   flag := 1;
   for y := (the first element) to (the last element) do
      if x·y ≠ y·x then flag := 0;
   if flag = 1 then C := C∪{x}
end
```

THEOREM 1.15   The decision problem whether a given first-order sentence with possible occurrences of $<$ yields an invariant global relation, is undecidable.

Proof   Let α range over first-order sentences without occurrences of $<$. The validity of α on all finite structures is undecidable (64), hence the validity of α on all finite structures with at least two elements is undecidable. Let P be a unary predicate symbol that does not occur in α, and let β be a first-order sentence of signature $\{P, <\}$ asserting that $<$ is a linear order and that the first element in that order belongs to P whereas the last element does not. Then α is valid on all finite structures with at least two elements if and only if the disjunction $(\alpha$ or $\beta)$ is invariant.   ∎

REMARK   Theorem 1.15 may be strengthened by means of different syntactic requirements on the given first-order formula: use numerous known strengthenings of Trakhtenbrot's theorem.

THEOREM 1.16   There is a first-order sentence φ such that the decision problem whether φ is invariant on a given ordered structure, is coNP complete.

Proof   We consider a restriction of the 3-colorability problem which is a known NP complete problem (25). Let H be the graph with vertices 0, 1, 2, 3 and the edges $\{0,1\}$, $\{1,2\}$, $\{2,3\}$, $\{3,0\}$ and $\{0,2\}$; H is a cycle of length 4 plus one additional edge. H is 3-colorable, and every 3-coloring of H assigns the same color to vertices 1 and 3. Let Γ be the set of graphs that include H as a component. It is assumed—with respect to the proviso of Section 1—that the vertices of any member of Γ form an initial segment of natural numbers. It is easy to see that the restriction of 3-colorability problem to Γ is NP complete. For every graph G in Γ let G^* be the enrichment of G by means of the natural order of vertices.

The desired φ speaks about ordered graphs. It asserts that there are vertices $x < y$ such that the segments $\{v: v < x\}$, $\{v: x \le v < y\}$ and $\{v: y \le v\}$ constitute a 3-coloring. It suffices to prove that an arbitrary member G of Γ is 3-colorable if and only if φ is not invariant on G^*. If G is not 3-colorable then φ fails on any ordered version of G and, therefore, is invariant on G^*.

Suppose G is 3-colorable. Fix a 3-coloring of G. Let $G1$ be any ordered version of G where the vertices of color 1 form an initial segment and the vertices of color 3 form a final segment. Let $G2$ be an ordered version of G where vertex 1 is the first and vertex 3 is the last. It is easy to see that φ holds on $G1$ and fails on $G2$; hence G is not invariant on G^*.   ■

SECTION 8.   IS THERE A LOGIC FOR NP∩coNP or R?

We give some evidence that no logic captures NP∩coNP global relations or exactly R (random polynomial time recognizable) global relations. The argument is an elaboration of a remark in (28) and uses Sipser's result (59) that each of the two classes fails to have a complete problem (with respect to polynomial time reductions) under an appropriate oracle. The notion of logics was defined in the previous section. In connection with this section see a recent paper of Hartmanis and Immerman (40).

First we consider class NP∩coNP. Nondeterministic Turing machines M, N and a polynomial f will be said to *witness* that a class K of structures of some signature σ is NP∩coNP if for every n and every σ-structure S of cardinality n, (i) S belongs to K if and only if M accepts S within time $f(n)$, and (ii) S does not belong to K if and only if N accepts S within time $f(n)$.

DEFINITION 1.21   A logic L *captures* NP∩coNP if:

1. For each L-sentence φ, the class $\mathrm{MOD}(\varphi)$ is $\mathrm{NP} \cap \mathrm{coNP}$; moreover, for every signature σ there is a Turing machine that, given an L-sentence φ of signature σ, produces a triple (M, N, f) witnessing that $\mathrm{MOD}(\varphi)$ is $\mathrm{NP} \cap \mathrm{coNP}$; and

2. Every $\mathrm{NP} \cap \mathrm{coNP}$ class of structures of a fixed signature is definable by an L-sentence.

THEOREM 1.17   If a logic L captures $\mathrm{NP} \cap \mathrm{coNP}$ then $\mathrm{NP} \cap \mathrm{coNP}$ has a complete problem with respect to polynomial time reducibility.

Proof   Let σ be a signature comprising one unary predicate symbol. Fix a Turing machine A that generates all L-sentences of signature σ, and a Turing machine B that, given an L-sentence φ of signature σ, generates a triple witnessing that $\mathrm{MOD}(\varphi)$ is $\mathrm{NP} \cap \mathrm{coNP}$. Let Q be the set of tuples $(\alpha,\ \varphi,\ \beta,\ M,\ N,\ f,\ S,\ 1^{f(n)})$ such that (i) α is a computation of A, φ is an L-sentence generated by α, β is the computation of B on φ, (M, N, f) is the output of β, S is a σ-structure, n is the cardinality of S, $1^{f(n)}$ is a string of 1's of length n, and (ii) S satisfies φ.

The condition (i) is polynomial time checkable. The condition (ii) is NP (respectively coNP): guess a computation of M (respectively N) on S of length $f(n)$ and verify that the computation is accepting. Thus the decision problem for Q is $\mathrm{NP} \cap \mathrm{coNP}$. To show that this decision problem is $\mathrm{NP} \cap \mathrm{coNP}$ hard, we reduce to Q the decision problem for an arbitrary $\mathrm{NP} \cap \mathrm{coNP}$ class X of binary words. If w is a binary word $\alpha_1 \ldots \alpha_n$ let S_w be the σ-structure with universe $\{0, 1, \ldots, n\}$ and relation $\{i: \alpha_i = 1\}$. (The universe contains $n + 1$ elements because it should be nonempty whereas n may be equal to 0.) Since L captures $\mathrm{NP} \cap \mathrm{coNP}$, there is an L-sentence φ with $\mathrm{MOD}(\varphi) = \{S_w: w \varepsilon X\}$. Let α be a computation of A that outputs φ, β be the computation of B on φ, and (M, N, f) be the output of β. Obviously, $w \varepsilon X$ iff $S_w \varepsilon \mathrm{MOD}(\varphi)$ iff $(\alpha,\ \varphi,\ \beta,\ M,\ N,\ f,\ S_w,\ 1^{f(n+1)})$ belongs to Q.   ∎

Theorem 1.17 contrasts with Sipser's result (59) that, relative to some oracle Δ, $\mathrm{NP} \cap \mathrm{coNP}$ does not possess a complete problem. (Certainly no logic captures $\mathrm{NP} \cap \mathrm{coNP}$ under the oracle Δ because the proof of Theorem 1.17 relativizes.) We conjecture that if some logic captures $\mathrm{NP} \cap \mathrm{coNP}$ then something drastic happens like $\mathrm{NP} \cap \mathrm{coNP} = P$ or $\mathrm{NP} = \mathrm{coNP}$. It may be desirable to restrict further the notion of a logic capturing $\mathrm{NP} \cap \mathrm{coNP}$. For example, one may request that L-sentences are polynomial time recognizable.

REMARK   The converse of Theorem 1.17 is true to the extent that, given an $\mathrm{NP} \cap \mathrm{coNP}$ complete problem Q, one can construct a set of "sentences" and a satisfaction relation that capture $\mathrm{NP} \cap \mathrm{coNP}$. Define sentences of signature σ as triples (M, f, σ) where M is a deterministic Turing machine able to take σ-

structures as inputs, and f is a polynomial. Say that a σ-structure S of cardinality n satisfies $\varphi = (M, f, \sigma)$ if M halts on inputs S within time $f(n)$, and the result $M(S)$ belongs to Q.

Definition 1.21 and Theorem 1.17 generalize to some other classes with well defined witnesses. We turn now to random polynomial time. Recall that a set K of strings in an alphabet Σ is R if and only if there are a deterministic Turing machine M and polynomials f, g such that for every n and every string $s \varepsilon \Sigma^*$ of length n the following are equivalent:

1. The string s belongs to K,
2. There is a string t in $\{0, 1\}^{g(n)}$ such that M accepts the pair (s, t) within time $f(n)$, and
3. For at least one half of strings t in $\{0, 1\}^{g(n)}$, M accepts the pair (s, t) within time $f(n)$.

We say that (M, f, g) *witnesses* that K belongs to R. Without loss of generality, we may suppose that $fn \geq gn$ for all n. The definition obviously generalizes to the case when K is a class of structures of a fixed signature.

DEFINITION 1.22   A logic L *captures* R if:

1. For each L-sentence φ, $\text{MOD}(\varphi)$ is R; moreover, for every signature σ there is a Turing machine that, given an L-sentence φ of signature σ, produces a triple (M, f, g) witnessing that $\{S: S \text{ satisfies } \varphi\}$ is R; and
2. Every R class of structures of a fixed signature is definable by an L-sentence.

THEOREM 1.18   If a logic L captures R then R has a complete problem with respect to polynomial time reducibility.

Proof   Similar to that of Theorem 1.17.   ∎

Theorem 1.18 contrasts with Sipser's result (59) that, relative to some oracle, there is no complete problem for R with respect to polynomial time reducibility.

SECTION 9.   MISCELLANY

9.1   Sequences of Bounded-Depth Circuits

We suppose here that signatures comprise only predicate symbols, and boolean circuits have unique output gates. Recall that, according to the proviso of Section 1, the universes of structures are proper initial segments of natural numbers.

DEFINITION 1.23   A boolean circuit C is *formatted* with respect to a signature σ and a positive integer n if input gates of C are labeled by sentences $Q(i_1, \ldots, i_r)$ where Q belongs to σ, r is the arity of Q, and every $i_p < n$. (Every input gate has exactly one label; hence, the number of input gates is bounded by the number of sentences $Q(i_1, \ldots, i_r)$.)

DEFINITION 1.24   A circuit C, formatted with respect to σ and n, *accepts* a σ-structure S of cardinality n if C outputs 1 when the input gates of C are set with respect to S (an input gate labeled $Q(i_1, \ldots, i_r)$ gets value 1 if S satisfies $Q(i_1, \ldots, i_r)$, and value 0 otherwise).

DEFINITION 1.25   A class K of σ-structures is *definable* by a sequence of circuits $C_1, C_2, \ldots$ if every C_n can be formatted with respect to σ and n in such a way that the formatted circuit accepts a σ-structure S of cardinality n if and only if S belongs to K.

LEMMA 1.5   Let σ be a signature, φ be a first-order σ-sentence, and n be a positive natural number. There is a circuit C_n formatted with respect to σ and n in such a way that the depth of C_n is the logical depth of φ, and C_n accepts a σ-structure S of cardinality n if and only if S satisfies φ.

Proof   Let σ_n be the extension of σ by individual constants $0, 1, \ldots, n-1$. By induction, turn any sentence α, whose signature is included into σ_n, into a formatted circuit α_n. If α is atomic then α_n is the circuit comprising one gate labeled α. The cases of conjunction, disjunction and negation are obvious. If α is $\exists x \beta(x)$ (respectively $\forall x \beta(x)$) then join the circuits $\beta(0)_n, \beta(1)_n, \ldots, \beta(n-1)_n$ by an additional OR (respectively AND) gate. Finally, φ_n is the desired C_n. ∎

   The sequence of circuits, constructed in the previous paragraph, is very uniform. In particular, it is log-space constructible i.e. there is a log-space bounded Turing machine that, given the unary notation for n, produces (the standard code for) C_n.

   Let L_0 be a logic that captures exactly log-space recognizable global relations of the empty vocabulary. L_0 can be the fragment of logic FO + DTC + < (see Section 3) whose formulas contain no individual constants, no function symbols and no predicate symbols except for <. L_0 can be the calculus of primitive recursive functions of the empty vocabulary (see Section 6); in this case the formulas are equations $t = 0$. Let FO + L_0 be the extension of first-order logic by L_0 whose formulas are built from first-order formulas and formulas in L_0 by first-order means (boolean connectives and quantifiers $\forall, \exists$); the global function semantics for FO + L_0 is obvious.

THEOREM 1.19   (35)   Let K be a class of structures of some signature σ. The following are equivalent:

1. K is definable by a log-space constructible sequence of circuits of bounded depth,
2. K is definable by a sentence in FO $+ L_0$.   ■

We skip the proof here. The theorem generalizes for many other complexity classes (35).

Logic FO $+ L_0$ and many other extensions of first-order logic, considered above, were specially tailored to capture respective complexity classes. Logic FO $+ L_0$ is the most modest of these extensions. An interesting question arises whether first-order logic itself captures any complexity class. Well, the answer to this question depends on the definition of complexity classes. The problem of the definition of complexity classes is a deep one, and we are not going to tackle it here. Let us only mention that Denenberg, Gurevich, and Shelah (17) have characterized first-order definable sequences of bounded-depth circuits by means of symmetry and uniformity conditions.

9.2   A Note on Topology on Finite Sets

There is a definite analogy between (i) classes of unary global relations definable by sequences of circuits of bounded depth and polynomially bounded size, and (ii) Borel subsets of the Cantor discontinuum. This analogy was exploited by Sipser in (60). Reading Ajtai's paper (3), we found it useful to think in terms of Borel subsets of finite topological spaces. The definition of Borel subsets of finite topological spaces is given in this subsection.

Recall that a topology is T_1 (50) if all one-point subsets are closed; we are not interested here in topologies that are not T_1. Every finite T_1 topological space is discrete, i.e., every subset is both closed and open. Thus, the theory of finite T_1 topological spaces seems to be quite trivial. However, one may ask how many intersections and unions does it take to express a given point-set in terms of sub-basic open sets. This leads to a generalization of the Borel hierarchy to finite topological spaces.

DEFINITION 1.26 X_n is the topological space whose points are subsets of $\{0, 1, \ldots, n-1\}$ and whose sub-basis comprises the n point-sets $\{P : i \in P\}$.

The analogous definition with the set ω of natural numbers instead of $\{0, 1, \ldots, n-1\}$ results in a topological space X_ω homeomorphic to the Cantor Discontinuum [(50), §3, IX]. Borel subsets of X_ω form the closure of the sub-basis under complements, countable intersections and countable unions. This suggests the following:

DEFINITION 1.27   A subset of X_n is Borel of *level* 0 if it is sub-basic. It is Borel of *level d*, where $d > 0$, if it is the intersection of at most n Borel sets of levels less than d, or the union of at most n Borel sets of levels less than d, or the complement of a Borel set of a level less than d.

There is an obvious connection between Borel point-sets and boolean circuits with unique output gates. Suppose that C is a circuit with n input gates labeled by integers $0, \ldots, n-1$. In the obvious way, the input of C represents a point in X_n. C is said to *accept* a point P if the corresponding output is 1. C is said to *recognize* the set $\{P: C$ accepts $P\}$.

CLAIM 1   Let A be a subset of X_n, and d be a natural number. The following are equivalent:

1. F is Borel of level d,
2. There is a circuit C with n input gates labeled by integers $0, \ldots, n-1$ such that the depth of C is at most d, the fan-in of C-gates is bounded by n, and C recognizes A.

Proof   is clear.   ■

DEFINITION 1.28   A *global point-set* π assigns a subset of X_n to each X_n. If there is a natural number d such that the specification of π on each X_n is Borel of level d then π is *Borel* (of level d).

CLAIM 2   The following are equivalent:

1. π is Borel,
2. There is a bounded-depth polynomially-bounded-size sequence of circuits C_n such that each C_n recognizes the specialization of π on X_n.

Proof   is clear.   ■

Let P be a unary predicate symbol. A first-order sentence $\varphi(P)$ in signature $\{P\}$ defines a Borel global point-set $\{P: \varphi(P)\}$ of level d where d is the logical depth of $\varphi(P)$. First-order definable point-set π are symmetric in the following sense: if P_1 and P_2 are subsets of X_n of the same cardinality then P_1 belongs to is the specialization of π on X_n if and only if P_2 does. Some Borel global point-sets are symmetric in that sense but not first-order definable (17, 22).

PART 2. DYNAMIC STRUCTURES WITH BOUNDED RESOURCES

One finds a great many formal languages in computer science: programming languages, query languages, etc. It is natural for a logician to ask what structures are suited to model those formal languages. For example, what are models for Pascal? Of course, it is not necessary to start with formal languages. One can ask what structures are appropriate to formalize machines, databases and other objects of interest in computer science. We adopt the unspoken assumption of mathematicians that in principle there are appropriate structures; the problem is to find them.

SECTION 10. DYNAMIC STRUCTURES WITH BOUNDED RESOURCES, AND TURING'S THESIS

This section develops the ideas presented first in technical report (31) and is sort of an extended abstract for (34). I am thankful to Kit Fine for his comments on the report, and to Andreas Blass for many useful discussions.

10.1 Abstract Machines with Bounded Resources

The popular and useful abstraction of unbounded resources may be inappropriate under certain circumstances. For example, one may be reluctant to idealize his/ her computer as a machine with unbounded memory if the computer keeps running out of memory all the time.

In (31) and (33) we discussed a new kind of abstract machines, called dynamic structures or dynamic algebras, whose resources may be bounded. Sometimes it is easier to express one's arguments in a discussion. Please allow me the liberty of introducing an opponent (a skeptical graduate student).

OBJECTION 1   There is already a very well worked out formalization of machines with bounded resources. I mean finite state machines. Your dynamic structures with bounded resources are finite state machines too, aren't they?

Answer   Yes, dynamic structures with bounded resources are finite state machines. But their theory does not reduce to the classical theory of finite state machines because the number of states may be overwhelming. Dynamic structure with bounded resources may capture the behavior of real computers (like PDP-11 or Macintosh) or model real programming languages (like Pascal or Small-talk). It is not feasible to draw the diagram or to write down the transition table (or a regular expression) for such a finite state machine.

OBJECTION 2 I do not understand how a machine with bounded resources can model Pascal. Consider a Pascal program for computing factorials. A machine with unbounded resources is needed to provide an operational meaning to the program. Every machine with bounded resources fails to compute the factorial of some sufficiently large integer; it cannot give an adequate operational meaning to the program.

Answer A good point. The meaning will be given by a family of finite machines (in the same way as the meaning of a first-order formula is given by a family of first-order structures). A family of finite Pascal machines will be briefly sketched below. Here is a simpler example of a family: bounded-tape versions of a given Turing machine T with special end-of-tape marks.

OBJECTION 3 Let me ignore the end-of-tape marks (I guess that bounded-tape versions of T without end-of-tape marks form a legitimate family too). Then the computation of any bounded-tape version of T is an initial segment of the computation of T, and the cut-off point is irrelevant to the meaning of the program. I would prefer to consider the computation of T itself rather than a pretty arbitrary collection of initial segments of the computation.

Answer Yes, in many cases, a machine with unbounded resources gives a cleaner operational semantics. But not always. The end-of-tape marks were there for a reason. Machines with bounded resources may know their resources and utilize this knowledge. A program for bounded-tape machines may use the end-of-tape mark for different purposes; for example, the end-of-tape mark may be used for dividing the tape equally into a left and a right part and executing two different processes in a time-sharing fashion. More convincing examples of how abstract machines with bounded resources may use their knowledge of bounded resources come from real life. Think about operating systems. In particular, think about an operating system which may run on many computers and which starts with an inventory of the available resources. Of course, this program (the operating system) can be modelled by a machine with unbounded resources, but this is not necessarily the best way to provide an operational semantics to the program.

10.2 Dynamic Structures

The usual mathematical structures, and in particular first-order structures, are static. They do not change in time. Mathematicians tend to formalize dynamic situations in a static way. Given a dynamic process in an n-dimensional space, a mathematician introduces an additional dimension for time and studies the resulting $(n + 1)$-dimensional body which represents all states of the original n-dimensional process at once.

Typical objects of computer science—machines, databases—are dynamic. They evolve in time. Of course, the same trick of representing all states at once can be used. This is exactly what you do when you draw the diagram of a finite automaton. Often, the trick does not work well. We believe that the difficulties are related to the overwhelming complexity of computing processes (versus, say, abstracted physical processes). There is no simple system of equations describing the behavior of a large time-sharing computer system. On the other hand, computing processes often have a certain simplicity in them: they evolve in discrete time and the states as well as atomic transitions are relatively simple.

The dynamic structure approach attempts to utilize the simple features of computing processes. A dynamic structure is a static structure (the initial configuration of the dynamic structure) evolving in discrete time with respect to specified transition rules. To specify a dynamic structure one needs to specify a static structure and transition rules.

The notion of dynamic structure may strike as an old news. There are similar notions in the literature; let me mention only transition systems in Gordon Plotkin's report (55). We see the main novelty in the intended use of dynamic structures. The configuration of discourse is going to play a greater role than the set of all configurations; from that point of view logic of dynamic structures is similar to temporal logic. Configurations are full-fledged static structures which have usually several universes. Here are some relevant questions. Do the universes change? Can new universes appear? Can old universes disappear? Does the signature change? What is the form of transition rules? Some other important notions are: bounded resources, families of dynamic structures, the dynamic structure of discourse.

Only special classes of static structures are defined formally in mathematical logic: usual first-order structures, many-sorted first-order structures, standard second-order structures, nonstandard second-order structures, etc. The general notion of static structures remains informal. Similarly, we leave the general notions of dynamic structures informal and define formally only special classes of dynamic structures. The notion of a family of dynamic structures is left informal too. We require however that all members of a family have the same transition rules.

To have a nontrivial example of a dynamic structure, one may formalize a modest computing device (on some level of abstraction). In connection with (33), my student, Bob Blakley, has worked out a formalization of PDP-11/04, the smallest machine using DEC's well-known PDP-11 architecture. The resulting dynamic structure is an evolving many-sorted first-order structure with static universes, static signature and transition rules of a very simple form.

Universes of the formalized PDP-11/04 are Registers $= \{R0, \ldots, R7\}$, Addresses $\subseteq \{0,1\}^{16}$, Words $= \{0,1\}^{16}$, Opcodes, etc. Elements of Registers represent the 8 registers of the computer. PDP-11/04 uses register $R7$ as the instruction pointer. Elements of Opcodes represent legal assembly-language instructions in the PDP-11/04 instruction set. The set of addresses varies from one implementation of PDP-11 to another. To reflect this fact, the extent of Addresses is not fixed in Blakley's formalization.

Many basic functions of the dynamic structure are static: arithmetical operations, the eight zero-ary functions (i.e. distinguished elements) $R1$–$R7$ of type Registers, a function Addrtranslate from Words to (Addresses $\cup$ {Error}), a function Getop from Words to Opcodes, etc. Addrtranslate converts words (elements of Words) to addresses (elements of Addresses). If a word w is an address then Addrtranslate$(w) = w$, otherwise Addrtranslate$(w) =$ Error. The analog of Addrtranslate for some other computers may be more complicated; one reason is that words may be longer than addresses.

Some dynamic basic functions of the formalized PDP-11 are

Regcontents: Registers $\to$ Words,
Contents: Addresses $\to$ Words,
Currentop, a distinguished element of Opcodes.

The following transition rule is self-explanatory:

Currentop $\leftarrow$ Getop(Contents(Addrtranslate(Regcontents($R7$)))).

REMARK   The idea of bounded resources and the idea of dynamic character are independent. One can study infinite static structures, finite static structures, dynamic structures with unbounded resources, and dynamic structures with bounded resources.

10.3   Turing's Thesis and Finite Dynamic Structures

A strong form of Turing's thesis states that every computing device can be simulated by an appropriate Turing machine (24). The thesis loses some appeal if one restricts attention to computing devices with bounded resources because the resources of Turing machines are unbounded. This brings us to the question of an analog of Turing's thesis for the case of machines with bounded resources.

New thesis problem (first draft formulation).   Define a modest class U (for 'universal') of abstract machines with bounded resources such that every computing device with bounded resources can be closely simulated by a U-machine of comparable specification and information sizes, and every family of computing devices with bounded resources can be appropriately simulated by a family of U-machines.

We speak about a modest class, close simulations and comparable sizes in order to exclude some unsatisfactory solutions. Let us explain that.

The computing devices in question are supposed to be real devices satisfying some minimal assumptions. (Actually, it is a little more complicated. We should be talking about a computing device and a fixed level of abstraction, of omitting details.) A part of the desired solution is that U-machines are dynamic structures. This is not a complete solution. First, the notion of dynamic structures was left informal. Second, dynamic structures may be used as virtual machines (for example, to model higher level programming languages) and therefore may be more complex than needed for the thesis. *The desired class U should be well-defined and as simple as possible.*

It is reasonable to assume that a computing device with bounded resources can be step-by-step simulated by a finite state transducer. (A finite state transducer is a finite automaton with output; a simulation is step-by-step if every step of the simulated machine corresponds to one step of the simulating machine.) Even if we ignore the question of families of finite state transducers, the reduction to finite state transducers should be treated with caution: the transition table of the simulating transducer may be much bigger than the description of the simulated device. *The specification size of the simulating machine should be severely bounded in terms of the specification size of the simulated machine.*

It would also be unsatisfactory if the number of states of the simulating machine too greatly exceeds the number of states of the simulated machine. The logarithm of number of states can be called the information size (9). *Thus, the information size of the simulating machine should be severely bounded in terms of the information size of the simulated machine.*

Bounded-tape versions of Turing machines with end-of-tape marks constitute one possible solution for the new thesis problem (31). An argument similar to Turing's informal proof of his thesis (66) establishes that for every computing device D with bounded resources there is an appropriate bounded-tape Turing machine that simulates D. This solution is unsatisfactory even if we put aside the question of the specification and information sizes: the simulations may be too complex and indirect. (Imagine, for example, that D is Apple's Macintosh in any of its incarnations.)

REMARK   One may argue that Turing's thesis itself has the same drawback. We agree; Turing machines are clumsy simulators. But who said that Turing's thesis cannot be improved? An early improvement of Turing's thesis was worked out by Kolmogoroff and Uspenski (48). So-called random access machines (1) are very popular. Very interesting machines were introduced by Schoenhage (58).

Which simulations should be permissible? Step-by-step simulations are ideal. Are they too restrictive? Recall that, in the case of machines with unbounded resources, a simulation is called real-time if one step of the simulated machine corresponds to at most c steps of the simulating machine where c is a constant. One can adapt this definition to the case of machines with bounded resources by imposing a restriction on the constant c in terms of the specification and information sizes of the simulated machine. Then one can require that *only real-time simulations are permissible*.

In (34) we intend to discuss more interesting solutions for the new thesis problem: Kolmogoroff-Uspenski machines with bounded resources, Schoenhage machines with bounded resources, random access machines with bounded resources and the solution proposed in (33). Andreas Blass and the author continue to work on the problem (9); the joint work has greatly influenced this section.

SECTION 11. MODELS FOR PASCAL

This section can be read independently.

11.1 Preliminaries

Imagine that you read a Pascal program and come across an assignment $x := x$. What a silly thing to write, you may think. The assignment is obviously superfluous. Or is it there for a reason? Maybe it appears in the definition of a function procedure x in order to trigger the side effects of procedure x? You check and find out that x is a variable of type INTEGER. If there were several processes, then the purpose of the assignment could be related to synchronization or claiming a shared variable. But no, this is standard Pascal with only one process. You can think up some other possible effects of the assignment in some other languages, but all that seems to be irrelevant to Pascal. You become convinced that the assignment can be deleted. But the deletion changes the program and its execution somewhat. Maybe the right reason for the assignment just did not pop up in your mind. You would like to be able to *prove* that the deletion does not change your program in any essential way. Your semantics of Pascal should facilitate easy proofs of such simple facts.

Semantics of programming languages is a very rich field (some of our sources appear in the list of references). Still it seems to us that no known formal semantics is sufficiently convenient to deal with real-life imperative languages. "Unfortunately, all of the formal approaches to semantic definition require a great deal of sophisticated effort and produce a result which is impossible to read without extensive study," writes Ellis Horowitz in his *Fundamentals of Programming Languages* (43).

We would like to model programming languages, and in particular Pascal, by means of dynamic structures with bounded resources. Recall that dynamic structures are generalizations of the many-sorted static structures used in mathematical logic. They evolve in discrete time; every configuration of a dynamic structure is a static structure. To specify a dynamic structure one should specify its initial configuration and transition rules. Recall also that dynamic structures with finite resources are finite state machines (rather than potentially infinite machines), and that semantics of a programming language is supposed to be given by a family of resource-bounded dynamic structures with the same language of initial configurations and the same finite set of transition rules.

The desired Pascal models are ideal Pascal machines that directly execute Pascal programs. Many questions arise immediately. In what form should Pascal programs be given? What is the language of initial configurations? Should subsequent configurations have the same language or should the language of configurations evolve? How much can be executed in one step? How simple should the transition rules be? How should one impose a bound on the memory? And so on, and so on. This section was written with the active participation of my graduate student Jim Morris. To answer the above questions, we tried to use rich experience of real-world Pascal implementations, the insight and achievements of present-day semantics of programming languages, and analogies in classical logic.

A family of Pascal models is sketched in Section 11.2. Answering our solicitation of problems, Albert Meyer sent us a number of simple claims about Pascal including the claim about the superfluousness of the assignment $x := x$ where x is an integer variable. In Section 11.3 we sketch proofs of three of Meyer's claims in our semantics. In the final Section 11.4, we discuss in particular the question of when two Pascal programs have the same meaning.

We barely touch upon the issue of bounded resources in this section. That issue and others (possible applications of semantics of programming languages go far beyond proving simple claims about existing programming languages) will be addressed in (36) and elsewhere.

Acknowledgements   I am thankful to Jim Morris for help, to Albert Meyer for sending the problems, to Albert Meyer, David Gries, and my Michigan colleagues Andreas Blass, Bernie Galler, and others for useful discussions.

11.2   Models for Pascal

We shall outline a finite dynamic structure $M(\text{Prog})$ where Prog is a Pascal program. Some parts of $M(\text{Prog})$ depend on Prog and some do not. One can abstract the underlying machine M which is a Pascal interpreter of a sort. For the sake of brevity, we will stress here the machine-like (rather than algebraic) aspects of $M(\text{Prog})$.

The initial configuration of $M(\text{Prog})$ is a finite many-sorted static structure. Some of the universes do not depend on Prog: an interval of integer numbers, a set of real numbers, the boolean universe {true, false}, a set of identifiers, and so on. The interval of integer numbers is equipped with the usual linear order, (the restrictions of) the usual arithmetical operations, distinguished elements MAXINT and MININT. We treat relations as boolean-valued functions. The only basic function defined on identifiers is the boolean function of equality. (Thus, identifiers are seen as mere tokens. In practice the token are represented by strings of letters and digits starting with a letter. Several strings may represent the same token. It may be, for example, that two strings of length 16 or more represent the same token if they have the same initial segment of length 16.)

The program Prog is given in the form of a decorated[1] parse tree which constitutes a universe in the initial configuration. Each type declared in Prog constitutes a universe of $M(\text{Prog})$. Many universes and many basic functions of $M(\text{Prog})$ are static; they are part of the initial configuration and do not change during the evolution of $M(\text{Prog})$.

One semantical complication is related to the fact that Pascal allows the programmer to reuse identifiers and labels. The name of a procedure, a variable, etc. may not identify the corresponding declaration uniquely. In order to provide unique names to different procedures, types and variables, we adopt a common convention. If a program Prog declares a procedure $P1$ which declares a procedure $P2$ which declares a procedure $P3$ (so that the procedures $P1$, $P2$ and $P3$ are of levels 1, 2 and 3, respectively, in Prog) then we will call the procedures (and the corresponding blocks) $P1$, $P1.P2$, $P1.P2.P3$ or Prog.$P1$, Prog.$P1.P2$, Prog.$P1.P2.P3$, respectively. If a Pascal variable x is declared in a block B (so that B is the smallest block containing the declaration), it will be called $B.x$. The denotation of $B.x$ will be called a *raw variable* because in general the block B may be called recursively, and $B.x$ may have several incarnations which are variables in their own right.

The complication arising from the reuse of identifiers and labels is not serious. Whenever one comes across a node of the parse tree decorated with an identifier, it is always clear which declaration of the identifier is relevant. To reveal this information, we use a special static function *Decl* which allows us to compute the *Signification* of the identifier in question. In the case of a variable name, Signification indicates the relevant raw variable. Signification is a dynamic function which solves, in particular, the aliasing problem (63).

REMARK   One may prefer to create the types and to compute the necessary values of the Decl function during the evolution of the machine. For some languages that may be the only alternative, but Pascal programs explicitly declare

---

[1]The decoration reflects the so-called static semantics of the program.

new types and use static binding of variables, which allows us to have all types and the Decl function from the beginning. Applying the principle of separation of concerns (26), we would like to get some relatively easy syntactical things out of the way by incorporating them into the initial configuration.

Transition rules of M specify the evolution from a given state to the next one. They do not depend on the given program. Let us perform an imaginary experiment. Imagine that you (rather than a computer) execute a Pascal program. What information should you keep in mind (or on paper)? You should know where you are currently in the program and where you should return after executing a procedure. You should know which variables exist and what their values are. You may need to remember the results of different subcomputations, in particular the values of different expressions and subexpressions; etc.

To record the current position in the program, M(Prog) has a 0-ary dynamic function (i.e. a dynamic distinguished element) called the *active node*, or *control*, whose possible values are nodes of the parse tree. Usually, one transition takes the control to a child or the parent of the currently active node. The exceptions are related to goto statements and procedure calls.

To record procedure calls and where to return from them, M(Prog) has a stack that will be called the *procedure stack*. The restriction allows us to get away with a simpler procedure stack. Formally speaking, the procedure stack is function from an initial segment of natural numbers to nodes of the parse tree. When a procedure is called at some node N of the parse tree, M(PROG) "pushes" N onto the stack and the control is transferred to Signification(N). When the execution of the procedure is finished, N is "popped off" the stack and control returns to N.

To record values of Pascal variables, M uses a dynamic function V-*val*. The domain of V-val contains all raw variables. To record the values of all incarnations of $B.x$, V-val maintains a special $B.x$-stack, a function from an initial segment of natural numbers to an appropriate type augmented with an additional value 'uninitialized.' Whenever control enters the block B, the value 'uninitialized' is pushed onto the $B.x$-stack; and when the execution of B is finished, the top of the $B.x$-stack is popped off.

A dynamic function N-*val* records (on appropriate nodes of the parse tree) the results of different subcomputations, in particular the values of different expressions and subexpressions. We use "OK" to indicate the successful execution of a command. (Another *a priori* possible result of the execution of a command is "Error.") Since procedures may be called recursively, N-val assigns a stack of values to a node. Consider for example the evaluation of $(a+b) + f(c)$ in the body of a function procedure f. The value of $a+b$ is "hanged" on some node N if "$a+b$" is evaluated during the first call on f, then a new value of

$a + b$ may be "hanged" on the same node N on top of the previous values each time the recursive call on f is executed, and so on.

There is also a universe called *Space* whose elements are called *units*. In implementations, a unit may correspond to one byte, to two bytes, or even to a single bit. A static function *Size* tells how many units of Space are needed for this or that purpose, and a dynamic function *Available* tells how many units of Space are available.

That ends our incomplete sketch of M(Prog). We did not specify any transition rules, did not discuss the parameter mechanism, did not discuss how the input is provided, etc. The details—for Modula-2 rather than Pascal—will appear in (36).

Notice that we are talking about a whole class *PM* of Pascal models. What may distinguish one member of *PM* from another? The interval of integers, the set of identifiers, etc. All members have literally the same transition rules. (Transition rules are given syntactically; they are written once for all members of *PM*.) The meaning of a Pascal program Prog is given by dynamic structures M(Prog) where M varies over those members of *PM* which contain all identifiers used in Prog. This is similar to the situation in mathematical logic where the global meaning of a first-order formula is given by the local meanings of the formula on those structures whose signatures include that of the formula.

11.3   Three Simple Problems of Meyer

For expository purposes, we allowed ourselves slight modifications of the original problems. In this subsection, a program means a Pascal program.

CLAIM 1   (The case of the superfluous statement.)

Let Prog2 be the result of deleting an assignment $x := x$, where x is an INTEGER variable, in a program Prog1. Then Prog2 is equivalent to Prog1.

CLAIM 2   (The case of the superfluous variable declaration.)

Suppose that a program Prog1 contains a procedure Prog1.P with declaration

```
PROCEDURE P;
VAR x: INTEGER;
BEGIN
  . . .
END;
```

where the body does not mention x. Let Prog2 be the result of deleting the declaration of $P.x$ in Prog1. Then Prog2 is equivalent to Prog1.

Claim 3   (The case of the superfluous procedure declaration.)

Suppose that a Pascal program Prog1 has parameter-free procedures Prog1.P, Prog1.Q and Prog1.Q:P such that the declarations of P and $Q.P$ are identical and the free identifiers of $Q.P$ are not captured within Q. Let Prog2 be the result of deleting the declaration of $Q.P$ in Prog1. Then Prog2 is equivalent to Prog1.

Clarification 1   What does it mean to delete an assignment, a variable declaration or a procedure declaration? To simplify the exposition, we suppose that we are allowed to use the empty statement, the empty variable declaration and the empty procedure declaration. Then the deletions can be interpreted as replacements with appropriate empty objects. Notice that if the assignment was labelled then the new empty statement is labelled.

Clarification 2   What does it mean that two Pascal programs are equivalent? This is a complicated question; it will be addressed in the next subsection. In this subsection two programs will be called equivalent if, provided the necessary resources, they exhibit the same input-output behavior. In other words, programs Prog1 and Prog2 are equivalent if they have the same input domain D, and for every Pascal model M and every input X in D the following condition is satisfied. If M contains all identifiers that occur in Prog1 or Prog2 and if $M(\text{Prog1})$, $M(\text{Prog2})$ do not run out of memory on X then either both structures $M(\text{Prog1})$, $M(\text{Prog2})$ converge on X or both structures diverge on X, but in either case the structures produce identical outputs on X.

Claim 1 was already discussed informally. Now let us discuss informally Claims 2 and 3.

The case of the superfluous variable declaration. Even though x does not occur in the body of P, some procedure Q with a free integer variable x may be called during the execution of P. The free variable x of the procedure Q will be interpreted as $B.x$ where B is the least block that contains the appropriate declaration of Q and declares an integer variable x. Obviously, B is different from the block of P, and $B.x$ is different from $P.x$. So the deletion of the declaration of $P.x$ won't matter.

The case of the superfluous procedure declaration. Deleting $Q.P$ means that calls on $Q.P$ in Prog1 will be interpreted as calls on P in Prog2. Since P and $Q.P$ are parameterless procedures with identical declarations, the execution of P can differ from the execution of $Q.P$ only if the binding declaration of some free identifier I of P differs from the binding declaration of the free identifier I of $Q.P$, which means that Q contains a declaration of I, which means that I is captured within Q, which is impossible.

Proof Sketch for Claim 1   Given a machine M, let $Mi = M(\text{Prog}i)$ and Ti be the parse tree of $\text{Prog}i$. $T2$ is obtained from $T1$ by replacing the subtree $t1$ of an assignment $x := x$ with a single-node tree $t2$ corresponding to the empty statement. Let T be the common part of $T1$ and $T2$.

Call a state of Mi black if its active node is in T, otherwise call it red. (The terms "black" and "red" are related to the expressions "to be in the black" and "to be in the red.") Say that a state $S1$ of $M1$ and a state $S2$ of $M2$ agree if

1. the active nodes of $S1$ and $S2$ coincide (which means in particular that both states are black),
2. the procedure stacks and the V-vals coincide, and
3. the N-vals coincide on T.

Say that a sequence of states of $M1$ and a sequence of states of $M2$ agree if erasing all red states in both sequences results in two sequences of the same (finite or infinite) length where the corresponding members agree. It suffices to prove that the computations (viewed as sequences of states) of $M1$ and $M2$ on the same input agree.

In the initial states, the active nodes are the roots of the respective parse trees, and the procedure stacks and the functions V-val, N-val are empty; thus the initial states agree. Suppose that Si is a black state of Mi, and the states $S1$, $S2$ agree. Then

1. $S1$ is final (halting) if and only if $S2$ is so,
2. the successor of $S1$ is black if and only if the successor of $S2$ is so,
3. if the successors are black then they agree, and
4. if the successors are red then for neither i is Si the last black state of Mi.

It remains to prove that if the successors of $S1$, $S2$ are red then the first black state after $S1$ agrees with the first black state after $S2$. Let us see what happens when each Mi goes through the red states following Si. The active node X of Si is either the parent of $\text{root}(ti)$ or the root of the subtree of a goto statement. In either case the control leaves X without changing the N-val at X. No procedure is called or exited when Mi goes through the red states, therefore the procedure stack does not change. The V-val does not change because the only relevant raw variable is $B.x$, where B is the block of ti, and the $B.x$-stack does not change. The restriction of the N-val to T does not change because, in the absence of procedure calls, the N-val changes only at the active node. Eventually the control finds its way to the parent of $\text{root}(ti)$, and Mi arrives to some black state Si'. Obviously, $S1'$ and $S2'$ agree.

REMARK   One may wonder whether there is any difference between Si and Si'. The answer is yes. In Si, the top value of the N-val at root(ti) is "undefined"; whereas in Si', the top value of the N-val at root(ti) is "OK."

Proof Sketch for Claim 2   The proof is similar to that of Claim 1. There are only two important differences. One is related to the definition of agreeing states. The requirement that the two V-vals coincide is replaced by the requirement that the two V-vals coincide on the domain of V-vals of $M2$. The modification is necessary because the domain of V-vals of $M1$ contains an additional raw variable $P.x$.

The second difference of importance is related to the verification that the black successors of agreeing states agree. The transition may deal with an integer variable x, but—as we explained above in the informal discussion—Prog1 will never interpret that x as $P.x$. Moreover, the two programs will interpret x in the same way. What we need is a separate simple lemma that the two Decl functions coincide on the common part of the parse trees.   ∎

Proof Sketch of Claim 3   Again, the proof is similar to that of Claim 1. Let $Mi = M(\text{Prog}i)$ and Ti be the parse tree of Prog$i$. $T2$ is obtained from $T1$ by replacing the subtree $t(Q.P)$ of the declaration of $Q.P$ with a single-node tree corresponding to the empty procedure declaration. Let $t(P)$ be the subtree of the declaration of P, and let T be the common part of $T1$ and $T2$.

This time we do not need red states: when the active node of $M1$ traverses $t(Q.P)$, the active node of $M2$ traverses $t(P)$. One little complication in the proof is that the corresponding states of $M1$ and $M2$ may have somewhat different V-vals (even though the V-vals have the same domain) and somewhat different restrictions of the N-vals to T. To overcome this difficulty, we introduce extended stacks. The extended stacks are imaginary, they are not parts of our Pascal models.

Let $B.x$ be an arbitrary raw variable of an arbitrary $M(\text{Prog})$. The V-val of $M(\text{Prog})$ maintains a $B.x$-stack. The *extended $B.x$-stack* is the $B.x$-stack possibly "diluted" with copies of a new item 'empty'. Whenever a block different from B is called, a copy of 'empty' is pushed on the extended $B.x$-stack, and whenever any block is exited, the top of the extended $B.x$-stack is popped off. The N-val assigns stacks of values to nodes; the corresponding extended stacks are defined in a similiar way.

Consider the extended stacks of two raw variables $B1.x$ and $B2.x$, where the blocks $B1$ and $B2$ are different. It is impossible that for some i, the extended stacks have i-th items that are both different from 'empty'. This allows us to merge the two extended stacks into a new stack whose height is the minimum of the heights of the two given stacks. Suppose that u is the i-th item of the extended $B1.x$-stack and v is the i-th item of the extended $B2.x$-stack. What is the i-th item w in the new stack? If u differs from 'empty' then $w = u$; if v differs from 'empty' then $w = v$; otherwise w is 'empty.'

Now we are ready to define agreeing states. A state $S1$ of $M1$ agrees with a state $S2$ of $M2$ if the following conditions (a)–(d) are satisfied.

(a) Either the active node of $S1$ coincides with the active node of $S2$, or the active node of $S1$ is in $t(Q.P)$ and the corresponding node of $t(P)$ is active in $S2$.

(b) The procedure stacks of $S1$ and $S2$ coincide.

(c) For every raw variable $B.x$, declared within the block of P, the extended $B.x$-stack of $S2$ is the merger of the exttended $B.x$-stack and the extended $Q.B.x$-stack of $S1$. For every other raw variable $C.y$, the $C.y$-stacks of $S1$ and $S2$ coincide.

(d) For every node N in $T\text{-}t(P)$, the N-stacks of $S1$ and $S2$ coincide. If N belongs to $t(P)$ and N' is the corresponding node in $t(Q.P)$ then the extended N-stack of $S2$ is the merger of the extended N-stack of $S1$ and the extended N'-stack of $S1$.

It is easy to check now that for every input I, the computation of $M1$ on I and the computation of $M2$ on I have the same length, and the corresponding members agree. It follows that Prog1 and Prog2 are equivalent. ∎

11.4 Final Remarks

11.4.1 Equivalent Programs

Let us address the question

     (*) When do two Pascal programs have the same meaning?

The equivalence relation of Section 11.3 is one answer to (*). Under certain circumstances it may be unsatisfactory. Imagine that Prog1 and Prog2 solve the same NP problem and are equivalent in the sense of Section 11.3, but Prog1 works in linear time whereas Prog2 works in exponential time. It does not seem right to consider them as having the same meaning. One may refine the equivalence relation of Section 11.3 to give different answers to (*). One may require, for example, that the computations of Prog1 and Prog2 simulate each other in real time, or that the histories of global variables are identical. (The proof of each of the three claims above establishes both stronger equivalences.)

We think that there are many reasonable answers to (*) and that an appropriate answer depends on the circumstances.

It is interesting to compare question (*) with the similar question for first-order formulas. The standard answer to the latter question is that two first-order formulas have the same meaning if and only if they are logically equivalent (i.e., define the same global relation). This ignores the computational aspect of formulas, in particular the cost of computing corresponding relations.

11.4.2 Distinguishing Features of the Proposed Semantics

Ellis Horowitz writes [(43), Section 2.1]: "*Interpretative* semantics begins by defining an abstract machine. This machine supports a simple set of operations and data structures. Then the semantics of the language being defined is given by a set of rules which show how programs will be translated onto the abstract machine. The Vienna Definition Language (70), which was developed as a means for formally defining PL/1, is the prime example of this approach." Our semantics is interpretative (or operational) because of the use of abstract machines, but it is somewhat different.

1. We define a family of abstract machines with bounded resources rather than one abstract machine with unbounded resources. Each machine gives a local meaning to a program, and the family gives the global meaning. (From that point of view, the semantics can be called global or multi-model.) Multi-model semantics is especially appropriate to handle implementation defined constants. (If your Pascal model has all integers then what is the meaning of MAXINT?) As a matter of fact, the presence of implementation defined constants makes modelling easier.

2. We tailor our machines to the given language (rather than translate the given language to the fixed language of a unique abstract machine). In this section, we described Pascal machines. We considered also models for different variations and extensions of Pascal (in particular, to check that passing a simple variable by name has the same effect as passing it by reference). In (36), we describe Modula-2 machines. We intend to model languages for parallel and distributing computing, and different other languages.

3. Our machines are algebraic structures of a sort, namely dynamic structures. (We would call the proposed semantics algebraic if the term were not taken (27).) To explain what we mean by the algebraic character of our models, let us point out the difference between usual algebraic structures, say graphs, and their representations. One does not care about the nature of the vertices, may not have unique names for the vertices, does not distinguish between isomorphic graphs. Similarly, we do not care about the nature of the elements of our models, may not have unique names for the elements, do not distinguish between isomorphic models. (For example, for any member M of the class PM of Pascal models, any permutation of identifiers gives rise to an automorphism of M.)

11.4.3   Solicitation

The examples above suggest using the proposed semantics for proving general properties of programs and correctness of different transformations (like source-to-source transformations employed by optimizing compilers). Dealing with two models of different levels of abstraction, we use the approach for proving correctness of source-to-target transformations (36). A related theoretical problem is to work out a useful notion of homomorphism of dynamic structures.

We are soliciting interesting and challenging problems about Pascal or other (real or imaginary) imperative languages. We are especially interested in problems related to limited resources.

APPENDIX.   TWO-WAY MULTIHEAD AUTOMATA

A two-way multihead automaton can be described as a multihead Turing machine without any work tape. It is well-known that, as recognizing devices, deterministic (respectively, nondeterministic) two-way multihead automata are equivalent to deterministic (respectively nondeterministic) log-space bounded Turing machines. Hartmanis and Hunt say in their 1974 paper (39) that this is a well-known fact and refer for a more complete proof to a 1972 paper of Hartmanis. It is also well-known that the equivalence survives if alternation is allowed. For reader's convenience, we prove here these facts.

REMARK   To accommodate naturally standard representations of structures (see §1), we allow Turing machines and two-way multihead finite automata to have several input tapes. One of these input tapes is the universe tape that contains the unary notation for the cardinality of the given structure. We will ignore structures of cardinality 1, and will suppose that the end-cells of the universe tape are specially marked.

THEOREM 1.20   A global relation is recognizable in log-space by a deterministic (respectively nondeterministic, alternating) Turing machine if and only if it is recognizable by a deterministic (respectively nondeterministic, alternating) two-way multihead finite automaton.

Proof   The "if" implication is easy (and will not be used): record the current positions of the automaton heads on a work tape.

To prove the "only if" implication, suppose that a log-space bounded Turing machine M recognizes the global relation in question. Let n be the length of the universe tape. Without loss of generality, we can assume the following about

M: it has only one work tape, on each step the work tape head either writes or moves but not both, the work tape alphabet is $\{0, 1\}$ where 0 is also the blank, the end cells of the work tape never hold zeros, initially the head of the work tape is in the leftmost position, and a configuration of M is accepting if and only if the corresponding internal state is one of the specially designated accepting states.

Let u be the content of the initial segment of the current work tape up to and including the position of the head, v^* be the content of the corresponding final segment, and v be the reverse of v^*. The strings u and v are binary notations for some numbers that uniquely define the content of work tape. The symbol observed by the work tape head is exactly the parity of u (0 if u is even and 1 otherwise). If the work tape head changes 0 to 1 (respectively 1 to 0) then $u := u + 1$ (respectively $u := u - 1$) and v does not change. If the work tape head moves to the right then $u := 2u + \delta$ and $v := (v - \delta)/2$ where δ is the parity of v. If the work tape head moves to the left then $u := (u - \delta)/2$ and $v := 2v + \delta$ where δ is the parity of u.

Since the length of the work tape is bounded by a multiple of $\log n$, the numbers u and v are bounded by some n^k. Thus,

$$u = \sum_{i<k} \alpha_i n^i \quad \text{and} \quad v = \sum_{i<k} \beta_i n^i$$

where $\alpha_i, \beta_i < n$ for each i. The desired two-way multihead automaton A represents u and v by $2k$ heads on the universe tape. Using a few auxiliary heads, A is able to compute the parities of u, v and to perform the operations $u := u + 1$, $u := u - 1$, $u := 2u + \text{parity}(v)$, $v := [v - \text{parity}(v)]/2$, etc. mentioned above.

Some internal states of A code the internal states of M, in addition A has auxiliary internal states. When A is in the internal state q' coding an internal state q of M, the configuration of A codes a configuration of M; if q is existential (respectively universal) then so is q'. The auxiliary internal state of A are deterministic. If M starts in the initial configuration C_0 and goes through subsequent configurations C_1, C_2, etc. then A starts in the initial configuration coding C_0, goes through a series of configurations with auxiliary internal states and arrives to the configuration coding C_1, goes through a series of configurations with auxiliary internal states and arrives to the configuration coding C_2, etc. A configuration of A is accepting if and only if it codes an accepting configuration of M. It is easy to see that A accepts a given structure if and only if M accepts it.   ■

COROLLARY   A global relation is polynomial time recognizable if and only if it is recognizable by an alternating two-way multihead finite automaton.

Proof   Polynomial time equals alternating log-space (13).   ■

Let us consider more closely the computation of a two-way multihead automaton A that recognizes a global relation ρ. A can be deterministic, nondeterministic or alternating. Represent the position of a head h on a tape of length n^p by a p-tuple $x_{h0}, \ldots, x_{h(p-1)}$ with the intended interpretation $\Sigma x_{hi} \cdot n^i$. Here n is the length of the universe tape and each x_{hi} is a natural number $<n$. Further, represent the j-th internal state of the automaton by a q-tuple $y_1, \ldots, y_q$ where q is the number of internal states, $y_j = 1$ and $y_i = 0$ for $i \neq j$. Thus there is an r such that every configuration of A is represented by an r-tuple of natural numbers $<n$. Without loss of generality, we may assume that A has a unique accepting configuration and that both in the initial and in the accepting configuration of A all heads are in the leftmost positions. Then the r-tuples Initial and Final, representing the initial and the final configurations respectively, consist of zeros and ones.

CLAIM   There is an FO $+$ $<$ formula Next satisfying the following. Let S be a structure in the domain of ρ, w be a tuple of elements of S whose length equals the arity of ρ, and x,y be r-tuples of elements of the universe of S. Then $\text{Next}(w,x,y)$ holds in S if and only if x,y represent configurations of A on inputs (S,w) and A is able to go from configuration x to configuration y in one step.

Proof   The desired formula Next is a conjunction where each conjunct describes (in the obvious way) one instruction of A. (The variables w appear since there are reading heads on the corresponding input tapes.) ∎

REMARK   The formula Next is especially simple if one uses the successor function (rather than order) and individual constants 0 and End. If the universe is $\{0, \ldots, n-1\}$ then End is interpreted as $n-1$. To make the successor function total, define $\text{Successor}(\text{End}) = 0$ or $\text{Successor}(\text{End}) = \text{End}$.

In the rest of Appendix, a global function is a partial σ-global function of type $\text{Universe}^p \to \text{Universe}^q$ for some σ, p, q; such global function assigns to each σ-structure S a p-ary q-coary operation on the universe of S. Two-way multihead automata were defined as Turing machines without working tapes. They may have output tapes however.

THEOREM 1.21   A global function is computable by a deterministic log-space bounded Turing machine if and only if it is computable by a deterministic two-way multihead automaton.

Proof   Essentially the same proof as that of Theorem 1.20. If the simulated Turing machine M writes on an output tape in a configuration x then the simulating automaton A does the same in the configuration that codes x. ∎

REFERENCES

1. Aho, A. V., J. E. Hopcroft and J. D. Ullman, *The Design and Analysis of Computer Algorithms*, Addison-Wesley, 1974.

2. Aho, A. V. and J. D. Ullman, "Universality of data retrieval languages," *6th POPL Symp.*, ACM, 1979, 110–117.

3. Ajtai, M., "Σ_1^1-formulae on finite structures," *Annals of Pure and Applied Logic 24* (1983), 1–48.

4. Ajtai, M. and Y. Gurevich, "Monotone versus positive," *Journal of ACM*, to appear.

5. Arvind, V. and S. Biswas, "Expressibility of first-order logic with a nondeterministic inductive operator," Manuscript, Indian Institute of Technology, Kanpur, India, May 1986.

6. de Bakker, J. W., *Mathematical Theory of Program Correctness*. Prentice-Hall, 1980.

7. Blass, A., *Private communication*.

8. Blass, A. and Y. Gurevich, "Henkin quantifiers and complete problems," *Annals of Pure and Applied Logic*, 32 (1986), 1–16.

9. Blass, A. and Y. Gurevich, "A new thesis" (tentative title), in preparation.

10. Blass, A., Y. Gurevich and D. C. Kozen, "A zero-one law for logic with a fixed-point operator," *Information and Control 67* (1985), 70–90.

11. Börger, E. and Y. Gurevich, "On fixed-point extensions of first-order logic" (tentative title), in preparation.

12a. Chandra A. K. and D. Harel, "Computable queries for relational data bases," *J. Comput. and System Sciences 21* (1980), 156–178.

12b. Chandra, A. K. and D. Harel, "Structure and complexity of relational queries," *J. Comput. and System Sciences 25* (1982), 99–128.

13. Chandra, A. K., D. C. Kozen and L. J. Stockmeyer, "Alternation," *J. of Association for Computing Machinery 28* (1981), 114–133.

14. Church, A., "An unsolvable problem of elementary number theory," *American Journal of Mathematics 58* (1936), 345–363.

15. Codd, E. F., "Relational completeness of database sublanguages," in *Database Systems* (ed. R. Rustin), Prentice-Hall, 1972, 65–98.

16. Compton, K., "The computational complexity of asymptotic problems I: partial orders," *Information and Control*, to appear.

17. Denenberg, L., Y. Gurevich and S. Shelah, "Cardinalities defined by constant depth polynomial size circuits," *Information and Control 70* (1986), 216–240.

18. Ebbinghaus, H.-D., J. Flum and W. Thomas, *Mathematical Logic*, Springer-Verlag, New York, 1984.

19. Ehrenfeucht, A., "An application of games to the completeness problem for formalized theories," *Fund. Math. 49* (1961), 129–141.

20. Fagin, R., "Generalized first-order spectra and polynomial time recognizable sets," *SIAM-AMS Proc. 7* (1974), 43–73.

21. Fagin, R., "Monadic generalized spectra," *Zeitschrift für Math. Logik und Grundlagen der Mathematik 21* (1975), 89–96.

22. Fagin, R., M. Klawe, N. J. Pippenger, and L. Stockmeyer, "Bounded depth polynomial size circuits for symmetric functions," *Theoretical Computer Science*, April 1985, 239–250.

23. Gaifman, H. and M. Vardi, "A simple proof that connectivity of finite graphs is not first-order definable," *Bulletin of European Assoc. for Theoretical Computer Science*, June 1985, 43–45.

24. Gandy, R., "Church's thesis and principles for mechanisms," in: *The Kleene Symposium* (ed. J. Barwise et al.), North-Holland, 1980, 123–148.

25. Garey, M. R. and D. S. Johnson, *Computers and Intractability: A Guide to the Theory of NP Completeness*, Freeman, 1979.

26. Gries, D., *The Science of Programming*, Springer-Verlag, 1981.

27. Guessarian, I., "Algebraic semantics," *Lecture Notes in Computer Science 99*, Springer-Verlag, 1981.

28. Gurevich, Y., "Algebras of feasible functions," *24th Symposium on Foundations of Computer Science*, IEEE Computer Society Press, 1983, 210–214.

29. Gurevich, Y., "Toward logic tailored for computational complexity," in *Computation and Proof Theory* (Ed. M. M. Richter et al.), Springer Lecture Notes in Math. 1104 (1984), 175–216.

30. Gurevich, Y., "Monadic second-order theories," in *Model-Theoretical Logics* (ed. J. Barwise and S. Feferman), Springer-Verlag, 1985, 479–506.

31. Gurevich, Y., "Reconsidering Turing's thesis (toward more realistic semantics of programs)," *Technical Report CRL-TR-36-84*, University of Michigan, Sep. 1984.

32. Gurevich, Y., "Logic and the challenge of computer science," *Technical Report CRL-TR-10-85*, University of Michigan, Sep. 1985.

33. Gurevich, Y., "A new thesis," *AMS Abstracts*, Aug. 1985, p. 317.

34. Gurevich, Y., "Algorithms in the world of bounded resources," in *The Universal Turing Machine—A Half-Century Survey* (ed. R. Herken), Oxford University Press, to appear.

35. Gurevich, Y. and H. R. Lewis, "A logic for constant-depth circuits," *Information and Control 61* (1984), 65–74.

36. Gurevich, Y. and J. M. Morris, *"Pragmatic semantic for Modula-2,"* (tentative title), in preparation.

37. Gurevich, Y. and S. Shelah, "Fixed-point extensions of first-order logic," *Annals of Pure and Applied Logic 32* (1986), 265–280.

38. Gurevich, Y. and S. Shelah, "Fixed-point extensions of first-order logic," *26th Annual Symp. on Foundation of Computer Science*, IEEE Computer Society Press, 1985, 346–353.

39. Hartmanis, J. and H. B. Hunt, "The LBA problem and its importance in the theory of computing," *SIAM-AMS Proc.*, vol. 7 (1974), 1–26.

40. Hartmanis, J. and N. Immerman, "On complete problems for NP $\cap$ coNP," *Lecture Notes in Computer Science 194* (1985), Springer-Verlag, 250–259.

41. Hayes, J. P., "Uncertainty, energy, and multiple-valued logics," *IEEE Trans. on Computers*, vol. C-35 (1986), 107–114.

42. Henkin, L., "Some remarks on infinitely long formulas," in *Infinitistic Methods*, Warsaw, 1961, 167–183.

43. Horowitz, E., *Fundamentals of Programming Languages*, Computer Science Press, 1983.

44. Immerman, N., "Relational queries computable in polynomial time," *14th Symposium on Theory of Computing*, Association for Computing Machinery, 1982, 147–152.

45. Immerman, N., "Languages which capture complexity classes," *15th Symposium on Theory of Computing*, Association for Computing Machinery, 1983, 347–354.

46. Jensen, K. and N. Wirth, *Pascal, User Manual and Report*, Springer-Verlag, 2nd edition, 1978.

47. Kleene, S. C., *Introduction to Metamathematics*, D. Van Nostrand, New York, Toronto, 1952.

48. Kolmogoroff, A. N. and V. A. Uspenski, "On the definition of an algorithm," *Uspekhi Mat. Nauk 13* (1958), 3–28 (Russian), AMS Transl. 29 (1963), 217–245.

49. Krom, M. R., "The decision problem for a class of first-order formulas in which all disjunctions are binary," *Zeitschrift für math. Logik und Grundlagen der Mathematik 13* (1967), 15–20.

50. Kuratowski, K., *Topology, volume 1*, Academic Press, 1966.

51. Lindström, P., "On extensions of elementary logic," *Theoria 35* (1969), 1–11.

52. Livchak, A., "The relational model for process control," *Automatic Documentation and Mathematical Linguistics 4* (1983), 27–29.

53. Lyndon, R., "An interpolation theorem in the predicate calculus," *Pacific J. Math. 9* (1959), 155–164.

54. Moschovakis, Y. N., *Foundations of the Theory of Algorithms, I*, Manuscript, University of California, Los Angeles, 1986.

55. Plotkin, G. D., "Structural approach to operational semantics," *Technical report DAIMI FN-19*, Computer Science Department, Aarhus University, Denmark, Sept. 1981.

56. Reynolds, J. C., *The Craft of Programming*, Prentice-Hall, 1981.

57. Sazonov, V. Y., "Polynomial computability and recursivity in finite domains," *Elektronische Informationverarbeitung und Kybernetik 16* (1980), 319–323.

58. Schoenhage, A., "Storage modification machines," *SIAM J. on Computing 9* (1980), 490–508.

59. Sipser, M., "On relativization and the existence of complete sets," *ICALP* 1982, 523–531.

60. Sipser, M., "Borel sets and circuit complexity," *15th ACM Symposium on Theory of Computing* (1983), 61–69.

61. Stoy, J. E., "*Denotational semantics*: The *Scott-Strachey Approach* to Programming Language Theory," MIT Press, Cambridge, Mass., 1977.

62. Tarski, A., "Some notions and methods on the borderline of algebra and metamathematics," *Proc. 1950 International Congress of Mathematicians*, Cambridge, MA, AMS, 1952, 705–720.

63. Tennent, R. D., *Principles of Programming Languages*, Prentice-Hall International, 1981.

64. Trakhtenbrot, B. A., "Impossibility of an algorithm for the decision problem on finite classes," *Doklady 70* (1950), 569–572.

65. Trakhtenbrot, B., J. Y. Halpern and A. R. Meyer, "From denotational to operational and axiomatic semantics for ALGOL-like languages: an overview," *Lecture Notes in Computer Science*, Volume 164, Springer-Verlag, 1983.

66. Turing, A. M., "On computable numbers, with an application to the Entscheidungs-problem," *Proc. of London Mathematical Society 2*, no. 42 (1936), 230–236, and no. 43 (1936), 544–546.

67. Ullman, J. D., *Principles of Database Systems*, Computer Science Press, 1982.

68. Vardi, M., "Complexity of relational query languages," *14th Symp. on Theory of Computing*, ACM, 1982, 137–146.

69. Walkoe, W., "Finite partially-ordered quantification," *Journal of Symbolic Logic 35* (1970), 535–555.

70. Wegner, P., "The Vienna Definition Language," *ACM Computing Surveys 4* (1972), 5–63.

71. Wirth, N., *Programming in Modula-2, 3rd edition*, Springer-Verlag, 1985.

Chapter 2

Logic as Machine:
Complexity Relations Between Programs and Formulae*

E. BÖRGER

Abstract—In this chapter a method for logical implementations of machine programs is presented which preserves many complexity properties in going from programs to formulae. This method of defining the semantics of programs by logical formulae reveals deep structural and combinatorial similarities between computations and logic deductions. These similarities bring out explicitly the fundamental and uniform reason for many completeness results of both combinatorial and logical decision problems.

In particular, PROLOG interpretations of bounded and unbounded computations of various machines are discussed. These interpretations obtain characterizations of standard complexity classes by decision problems of syntactically restricted classes of formulae over arbitrary respectively finite domains.

---

*Part of this material comes from a complete revision of a lecture series delivered by the author to the post-graduate school, "Foundations of Computation Theory." The school was organized by Professors M. Karpinski (Poznan/Bonn), V. Kirin (Zagreb), and H. Rasiowa (Warszawia) at the Inter-University Center in Dubrovnik (Yugoslavia) from 17.1–28.1.1983. A survey of the main ideas developed here on the interplay between logical and computational complexity of PROLOG programs was presented by the author to the "FESTKOLLOQUIUM aus Anlaß der 100. Wiederkehr des Geburtstages von Heinrich Scholz" held at the Institut für mathematische Logik und Grundlagenforschung of the University of Münster/Westf. on February 8–9, 1985.

2.1 INTRODUCTION

In this chapter we present a logical implementation method for machine programs, which has found many applications in logic, recursion, and complexity theory.

The spirit of the method goes back to Turing (1937) where it was introduced to show the undecidability of first order logic. Twenty-five years later Büchi (1962) combined Turing's idea with the use of Herbrand interpretations of first-order formulae, thus opening the way to a solution of the long-standing prefix and prefix-similarity problem of classical reduction theory by Kahr (1962), Kostyrko (1964), Genenz (1965), Gurevich (1966). For a more detailed account, see Börger (1984). In Aanderaa (1971) and Börger (1971), a further refinement of the Turing-Büchi-method was developed which allowed, in addition to quantifier restrictions, propositional constraints in logical descriptions of machine computations, namely to Krom formulae (i.e. formulae in prenex normal form with a matrix in conjunctive normal form, where the disjunctions are at most binary; named after Krom 1967); and to Horn formulae (i.e. formulae which essentially have the logical form of a PROLOG program). Variations of this method revealed an intimate and natural link between the complexity of machine halting problems and the complexity of the logical decision problems of the formulae describing those machine problems. This holds in the realm of unlimited halting resp. recursively unsolvable decision problems as well as between time or space bounded halting resp. logical decision problems which are complete in the given computational complexity class. Furthermore, in the Aanderaa-Börger-method, the logical implementations of the machine computations show that there is a one-to-one correspondence between the steps of the machine computation and the logical deductions steps. Thus, by turning logic into a (suitably programmed) machine, we can show how computational hierarchy results find their natural analogues in logical terms. This will be discussed below for the particularly interesting case of resolution-based implementations of PROLOG programs which describe given machine computations.

In the following sections we give details of logical implementations of machine programs for three typical cases (which are useful also in connection with the chapters of Y. Gurevich and M. Vardi in this volume). In Section 2.2 we give a Horn description of unbounded computations. This yields small universal PROLOG programs, sharp normal forms for PROLOG programs, and a natural correspondence between small universal programs and minimal reduction classes (i.e., with a decision problem which is complete for the recursively enumerable sets). As a by-product we also obtain uniform and simple proofs for some classical impossibility results such as (1) the stumbling block of data base theory that the class of first order formulae valid over finite domains is not recursively axiomatizable (Trachtenbrot, 1950), (2) consistent PROLOG programs without recursive models resp. constituting an essentially undecidable and therefore incomplete theory, and (3) impossibility of recursive interpolation (Kreisel, 1961) or of recursive bounds on the explication of implicitly defined predicates in first-order logic (Friedman, 1976) even when restricted to finite structures (Gurevich, 1984).

In Section 2.3 we present a logical complexity measure for Boolean functions which is defined in Aanderaa & Börger (1979) and is motivated by the "almost" Horn structure of the propositional logic interpretation of our reduction formulae in Section 2.2 for the case of polynomial time bounded computations. (For the computations of a nondeterministic polynomial time bounded Turing machine program, this reinterpretation gives Cook's 1971 theorem on the *NP*-completeness of the satisfiability problem of propositional logic.) By an "almost" Horn description of networks of Boolean functions by propositional formulae we show the polynomial equivalence of network complexity and the above-mentioned Horn complexity for Boolean functions.

We also discuss in this context an algorithm by Henschen & Wos (1974) which shows that unit resolution is a complete proof procedure for first-order Horn formulae. In the case of propositional logic, this yields a polynomial time algorithm for the decision problem of Horn formulae and also for the construction of Horn interpolants (by an observation of Dahlhaus et al. 1984).

In Section 2.4 we study logical descriptions of bounded computations over finite structures to obtain characterizations of given complexity classes by the decision problem of syntactically restricted classes of formulae. Here again a reinterpretation of our reduction formulae in Section 2.2 in terms of higher order logic proves (the lower complexity part of) the theorem that the class of spectra of n-th order logic coincides with the class of sets of positive integers which can be accepted by a nondeterministic Turing machine program in n-fold exponential time. A special case is Fagin's 1974 characterization of *NP* by generalized spectra. Another reinterpretation of our reduction formulae of Section 2.2 yields the hardness part of the PSPACE-completeness of the decision problem of PROLOG programs where no terms other than variables and individual constants occur and where all clauses are binary (Plaisted, 1984 and Denenberg & Lewis, 1984). Without this last restriction, one has EXPTIME-completeness (Plaisted, 1984) and without the restriction to Horn formulae, NEXPTIME-completeness (Lewis, 1980). An application of our reduction technique to alternating pushdown automata shows the hardness part of the EXPTIME-completeness of the decision problem of the so-called Ackermann prefix class (Lewis, 1980). Many characterizations of complexity classes by suitable logics restricted to finite structures use reductions which are reminiscent of the ones we give in Section 2.4; see especially the chapter by Y. Gurevich in this volume.

For unexplained terminology, notations, and standard results borrowed from logic, recursion, or complexity theory refer to Rogers (1967), Shoenfield (1967), Machtey & Young (1978), Hopcroft & Ullman (1979), and Börger (1985). For the fundamentals of logic programming (Herbrand models, procedural interpretation of Horn clauses as PROLOG programs, resolution and SLD-resolution) refer in particular to §DIII3 of Börger (1985) or to Lloyd (1984).

It is assumed that the reader is familiar with the basic notions and facts of computation theory and logic, including the fundamentals of logic programming.

2.2 PROLOG INTERPRETATION OF UNBOUNDED COMPUTATIONS

In Section 2.2.1 a natural and simple PROLOG implementation of structured programs in a computation universal programming language is shown. Because this PROLOG simulation of arbitrary computations is step-by-step, complexity theoretic properties of programs are preserved by this translation. In Section 2.2.2 we show how logical program semantics relates the minimality of reduction classes of the decision problem of first-order logic to sharp (i.e., not improvable) normal forms for PROLOG programs. In Section 2.2.3 characteristic examples are given for the preservation of (sub-) recursive inseparability properties in going from halting problems of programs to model construction problems of their PROLOG descriptions.

2.2.1 A Small Universal PROLOG Program

Consider a computation universal language L of structured programs. To be specific, let these programs be built up from a finite number of elementary programs e by use of concatenation MN ("first M, then N") and WHILE-iteration WHILE $x_i \neq$ nil DO M with respect to a finite number $x_1, \ldots, x_n$ of "registers" containing arbitrary data. The following first-order formula U describes the semantics of L; since U is a definite Horn formula, we can say also that U as a PROLOG program interprets the programs of L.

DEFINITION 2.1   Let Conf be a $n + 1$-ary relational predicate symbol (with Conf(M, $x_1, \ldots, x_n$) intended to mean that the configuration consisting of the program M together with the data $x_1, \ldots, x_n$ on which M has to be executed will eventually lead to an accepting halting configuration.) Let M, N be individual variables (to be interpreted by structured L-programs), $*$ a binary function symbol (standing for the concatenation of structured programs), and ( )$_i$ a monadic function symbol (which applied to M is meant to represent the WHILE-program WHILE $x_i \neq$ nil DO M) for $1 \leq i \leq n$. Let e be individual constants (denoting the elementary L-programs). Let $\vec{x} = (\vec{y}, x_i, \vec{z}) = (x_1, \ldots, x_n)$ with individual variables $x_1, \ldots, x_n$, u (standing for data contained in the registers) and $\cdot$ a binary function symbol (used to denote concatenation of data). Let nil denote an individual constant (standing for the empty string (of data or of programs)). We define U as the following set (read: conjunction) of clauses (where we use the PROLOG notation $F \leftarrow F_1, \ldots, F_n$ for the logical implication $F_1 \& \ldots \& F_n \rightarrow F$ which the reader should think about as universally closed first-order formula):

$\mathrm{Conf}(e * M, \vec{x}) \leftarrow \mathrm{Conf}(M, e(\vec{x}))$) for e elementary

> where $e(\vec{x})$ is shorthand for (a logical representation of) the result of executing program e on data $\vec{x}$

read: to execute program $e * M$ on data $\vec{x}$ means to execute program M on the data resulting from applying the elementary program e on $\vec{x}$.

$(U) \qquad \mathrm{Conf}((M)_i * N, \vec{y}, u \cdot x_i, \vec{z}) \leftarrow \mathrm{Conf}(M * (M)_i * N, \vec{y}, u \cdot x_i, \vec{z})$

$\mathrm{Conf}(. \ldots \ldots \ldots, \mathrm{nil}, . .) \leftarrow \mathrm{Conf}(N, \vec{y}, \mathrm{nil}, \vec{z})$ for $1 \le i \le n$

read: to execute program (WHILE $x_i \ne \mathrm{nil}$ DO M) $* N$ on data $\vec{x}$ means to execute N on $\vec{x}$ (if $x_i = \mathrm{nil}$) respectively to execute once M on $\vec{x}$ and then again $(M)_i * N$ on the data obtained from computing M on $\vec{x}$ (if the i-th register contains compound data, i.e. of the form $u \cdot x_i \ne \mathrm{nil}$).

$$\mathrm{Conf}(\mathrm{nil}, \vec{x}) \leftarrow \qquad (\text{``Halting clause''})$$

read: The empty program together with arbitrary data represents by definition an accepting configuration; nothing has to be computed any more. The resolution calculus simulation of computations of L-programs will terminate by producing the empty clause from a halting configuration goal $\leftarrow \mathrm{Conf}(\mathrm{nil}, \vec{t})$ and the halting clause.

THEOREM 2.1   For $n \ge 2$ the above defined PROLOG program U is computation universal, i.e., for every (e.g. Turing machine) program M and every input A for M one has for some L-program m (expressing M) and data a (representing A) the equivalence:

$$M \text{ accepts } A \quad \text{iff} \quad U \text{ accepts } \leftarrow\mathrm{Conf}(m, a).$$

Here acceptance of the input clause $\leftarrow\mathrm{Conf}(m, a)$ (so called goal clause) by U means that using the resolution rule, one can derive the empty clause from the union of U with $\leftarrow\mathrm{Conf}(m, a)$.

Proof   By our assumption that L is computation universal we can encode Turing machine programs M and tapes A of M into structured L-programs m and data a on which m simulates the behavior of M on A. This is a version of Böhm's 1964 theorem. For a short direct proof see §AI1 in Börger 1985. By construction of U, the computation of m on a is simulated by the (resolution calculus computation of) program U started with the goal clause $\leftarrow$Conf(m, a). This computation in the resolution calculus will terminate successfully (by producing the empty clause) iff it uses the unique halting clause Conf(nil, $\vec{x}$)$\leftarrow$ of U at least once. This is the case iff m on input a will terminate successfully. The condition $2 \leq n$ is fulfilled by Minsky's 1961 theorem that two registers suffice to compute arbitrary partial recursive functions.

COROLLARY 2.1   Let U' be the PROLOG program obtained from U by contraposition (i.e. substitution of $\alpha \leftarrow \beta$ by $\neg\beta \leftarrow \neg\alpha$) followed by replacement of $\neg$Conf by a new predicate symbol Conf$'$. Then U' is equivalent to U and deterministic as PROLOG program (in the sense of Clocksin & Mellish, 1981).

Proof   The determinism of U' as PROLOG program results from the determinism of L-programs: for every clause C in U' and every ground instance p of a procedure call (logically speaking of a premise) of C—p represents a given configuration—there is at most one clause D in U' such that the procedure name (logically speaking the conclusion) c of D—which represents the uniquely determined next configuration—is unifiable with p. Trivially every variable occurring in the procedure body of a clause of U' occurs also in the corresponding procedure name.

REMARK 2.1   From the construction of U, it is obvious that in Theorem 2.1, the resolution calculus can be restricted to so-called positive unit resolution, where at each application of the resolution rule at least one of the two clauses involved is a prime formula (i.e., a literal without negation sign). A direct proof for this completeness of (positive) unit resolution for (definite) Horn clauses has been given by Henschen & Wos, 1974, see Section 2.3. It is also obvious from the construction of U that to each computation step of the given structured program m corresponds exactly one (positive unit) resolution step in the simulation of m by U, and vice versa. Thus, by our reduction technique (which is an elaboration of the register machine simulation technique invented in Aanderaa 1971 and Börger 1971) hierarchy results of computational complexity theory directly find natural logical analogues, namely, interpretation in terms of complexity questions for logical calculi (in particular resolution-based systems).

2.2.2   Normal Forms and Reduction Classes

We now show that the computation universality of U as a program is related to the universality with respect to Hilbert's Entscheidungsproblem of the decision problem of the class of computation formulae defined by U, namely:

$$\overline{U} := \{\Lambda(U, \leftarrow\text{Conf}(m, a)) \mid m \text{ program}, a \text{ input data}\}.$$

Here ΛF denotes the universal closure of F.

In order to formulate and to prove this connection precisely, let us recall the fundamental notion of logical reduction theory. A class R of first-order formulae is called a *reduction class* (with respect to satisfiability) iff there is some recursive function associating to each first order formula F a formula $\overline{F}$ which is element of R and such that: F is satisfiable iff $\overline{F}$ is satisfiable. R is called a conservative reduction class if F has a finite model iff $\overline{F}$ has a finite model.

There is a huge body of literature investigating classes of formulae to determine whether they are reduction classes (and therefore with a decision problem to which the whole Entscheidungsproblem can be effectively reduced) or whether they have a recursively solvable decision problem (see the books Ackermann (1954); Suranyi (1959); Lewis (1979); Dreben & Goldfarb (1979); and for a modern survey Börger (1984)). We want to show explicitly that the computation universality of U as a program with inputs $\leftarrow$Conf(m, a) relates to the universality of the decision problem of the related class of computation formulae $\Lambda(U, \leftarrow$Conf$(m, a))$ (remember that the comma stands here for logical conjunction):

COROLLARY 2.2   The class $\overline{U} := \{\Lambda(U, \leftarrow$Conf$(m, a)) | m$ program, a input data$\}$ of computation formulae defined by the (program) formula U is a reduction class of first-order logic.

Proof   By Gödel's completeness theorem one can compute for each first-order formula F a (structured Turing machine) program m_F which accepts the empty input nil iff F is not satisfiable. Therefore:

$$F \text{ is satisfiable } \text{ iff } m_F \text{ does not accept the input nil}$$
$$\text{iff } U \text{ does not accept } \leftarrow\text{Conf}(m_F, \text{ nil})$$
$$\text{iff } \Lambda(U, \leftarrow\text{Conf}(m_F, \text{ nil})) \text{ is satisfiable.}$$

The last equivalence is due to the completeness of resolution for first-order logic.

The computation universality of U incorporates a normal form for PROLOG programs corresponding to the normal form of the Entscheidungsproblem represented by $\overline{U}$:

a) U has only binary clauses—Reynolds, 1969 and Krom, 1970 seem to be the first to have proved the r.e. completeness of the decision problem for sets of binary clauses by reducing to it Post's correspondence problems respectively Post's Tag systems.

b) besides function symbols for concatenation, for the WHILE-constructs and for the elementary programs, U does not need any other auxiliary constants or functions for encoding computations, a theme which has been investigated more precisely in Andreka & Nemeti, 1976 and Tärnlund, 1977.

c) U uses only one relation symbol.

By more careful choice of the simulated universal programming language and by writing down logically the meaning of its programs and data, one can obtain in a natural way much stronger normal forms for PROLOG programs. The latter not only sharpen the above cited results (and also rediscoveries of similar results in other papers, see Hill (1974), Sebelik & Stepanek (1982), Itai & Makowsky (1983)), but also they correspond to the syntactical form of so-called minimal reduction classes and therefore, in a precise sense cannot be improved.

DEFINITION 2.2   To come up with our favorite example (found as reduction class by Aanderaa (1971) and Börger (1971)) it suffices to read $\mathrm{Conf}(i, \vec{x})$ in U as binary relation with variables x_1, x_2 ranging over natural numbers and with i interpreted as "instruction parameter"; then our PROLOG-program $U(M)$— which now depends on a given program M (on the Minsky (1961) machine with only two number registers) and defines its interpretation—consists of the following binary clauses containing only number terms $x, y, 0$ (for zero), Sx (for successor $x + 1$ of x):

$$\mathrm{Conf}_i(x, y) \leftarrow \mathrm{Conf}_j(Sx, y) \text{ for } M\text{-instructions } (i: \mathrm{DO\ add_1\ GOTO}\ j)$$

$$\left. \begin{array}{l} \mathrm{Conf}_i(0, y) \leftarrow \mathrm{Conf}_j(0, y) \\[2ex] \mathrm{Conf}_i(Sx, y) \leftarrow \mathrm{Conf}_k(x, y) \end{array} \right\} \begin{array}{l} \text{for } M\text{-instructions} \\ (i: \mathrm{IF}\ x_1\ =\ 0\ \mathrm{GOTO}\ j\ \mathrm{ELSE} \\ \mathrm{DO\ sub_1\ GOTO}\ k) \end{array}$$

Symmetrically for $\mathrm{add_2}$- and $\mathrm{test_2}/\mathrm{subtract_2}$-instructions with respect to the second register interchanging first and second component.

$$\mathrm{Conf}_1(x, y) \leftarrow \text{ for the accepting state (say) 1 of } M$$

COROLLARY 2.3   (Aanderaa, 1971; Börger, 1971; Aanderaa & Lewis, 1973). Every PROLOG program can be brought into the normal form $U(M)$ of Definition 2.2 (for some M) containing only number terms x, y, 0, Sx, binary relation symbols, and binary clauses. This normal form cannot be improved furthermore by leaving out either one variable or the individual constant or the function symbol or by allowing only monadic predicates or only literals.

If M is universal on the Minsky machine, then $U(M)$ is a computation universal PROLOG program. The class $\overline{U}(M) := \{\Lambda(U, \leftarrow\mathrm{Conf}_o(a, b)) | a, b \varepsilon N\}$ of U-computation formulae is a minimal reduction class for each computation universal M.

Proof   The normal form claim follows from Theorem 2.1 and Minsky's 1961 theorem that the register machine with only two number registers is computation universal. For the reduction class claim, apply the reasoning of the proof of Corollary 2.2 to an arbitrary but fixed 2-register machine program M which enumerates first-order logic as follows (where F is an arbitrary formula and $\overline{F}$

an encoding of F as register input to M using 0 and S): F is satisfiable iff M does not accept the input $\overline{F}$, iff $U(M)$ does not accept $\leftarrow\text{Conf}_o(\overline{F})$, and iff $\Lambda(U(M), \leftarrow\text{Conf}_o(\overline{F}))$ is satisfiable. The minimality part follows from the decidability of the decision problem for those classes of formulae which result from leaving out one of the above indicated syntactical components of $U(M)$ (see Aanderaa & Lewis, 1973).

REMARK 2.2   Another result which is particularly interesting when interpreted in terms of PROLOG programs is the theorem of Gurevich (1976) that the class of purely universal Horn formulae is a reduction class even if restricted to formulae containing only one variable and as atomic formulae only equations between terms built up using only monadic function symbols. This can be proved by encoding the clauses of $U(M)$ into equations, (see Börger, 1978 or Exercise 1 to Corollary 1 in §FI1 of Börger, 1985).

REMARK 2.3   The smoothness of formulae $U(M)$ as universal computation model can be put into use also in the context of more classical computation formalism like Thue systems, Markov algorithms, Post canonical (normal) calculi, etc. As observed already in Börger 1975, a simple rewriting visualizes a fruitful interpretation of $U(M)$ as semi-Thue system or Markov algorithm. First reverse the arrows—this means that we switch from the refutation-oriented (procedural) PROLOG interpretation of $U(M)$ to its deductive proof-oriented interpretation; i.e., $\text{Conf}_i(\vec{x})$ instead of meaning ''from the configuration $(i, \vec{x})$ an *a priori* given final configuration will eventually be reached'' now expresses ''the configuration $(i, \vec{x})$ will eventually be reached from an *a priori* given initial configuration.'' After having reversed the arrows in $U(M)$, imagine the atomic formulae $\text{Conf}_i(s, t)$ with terms $s, t \ \varepsilon \ \{x, y, 0, Sx\}$ written in the form $s\text{Conf}_i t$, interpret the relational symbols Conf_i as well as the function symbols 0 and S as letters of a finite alphabet and cancel the variables x, y (as well as the unit clause $xK_1 y \leftarrow$).

As a result of this rewriting, $U(M)$ is a Semi-Thue system (and for deterministic programs M even a Markov algorithm) which obviously simulates step-by-step the computation of the given program M. Thus, $U(M)$ as a substitution algorithm or as a program formula ''are the same'' except for a notationally different viewpoint. In particular $U(M)$ as a semi-Thue system respectively Markov algorithm or as a PROLOG program share the same computational properties. Because of the smooth step-by-step simulation of M by $U(M)$, the many-one degrees and in most cases even the recursive isomorphism types of corresponding decision problems of M and of $U(M)$ are the same. With minor natural changes in the (way of interpreting or writing) rules of $U(M)$, this degree preserving property of our simulation of M by $U(M)$ holds also in terms of other classical computation formalisms like Post normal calculi, restricted Post canonical systems, Post correspondence problems, partial implication propositional calculi,

Wang's nonerasing Turing machines, Aanderaa's modular machines, ordered
Petri nets or vector addition systems (i.e., commutative Markov algorithms).
For details see Börger (1979, 1983), Börger & Heidler (1976), Börger & Kleine
Büning (1980), Cohen (1980).

2.2.3 Preservation of Inseparability Properties

The step-by-step simulation of M by $U(M)$ transforms recursive inseparabilities
of M-halting problems into recursive inseparability properties of corresponding
logical $U(M)$-decision problems. Our first example shows how the recursive
inseparability of two halting problems of M—defined by two designated halting
states, say 1 and 2—via the translation of M into $U(M)$ results in recursive
inseparability of the finitely satisfiable and the contradictory (respectively the
infinity axioms) among the reduction formulae. To obtain this from Theorem
2.1 it suffices to add to the formula $U(M)$ an auxiliary set Data Ord(M) of clauses
which provides for a linear order of the (model representation of the) data of
the M-computations in such a way that arbitrarily large data are represented by
arbitrary large objects with respect to that order. This observation is the key to

COROLLARY 2.4   Let M be a program with two recursively inseparable halting
problems (for say $i = 1,2$)

$$H_i := \{x | M \text{ started with input } x \text{ eventually reaches state } i$$
$$\text{(without loss of generality with empty registers)}\}.$$

Assume that M started (in its initial state 0) with input x either halts in one of
its accepting states 1 and 2 or goes into a computation which does not become
periodic. Then the sets of contradictory respectively finitely satisfiable among
the M-computation formulae $U(M)$, $\leftarrow$Conf$_o(\bar{x})$ (where $\bar{x}$ represents an encoding
of input x to M in terms of $0, S$) are also recursively inseparable.

In particular, the sets of contradictory respectively finitely satisfiable respectively satisfiable formulae without finite models are pairwise recursively inseparable and the set of formulae which are valid over finite domains is not recursively
enumerable (Trachtenbrot 1950, 1953).

Proof   For the first inseparability claim, it suffices to show that for the above-
defined clause set Data Ord(M), the following two equivalences are true for
arbitrary x:

(i) $x \varepsilon H_1$ iff $\Lambda(U(M), \leftarrow$Conf$_o(x)$, Data Ord$(M))$ is contradictory
(ii) $x \varepsilon H_2$ .... has a finite model.

Without Data Ord(M) equivalence (i) holds as in the proof of Corollary 2.3; the
same for (ii) from left to right (e.g., by interpreting Conf$_i(\bar{a})$ as meaning that

from the configuration defined by state i and data a, M will not reach state 2). These two facts remain true if we add the following set Data Ord(M) of clauses (for some binary predicate symbol K with the intended meaning $<$):

$K(x,x) \leftarrow$ (irreflexivity)

$K(y,Sx) \leftarrow K(y,x)$ read: if y is smaller than x, then it is also smaller than the successor Sx

$K(x,Sx) \leftarrow \text{Conf}_i(x,y)$ } read: arbitrary data which occur during the
$K(x,Sx) \leftarrow \text{Conf}_i(y,x)$ }   computation have bigger successors (for
                                         each M-state i)

Now let us assume $x \notin H_2$; we want to show that the universal closure of $U(M)$, $\leftarrow \text{Conf}_o(\bar{x})$, Data Ord($M$) has no finite model. In case $x \in H_1$ this is obvious from (i); otherwise the M-computation started with input x does not become periodic, therefore arbitrarily large numbers must appear in it as data which (as a result of Data Ord(M)) must be represented in every model of our formulae by arbitrarily K-large objects.

To infer Trachtenbrot's result, we only have to specialize M to an appropriate program which looks for refutations respectively finite models of its input formulae. (Note that the recursive inseparability of the sets of infinity axioms respectively of contradictory formulae follows already from the undecidability of first-order logic and the recursive enumerability of the contradictory and the finitely satisfiable formulae.)

REMARK 2.4   Our proof shows that the description of M by $U(M)$ preserves inseparability properties also with respect to arbitrary (sub-) recursive complexity of the halting respectively satisfiability problems.

REMARK 2.5   The formulae used to obtain equivalences (i) and (ii) in Corollary 2.4 show that the reduction classes in Corollaries 2.2 and 2.3 (augmented by the Data Ord(M)-part) are even conservative. See also, Aanderaa & Börger & Lewis, 1982.

Our second example shows that the recursive inseparability of M-halting problems H_1, H_2 makes the first-order theory of a PROLOG implementation of M with only binary clauses essentially undecidable (therefore incomplete) and both this PROLOG description as well as a variant without function symbols simple and natural examples for satisfiable formulae without recursive models (for previous set theoretic examples confirming a conjecture by Hilbert & Bernays, 1939, see Kreisel, 1953; Mostowski, 1953; Rabin, 1958).

COROLLARY 2.5   (Aanderaa 1971, Börger 1975a)   For M as in the premise of Corollary 2.4, the PROLOG implementation $T(M)$ of M defined below (using only binary clauses) together with the stop formulae $\leftarrow\mathrm{Conf}_1(\bar{0})$ and $\mathrm{Conf}_2(\bar{0})\leftarrow$ constitute the nonlogical axiom of an essentially undecidable (therefore incomplete) theory. They form a consistent formula without recursive models and the same holds for the variant defined below without using the function symbols $0, S$.

Proof Let $T(M)$ be the Thue version of $U(M)$ (i.e., the formula obtained from $U(M)$ by replacing arrows $\leftarrow$ by equivalences $\leftrightarrow$ (and deleting the unit clause $K_1 xy\leftarrow$). $T(M)$ expresses the symmetric closure of the transition relation programmed by M. Technically speaking this comes up to the following strengthened simulation property for arbitrary M-configurations C (where $\bar{C}$ is $\mathrm{Conf}_i(\bar{x})$ for $C = (i, x)$ consisting of state i and data x):

$$\text{(i)} \quad C\vdash_{\overline{M}}(1,\bar{0}) \quad \text{iff} \quad (T(M),\ \leftarrow\mathrm{Conf}_1(\bar{0}),\ \mathrm{Conf}_2(\bar{0})\leftarrow)\Big|_{\overline{\mathrm{Res}}}\ \neg\bar{C}$$

$$\text{(ii)} \quad \dots\dots.2\ \dots\dots\dots\dots\dots\dots\dots\dots\dots\dots\dots\dots\dots\dots\dots\dots\dots \quad \bar{C}$$

These equivalences are easily proved paraphrasing the arguments given for Corollaries 2.2 and 2.4.

By (i) and (ii) the recursive inseparability is induced from H_1 and H_2 on the sets $\{F|\ \vdash_T F\}$ of provable respectively $\{F|\ \vdash_T \neg F\}$ of refutable sentences in the first order theory T with only nonlogical axiom

$$A(M) :\equiv \Lambda(T(M),\ \leftarrow\mathrm{Conf}_1(\bar{0}),\ \mathrm{Conf}_2(\bar{0})\leftarrow).$$

Consequently this theory has no recursive supertheory.

Similarly in every model of $A(M)$, the refutation set of all inputs x such that $\mathrm{Conf}_o(\bar{x})$ does not hold in the model separates H_1 and H_2 by (i) and (ii). This excludes recursive models if H_1 and H_2 are recursively inseparable.

The use of function symbols 0 and S can be avoided by appropriate ''prenexing'': collect all clauses where 0 appears, substitute 0 by an individual variable u and add the quantifier $\underset{u\ x}{V\ \Lambda}$; add the successor axiomatization $\underset{x\ v}{\Lambda\ V}\ N(x, v)$ for a new relation symbol N, substitute Sx in all clauses where it appears by v and replace the resulting conjunction F by (a Horn formula equivalent to) $\underset{x\ v\ y}{\Lambda\ \Lambda\ \Lambda}(N(x, v) \rightarrow F)$. Let the resulting formula be $A'(M)$. A recursive model of $A'(M)$ would yield a recursive model for $A(M)$ by restricting the given model to a subset $\{u_k|k\varepsilon N\}$ with u_o taken to fulfill the $\underset{u\ x}{V\ \Lambda}$—part of $A'(M)$ and u_{k+1} such that $N(u_k, u_{k+1})$ is true.

REMARK 2.6   From Corollary 2.5 one can conclude by an argument of Kreisel, 1961 that the well-known interpolation procedure in first-order logic cannot be realized by a total recursive function; also by making the $U(M)$-description of M unique up to isomorphism, the result by Friedman (1976) can be obtained in the finitary form proved by Gurevich (1984). He proved that there is no recursive way to bound the length of explications of implicitly defined predicates respectively the length of interpolants with respect to validity over finite first-order structures. For details, the interested reader may consult §FI1 in Börger (1985).

2.3 HORN STRUCTURE AND COMPLEXITY MEASURES FOR BOOLEAN FUNCTIONS

We show in Section 2.3.1 (*NP*-completeness of propositional logic) that in the case of polynomial time-bounded computations, a natural reinterpretation of our program reduction formulae of Section 2.2 in terms of propositional instead of first-order logic proves Cook's 1971 theorem on the *NP*-completeness of propositional logic. The Horn structure of the reduction formulae for deterministic programs is affected only by possible nondeterministic choices in nondeterministic programs. Since the satisfiability problem for propositional Horn formulae is in P, it is therefore natural to introduce in Section 2.3.2 (Horn complexity of Boolean functions), a complexity measure for Boolean functions f which considers the shortest definition of f by a (almost) Horn formula. It is shown in the theorem of Aanderaa & Börger, 1979 that this Horn complexity is polynomially related to the network complexity of Boolean functions. For sake of motivation, in Section 2.3.3 (Horn formulae and unit resolution), we prove the theorem of Henschen & Wos, 1974 that unit resolution is a complete proof procedure for first-order Horn formulae and show that in the propositional case, the underlying algorithm yields an efficient (polynomial time-bounded) decision resp. interpolation procedure.

2.3.1 *NP*-Completeness of Propositional Logic

Since polynomial time-bounded computations are finite, it is natural to try a translation of such computations into propositional logic by substituting in their first-order description of Section 2.2 the quantifications by conjunctions. Essentially this idea turns the result of Section 2.2 about the Σ_1-completeness of Hilbert's Entscheidungsproblem and Trachtenbrot's version of it for finite domains into the *NP*-completeness of the decision problem of propositional logic.

In the adaption of the reduction method of Section 2.2, in regard to the context of polynomial time complexities, there is only a small technical problem to assure that the construction of the reduction formula itself is computable in polynomial time. Our formulae in Section 2.2 describe the execution of every instruction (or elementary program) by referring to a logical encoding of the whole given configuration instead of referring just to that specific local part of it which is directly affected by the execution of the instruction. In this way we succeeded in giving a compact implementation of programs into short and syntactically restricted formulae and in trivializing the correctness proof for our construction. In the case of a translation of finite computations into propositional logic, such a global description of single computation steps would result in exponential length of the reduction formulae with respect to program and computation length. Note that for bounded computations, the latter becomes an explicit parameter of the formulae. Therefore, we modify our global description technique to a local one where we formulate that, except for the explicit expression of the local changes affected by single instructions, everything else remains unchanged.

Except for this technical point, both in this section and the next we follow the same schema of implementing programs by logical formulae as in Section 2.2. What changes are the resource restrictions on the computations and correspondingly the syntactical restrictions in and the interpretations of the logical reduction formula. For a better understanding of the core of the different constructions, we make the general pattern explicit in the following

Schema of Minimal Logical Implementation of Turing Machines
(Börger 1984a):

(i) To every deterministic or nondeterministic Turing machine program M and every M-configuration C, we associate a configuration formula $\overline{C}$ and a program formula Π_M which describes the meaning of M on C in the sense of the following *Simulation Property*: Let A be any model for Π_M. Let C be any M-configuration and t an arbitrary natural number. If $\overline{C}$ is true in A, then also $\overline{D}$ is true in A for at least one of the configurations D, which M may reach after precisely t computation steps started in C.

(ii) To every instance of a given M-halting problem H, we associate an input formula α and a stop formula ω with a corresponding logical decision problem D which describes H in the sense of the following *Reduction Property*: Any instance of the M-halting problem H has a positive answer iff the decision problem D for the corresponding formula $\Pi_M \wedge \alpha \wedge \omega$ has a positive answer.

For the definition of Π_M, we use logical formulae $S(t,t')$, $I_i(t)$, $P(t,u)$, $T_j(t,v)$ with the following intended meaning:

> $I_i(t)$ iff at time t the program M is in state i (instruction label)
> $P(t,u)$ iff .... is scanning the u-th tape cell
> $T_j(t,v)$ iff .... the content of the v-th tape cell is j
> $S(t,t')$ iff t' is immediate successor of (time moment) t

Let M be given by a program of instructions $(i,j,k,\pm 1,l)$ for states i,l and tape symbols j,k of M with the meaning: if in state i symbol j is scanned under the reading head, then M may print symbol k, move the reading head one position to the right $(+1)$ respectively to the left (-1) and go to the successive state l. (For easier formulation but without loss of generality, we assume that M contains for any instruction entry (i,j) either only right-movement or only left-movement instructions.) Π_M defines the meaning of these M-instructions for transforming given configurations at time t into successive configurations at time t' by the (finite or infinite) conjunction over all parameters of the following implications:

$$
\begin{aligned}
I_i(t) \wedge S(t,t') \wedge S(x,x') & \\
\wedge P(t,x) \wedge T_j(t,x) \quad \to \quad & \bigvee_{(i,j,k,+1,l)\,\epsilon\, M} P(t',x') \wedge T_k(t',x) \wedge I_l(t')
\end{aligned}
$$

$$\ldots\ldots\ldots x' \ldots\ldots\ldots x' \ldots\ldots\ldots -1 \ldots\ldots\ldots x \ldots\ldots\ldots x' \ldots\ldots\ldots$$

$$P(t,y) \wedge x \neq y \wedge T_j(t,x) \wedge S(t,t') \to T_j(t',x)$$

(read: outside the reading head position the tape symbols remain unchanged.)

$\overline{C}$ is defined in the obvious way to describe C using the auxiliary formulae $I_i(0)$, $P(0,0)$, $T_j(0,v)$ for initial state 0, reading head position (say) 0 and tape content at time moment 0.

From the definition it is obvious that Π_M and $\overline{C}$ satisfy the simulation property. (If your intuition needs help from a formal proof, try an induction on the computation length t: for $t = 0$ take $D = C$. For $t + 1$ one knows by induction hypothesis that $\overline{E}$ is true in the given model for at least one M-configuration E reached at time t from C; truth of $\overline{E}$ assures truth of corresponding Π_M-premises so that from the truth of Π_M one obtains the truth of one possible successive configuration D of E defined by the corresponding conclusions.)

REMARK 2.7 Note that in Π_M and in $\overline{C}$ (as already in U and $U(M)$ of Section 2.2) there is no formulation of assumptions about unique state, unique reading head position, or uniqueness of tape content. Π_M expresses only the local changements of data effected by an instruction and that all other tape positions which are not under actual control of the reading head remain unchanged. Accordingly $\overline{C}$ consists of only positive statements expressing an initial state (say 0), an initial reading head position (say 0), and through statement $T_j(0,v)$ that initially a content of the v-th cell is j. For this reason Π_M is a Horn formula if M is deterministic and if the clause $y \neq x$ can be expressed by some positive statement.

In order to simplify our *notation* but without loss of generality we assume for the following that the machines M are equipped with a tape which is infinite in one direction, say to the right, with cells numbered $0, 1, 2, \ldots$. Let us agree on 0 as initial state, cell 0 as initial position of the reading head, and 1 as (accepting) halting state. We assume that in a halting state the machine computation becomes constant, say because no program contains an instruction with a label which is a halting state.

An interpretation of Π_M in terms of propositional logic yields the hardness part of Cook's 1971 theorem on *NP*-completeness of propositional logic (which corresponds to the Σ_1-completeness of the first-order decision problem obtained from the obvious quantifier logic interpretation of Π_M). We only have to specify our auxiliary formulae, the reduction property and the input and stop formulae as follows.

The reduction property reads for all inputs q: M accepts $q \varepsilon \{0, 1\}^n$ in l steps iff $\Pi_{M,l} \wedge \alpha_{M,n}(q) \wedge \omega_{M,l}$ is satisfiable where $\Pi_M \wedge \alpha \wedge \omega$ is polynomial time bound computable from n, and l is a polynomial in the length n of the input q.

In Π_M the auxiliary formulae $I_i(t)$, $P(t,u)$, $T_j(t,v)$ have to be read as propositional variables for t, u, $v \leq l$ and with $u \neq v$, Stt', Suu' deleted from the formula but added as external conditions $u \neq v$, $t' = t + 1$, $u' = u + 1$ on the parameters.

The input formula α is defined as conjunction of the following formulae for $0 \leq j < n$, $n \leq k \leq l$ (with blank symbol 2 and new propositional variables x_j which are substituted by $q_j \varepsilon \{0, 1\}$ to obtain $\alpha(q)$):

$$T_o(0, j) \leftrightarrow \neg x_j \quad T_1(0, j) \leftrightarrow x_j \quad T_2(0, k) \quad I_o(0) \quad P(0, 0).$$

The stop formula ω expresses acceptance in state 1 in a nondeterministic milieu by saying that in the last step l, no nonaccepting state is true:

$$\omega :\equiv \bigwedge_{i \neq 1} \text{ not } I_i(l).$$

2.3.2 Horn Complexity of Boolean Functions

For deterministic programs M, the above formulae $\Pi_M \wedge \alpha \wedge \omega(q)$ are trivially equivalent to Horn formulae for each 0-1-sequence q substituted for the x-variables. Since the satisfiability problem for propositional Horn formulae is in P (see below Section 2.3.3), this propositional Horn description of finite deterministic computations makes it particularly interesting in the context of the $P = NP$-problem to study the effect which results from a restriction to Horn structure in the definition of Boolean functions. This motivates the following notion introduced by Aanderaa & Börger (1979).

DEFINITION 2.3   Let α be a propositional formula, $x = x_1, \ldots, x_n$ a sequence of (not necessarily all) propositional variables occurring in α. For a Boolean function f: $\{0, 1\}^n \rightarrow \{0, 1\}$ one says that α defines f with respect to x iff

For all $q = (q_1, \ldots, q_n) \varepsilon \{0, 1\}^n$: $f(q) = 1$ iff $\alpha[x/q]$ is satisfiable.

Here $\alpha[x/q]$ denotes the result of substituting q_i for x_i in α. We call the x_i input variables of α and all other variables in α working variables. We say that α is a *Horn formula in its working variables* iff one obtains a Horn formula if every literal with an input variable x_i is replaced by a new variable u. Finally we define the *Horn complexity $C_H(f)$ of* f as the minimal length of a formula which defines f and is Horn in its working variables.

From the Horn description of deterministic computations in Section 2.2.1 we obtain as easy corollary *a polynomial bound for Horn complexity*:

PROPOSITION 2.1 One can exhibit a polynomial p such that for every n-ary Boolean function f and any deterministic Turing machine M computing f holds:

$$C_H(f) \leq p \text{ (program size } (M), n, \text{ maximal run time of } M \text{ on inputs in } \{0,1\}^n)$$

where the program size of M is the number of instructions in M and the maximal run time $l_{M,n}$ of M on inputs in $\{0,1\}^n$ the maximal length of M-computations starting with input q for arbitrary 0-1-sequences q of length n.

Proof For deterministic M computing f, $l = l_{M,n}$ and $q \varepsilon \{0,1\}^n$ we have:

$$f(q) = 1 \text{ iff } M \text{ started with input } q \text{ accepts in } l \text{ steps}$$
$$\text{iff } \Pi_{M,l} \wedge \alpha_{M,n}(q) \wedge \omega_{M,l} \text{ is satisfiable.}$$

Therefore $F :\equiv \Pi_{M,l} \wedge \alpha_{M,n} \wedge \omega_{M,l}$ defines f, and since it is Horn in its working variables and by the theorem of length bounded by some polynomial p in the program size of M, n, and l it follows

$$C_H(f) \leq \text{ length of } F \leq p \text{ (program size } (M), n, l_{M,n}).$$

The above proposition shows that the Horn complexity of a Boolean function is not essentially bigger than its computational complexity in terms of program size, input length, and computation time. By a similar argument, it can be shown that if in the logical definitions of Boolean functions, the restriction to formulae, which are Horn at least in their working variables, increases for at least one f the logical complexity (i.e., minimal length of f-defining formulae) more than by an arbitrary previously given polynomial p, then $P \neq NP$:

PROPOSITION 2.2 *If for every polynomial p there is a Boolean function f such that $C_H(f) > p(C(f))$, then $P \neq NP$. ($C(f)$ denotes the minimal length of a formula defining f.)*

Proof Assume $P = NP$. Then some deterministic Turing machine M decides satisfiability for propositional formulae in some polynomial time bound p. For any Boolean function f, any β of minimal length defining f and any $q \varepsilon \{0,1\}^n$ therefore holds (abbreviate $l(\beta) = $ length of β):

$$f(q) = 1 \text{ iff } \beta(q) \text{ is satisfiable}$$
$$\text{iff } M \text{ accepts } \beta(q) \text{ in } p(l(\beta)) \text{ steps}$$
$$\text{iff } \Pi_{M,p(l(\beta))} \wedge \alpha_{M,n}(q) \wedge \omega_{M,p(l(\beta))}$$

Since the last formula is Horn in its working variables and of length polynomially bounded in $M, p(l(\beta))$ and n, we have $C_H(f) \leq p_1(l(\beta)) = p_1(C(f))$ for some polynomial p_1 independent from f.

The above two propositions refer to a strong connection of Horn complexity for Boolean functions to the $P = NP$-problem. Indeed, we now show by adaption of our logical description method to logical networks that *Horn complexity and network complexity for Boolean functions are the same up to a polynomial*, illuminating thereby the naturalness of the complexity measures involved.

Before proceeding to a proof of this fact, let us recall that a *logical network* N is a finite acyclic graph with labelled nodes such that

1) every node n of N has either 0 or 2 entering edges. The nodes without entering edges are called entries of N,

2) every entry n of N is labelled with a propositional variable $op(n)$,

3) every nonentry n of N is labelled with a binary operation $op(n)$. The entering edges of n correspond in a fixed way to the arguments of $op(n)$.

To every node n of N with entries labelled with $x_1, \ldots, x_m$ is associated the computed m-ary Boolean function $f_{N,n}$ of $q_1, \ldots, q_m$ defined recursively by applying $op(n)$ to the values computed for the preceeding nodes, whereas for every entry n labelled with $x_i (1 \leq i \leq m) f_{N,n}$ takes as value $f_{N,n}(q_1, \ldots, q_m)$ the value q_i associated to the variable x_i. The network complexity $C_N(f)$ of an m-ary Boolean function f is defined as the minimal number of binary Boolean operations in any logical network N with entries $x_1, \ldots, x_m$ which computes f (i.e., with $f = f_{N,n}$ for some node n).

THEOREM 2.2   (Aanderaa & Börger 1981). *Horn and network complexity of Boolean functions are polynomially equivalent.* Indeed for every Boolean function f holds:

$$(1) \quad C_H(f) \leq 0(C_N(f)) \qquad\qquad (2) \quad C_N(f) \leq 0(C_H(f)^2(\lg C_H(f))^3)$$

Proof   We first show (1) for arbitrary f. Since $C_N(f)$ can be bounded by some linear expression in the network complexity of f with respect to logical networks built up with any complete set of binary Boolean operations, we need to consider only networks computing f with binary operations say $\wedge$, $\vee$ and $|$ (Sheffer's stroke). We show how one can associate to an arbitrary such logical network N (computing a Boolean function f) a Horn network formula σ_N, a Krom input formula α_n which is Horn in the input variables, and a simple output formula ω such that $\sigma_N \wedge \alpha_n \wedge \omega$ defines f with respect to its input variables and is of length linearly bounded by the complexity of N. By such a construction (1) is proved.

Let N be an arbitrary logical network with nodes $N_o, \ldots, N_m$ where $N_1, \ldots, N_n$ are the entries, N_o is the node with respect to which N computes f and the nonentries are labeled with $\wedge$, $\vee$ or $|$. Every node N_k is encoded by variables y_k, u_k with the *intended interpretation*

$$y_k = f_{N, N_k(q)} \quad \text{and} \quad u_k \leftrightarrow \neg y_k$$

for previously given values q to the input variables $y_1, \ldots, y_n$. Define, therefore, σ_N as conjunction of the following formulae for every node N_k labelled with $op(N_k)$ applied to the directly preceeding nodes N_i, N_j in this order $-0 \leq i, j, k \leq m-$, describing the computation at node N_k for the arguments computed at N_i, N_j:

Case 1. $op(N_k) = \wedge$:

$$(y_i \wedge y_j) \rightarrow y_k \qquad u_i \rightarrow u_k \qquad u_j \rightarrow u_k$$

Case 2. $op(N_k) = \vee$:

$$y_i \rightarrow y_k \qquad y_j \rightarrow y_k \qquad (u_i \wedge u_j) \rightarrow u_k$$

Case 3. $op(N_k) = |$:

$$u_i \wedge u_j \rightarrow y_k \qquad y_i \rightarrow u_k \qquad y_j \rightarrow u_k$$

Define α_n as conjunction of all $y_i \leftrightarrow x_i$ and $u_i \leftrightarrow \neg x_i$ for $1 \leq i \leq n$ and $\omega :\equiv y_o \wedge \neg u_o$. The *reduction property* for all $q \varepsilon \{0, 1\}^n$ reads:

$f_{N, N_o}(q) = 1$ iff $\sigma_N \wedge \alpha_n(q) \wedge y_o \wedge \neg u_o$ is satisfiable where as before $\alpha_n(q)$ denotes α_n after substitution of q_i for x_i.

The proof of the reduction property follows the now well-established pattern: from left to right the above indicated intended interpretation satisfies $\sigma_N \wedge \alpha_n(q) \wedge \omega$. Conversely, any truth assignment for which that formula is true simulates the network computation in the sense that for every node N_k of N:

$$(1) \quad f_{N, N_k}(q) = 1 \quad \text{implies} \quad A(y_k) = 1$$

$$(2) \quad f_{N, N_k}(q) = 0 \quad \text{implies} \quad A(u_k) = 1$$

from which $f_{N, N_o}(q) = 1$ follows because $A(u_o) = 0$ by ω.

The simulation property is shown by induction along the computation process of N: the base of the induction at entries $N_i (1 \leq i \leq n)$ is assured by $\alpha_n(q)$, whereas for every node N_k with directly preceding nodes N_i, N_j in this order, the claim follows from the inductive hypothesis, the formulae corresponding to this node and $f_{N, N_k}(q) = op(N_k)(f_{N, N_i}(q), f_{N, N_j}(q))$.

Instead of an explicit transformation of minimal definitions of f by formulae which are Horn in their input variables into a normal form suited for the construction of a logical network defining f, we base our *proof of inequality (2)* on the following:

Fact 1.   The satisfiability problem for Horn formulae can be decided by a deterministic Turing machine within time bound $0(l \ lg \ l)^2$ in the length l of the input.

Fact 2.   For all 0-1-Turing machines M and every number m there are logical networks N_m simulating m steps of M with magnitude $\|N_m\| = 0(m \ lg \ m)$.

Fact 1 will be shown below, for fact 2 we refer the reader to Schnorr, 1976.

For an arbitrary Boolean function f, let α_f be a formula of minimal length m that defines f and that is Horn in its working variables. Then the following equivalences hold for all 0-1-sequences q:

$$f(q) \ = \ 1 \quad \text{iff} \quad \alpha_f(x|q) \text{ is satisfiable (since } \alpha_f \text{ defines } f)$$
$$\text{iff} \quad M \text{ accepts } \alpha_f(x|q) \text{ in } 0(m \ lg \ m)^2 \text{ steps (fact 1)}$$
$$\text{iff} \quad N_{0(m \ lg \ m)^2}(\alpha_f(x|q)) \ = \ 1 \text{ (fact 2).}$$

Therefore,

$$C_N(f) \leqq \|N_{0(m \ lg \ m)^2}\| \leqq 0(0(m \ lg \ m)^2 \cdot lg(0(m \ lg \ m)^2))$$
$$\leqq 0(C_H(f)^2 \cdot lg(C_H(f))^3)$$

2.3.3   Horn Formulae and Unit Resolution

The interest for Horn structure in descriptions of machine programs derives also from the computational simplicity of the decision problem for Horn formula as is shown in the following

THEOREM 2.3   (Henschen & Wos 1974).   The (even positive) unit resolution calculus is complete for Horn formulae, i.e., for every first order formula α holds:

(1) α is contradictory iff the empty clause $\square$ can be derived from α by resolution steps which are applied each time to an atomic formula Π and a Horn clause $\neg\Pi \lor \sigma$ to yield a resolvent σsub for some substitution sub.

COROLLARY 2.6   For propositional Horn formulae the (positive) unit resolution calculus is a polynomial time decision procedure.

COROLLARY 2.7   (Dahlhaus et al., 1984).   There is a polynomial time computable interpolation procedure for propositional Horn formulae.

Proof   We describe an algorithm which for the Horn clause set α of a given first order formula in Skolem normal form as input enumerates two sets L_o, L_1 of atomic formulae such that every element of L_1 respectively L_o follows respectively is refuted logically from α and furthermore:

(2) α is satisfiable iff there is no unifiable pair $\Pi_i \varepsilon L_i$.

The idea of the algorithm is natural: the sets L_i are enumerated in steps starting from $L_{i,o} := \emptyset$. In step $t+1$ we roughly speaking add to $L_{i,t}$ all conclusions of implications in α all of which premises are in $L_{1,t}$. (This is the usual procedure to approximate the least Herbrand model of α for satisfiable α.)

Formally, we set $L_{i,o} := \emptyset$. At step $t+1$ we consider every clause $\Pi_1 \ldots \Pi_n \to \lambda$ in α with atomic Π_i and literal $\lambda \varepsilon \{\Pi, \neg\Pi\}$. Check if there are substitutions sub_i ($i \le n$) with $\mathrm{sub}_o =$ identity and atomic formulae $\sigma_i \varepsilon L_{1,t}$ such that for all $i \le n$ one has: $(\Pi_{i+1} \wedge \ldots \wedge \Pi_n \to \lambda)\mathrm{sub}_i$ is a first order resolvent of $(\Pi_i \wedge \ldots \wedge \Pi_n \to \lambda)\mathrm{sub}_{i-1}$ and σ_i. If yes, then add $\Pi\mathrm{sub}_n$ to $L_{1,t}$ (if $\lambda \equiv \Pi$) respectively $\Pi\mathrm{sub}_n$ to $L_{o,t}$ (if $\lambda \equiv \neg\Pi$) to form $L_{i,t+1}$.

If there is a unifiable pair α_o, α_1 of $\alpha_i \varepsilon L_{i,t+1}$, then the algorithm terminates with $L_i := L_{i,t+1}$ and α is contradictory. Also, check whether $L_{i,t} = L_{i,t+1}$ for $i = 0$ and $i = 1$. In the positive case, the algorithm terminates with $L_i := L_{i,t+1}$ and the set of closed atomic formulae obtained from the elements of L_1 by substituting terms of the Herbrand domain of α for variables is the minimal Herbrand model for α. Otherwise, the algorithm proceeds with the next step.

If this algorithm does not terminate, we set $L_i := \bigcup_t L_{i,t}$.

From the definition of the above algorithm we have for all time moments t:

(3) For all $\Pi \varepsilon L_{1,t}$: Π is derivable from α by (positive) unit resolution

$$\ldots\ldots\ldots\ldots L_{o,t}\colon \neg\Pi \ldots\ldots\ldots\ldots\ldots\ldots\ldots\ldots\ldots$$

From (3) one obtains easily (2) as follows: If α is satisfiable, then by the correctness of the resolution rule, there is no unifiable pair of atomic formulae $\Pi_i \varepsilon L_i$. If there is no such pair, then the algorithm produces the core of the minimal Herbrand model of α, therefore, α is satisfiable. (2) and (3) obviously yield (1).

Proof of Corollary 2.6   In the case of a propositional input α, the above algorithm terminates after at most n steps (for the number n of variables of α).

Proof of Corollary 2.7   For contradictory Horn formulae $\alpha \wedge \beta$, we have to produce an interpolant δ, i.e., such that $\alpha \to \delta, \delta \to \beta$ are valid and δ contains only variables occurring in both α and β. Extend the above algorithm to compute also the set C of clauses which are used to assign truth values to variables; without loss of generality take only one such clause for each computed variable.

For simplicity of formulation assume that clauses $p \to \neg x$ have been substituted by $(p \to x) \wedge x \to \square$ with $\square$ standing for the empty clause (falsum). Assume the algorithm to be modified accordingly.

Apply the algorithm to the given $\alpha \wedge \beta$. After termination determine the variables $x_1, \ldots, x_m$ that occur in α and C but not in β and get truth value 1 assigned by the algorithm. Starting from $I_o := \alpha \cap C$ form I_{i+1} by substituting in each I_i-formula each occurrence of x_{i+1} by its premise p in the C-clause $p = x_{i+1}$, followed by deletion of that clause.

By definition I_m contains only variables common to α and β, $I_m \wedge \beta$ is still contradictory if $\alpha \wedge \beta$ was, and α implies I_m.

2.4 DESCRIPTIONS OF BOUNDED COMPUTATIONS OVER FINITE STRUCTURES

We present characterizations of some well-known complexity classes by logical decision problems of classes of syntactically restricted formulae to be interpreted over finite domains. In Section 2.4.1 (spectra and nondeterministic n-fold exponential time complexity) we give a reinterpretation of the schema in Section 2.3 in terms of n-th order logic and obtain thereby a characterization of deterministic n-fold exponential time-bounded halting problems as spectra of n-th order formulae; as a corollary the emptiness resp. infinity problem for first order spectra can be shown to be Π_1- resp. Π_2-complete. In Section 2.4.2 (Horn prefix classes and complexity classes) we apply the logical reduction technique to Turing respectively alternating pushdown automata to characterize PSPACE resp. EXP-TIME by the satisfiability problem of syntactically restricted PROLOG programs corresponding to the classical decidable prefix classes $V^*\Lambda^*$ of Bernays & Schön-finkel with only binary clauses respectively $V^*\Lambda V^*$ of Ackermann.

2.4.1 Spectra and Nondeterministic n-fold Exponential Time Complexity Classes

The spectrum of a formula α is defined as the set of all finite cardinalities of models of α:

$$spectrum(\alpha) := \{k \mid \alpha \text{ is satisfiable over } k = \{0, 1, \ldots, k-1\}\}.$$

Let SPECTRA_n for $0 < n$ be the class of all spectrum (α) for formulae α of logic of order n (without function symbols but with equality).

The restriction to formulae with equality but without function symbols and to cardinalities of finite models of them is imposed by well-known properties of first-order logic. Function symbols can be eliminated by predicate symbols describing their graph. A formula without identity that admits a model of cardinality n admits models of any bigger cardinality. By the Löwenheim-Skolem and the compactness theorem, any denumerable first-order theory either has no infinite model or models of any infinite cardinalities; and in the first case, it can have finite models (if any) only over domains of a finite number of cardinalities. Admitting infinitely many axioms would make the Spektralproblem (i.e., to characterize the class of spectra) trivial since any finite number n can be characterized by an equational formula α_n—saying that there are precisely (i.e., at least and not more than) n elements in the domain—and therefore be excluded as possible domain cardinality by the negation of α_n.

A natural interpretation of the basic formulae in our implementation schema of Section 2.3 in terms of type logic of n-th order yields the hardness part of the following characterization of $\mathrm{SPECTRA}_n$ by the nondeterministic n-fold exponential time complexity class (Bennett 1962, Rödding & Schwichtenberg 1972, Jones & Selman 1974, Christen 1974; for an exact history see §1 in Börger 1984a):

Characterization theorem for SPECTRA of n-th order.
$\mathrm{SPECTRA}_n = \mathrm{NTIME}(\alpha_3^n \circ 0)$ for all $n \geq 1$, where $\alpha_3 = \lambda x.2^x$ and $\alpha_3^n = \alpha_3 \circ \ldots \circ \alpha_3$ n-times, $\alpha_3^0 = $ identity.

Proof (of the hardness part). We *specify the reduction property* of the schema in Section 2.3 as follows: to an arbitrary Turing-machine program M and arbitrary constant $c > 0$, we define an ordering axiom $\mathrm{Ord}_K(Z, S)$—for a linear order K with zero predicate Z and immediate successor relation S—and program, input and stop formulae $\Pi_{M,c}$, α_c, $\omega_{M,c}$ such that for all unary inputs $k = 11 \ldots 1 \geq 2$ holds:

M accepts k in $\leq \alpha_3^n(k^c)$ steps

iff $\mathrm{Ord}_K(Z, S) \wedge \Pi_{M,c} \wedge \alpha_c \wedge \omega_{M,c}$ has a model over $k = \{0, 1, \ldots, k-1\}$.

(This yields the claim of the hardness part because a polynomial bound k^c in the length k of a unary input corresponds to an exponential bound in the length of the binary representation of k.)

To describe over a domain with k elements, say $k := \{0, 1, \ldots, k-1\}$, the M-computation of length $\alpha_3^n(k^c)$ started with input k, we need an encoding of $\alpha_3^n(k^c)$ many successive "time moments" together with the corresponding situation of the computation. The *idea* is to *create by successive power set construction*—starting from the c-ary cartesian product over k—the needed $\alpha_3^n(k^c)$ objects of a type σ_n of order n, to *order these objects in a linear way* and then to describe the M-computation in the same way as done in Section 2.3 but using a zero predicate Z and a successor relation S relative to the previously defined linear ordering K, and an embedding F of k into a segment of these σ_n-type objects for description of the input.

Remember that *types* are inductively defined by: ι is a type (of domain elements) of order $|\iota| := 0$, and with $\tau_1, \ldots, \tau_s$ also $(\tau_1, \ldots, \tau_s)$ is a type (of s-ary predicates) of order $|(\tau_1, \ldots, \tau_s)| := \max\{|\tau_i| \mid 1 \leq i \leq s\} + 1$. For any type τ, there are countably many variables x^τ, y^τ, $\ldots$ (for objects) of type τ from which *formulae* are inductively defined by saying that any

$$x^{(\tau_1, \ldots, \tau_s)} \, y^{\tau_1} \ldots y^{\tau_s} \quad \text{and} \quad x^\tau = y^\tau$$

are formulae (the "atomic" formulae) and with α, β also $\neg\alpha$, $(\alpha \wedge \beta)$, $\bigwedge_{x^\tau} \beta$ for

any type τ. α is said of *order n* if all bounded variables in α have types of order $\leq n-1$ and all free occurring variables in α have types of order $\leq n$.

Formally the *power set types* over k^c are defined by

$$\sigma_1 := \underbrace{(\iota \ \ldots \ \iota)}_{c\text{-times}} \qquad \sigma_{i+1} := (\sigma_i) \qquad |\sigma_n| = n$$

Over $k = \{0, \ldots, k-1\}$, there are exactly $\alpha_3^n(k^c)$ objects of type σ_n where by objects of type σ_o we understand c-tuples of elements from k. We use x, y, z as variables of type ι and $t, u, v, w, t', u', \ldots$ as variables of type σ_n for $n \geq 1$ respectively as c-tuples of variables of type ι for $n = 0$ (using $u = v$ as abbreviation for $u_1 = v_1 \wedge \ldots \wedge u_c = v_c$, similarly $\bigwedge\limits_u$, etc.).

Define the formula $\mathrm{Ord}_K(Z, S)$ of order $n+1$—expressing that Z represents "zero" (the first element) and S the "successor" relation with respect to a linear ordering K of all type-σ_n objects over any (finite) domain—as conjunction of the following formulae:

$$\bigwedge\limits_u \bigwedge\limits_v \bigwedge\limits_w \ ((Kuv \vee Kvu \vee u = v) \wedge \neg Kuu \wedge (Kuv \wedge Kvw \to Kuw))$$

$$\bigvee\limits_u Zu \wedge \bigwedge\limits_u (Zu \to \neg \bigvee\limits_u Kvu) \quad \{\text{``zero'' has no ``predecessor''}\}$$

$$\bigwedge\limits_u \bigwedge\limits_v (Suv \leftrightarrow (Kuv \wedge \neg \bigvee\limits_w (Kuw \wedge Kwv))) \quad \{\text{no element between successors}\}$$

Using $\mathrm{Ord}(Z, S)$, we can define the program formula $\Pi_{M,c}$ as in the preceding sections using Z respectively S for 0 resp. $t+1$ and (almost) the same *intended meaning for the* (predicate) variables I_i, P and T_j *encoding* over any domain $k = \{0, \ldots, k-1\}$ respectively state i, the pointer (reading head) position and tape cell inscription a_j for any time moment t and any tape position u of any M-computation started with input k (let $-l$ be the number of the leftmost cell visited during the given computation and $|t|$ the order number of t in the given ordering K):

$I_i t$ is true iff at time $|t|$ instruction i is executed
Ptu is true iff $|u| = $ pointer position at time $|t|$
$T_j tu$ is true iff at time $|t|$ the tape cell with number $|u|$ contains letter a_j

To define the input representation, we make use of the following *embedding formula* stating that the given domain (namely $k = \{0, \ldots, k-1\}$ for some k) is embedded into a segment of the ordering of the σ_n-objects by some function (with graph) F:

$$\bigwedge\limits_x \bigvee\limits_u Fxu \ \{\text{existence}\} \wedge \bigwedge\limits_x \bigwedge\limits_u \bigwedge\limits_v (Fxu \wedge Fxv \to u = v) \ \{\text{uniqueness}\}$$

$$\wedge \bigwedge\limits_x \bigwedge\limits_y \bigwedge\limits_u (Fxu \wedge Fyu \to x = y) \ \{\text{injectivity}\}$$

$$\wedge \bigwedge\limits_u \bigwedge\limits_v \bigwedge\limits_w \bigwedge\limits_y \bigwedge\limits_x (Kuv \wedge Kvw \wedge Fxu \wedge Fyw \to \bigvee\limits_z Fzv) \ \{\text{range is a segment}\}$$

Define the *input formula* α_c as conjunction of the above embedding formula and the following formulae:

$$\bigwedge_t (Zt \to I_1 t) \quad \{\text{read: at time point 0 instruction 1 is to be executed}\}$$

$$\bigwedge_t (Zt \to \underset{u}{V} \underset{x}{V}(Ptu \wedge Fxu \wedge \bigwedge_v (Kvu \to \neg \underset{y}{V} Fyv)))$$

{read: at time 0 the pointer position is encoded by the first F-value}

$$\bigwedge_t (Zt \to \bigwedge_u ((\underset{x}{V} Fxu \to T_1 tu) \wedge ((\neg \underset{x}{V} Fxu) \to T_o tu))$$

{read: at time 0 every tape cell (with number) in the range of F has tape
inscription $a_1 = 1$ and any other the blank symbol $a_o = b$.}

Define the *stop formula* $\omega_{M,c}$ by saying that at the last moment no instruction different from the accepting-state-instruction I_o can be executed:

$$\bigwedge_t ((\neg \underset{u}{V} Ktu) \to \neg I_1 t \wedge \ldots \wedge \neg I_r t)$$

From the simulation property of the implementation scheme in Section 2.3, it follows that the conjunction

$$\alpha :\equiv \mathrm{Ord}(Z, S) \wedge \Pi_{M,c} \wedge \alpha_c \wedge \omega_{M,c}$$

of program, start and stop formulae with respect to the zero-successor-structure defined by $\mathrm{Ord}_K(Z, S)$ fulfills the reduction property.

If we adapt the axiomatization method of the main construction directly to rudimentary predicates instead of polynomially time-bounded machine computations, we can derive from it and classical results about normal forms for partial recursive functions Büchi's strengthening of Trachtenbrot's theorem giving for first-order spectra *the exact determination of the arithmetical complexity of the emptiness* (incidentally the same comes out also for *the infinity*) *problem*:

COROLLARY 2.8 *Every rudimentary predicate has a first-order representation in finite domains*. Therefore, for first order spectra the emptiness problem is Π_1-complete and the infinity problem Π_2-complete.

Remember that the *rudimentary predicates* are those number theoretical relations which can be defined explicitly from the graphs of "$+$" and "$\cdot$" using Boolean operations and bounded quantifications ("explicitly" means that identification or permutation of variables and substitution of number constants are allowed). A number theoretical predicate R is said to have a *first order representation in finite domains* iff some first order formula $\alpha_{\bar{R}}$ (containing in particular a predicate symbol $\bar{R}$ of the same arity as R and eventually a binary predicate symbol K) is satisfiable over every domain $k := \{0, 1, \ldots, k-1\}$ with K

interpreted as $<$ and in every such model of $\alpha_{\overline{R}}$ the interpretation of $\overline{R}$ is the restriction of R to k.

Proof of Corollary 2.8   The zero predicate $\lambda x \cdot x = 0$ and the successor relation $\lambda x, y \cdot y = x + 1$ have representation $\mathrm{Ord}(Z, S)_Z$ resp. $\mathrm{Ord}(Z, S)_S$ with $\mathrm{Ord}(Z, S)$ as defined in the main construction. From this, one obtains by a straightforward induction {*Exercise!*} a representation $\alpha_{\overline{R}}$ for every rudimentary predicate R starting with $\alpha_{\overline{R}} :\equiv \mathrm{Ord}(Z, S) \wedge \mathrm{add}$ for $R = G_+ := \lambda x, y, z \cdot x + y = z$ and $\alpha_{\overline{R}} :\equiv \mathrm{Ord}(Z, S) \wedge \mathrm{add} \wedge \mathrm{mult}$ for $R = G$. where add and mult are the recursive definitions of " $+$ " respectively " $\cdot$ " from Z, S:

$$\mathrm{add} :\equiv \bigwedge_x \bigwedge_y \bigwedge_z (Zy \rightarrow (\overline{G}_+ xyz \leftrightarrow x = z)) \quad \{\text{read: } x + 0 = x\}$$

$$\wedge \bigwedge_x \bigwedge_{y'} \bigwedge_{z'} \bigwedge_y (Syy' \rightarrow (\overline{G}_+ xy'z' \leftrightarrow \underset{z}{V}(\overline{G}_+ xyz \wedge Szz')))$$

$$\{x + y' = (x + y)'\}$$

$$\mathrm{mult} :\equiv \bigwedge_x \bigwedge_y \bigwedge_z (Zy \rightarrow (\overline{G}.xyz \leftrightarrow y = z))) \quad \{\text{read: } x0 = x\}$$

$$\wedge \bigwedge_x \bigwedge_{y'} \bigwedge_{z'} \bigwedge_y (Syy' \rightarrow (\overline{G}.xy'z' \leftrightarrow \underset{z}{V}(\overline{G}.xyz \wedge \overline{G}_+ zxz')))$$

$$\{xy' = xy + x\}$$

Since Kleene's T-predicate can be constructed as rudimentary predicate (see Smullyan, 1961) there is in particular a first order representation $\alpha_{\overline{T}}$ of T in finite domains where furthermore $T(i, x, y)$ implies $i, x < y$. Therefore, the Σ_1-complete nonemptiness problem $\{i | \underset{x}{V} \underset{y}{V} T(i, x, y)\}$ for the r.e. sets $W_i = \{x | \exists y T(i, x, y)\}$ respectively their Π_2-complete infinity problem $\{i | \overset{\infty}{\exists} x \exists y T(i, x, y)\}$ is 1-1-reduced to the nonemptiness respectively infinity problem for spectrum (nonempty$_i$) respectively spectrum (inf$_i$) where

$$\mathrm{nonempty}_i :\equiv \underset{z}{V} \underset{x}{V} \underset{y}{V} ((\alpha_{\overline{\lambda z \cdot z = i}} \wedge \overline{z = i}) \wedge (\alpha_{\overline{T}} \wedge \overline{T}zxy))$$

{read: machine i for some input x has an accepting computation y}

$$\mathrm{inf}_i :\equiv \text{machine } i \text{ for some } x \text{ has an accepting computation } y$$

$$\wedge \bigwedge_{y_1} \neg Kyy_1 \quad \{y \text{ is the last element in the model}\}$$

$$\wedge \bigwedge_{y_1} (\overline{T}zxy_1 \rightarrow \neg Ky_1y) \quad \{\text{no accepting computation for input } x \text{ is shorter than } y\}$$

The characterization of spectra applies equally well to finitely axiomatizable classes of finite structures: one only needs to add to the construction an appropriate encoding of subsets of finite sets. Remember that a finitely (first order) axiomatizable *projective class* of finite type in the sense of Tarski is a class of precisely those finite structures (i.e., with finite domain and finitely many finite relations (without loss of generality we treat functions as graph predicates) over that domain) which are models of a formula $\underset{P_1}{V} \ldots \underset{P_c}{V} \alpha$ without free individual variables, with the bounded predicate variables $P_1, \ldots, P_c$ and some free occurring predicate symbols $R_1, \ldots, R_d$; sometimes such a class is also called $\{R_1, \ldots, R_d\}$-spectrum of $\underset{P_1}{V} \ldots \underset{P_c}{V} \alpha$ or simply *generalized* (first-order) *spectrum*. We tacitly assume in the following that all model classes we are talking about are closed under isomorphisms, what in this context is equivalent to saying that we can restrict our attention to structures over $k := \{0, 1, \ldots, k-1\}$ with the usual ordering $<$, the initial element 0 and the successor relation $\lambda x, y \cdot y = x+1$. (formally: satisfying $\mathrm{Ord}(Z_o, S_o)$ with respect to K_o for predicate symbols Z_o respectively K_o, S_o of type (ι) respectively $(\iota\iota)$).

Formally define the *encoding $e(S)$ of a structure $S = (k; R_1, \ldots, R_d)$* as concatenation of encodings $e(R_1), \ldots, e(R_d)$ of $R_1, \ldots, R_d$ where for r-ary R $e(R)$ is defined as $\{a_1, a_2\}$-word of length k^r which has i-th digital a_2 respectively a_1 if R is true respectively false for the i-th element of k^r with respect to lexicographical ordering. (Note that since we assume here $0 < d$, the domain cardinality k need not to be encoded since it can be computed nondeterministically in polynomial time from $e(S)$. *Exercise*: Prove this observation.) For a class C of structures let $e(C) = \{e(S)|S \varepsilon C\}$.

The characterization of spectra of first order extends by the same construction to generalized spectra as has been observed by Fagin:

COROLLARY 2.9 (Fagin 1974). *The* (encodings of) *generalized spectra are precisely the NP-sets* (of nonempty words).

Proof The trivial inclusion that any generalized spectrum is in *NP* is left as exercise. For any $L \varepsilon NP$ not containing the empty word holds $L = e(\{I\}\text{-spec-trum}(\alpha))$ where α is the formula defined in the preceding theorem for a non-deterministic Turing machine M accepting L in time k^c, but with additionally $\mathrm{Ord}(0, \lambda x, y \cdot y = x+1)$, in order to restrict attention to models over $k = \{0, 1, \ldots, k-1\}$, and the following replacements in the input formula $\alpha_{M,c}$: replace the embedding formula by the *new embedding formula* expressing that the domain $k = \{0, 1, \ldots, k-1\}$ is embedded via F in an order preserving way into a segment of the c-tuples:

$$\underset{x}{\bigwedge} \underset{u}{V} Fxu \wedge \underset{x}{\bigwedge} \underset{y}{\bigwedge} \underset{v}{\bigwedge} \underset{w}{\bigwedge} (Fxv \wedge Fyw \rightarrow (S_o xy \leftrightarrow Svw))$$

{Note that the order-preservation implies uniqueness and injectivity of F and the fact that the range of F is a K-segment}; replace the initial-tape-description by the following *new initial-tape-formula* expressing that M starts at time 0 with the encoding of the monadic "input" predicate I, which is of length k and is inscribed in the tape cells numbered by F-values u:

$$\bigwedge_t (Zt \to \bigwedge_x \bigwedge_u (Fxu \to ((Ix \to T_2 tu) \land (\neg Ix \to T_1 tu)))$$

$$\land \bigwedge_t (Zt \to \bigwedge_u ((\neg \lor_x Fxu) \to T_o tu)) \quad \{\text{blank } a_o \text{ outside range } (F)\}$$

Finally, bound all predicate symbols except I by an existential quantifier.

REMARK 2.8   Corollaries $1, 2$ illuminate the connection of the Spektral problem to Cook's problem whether $P = NP$. A positive solution to *Asser's problem* (whether the complement of every first-order spectrum is again a first-order spectrum) for example would imply that also unary-represented NP-sets are closed under complementation, whereas a negative solution would imply that also NP is not closed under complementation and thereby $P \neq NP$. If $P = NP$, then every first-order spectrum can be decided by a deterministic Turing machine in polynomial time with unary representation respectively in exponential time with binary representation.

References and Further Readings

The Spektralproblem has been formulated by Heinrich Scholz: Ein ungelöstets Problem in der symbolischen Logik, in *The Journal of Symbolic Logic 17*, 1952, pg. 160.

Asser's problem has been formulated in G. Asser: Das Repräsentantenproblem im Prädikatenkalkül der ersten Stufe mit Identität, in *Zeitschr. f. math. Logik und Grundlagen der Mathematik 1*, 1956, 252–263. The results presented here have been found by: J. Bennett: On Spectra, Doctoral Dissertation, Princeton University, 1962 (Microfilm HO1: 63-496); D. Rödding & H. Schwichtenberg: Bemerkungen zum Spektralproblem, in: *Zeitschrift f. math. Logik und Grundlagen der Math. 18*, 1972, 1–12 (submitted 26.2.1971); N.D. Jones & A.L. Selman, "Turing Machines and the Spectra of First-order Formulas," in *The Journal of Symbolic Logic 39*, 1974, 139–150 (announced as "Automata theoretic solutions to a problem of H. Scholz" in: *Notices AMS 19,2* 1972; R. Fagin, "Generalized First-Order Spectra and Polynomial-Time Recognizable Sets," in *Complexity of Computation*, R. Karp (ed.), SIAM-AMS Proceedings 7, 1974, 43–73; C.A. Christen, 1973.

Fagin's 1974 paper contains more results about the relation of the Spektralproblem and of Asser's problem to Cook's problem; Asser's problem is investigated for generalized spectra of formulae with only monadic auxiliary predicate symbols—the P_i above—in three other papers by R. Fagin, "Monadic Generalized Spectra" in *Zeitschrift f. math. Logik und Grundl. d. Math. 21*, 1975,

89–96; "A two-cardinal Characterization of Double Spectra," ibid., 121–122; "A Spectrum Hierarchy," ibid., 123–134. See also J.F. Lynch, "Complexity Classes and Theories of Finite Models, in *Math. Systems Theory 15*, 1982, 127–144, where classes of particular finite models for closed monadic existential second-order formulae in the language of addition are investigated with respect to NTIME-bounded computations.

B. Scarpellini, "Complete second order spectra," *ZMLG 30*, 1984, 509–524, exhibits "universal" second-order spectra within given prefix classes, see also B. Scarpellini "Lower bound results on lengths of second order formulas," *Annals of Pure and Applied Logic 29*, 1985, 29–58.

For characterizations of complexity classes by classes of spectra of prenex first-order formulae with a fixed number of universal quantifiers see E. Grandjean, "Universal quantifiers and time complexity of random access machines," *Math. Systems Theory 18*, 1985, 171–187, and "The spectra of first-order sentences and computational complexity," *SIAM J. on Computing*, 1984.

2.4.2 Horn Prefix Classes and Complexity Classes

For polynomial space bounded Turing machine computations, we can reuse the global description technique of Section 2.2 without need to introduce monadic or higher function symbols: the arity of the configuration predicate encodes the computation space bound, and the content of a cell is presented by an individual constant. This reinterpretation transforms the characterization of recursively enumerable sets by the prefix class $V\Lambda V\Lambda$ of Krom formulae in Section 2.2 into a characterization of PSPACE by the prefix class $V^*\Lambda^*$ of Krom formulae (even when restricted to deterministic PROLOG programs):

THEOREM 2.4   (Plaisted 1984 and Denenberg & Lewis 1984). The satisfiability problem of (even deterministic) PROLOG programs with binary clauses and no other terms than variables and individual constants is PSPACE-complete.

Proof (of the hardness part).   Following the schema of Section 2.3 we specify the reduction property by: M accepts input v within space bound $k =$ (polynomial in the length of v) iff $\Pi \wedge \alpha \wedge \omega$ has no model.

We represent a configuration $\vec{x}$ of length k by a k-sequence of letters $j \leq s$ of the tape alphabet and of one pair (i,j) of state $i \leq r$ and tape symbol $j \leq s$ of M, the pair indicating the reading head position. These letters i and pairs (i,j) are logically treated as individual constants (read: existentially bounded variables). The global representation of configurations as given in Section 2.2 reads accordingly (in the proof oriented form):

$$\text{Conf}(\vec{x}) \text{ is true } \text{ iff } \vec{x} \text{ is reached by } M \text{ started with input } v.$$

For sake of completeness we indicate the corresponding variant of the program formula Π which now consists of clauses of form (with variable sequence xy of length $k-1$):

$$\text{Conf } x(i,j)y \rightarrow \text{Conf } x(i',j')y \qquad \text{for print instructions } (i,j,j',i') \text{ in } M$$
$$\text{Conf } x(i,j)j'y \rightarrow \text{Conf } xj(i',j')y \qquad \text{for right-movement instructions}$$
$$(i,j,+1,i) \text{ in } M$$

similarly for left-movement instructions in M.

The input formula α is $\text{Conf}(0,v_1)v_2 \ldots v_n0 \ldots 0$ for input $v = v_1 \ldots v_n$ and initial state 0. The stop formula ω is $\neg\text{Conf}(1,0)0 \ldots 0$ for accepting state 1 and acceptance with empty tape.

To transform the above formula for deterministic M into a PROLOG program which is deterministic it is sufficient to rewrite the formula with respect to fixed argument places for the description of the working head position (i,j) and its left and right neighbor cells a respectively b; cf. Corollary 2.1 to theorem 2.1 in Section 2.2.

REMARK 2.9   Plaisted 1984 has shown that PROLOG programs as in Theorem 2.4 but with ternary clauses allowed characterize the class of deterministic exponential time computable sets; the complexity jump is due to a binary encoding of big tape sections and time moments. Lewis (1980) had shown that without the Horn restriction, the prefix class $V^*\Lambda^*$ has a satisfiability problem which is complete for nondeterministic exponential time bounded computations.

REMARK 2.10   The possibility of having predicates of arbitrarily high rank to encode the computation space bounds is crucial in Theorem 2.4. A rather complete analysis of the complexity of PROLOG program classes as in Theorem 2.4 but also with fixed arity or fixed number of predicate symbols is given in Börger & Löwen 1987.

As further example we show how the application of our logical implementation technique to alternating pushdown automata transfer the deterministic exponential time completeness from the halting problem of these automata to the satisfiability problem of (the Horn formulae in) the so called Ackermann prefix class $V^*\Lambda V^*$:

THEOREM 2.5   (Lewis 1980).   The satisfiability problem of PROLOG programs with only one variable, individual constants, and monadic function symbols is complete for deterministic exponential time.

Proof   (of the hardness part) by reduction of the halting problem of alternating pushdown automata which is known to be deterministic exponential time complete (see R.E. Ladner & R.J. Lipton & L.J. Stockmeyer 1978: Alternating pushdown automata. FOCS 19, 92–106.) The reduction property in the schema of Section 2.3 is specified to:

(1) M does not accept input w iff $\Pi \wedge \alpha \wedge \omega$ is satisfiable. The logical representation of M-configurations (i, w, j, s) with state i, input w, reading head position $j \leq |w|$, content s of the pushdown store is realized by atomic formulae $\mathrm{Conf}_{i,j}(s)$ with the intended meaning that this configuration is an accepting one. $\mathrm{Conf}_{i,j}$ is a monadic predicate symbol, the store content s is interpreted as term built up from an individual constant 0 (representing the bottom of the pushdown store) by monadic function symbols for every symbol of the pushdown store alphabet.

The PROLOG interpretation Π of M with respect to acceptance of w follows the recursive definition of M-acceptance from the leaves to the root and is given by the following set of clauses (where x is an individual variable): For each *input tape read-instruction* (in state i, if the letter in the present input reading head position is a, then go to state i') of M take the clause (for each position $1 \leq j \leq |w|$ with letter a in w):

$$\mathrm{Conf}_{i,j}(x) \leftarrow \mathrm{Conf}_{i',j}(x).$$

For each *move-instruction* (in state i move the reading head on the input tape by ± 1 and go to state i') of M take the clause (for all $1 \leq j \pm 1 \leq |w|$):

$$\mathrm{Conf}_{i,j}(x) \leftarrow \mathrm{Conf}_{i',j \pm 1}(x).$$

For each *push-instruction* (in state i push symbol f on top of the present content of the pushdown store and go to state i') of M take the clause (for all $1 \leq j \leq |w|$):

$$\mathrm{Conf}_{i,j}(x) \leftarrow \mathrm{Conf}_{i',j}(f(x)).$$

In this clause f is interpreted as monadic function symbol.

For each *pop-instruction* (in state i pop the symbol which at present is on top of the pushdown store and go to state i') of M take the clause (for all $1 \leq j \leq |w|$ and every symbol f of the pushdown store alphabet):

$$\mathrm{Conf}_{i,j}(f(x)) \leftarrow \mathrm{Conf}_{i',j}(x).$$

For each *pushdown store read instruction* (in state i, if the symbol on top of the pushdown store is f (or if the pushdown store is empty), then go to state i') of M take for all $1 \leq i \leq |w|$ the clauses:

$$\mathrm{Conf}_{i,j}(f(x)) \leftarrow \mathrm{Conf}_{i',j}(f(x))$$
$$\mathrm{Conf}_{i,j}(0) \quad \leftarrow \mathrm{Conf}_{i',j}(0)$$

For *existential branch instructions* (in state i, go to one of the states $i_1, \ldots,$ i_r—at least one of which has to lead to acceptance in order to lead state i to acceptance) of M take the clauses (for $1 \le j \le |w|$):

$$\mathrm{Conf}_{i,j}(x) \leftarrow \mathrm{Conf}_{i_1,j}(x)$$

$$\vdots$$

$$\mathrm{Conf}_{i,j}(x) \leftarrow \mathrm{Conf}_{i_r,j}(x)$$

This expresses that the configuration with state i accepts if changing i to one of the possible successive states $i_1, \ldots, i_r$ defines an accepting configuration. The PROLOG interpreter reflects this nondeterminism by a nondeterministic choice of one of these clauses with same procedure name.

For *universal branch instructions* (in state i, go to one of the states $i_1, \ldots,$ i_r—all of which must lead to acceptance in order to lead i to acceptance) of M take the clause (for all $1 \le j \le |w|$):

$$\mathrm{Conf}_{i,j}(x) \leftarrow \mathrm{Conf}_{i_1,j}(x), \ldots, \mathrm{Conf}_{i_r,j}(x).$$

This expresses that a configuration with state i leads to acceptance if each of the configurations obtained by changing state from i to one of $i_1, \ldots, i_r$ leads to acceptance. The PROLOG interpreter reflects this situation by the fact that in order to execute successfully procedure $\mathrm{Conf}_{i,j}(x)$, all of the subprocedures $\mathrm{Conf}_{i_k,j}(x)$ occurring in its procedure body have to be executed successfully.

The *input formula* α to describe the start in state 0 with empty pushdown store and reading head position 1 is given by the clause

$$\leftarrow \mathrm{Conf}_{0,1}(0).$$

The *stop formula* ω expressing that state 1 is a final accepting state (where without loss of generality the final reading head position is supposed to be 1) is given by the clause

$$\mathrm{Conf}_{1,1}(x) \leftarrow$$

REMARK 2.11   Shapiro (1982) investigates an application of the above reduction technique to alternating Turing machines. It turns out that the complexity of the machine computations and of their PROLOG simulations are naturally and intimately related also in the alternating case. There are simultaneously linear relations between M-space and Π_M-goal-size, between M-tree-size and the product of length and goal-size of M, between M-time and the product of depth and goal-size of Π_M.

REMARK 2.12   Lewis (1980) gives also a description of alternating stack automata which yields a logical characterization by restricted first-order formulae of double exponential time complexity. Lewis (1975) contains interesting applications of the logical implementation technique to context free grammars, finite automata, stack automata, and pushdown automata. Börger & Kleine Büning (1980) study descriptions of various computation models (including Petri nets) in extended Skolem arithmetic; they obtain a sharp syntactical boundary between decidable and undecidable classes of formulae corresponding to the dichotomy between (undecidable) Petri nets with order and (decidable) Petri nets.

REFERENCES

1. Aanderaa, S.O., 1971. "On the decision problem for formulas in which all disjunctions are binary," *Proc. 2nd Scandinavian Logic Symposium*, 1–18.
2. Aanderaa, S.O., & E. Börger, 1979. "The Horn Complexity of Boolean Functions and Cook's Problem," *Proc. 5th Scand. Logic Symp.*, B. Mayoh & F. Jensen, editors, Aalborg University Press, 231–256.
3. Aanderaa, S.O., & E. Börger, 1981. "The equivalence of Horn and network complexity for Boolean functions," *Acta Informatica 15*, 303–307.
4. Aanderaa, S.O., & E. Börger, & H.R. Lewis, 1982. "Conservative reduction of Krom formula," *JSL 47*, 110–129.
5. Aanderaa, S.O., & H.R. Lewis, 1973. "Prefix classes of Krom formulas," *JSL 38*, 628–642.
6. Ackermann, W., 1954. "Solvable cases of the decision problem." Amsterdam. North-Holland Pub. Co.
7. Andreka, H., & I. Nemeti, 1976. "The generalized completeness of Horn predicate-logic as a programming language," *DAI Res. Rep. 21*, University of Edinburgh.
8. Bennett, J.H., 1962. "On spectra." *Doctoral Diss.*, Princeton University.
9. Böhm, C., 1964. "On a family of Turing machines and the related programming language." *ICC Bull. 3*, 3–12.
10. Börger, E., 1971. "Reduktionstypen in Krom- und Hornformeln." Dissertation, Universität Münster (s. Beitrag zur Reduktion des Entscheidungsproblems auf Klassen von Hornformeln mit kurzen Alternationen, AMLG 16, 1974, 67–84.)
    — 1975: Recursively unsolvable algorithmic problems and related questions reexamined. ISILC Logic Colloquium (Ed. G.H. Müller, A. Oberschelp, K. Potthoff), SLNM 499, 10–24.
    — 1975a: On the construction of simple first-order formulae without recursive models. Proc. Coloquio sobra logica simbolica, Madrid, 9–24.
    — 1978: Bemerkung zu Gurevich's Arbeit über das Entscheidungsproblem für Standardklassen. AMLG 19, 111–114.
    — 1979: A new general approach to the theory of many-one equivalence of decision problems for algorithmic systems. ZMLG 25, 135–162.
    — 1983: Undecidability versus degree complexity of decision problems for formal grammars. Report on the 1st GTI-workshop, Fb. Math.-Informatik, Universität-GH Paderborn, 44–55.

— 1984: Decision problems in predicate logic. Logic Colloquium '82 (Eds. G. Lolli, G. Longo, A. Marcja), North-Holland, 263–301.

— 1984a: Spektralproblem and completeness of logical decision problems. SLNCS 171, 333–356.

— & K. Heidler, 1976: Die m-Grade logischer Entscheidungsprobleme. AMLG 17, 105–112.

— & H. Kleine Büning, 1980: The r.e. complexity of decision problems for commutative semi-Thue systems with recursive rule set. ZMLG 26, 459–469.

— 1985: Berechenbarkeit, Komplexität, Logik. Vieweg, Braunschweig/Wiesbaden, pp. XVII + 469 (English translation in preparation).

— & U. Löwen, 1987: Logical Decision Problems and Complexity of Logic Programs. Fundamenta Informaticae X, 1–34.

11. Büchi, J.R., 1962. "Turing machines and the Entscheidungsproblem," *Math. Ann. 148*, 201–213.

12. Christen, C.-A., 1974. "Spektren und Klassen elementarer Funktionen," *Dissertation*. ETH Zürich, 88.

13. Clocksin, W.F., & C.S. Mellish, 1981. *Programming in Prolog*, Springer.

14. Cohen, D., 1980. "Degree problems for modular machines," *JSL 45*, 510–528.

15. Cook, S.A., 1971. "The complexity of theorem-proving procedures," *STOC*, 151–158.

16. Dahlhaus E., & A. Israeli, & J.A. Makowsky, 1984. "On the existence of polynomial time algorithms for interpolation problems in propositional logic," Technion, Israel Inst. of Technology, Haifa TR 320.

17. Denenberg, L.A., & H.R. Lewis, 1984. "The complexity of the satisfiability problem from Krom formulas," *TCS 30*, 319–341.

18. Dreben, B., & H.D. Goldfarb, 1979. "The decision problem: Solvable cases of quantificational formulas," Addison-Wesley.

19. Friedman, H., 1976. "The complexity of explicit definitions," *Advances in Mathematics 20*, 18–29.

20. Fürer, M., 1981. "Alternation and the Ackermann case of the decision problem," *L'Enseignement mathématique XXVII*, 1–2, pp. 137–162.

21. Genenz, J., 1965. Untersuchungen zum Entscheidungsproblem im Prädikatenkalkül der ersten Stufe. Dissertation. Institut für math. Logik und Grundlagenforschung der Universität Münster.

22. Gurevich, Yu., 1966. Über die effektive Entscheidbarkeit der Erfüllbarkeit von Formeln des engeren Prädikatenkalküls. (Russ.) Algebra y Logika, 25–55.

— 1976: "The decision problem for standard classes," *JSL* 41, 460–464.

— 1984: "Toward logic tailored for computational complexity," *Computation and Proof Theory*, SLNM 1104, 175–216.

23. Henschen, L., & L. Wos, 1974. "Unit refutations and Horn sets," *JACM* 21, 590–605.

24. Hilbert, D., & P. Bernays, 1939, 1970. *Grundlagen der Mathematik I, II*, Berlin.

25. Hill, R., 1974. "Lush resolution and its completeness," *DLC Memo 78*, University of Edinburgh.

26. Hopcroft, J.E., & J.D. Ullman, 1979. *Introduction to automata theory, languages and computation*, Addison-Wesley, Reading, Mass.

27. Itai, A., & J.A. Makowsky, 1983. *Unification as a complexity measure for logic programming*, Technion-Israel Inst. of Technology, TR 301.

28. Jones, N.D., & A.L. Selman, 1974. "Turing machines and the spectra of first-order formulas," *JSL* 39, 139–150.

29. Kahr, A.S., 1962. "Improved reductions of the Entscheidungsproblem to subclasses of AEA formulas," *Proc. Symp. on Math. Theory of Automata*, Brooklyn Polytechnic Institute, New York, 57–70.

30. Kostyrko, V.F., 1964. Klass svedeniya $\forall\exists^n\forall$. *Algebra y Logika*, 45–65.

31. Kreisel, G., 1953. "Note on arithmetic models for consistent formulae of the predicate calculus II," *Proc. XI-th Int. Congr. Philos.*, Vol. 14, 39–49.
   — 1961: *Techn. Report No. 3, Appl. Math. & Stat. Labs.*, Stanford University.

32. Krom, M.R., 1967. "The decision problem for a class of first-order formulas in which all disjunctions are binary," *ZMLG* 13, 15–20.
   — 1970: "The decision problem for formulas in prenex conjunctive normal form with binary disjunctions," *JSL* 35, 210–216.

33. Lewis, H.R., 1978. "Description of restricted automata by first-order formulae," *Math. Systems Theory* 9, 97–104.
   — 1979: *Unsolvable classes of quantificational formulas*, Addison-Wesley.
   — 1980: "Complexity results for classes of quantificational formulas," *JCSS* 21, 317–353.

34. Lloyd, J.W., 1984. *Foundations of Logic Programming*, Springer.

35. Machtey, M., & P. Young, 1978. *An introduction to the general theory of algorithms*, North-Holland, New York.

36. Minsky, M.L., 1961. "Recursive unsolvability of Post's problem of 'tag' and other topics in the theory of Turing machines," *Ann. of Math.* 74, 437–455.

37. Mostowski, A., 1953. "On a system of axioms which has no recursively enumerable model," *Fund. Math.* 40, 56–61.

38. Plaisted, D.A., 1984. "Complete problems in the first-order predicate calculus," *JCSS* 29, 8–35.

39. Rabin, M.O., 1958. "On recursively enumerable and arithmetic models of set theory," *JSL* 23, 408–416.

40. Reynolds, J.C., 1969. "Transformational systems and the algebraic structure of atomic formulas" in: *Machine Intelligence*, vol. 5 (Eds. B. Meltzer, D. Michie), American Elsevier, 135–151.

41. Rödding, D., & H. Schwichtenberg, 1972. "Bemerkungen zum Spektralproblem. *ZMLG* 18, 1–12.

42. Rogers, H., 1967. *Theory of recursive functions and effective computability*, McGraw Hill, New York.

43. Schnorr, C.P., 1976. The network complexity and the Turing machine complexity of finite functions, *Acta Informatica* 7, 95–107.

44. Shapiro, E.Y., 1982. "Alternation and the computational complexity of logic programs," *Proc. first int. logic programming conf.*, 154–163.

45. Shoenfield, J.R., 1967. *Mathematical logic*, Reading.

46. Suranyi, J., 1959. *Reduktionstheorie des Entscheidungsproblems im Prädikatenkalkül der ersten Stufe*, Budapest.

47. Tärnlund, S.-A., 1977. "Horn clause computability," *BIT* 17, 215–226.

48. Trachtenbrot, B., 1950. Impossibility of an algorithm for the decision problem in finite classes, *Dokl. Akad. Nauk SSSR* 70, 569–572 (Engl. transl. in: AMS Transl. Ser. 2, vol. 23 (1963) 1–5).

49. Trachtenbrot, B.A., 1953. O recursivno otdelimosti, *Dokl. Akad. SSSR* 88, 953–955.

50. Turing, A.M., 1937. "On computable numbers, with an application to the Entscheidungsproblem," *Proc. London Math. Soc.* (2) 42, 230–265. A Correction ibid. 43 (1937) 544–546.

Chapter 3

Polynomial Time Degrees of *NP*-Sets

KLAUS AMBOS-SPIES*

3.1 INTRODUCTION

It is a commonly accepted thesis that the class $\mathcal{P}$ of sets recognizable by deterministic Turing machines in polynomial time coincides with the class of the *feasibly* computable sets. By relativizing this thesis, the polynomial time bounded versions of the recursive reducibilities formalize the notion of feasibly computable reduction, thus providing a natural tool for measuring the relative complexity of solvable but intractable problems. The polynomial time reducibilities proved to be of particular value for classifying problems in the classes $\mathcal{NP}$ and PSPACE. See Garey and Johnson, (15).

Here we will study structural properties of the polynomial time bounded (p-) reducibilities. We will restrict ourselves to the two most important p-reducibilities, namely the polynomially bounded versions of Turing (T) and many-one (m) reducibility (Cook, 14 and Karp, 18). Structural questions about the (unbounded) recursive reducibilities have been first pursued by Post in the 1940s. Since then the analysis of the algebraic structure of these reducibilities has become one of the major areas in recursive function theory (see Rogers, 28, Lerman, 23 and Soare, 35). The investigation of the structure of the polynomial time bounded reducibilities on the recursive sets and, assuming $\mathcal{P} \neq \mathcal{NP}$, on the *NP*-sets has been initiated by Ladner in 1973 (19, 20). Since then particular attention has been paid to the possible relations with respect to these reducibilities among the *NP*-sets under the assumption that $\mathcal{P} \neq \mathcal{NP}$. In this chapter, we will present the main results and techniques of this area.

---

*Universität Dortmund

The equivalence classes induced by the polynomial time reducibilities are called polynomial time (p-) degrees. The problems contained in a p-degree are all of the same relative complexity. Therefore, structural questions about the p-reducibilities are generally structural questions about the induced orderings on the p-degrees. In other words, the algebraic structure of the partial orderings $(\mathbf{Rec}_r; \leqq_r)$ and $(\mathbf{NP}_r; \leqq_r)$ of the p-r-degrees of recursive sets and *NP*-sets, respectively, reflects the structural properties of the p-r-reducibilities on those sets ($r = m, T$).

In Section 3.2, we survey some elementary properties of the polynomial time reducibilities and degrees. Section 3.4 presents the variant of the delayed diagonalization technique used by Ladner (20) to prove the partial orderings of p-degrees of recursive sets and assuming $\mathcal{P} \neq \mathcal{NP}$, of *NP*-sets dense. Moreover, a refinement of this technique from Landweber, Lipton, and Robertson (22), based on diagonalizations over arbitrary recursively presentable classes of recursive sets, is introduced. The material required for this more general approach is provided in Section 3.3. In Section 3.5, using the technique of Landweber et al., a diagonalization lemma is proved which yields strong density results for the partial orderings $(\mathbf{Rec}_r; \leqq_r)$ and $(\mathbf{NP}_r; \leqq_r)$ and allows constructions of nontrivial joins (suprema) in arbitrary intervals of p-degrees. Section 3.6 contains results on minimal pairs, i.e., incomparable p-degrees with infimum $\mathbf{0}, \mathbf{0}$ the p-degree of the polynomial time computable problems, and more generally, on meets (infima) of incomparable p-degrees. These results are condensed in a simple, but quite general, meet lemma. Based on the diagonalization and meet lemmas, in Section 3.7 a general result on lattice embeddings into the partial ordering $(\mathbf{NP}_r; \leqq_r)$ is proved (assuming $\mathcal{P} \neq \mathcal{NP}$), which subsumes most of the previously obtained results on the p-r-degrees of *NP*-sets. Finally, in Section 3.8 limitations of the delayed diagonalization technique for studying the structure of $(\mathbf{NP}_r; \leqq_r)$ are discussed and some open problems are stated.

Although this paper is mainly a survey, some of the results presented here, such as Theorems 3.4 and 3.10, are new.

We assume familiarity with the basic concepts of recursive function theory and computational complexity theory (as presented for example in Garey and Johnson (15), or Hopcroft and Ullman (17)). In particular, the reader should be well acquainted with the oracle machine concept and the elementary properties of the polynomial time bounded reducibilities. The more advanced topics in Section 3.7 require acquaintance with the material presented in the previous sections, in particular that of Sections 3.5 and 3.6.

We conclude this section by explaining our terminology. Let Σ be the alphabet consisting of the two letters 0 and 1, and let Σ^* denote the set of strings over Σ. We denote elements of Σ^* by lower case letters from the end of the alphabet, while capital letters stand for *recursive* subsets of Σ^*. The terms *set*, *language*, and *problem* in general refer to recursive subsets of Σ^*. The symbol $|x|$ is the length of x, $|A|$ is the cardinality of A, $<$ is the natural ordering on Σ^*, i.e., $x < y$ if $|x| < |y|$ or $|x| = |y|$ and $x(n) < y(n)$ and $x(m) = y(m)$ for some $n < |x|$ and all $m < n$, where $x(n)$ denotes the $(n+1)$st letter in the string x. A set A is *tally* if $A \subseteq \{0\}^*$. $\overline{A}$ denotes the complement $\Sigma^* - A$ of A, xA is the set $\{xy: y \,\varepsilon\, A\}$, and $A \oplus B = 0A \cup 1B$. We write $A =^* B$ if the symmetrical difference $(A - B) \cup (B - A)$ of A and B is finite. In our notation, we do not distinguish between a set and its characteristic function. So $x \,\varepsilon\, A$ iff $A(x) = 1$ and $x \,\cancel{\varepsilon}\, A$ iff $A(x) = 0$. $A \restriction s$ denotes the restriction of (the characteristic function of) A to arguments of length less than s, i.e., $A \restriction s\,(x) = A(x)$ if $|x| < s$ and $A \restriction s(x) = 0$, otherwise.

$\mathbb{N}$ is the set of natural numbers. Lower case letters from the middle of the alphabet denote elements of $\mathbb{N}$, lower case Greek letters denote recursive subsets of $\mathbb{N}$. For $i,k \,\varepsilon\, \mathbb{N}$ and $\alpha \subseteq \mathbb{N}$, $k\alpha + i = \{k \cdot n + i: n \,\varepsilon\, \alpha\}$. Moreover, for $m,n \,\varepsilon\, \mathbb{N}$, $[\![m,n)\!)$ is the set of all strings of length at least m but less than n, i.e.,

$$[\![m,n)\!) = \{x \,\varepsilon\, \Sigma^*: m \leq |x| < n\}.$$

For a TM M the *step counting function* $f_M: \mathbb{N} \to \mathbb{N}$ of M is defined as follows: $f(n)$ is the least number m such that for any string x of length at most n the computation $M(x)$ takes at most m steps. Note that step counting functions are nondecreasing. A TM M is polynomial time bounded if $f_M(n) \leq p(n)$ for some polynomial p and all numbers n.

Classes of sets are denoted by script capital letters. For a class $\mathcal{C}$, we let co-$\mathcal{C} = \{\overline{A}: A \,\varepsilon\, \mathcal{C}\}$. $\mathcal{P}(\mathcal{NP})$ is the class of subsets of Σ^* which are recognized by nondeterministic Turing machines (TM) in polynomial time. $\mathcal{PF}$ is the set of deterministically polynomial time computable functions from Σ^* to Σ^*. If not stated otherwise $\{P_n: n \,\varepsilon\, \mathbb{N}\}$ and $\{f_n: n \,\varepsilon\, \mathbb{N}\}$ are recursive enumerations of $\mathcal{P}$ and $\mathcal{PF}$, respectively. $\mathcal{P}_{\mathbb{N}}$ is the class of subsets of $\mathbb{N}$ which are polynomial time computable with respect to unary representation. Note that by identifying a set $\alpha \subseteq \mathbb{N}$ with its representation $A_\alpha = \{0^n: n \,\varepsilon\, \alpha\}$, $\mathcal{P}_{\mathbb{N}} = \mathcal{P} \cap \{A: A \text{ tally}\}$.

We use $\langle\,,\,\rangle$ to denote polynomial time computable and invertible bijections from $\mathbb{N} \times \Sigma^*$ to Σ^* and from $\mathbb{N}^n$ to $\mathbb{N}$ ($n \geq 2$). $A^{(n)} = \{x: \langle n,x \rangle \,\varepsilon\, A\}$ and $A^{(\leq n)} = \{\langle m,x \rangle: m \leq n \,\&\, \langle m,x \rangle \,\varepsilon\, A\}$.

We let $\{M_e^X: e \,\varepsilon\, \mathbb{N}\}$ be a standard enumeration of the polynomial time bounded (deterministic) oracle Turing machines with oracle set X, and we let $\{p_e: e \,\varepsilon\, \mathbb{N}\}$ be a recursive sequence of polynomials such that p_e bounds the run time of M_e^X for each oracle set X. For a precise definition of oracle TMs we refer the reader to Hopcroft and Ullman (17). We write $x \,\varepsilon\, M_e^X$ or $M_e^X(x) = 1$ ($x \,\cancel{\varepsilon}\, M_e^X$ or $M_e^X(x) = 0$) if M_e^X accepts (refutes) x, i.e., M_e^X also stands for the language accepted by the machine M_e^X. Furthermore, sometimes we write $M_e(X)$ and $M_e(X)(x)$ instead of M_e^X and $M_e^X(x)$, respectively. Note that in the computation $M_e(X)(x)$, there are only queries "$y \,\varepsilon\, X$?" for strings y of length less than $p_e(|x|)$. So, for sets X and Y such that $X \restriction p_e(|x|) = Y \restriction p_e(|x|)$, $M_e(X)(x) = M_e(Y)(x)$.

Finally, recall that a partial ordering (p.o.) is a binary relation which is anti-symmetric, reflexive and transitive. A partially ordered (p.o.) set $\mathcal{L} = (L; \leqq)$ is a set L together with a partial ordering $\leqq$ on L. Further notions from lattice theory will be introduced in the following sections. A general reference for the lattice theoretic concepts used here is Grätzer (16).

3.2 POLYNOMIAL TIME REDUCIBILITIES AND DEGREES

In this section we introduce the basic notions we will deal with and prove some elementary results on them.

DEFINITION 3.1   (a) (Cook 14)   A set A is *polynomial time Turing* (*p-Turing* or *p-T* for short) *reducible* to a set B, $A \leq_T^p B$, if there is a polynomial time bounded deterministic oracle Turing machine M such that $A = M(B)$.

(b) (Karp 18)   A set A is *polynomial time many-one* (*p-many-one* or *p-m* for short) *reducible* to a set B, $A \leq_m^p B$, if there is a (deterministically) polynomial time computable function $f: \Sigma^* \to \Sigma^*$ such that $A = f^{-1}(B)$, i.e.,

$$\forall\, x\, \varepsilon\, \Sigma^* \quad (x\, \varepsilon\, A \leftrightarrow f(x)\, \varepsilon\, B).$$

If $A = M(B)$ $(A = f^{-1}(B))$, then we say A is *p-T* (*p-m*) reducible to B *via* $M(f)$.

Besides *p*-Turing and *p*-many-one reducibility, the polynomial versions of various other recursive reducibilities have been introduced (21, 33, 34, 38). As in the unbounded case, however, *p*-Turing and *p*-many-one seem to be the most natural and important reducibilities. By relativizing Cook's thesis that feasible computations are those which can be carried out by a deterministic TM in polynomial time, *p*-Turing reducibility formalizes the notion of feasibly computable reduction. The conceptually simpler, but more restrictive *p-m*-reducibility, turned out to be of particular value for the classification of natural problems. Most polynomial reductions among such sets are in fact *p-m*-reductions. See e.g., (18) and (15). Moreover, certain complexity classes, like $\mathcal{NP}$, are known to be closed under $\leqq_m^p$ while closure under $\leqq_T^p$ seems to be unlikely (see Proposition 3.8, below).

In the following, r will stand for either m or T. We write $A \not\leqq_r^p B$ if not $A \leqq_r^p B$; $A =_r^p B$ if $A \leqq_r^p B$ and $B \leqq_r^p A$; $A \neq_r^p B$ if not $A =_r^p B$; $A <_r^p B$ if $A \leqq_r^p B$ and $A \neq_r^p B$; and $A \mid_r^p B$ if $A \not\leqq_r^p B$ and $B \not\leqq_r^p A$. If $A =_r^p B$ we say A and B are *p-r-equivalent* and if $A \mid_r^p B$ we say A and B are *p-r-incomparable*.

We assume that the reader is familiar with the fundamental properties of the polynomial time reducibilities summarized in the next proposition. For a proof see, for example, Hopcroft and Ullman (17).

PROPOSITION 3.1

(i)   If $A \leq_m^p B$ then $A \leq_T^p B$.

(ii) The relation $\leq_r^p$ is a quasi ordering, i.e., $A \leq_r^p A$ (reflexivity) and $A \leq_r^p B$ and $B \leq_r^p C$ imply $A \leq_r^p C$ (transitivity).

(iii) If $A \in \mathcal{P}$ and $B \neq \emptyset, \Sigma^*$ then $A \leq_m^p B$. Furthermore, $\emptyset \mid_m^p \Sigma^*$.

(iv) If $A \in \mathcal{P}$ then $A \leq_T^p B$.

(v)   If $A \leq_r^p B$ and $B \in \mathcal{P}$ then $A \in \mathcal{P}$.

(vi) $A =_T^p \overline{A}$.

In the following, the above facts will be tacitly used quite frequently. Part (i) of the proposition can be improved. P-m-reducibility is a *proper* refinement of p-T-reducibility. There are recursive, in fact, exponential time computable sets A and B such that $A \leq_T^p B$, but $A \not\leq_m^p B$. This follows from (vi) above and Ladner, Lynch, and Selman's result that there is an exponential time computable set A such that $A \not\leq_m^p \overline{A}$ (21). It is not known, however, whether $\mathcal{P} \neq \mathcal{NP}$ implies that $\leq_m^p$ and $\leq_T^p$ disagree on $\mathcal{NP}$. For a discussion of this question see Selman (32).

By the second part of the proposition, p-r-equivalence is an equivalence relation. Its equivalence classes are called p-r-degrees.

DEFINITION 3.2   The class

$$\deg_r^p(A) = \{B : B =_r^p A\}$$

is called the *p-r-degree* of A.

We denote p-r-degrees of recursive sets by boldface lower case letters, and classes of p-r-degrees of recursive sets by boldface capital letters. The classes of p-r-degrees of recursive and NP-sets are denoted by $\mathbf{Rec}_r$ and $\mathbf{NP}_r$, respectively. We say that a p-r-degree $\mathbf{a}$ is less than or equal to a p-r-degree $\mathbf{b}$ and write $\mathbf{a} \leq_r \mathbf{b}$ if

$$\forall A \in \mathbf{a} \, \forall B \in \mathbf{b} \;\; (A \leq_r^p B).$$

Note that $\leq_r$ is the partial ordering induced by $\leq_r^p$ on the p-r-degrees. If no confusion can arise, we write $\leq$ in place of $\leq_r$. The relations $<$, $\not\leq$, $=$, $\neq$ and $\mid$ are defined in the obvious way.

PROPOSITION 3.2 $(\mathbf{Rec}_r; \leq_r)$ and $(\mathbf{NP}_r; \leq_r)$ are partial orderings. Moreover,

$$\deg_r^p(A) \leq_r \deg_r^p(B) \quad \text{iff} \quad A \leq_r^p B.$$

Proof By Proposition 3.1 (ii).   ∎

This paper is devoted to the study of the algebraic structures of the partial orderings $(\mathbf{Rec}_r; \leqq)$ and, in particular, $(\mathbf{NP}_r; \leqq)$. Note that, by Proposition 3.2, the structural properties of the polynomial reducibilities on the recursive and $\mathcal{NP}$-sets are reflected in these structures. Also note that $(\mathbf{NP}_r; \leqq)$ is a partial subordering of $(\mathbf{Rec}_r; \leqq)$ and that, for any set A, $\deg_m^p(A) \subseteq \deg_T^p(A)$. In the remainder of this section we present some elementary algebraic properties of the degree structures.

We first observe that, by Proposition 3.1 (iv) and (v), the class $\mathcal{P}$ constitutes a single p-T-degree, which moreover is the least element of $(\mathbf{Rec}_T; \leqq)$ and $(\mathbf{NP}_T; \leqq)$. In case of p-m-reducibility, the situation is slightly different. There the class $\mathcal{P}$ consists of three degrees, namely $\{\emptyset\}$, $\{\Sigma^*\}$, and $\mathcal{P}$-$\{\emptyset, \Sigma^*\}$. To avoid trivialities in case of p-m-reducibility, we will systematically ignore the sets $\emptyset$ and Σ^* so that $\mathcal{P}$ will again consist of a single degree, which also is the least element of $(\mathbf{Rec}_m; \leqq)$ and $(\mathbf{NP}_m; \leqq)$. For either reducibility we let $\mathbf{0}$ be the degree $\mathcal{P}$.

PROPOSITION 3.3   The partial orderings $(\mathbf{Rec}_r; \leqq)$ and $(\mathbf{NP}_r; \leqq)$ possess a least element $\mathbf{0}$, namely the degree of polynomial time computable sets.   ∎

In a partial ordering $(S; \leqq)$ the join (least upper bound) of two elements a and b is denoted by $a \vee b$, the meet (greatest lower bound) by $a \wedge b$. $(S; \leqq)$ is an upper semilattice (u.s.l.) if, for any two elements $a, b \; \varepsilon \; S$, $a \vee b$ exists. If moreover meets always exist then $(S; \leqq)$ is a lattice.

PROPOSITION 3.4   (Ladner 20). $\deg_r^p(A \oplus B) = \deg_r^p(A) \vee \deg_r^p(B)$.

Proof We consider $r = m$. The proof for $r = T$ is similar. Obviously, $A \leqq_m^p A \oplus B$ via $f(x) = 0x$ and $B \leqq_m^p A \oplus B$ via $g(x) = 1x$. So $\deg_m^p(A \oplus B)$ is an upper bound for $\deg_m^p(A)$ and $\deg_m^p(B)$. To show that it is the least upper bound, let $\deg_m^p(C)$ be any other upper bound for $\deg_m^p(A)$ and $\deg_m^p(B)$, say $A \leqq_m^p C$ via h_0 and $B \leqq_m^p C$ via h_1. Then $A \oplus B \leqq_m^p C$ via h where $h(ix) = h_i(x)$ $(i = 0, 1)$.   ∎

COROLLARY 3.1 $(\mathbf{Rec}_r; \leqq)$ and $(\mathbf{NP}_r; \leqq)$ are upper semilattices.

Proof By Proposition 3.4. Note that $\mathcal{NP}$ is closed under $\oplus$.   ∎

Ladner (20) has also shown that, in contrast to Proposition 3.4, meets of p-r-degrees not always exist, whence $(\mathbf{Rec}_r; \leqq)$ is not a lattice. It is not known, however, whether $\mathcal{P} \neq \mathcal{NP}$ implies that $(\mathbf{NP}_r; \leqq)$ is not a lattice too.

PROPOSITION 3.5 (Ladner).   Let $A \neq \Sigma^*$ be a recursive set and $B \; \varepsilon \; \mathcal{P}$. Then $A \cap B \leq_m^p A$, $A \cap \overline{B} \leq_m^p A$ and $(A \cap B) \oplus (A \cap \overline{B}) =_m^p A$.

Proof   Fix $x_0 \notin A$. Then $A \cap B \leq_m^p A$ via f, where

$$f(x) = \begin{cases} x & \text{if } x \; \varepsilon \; B \\ x_0 & \text{otherwise.} \end{cases}$$

Since $\mathcal{P}$ is closed under complementation, by symmetry $A \cap \overline{B} \leq_m^p A$ too and thus, by Proposition 3.4, $(A \cap B) \oplus (A \cap \overline{B}) \leq_m^p A$. Finally, $A \leq_m^p (A \cap B) \oplus (A \cap \overline{B})$ via g, where

$$g(x) = \begin{cases} 0x & \text{if } x \; \varepsilon \; B \\ 1x & \text{otherwise.} \end{cases} \qquad \blacksquare$$

Proposition 3.5, in particular, shows that any *subproblem* of a problem A (i.e., any restriction of A to some polynomial time computable set), is polynomially reducible to A. So p-degrees below a given p-degree $\mathbf{a}$ can be obtained by considering subproblems of any representative $\mathbf{a}$. This fact will be exploited in the following quite frequently. The question, for which p-r-degrees $\mathbf{a}$ and what sets $A \; \varepsilon \; \mathbf{a}$, *all* degrees below $\mathbf{a}$ are represented by subproblems of A is discussed in Ambos-Spies (2).

An element a of a partial ordering $(S; \leq)$ is called maximal if there is no element b of S such that $a < b$. Note that a u.s.l. has at most one maximal element, namely its greatest element if it exists.

PROPOSITION 3.6 (Ladner 20).   The partial ordering $(\mathbf{Rec}_r; \leq)$ has no maximal elements.

Proof   Since $(\mathbf{Rec}_r; \leq)$ is an u.s.l., it suffices to show that for any given recursive set A there is a recursive set B such that $B \not\leq_T^p A$. Such a set $B \subseteq \{0\}^*$ is obtained by setting $B(0^n) = 1 - M_n^A(0^n)$. $\blacksquare$

Note that, by Proposition 3.6, the structure $(\mathbf{Rec}_r; \leq)$ possesses infinite ascending sequences. Since on the other hand the p-r-degrees define a partition of the countable class of recursive sets into nonempty subclasses, it follows that $\mathbf{Rec}_r$ is countably infinite. By refining the diagonalization argument used in the proof of Proposition 3.6, we can show that the partial ordering $(\mathbf{Rec}_r; \leq)$ is not total.

THEOREM 3.1 (Ladner 20).   For any recursive set $B \notin \mathcal{P}$, there is a recursive set A such that $A \mid_T^p B$.

Proof　Given $B \not\in \mathcal{P}$ the desired set A is effectively constructed in stages. Simultaneously, with A we define a strictly increasing recursive (length) function $l: \mathbb{N} \to \mathbb{N}$, $l(s)$ being defined at stage s of the construction, such that, for

$$A_s = \{x: x \text{ is put into } A \text{ by the end of stage } s\},$$

$A_s = A \restriction l(s)$. I.e., for a string $x \varepsilon [\![l(s), l(s+1))\!)$, $x \varepsilon A$ iff x is put into A at stage $s+1$. This will ensure that A is recursive.

Now A has to satisfy $A \not\leq_T^p B$ and $B \not\leq_T^p A$. These conditions reduce to infinite sequences of simpler requirements, namely

$$R_e^0: \quad A \neq M_e(B) \quad (e \varepsilon \mathbb{N})$$

and

$$R_e^1: \quad B \neq M_e(A) \quad (e \varepsilon \mathbb{N}),$$

respectively. For the construction of A it is crucial that these requirements are finitary, i.e., given $e \varepsilon \mathbb{N}$ and the finite initial part $A_s = A \restriction l(s)$ of A built up to some stage s, we can effectively find an appropriate extension $A_{s+1} = A \restriction l(s+1)$, $l(s+1) > l(s)$, of A_s such that, no matter how A will be defined for strings of length $\geq l(s+1)$, A will satisfy requirement R_e^0 or R_e^1. Namely, to meet R_e^0, just let $l(s+1) = l(s)+1$ and set

$$A(x) = 1 - M_e(B)(x)$$

for all strings x of length $l(s)$. In case of R_e^1 the diagonalization is a little bit more complicated: Since $A_s = A \restriction l(s)$ is finite, $M_e(A_s)$ can be computed in polynomial time. On the other hand, $B \not\in \mathcal{P}$, whence $B \neq M_e(A_s)$. So, by recursiveness of B and $M_e(A_s)$ we can compute the least string x satisfying $B(x) \neq M_e(A_s)(x)$. We then let $l(s+1) = \max(l(s)+1, p_e(|x|))$ and $A_{s+1} = A_s$ (i.e., no string $y \varepsilon [\![l(s), l(s+1))\!)$ is taken into A). Since the computation $M_e(A_s)(x)$ queries its oracle only about strings of length less than $p_e(|x|)$, and since, by choice of A_{s+1} and $l(s+1)$, A and A_s agree on those strings, this will imply $M_e(A)(x) = M_e(A_s)(x)$, and thus $B \neq M_e(A)$.

The above arguments show that in the construction of A we can handle the requirements R_e^0 and R_e^1, $e \varepsilon \mathbb{N}$, one after the other. For this sake we order the requirements by setting $R_{2e} = R_e^0$ and $R_{2e+1} = R_e^1$. Then the following construction ensures that requirement R_s is met at stage s ($s \varepsilon \mathbb{N}$).

Construction of A and l

Let $l(-1) = 0$ and $A_{-1} = \varnothing$.

Stage $2s \geq 0$.　Let $\quad l(2s) = l(2s-1)+1 \quad$ and
$$A_{2s} = A_{2s-1} \cup \{x: |x| = l(2s-1) \ \& \ x \not\in M_s(B)\}.$$

Stage $2s + 1 > 0$. Let

$$l(2s+1) = \mu n \ (n > l(2s) \ \& \ \exists x \ (p_s(|x|) < n \ \& \ B(x) \neq$$
$$M_s(A_{2s})(x))) \text{ and}$$

$$A_{2s+1} = A_{2s}.$$

Obviously, the construction is effective. Moreover, using the observations preceding the construction, one can easily show by induction on s that $l(s)$ is defined, $l(s) > l(s-1)$, $A_s = A \restriction l(s)$, and requirement R_s is met.

This completes the proof of Theorem 3.1. ∎

Before turning to the structures $(\mathbf{NP}_r; \leq)$, we shortly look at an algebraic property distinguishing $(\mathbf{Rec}_T; \leq)$ from $(\mathbf{Rec}_m; \leq)$. An u.s.l. $(S; \leq)$ is distributive if, for $a, b, c \in S$

$$a \leq b \vee c \rightarrow \exists \ b_0, c_0 \ \varepsilon \ S \ (a = b_0 \vee c_0 \ \& \ b_0 \leq b \ \& \ c_0 \leq c).$$

For a lattice this definition coincides with the standard definition of distributivity.

THEOREM 3.2   (Ambos-Spies 1).   The u.s.l. $(\mathbf{Rec}_m; \leq)$ is distributive whereas $(\mathbf{Rec}_T; \leq)$ is not distributive.

Proof   Here we prove only the first part of the theorem. For a proof of the second part see (1).

Given p-m-degrees $\mathbf{a}$, $\mathbf{b}$, $\mathbf{c}$ such that $\mathbf{a} \leq \mathbf{b} \vee \mathbf{c}$, choose recursive sets $A \ \varepsilon \ \mathbf{a}$, $B \ \varepsilon \ \mathbf{b}$, $C \ \varepsilon \ \mathbf{c}$ and a function f which p-m-reduces A to $B \oplus C$. Moreover, let $D = \{x : f(x) \ \varepsilon \ 0\Sigma^*\}$, $B_0 = A \cap D$, $C_0 = A \cap \bar{D}$, $\mathbf{b}_0 = \deg_m^p(B_0)$ and $\mathbf{c}_0 = \deg_m^p(C_0)$. Obviously, $D \ \varepsilon \ \mathcal{P}$, whence, by Propositions 3.4 and 3.5, $\mathbf{a} = \mathbf{b}_0 \vee \mathbf{c}_0$. Moreover, $B_0 \leq_m^p B \oplus \emptyset$ via f and $C_0 \leq_m^p \emptyset \oplus C$ via f, whence $\mathbf{b}_0 \leq \mathbf{b}$ and $\mathbf{c}_0 \leq \mathbf{c}$. ∎

Ambos-Spies (7) and, independently, Yang (37) studied nondistributive sublattices of $(\mathbf{Rec}_T; \leq)$. Yang has shown that all efficiently representable lattices, in particular all finite lattices, can be embedded in $(\mathbf{Rec}_T; \leq)$. It is an open problem, however, whether, assuming $\mathcal{P} \neq \mathcal{NP}$, $(\mathbf{NP}_T; \leq)$ is distributive or not. On the other hand, distributivity of $(\mathbf{Rec}_m; \leq)$ is inherited by $(\mathbf{NP}_m; \leq)$. This follows by inspection of the above proof or directly by Theorem 3.2 and Proposition 3.7 below.

Cook (14) and Karp (18) have shown that the u.s.l. $(\mathbf{NP}_r; \leq)$ possesses a greatest element, i.e., that there are hardest problems among the problems in $\mathcal{NP}$. Recall that, for a class $\mathscr{C}$ of recursive sets, a set A is $\mathscr{C}$-r-*complete* if $A \ \varepsilon \ \mathscr{C}$ and $B \leq_r^p A$ for all elements B of $\mathscr{C}$. Note that any $\mathscr{C}$-m-complete problem is also $\mathscr{C}$-T-complete (but, in general, not vice versa). Also note that any two $\mathscr{C}$-r-complete problems are p-r-equivalent and that the p-r-degree of $\mathscr{C}$-r-complete problems is the greatest element in the partial ordering of the *p-r*-degrees of the sets in $\mathscr{C}$.

THEOREM 3.3   (Cook 14 and Karp 18).   There are *NP-m*-complete problems. Hence, the u.s.l. $(\mathbf{NP}_r; \leqq)$ possesses a greatest element.

The *p-r*-degree of the *NP-r*-complete problems will be denoted by $\mathbf{1}_r$ in the following.

Cook and Karp proved Theorem 3.3 by giving natural examples of *NP*-complete problems. Since then a great number of *NP*-complete problems has been found. For a survey see Garey and Johnson (15). For simplicity, we here construct an (artificial) *NP*-complete set.

Proof of Theorem 3.3   (Baker et al. 8).   Let $\{N_n : n \ \varepsilon \ \mathrm{I\!N}\}$ be a standard enumeration of the (unbounded) nondeterministic TMs. Then there is a *universal* nondeterministic TM U and a polynomial p such that $U(0^n 1x) \cong N_n(x)$ and, if N_n accepts x in $\leqq t$ steps, then U accepts $0^n 1x$ in $\leqq p(t)$ steps.

We claim that

$$K = \{0^n 1x 10^m : U \text{ accepts } 0^n 1x \text{ in } \leqq m \text{ steps}\}$$

is *NP-m*-complete. Obviously, K can be nondeterministically computed in linear time, i.e., $K \ \varepsilon \ \mathscr{NP}$. So fix $A \ \varepsilon \ \mathscr{NP}$ to show that $A \leqq_m^p K$. Since $A \ \varepsilon \ \mathscr{NP}$ there is an index n and a polynomial q such that $A = N_n$ and the run time of N_n is bounded by q. Hence, for any string x,

$$x \ \varepsilon \ A \leftrightarrow N_n \text{ accepts } x \text{ in } < q(|x|) \text{ steps}$$

$$\leftrightarrow U \text{ accepts } 0^n 1x \text{ in } < p(q(|x|)) \text{ steps}$$

$$\leftrightarrow 0^n 1x 10^{p(q(|x|))} \ \varepsilon \ K.$$

So the polynomial time computable function $f(x) = 0^n 1x 10^{p(q(|x|))}$ reduces A to K.   ■

By Theorem 3.3, Cook's problem whether $\mathscr{P} \neq \mathscr{NP}$ can now be formulated in terms of polynomial degrees as follows.

COROLLARY 3.2 $\mathscr{P} \neq \mathscr{NP}$ iff $\mathbf{NP}_r \neq \{\mathbf{0}\}$ iff $\mathbf{0} < \mathbf{1}_r$.

Proof   By Proposition 3.3 and Theorem 3.3.   ■

Given a partial ordering $(S; \leqq)$ and elements a, b of S such that $a \leqq b$, the closed and open intervals with endpoints a, b are defined by

$$[a, b] = \{c \ \varepsilon \ S : a \leqq c \leqq b\} \quad \text{and}$$

$$(a, b) = \{c \ \varepsilon \ S : a < c < b\},$$

respectively. These intervals are proper if $a < b$. In the sequel, the term interval will usually refer to proper interval. If S has a least element 0 (and $a > 0$) then $[0, a]$ is called a (proper) initial segment of S. Again, in the sequel initial segment will usually stand for proper initial segment.

Note that, by Theorem 3.3, $\mathbf{NP}_r$ is contained in the initial segment $[0, 1_r]$ of $(\mathbf{Rec}_r; \leqq)$. We will next show that $\mathbf{NP}_m$ and $[0, 1_m]$ in fact coincide while the question whether $\mathbf{NP}_T = [0, 1_T]$ is still open.

PROPOSITION 3.7 (Karp). $\mathcal{NP}$ is downwards closed under $\leqq_m^p$, i.e., for $A \ \varepsilon \ \mathcal{NP}$ and $B \leqq_m^p A$, $B \ \varepsilon \ \mathcal{NP}$ too. Hence, any degree in $\mathbf{NP}_m$ entirely consists of NP-sets.

Proof (idea)   Fix $A \ \varepsilon \ \mathcal{NP}$ and B such that $B \leqq_m^p A$, via f say. Then a nondeterministic polynomial time computation of B is as follows. Given x, first deterministically and in polynomial time compute $f(x)$. Then nondeterministically and in polynomial time in the length of $f(x)$ evaluate $A(f(x))$ and let $B(x) = A(f(x))$. Since the length of $f(x)$ is polynomially bounded in the length of x, the just described nondeterministic computation of B is polynomially bounded. ∎

COROLLARY 3.3 $(\mathbf{NP}_m; \leqq) = ([0, 1_m]; \leqq)$.

Proof   By Theorem 3.3 and Proposition 3.7. ∎

COROLLARY 3.4   (Ambos-Spies 1).   The u.s.l. $(\mathbf{NP}_m; \leqq)$ is distributive.

Proof   By Theorem 3.2 and Corollary 3.3, since obviously any initial segment of a distributive u.s.l. is distributive again. ∎

The fact that, by Corollaries 3.2 and 3.3, $\mathcal{P} \neq \mathcal{NP}$ implies that $\mathbf{NP}_m$ coincides with the proper initial segment $[0, 1_m]$ of $(\mathbf{Rec}_m; \leqq)$ has been exploited in all so far obtained results on the algebraic structure of the u.s.l. $(\mathbf{NP}_m; \leqq)$. To show that, assuming $\mathcal{P} \neq \mathcal{NP}$, the structure $(\mathbf{NP}_m; \leqq)$ has a certain property, one has shown that this property is shared by *all* proper initial segments of $(\mathbf{Rec}_m; \leqq)$.

In case of p-T-reducibility, it is not known whether $(\mathbf{NP}_T; \leqq)$ and $[0, 1_T]$ coincide or whether $\mathbf{NP}_T$ is properly contained in $[0, 1_T]$. This question is related to the open $NP = coNP$-problem as the following proposition shows.

PROPOSITION 3.8   (Selman 32).   The following are equivalent

(i) $\mathcal{NP} = co\mathcal{NP}$
(ii) $\mathcal{NP}$ is downwards closed under $\leqq_T^p$.

Proof (idea)   If $\mathcal{NP}$ is closed under $\leqq_T^p$, then, for any set $A \ \varepsilon \ \mathcal{NP}$, $\overline{A} \ \varepsilon \ \mathcal{NP}$ too, whence $co\mathcal{NP} \subseteq \mathcal{NP}$. $\mathcal{NP} \subseteq co\mathcal{NP}$ follows by symmetry. On the other hand, if $A \in \mathcal{NP}$ and $\overline{A} \in \mathcal{NP}$ and $B \leq_T^p A$, say via M, then oracle queries in the computations of $M(A)$ can be nondeterministically eliminated as follows: Replace a query "$y \in A$?" by simultaneous nondeterministic polynomially bounded computations of $A(y)$ and $\overline{A}(y)$, and let accepting branches of the computations of $A(y)$ and $\overline{A}(y)$ answer the query by "YES" and "NO," respectively. Obviously this yields an *NP*-computation of B. ■

The class of sets which can be *p-T*-reduced to some *NP*-set is denoted by Δ_2^p. (This refers to a level in the polynomial time hierarchy of Stockmeyer 36.) Obviously,

$$\mathcal{NP} \cup \mathrm{co}\mathcal{NP} \subseteq \Delta_2^p = \{A : \deg_T^p(A) \in [\mathbf{0}, \mathbf{1}_T]\}.$$

By the previous proposition, $\mathcal{NP} = \Delta_2^p$ iff $\mathcal{NP} = \mathrm{co}\mathcal{NP}$. Hence, $\mathcal{NP} = \mathrm{co}\mathcal{NP}$ implies $\mathbf{NP}_T = [\mathbf{0}, \mathbf{1}_T]$. It is not known, however, whether $\mathcal{NP} \neq \mathrm{co}\mathcal{NP}$ implies that $\mathbf{NP}_T \subsetneq [\mathbf{0}, \mathbf{1}_T]$. Some evidence for the latter is given by the next theorem, which says that, relative to some oracle, $\mathbf{NP}_T \subsetneq [\mathbf{0}, \mathbf{1}_T]$ holds. For a discussion of the concept of relativization in computational complexity theory we refer the reader to Baker et al. (8) and Balcazar (9).

THEOREM 3.4   There are recursive sets A and B such that $B \in \Delta_2^p(A)$ but

$$\forall C(C =_T^{p(A)} B \rightarrow C \notin \mathcal{NP}(A)). \tag{3.1}$$

In the statement of Theorem 3.4, $\Delta_2^p(A)$, $=_T^{p(A)}$ and $\mathcal{NP}(A)$ refer to the relativizations to A of Δ_2^p, $=_T^p$ and $\mathcal{NP}$, respectively (see Baker et al. 8). The proof of the theorem is based on the diagonalization technique of (8), a technique which will not be used in the sequel. So the reader not interested in relativization results might want to skip the proof.

Proof   We construct sets A and B with the desired properties in stages. The set B is obtained from A by

$$B = \{0^n : \exists x \, (x \in A \ \& \ |x| = 2n)$$

$$\& \ \forall y \, (|y| = 2n+1 \rightarrow y \notin A)\}.$$

As one can easily check this implies $B \in \Delta_2^p(A)$. Condition (3.1) is broken down into the following infinite list of simpler requirements

$$R_{\langle e,i,j\rangle} : \ B \neq M_i(A \oplus M_e(A \oplus B)) \quad \text{or}$$

$$M_e(A \oplus B) \neq N_j(A) \quad (e,i,j \in \mathbb{N}),$$

where $\{M_n(X) : n \in \mathbb{N}\}$ and $\{N_n(X) : n \in \mathbb{N}\}$ are standard enumerations of the polynomial time bounded deterministic respectively nondeterministic oracle Turing machines (with oracle X). That the requirements guarantee (3.1) is seen as follows: Suppose (3.1) fails, say $C =_T^{p(A)} B$ and $C \varepsilon \mathcal{NP}(A)$. Then there are numbers e, i, j such that $C = M_e(A \oplus B)$, $B = M_i(A \oplus C)$—whence $B = M_i(A \oplus M_e(A \oplus B))$—and $C = N_j(A)$. So requirement $R_{\langle e,i,j\rangle}$ is not met.

We use the following notation. A_s denotes the elements of A enumerated by the end of stage s. So $A_s \subseteq A_{s+1}$ and $A = \bigcup_{s \varepsilon \text{IN}} A_s$. A definition of the approximation B_s to B at stage s is obtained from the definition of B by replacing all occurrences of A by A_s. Simultaneously, with A we define a (length) function $l: \text{IN} \to \text{IN}$, $l(s)$ being defined at stage s, such that $l(s) < l(s+1)$ and

$$A_s = A \upharpoonright l(s). \tag{3.2}$$

In other words A_s contains only strings of length less than $l(s)$ and, for any string x of length less than $l(s)$, $x \varepsilon A$ iff $x \varepsilon A_s$. Effectiveness of the construction and (3.2) will guarantee that A is recursive. Moreover, by (3.2) and by definition of B and B_s,

$$B_s \subseteq \{0\}^* \upharpoonright \ulcorner l(s)/2 \urcorner \ \& \ \forall n \ (2n+1 < l(s) \to B_s(0^n) = B(0^n)). \tag{3.3}$$

Let $\{p_s : s \ \varepsilon \ \text{IN}\}$ be a recursive sequence of polynomials such that $p_s(n) > n$ and, for $s = \langle e,i,j \rangle$, p_s bounds the run times of M_e, M_i and N_j. Note that in computations $M_e(X)(x)$, $M_i(X)(x)$ and $N_j(X)(x)$ there occur only queries concerning strings of length $<p_s(|x|)$. So (3.2) and (3.3) ensure that we can preserve computations which occur at stage s by choosing $l(s)$ big enough:

$$\forall x \ (\text{If } s = \langle e,i,j \rangle \ \text{and} \ 2p_s(p_s(|x|)) \leq l(s) \ \text{then}$$

$$M_e(A_s \oplus B_s)(x) = M_e(A \oplus B)(x) \ \text{and} \tag{3.4}$$

$$M_i(A_s \oplus M_e(A_s \oplus B_s))(x) = M_i(A \oplus M_e(A \oplus B))(x) \ \text{and}$$

$$N_j(A_s)(x) = N_j(A)(x)).$$

We are now ready to give the construction of A. At stage s we ensure that requirement R_s is met. Note that, at the beginning of stage s, A_{s-1}, B_{s-1} and $l(s-1)$ are given, where $A_{-1} = B_{-1} = \emptyset$ and $l(-1) = 0$.

Stage $s \geq 0$. Fix e, i, j such that $s = \langle e,i,j \rangle$ and choose $n > l(s-1)$ minimal such that

$$p_s(n) \cdot p_s(p_s(n)) < 2^n, \tag{3.5}$$

and let $C_{s-1} = M_e(A_{s-1} \oplus B_{s-1})$. Then let $l(s) = 2p_s(p_s(p_s(n)))$. For the definition of A_s distinguish the following cases.

Case 1: $M_i(A_{s-1} \oplus C_{s-1})(0^n) = 1$ or $C_{s-1} \upharpoonright p_s(n) \neq N_j(A_{s-1}) \upharpoonright p_s(n)$.

Then let $A_s = A_{s-1}$.

{Comment: By (3.3), $B_{s-1}(0^n) = 0$. So, by (3.4), the choices of A_s and $l(s)$ ensure that $B(0^n) \neq M_i(A \oplus C)(0^n)$ or $C \neq N_j(A)$ for $C = M_e(A \oplus B)$, whence R_s is met.}

Case 2: Otherwise, i.e. $M_i(A_{s-1} \oplus C_{s-1})(0^n) = 0$ and $C_{s-1} \restriction p_s(n) = N_j(A_{s-1}) \restriction p_s(n)$.

Then distinguish the following subcases.

Case 2.1: $C_{s-1} \restriction p_s(n) = M_e(A_{s-1} \oplus B_{s-1} \cup \{0^n\}) \restriction p_s(n)$.

Then $M_i(A_{s-1} \oplus M_e(A_{s-1} \oplus B_{s-1} \cup \{0^n\}))(0^n) = M_i(A_{s-1} \oplus C_{s-1})(0^n) = 0$. Let

$$U = \{z: \text{The query ``}z \in A_{s-1}\text{?'' occurs in the computation}$$

$$M_i(A_{s-1} \oplus M_e(A_{s-1} \oplus B_{s-1} \cup \{0^n\}))(0^n).$$

Note that $|U| < p_s(n) + p_s(n)p_s(p_s(n))$. So, by (3.5), there is a string z such that $|z| = 2n$ and $z \notin U$. For the least such z let $A_s = A_{s-1} \cup \{z\}$.

{Comment: By choice of A_s, $B_s = B_{s-1} \cup \{0^n\}$ and $M_i(A_s \oplus M_e(A_s \oplus B_s))(0^n) = 0$. So $B_s \neq M_i(A_s \oplus M_e(A_s \oplus B_s))$ and, by (3.4) and by choice of $l(s)$, this disagreement is preserved.}

Case 2.2: Otherwise.

Then fix the least y, $|y| < p_s(n)$, such that $M_e(A_{s-1} \oplus B_{s-1})(y) \neq M_e(A_{s-1} \oplus B_{s-1} \cup \{0^n\})(y)$, and distinguish the following subcases.

Case 2.2.1: $N_j(A_{s-1})(y) = 1$.

Then fix an accepting branch of the computation of $N_j(A_{s-1})(y)$ and let V be the set of strings used in oracle queries on this branch. Note that $|V| < p_s(|y|) < p_s(p_s(n))$. Moreover, let V' be the set of strings y such that $0y$ is used in the computation $M_e(A_{s-1} \oplus B_{s-1} \cup \{0^n\})(y)$. Again $|V'| < p_s(|y|) < p_s(p_s(n))$. So, by (3.5), there is a string z such that $|z| = 2n$ and $z \notin V \cup V'$. For the least such z let $A_s = A_{s-1} \cup \{z\}$.

{Comment: By choice of A_s, $B_s = B_{s-1} \cup \{0^n\}$ and $M_e(A_s \oplus B_s)(y) = M_e(A_{s-1} \oplus B_{s-1} \cup \{0^n\})(y) \neq M_e(A_{s-1} \oplus B_{s-1})(y) = N_j(A_{s-1})(y) = N_j(A_s)(y) = 1$. Again, this disagreement is preserved by choice of $l(s)$.}

Case 2.2.2: $N_j(A_{s-1})(y) = 0$.

Then let W be the set of strings z such that $0z$ is used in a query of $M_e(A_{s-1} \oplus B_{s-1})(y)$ or $M_e(A_{s-1} \oplus B_{s-1} \cup \{0^n\})(y)$. Note that $|W| < 2p_s(p_s(n))$. Distinguish the following subcases.

Case 2.2.2.1: $\exists z\,(|z| = 2n\ \&\ z \notin W\ \&\ N_j(A_{s-1} \cup \{z\})(y) = 1)$.

Then fix the least such z, fix an accepting branch in the computation $N_j(A_{s-1} \cup \{z\})(y)$ and let W' be the set of strings used in queries on that branch. $|W'| < p_s(p_s(n))$. So, by (3.5), there is some string z' of length $2n+1$ such that $z' \notin W \cup W'$. Fix the least such z' and let $A_s = A_{s-1} \cup \{z, z'\}$.

{Comment: By choice of A_s, $B_s = B_{s-1}$, $N_j(A_s)(y) = N_j(A_{s-1} \cup \{z\})(y) \neq N_j(A_{s-1})(y) = M_e(A_{s-1} \oplus B_{s-1})(y) = M_e(A_s \oplus B_s)(y)$, and this disagreement will be preserved.}

Case 2.2.2.2: Otherwise.

Then fix z minimal such that $|z| = 2n$ and $z \notin W$, and let $A_s = A_{s-1} \cup \{z\}$.

{Comment: By choice of A_s, $B_s = B_{s-1} \cup \{0^n\}$ and $M_e(A_s \oplus B_s)(y) = M_e(A_{s-1} \oplus B_{s-1} \cup \{0^n\})(y) \neq M_e(A_{s-1} \oplus B_{s-1})(y) = N_j(A_{s-1})(y) = N_j(A_s)(y)$, and the disagreement is preserved.}

This completes the construction. The correctness easily follows from the remarks accompanying the cases of the construction. ∎

Baker et al. (8) have constructed an oracle C relative to which $\mathcal{P} \neq \mathcal{NP}$ but $\mathcal{NP} = \text{co}\mathcal{NP}$. Since Proposition 3.8 relativizes, this and Theorem 3.4 show that the question whether $\mathcal{P} \neq \mathcal{NP}$ implies that $\mathbf{NP}_T \subsetneq [\mathbf{0}, \mathbf{1}_T]$ is oracle dependent, i.e., it has for some oracle sets a positive answer (namely for the set A of the theorem) for others, however, a negative answer (namely for the set C above).

The above results show that, in contrast to *p-m*-reducibility, the analysis of the structure of $\mathbf{NP}_T$ cannot be reduced to the study of initial segments of $\mathbf{Rec}_T$. Still $\mathbf{NP}_T$ can be characterized in terms of pseudo initial segments by mixing our two reducibility notions.

DEFINITION 3.3   For any recursive set A let

$$\mathbf{Rec}_{T,m}(\leq A) = \{\deg_T^p(B) : B \leq_m^p A\}.$$

For $A \notin \mathcal{P}$ we call $\mathbf{Rec}_{T,m}(\leq A)$ a *mixed initial segment* of $\mathbf{Rec}_T$. Note that $\mathbf{Rec}_{T,m}(\leq A) \subseteq [\mathbf{0}, \deg_T^p(A)]$.

PROPOSITION 3.9   Let A be *NP-m*-complete. Then $\mathbf{NP}_T = \mathbf{Rec}_{T,m}(\leq A)$.

Proof $\mathbf{NP}_T \subseteq \mathbf{Rec}_{T,m}(\leq A)$ by definition of *NP-m*-completeness. $\mathbf{Rec}_{T,m}(\leq A) \subseteq \mathbf{NP}_T$ by Proposition 3.7. ∎

Again, all results obtained so far on the structure of $(\mathbf{NP}_T; \leqq)$ are under the assumption that $\mathscr{P} \neq \mathscr{NP}$ and they have been proved by showing them for all mixed initial segments of $\mathbf{Rec}_T$.

The only information on the structure of $(\mathbf{NP}_r; \leqq)$ under the assumption that $\mathscr{P} \neq \mathscr{NP}$ that can be deduced from the above described results is the fact that $(\mathbf{NP}_r; \leqq)$ consists of at least two elements, namely a least element $\mathbf{0}$ consisting of the polynomial time computable sets and a greatest element $\mathbf{1}_r$ containing the *NP-r*-complete problems. So it is natural to ask whether, assuming $\mathscr{P} \neq \mathscr{NP}$, there are problems in $\mathscr{NP}$ of intermediate complexity degree, i.e., problems which are neither *NP-r*-complete nor in $\mathscr{P}$. In Section 3.4 we will show that this is indeed the case. In Sections 3.5–3.7 we will then systematically study basic algebraic properties of the u.s.l. $(\mathbf{NP}_r; \leqq)$ under the assumption of $\mathscr{P} \neq \mathscr{NP}$.

In contrast to the observation that $\mathbf{NP}_r$ possesses a greatest element, which was originally established by analyzing natural problems, such an analysis did not provide any deeper insight into the structure of $(\mathbf{NP}_r; \leqq)$. Up to now no natural problem in $\mathscr{NP}$ has been proven to be neither *NP-m*-complete nor in $\mathscr{P}$ (still assuming $\mathscr{P} \neq \mathscr{NP}$). So the subsequent results are obtained by a *structural approach*, i.e., by *constructing NP-sets* with the desired properties. The fundamental method underlying this approach is the so called *delayed diagonalization* technique. In Section 3.4 we introduce the variant of this technique which was first applied to the analysis of polynomial degrees by Ladner (19, 20). In the subsequent sections, a quite elegant simplification of the delayed diagonalization technique shown by Landweber, Lipton and Robertson (22) will be presented. Some notions required by the latter will be introduced in the next section.

3.3 RECURSIVELY PRESENTABLE CLASSES AND POLYNOMIALLY HONEST FUNCTIONS

Landweber, Lipton and Robertson (22) have observed that recursively presentable classes of recursive sets and classes of recursive sets which are closed under finite variants play an important role in the study of the polynomial time degrees. Here we review these notions summarizing some fundamental facts. Also some properties of polynomially honest functions are studied. Some of the material presented here is taken from the literature (13, 22, 27, 29, 30). The presentation follows (4).

In the subsequent sections the results of this section will be applied without giving explicit references.

DEFINITION 3.4   A class $\mathscr{C}$ of recursive sets is *closed under finite variants* (*c.f.v.*) if

$$\forall A \; \varepsilon \; \mathscr{C} \; \forall B \; (A =^* B \to B \; \varepsilon \; \mathscr{C}),$$

where $A =^* B$ says that the symmetric difference $(A - B) \cup (B - A)$ of A and B is finite.

PROPOSITION 3.10   For any recursive set A, $\deg_r^p(A)$ is closed under finite variants.

Proof   Let A, B be given such that $A =^* B$. It suffices to show $A \leq_m^p B$. Fix n such that, for all strings x of length greater than n, $A(x) = B(x)$. Moreover, since by our convention $B \neq \emptyset, \Sigma^*$, we may choose strings y and z such that $y \, \varepsilon \, B$ and $z \notin B$. Then the following function f reduces A to B:

$$f(x) = \begin{cases} y & \text{if } |x| \leq n \text{ and } x \, \varepsilon \, A \\ z & \text{if } |x| \leq n \text{ and } x \notin A \\ x & \text{otherwise.} \end{cases} \qquad \blacksquare$$

By Proposition 3.10, any class which is closed under p-r-equivalence (i.e., which is the union of p-r-degrees), is closed under finite variants. In particular, the classes $\mathcal{P} = \mathbf{0}$, $\mathcal{NP} = \{A : \deg_m^p(A) \, \varepsilon \, [\mathbf{0}, \mathbf{1}_m]\}$, and $\Delta_2^p = \{A : \deg_T^p(A) \, \varepsilon \, [\mathbf{0}, \mathbf{1}_T]\}$ are c.f.v. Also note that for c.f.v. classes $\mathcal{C}$ and $\mathcal{D}$ the classes $\mathcal{C} \cup \mathcal{D}$, $\mathcal{C} \cap \mathcal{D}$ and co-$\mathcal{C}$ are c.f.v. too.

A class $\mathcal{C}$ of recursive sets is called recursively presentable if it is empty or there is a recursive sequence $\langle C_n : n \, \varepsilon \, \mathbb{N} \rangle$ of recursive sets such that $\mathcal{C} = \{C_n : n \, \varepsilon \, \mathbb{N}\}$. By effectively coding the sequence $\langle C_n : n \, \varepsilon \, \mathbb{N} \rangle$ into a single rescursive set U, we obtain the following equivalent definition.

DEFINITION 3.5   A class $\mathcal{C}$ of recursive sets is *recursively presentable* (*r.p.*) if $\mathcal{C} = \emptyset$ or there is a recursive set U such that $\mathcal{C} = \{U^{(n)} : n \, \varepsilon \, \mathbb{N}\}$. In the latter case U is called a *universal set* for $\mathcal{C}$.

In the literature r.p. classes are sometimes also called *recursive* classes and usually they are required to be nonempty. Inclusion of the empty class here is purely for convenience. We next observe that r.p. classes are bounded; whence for example, the class of all recursive sets is not r.p.

PROPOSITION 3.11   Let $\mathcal{C}$ be recursively presentable. There is a recursive set A such that $\mathcal{C} <_r^p A$ for all elements C of $\mathcal{C}$.

Proof   W.l.o.g. $\mathcal{C} \neq \emptyset$. Then, for any universal set U of $\mathcal{C}$, $C \leq_m^p U$ for all sets $C \, \varepsilon \, \mathcal{C}$. So the claim follows with Proposition 3.6. $\blacksquare$

PROPOSITION 3.12   Let $\mathcal{C}$ be finite. Then $\mathcal{C}$ is r.p.

Proof   Immediate. $\blacksquare$

The next theorem, which summarizes some closure properties of the family of r.p. classes, requires some notation. Let $\mathscr{C}$ and $\mathscr{D}$ be classes of recursive sets. The closure under finite variants of $\mathscr{C}$ is defined by

$$\mathscr{C}^{\mathrm{Fin}} = \{A : \exists C \; \varepsilon \; \mathscr{C} \; (A =^* C)\},$$

the closure under *p-r*-equivalence of $\mathscr{C}$ by

$$\mathscr{D}_r(\mathscr{C}) = \{A : \exists C \; \varepsilon \; \mathscr{C} \; (A =^p_r C)\},$$

and the *p-r*-interval of $\mathscr{C}$ and $\mathscr{D}$ by

$$[\mathscr{C},\mathscr{D}]_r = \{A : \exists C \; \varepsilon \; \mathscr{C} \; \exists D \; \varepsilon \; \mathscr{D} \; (C \leq^p_r A \leq^p_r D)\}.$$

Finally, for a class $\mathbf{C}$ of *p-r*-degrees of recursive sets, $\mathscr{S}(\mathbf{C})$ denotes the union of the elements of $\mathbf{C}$, i.e.,

$$\mathscr{S}(\mathbf{C}) = \{C : \deg^p_r(C) \; \varepsilon \; \mathbf{C}\}.$$

Note that $\mathscr{C}^{\mathrm{Fin}}$ and, by Proposition 3.10, $\mathscr{D}_r(\mathscr{C})$, $[\mathscr{C},\mathscr{D}]_r$ and $\mathscr{S}(\mathbf{C})$ are c.f.v.

THEOREM 3.5   Let $\mathscr{C}$ and $\mathscr{D}$ be r.p. classes of recursive sets.

(a) $\mathscr{C} \cup \mathscr{D}$ is r.p.
(b) If $\mathscr{C}$ and $\mathscr{D}$ are c.f.v. then $\mathscr{C} \cap \mathscr{D}$ is r.p.
(c) $\mathscr{C}^{\mathrm{Fin}}$ is r.p. Hence, in particular the classes $\{\varnothing\}^{\mathrm{Fin}}$ of finite sets and $\{\Sigma^*\}^{\mathrm{Fin}}$ of cofinite sets are r.p.
(d) $\mathscr{D}_r(\mathscr{C})$ is r.p.
(e) $[\mathscr{C},\mathscr{D}]_r$ is r.p.
(f) co-$\mathscr{C}$ is r.p.

Proof   W.l.o.g. we may assume that $\mathscr{C}$ and $\mathscr{D}$ are nonempty, say U and V are universal sets for $\mathscr{C}$ and $\mathscr{D}$, respectively.

(a) The set W defined by $\langle 2n,x \rangle \; \varepsilon \; W$ iff $\langle n,x \rangle \; \varepsilon \; U$ and $\langle 2n+1,x \rangle \; \varepsilon \; W$ iff $\langle n,x \rangle \; \varepsilon \; V$ is universal for $\mathscr{C} \cup \mathscr{D}$.
(b) W.l.o.g. $\mathscr{C} \cap \mathscr{D} \neq \varnothing$, say $C \; \varepsilon \; \mathscr{C} \cap \mathscr{D}$. Define a recursive set X by

$$X^{(\langle m,n \rangle)}(x) = \begin{cases} U^{(m)}(x) & \text{if } \forall y < x \; (U^{(m)}(y) = V^{(n)}(y)) \\ C(x) & \text{otherwise.} \end{cases}$$

Then $X^{(\langle m,n \rangle)} = U^{(m)}$ if $U^{(m)} = V^{(n)}$ and $X^{(\langle m,n \rangle)} =^* C$ otherwise. Hence, X is universal for $\mathscr{C} \cap \mathscr{D}$.
(c) We first show that $\{\varnothing\}^{\mathrm{Fin}}$ is r.p. Let x_n denote the nth string w.r.t. the natural ordering of Σ^*. Then the set F, defined by $x_n \; \varepsilon \; F^{(m)}$ iff the binary representation of m has length greater than n and the nth digit of it equals one, is universal for $\{\varnothing\}^{\mathrm{Fin}}$. It follows that the set Y defined by

$$Y^{(\langle k, m, n\rangle)}(x) = \begin{cases} U^{(k)}(x) & \text{if } |x| \geqq m \\ F^{(n)}(x) & \text{otherwise,} \end{cases}$$

enumerates all finite variants of sets in $\mathscr{C}$.

(d) We consider the case $r = m$ and leave the similar case $r = T$ to the reader. Define Z by

$$Z^{(\langle k, m, n\rangle)}(x) = \begin{cases} U^{(k)}(f_m(x)) & \text{if } \forall y < x (f_n(y) < x \rightarrow \\ & \qquad U^{(k)}(y) = Z^{(\langle k, m, n\rangle)}(f_n(y))) \\ U^{(k)}(x) & \text{otherwise.} \end{cases}$$

Obviously Z is recursive. Moreover, if there is a set A such that $A \leqq_m^p U^{(k)}$ via f_m and $U^{(k)} \leqq_m^p A$ via f_n then $Z^{(\langle k, m, n\rangle)} = A$; otherwise $Z^{(\langle k, m, n\rangle)} =^* U^{(k)}$ (and thus $Z^{(\langle k, m, n\rangle)} \varepsilon \mathscr{D}_m(\mathscr{C})$ by Proposition 3.10). Hence, Z is universal for $\mathscr{D}_m(\mathscr{C})$.

(e) The proof is similar to that of part (d). See (4).

(f) Obviously $\overline{U}$ is universal for co-$\mathscr{C}$. ∎

The above results easily imply recursive representability of the standard complexity classes extending $\mathscr{P}$. We give a few examples which we will need later on.

COROLLARY 3.5   Let A and B be recursive sets. The following classes are r.p. and c.f.v.

(i) $\deg_r^p(A)$

(ii) $\{C : C \leqq_r^p A\}$

(iii) $\{C : A \leqq_r^p C \leqq_r^p B\}$

(iv) $\mathscr{P}$

(v) $\mathscr{NP}$

(vi) $\{C : C \text{ is } NP\text{-}r\text{-complete}\}$

Proof   Closure under finite variants is immediate by Proposition 3.10. For a proof of recursive presentability, note that $\deg_r^p(A) = \mathscr{D}_r(\{A\})$, $\{C : C \leqq_r^p A\} = [\{\{0\}\}, \{A\}]_r$, and $\{C : A \leqq_r^p C \leqq_r^p B\} = [\{A\}, \{B\}]_r$. So (i)–(iii) are immediate by Proposition 3.12 and Theorem 3.5. The remainder of the corollary follows using the following equations: $\mathscr{P} = \deg_T^p(\emptyset)$ and, for A being any NP-m-complete set, $\mathscr{NP} = \{C : C \leqq_m^p A\}$ and $\{C : C \text{ is } NP\text{-}r\text{-complete}\} = \deg_r^p(A) \cap \mathscr{NP}$. ∎

The following definition extends the concept of recursive representability to classes of polynomial degrees.

DEFINITION 3.6　A class $\mathbf{C}$ of *p-r*-degrees of recursive sets is *recursively presentable* (*r.p.*) if $\mathbf{C}$ is empty or there is a recursive set U such that $\mathbf{C} = \{\deg_r^p(U^{(n)}): n \; \varepsilon \; \mathbb{N}\}$. In the latter case, U is called a *universal set* for $\mathbf{C}$.

In other words, the class $\mathbf{C}$ is r.p. if there is an r.p. class $\mathscr{C}$ of recursive sets such that $\mathbf{C} = \{\deg_r^p(C): C \; \varepsilon \; \mathscr{C}\}$. Hence, by Proposition 3.12, any finite set of *p-r*-degrees is r.p.

PROPOSITION 3.13　Let $\mathbf{C}$ be a finite class of *p-r*-degrees of recursive sets. Then $\mathbf{C}$ is recursively presentable.

By applying the results on r.p. classes of recursive sets, we obtain further representability results for polynomial degrees.

COROLLARY 3.6

(a) Any closed interval of *p-r*-degrees is r.p. In fact, any finite union of such intervals is r.p.
(b) For any recursive set A, $\mathbf{Rec}_{T,m}(\leqq A)$ is r.p.
(c) $\mathbf{NP}_r$ is r.p.
(d) For any r.p. class $\mathbf{C}$, $\mathbf{C} \cap \mathbf{NP}_r$ is r.p. In particular, for any interval $[\mathbf{a},\mathbf{b}]$, $[\mathbf{a},\mathbf{b}] \cap \mathbf{NP}_r$ is r.p.

Proof　Parts (a) and (b) are immediate by Corollary 3.5(ii),(iii) and Theorem 3.5(a). (c) is a consequence of (a) and (b). Finally, (d) follows from (a), (c) and from part (b) of Theorem 3.5.　　　　　　　　　　　　　　　　■

COROLLARY 3.7　Let $\mathbf{C}$ be a recursively presentable class of *p-r*-degrees. Then the class $\mathscr{S}(\mathbf{C})$ is r.p. and c.f.v.

Proof　Let $\mathscr{C}$ be a r.p. class such that $\mathbf{C} = \{\deg_r^p(C): C \; \varepsilon \; \mathscr{C}\}$. Then $\mathscr{S}(\mathbf{C}) = \mathscr{D}_r(\mathscr{C})$. So the claim follows from Theorem 3.5 and Proposition 3.10.　　　　■

In the remainder of this section, we review some notions concerning recursive functions on natural numbers. Let $g\colon \mathbb{N} \to \mathbb{N}$ and $h\colon \mathbb{N} \to \mathbb{N}$ be recursive functions. We say h *dominates* g if $h(n) > g(n)$ for all numbers n. The *n*th *iteration* $g^n\colon \mathbb{N} \to \mathbb{N}$ of g is inductively defined by $g^0(m) = m$ and $g^{n+1}(m) = g(g^n(m))$. The $(n+1)$st g-interval $I_n^g \subseteq \Sigma^*$ is given by

$$I_n^g = [\![g^n(0), g^{n+1}(0))\!]$$

$$= \{x \; \varepsilon \; \Sigma^*: g^n(0) \leqq |x| < g^{n+1}(0)\}.$$

For a function g dominating the identity function, the g-intervals define a partition of Σ^*.

PROPOSITION 3.14   Let $g(n) > n$ for all n. Then, $\Sigma^* = \cup\{I_n^g: n \in \mathbb{N}\}$ and, for $n \neq m$, $I_n^g \cap I_m^g = \emptyset$.

Proof   Straightforward.   ∎

For $\alpha \subseteq \mathbb{N}$ we abbreviate $\cup\{I_n^g: n \in \alpha\}$ by I_α^g. Note that, for $g(n) > n$, $\alpha \cap \beta = \emptyset$ iff $I_\alpha^g \cap I_\beta^g = \emptyset$, and α is finite iff I_α^g is finite.

Obviously the complexity of a collection of g-intervals depends on both the complexity of the function g and the complexity of the index set α. We now define a class of functions which yields polynomial time computable interval sets for polynomial time computable indices.

DEFINITION 3.7   A recursive function $g: \mathbb{N} \to \mathbb{N}$ is *polynomially honest* if there is a polynomial p and a deterministic TM M such that M computes $g(n)$ in $p(g(n))$ steps.

We first note that there are arbitrarily large polynomially honest functions.

PROPOSITION 3.15   Let $f: \mathbb{N} \to \mathbb{N}$ be recursive. There is a strictly increasing and polynomially honest function g which dominates f.

Proof   Let M be a deterministic TM which on input 0^n computes $0^{f(n)}$, and let $g'(n)$ be the run time of M on input 0^n. Obviously, g' is polynomially honest and dominates f. It follows that g, defined by $g(n) = \max\{g'(m): m \leq n\} + n$ has the desired properties.   ∎

LEMMA 3.1   Let $g: \mathbb{N} \to \mathbb{N}$ be a strictly increasing polynomially honest function and let $\alpha \in \mathcal{P}_{\mathbb{N}}$. Then $\cup\{[\![g(n), g(n+1))\!): n \in \alpha\} \in \mathcal{P}$.

Proof   Let p be a polynomial witnessing honesty of g. The following algorithm decides $G_\alpha = \cup\{[\![g(n), g(n+1))\!): n \in \alpha\}$ in polynomial time. Given x, for each $n \leq |x| + 1$ compute $g(n)$ for up to $p(|x| + 1)$ steps, and let n_0 be the least n such that $|x| < g(n)$ or the computation of $g(n)$ does not terminate in $p(|x|)$ steps. Note that, by strict monotonicity of g, $|x| < g(|x| + 1)$, whence, $n_0 \leq |x| + 1$ does exist. Moreover, $x \in [\![g(n_0 - 1), g(n_0))\!)$ (where $g(-1) = 0$). Hence, $x \in G_\alpha$ iff $n_0 - 1 \in \alpha$.   ∎

COROLLARY 3.8   Let g be a polynomially honest function such that $g(n) > n$ and let $\alpha \in \mathcal{P}_{\mathbb{N}}$. Then $I_\alpha^g \in \mathcal{P}$.

Proof. By Lemma 3.1, since the function $\lambda n.g^n(0)$ is strictly increasing and polynomially honest. ∎

DEFINITION 3.8   Let $g: \mathbb{N} \to \mathbb{N}$ be recursive and $g(n) > n$, and let A and B be recursive subsets of Σ^*. A and B are *g-similar* if

$$A \cap [\![n, g(n)]\!] = B \cap [\![n, g(n)]\!]$$

for infinitely many numbers n.

Note that, by Corollary 3.8, for polynomially honest g, $g(n) > n$, and $\alpha \ \varepsilon \ \mathcal{P}_{\mathbb{N}}$, $A \cap I_\alpha^g$ is a subproblem of A, whence, by Proposition 3.5, $A \cap I_\alpha^g \leq_m^p A$. Also note that, for infinite α, A and $A \cap I_\alpha^g$ are g-similar. In Section 3.5 we will show that, given a r.p. and c.f.v. class $\mathscr{C}$ and $A \ \not\varepsilon \ \mathscr{C}$, for any sufficiently large function g, no set g-similar with A belongs to the class $\mathscr{C}$.

3.4   DELAYED DIAGONALIZATION

The fundamental technique for analyzing the structure of $(\mathbf{NP}_r; \leq)$ under the assumption that $\mathscr{P} \neq \mathcal{NP}$ is the delayed diagonalization method. In this section, we introduce the variant of this technique which was first applied to polynomial reducibilities by Ladner (19, 20). To illustrate this technique we give an outline of Ladner's proof that there are no intractable problems of minimal relative polynomial complexity. By analyzing this proof, we will discover the role played by r.p. and c.f.v. classes in our investigations. Moreover, we will hint at a quite elegant variant of the delayed diagonalization technique shown in Landweber et al. (22), which will be systematically developed in the next section.

THEOREM 3.6   (Ladner 20).   Let B be a recursive set such that $B \ \not\varepsilon \ \mathscr{P}$. There is a recursive set A such that $A \ \not\varepsilon \ \mathscr{P}$, $A \leq_m^p B$ and $B \ \not\leq_T^p A$.

Before turning to the proof, we state some corollaries.

COROLLARY 3.9   For any recursive *p-r*-degree $\mathbf{b} > \mathbf{0}$ there is a *p-r*-degree $\mathbf{a}$ such that $\mathbf{0} < \mathbf{a} < \mathbf{b}$. If moreover, $\mathbf{b} \ \varepsilon \ \mathbf{NP}_r$ then $\mathbf{a}$ can be chosen to be in $\mathbf{NP}_r$ too. Hence, neither $(\mathbf{Rec}_r - \{\mathbf{0}\}; \leq)$ nor $(\mathbf{NP}_r - \{\mathbf{0}\}; \leq)$ possesses minimal elements.

Proof   Given $\mathbf{b} > \mathbf{0}$ (with $\mathbf{b} \ \varepsilon \ \mathbf{NP}_r$), choose $B \ \varepsilon \ \mathbf{b}$ (with $B \ \varepsilon \ \mathcal{NP}$), apply Theorem 3.6 to B, and, for the resulting set A, let $\mathbf{a} = \deg_r^p(A)$. Then $\mathbf{0} < \mathbf{a} < \mathbf{b}$ and, since $A \leq_m^p B$, $B \ \varepsilon \ \mathcal{NP}$ implies $A \ \varepsilon \ \mathcal{NP}$ too. ∎

Recall that, assuming $\mathcal{P} \neq \mathcal{NP}$, $\mathbf{0} < \mathbf{1}_r$. So, by iterated applications of Corollary 3.9 we obtain Corollary 3.10.

COROLLARY 3.10 Assume $\mathcal{P} \neq \mathcal{NP}$. There exists a strictly descending infinite sequence of degrees in $(\mathbf{NP}_r; \leqq)$. In particular, $\mathbf{NP}_r$ is (countably) infinite.

Proof of Theorem 3.6 The proof is a refinement of that of Theorem 3.1. Rather than giving a precise and formal argument, we will develop the ideas underlying the proof.

We will construct a set A satisfying the following three conditions:

(1) $A \not\in \mathcal{P}$

(2) $B \not\leq^p_T A$

(3) $A \leqq^p_m B$.

As in the proof of 3.1, Conditions (1) and (2) can be replaced by the finitary requirements

$$R^0_e: A \neq P_e \qquad (e \ \varepsilon \ \mathbb{N})$$

and

$$R^1_e: B \neq M_e(A) \ (e \ \varepsilon \ \mathbb{N}),$$

respectively. In the proof of Theorem 3.1, we have shown how to build a recursive set A to meet these requirements. (In case of requirement R^0_e, just substitute P_e for $M_e(B)$.) The thus constructed set A, however, does not satisfy Condition (3).

In order to guarantee Condition (3) we will make A a subproblem of B, i.e., we will construct a set $C \ \varepsilon \ \mathcal{P}$ such that $A = B \cap C$. This additional requirement, however, limits our freedom in choosing the values for $A(x)$ so that we succeed in the diagonalizations ensuring the requirements R^i_e ($i \leq 1$, $e \ \varepsilon \ \mathbb{N}$). Namely, for any string x, we now can only let $A(x) = B(x)$ (by taking x into C) or $A(x) = \emptyset(x) = 0$ (by keeping x out of C). If we analyze the strategies for meeting the requirements R^0_e and R^1_e used in the proof of Theorem 3.1, then we note that the strategy for meeting R^1_e goes along with these constraints: There, given some finite initial part $A_s = A \upharpoonright l(s)$ of A, we have chosen $l(s+1) > l(s)$ so that restraining all strings of the interval $[\![l(s), l(s+1))\!]$ from A, which we can now guarantee by restraining this interval from C, ensured that R^1_e was met. The strategy for meeting the requirements R^0_e, however, has to be changed. We now use a strategy quite similar to the one for R^1_e, but with the roles of B and $\emptyset$ interchanged: Since $B \not\in \mathcal{P}$ and $\mathcal{P}$ is closed under finite variants, $B(x) \neq P_e(x)$ for infinitely many strings x. So, given $A_s = A \upharpoonright l(s)$, we can effectively find the least string x, $|x| \geqq l(s)$, such that $B(x) \neq P_e(x)$. Then by setting $l(s+1) =$

$|x| + 1$ and letting A look like B on the interval $[\![l(s), l(s+1))\!)$, i.e., by entirely putting this interval into C, we can ensure that $A \neq P_e$.

Summing up, given any finite initial part $A_s = A \upharpoonright l(s)$ of A, $A = B \cap C$, we can effectively meet R_e^0 or R_e^1 by appropriately choosing $l(s+1) > l(s)$ and ensuring $[\![l(s), l(s+1))\!) \subseteq C$ or $[\![l(s), l(s+1))\!) \subseteq \overline{C}$, respectively. So, by ordering the requirements by setting $R_{2e} = R_e^0$ and $R_{2e+1} = R_e^1$, as in the proof of Theorem 3.1, we can meet the requirements one by one by defining a strictly increasing recursive function $l: \mathbb{N} \to \mathbb{N}$ and by taking $[\![l(s), l(s+1))\!)$ into C for odd s, i.e., by letting

$$A \cap [\![l(s), l(s+1))\!) = \begin{cases} B \cap [\![l(s), l(s+1))\!) & \text{if } s \text{ is odd} \\ \emptyset \cap [\![l(s), l(s+1))\!) = \emptyset & \text{otherwise.} \end{cases}$$

In other words, the set A is built from intervals of B alternating with empty intervals as shown in Figure 3.1 below.

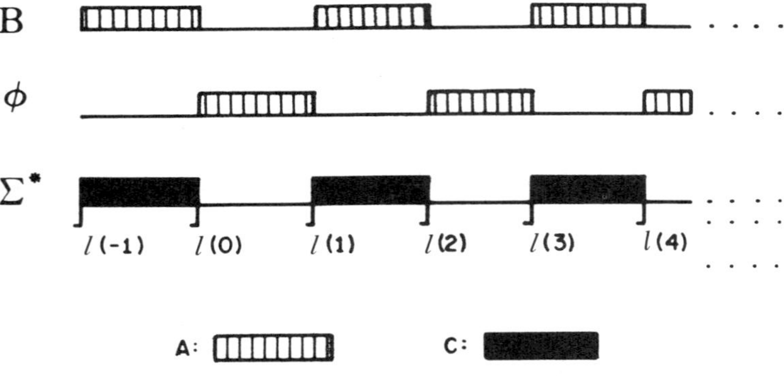

Figure 3.1

More formally, a strictly increasing function l defining the endpoints of the intervals of A is inductively defined by

$$l(-1) = 0$$

and, for $s \geq 0$,

$$l(2s) = \mu n > l(2s-1)(\exists x \in [\![l(2s-1), n)\!) \, (B(x) \neq P_s(x)))$$

and

$$l(2s+1) = \mu n > l(2s) \, (\exists x (p_s(|x|) \leq n \ \& \ B(x) \neq M_s(A_{2s})(x)),$$

where $A_{2s} = B \cap (\cup\{[\![l(2t-1), l(2t))\!) : 0 \leq t \leq s\})$.

By the preceding observations, a straightforward induction shows that the function l is strictly increasing, total and recursive, and that, for

$$C = \cup\{[\![l(2s-1),l(2s))\!) : s \geq 0\} \quad \text{and} \quad A = B \cap C,$$

A meets the requirements R_s, $s \; \varepsilon \; \mathbb{N}$.

It remains to be shown that $C \; \varepsilon \; \mathcal{P}$. Since l is strictly increasing, by Lemma 3.1 this amounts to proving that l is polynomially honest. Unfortunately, this is not the case: By construction, $l(s)$ is the least number n greater than $l(s-1)$ such that R_s is witnessed by some string x of length less than n, and there is no polynomial time algorithm for determining for given x and s whether x witnesses that R_s is met.

This difficulty is overcome by increasing l, i.e. by extending the intervals $[\![l(s),l(s+1))\!)$ as follows. After having a diagonalization witness for R_s we do not immediately close the interval $[\![l(s),l(s+1))\!)$ and turn to the next requirement, but the diagonalization is *delayed* by not closing the interval until a length $l(s+1)$ is reached such that by *looking back* to the strings of smaller length a diagonalization witness (of length $\geq l(s)$ for even s) for R_s can be found in $l(s+1)$ steps. Testing strings in increasing order such a number $l(s+1)$ must be eventually reached, and, since now, knowing $l(s)$, $l(s+1)$ can be computed in $0(l(s+1))$ steps, the strictly increasing function l is polynomially honest.

Diagonalizations based on this idea are called *delayed diagonalizations*. Sometimes also the notion *looking back technique* is used.

Summing up the above arguments, we conclude the proof with giving an informal construction enumerating the graph of a polynomially honest function l in increasing order such that, for $C = \cup\{[\![l(2s-1),l(2s))\!) : s \; \varepsilon \; \mathbb{N}\}$ and $A = B \cap C$, the set A satisfies Conditions (1)–(3).

Stage 0. Let $l(-1) = 0$.

Stage $s+1$. The stage consists of two substages.
Substage 1. Find n maximal such that $l(n)$ has been defined at a previous stage, and compute $l(-1), \ldots, l(n)$.
Substage 2. For up to $s+1$ steps carry out the following subroutine. If the procedure yields FOUND, let $l(n+1) = s+1$.

 if $n+1 = 2e$ *then*
  begin
   $x := 0^{l(n)}$;
   while $|x| < s+1$ *do*
    begin
     compute $B(x)$;
     compute $P_e(x)$;

$$\textit{if } B(x) \ne P_e(x) \textit{ then } \text{FOUND} \textit{ else } x := \text{successor}(x)$$
$$\textit{end}$$
$$\textit{end};$$
$$\textit{if } n+1 = 2e+1 \textit{ then}$$
$$\textit{begin}$$
$$x := 0^0;$$
$$\textit{while } p_e(|x|) < s+1 \textit{ do}$$
$$\textit{begin}$$
$$\text{compute } B(x);$$
$$\text{compute } M_e(A_n)(x),$$
$$\text{where } A_n = B \cap (\cup\{[\![l(2t-1), l(2t)]\!] : 0 \le 2t \le n\});$$
$$\textit{if } B(x) \ne M_e(A_n)(x) \textit{ then } \text{FOUND} \textit{ else } x := \text{successor}(x)$$
$$\textit{end}$$
$$\textit{end}$$

This completes the construction. For a proof of correctness, note that in substage 2 of stage $s+1$, $l(n+1) = s+1$ iff in $s+1$ steps a string x can be found such that, for $n+1 = 2e$, $x \in [\![l(n), l(n+1))\!]$ and $B(x) \ne P_e(x)$ (whence, by definition of A, $A(x) \ne P_e(x)$), while, for $n+1 = 2e+1$, $p_e(|x|) < l(n+1)$ and $B(x) \ne M_e(A \restriction l(n))(x)$ (whence, by definition of A, $B(x) \ne M_e(A \restriction l(n))(x) = M_e(A \restriction l(n+1))(x) = M_e(A)(x)$). So in either case, $l(n+1) = s+1$ indicates that fulfillment of requirement R_{n+1} is guaranteed by $A \restriction l(n+1)$. Moreover, we can argue as before that l is total and strictly increasing. Hence, A meets all requirements R_n, $n \in \mathbb{N}$. Finally, substage 2 of stage $s+1$ requires $0(s+1)$ steps, whence, by successively performing substage 2 of the previous stages, substage 1 of stage $s+1$ can be carried out in $0((s+1)^2)$ steps. So $l(s)$ can be computed in $0((l(s)^2)$ steps, whence l is polynomially honest. It follows that $C \in \mathcal{P}$ (by Lemma 3.1) and thus $A \le_m^p B$ (by Proposition 3.5).

This completes the proof. ∎

If we analyze the strategy for meeting the requirements R_e^0 in the proof of Theorem 3.6, then we observe that we only used that $\langle P_e : e \in \mathbb{N}\rangle$ is a recursive sequence of recursive sets such that, for all e, not $B =^* P_e$. So if $\mathcal{C}$ is a recursively presentable class and $\langle C_e : e \in \mathbb{N}\rangle$ is a recursive presentation of $\mathcal{C}$ (i.e., $C_e = U^{(e)}$ for some universal set U for $\mathcal{C}$), then, by substituting C_e for P_e, the above proof shows that, for any r.p. and c.f.v. class $\mathcal{C}$ and $B \notin \mathcal{C}$, there is a set $A \notin \mathcal{C}$ such that $A \le_m^p B$ and $B \not\le_T^p A$. This result can be further generalized as follows: Given r.p. and c.f.v. classes $\mathcal{C}$ and $\mathcal{C}'$ and recursive sets $B \notin \mathcal{C}$ and $B' \notin \mathcal{C}'$, we may choose recursive representations $\langle C_e : e \in \mathbb{N}\rangle$ and $\langle C'_e : e \in \mathbb{N}\rangle$ of $\mathcal{C}$ and $\mathcal{C}'$, respectively, and then using the strategy for meeting the requirements R_e^0 above, we can meet the requirements

$$\bar{R}_e : A \ne C_e \quad \text{and} \quad \bar{R}'_e : A \ne C'_e$$

by letting A look like B and B', respectively, on certain intervals. To be more precise, proceeding as in the proof of Theorem 3.6, we can define a polynomially honest and strictly increasing function l such that, for any set A,

$$A \cap [\![l(2e-1), l(2e))\!] = B \cap [\![l(2e-1), l(2e))\!] \to \overline{R}_e \text{ is met} \qquad (3.6a)$$

and

$$A \cap [\![l(2e), l(2e+1))\!] = B' \cap [\![l(2e), l(2e+1))\!] \to \overline{R}'_e \text{ is met} \qquad (3.6b)$$

hold (i.e. if A is built from intervals of B alternating with intervals of B' as illustrated by Figure 3.1 when $\emptyset$ is replaced with B', then $A \not\in \mathscr{C} \cup \mathscr{C}'$). Moreover, since, by honesty of l, $C = \cup\{[\![l(2e+1), l(2e))\!] : e \in \mathbb{N}\}$ is polynomial time computable and $A = (B \cap C) \cup (B' \cap \overline{C})$, $A \leq^p_m B \oplus B'$. So the strategy developed for handling the R^0_e requirements above suffices to prove the following variant of Schöning's diagonalization lemma (30).

THEOREM 3.7   Let $\mathscr{C}$ and $\mathscr{C}'$ be r.p. and c.f.v. classes of recursive sets and let B and B' be recursive sets such that $B \not\in \mathscr{C}$ and $B' \not\in \mathscr{C}'$. There is a recursive set A such that $A \not\in \mathscr{C} \cup \mathscr{C}'$ and $A \leq^p_m B \oplus B'$.

Since the union of two r.p. and c.f.v. classes is r.p. and c.f.v. again, by iterated applications Theorem 3.7 extends to arbitrary finite collections of r.p. and c.f.v. classes, i.e., given $n \geq 1$, r.p. and c.f.v. classes $\mathscr{C}_i$ and recursive sets $B_i \not\in \mathscr{C}_i$ ($i \leq n$), there is a recursive set A such that $A \not\in \mathscr{C}_0 \cup \ldots \cup \mathscr{C}_n$ and $A \leq^p_m B_0 \oplus \ldots \oplus B_n$. So, intuitively, Theorem 3.7 says that given any diagonals for (r.p. and c.f.v.) complexity classes, there is a diagonal for the union of these classes whose complexity is bounded by the sum of the diagonals for the individual classes. Numerous results proved by delayed diagonalization can be reduced to Theorem 3.7 (see Schöning (30)). In particular, Theorem 3.6 can be deduced from Theorem 3.7 as follows. Given $B \not\in \mathscr{P}$, apply Theorem 3.7 to $\mathscr{C} = \mathscr{P}$, $\mathscr{C}' = \deg^p_T(B)$, B and $B' = \emptyset$. Then, for the resulting set A, Conditions (1) and (3) are immediate since $B =^p_m B \oplus \emptyset$. Condition (2) follows from Condition (3) together with the fact that $A \not\in \deg^p_T(B)$.

The fact that Theorem 3.7 entails Theorem 3.6 shows that the more sophisticated requirements of type R^1 can be replaced by appropriate requirements of type R^0, i.e., the latter type of requirement suffices. Though the strategies for these two types of requirements are similar, there is a crucial point in which they differ. While, given some initial part $A_s = A \upharpoonright l(s)$, in the strategy for meeting a requirement R^1_e by finding some appropriate extension $A_{s+1} = A \upharpoonright l(s+1)$ of A_s witnessing R^1_e, the value of $l(s+1)$ depends on the previously generated part A_s of A (recall that we have to diagonalize over computations of the form $M_e(A_s)(x)$ and then preserve these computations by choice of $l(s+1)$), in the strategy of meeting a requirement R^0_1 the computation of $l(s+1)$ such that $A \cup$

$[\![l(s), l(s+1)]\!]$ contains a witness for R_1^0 depends only on $l(s)$ but *not* on A_s (cf. (3.6a) and (3.6b) above). Hence, while in the definition of the intervals of A ensuring that the R^1 requirements are met one has to proceed inductively, for the R^0 requirements this is not necessary, i.e., for each e, we can effectively define a recursive function g_e such that, for any n,

$$A \cap [\![n, g_e(n)]\!] = B \cap [\![n, g_e(n)]\!] \to R_e^0 \text{ is met.} \tag{3.7}$$

(We can handle R^1 requirements in a similar way. But then we have to consider *all* possible values of $A \upharpoonright n$, since no reference to the actual value of $A \upharpoonright n$ is made.) In (3.7) as in the proof of Theorem 3.6, each interval is concerned with a single requirement. By letting $g(n) = \max\{g_0(n), \ldots, g_n(n)\}$, we can handle more requirements simultaneously, namely (3.7) implies, for any n,

$$A \cap [\![n, g(n)]\!] = B \cap [\![n, g(n)]\!] \to R_0^0, \ldots, R_n^0 \text{ are met.}$$

Hence, for any set A which is g-similar to B (cf. Definition 3.8), all requirements R_n^0, $n \ \varepsilon \ \mathrm{IN}$, are met. The advantage of this modification is that now we do not have to worry about making g polynomially honest: since g'-similarity implies g-similarity for all functions g' dominating g, we may just replace g by *any* polynomially honest g' dominating g (cf. Proposition 3.15).

The observations of the preceding paragraphs are due to Landweber, Lipton and Robertson (22). Their variant of the delayed diagonalization technique based here on will be systematically developed in the next section.

3.5 A DIAGONALIZATION LEMMA

In the preceding section we introduced the delayed diagonalization technique and discussed some variants of it. Here we systematically develop the structural variant of this technique first proposed by Landweber et al. (22) which we described briefly at the end of the last section. Using this technique various quite similar lemmas on complexity bounded diagonalizations over (pairs of) r.p. and c.f.v. classes have been proved. See Landweber et al. (22), Chew and Machtey (13), Regan (27), Schmidt (29), Schöning (30). Here, we present a diagonalization lemma, taken from Ambos-Spies (4), which is especially designed for applications to the theory of the polynomial degrees. As we will show, all density and splitting theorems on p-degrees in the literature are direct consequences of this lemma.

Though Section 3.4 motivates the approach to the structural delayed diagonalization method taken here, this section does not depend on it. It will be based, however, on the material presented in Section 3.3.

The following observation is the key to all of the diagonalization lemmas mentioned above.

LEMMA 3.2   Let C be a recursive set and let $\mathscr{C}$ be a recursively presentable and c.f.v. class of recursive sets such that $C \notin \mathscr{C}$. Then there is a total recursive function $g_0 \colon \mathbb{N} \to \mathbb{N}$ such that $g_0(n) > n$ and, for every recursive function g dominating g_0, the following holds: If A is a recursive set such that A and C are g-similar, i.e.,

$$\overset{\infty}{\exists}\, n\, (A \cap [\![n, g(n)]\!]) = C \cap [\![n, g(n)]\!]), \tag{3.8}$$

then $A \notin \mathscr{C}$.

Proof   W.l.o.g. $\mathscr{C} \neq \varnothing$, say U is a universal set for $\mathscr{C}$. Then let

$$g_0(n) = \mu m > n\, (\forall\, i \leq n\, \exists\, x\, (n \leq |x| < m\ \&\ U^{(i)}(x) \neq C(x))).$$

Obviously, g_0 is partial recursive. Moreover, since $C \notin \mathscr{C}$ and $\mathscr{C}$ is c.f.v., for each i there are infinitely many strings x such that $U^{(i)}(x) \neq C(x)$. Hence, g_0 is total. Trivially, $g_0(n) > n$.

To see that g_0 has the desired properties, fix g dominating g_0 and a set A satisfying (3.8). We have to show that, for given i, $A \neq U^{(i)}$. To do so, by (3.8), fix n such that $n \geq i$ and $A \cap [\![n, g(n)]\!]) = C \cap [\![n, g(n)]\!])$. Since $[\![n, g_0(n)]\!])\subseteq [\![n, g(n)]\!])$, it follows by definition of g_0, that there is a string x, $x \in [\![n, g_0(n)]\!])$, such that $U^{(i)}(x) \neq C(x) = A(x)$. $\blacksquare$

Note that Theorem 3.7 can be deduced from Lemma 3.2 as follows: Given $B, B', \mathscr{C}, \mathscr{C}'$ as in the premise of Theorem 3.7, apply Lemma 3.2 to $B, \mathscr{C}$ and $B', \mathscr{C}'$ and let g_0 and g_0', respectively, be the resulting functions. Then, by Proposition 3.15, let g be a polynomial honest function dominating g_0 and g_1, and set $A = (B \cap I^g_{2\mathbb{N}}) \cup (B' \cap I^g_{2\mathbb{N}+1})$ (note that $I^g_{2\mathbb{N}+1} = \overline{I^g_{2\mathbb{N}}}$). Then the pairs A, B and A, B' are g-similar, whence, by Lemma 3.2, $A \notin \mathscr{C} \cup \mathscr{C}'$. Finally, by honesty of g, $I^g_{2\mathbb{N}} \in \mathscr{P}$ (Corollary 3.8), whence $A \leq^p_m B \oplus B'$.

The following diagonalization lemma will be the basis for all of the subsequent results on p-r-degrees.

THEOREM 3.8 (Diagonalization lemma, (4)).   Let C_0, C_1 be recursive sets and let $\mathscr{C}_0, \mathscr{C}_1$ be r.p. and c.f.v. classes of recursive sets such that $C_0 \cup C_1 \notin \mathscr{C}_0$ and $C_1 \notin \mathscr{C}_1$. Then there is a recursive function $g_1 \colon \mathbb{N} \to \mathbb{N}$ such that $g_1(n) > n$ for all n and the following holds. If g is a function which dominates g_1 and if α is an infinite and coinfinite set of natural numbers then

$$(C_0 \cap I^g_\alpha) \cup C_1 \notin \mathscr{C}_0 \cup \mathscr{C}_1. \tag{3.9}$$

Proof   Apply Lemma 3.2 twice, once to the set $C_0 \cup C_1$ and the class $\mathscr{C}_0$, and once to the set C_1 and the class $\mathscr{C}_1$, and let g_1 be a recursive function dominating the resulting functions g_0 and g_0', respectively.

Now given a recursive function g dominating g_1 and an infinite and coinfinite set $\alpha \subseteq \mathbb{N}$, let $A = (C_0 \cap I_\alpha^g) \cup C_1$. To show that $A \not\in \mathscr{C}_0 \cup \mathscr{C}_1$, first recall that $I_n^g = [\![g^n(0), g(g^n(0))]\!]$. So, for $n \, \varepsilon \, \alpha$,

$$A \cap [\![g^n(0), g(g^n(0))]\!] = (C_0 \cup C_1) \cap [\![g^n(0), g(g^n(0))]\!]$$

whereas, for $n \not\in \alpha$,

$$A \cap [\![g^n(0), g(g^n(0))]\!] = C_1 \cap [\![g^n(0), g(g^n(0))]\!].$$

By injectivity of $\lambda n . g^n(0)$, infinity of α, and coinfinity of α, it follows that $A, C_0 \cup C_1$ and A, C_1 are g-similar. So, by Lemma 3.2, $A \not\in \mathscr{C}_0$ and $A \not\in \mathscr{C}_1$. ∎

The diagonalization lemma is tailored for applications to lattice embeddings in the p-r-degrees (see Section 3.7 below and (4)). For density and splitting type results a special case suffices.

COROLLARY 3.11   Let C_0, C_1 be recursive sets and let $\mathscr{C}_0, \mathscr{C}_1$ be r.p. and c.f.v. classes such that $C_0 \cup C_1 \not\in \mathscr{C}_0$ and $C_1 \not\in \mathscr{C}_1$. There is a set $D \, \varepsilon \, \mathscr{P}$ such that

$$(C_0 \cap D) \cup C_1 \not\in \mathscr{C}_0 \cup \mathscr{C}_1 \qquad (3.10)$$

and

$$(C_0 \cap \overline{D}) \cup C_1 \not\in \mathscr{C}_0 \cup \mathscr{C}_1. \qquad (3.11)$$

Proof   By Theorem 3.8 choose a polynomially honest function g, $g(n) > n$, such that, for any infinite and coinfinite subset α of $\mathbb{N}$, (3.9) holds. Then, for $D = I_{2\mathbb{N}}^g$, $D \, \varepsilon \, \mathscr{P}$ by Corollary 3.8. Moreover, $\overline{D} = I_{2\mathbb{N}+1}^g$. So (3.10) and (3.11) are immediate by (3.9). ∎

Corollary 3.11 can be reformulated for polynomial time degrees as follows.

COROLLARY 3.12   Let $\mathbf{c}_0, \mathbf{c}_1 \, \varepsilon \, \mathbf{Rec}_r \, (\mathbf{NP}_r)$ and let $\mathbf{C}_0, \mathbf{C}_1$ be r.p. classes of p-r-degrees such that $\mathbf{c}_0 \vee \mathbf{c}_1 \not\in \mathbf{C}_0$ and $\mathbf{c}_1 \not\in \mathbf{C}_1$. There are degrees $\mathbf{d}_0, \mathbf{d}_1 \, \varepsilon \, \mathbf{Rec}_r \, (\mathbf{NP}_r)$ such that $\mathbf{c}_1 \leq \mathbf{d}_i \leq \mathbf{c}_0 \vee \mathbf{c}_1$, $\mathbf{d}_0 \vee \mathbf{d}_1 = \mathbf{c}_0 \vee \mathbf{c}_1$, and $\mathbf{d}_i \not\in \mathbf{C}_0 \cup \mathbf{C}_1$ $(i = 0, 1)$.

Proof   Choose $C_0 \, \varepsilon \, \mathbf{c}_0$ and $C_1 \, \varepsilon \, \mathbf{c}_1$ such that $C_0 \subsetneq 0\Sigma^*$ and $C_1 \subsetneq 1\Sigma^*$ (and $C_0, C_1 \, \varepsilon \, \mathscr{NP}$), and let $\mathscr{C}_0 = \mathscr{P}(\mathbf{C}_0)$ and $\mathscr{C}_1 = \mathscr{P}(\mathbf{C}_1)$. Note that, by choice of C_0 and C_1,

$$(C_0 \cap E) \cup C_1 =_m^p (C_0 \cap E) \oplus C_1 \qquad (3.12)$$

for any set E. So $C_0 \cup C_1 \, \varepsilon \, \mathbf{c}_0 \vee \mathbf{c}_1$, whence $C_0, C_1, \mathscr{C}_0, \mathscr{C}_1$ satisfy the premise of Corollary 3.11, and we may choose $D \, \varepsilon \, \mathscr{P}$ satisfying (3.10) and (3.11). Now let $D_0 = (C_0 \cap D) \cup C_1$, $D_1 = (C_0 \cap D) \cup C_1$, and $\mathbf{d}_i = \deg_r^p(D_i)$, $i = 0, 1$. Then, by (3.10) and (3.11), $\mathbf{d}_0, \mathbf{d}_1 \not\leq C_0 \cup C_1$. Moreover, by (3.12) and Proposition 3.5,

$$C_1 \leq_m^p D_i \leq_m^p C_0 \oplus C_1 \quad (i = 0, 1)$$

(whence $D_0, D_1 \; \varepsilon \; \mathcal{NP}$ and thus $\mathbf{d}_0, \mathbf{d}_1 \; \varepsilon \; \mathbf{NP}_r$) and

$$D_0 \oplus D_1 =_m^p C_0 \oplus C_1.$$

It follows that $\mathbf{c}_1 \leq \mathbf{d}_0, \mathbf{d}_1 \leq \mathbf{c}_0 \vee \mathbf{c}_1$ and $\mathbf{d}_0 \vee \mathbf{d}_1 = \mathbf{c}_0 \vee \mathbf{c}_1$. ∎

We conclude this section with some density and splitting theorems implied by Corollary 3.12.

COROLLARY 3.13 (Density theorem, Ladner (20)). Let $\mathbf{a}, \mathbf{b} \; \varepsilon \; \mathbf{Rec}_r \; (\mathbf{NP}_r)$ be given such that $\mathbf{b} < \mathbf{a}$. There is a degree $\mathbf{d} \; \varepsilon \; \mathbf{Rec}_r \; (\mathbf{NP}_r)$ such that $\mathbf{b} < \mathbf{d} < \mathbf{a}$.

Proof Apply Corollary 3.12 to $\mathbf{c}_0 = \mathbf{a}$, $\mathbf{c}_1 = \mathbf{b}$, $\mathbf{C}_0 = \{\mathbf{b}\}$ and $\mathbf{C}_1 = \{\mathbf{a}\}$. Then, for $\mathbf{d} = \mathbf{d}_0$, $\mathbf{b} \leq \mathbf{d} \leq \mathbf{b} \vee \mathbf{a} = \mathbf{a}$ and $\mathbf{d} \not\leq \{\mathbf{a}, \mathbf{b}\}$, i.e., $\mathbf{b} < \mathbf{d} < \mathbf{a}$. ∎

Corollary 3.13 shows that any proper interval $[\mathbf{b}, \mathbf{a}]$ of $\mathbf{Rec}_r \; (\mathbf{NP}_r)$ is a dense partial ordering, whence any countable total ordering can be order embedded into it. In particular, if $\mathcal{P} \neq \mathcal{NP}$, i.e., if $\mathbf{0} < \mathbf{1}_r$ then $\mathbf{NP}_r$ is a countably infinite dense partial ordering.

Recall that an element a of a partial ordering $(S; \leq)$ is join-reducible (in S) if $a = b \vee c$ for elements $b, c < a$ of S. Otherwise a is join-irreducible. Note that, for a, b, c as above, $b \mid c$. So a partial ordering possessing join-reducible elements is not total.

COROLLARY 3.14 (Splitting theorem, Ladner (20)). Every nonzero element of $\mathbf{Rec}_r \; (\mathbf{NP}_r)$ is join-reducible. In fact, given $\mathbf{a}, \mathbf{b} \; \varepsilon \; \mathbf{Rec}_r \; (\mathbf{NP}_r)$ such that $\mathbf{b} < \mathbf{a}$ there are degrees $\mathbf{d}_0, \mathbf{d}_1 \; \varepsilon \; \mathbf{Rec}_r \; (\mathbf{NP}_r)$ such that $\mathbf{d}_0, \mathbf{d}_1 \; \varepsilon \; (\mathbf{b}, \mathbf{a})$ and $\mathbf{a} = \mathbf{d}_0 \vee \mathbf{d}_1$.

Proof Apply Corollary 3.12 to $\mathbf{c}_0 = \mathbf{a}$, $\mathbf{c}_1 = \mathbf{b}$, $\mathbf{C}_0 = \{\mathbf{b}\}$ and $\mathbf{C}_1 = \{\mathbf{a}\}$. ∎

COROLLARY 3.15 (20). If $\mathcal{P} \neq \mathcal{NP}$ then the partial ordering $(\mathbf{NP}_r; \leq)$ is not total. ∎

Schmidt (29) has shown that, assuming $\mathcal{P} \neq \mathcal{NP}$, there are infinitely many mutually incomparable degrees in $\mathbf{NP}_r$, while Balcazar and Diaz (9) have proved, that for any degree $\mathbf{a} \; \varepsilon \; \mathbf{NP}_r - \{\mathbf{0}, \mathbf{1}_r\}$ there is a degree $\mathbf{b} \; \varepsilon \; \mathbf{NP}_r$ incomparable with $\mathbf{a}$. We can deduce these results from the following extension of Corollary 3.14.

Corollary 3.16   Let $\mathbf{a}, \mathbf{b} \; \varepsilon \; \mathbf{Rec}_r \; (\mathbf{NP}_r)$ such that $\mathbf{b} < \mathbf{a}$ and let $\mathbf{C}$ be a r.p. class of p-r-degrees such that

$$\forall \; \mathbf{c} \; \varepsilon \; \mathbf{C} \; (\mathbf{c} \nleq \mathbf{b} \; \& \; \mathbf{a} \nleq \mathbf{c}). \tag{3.13}$$

There are degrees $\mathbf{d}_0, \mathbf{d}_1 \; \varepsilon \; \mathbf{Rec}_r \; (\mathbf{NP}_r)$ such that, for $i = 0, 1$, $\mathbf{d}_i \; \varepsilon \; (\mathbf{b}, \mathbf{a})$, $\mathbf{d}_i \mid \mathbf{c}$ for all $\mathbf{c} \; \varepsilon \; \mathbf{C}$, and $\mathbf{a} = \mathbf{d}_0 \vee \mathbf{d}_1$.

Note that (3.13) is satisfied by any subset $\mathbf{C}$ of $(\mathbf{b}, \mathbf{a})$.

Proof.   Apply Corollary 3.12 to $\mathbf{c}_0 = \mathbf{a}$, $\mathbf{c}_1 = \mathbf{b}$, $\mathbf{C}_0 = \{\mathbf{b}\} \cup \{\deg_r^p(D) : D \; \varepsilon \; [\mathbf{b}, \mathscr{S}(\mathbf{C})]\}$ and $\mathbf{C}_1 = \{\mathbf{a}\} \cup \{\deg_r^p(D) : D \; \varepsilon \; [\mathscr{S}(\mathbf{C}), \mathbf{a}]_r\}$.   ∎

Call a set $\mathbf{C}$ of mutually incomparable degrees an anti-chain. An anti-chain $\mathbf{C} \subseteq \mathbf{D}$ is maximal in $\mathbf{D}$ if no degree in $\mathbf{D} - \mathbf{C}$ is incomparable with all elements of $\mathbf{C}$.

Corollary 3.17

(a) Let $\mathbf{a}, \mathbf{b} \; \varepsilon \; \mathbf{Rec}_r \; (\mathbf{NP}_r)$ such that $\mathbf{b} < \mathbf{a}$. No r.p., and thus no finite, anti-chain of $(\mathbf{b}, \mathbf{a}) \; (\cap \; \mathbf{NP}_r)$ is maximal in $(\mathbf{b}, \mathbf{a}) \; (\cap \; \mathbf{NP}_r)$.

(b) Assume $\mathscr{P} \neq \mathscr{NP}$. No r.p. anti-chain of $\mathbf{NP}_r - \{\mathbf{0}, \mathbf{1}_r\}$ is maximal in $\mathbf{NP}_r$.

(c) (Mehlhorn 25)   No r.p. anti-chain of $\mathbf{Rec}_r - \{\mathbf{0}\}$ is maximal in $\mathbf{Rec}_r$.

(d) (Schmidt 29)   Let $\mathbf{a}, \mathbf{b} \; \varepsilon \; \mathbf{Rec}_r \; (\mathbf{NP}_r)$ such that $\mathbf{b} < \mathbf{a}$. Then $(\mathbf{b}, \mathbf{a}) \; (\cap \; \mathbf{NP}_r)$ contains an infinite anti-chain.

Proof   (a) By Corollary 3.16. (b) is a special instance of (a). (c) Given a r.p. anti-chain $\mathbf{C}$ of $\mathbf{Rec}_r - \{\mathbf{0}\}$, fix $\mathbf{a} \; \varepsilon \; \mathbf{Rec}_r$ such that $\mathbf{c} < \mathbf{a}$ for all $\mathbf{c} \; \varepsilon \; \mathbf{C}$, and apply (a) to the interval $(\mathbf{0}, \mathbf{a})$. (d) follows from (a).   ∎

We conclude with the observation that no interval of p-r-degrees can be split into two nonempty r.p. classes of p-r-degrees. Schmidt (29) has shown that this observation applies to most reasonable complexity classes in place of intervals of degrees.

Corollary 3.18   Let $\mathbf{b} < \mathbf{a}$, $\mathbf{C}_0, \mathbf{C}_1 \neq \varnothing$, $\mathbf{C}_0 \cap \mathbf{C}_1 = \varnothing$ and $\mathbf{C}_0 \cup \mathbf{C}_1 = [\mathbf{b}, \mathbf{a}]$. Then $\mathbf{C}_0$ or $\mathbf{C}_1$ is not recursively presentable.

Proof   For a contradiction assume that both $\mathbf{C}_0$ and $\mathbf{C}_1$ are r.p. By symmetry, w.l.o.g. $\mathbf{a} \notin \mathbf{C}_0$. So we may choose $\mathbf{c}$ with $\mathbf{b} \leq \mathbf{c} < \mathbf{a}$ and $\mathbf{c} \notin \mathbf{C}_1$. Now apply Corollary 3.12 to $\mathbf{c}_0 = \mathbf{a}$, $\mathbf{c}_1 = \mathbf{c}$, $\mathbf{C}_0$ and $\mathbf{C}_1$. This yields a degree $\mathbf{d}$ such that $\mathbf{c} \leq \mathbf{d} \leq \mathbf{a}$ and $\mathbf{d} \notin \mathbf{C}_0 \cup \mathbf{C}_1$. Since $[\mathbf{c}, \mathbf{a}] \subseteq [\mathbf{b}, \mathbf{a}] = \mathbf{C}_0 \cup \mathbf{C}_1$, this is impossible.   ∎

Note that, by Corollary 3.18, for $\mathbf{b} < \mathbf{a}$, in contrast to $[\mathbf{b},\mathbf{a}]$, neither $(\mathbf{b},\mathbf{a})$ nor $(\mathbf{b},\mathbf{a}]$ nor $[\mathbf{b},\mathbf{a})$ is recursively presentable. By applying this observation to the interval $[\mathbf{0},\mathbf{1}_m]$, we see that, assuming $\mathcal{P} \neq \mathcal{NP}$, neither $\mathcal{NP} - \mathcal{P}$ nor $\mathcal{NP} - \mathcal{NPC}_r$ nor $\mathcal{NP} - (\mathcal{P} \cup \mathcal{NPC}_r)$, where $\mathcal{NPC}_r = \{A \colon A \text{ is } NP\text{-}r\text{-com-}$ plete$\}$, is r.p. (22). These results are also direct consequences of Theorem 3.7 above (see Schöning (30)).

3.6   A MEET LEMMA

The diagonalization lemma enables us to realize nontrivial joins in arbitrary intervals of $\mathbf{Rec}_r$ and $\mathbf{NP}_r$, and thus, to obtain a series of density and splitting theorems for polynomial degrees. It does not give us, however, any information about nontrivial meets in $\mathbf{Rec}_r$ and $\mathbf{NP}_r$. Ladner has shown that $\mathbf{Rec}_r$ possesses *minimal pairs*, i.e. degrees $\mathbf{a},\mathbf{b} > \mathbf{0}$ such that $\mathbf{a} \wedge \mathbf{b} = \mathbf{0}$. By refining his argument, Breidbart (12) and, independently, Landweber et al. (22) proved that every nonzero degree $\mathbf{a} \; \varepsilon \; \mathbf{Rec}_r$ ($\mathbf{NP}_r$) bounds a minimal pair (in $\mathbf{NP}_r$). Moreover, they noticed that their argument can be extended to prove that, for any p-r-degrees $\mathbf{b} < \mathbf{a}$, $\mathbf{b}$ is *meet-reducible* in $[\mathbf{b},\mathbf{a}]$, i.e. $\mathbf{b} = \mathbf{c} \wedge \mathbf{d}$ for degrees $\mathbf{c},\mathbf{d} \; \varepsilon$ $(\mathbf{b},\mathbf{a})$.

In this section, we prove a meet lemma which, together with the diagonalization lemma, allows us to construct meets in arbitrary intervals of degrees. Like the diagonalization lemma, this lemma is tailored for lattice embeddings into intervals of polynomial degrees. A similar lemma designed for applications to minimal pairs can be found in Schöning (31). Since the proof of the meet lemma is based on Landweber, Lipton and Robertson's construction of a minimal pair below a given nonzero degree, we will start with describing this argument. See also Chew and Machtey (13).

Given a recursive set $A \; \not\varepsilon \; \mathcal{P}$, we want to construct sets $B,C \leqq^p_m A$ such that $B,C \; \not\varepsilon \; \mathcal{P}$ and

$$\forall D \; (D \leqq^p_T B \; \& \; D \leqq^p_T C \; \rightarrow \; D \; \varepsilon \; \mathcal{P}). \tag{3.14}$$

To ensure $B,C \leqq^p_m A$, we will make B and C subproblems of A. The basic idea for meeting (3.14) is to separate B and C by long *gaps*. To be more precise, we will take a polynomially honest function g, $g(n) > n$, and let

$$B = A \cap I^g_{4\mathbb{N}} \quad \text{and} \quad C = A \cap I^g_{4\mathbb{N}+2}. \tag{3.15}$$

So the end of a relevant g-interval of B and the beginning of the next relevant g-interval for C (or vice versa) is separated by another g-interval, on which both B and C are empty (see Figure 3.2).

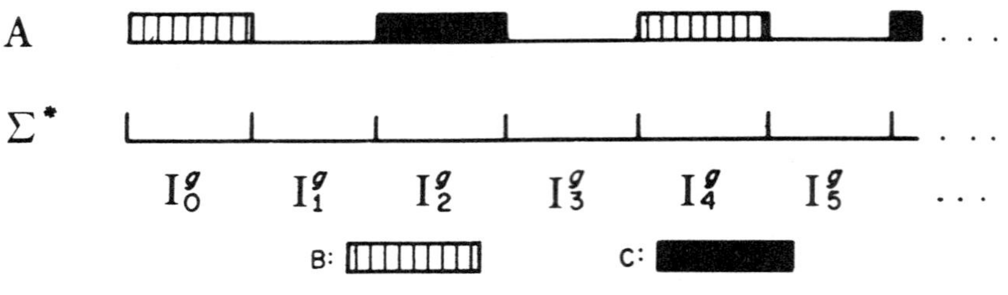

Figure 3.2

As we will show now, this will suffice to ensure (3.14) provided g dominates the step counting function of some deterministic TM computing A.

Given a set D such that $D \leq_T^p B$ and $D \leq_T^p C$, choose oracle machines M and M' such that $D = M(B) = M'(C)$ and a polynomial p such that the run times of M and M' are bounded by p. Then a polynomial time algorithm for computing D is as follows.

Given x, by honesty of g, we can efficiently compute n such that $0^{p(|x|)} \varepsilon$ I_n^g. Note that, since p bounds M and M', in the computations $M(B)(x)$ and $M'(C)(x)$ only strings in $I_0^g \cup \ldots \cup I_n^g$ are queried. Now fix $m \varepsilon$ IN and $i \leq 3$ such that $n = 4m + i$, and distinguish the following two cases.

Case 1: $i \varepsilon \{0,1\}$.   Then we compute $D(x)$ by computing $M'(C)(x)$ where any oracle query "$y \varepsilon C$?" is replaced by the following subroutine:

Decide whether $y \varepsilon I_{4\mathrm{IN}+2}^g$. If so, compute $A(y)$ and answer YES if $y \varepsilon A$.

In all other cases answer NO.

Since $C = A \cap I_{4\mathrm{IN}+2}^g$ this subroutine returns the correct answer to the question "$y \varepsilon C$?" Moreover, by honesty of g, the decision whether $y \varepsilon I_{4\mathrm{IN}+2}^g$ can be made in time polynomial in $|y| < p(|x|)$ and thus in time polynomial in $|x|$. Furthermore, if $y \varepsilon I_{4\mathrm{IN}+2}^g$ then, since $y \varepsilon I_0^g \cup \ldots \cup I_{4m+1}^g$, there is a number $m' < m$ with $y \varepsilon I_{4m'+2}^g$. So, since $|y| < g^{4m'+3}(0)$, since g dominates the step counting function of some deterministic TM computing A, and since step counting functions are nondecreasing, $A(y)$ can be computed in $g(g^{4m'+3}(0))$ steps and, by $g(n) > n$, $g(g^{4m'+3}(0)) = g^{4m'+4}(0) \leq g^{4m}(0) \leq g^n(0) \leq p(|x|)$. It follows that the above subroutine answers any call of the oracle in the computation of $M'(C)(x)$ in time polynomial in $|x|$, whence the time required to compute $D(x)$ is polynomially bounded (in $|x|$).

Case 2: $i \varepsilon \{2,3\}$.   Then $D(x)$ is computed by simulating the computation $M(B)(x)$ by answering each oracle query "$y \varepsilon B$?" with YES if $y \varepsilon I_{4\mathrm{IN}}^g$ and

$A(y) = 1$ and with NO otherwise. Like in the first case one easily checks that for each admissible string y with $|y| < p(|x|)$ the answer to the question "$y \in B$?" can be found in time polynomial in $|x|$, whence again the computation time of $D(x)$ is polynomially bounded.

This completes the proof that, for any polynomially honest g dominating the step counting function of some computation of A and for sets B and C defined by (3.15), condition (3.14) is satisfied. Finally, since A and B respectively A and C are g-similar and since $A \not\in \mathcal{P}$, we can ensure $B, C \not\in \mathcal{P}$ by choosing g sufficiently large (see Lemma 3.2).

In the above argument showing that (3.14) holds, we exploited the fact that, for a set D p-r-reducible to both B and C, some part of D is trivial by existence of a reduction to B (namely $D \cap \{x: 0^{p(|x|)} \in I^g_{4\mathbb{N}+2} \cup I^g_{4\mathbb{N}+3}\}$) while the complementary part is trivial by existence of a reduction to C. The following lemma applies this observation to a more general setting.

LEMMA 3.3   Let A be a recursive set and let g, $g(n) > n$, be a polynomially honest function dominating the step counting function of some deterministic TM T computing A. Moreover, let $\alpha \in \mathcal{P}_{\mathbb{N}}$ and let D and E be recursive sets such that $D \leq^p_r (A \cap I^g_\alpha) \oplus E$.

Then there is a polynomial p_0 such that, for any polynomial p dominating p_0,

$$D \cap \{x: 0^{p(|x|)} \not\in I^g_\alpha \cup I^g_{\alpha+1}\} \leq^p_r E. \tag{3.16}$$

Proof   We give the proof for $r = T$ and leave the similar proof for $r = m$ to the reader. Fix M and p such that $D = M((A \cap I^g_\alpha) \oplus E)$ and p is a polynomial bounding the run time of M. Moreover, let

$$D' = D \cap \{x: 0^{p(|x|)} \not\in I^g_\alpha \cup I^g_{\alpha+1}\}.$$

Then a p-T-reduction of D' to E can be obtained by formalizing the following algorithm.

input x:
if $0^{p(|x|)} \in I^g_\alpha \cup I^g_{\alpha+1}$
   then $D'(x) = 0$
   else simulate the computation $M((A \cap I^g_\alpha) \oplus E)(x)$ by replacing any
           oracle query as follows:
               for query "$0y \in (A \cap I^g_\alpha) \oplus E$?" with $y \not\in I^g_\alpha$: answer NO
               for query "$0y \in (A \cap I^g_\alpha) \oplus E$?" with $y \in I^g_\alpha$: compute $T(y)$ and
                    answer YES if $T(y) = 1$ and NO otherwise
               for query "$1y \in (A \cap I^g_\alpha) \oplus E$?": compute $E(y)$ and answer YES
                    if $E(y) = 1$ and NO otherwise.

Obviously, this algorithm correctly computes $D'(x)$ from E. Moreover, since $I^g_\alpha, I^g_{\alpha+1} \in \mathcal{P}$ and since in the computation $M((A \cap I^g_\alpha) \oplus E)(x)$ the oracle is queried only about strings of length $< p(|x|)$, the algorithm will be polynomial time bounded, provided that for given x and y such that $0^{p(|x|)} \notin I_\alpha^g \cup I_{\alpha+1}^g$, $|y| < p(|x|)$ and $y \; \varepsilon \; I_\alpha^g$, the computation time of $T(y)$ is polynomially bounded in $|x|$. So fix such x and y. Then there are numbers n and m such that $y \; \varepsilon \; I_n^g$, $0^{p(|x|)} \; \varepsilon \; I_m^g$ and $n+1 < m$. Hence,

$$|y| < g^{n+1}(0) < g(g^{n+1}(0)) = g^{n+2}(0) \leqq g^m(0) \leqq p(|x|).$$

Now, since g dominates the step counting function of T and since, by our convention, step counting functions are nondecreasing, $T(y)$ can be computed in $g(g^{n+1}(0)) \leqq p(|x|)$ steps.

This completes the proof. ∎

To state the meet lemma, which will be an easy consequence of Lemma 3.3, we require the following notion. Call two sets $\alpha_0, \alpha_1 \subseteq \mathbb{N}$ *strongly disjoint* if

$$\forall \; i \leqq 1 \; \forall \; n \; \varepsilon \; \mathbb{N} \; (n \; \varepsilon \; \alpha_i \; \rightarrow \; \{n, n+1\} \cap \alpha_{1-i} = \emptyset). \tag{3.17}$$

Intuitively, for any two elements n and m of two strongly disjoint sets α_0 and α_1, respectively, n and m are separated by a number which neither belongs to α_0 nor to α_1.

THEOREM 3.9   (Meet lemma).   Let A be a recursive set. There is a recursive function $g_2 \colon \mathbb{N} \to \mathbb{N}$, $g_2(n) > n$, such that for any polynomially honest function g which dominates g_2 the following holds. If $\alpha, \beta \; \varepsilon \; \mathcal{P}_{\mathbb{N}}$ are strongly disjoint and $E \subseteq \Sigma^*$ is recursive, then

$$\deg_r^p(E) = \deg_r^p((A \cap I_\alpha^g) \oplus E) \wedge \deg_r^p((A \cap I_\beta^g) \oplus E). \tag{3.18}$$

Proof   Let g_2 be any recursive function such that $g_2(n) > n$ and g_2 dominates the step counting function of some deterministic TM computing A. Moreover, let g be a polynomially honest function dominating g_2, let $\alpha, \beta \; \varepsilon \; \mathcal{P}_{\mathbb{N}}$ be strongly disjoint and let E be recursive. Since, obviously

$$E \leqq_m^p (A \cap I_\alpha^g) \oplus E \quad \text{and} \quad E \leqq_m^p (A \cap I_\beta^g) \oplus E,$$

for a proof of (3.18) it suffices to show that, for any set D satisfying

$$D \leqq_r^p (A \cap I_\alpha^g) \oplus E \quad \text{and} \quad D \leqq_r^p (A \cap I_\beta^g) \oplus E, \tag{3.19}$$

$D \leqq_r^p E$ holds. So fix D satisfying (3.19). Then by Lemma 3.3, $D \cap J_\alpha \leqq_r^p E$ and $D \cap J_\beta \leqq_r^p E$ for $J_\alpha = \{x \colon 0^{p(|x|)} \notin I_\alpha^g \cup I_{\alpha+1}^g\}$ and $J_\beta = \{x \colon 0^{p(|x|)} \notin I_\beta^g \cup I_{\beta+1}^g\}$. Moreover, $J_\alpha, J_\beta \; \varepsilon \; \mathcal{P}$ and, by strong disjointness of α and β, $J_\alpha \cup J_\beta = \Sigma^*$. Hence, $D \leqq_r^p E$. ∎

The meet lemma in combination with the diagonalization lemma provides us with the means for constructing meets in the p-r-degrees. Note that $4\mathbb{N}$ and $4\mathbb{N}+2$ are strongly disjoint. So, given a recursive set A, an application of the meet lemma to $\alpha = 4\mathbb{N}$, $\beta = 4\mathbb{N}+2$ and some set $E \ \varepsilon \ \mathscr{P}$ shows that, for sets B and C defined by (3.15), (3.14) holds. By letting E vary over the sets p-r-reducible to A, we see that, for any p-r-degrees $\mathbf{b} < \mathbf{a}$, $\mathbf{b}$ is meet reducible in $(\mathbf{b}, \mathbf{a})$. See Breidbart (12), Landweber et al. (22). In fact, we obtain a result for meets dual to the result for joins stated in Corollary 3.16 above.

CUROLLARY 3.19   Let $\mathbf{a}, \mathbf{b} \ \varepsilon \ \mathbf{Rec}_r \ (\mathbf{NP}_r)$ such that $\mathbf{b} < \mathbf{a}$ and let $\mathbf{C}$ be a r.p. class of p-r-degrees such that

$$\forall \ \mathbf{c} \ \varepsilon \ \mathbf{C} \ (\mathbf{c} \not\leq \mathbf{b} \ \& \ \mathbf{a} \not\leq \mathbf{c}).$$

There are degrees $\mathbf{d}_0, \mathbf{d}_1 \ \varepsilon \ \mathbf{Rec}_r \ (\mathbf{NP}_r)$ such that, for $i = 0, 1$, $\mathbf{d}_i \ \varepsilon \ (\mathbf{b}, \mathbf{a})$, $\mathbf{d}_i \ | \ \mathbf{c}$ for all $\mathbf{c} \ \varepsilon \ \mathbf{C}$, and $\mathbf{b} = \mathbf{d}_0 \wedge \mathbf{d}_1$.

Proof   Choose sets $A \ \varepsilon \ \mathbf{a}$ and $B \ \varepsilon \ \mathbf{b}$ such that $A \not\subseteq 0\Sigma^*$ and $B \not\subseteq 1\Sigma^*$ (and $A, B \ \varepsilon \ \mathscr{NP}$). Then apply the diagonalization lemma to $C_0 = A$, $C_1 = B$, $\mathscr{C}_0 = \mathbf{b} \cup [\mathbf{b}, \mathscr{S}(\mathbf{C})]_r$ and $\mathscr{C}_1 = \mathbf{a} \cup [\mathscr{S}(\mathbf{C}), \mathbf{a}]_r$, and the meet lemma to A. Let g be a polynomially honest function dominating the resulting functions g_1 and g_2, respectively, define D_i by $D_i = (A \cap I^g_{4\mathbb{N}+2i}) \cup B$, and let $\mathbf{d}_i = \deg^p_r(D_i)$ $(i = 0, 1)$. Then

$$B \leq^p_m D_i =^p_m (A \cap I^g_{4\mathbb{N}+2i}) \oplus B \leq^p_m A,$$

whence $\mathbf{b} \leq \mathbf{d}_i \leq \mathbf{a}$ (and $\mathbf{d}_i \ \varepsilon \ \mathbf{NP}_r$). Since, by the diagonalization lemma, $D_i \not\leq \mathscr{C}_0 \cup \mathscr{C}_1$, this implies $\mathbf{b} < \mathbf{d}_i < \mathbf{a}$ and $\mathbf{d}_i \ | \ \mathbf{c}$ for all $\mathbf{c} \ \varepsilon \ \mathbf{C}$ $(i = 0, 1)$. Finally, by the meet lemma, $\mathbf{b} = \mathbf{d}_0 \wedge \mathbf{d}_1$.   ■

For the next section we need the following more general formulation of the meet lemma.

CUROLLARY 3.20   Let A be a recursive set. There is a recursive function g_2: $\mathbb{N} \to \mathbb{N}$, $g_2(n) > n$, such that for any polynomially honest function g which dominates g_2 the following holds. If $\alpha, \beta \ \varepsilon \ \mathscr{P}_{\mathbb{N}}$ such that $\alpha - \beta$ and β are strongly disjoint and $E \subseteq \Sigma^*$ is recursive, then

$$\deg^p_r((A \cap I^g_{\alpha \cap \beta}) \oplus E) = \deg^p_r((A \cap I^g_{\alpha}) \oplus E) \wedge \deg^p_r((A \cap I^g_{\beta}) \oplus E). \quad (3.20)$$

Proof   Note that

$$(A \cap I^g_{\alpha}) \oplus E =^p_m (A \cap I^g_{\alpha - \beta}) \oplus ((A \cap I^g_{\alpha \cap \beta}) \oplus E)$$

and

$$(A \cap I_\beta^g) \oplus E \; =_m^p \; (A \cap I_\beta^g) \oplus ((A \cap I_{\alpha \cap \beta}^g) \oplus E).$$

So the claim follows by applying the meet lemma to $\alpha - \beta$, β and $(A \cap I_{\alpha \cap \beta}^g) \oplus E.$ ∎

3.7 SUBLATTICES OF THE POLYNOMIAL DEGREES

The density, splitting and minimal pair theorems of the preceding sections can be interpreted as results on lattice embeddings into intervals of polynomial degrees. The strongest splitting and minimal pair results we have stated, namely Corollaries 3.16 and 3.19, will follow if we can embed the four-element Boolean lattice in any interval $[\mathbf{b}, \mathbf{a}]$ of *p-r*-degrees by maps which preserve the greatest element (Corollary 3.16) and least element (Corollary 3.19), respectively, and which in addition avoid a given r.p. subclass of $\mathbf{Rec}_r - \{\mathbf{d}\colon \mathbf{d} \leq \mathbf{b}$ or $\mathbf{a} \leq \mathbf{d}\}$. Here we show that any finite distributive lattice which is nowhere complemented can be embedded in any interval of *p-r*-degrees by a map which preserves both the least and the greatest elements. As a consequence, any finite distributive lattice has embeddings which preserve the least respectively greatest elements.

We start with recalling some notions from lattice theory. An *order embedding* of a p.o. set $\mathscr{L}_1 = (L_1; \leq_1)$ into a p.o. set $\mathscr{L}_2 = (L_2; \leq_2)$ is a one-to-one map $f\colon L_1 \to L_2$ such that, for all $a, b \; \varepsilon \; L_1$, $a \leq_1 b$ iff $f(a) \leq_2 f(b)$. An order embedding of a lattice $\mathscr{L}_1$ into an upper semilattice $\mathscr{L}_2$ is a *(lattice) embedding* if

$$\forall \; a, b \; \varepsilon \; L_1 \quad (f(a \vee b) = f(a) \vee f(b),\; f(a) \wedge f(b) \text{ exists, and}$$

$$f(a \wedge b) = f(a) \wedge f(b)).$$

If $\mathscr{L}_1$ is embeddable in $\mathscr{L}_2$ then we also say that $\mathscr{L}_1$ is a *sublattice* of $\mathscr{L}_2$ (up to isomorphisms). The least (greatest) element of a p.o. set $\mathscr{L}$ is denoted by $0_\mathscr{L}$ $(1_\mathscr{L})$ or, if no confusion can arise, simply by 0 (1). We say an embedding f of $\mathscr{L}_1$ into $\mathscr{L}_2$ *preserves the least element* or 0 (*greatest element* or 1) if $f(0_{\mathscr{L}_1}) = 0_{\mathscr{L}_2}$ $(f(1_{\mathscr{L}_1}) = 1_{\mathscr{L}_2})$. A lattice $\mathscr{L} = (L; \leq)$ is *distributive* if

$$\forall \; a, b, c \; \varepsilon \; L \quad ((a \vee b) \wedge (a \vee c) = a \vee (b \wedge c)).$$

A u.s.l. $\mathscr{L} = (L; \leq)$ possessing least and greatest elements is *somewhere complemented* if $|L| = 1$ or there are intermediate elements of L which possess a complement, i.e. elements a and $\bar{a}$ of $L - \{0, 1\}$ such that $a \vee \bar{a} = 1$ and $a \wedge \bar{a} = 0$. Otherwise $\mathscr{L}$ is *nowhere complemented*. Finally, an element a of a lattice $(L; \leq)$ with least element 0 is an *atom* if a is a minimal element of $(L - \{0\}; \leq)$.

THEOREM 3.10   Let $\mathcal{L} = (L; \leq)$ be a finite distributive lattice which is nowhere complemented, let $\mathbf{a}, \mathbf{b} \ \varepsilon \ \mathbf{Rec}_r$ such that $\mathbf{b} < \mathbf{a}$, and let $\mathbf{C}$ be a r.p. class of p-r-degrees such that

$$\forall \ \mathbf{c} \ \varepsilon \ \mathbf{C} \ (\mathbf{c} \nleq \mathbf{b} \ \& \ \mathbf{a} \nleq \mathbf{c}).$$

There is an embedding $f^*: L \rightarrow [\mathbf{b}, \mathbf{a}]$ of $\mathcal{L}$ into $([\mathbf{b}, \mathbf{a}]; \leq)$ which preserves 0 and 1 and such that

$$\forall \ x \ \varepsilon \ L - \{0, 1\} \ \forall \ \mathbf{c} \ \varepsilon \ \mathbf{C} \ (f^*(x) \mid \mathbf{c}).$$

Moreover, if $\mathbf{a}, \mathbf{b} \ \varepsilon \ \mathbf{NP}_r$ then the range of f^* is contained in $\mathbf{NP}_r$.

The proof of Theorem 3.10 requires appropriate representations of finite distributive lattices. Recall that a *ring* over $\{1, \ldots, n\}$ ($n \geq 1$) is a subset S of the power set $\mathcal{P} \ (\{1, \ldots, n\})$ of $\{1, \ldots, n\}$ such that S is closed under union and intersection. We identify a ring S with the lattice $\mathcal{S} = (S; \subseteq)$. Note that in $\mathcal{S}$ joins and meets coincide with unions and intersections, respectively. We say that a ring $\mathcal{S} = (S; \subseteq)$ over $\{1, \ldots, n\}$ is *normal* if there is some k, $1 \leq k \leq n$, and a sequence $\alpha_1, \ldots, \alpha_n$ of pairwise different elements of S such that the following holds

$\emptyset$ is the least element of S and $\{1, \ldots, n\}$ is the greatest   (3.21)
element of S.

α_i, $1 \leq i \leq n$, are the join irreducible elements $\neq \emptyset$ of $\mathcal{S}$ and   (3.22)
α_i, $1 \leq i \leq k$, are the atoms of $\mathcal{S}$.

For $1 \leq i \leq n$,   (3.23)
$$\alpha_i = \cup\{\beta \ \varepsilon \ S: \beta \subset \alpha_i\} \cup \{i\}$$
and, for join reducible $\alpha \ \varepsilon \ S$,
$$\alpha = \cup\{\beta \ \varepsilon \ S: \beta \subset \alpha\}.$$

Note that $\{1\}, \ldots, \{k\}$ are the atoms of $\mathcal{S}$. Moreover, for $\alpha \ \varepsilon \ S$ and $1 \leq i \leq n$, if $i \ \varepsilon \ \alpha$ then $\alpha_i \subseteq \alpha$.

The following lemma is well known from lattice theory (Grätzer (16), Ch. II, §1).

LEMMA 3.4   Let $\mathcal{L} = (L; \leq)$ be a finite distributive lattice with at least two elements. Then $\mathcal{L}$ is isomorphic to a normal ring over $\{1, \ldots, n\}$, where n is the number of nonzero join irreducible elements of $\mathcal{L}$.

By this lemma, in a proof of Theorem 3.10 it suffices to consider normal rings over $\{1, \ldots, n\}$ (for some $n \geq 1$) which are nowhere complemented. The next lemma and its corollary give a property of such rings which will be crucial for the proof.

LEMMA 3.5   Let $\mathcal{S} = (S;\subseteq)$ be a normal ring over $\{1,\ldots,n\}$ which is nowhere complemented and let $k \leq n$ and $\alpha_1,\ldots,\alpha_n \in S$ be given such that (3.21)–(3.23) hold. Then for i,j such that $1 \leq i < j \leq k$ there are atoms $\beta_1,\ldots,\beta_n$ of $\mathcal{S}$ and join irreducible elements $\gamma_1,\ldots,\gamma_{n-1}$ of $\mathcal{S}$ such that

$$\alpha_i = \beta_1, \quad \beta_m,\beta_{m+1} \subseteq \gamma_m \ (1 \leq m < n) \quad \text{and} \quad \beta_n = \alpha_j.$$

Proof   Fix i and j such that $1 \leq i < j \leq k$ and inductively define

$$A_1 = \{i\}$$

$$A_{m+1} = \{p: 1 \leq p \leq k \ \& \ \exists q \in A_m \, \exists r \leq n \, (\alpha_p,\alpha_q \subseteq \alpha_r)\}.$$

Note that $A_m \subseteq A_{m+1} \subseteq \{1,\ldots,k\}$. Moreover, if $A_m = A_{m+1}$ then $A_m = A_{m'}$, for all $m' > m$. Let $A = A_{m_0}$ where m_0 is the least m such that $A_m = A_{m+1}$. Note that $m_0 \leq k$. We will show that $j \in A$. Then, by definition of A, there are atoms $\beta_1,\ldots,\beta_{m_0}$ and join irreducible elements $\gamma_1,\ldots,\gamma_{m_0-1}$ of S such that $\alpha_i = \beta_1$, $\beta_m,\beta_{m+1} \subseteq \gamma_m \ (1 \leq m \leq m_0-1)$ and $\beta_{m_0} = \alpha_j$. So we obtain the desired elements of S by adding $\beta_m = \gamma_{m-1} = \alpha_j$ for $m_0 < m \leq n$.

Now, for a contradiction, assume that $j \notin A$. Let

$$\alpha = \{q \leq n: q \in A \quad \text{or} \quad \exists r \in A \ (\alpha_r \subset \alpha_q)\}$$

and let $\overline{\alpha} = \{1,\ldots,n\} - \alpha$. Note that $\alpha \notin \{0_{\mathcal{S}}, 1_{\mathcal{S}}\}$, since $i \in \alpha$ and $j \in \overline{\alpha}$. So it suffices to show that α and $\overline{\alpha}$ belong to S, thus proving S to be somewhere complemented contrary to assumption. We claim

$$\forall \, m_1,m_2 \leq n \ (m_1 \in \alpha \ \& \ \alpha_{m_1} \subseteq \alpha_{m_2} \rightarrow m_2 \in \alpha) \quad \text{and} \tag{3.24}$$

$$\forall \, m_1,m_2 \leq n \ (m_2 \in \alpha \ \& \ \alpha_{m_1} \subseteq \alpha_{m_2} \rightarrow m_1 \in \alpha). \tag{3.25}$$

The first claim is immediate by definition of α. For a proof of the second claim, fix $m_1,m_2 \leq n$ such that $\alpha_{m_1} \subseteq \alpha_{m_2}$ and $m_2 \in \alpha$. Then there are atoms $\alpha_{p_1},\alpha_{p_2}$ such that $\alpha_{p_1} \subseteq \alpha_{m_1}$, $\alpha_{p_2} \subseteq \alpha_{m_2}$ and $p_2 \in A$. Since $\alpha_{m_1} \subseteq \alpha_{m_2}$, this implies $\alpha_{p_1},\alpha_{p_2} \subseteq \alpha_{m_2}$ and thus $p_1 \in A$ by definition of A. It follows $m_1 \in \alpha$. So (3.25) holds.

Now, by (3.24) and (3.25), $\alpha = \bigcup\{\alpha_r: 1 \leq r \leq n \ \& \ r \in \alpha\}$ and $\overline{\alpha} = \bigcup\{\alpha_r: 1 \leq r \leq n \ \& \ r \notin \alpha\}$, whence $\alpha,\overline{\alpha} \in S$.   ∎

COROLLARY 3.21   Let $\mathcal{S},n,k,\alpha_1,\ldots,\alpha_n$ be given as in Lemma 3.5. There is a polynomial time computable function $h: \text{IN} \rightarrow \{1,\ldots,n\}$ such that

(i) $\forall \, m \in \text{IN} \ (h(2m) \leq k \ \& \ \alpha_{h(2m)} \subseteq \alpha_{h(2m+1)},\alpha_{h(2m-1)})$ and

(ii) $\forall \, p \leq n \, \overset{\infty}{\exists} \, m \in \text{IN} \ (h(m) = p)$.

Proof   We define a function $h': \{0,\ldots,4nk-1\} \rightarrow \{1,\ldots,n\}$ such that h' is onto, $h'(0) = h'(4nk-1)$ and

$$\forall\, m\ (2m < 4nk - 1 \rightarrow \alpha_{h'(2m)} \subseteq \alpha_{h'(2m+1)}, \alpha_{h'(2m \div 1)}).$$

Then the function h defined by

$$h(4nkm + p) = h'(p) \quad (m \ \varepsilon \ \mathbb{N},\ p \leq 4nk - 1)$$

has the desired properties.

For the definition of h', by Lemma 3.5 choose numbers $a(i,m)$ and $b(i,m)$ $(1 \leq i \leq k,\ 1 \leq m \leq n)$ such that

$$1 \leq a(i,m) \leq k$$

$$1 \leq b(i,m) \leq n$$

$$a(i,1) = i$$

$$\alpha_{a(i,m)}, \alpha_{a(i,m+1)} \subseteq \alpha_{b(i,m)} \quad (m < n)$$

$$a(i,n) = \textit{if } i < k \textit{ then } i + 1 \textit{ else } 1$$

$$b(i,n) = a(i,n).$$

Furthermore, for $1 \leq i \leq k$ and $1 \leq m \leq n$ let

$$c(i,m) = \begin{cases} m & \text{if } \alpha_i \subseteq \alpha_m \\ i & \text{otherwise.} \end{cases}$$

Now h' is defined by

$$h'(4ni + 2m) = i + 1$$

$$h'(4ni + 2m + 1) = c(i+1, m+1) \qquad (i < k,\ m < n)$$

$$h'(4ni + 2n + 2m) = a(i+1, m+1)$$

$$h'(4ni + 2n + 2m + 1) = b(i+1, m+1).$$

Note that for j such that $k < j \leq n$ there is some i, $1 \leq i \leq k$, such that $\alpha_i \subset \alpha_j$, i.e. $c(i,j) = j$. Since, for $1 \leq i \leq k$, $a(i,1) = i$, this implies that h' is onto. The other desired properties of h' follow from choice of $a(i,m)$, $b(i,m)$ and $c(i,m)$. ∎

We are now ready to prove the theorem.

Proof of Theorem 3.10 By Lemma 3.4, w.l.o.g. we may assume that $\mathcal{L}$ is a normal nowhere complemented ring $\mathcal{S} = (S; \leq)$ over $\{1, \ldots, n\}$. Fix $k \leq n$ and α_i, $1 \leq i \leq n$, such that (3.21)–(3.23) hold. Furthermore, choose $A \ \varepsilon \ \mathbf{a}$ and $B \ \varepsilon \ \mathbf{b}$ (with $A, B \ \varepsilon \ \mathcal{NP}$ if $\mathbf{a}, \mathbf{b} \ \varepsilon \ \mathbf{NP}_r$). In order to obtain the desired embedding f^* of $\mathcal{S}$ into $[\mathbf{b}, \mathbf{a}]$, first apply the diagonalization lemma to $C_0 = A \oplus \emptyset$, $C_1 = \emptyset \oplus B$, $\mathcal{C}_0 = \mathbf{b} \cup [\mathbf{b}, \mathcal{S}(\mathbf{C})]_r$, and $\mathcal{C}_1 = \mathbf{a} \cup [\mathcal{S}(\mathbf{C}), \mathbf{a}]_r$, and Corollary 3.20 to A, and let g be a polynomially honest function dominating the resulting functions

g_1 and g_2. Then choose h as in Corollary 3.21 and define a function f from the power set of $\{1, \ldots, n\}$ into the class of sets over Σ by letting, for $\alpha \subseteq \{1, \ldots, n\}$,

$$f(\alpha) = (A \cap I^g_{h^{-1}(\alpha)}) \oplus B,$$

where $h^{-1}(\alpha) = \{m \ \varepsilon \ \mathbb{N} : h(m) \ \varepsilon \ \alpha\}$. Finally let $f^*(\alpha) = \deg^p_r(f(\alpha))$.

Note that for $\alpha, \beta \subseteq \{1, \ldots, n\}$,

$$I^g_{h^{-1}(\alpha)} \ \varepsilon \ \mathscr{P},$$

$$I^g_{h^{-1}(\varnothing)} = \varnothing \quad \text{and} \quad I^g_{h^{-1}(\{1, \ldots, n\})} = \Sigma^*,$$

$$I^g_{h^{-1}(\alpha \cup \beta)} = I^g_{h^{-1}(\alpha)} \cup I^g_{h^{-1}(\beta)},$$

$$I^g_{h^{-1}(\alpha \cap \beta)} = I^g_{h^{-1}(\alpha)} \cap I^g_{h^{-1}(\beta)},$$

and, by Corollary 3.21,

$$I^g_{h^{-1}(\alpha)} \text{ is infinite and coinfinite if } \alpha \neq \varnothing, \{1, \ldots, n\}. \tag{3.26}$$

These observations imply

$$B =^p_m f(\varnothing) \leq^p_m f(\alpha) \leq^p_m f(\{1, \ldots, n\}) =^p_m A \oplus B, \tag{3.27}$$

$$f(\alpha \cup \beta) =^p_m f(\alpha) \oplus f(\beta) \qquad \text{and} \tag{3.28}$$

$$f(\alpha) \leq^p_m f(\beta) \text{ if } \alpha \subseteq \beta. \tag{3.29}$$

Moreover, if $\alpha \not\subseteq \beta$, say $i \ \varepsilon \ \alpha - \beta$, then, as in the proof of Corollary 3.12, we can deduce from the diagonalization lemma that $f(\{i\})$ and $f(\{1, \ldots, n\} - \{i\})$ are p-r-incomparable. Since $f(\{i\}) \leq^p_m f(\alpha)$ and $f(\beta) \leq^p_m f(\{1, \ldots, n\} - \{i\})$, this implies $f(\alpha) \not\leq^p_r f(\beta)$. Together with (3.29) this yields

$$\alpha \neq \beta \quad \rightarrow \quad f(\alpha) \neq^p_r f(\beta). \tag{3.30}$$

Facts (3.27)–(3.30) show that f^* is an order embedding of $(\mathscr{P}(\{1, \ldots, n\}); \subseteq)$ into $([\mathbf{b}, \mathbf{a}]; \leq)$ which preserves $0, 1$ and joins. Moreover, by (3.27), if $\mathbf{a}, \mathbf{b} \ \varepsilon \ \mathbf{NP}_r$ then the range of f^* is contained in $\mathbf{NP}_r$ also. Therefore, it only remains to show that the restriction of f^* to S also preserves meets and that

$$\forall \ \alpha \ \varepsilon \ S - \{\varnothing, \{1, \ldots, n\}\} \ \forall \ \mathbf{c} \ \varepsilon \ \mathbf{C}(f^*(\alpha) \mid \mathbf{c}). \tag{3.31}$$

For a proof of the former fix $\alpha, \beta \ \varepsilon \ S$. We have to show $f^*(\alpha \cap \beta) = f^*(\alpha) \wedge f^*(\beta)$, i.e.,

$$\deg^p_r((A \cap I^g_{h^{-1}(\alpha \cap \beta)}) \oplus B) = \deg^p_r((A \cap I^g_{h^{-1}(\alpha)}) \oplus B)$$

$$\wedge \deg^p_r((A \cap I^g_{h^{-1}(\beta)}) \oplus B).$$

Since $I^g_{h^{-1}(\alpha \cap \beta)} = I^g_{h^{-1}(\alpha) \cap h^{-1}(\beta)}$, this will follow from Corollary 3.20, provided that $h^{-1}(\alpha)$ and $h^{-1}(\beta) - h^{-1}(\alpha)$ are strongly disjoint. To prove this we have to show for all $e \ \varepsilon \ \mathbb{N}$

$$\exists\, i \leq 1 \; (e + i \,\varepsilon\, h^{-1}(\alpha) \;\; \& \;\; e + (1-i) \,\varepsilon\, h^{-1}(\beta)) \;\rightarrow$$

$$\rightarrow \; (e \,\varepsilon\, h^{-1}(\alpha \cap \beta) \;\; \text{or} \;\; e+1 \,\varepsilon\, h^{-1}(\alpha \cap \beta)). \qquad (3.32)$$

To verify (3.32) fix e satisfying the premise. W.l.o.g. we may assume that $e \,\varepsilon\, h^{-1}(\alpha)$, $e+1 \,\varepsilon\, h^{-1}(\beta)$ and e is even (the other cases follow by symmetry). Then, by Corollary 3.21(i),

$$1 \leq h(e) \leq k \quad \text{and} \quad \alpha_{h(e)} \subseteq \alpha_{h(e+1)}. \qquad (3.33)$$

Recall that, by definition of α_m, $\alpha_m \subseteq \gamma$ for each $\gamma \,\varepsilon\, S$ such that $m \,\varepsilon\, \gamma$ ($1 \leq m \leq n$) and that, for $1 \leq m \leq k$, $\alpha_m = \{m\}$. So, since $h(e) \,\varepsilon\, \alpha$ and $h(e+1) \,\varepsilon\, \beta$, (3.33) implies

$$\{h(e)\} = \alpha_{h(e)} \subseteq \alpha \quad \text{and} \quad \{h(e)\} = \alpha_{h(e)} \subseteq \alpha_{h(e+1)} \subseteq \beta.$$

Hence, $h(e) \,\varepsilon\, \alpha \cap \beta$ and thus $e \,\varepsilon\, h^{-1}(\alpha \cap \beta)$. This completes the proof that f^* preserves meets.

Finally, by the diagonalization lemma, $(A \cap I^g_{h^{-1}(\alpha)}) \oplus B \not\leq \mathscr{C}_0 \cup \mathscr{C}_1$ for $\varnothing \subsetneq \alpha \subsetneq \{1, \ldots, n\}$. By choice of $\mathscr{C}_0, \mathscr{C}_1$ and definition of f^* this implies (3.31), thus completing the proof of the theorem. $\blacksquare$

As we have shown in (5), in general Theorem 3.10 does not extend to somewhere complemented lattices. If we consider embeddings preserving only the least *or* the greatest element, however, then we capture *all* finite distributive lattices.

COROLLARRY 3.22   Let $\mathscr{L} = (L; \leq)$ be a finite distributive lattice, let $\mathbf{a}, \mathbf{b} \,\varepsilon\, \mathbf{Rec}_r$ such that $\mathbf{b} < \mathbf{a}$, and let $\mathbf{C}$ be a r.p. class of p-r-degrees such that

$$\forall\, \mathbf{c} \,\varepsilon\, \mathbf{C} \; (\mathbf{c} \not\leq \mathbf{b} \;\; \& \;\; \mathbf{a} \not\leq \mathbf{c}).$$

There are embeddings f_i^*, $i = 0, 1$, of $\mathscr{L}$ into $([\mathbf{b}, \mathbf{a}]; \leq)$ such that $f_0^*(0) = \mathbf{b}$, $f_1^*(1) = \mathbf{a}$, and

$$\forall\, x \,\varepsilon\, L - \{i\} \; \forall\, \mathbf{c} \,\varepsilon\, \mathbf{C} \; (f_i^*(x) \mid \mathbf{c}).$$

Moreover, if $\mathbf{a}, \mathbf{b} \,\varepsilon\, \mathbf{NP}_r$ then range $(f_i^*) \subseteq \mathbf{NP}_r$.

Proof   Apply Theorem 3.10 to the nowhere complemented lattices $\mathscr{L}_i = (L \cup \{x_i\}; \leq_i)$, $i = 0, 1$, obtained by adding a new least respectively greatest element to $\mathscr{L}$; i.e., for $x, y \,\varepsilon\, L$, $x <_1 x_1$, $x_0 <_0 x$, and $x \leq_i y$ iff $x \leq y$. $\blacksquare$

In (4) we have shown that Corollary 3.22 extends to countable lattices. Since any finite (countable) partial ordering can be order embedded in some finite (countable) distributive lattice, it follows that any such partial ordering can be

embedded into arbitrary intervals of *p-r*-degrees. See Breidbart (12) and Mehlhorn (26).

As noted above, Corollary 3.22 applied to the four-element Boolean lattice
establishes Corollaries 3.16 and 3.19. We conclude with a further application
of Theorem 3.10 extending a result of Breidbart (12). Call *p-r*-degrees c_1, c_2, c_3
totally incomparable if, for $\{i,j,k\} = \{1,2,3\}$, $c_j \wedge c_k$ exists, $c_i \mid c_j \wedge c_k$ and
$c_i \mid c_j \vee c_k$.

COROLLARY 3.23   Let $\mathbf{a}, \mathbf{b} \; \varepsilon \; \mathbf{Rec}_r \; (\mathbf{NP}_r)$ be given such that $\mathbf{b} < \mathbf{a}$. There are
totally incomparable degrees $c_1, c_2, c_3 \; \varepsilon \; [\mathbf{b}, \mathbf{a}] \; (\cap \; \mathbf{NP}_r)$ such that $\sup\{c_1, c_2, c_3\}$
$= \mathbf{a}$ and $\inf\{c_1, c_2, c_3\} = \mathbf{b}$.

Proof   Apply Theorem 3.10 to the nowhere complemented distributive lattice
shown in Figure 3.3 below.   ■

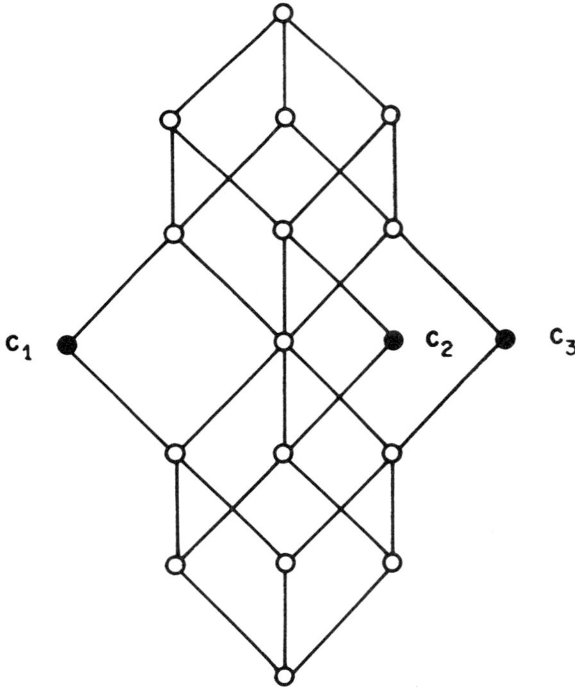

Figure 3.3

3.8 FURTHER RESULTS AND OPEN PROBLEMS

As pointed out above, most results in the literature on the polynomial time degrees of *NP*-sets are covered by the embedding results of Section 3.7 and (4). Some recent results not subsumed by these theorems can be found in Ambos-Spies (3). Assuming $\mathcal{P} \neq \mathcal{NP}$, the partial ordering $(\mathbf{NP}_r; \leq)$ is not complete, i.e., there are strictly increasing sequences of *p-r*-degrees of *NP*-sets which have no least upper bound (in $\mathbf{NP}_r$). In fact no r.p. ascending sequence of *p-r*-degrees possesses a minimal upper bound. Moreover, still assuming $\mathcal{P} \neq \mathcal{NP}$, the u.s.l. $(\mathbf{NP}_r; \leq)$ is not complemented, i.e. there is a degree $\mathbf{a} \; \varepsilon \; \mathbf{NP}_r$ such that, for no degree $\bar{\mathbf{a}} \; \varepsilon \; \mathbf{NP}_r$, $\mathbf{a} \vee \bar{\mathbf{a}} = \mathbf{1}_r$ and $\mathbf{a} \wedge \bar{\mathbf{a}} = \mathbf{0}$. This is a consequence of the following stronger result in (3): Given a degree $\mathbf{a} \; \varepsilon \; \mathbf{Rec}_r \; (\mathbf{NP}_r)$ such that $\mathbf{a} \neq \mathbf{0}$ there is a degree $\mathbf{b} \; \varepsilon \; \mathbf{Rec}_r \; (\mathbf{NP}_r)$ such that $\mathbf{0} < \mathbf{b} < \mathbf{a}$ and $\mathbf{b}$ does not *help* $\mathbf{a}$, i.e.,

$$\forall \mathbf{c} \; (\mathbf{a} \leq \mathbf{b} \vee \mathbf{c} \; \rightarrow \; \mathbf{a} \leq \mathbf{c}).$$

Like all the previous results on $(\mathbf{NP}_r; \leq)$, these results are obtained by *global arguments*. That is to show that, assuming $\mathcal{P} \neq \mathcal{NP}$, $(\mathbf{NP}_r; \leq)$ has a certain property Q, we show that *every* proper initial segment $[\mathbf{0}, \mathbf{a}]$ of $\mathbf{Rec}_m$ (for $r = m$) respectively every mixed initial segment $\mathbf{Rec}_{T,m}(\leq A)$, $A \nleq \mathcal{P}$, of $\mathbf{Rec}_T$ (for $r = T$) has this property whence Q is shared by the initial segment $\mathbf{NP}_m = [\mathbf{0}, \mathbf{1}_m]$ and $\mathbf{NP}_T = \mathbf{Rec}_{T,m}(\leq B)$, B some *NP-m*-complete problem, respectively. This led to the conjecture that any two initial segments of $(\mathbf{Rec}_r; \leq)$ in fact any two intervals of it, are isomorphic. See Breidbart (12). This homogeneity conjecture, however, has been refuted in Ambos-Spies (5, 6). In (6) we have shown that there is a recursive set $A \nleq \mathcal{P}$ such that

$$([\mathbf{0}, \deg_m^p(A)]; \leq) \; \cong \; ([\mathbf{0}, \deg_T^p(A); \leq) \; \cong \; (\mathbf{Rec}_{T,m}(\leq A); \leq)$$

and $([\mathbf{0}, \deg_m^p(A)]; \leq)$ (and thus the other two structures above too) is a distributive lattice. On the other hand, as noted earlier, Ladner (20) has shown that $(\mathbf{Rec}_r; \leq)$ is not a lattice and we (1) have shown that the u.s.l. $(\mathbf{Rec}_T; \leq)$ is not distributive. So there are recursive sets $B, C \nleq \mathcal{P}$ such that neither $([\mathbf{0}, \deg_r^p(B)]; \leq)$ nor $(\mathbf{Rec}_{T,m}(\leq B); \leq)$ is a lattice, and neither $([\mathbf{0}, \deg_T^p(C)]; \leq)$ nor $(\mathbf{Rec}_{T,m}(\leq C); \leq)$ is distributive. Hence, for instance, $([\mathbf{0}, \deg_r^p(A)]; \leq) \; \ncong \; ([\mathbf{0}, \deg_r^p(B)]; \leq)$ and $(\mathbf{Rec}_{T,m}(\leq A); \leq) \; \ncong \; (\mathbf{Rec}_{T,m}(\leq B); \leq)$, thus refuting the homogeneity conjecture. Moreover, $([\mathbf{0}, \deg_m^p(C)]; \leq) \; \ncong \; (\mathbf{Rec}_{T,m}(\leq C); \leq)$ by Theorem 3.2.

The just listed inhomogeneities imply that the following open problems regarding the structure of $(\mathbf{NP}_r; \leq)$ under the assumption that $\mathcal{P} \neq \mathcal{NP}$, cannot be solved by global arguments.

Problem 1.   ($\mathcal{P} \neq \mathcal{NP}$)   Are the partial orderings $(\mathbf{NP}_T; \leqq)$ and $(\mathbf{NP}_m; \leqq)$ isomorphic?

Problem 2.   ($\mathcal{P} \neq \mathcal{NP}$)   Is the u.s.l. $(\mathbf{NP}_T; \leqq)$ distributive?

Problem 3.   ($\mathcal{P} \neq \mathcal{NP}$)   Is the u.s.l. $(\mathbf{NP}_r; \leqq)$ a lattice?

A further problem not solvable by global arguments (see (5)) is:

Problem 4.   ($\mathcal{P} \neq \mathcal{NP}$)   Is $\mathbf{1}_m$ the join of a minimal pair, i.e., are there degrees $\mathbf{a}, \mathbf{b} \; \varepsilon \; \mathbf{NP}_m - \{\mathbf{0}\}$ such that $\mathbf{1}_m = \mathbf{a} \vee \mathbf{b}$ and $\mathbf{0} = \mathbf{a} \wedge \mathbf{b}$?

Problem 4 is open for *p-T*-degrees too. There we do not know, however, whether global arguments must fail (cf.(5)).

The next step in the study of the *p-r*-degrees of *NP*-sets under the assumption that $\mathcal{P} \neq \mathcal{NP}$ should be an attack on the above problems. Such an attack requires to learn about specific properties of *NP*-complete sets, i.e., properties Q such that some *NP*-complete problems have these properties though there are nonzero degrees not containing any set with property Q. An example of such a property is a certain self-reducibility property shared by the common *NP*-complete sets (see e.g. 24). This property has been exploited by P. Berman (11) and Mahaney (24) to show that, assuming $\mathcal{P} \neq \mathcal{NP}$, no tally, in fact no sparse set is *NP-m*-complete, thus giving more specific properties of the degree $\mathbf{1}_m$.

3.9 REFERENCES

1. K. Ambos-Spies, "On the structure of polynomial time degrees," in *STACS 84, Symp. on Theor. Aspects of Comp. Sci.* (M. Fontet and K. Mehlhorn, Eds.), Lect. Notes Comp. Sci. 166 (1984) 198–208, Springer Verlag.

2. ______, "On the relative complexity of subproblems of intractable problems," in *STACS 85, 2nd Ann. Symp. on Theor. Aspects of Comp. Sci.* (K. Mehlhorn, Ed.), Lect. Notes Comp. Sci. 182 (1985) 1–12, Springer Verlag.

3. ______, "Three theorems on polynomial degrees of *NP*-sets," *Proc. 26th Symp. Foundations Comp. Sci.*, 1985, 51–55.

4. ______, "Sublattices of the polynomial time degrees," *Inform. Control* 65 (1985) 63–84.

5. ______, "An inhomogeneity in the structure of Karp degrees," *SIAM J. Computing,* 15 (1986) 958–963.

6. ______, Inhomogeneities in the polynomial time degrees: the degrees of super sparse sets." *Inf. Proc. Letters* 22 (1986) 113–117.

7. ______, "On the structure of the polynomial time degrees of recursive sets (Habilitationsschrift)," *Tech. Rep. 206* (1985), Abteilung Informatik, Universität Dortmund.

8. T. Baker, J. Gill and R. Solovay, "Relativizations of the $P = ?NP$ question," *SIAM J. Computing 4* (1975) 431–442.

9. J. L. Balcazar, "Separating, strongly separating and collapsing relativized complexity classes," in *Math. Foundations of Comp. Sci. 1984*, (M. P. Chytil and V. Koubek, Eds.), Lect. Notes Comp. Sci. 176 (1984) 1–16, Springer Verlag.

10. J. L. Balcazar and J. Diaz, "A note on a theorem by Ladner," *Inform. Proc. Letters 15* (1982) 84–86.

11. P. Berman, "Relationship between density and deterministic complexity of *NP*-complete languages," in *Fifth International Colloquium on Automata, Languages, and Programming*, Lect. Notes Comp. Sci. 62 (1978) 63–71, Springer Verlag.

12. S. I. Breidbart, "The structure of complexity classes and degrees," Dissertation, University of California, Santa Barbara, 1977.

13. P. Chew and M. Machtey, "A note on structure and looking back applied to the relative complexity of computable functions," *J. Comput. System Sci. 22* (1982) 53–59.

14. S. A. Cook, "The complexity of theorem proving procedures," *Proc. Third Annual ACM Symp. on Theory of Comp.*, 1971, 151–158.

15. M. R. Garey and D. S. Johnson, *Computers and Intractability: A Guide to the Theorey of NP-Completeness*, H. Freeman, San Francisco, 1978.

16. G. Grätzer, *General Lattice Theory*, Birkhäuser Verlag, Basel and Stuttgart, 1978.

17. J. E. Hopcroft and J. D. Ullman, *Introduction to Automata Theory, Languages and Computation*, Reading, MA, 1979.

18. R. M. Karp, "Reducibility among combinatorial problems," in *Complexity of Computer Computations* (R. E. Miller and J. W. Thatcher, Eds.) Plenum, New York, 1972, 85–103.

19. R. E. Ladner, "Polynomial time reducibility," *Proc. Fifth Annual ACM Symp. on Theory of Comp.*, 1973, 122–129.

20. _____, "On the structure of polynomial time reducibility," *J. ACM 22* (1975) 155–171.

21. R. E. Ladner, N. Lynch and A. L. Selman, "A comparison of polynomial time reducibilities," *Theor. Comp. Sci. 1* (1975) 103–123.

22. L. H. Landweber, R. J. Lipton and E. L. Robertson, "On the structure of sets in *NP* and other complexity classes," *Theor. Comp. Sci. 15* (1981) 181–200.

23. M. Lerman, *Degrees of Unsolvability*, 1983, Springer Verlag, Berlin.

24. S. R. Mahaney, "Sparse complete sets for *NP*: Solution of a conjecture of Berman and Hartmanis," *J. Comput. System Sci. 24* (1982) 130–143.

25. K. Mehlhorn, "On the size of sets of computable functions," *Tech. Rep. TR 72-164* (1973), Dept. Comp. Sci., Cornell University.

26. _____, "Polynomial and abstract subrecursive classes," *J. Comput. System Sci. 12* (1976) 147–178.

27. K. W. Regan, "On diagonalization methods and the structure of language classes," in *Foundations of Computation Theory* (M. Karpinski, Ed.) Lect. Notes Comp. Sci. 158 (1983) 368–380.

28. H. Rogers, Jr., *Theory of Recursive Functions and Effective Computability*, McGraw Hill, New York, 1967.

29. D. Schmidt, "On the complement of one complexity class in another," in *Logic and Machines: Decision Problems and Complexity* (E. Börger et al., Eds.), Lect. Notes Comp. Sci. 171 (1984) 77–87.

30. U. Schöning, "A uniform approach to obtain diagonal sets in complexity classes," *Theor. Comp. Sci.* 18 (1982) 95–103.

31. _____, "Minimal pairs for *P*," *Theor. Comp. Sci. 31* (1984) 41–48.

32. A. L. Selman, "*P*-selective sets, tally languages, and the behavior of polynomial time reducibilities on *NP*," *Math. Systems Theory 13* (1979) 55–65.

33. _____, "Reductions on *NP* and *p*-selective sets," *Theor. Comp. Sci.* 19 (1982) 287–304.

34. _____, "Analogues of semirecursive sets and effective reducibilities to the study of *NP* complexity," *Inform. Control* 52 (1982) 36–51.

35. R. I. Soare, *Recursively Enumerable Sets and Degrees: The Study of Computable Functions and Computably Generated Sets*, Springer Verlag, Berlin 1987.

36. L. J. Stockmeyer, "The polynomial-time hierarchy," *Theor. Comp. Sci.* 3 (1977) 1–22.

37. D. Yang, "On the embedding of polynomial time constructable lattices into the recursive polynomial Turing degrees," to appear in the proceedings of the *Conference on Effective Algebra and 5th Generation Languages at Monash (Australia)*, 1984.

38. P. Young, "Some structural properties of polynomial reducibilities and sets in *NP*," *Proc. Fifteenth Annual ACM Symp. on Theory of Comp.*, 1983, 392–401.

Chapter 4

Application of Logic and Combinatorics to Enumeration Problems

E. SPECKER

4.1 INTRODUCTION

This work originated from the disturbing fact that the number of elements of a certain finite set T (the set of topologies on $\{1,2,3,4,5\}$) is determined to be 7181 in [11] and 6942 in [5]. It seemed desirable to have an algorithm which provides us with an element t of $\{7181,6942\}$ and a proof of $t \neq \#T$ ($\#T$ is the number of elements of T). Such an algorithm does exist. It consists of computing the residue class r of $\#T$ mod 5; r being equal to 2, we have a proof of $\#T \neq 7181$.

The method used in the computation of r can be extended to a general class of cases; this has been done in [1], [2], [3]. The main result is as follows: Let A be an axiom expressible in the language of monadic second order logic (in binary predicates), let $C_n(A)$ be the set of models of A on the set $\{1,2,\ldots,n\}$, and let f be the function defined by

$$f(n) \ = \ \# \, C_n(A).$$

Then f satisfies modular linear recurrence relations, i.e., for every positive integer m, there exist integers d, $a_1,\ldots,a_d$ such that

$$f(n) \equiv \sum_{i=1}^{d} a_i f(n-i) \ (\mathrm{mod} \ m).$$

In many known cases, these modular relations are consequences of polynomial recurrence relations of the following type:

$$f(n) = \sum_{i=1}^{d} P_i(n)f(n-i)$$

(P_i being polynomials; cf. [8], [12].)

It would be interesting to have general conditions on axioms A implying such a recurrence relation.

4.2 STRUCTURES AND PERMUTATIONS

A structure is an object

$$\langle S; R_1, \ldots, R_k \rangle$$

where S is a finite nonempty set and R_i, $i = 1, \ldots, k$, are relations on S, i.e., for some integer m_i, $m_i \in N$,

$$R_i: S^{m_i} \Rightarrow \{\text{true, false}\}.$$

(R_i is called an m_i-ary relation, $\vec{m} = \langle m_1, \ldots, m_k \rangle$ is the "type" of the structure.) In most cases, we will have $k = 1$ and $m_1 = 2$ (binary case). The following are typical examples:

Example 1 ($k = 1$, $m_1 = 2$) R is irreflexive and symmetric:

$$\neg R(a,a),\ R(a,b) \rightarrow R(b,a).$$

Such a structure is called a "graph."

Example 2 ($k = 1$, $m_1 = 2$) R is an order relation, i.e., R satisfies

D_1: $R(a,b) \wedge R(b,c) \rightarrow R(a,c)$

D_2: $R(a,b) \wedge R(b,a) \rightarrow a = b$

D_3: $R(a,b) \vee R(b,a)$

(D_3': $R(a,a)$; D_3' is a consequence of D_3)

Example 3 R is a partial order: D_1, D_2, D_3'.

Example 4 R is a preorder: D_1, D_3'.

Example 5 R is an equivalence relation:

D_1, D_3' and $R(a,b) \leftrightarrow R(b,a)$.

Example 6 The notion of $n \times n$-matrices a with row and column sum k over the non-negative integers can be formalized in our framework as follows: ($m_1 = m_2 = \ldots = m_k = 2$) $S = \{1, 2, \ldots, n\}$; $R_j(h, i)$ ($1 \leq j \leq k$; $1 \leq h, i \leq n$) holds iff $a(h, i) = j$. ($a(h, i) = 0$ corresponds to $\neg R_j(h, i)$ for $j = 1, \ldots, k$.)

For all k, the conditions on $R_1, \ldots, R_k$ corresponding to the postulates

$$\sum_{h=1}^{n} a(h, i) = k, \quad \sum_{i=1}^{n} a(h, i) = k$$

can be expressed by formulas in $R_1, \ldots, R_k$ of first order predicate logic not depending on n.

All of these classes of structures have the property of being closed under isomorphism: If a structure belongs to the class, so does every isomorphic structure. With such a class C of structures, there are two associated functions f^C and f_1^C from N^+ to N. $f^C(n)$ is the number of structures on the set $\{1, 2, \ldots, n\}$ belonging to C, two structures being counted as different (Ex. 6) iff for some j, h, i the values associated to $R_j(h, i)$ are different. (If structures are counted in this way, they are sometimes called "labeled structures.") $f_1^C(n)$ is the number of isomorphism types of structures on the set $\{1, 2, \ldots, n\}$ belonging to C. It is the function f^C we shall be interested in.

For the class G of graphs we have

$$f^G(n) = 2^{\binom{n}{2}}.$$

(There are $\binom{n}{2}$ unordered pairs of elements of $\{1, 2, \ldots, n\}$, for each such pair $\{i, j\}$ the relations $R(i, j)$, $R(j, i)$ either hold or do not hold.)

For the class O of orders, we have

$$f^O(n) = n!.$$

The number of partial orders on $\{1, 2, \ldots, n\}$ has been determined for $n \leq 7$. We know very little about the behavior of the corresponding counting function [5]. The number of preorders on a set S has been studied in some detail because this number is equal to the number of topologies on S (we assume S finite). In order to see this, define a topology on S by the closure operation Cl defined on the power set P of S with values in P and satisfying

1. $Cl(\wedge) = \wedge$ ($\wedge$ empty)
2. $X \subseteq Cl(X)$
3. $Cl(Cl(X)) \subseteq Cl(X)$
4. $Cl(X \cup Y) = Cl(X) \cup Cl(Y)$

Defining a map $cl: S \Rightarrow P$ by

$$cl(x) = Cl(\{x\}),$$

Conditions (1) and (4) are equivalent to

$$Cl(X) = \bigcup_{x \in X} cl(x). \tag{4.1}$$

Defining Cl by (4.1), Conditions (2) and (3) follow from their special cases where X is a one-element set $\{x\}$:

(2a) $x \in cl(x)$,   (3a) $Cl(cl(x)) \subseteq cl(x)$.

According to (4.1), $z \in Cl(cl(x))$ is equivalent to: There is a y such that

$$z \in cl(y) \quad \text{and} \quad y \in cl(x).$$

(3a) is, therefore, equivalent to

(3b)   :   For all x, y, z:

$$z \in cl(y) \wedge y \in cl(x) \to z \in cl(x).$$

Defining $a \in cl(b)$ as $a \leq b$ we see that (2a) is $a \leq a$ and (3b) transitivity, i.e., cl defines a topology iff the relation $a \in cl(b)$ is a preorder. The notion of equality being the same for preorders and topologies, we have established that the number of preorders and topologies on a finite set is the same. The number of topologies on a set with n element has been computed for $n \leq 6$ in [11], for $n \leq 7$ in [5]. The values found coincide up to 4; for $n = 5$, [11] finds $7'181$, while [5] obtains $6'942$.

It is desirable to have a method which permits one to prove that one of the numbers $6'942$, $7'181$ is wrong. Such a method exists, it consists of computing the rest mod 5; it turns out that this rest is 2, from which it follows that $7'181$ is wrong, whereas $6'942$ is "possible."

Next, we explain the general method in the case of equivalence relations on the set $\{1, 2, \ldots, n\}$. The number of these relations is called the "Bell number B_n". The first values are

$$B_1 = 1; \quad B_2 = 2; \quad B_3 = 5.$$

The five equivalence relations on $\{1, 2, 3\}$ are defined by their equivalence classes as follows

$$\equiv_1: \{1\} \quad \{2\} \quad \{3\}$$

$$\equiv_2: \{1\} \quad \{2, 3\}$$

$$\equiv_3: \{2\} \quad \{1, 3\}$$

$$\equiv_4: \{3\} \quad \{1, 2\}$$

$$\equiv_5: \{1, 2, 3\}.$$

In order to determine the parity of B_n, we define a permutation π on $\{1, 2, \ldots, n\}$

(assuming $2 \leq n$) as follows: For $i \leq n - 2$: $\pi(i) = i$; $\pi(n-1) = n$; $\pi(n) = (n-1)$. π induces an operation on equivalence relations on $\{1, \ldots, n\}$ by

$$a \overset{\pi}{\equiv} b \leftrightarrow \pi(a) \equiv \pi(b).$$

The five equivalence relations on $\{1,2,3\}$ are permuted by π as follows: $\overset{\pi}{\equiv}_1$ is $\equiv_1$, $\overset{\pi}{\equiv}_2$ is $\equiv_2$, $\overset{\pi}{\equiv}_3$ is $\equiv_4$, $\overset{\pi}{\equiv}_4$ is $\equiv_3$ and $\overset{\pi}{\equiv}_5$ is $\equiv_5$, the permutation induced is $\left(\begin{smallmatrix} 1 & 2 & 3 & 4 & 5 \\ 1 & 2 & 4 & 3 & 5 \end{smallmatrix}\right)$.

In general, we can distinguish the two following cases:

(1) $\overset{\pi}{\equiv}$ is $\equiv$.
(2) $\overset{\pi}{\equiv}$ is different from $\equiv$;
$\overset{\pi}{\equiv}$ and $\equiv$ are interchanged by π; i.e., if $\overset{\pi}{\equiv}$ is $\equiv'$, $\overset{\pi}{\equiv}{}'$ is $\equiv$.

The fundamental idea is the following: The parity of B_n is equal to the parity of the number of equivalence relations $\equiv$ on $\{1,2,\ldots,n\}$ such that $\overset{\pi}{\equiv}$ is equal to $\equiv$ ("$\equiv$ is invariant").

How many invariant equivalence relations are there on $\{1,2,\ldots,n\}$? We distinguish two cases:

1. n is in a class by itself. Then, $(n-1)$ has also to be in a class by itself. All such equivalence relations are invariant; there are B_{n-2} of these.
2. n is not in a class by itself. We want to show that $(n-1)$ and n are in the same class; assume that a is in the class of n, $a \neq n-1$. We have $a \equiv n$, $\pi(a) \equiv \pi(n)$, i.e., $a \equiv n-1$ and by transitivity $(n-1) \equiv n$. An equivalence relation for which $(n-1)$ and n are in the same class is π-invariant; there are B_{n-1} of these.

We have shown

$$B_n \equiv B_{n-2} + B_{n-1} \pmod{2}.$$

By a similar argument it is possible to prove the result of J.M. Touchard [13]:

$$B_n \equiv B_{n-p} + B_{n-p+1} \bmod p \quad (p \text{ prime}).$$

As a last example, we count the number of preorders on $\{1,2,3,4,5\}$ mod 5. $\leq$ being a preorder, let $\overset{\pi}{\leq}$ be defined as follows:

$$a \overset{\pi}{\leq} b: a+1 \leq b+1$$

(Addition mod 5, i.e., $5+1 = 1$)

π permutes the preorders on $\{1,2,3,4,5\}$.

We first show that there are exactly two invariant preorders

1. $a \leq b$ for all a,b
2. $a \leq b$ iff $a = b$.

These preorders are invariant and different. We show that they are the only invariant preorders. Let $\leq$ be an invariant preorder; u, v elements such that $u \leq v$ and $u \neq v$. $\leq$ being invariant, we have $u+1 \leq v+1, \ldots, u+j \leq v+j$ (all j). Because of $u \neq v$, there exists k, $1 \leq k \leq 4$, such that $v = u+k$; we have $u \leq u+k$, $u+k \leq u+2k$, i.e., $u \leq u+2k$ and in general $u \leq u+hk$; for every i there exists h such that $i = h \cdot k$, i.e., $u \leq w$ for all w and also $a \leq b$ for all a, b.

Preorders (1) and (2) are, therefore, the only invariant preorders. We define an equivalence relation on the set of all preorders: $\leq$ is equivalent to $\leq'$ iff there exists k ($0 \leq k \leq 4$) such that for all a, b

$$a \leq' b \quad \text{iff} \quad a+k \leq b+k.$$

If $\leq$ is a preorder, let $\leq_k$ be the preorder defined by

$$a \leq_k b \quad \text{iff} \quad a+k \leq b+k.$$

We have: $\leq_0$ is $\leq$ and the preorders of an equivalence class are: $\leq$, $\leq_1$, $\leq_2$, $\leq_3$, $\leq_4$. If $\leq$ is invariant, i.e., $a \leq b$ iff $a+1 \leq b+1$, then all preorders in the class of $\leq$ are the same. We show that this is the case if not all of the preorders are different. Assume, therefore, $\leq_h$ to be equal to $\leq_i$, $0 \leq h < i \leq 4$; putting $j = i-h$, the preorder $\leq$ and $\leq_j$ are equal, i.e., $a \leq b$ iff $a+j \leq b+j$ and also $a \leq b$ iff $a+2j \leq b+2j$, and, in general, $a \leq b$ iff $a+mj \leq b+mj$; because of $j \neq 0$, there is m such that $mj = 1$ (counted mod 5) which shows that the preorder $\leq$ is invariant. We have shown that an equivalence class contains either one or five elements and that there are exactly two invariant preorders. From this we conclude that the number of preorders on the set $\{1, 2, 3, 4, 5\}$ is congruent to 2 mod 5.

We recall the notion of isomorphism: Let $\langle S; R_1, \ldots, R_k \rangle$ and $\langle S'; R'_1, \ldots, R'_k \rangle$ be two structures of the same type (i.e., R_i, R'_i are m_i-ary relations for some m_i, $i = 1, \ldots, k$).

A surjective map f

$$f: S \Rightarrow S'$$

is an isomorphism iff for all a, b in S:

$$a = b \leftrightarrow f(a) = f(b)$$

$$R_i(a, b) \leftrightarrow R'_i(f(a), f(b)) \quad (i = 1, \ldots, k).$$

Let $\langle S; R_1, \ldots, R_k \rangle$ be a structure and f be a bijective map

$$f: S \Rightarrow S'.$$

Then there exists exactly one structure $\langle S'; R'_1, \ldots, R'_k \rangle$ on S' such that f is an isomorphism. R'_i is defined as

$$R'_i(u_1, \ldots, u_{m_i}) = R_i(f^{-1}(u_1), \ldots, f^{-1}(u_{m_i})) \quad i = 1, \ldots, k.$$

We denote R_i' by ${}^f R_i$. A case of special interest is $S' = S$. Bijective maps from S to S are called permutations. If π_1, π_2 are permutations of S and R is a relation on S, we have

$$\pi_2({}^{\pi_1}R) = {}^{(\pi_2\pi_1)}R.$$

Let $\vec{m} = \langle m_1, \ldots, m_k \rangle$ be a sequence of non-negative integers (a "type") and S a finite set. $\Sigma(S, \vec{m})$ is the set of all structures $\langle S; R_1, \ldots, R_k \rangle$ on S, the relations R_i $(i = 1, \ldots, k)$ being m_i-ary. Defining $\bar{\pi}(\langle S; R_1, \ldots, R_k \rangle)$—$\pi$ a permutation on S—to be the structure

$$\langle S; {}^{\pi}R_1, \ldots, {}^{\pi}R_k \rangle$$

we have defined a map h—$h(\pi) = \bar{\pi}$—associating a permutation of $\Sigma(S, \vec{m})$ to a permutation of S. Because of ${}^{\pi_1}({}^{\pi_2}R) = {}^{(\pi_1\pi_2)}R$ this map h is a homomorphism.

Let M be a set and G a group of permutations on M. An equivalence relation $\equiv$ is defined on M as follows:

$$a \equiv b \quad \text{if there exists } \pi \text{ in } G$$
$$\text{such that } b = \pi(a).$$

For fixed a, the elements π of G such that $\pi(a) = a$ form a subgroup $H(a)$ of G; we have $\pi_1(a) = \pi_2(a)$ iff $\pi_1^{-1}\pi_2 \in H(a)$. The number of elements in the equivalence class of a is, therefore, equal to the index of $H(a)$ in G; it is a divisor of the order of G. We shall only apply this in the following case: G is a cyclic group of prime order p; then the equivalence classes contain either 1 or p elements.

LEMMA 4.1   Let C be a class of structures of fixed type, closed under isomorphism, and let p be a prime. Assume $p \leq n$ and let π be a permutation of $\{1, 2, \ldots, n\}$, fixing $n - p$ elements and permuting the remaining p elements cyclically. Then the number of structures on $\{1, 2, \ldots, n\}$ belonging to C is congruent modulo p to the number of structures on $\{1, \ldots, n\}$ belonging to C and invariant under π (i.e., ${}^{\pi}R = R$ for all relations).   ∎

Proof   Let $\Sigma(S, \vec{m})$ be the class of all structures on the set $S = \{1, 2, \ldots, n\}$ of the given type $\vec{m}$, and let $\bar{\pi}$ be the permutation on $\Sigma(S, \vec{m})$ induced by π on the underlying set. $\bar{\pi}$ is of order p (except in the case $m_1 = \ldots = m_k = 0$, in which case all structures are invariant); let G be the group of order p generated by $\bar{\pi}$. C being closed under isomorphism, G-equivalence classes either are subsets of C or disjoint of C. If such a class does not have p elements, it contains exactly one and this element is an invariant structure.

We consider some examples:

Example 4.1 Let $\vec{m} = \langle 1,\ldots,1\rangle$ and let C be the class of structures $\langle S;R_1,\ldots,R_k\rangle$ such that for every element a of S exactly one relation $R_1(a),\ldots,R_k(a)$ holds. ("The elements of S are colored by colors $1,\ldots,k$.") We have k^n possibilities of coloring the elements of $\{1,2,\ldots,n\}$, i.e.,

$$f^C(n) = k^n.$$

Assume $p \leq n$ and let the permutation π permute cyclically p elements and fix the rest. Clearly, there are $k \cdot k^{n-p}$ possibilities for invariant coloring (k possibilities for the p elements in the cycle, k^{n-p} for the rest). Therefore,

$$k^n \equiv k^{n-p+1} \mod p.$$

Putting $n = p$:

$$k^p \equiv k \mod p.$$

(k prime to p: $k^{p-1} \equiv 1 \mod p$, a relation known as Fermat's theorem.)

Example 4.2 Consider the class C of binary structures $\langle S,R\rangle$ such that

(a) $R(x,x)$ for all x in S.
(b) For all x in S there is exactly one y in S such that $R(x,y)$.
(c) If S' is a subset of S closed under R (i.e. if $x \in S'$ and $R(x,y)$ then $y \in S'$) then S' is empty or $S' = S$.

Representing the fact that $R(x,y)$ holds by an arrow from x to y a structure of C is a closed oriented circle

The number of C-structures on $\{1,\ldots,n\}$ is equal to $(n-1)!$ (Start from 1: there are $(n-1)$ possible successors of 1; there are $(n-2)$ possibilities for a successor of this successor, etc.) We assume n to be a prime p, define π to be the permutation $\pi(k) = k+1 \pmod p$ and we want to determine the number of π-invariant structures on $\{1,2,\ldots,p\}$. We show that for every j, $2 \leq j \leq p$, there is exactly one π-invariant structure such that $R(1,j)$ holds. If R is invariant and $R(1,j)$ holds, then also does $R(2,j+1)$, $R(3,j+2)$, $\ldots$, i.e., in general $R(i,k)$ for $k-i = j-1 \mod p$. Conversely, the relation $R(i,k) \leftrightarrow k-i = j-1 \mod p$ satisfies our conditions ($j = 2,\ldots,p$) and is invariant. Therefore, $(p-1)! \equiv (p-1) \mod p$, or $(p-1)! \equiv -1 \mod p$ (Wilson).

Examples k ($k = 3,\ldots$) Let G_k be the class of binary structures that are graphs containing no k element, all of which are in the relation R. (A graph of G_k does not contain a complete subgraph of k elements.) Putting $f^{G_k}(n) = g_k(n)$, we have

$$n < k: \quad g_k(n) = 2^{\binom{n}{2}}$$

$$g_k(k) = 2^{\binom{k}{2}} - 1.$$

For $k = 3$, therefore: $g_3(1) = 1$, $g_3(2) = 2$, $g_3(3) = 7$. $g_3(4)$ is $41 = 64 - 23$, for there are 64 graphs on a set of four elements; one—the complete graph—has four triangles; there are six graphs of type

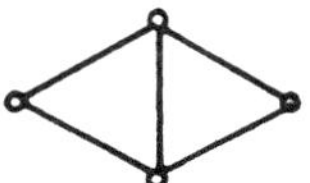

with two triangles and 16 with one triangle, these being of the types

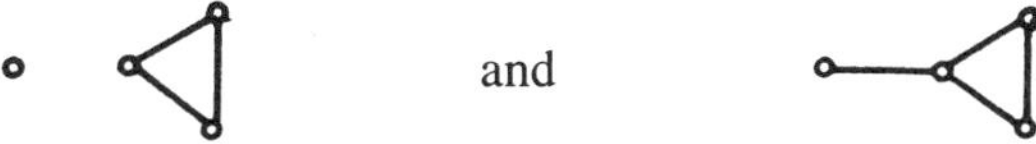

We want to study $g_3(n)$ mod 5. We first ask which graphs on the set $\{1,2,3,4,5\}$ are invariant under the permutation π,

$$\pi(i) = i+1 \quad (\text{mod } 5).$$

There are four such graphs

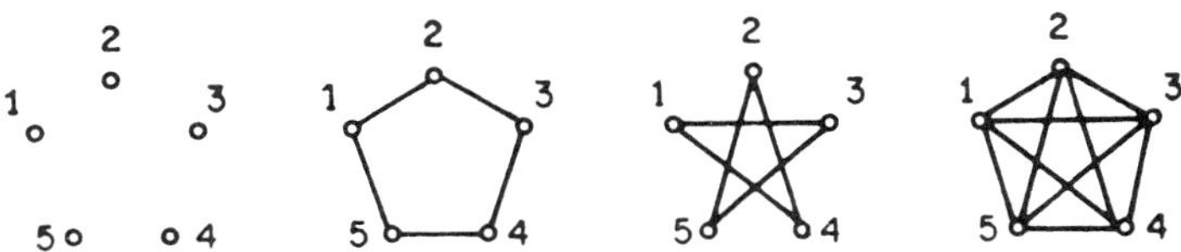

The first three of these do not contain a triangle.

According to our lemma, $g_3(5) \equiv 3$ mod 5. We now assume $5 < n$ and let π be permuting cyclically the first five elements and fixing the rest.

We count the π-invariant graphs on $\{1,\ldots,n\}$ by distinguishing two cases:

(a) The subgraph on $\{1,2,\ldots,5\}$—which is invariant!—has no edge. Then a graph on $\{1,2,\ldots,5,6,\ldots,n\}$ has no triangle iff the subgraph on $\{1,6,\ldots,n\}$ has no triangle. Conversely, to a graph on $\{1,6,\ldots,n\}$ without a triangle there is exactly one extension to a graph on $\{1,2,\ldots,5,\ldots,n\}$ which is invariant, has no triangle, and the subgraph on $\{1,2,\ldots,5\}$ has no edge. (For $1 \le i \le 5$, $6 \le j \le n$ the relation $R(i,j)$ holds iff $R(1,j)$ holds.) The number of invariant graphs on $\{1,\ldots,n\}$ without edges on $\{1,\ldots,5\}$ is $g_3(n-4)$.

(b) The subgraph on $\{1,2,3,4,5\}$ has edges. Being invariant, it is

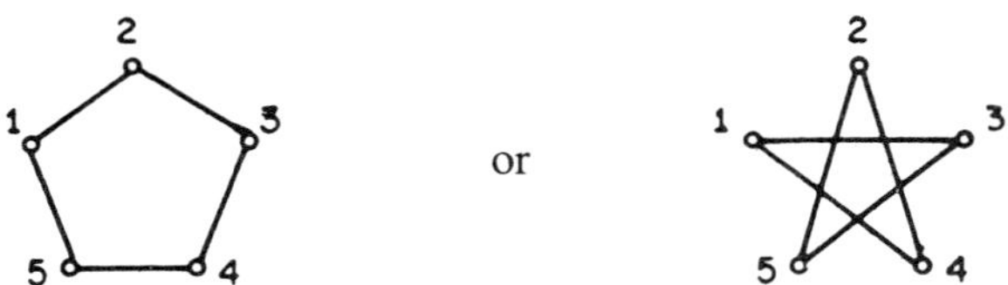

The graph on $\{6,\ldots,n\}$ is arbitrary, but none of the points of $\{1,\ldots,5\}$ is connected to a point of $\{6,\ldots,n\}$ as otherwise there would be a triangle. There are $2 \cdot g_3(n-5)$ graphs of this type and we have

$$g_3(n) \equiv g_3(n-4) + 2g_3(n-5) \mod 5.$$

Knowing the values of $g_3(n) \mod 5$ for $1 \le n \le 5$, we can compute all of the values of $g_3(n) \mod 5$. It is interesting to remark that the recurrence formula holds for $n = 5$ if we put $g_3(0) = 1$.

The case of graphs without triangles does not exhibit enough of the difficulties of establishing a recurrence relation. We, therefore, consider the class of graphs without a "tetrahedron," i.e., a 4-complete subgraph.

We have

$$g_4(1) = 1, \quad g_4(2) = 2,$$

$$g_4(3) = 8, \quad g_4(4) = 63;$$

for $n = 5$, an invariant subgraph without a triangle is without a tetrahedron, and therefore, $g_4(5) \equiv 3 \mod 5$.

We study the recurrence by introducing the same permutation and distinguishing the same cases:

(a) The subgraph on $\{1,2,3,4,5\}$ has no edge. This corresponds to $g_4(n-4)$ graphs on $\{1,2,\ldots,n\}$ elements just as in the case of graphs without triangles.

(b) The invariant subgraph on $\{1,2,3,4,5\}$ has an edge; there are two cases, viz.

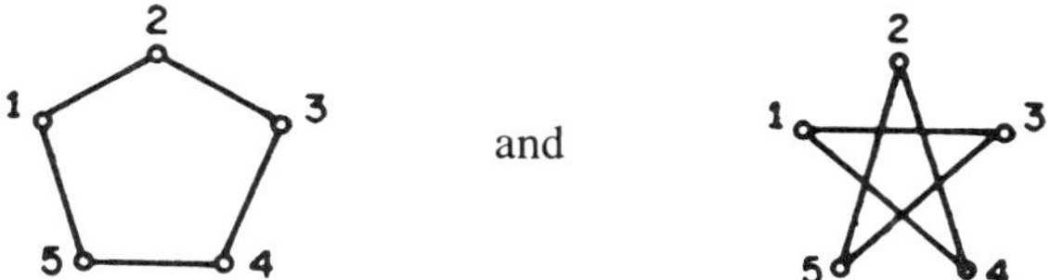

which give rise to the same number of graphs.

What are the conditions on the subgraph on $\{1,6,7,\ldots,n\}$? If 1 is isolated, there is no problem as in the previous case. But this is not necessary, as the following graph on $\{1,\ldots,6\}$ shows

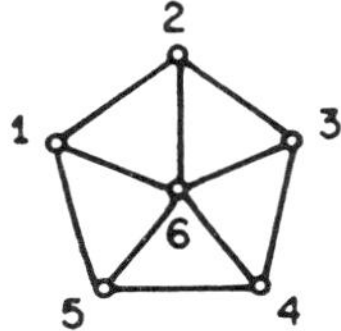

It is, however, impossible that 1 is connected to two elements—say $6,7$—which are connected:

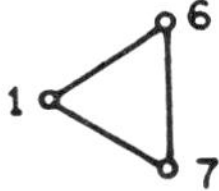

Such a situation corresponds in the graph on $\{1,2,\ldots,n\}$ to a tetrahedron $1,2,6,7$:

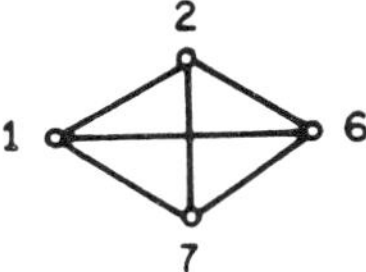

On the other hand, G being a graph on $\{1,6,\ldots,n\}$ such that there is no tetrahedron in the subgraph on $\{6,\ldots,n\}$ and that 1 is in no triangle, there are exactly two graphs on $\{1,\ldots,n\}$ without tetrahedra, invariant under π and having edges on $\{1,\ldots,5\}$. They are obtained from G by blowing up 1 to one of the two invariant graphs on $\{1,2,3,4,5\}$ with five edges. In order to arrive at a recurrence, we have to count graphs on $\{1,6,\ldots,n\}$ with the property mentioned. This problem will lead in turn to new cases and the real problem is, therefore, to find a class of problems such that our recurrence does not lead outside. We consider this problem in the next section.

4.3 SUBSTITUTION OF STRUCTURES

In our attempt to establish a modular recurrence formula for the number of graphs without tetrahedra on an n-element set, we have been confronted with the problem of counting the number of graphs G with a distinguished vertex x such that the graph G' obtained from G by replacing x by a pentagon is a graph without tetrahedra.

The general notion of "replacing" an element of a structure by a structure shall be explained for structures with one binary relation. The generalization to an arbitrary number of binary relations is immediate. It is, however, not known whether there is an analogous notion for ternary relations.

Let $\underline{S}, \underline{E}$ be two binary structures, $\underline{S} = \langle S, R^S \rangle$, $\underline{E} = \langle E, R^E \rangle$, and x an element of S. The structure $\underline{S}(x|\underline{E})$ (obtained by substituting $\underline{E}$ for x) is the following structure $\langle S^+, R^+ \rangle$:

$$S^+ = S \setminus \{x\} \mathbin{\dot{\cup}} E.$$

The relation R^+ is defined according to the following cases:

(1) Both elements are in $S \setminus \{x\}$

$$R^+(a,b) \leftrightarrow R^S(a,b)$$

(2) One element—a say—is in $S \setminus \{x\}$, the other is in E

$$R^+(a,b) \leftrightarrow R^S(a,x)$$

$$R^+(b,a) \leftrightarrow R^S(x,a)$$

(3) Both elements a, b are in E and they are different

$$R^+(a,b) \leftrightarrow R^E(a,b)$$

(4) $a = b$ and $a \in E$

$$R^+(a,b) \leftrightarrow R^S(x,x)$$

(At first sight, it seems, perhaps, more natural to subsume Case 4 under Case 3. The above definition has been chosen because the main theorem turns out to be stronger under this definition.)

If the two structures are graphs, substitution is the following operation: A vertex x of $\langle S, R^S \rangle$ is replaced by the graph $\langle E, R^E \rangle$ and vertices of E are connected to the outside $S \setminus \{x\}$ as x is in the graph $\langle S, R^S \rangle$.

Obviously, the isomorphism type of the resulting structure depends only on the isomorphism type of the given structures. We shall write this as follows: If the structures $\underline{E}$ and $\underline{E}'$ are isomorphic, so are

$$\underline{S}(x|\underline{E}) \quad \text{and} \quad \underline{S}(x|\underline{E}').$$

Let C be a class of binary structures, closed under isomorphism. (Example: C is the class of graphs without triangles.) C induces an equivalence relation ρ_c in the class of all binary structures (not just in C!) by the following definition

$$\underline{E} \; \rho_C \; \underline{E}'$$

iff for all binary structures $\underline{S}$ and all x in the underlying set:

$$\underline{S}(x|\underline{E}) \in C \leftrightarrow \underline{S}(x|\underline{E}') \in C.$$

ρ_C is an equivalence relation. If the structures $\underline{E}, \underline{E}'$ are isomorphic, so are $\underline{S}(x|\underline{E})$, $\underline{S}(x|\underline{E}')$ and, therefore,

$$\underline{E} \; \rho_C \; \underline{E}'.$$

We make some remarks.

REMARK 4.1   Let $\underline{E}, \underline{E}'$ be two structures on the same set and identical on pairs of distinct elements (i.e., for $a \neq b$: $R^{\underline{E}}(a,b) \leftrightarrow R^{\underline{E}'}(a,b)$). The structures $\underline{S}(x|\underline{E})$ and $\underline{S}(x|\underline{E}')$ then coincide and we have

$$\underline{E} \; \rho_C \; \underline{E}'.$$

If we define $\hat{\underline{E}}$ to be the structure on the underlying set of $\underline{E}$ coinciding with $\underline{E}$ on pairs of distinct elements and satisfying $\neg R^{\hat{\underline{E}}}(a,a)$, we have:

$$\underline{E}_1 \; \rho_C \; \underline{E}_2 \quad \text{iff} \quad \hat{\underline{E}}_1 \; \rho_C \; \hat{\underline{E}}_2.$$

REMARK 4.2   Let C be a class of graphs (closed under isomorphism). Then

$$\underline{E}_1 \; \rho_C \; \underline{E}_2 \quad \text{iff}$$

for all graphs $\underline{S}$

$$\underline{S}(x|\hat{\underline{E}}_1) \in C \leftrightarrow \underline{S}(x|\hat{\underline{E}}_2) \in C.$$

One direction is trivial as we have

$$\hat{\underline{E}}_i \; \rho_C \; \underline{E}_i \quad (i = 1, 2).$$

Assume that $\underline{S}$ is not a graph; then there is either an element a in the set such that $R(a,a)$ or there are elements a,b such that $R(a,b)$ and $\neg R(b,a)$. The same then holds for $\underline{S}(x|\underline{E})$. (If a,b are different from x we just choose the same elements; if $a = x$ or $b = x$, choose a' or b' to be a fixed element of $\underline{E}$.)

We shall study an example in detail and choose the class T of trees; i.e., connected graphs without "circles" (a sequence of distinct vertices $v_0,v_1,\ldots,v_k$—$2 \le k$—such that for all i, $0 \le i < k$, $R(v_i,v_{i+1})$ and $R(v_k,v_0)$). We want to show that the equivalence classes of ρ_T (within the class of irreflexive structures) are the following:

(K_1) The one element structure $\{e\}$.

(K_2) The graphs consisting of two or more isolated points.

(K_3) The class T of trees except $\{e\}$.

(K_4) All of the rest.

Consider the following structures $\underline{S}_1, \underline{S}_2$:

$$\underline{S}_1 : \ \{x\}$$

$$\underline{S}_2 : \ \text{O----O}$$
$$x$$

$\underline{S}_1(x|\underline{E})$ is $\underline{E}$; an element of $K_1 \cup K_3$ is not in the same class as an element of $K_2 \cup K_4$.

$\underline{S}_2(x|\underline{E})$ is a tree iff there are no connected elements in $\underline{E}$; an element of $K_1 \cup K_2$ is not in the same class as an element of $K_3 \cup K_4$.

Next, we must show that any two elements of a class K_i ($i = 1,2,3,4$) are ρ_T-equivalent. The case of K_1 is trivial.

K_2: If $\underline{E}$ is a graph of two or more isolated points, $\underline{S}(x|\underline{E})$ is a tree if and only if x is connected to one element and $\underline{S}$ is a tree.

K_3: If $\underline{E}$ is a tree with more than one element, $\underline{S}(x|\underline{E})$ is a tree iff $\underline{S}$ is the one element structure. (If x is connected to no other element and $\underline{S}$ is not $\{x\}$, then $\underline{S}(x|\underline{E})$ is not connected; if x is connected to an element, $\underline{S}(x|\underline{E})$ contains a triangle.)

K_4: There is no structure in K_4 such that $\underline{S}(x|\underline{E})$ is a tree.

This completes the proof that ρ_T has the four classes K_1, K_2, K_3, K_4: $\underline{E}_1 \ \rho_T \ \underline{E}_2 \leftrightarrow (\exists i)(\underline{E}_1 \in K_i \wedge \underline{E}_2 \in K_i)$.

As a second example let C be the class of graphs which are, for some n, $n \in N^+$, isomorphic to the following graph $\underline{S}_n$ on the set $\{1,\ldots,n,\ldots,2n\}$: For i,j ($i \ne j$) $R(i,j)$ iff

$$(1 \le i \le n \quad \text{and} \quad 1 \le j \le n) \quad \text{or}$$

$$(n+1 \leq i \leq 2n \quad \text{and} \quad n+1 \leq j \leq 2n)$$

($\underline{S}_n$ consists, therefore, of two components, both being complete graphs and having the same number of elements.)

For $n \in N^+$, let $\underline{T}_n$ be the graph on $\{1, 2, \ldots, n+1\}$ defined by

$$R(i,j) \quad \text{iff} \quad (i \leq n \quad \text{and} \quad j \leq n)$$

(i.e., all of the vertices $1, 2, \ldots, n$ are connected in $\underline{T}_n$; $n+1$ is isolated), and let $\underline{U}_n$ be the complete graph on $\{1, 2, \ldots, n\}$.

The graph $\underline{T}_n((n+1)|\underline{U}_n)$ is the graph $\underline{S}_n$ (and belongs, therefore, to C), whereas for $m \neq n$ the graph $\underline{T}_n((n+1)|\underline{U}_m)$ does not belong to C. Therefore, the graphs $\underline{U}_1, \underline{U}_2, \ldots$ are all ρ_C-inequivalent.

We now give the fundamental definition.

DEFINITION 4.1   A class C of binary structures (closed under isomorphism) is of finite character iff the equivalence relation ρ_C has only a finite number of equivalence classes. ∎

Before stating the main theorem, we repeat the definition of f^C: $f^C(n)$ is the number of labeled structures on the set $\{1, 2, \ldots, n\}$ belonging to C.

THEOREM 4.1   For a class C of finite character, the function f^C satisfies for all m, $m \in N^+$, a linear recurrence relation mod m.

In detail: For such a class C and for m, $m \in N^+$, there exist k, $k \in N^+$, $a_1, \ldots, a_k$ ($a_i \in N$) such that for all n, $k+1 \leq n$,

$$f^C(n) \equiv \sum_{j=1}^{k} a_j f^C(n-j) \mod m. \qquad ∎$$

COROLLARY 4.1   For a class C of finite character, the function f^C is periodic mod m for large arguments.

In detail: For positive m there exist positive t, n_o such that for all n, $n_o \leq n$,

$$f^C(n+t) \equiv f^C(n) \mod m. \qquad ∎$$

4.4   FINITE CHARACTER AND MONADIC LOGIC

In most cases, classes of structures are defined by axioms. It is, therefore, natural to look for a property of axiom systems implying that the corresponding class of structures is of finite character. In order to define such a property, we have to define the notion of "sentence of monadic second order logic." A sentence is a formula without free variables and we define, therefore, the notion of "formula of monadic second order logic." Assume given

1. $x_0, x_1, \ldots$:   sequence of individual variables.
2. $X_0, X_1, \ldots$:   sequence of set variables.
3. $R_0, R_1, \ldots$:   sequence of m_i-ary ($i = 0, \ldots$) predicate signs.
4. equality sign: $=$

The following then are formulas:

(I) $R_i(x_{j_1}, \ldots, x_{j_{m_i}}), \ x_{j_1} = x_{j_2},$

$$x_{j_1} \in X_{j_2} \ (j_1, j_2 \in N)$$

(II)   If φ, ψ are formulas, so are

$$(\varphi \wedge \psi), \ (\varphi \rightarrow \psi), \ (\varphi \vee \psi), \ (\varphi \leftrightarrow \psi),$$

$$\neg \varphi, \ (\exists x_j)\varphi, \ (\forall x_j)\varphi, \ (\exists X_j)\varphi, \ (\forall X_j)\varphi.$$

"Second order" refers to the presence of variables $X_0, \ldots$; "monadic" to the restriction to sets (excluding, e.g., binary predicates). Formulas where no subformula of the types $x_{j_1} \in X_{j_2}$, $(\exists X_j)\varphi$, $(\forall X_j)\varphi$, occurs are formulas of "first order logic." We define some of the classes we have considered by an axiom system consisting of a finite number of sentences.

1. *Graphs without triangles:*
   $R(x_1, x_2)$: binary predicate sign.
   Axioms:

$$(\forall x_1) \ \neg R(x_1, x_1)$$

$$(\forall x_1) \ (\forall x_2) \ (R(x_1, x_2) \rightarrow R(x_2, x_1))$$

(These two axioms define the notion of graph)

$$(\forall x_1)(\forall x_2)(\forall x_3) \ \neg((R(x_1, x_2) \wedge$$

$$R(x_1, x_3)) \wedge R(x_2, x_3)) \ \text{(no triangle!)}$$

In the same way, graphs without tetrahedra, etc. can be defined. What about the notion of graph without circle? We show how to define this notion in monadic second order logic.

2. *Graphs without circle:*
   We first give a formula expressing the notion "X_0 is a subgraph the elements of which have exactly two neighbors":

$$(\forall x_1)(\exists x_2)(\exists x_3)(x_1 \in X_0 \to$$

$$(((x_2 \in X_0 \wedge x_3 \in X_0) \wedge \neg x_2 = x_3)$$

$$\wedge (\forall x_4)((R(x_1,x_4) \wedge x_4 \in X_0) \leftrightarrow$$

$$(x_4 = x_2 \vee x_4 = x_3))))$$

("x_2, x_3 are different elements in X_0; x_4 is a neighbor of x_1 in X_0 iff x_4 is either x_2 or x_3.")

A graph is without circle iff it does not contain a (non-empty) subgraph X_0 of the above type:

$$(\forall X_0)((\exists x_0)x_0 \in X_0 \to \neg\psi)$$

(ψ being the above formula.)

3. *Trees:* A tree is a connected graph without circle. We give a sentence Γ such that a graph without circles satisfies Γ iff it is a tree. Γ expresses the fact that the binary relation R is connected, i.e., that the only sets closed under R are the empty set and the whole set:

$$(\forall X_0)((\forall x_1)(\forall x_2)$$

$$((x_1 \in X_0 \wedge R(x_1,x_2)) \to x_2 \in X_0) \to$$

$$((\exists x_3)x_3 \in X_0 \to (\forall x_3)x_3 \in X_0)).$$

4. We give an example of a class of structures definable in second order logic but not in monadic logic: it is the class C considered on page 145; its structures are the graphs consisting of two isomorphic copies of complete graphs. A second order characterization is immediate: On the one hand, one expresses the fact that the graph has two components which are complete graphs; this can be done in first order logic. On the other hand, one postulates the existence of an automorphism f such that x and $f(x)$ are not in relation R. We prove the following:

LEMMA 4.2 The number $f^C(n)$ is odd iff n is even and a power of 2, i.e., $n = 2,4,8,\ldots$. ∎

Proof $f^C(n)$ is the number of ways the set $\{1,2,\ldots,n\}$ splits into two equal parts. Clearly, $f^C(n) = 0$ for n odd. Assume n even and let h be the map interchanging i and $n/2 + i$ ($i = 1,\ldots,n/2$). If A,B is a splitting of $\{1,\ldots,n\}$ into two equal parts, so is $h(A),h(B)$. The parity of $f^C(n)$ is equal to the parity of numbers of splittings A,B such that $h(A),h(B)$ is the same splitting as A,B.

We put

$$A' = \{1,\ldots,n/2\} \cap A,$$

$$B' = \{1,\ldots,n/2\} \cap B.$$

and distinguish two cases:

1. $h(A) = A,\ h(B) = B.$
   We have $\quad A = A' \cup h(A')$
   $$\qquad\qquad B = B' \cup h(B')$$
   and A',B' is a splitting of $\{1,\ldots,n/2\}$ into two equal parts. The number of such splittings is $f^C(n/2)$.

2. $h(A) = B,\ h(B) = A.$
   We have $\quad A = A' \cup h(B')$
   $$\qquad\qquad B = B' \cup h(A').$$

   For every subset A' of $\{1,\ldots,n/2\}$, there is exactly one such splitting. Two subsets of $\{1,\ldots,n/2\}$ define the same splitting iff one is the complement of the other. The number of such splittings is $2^{n/2-1}$.

   We have

$$f^C(n) = 0 \ \text{ for } n \text{ odd}$$

$$f^C(2n) \equiv f^C(n) + 2^{n-1} \pmod 2, \text{ i.e.}$$

$$f^C(2n) \equiv f^C(n) \ \bmod 2 \ (2 \leq n)$$

$$f^C(2) \equiv 1 \ \bmod 2.$$

These relations imply

$$f^C(2^m) \equiv 1 \ \bmod 2 \ (1 \leq m)$$

$$f^C(2^m \cdot u) \equiv 0 \ \bmod 2, \ u \text{ odd}, \ 1 < u;$$

This finishes the proof of the lemma.

The function f^C is not periodic mod 2 for large arguments; as a consequence of the theorem, we conclude that the class C cannot be defined by axioms of monadic second order logic.

THEOREM 4.2   (MF)   If the class C of binary structures is defined by a sentence of monadic second order logic then C is of finite character.   ■

Proof   Given two structures of the same type—say $\langle S_1,R_1\rangle$, $\langle S_2,R_2\rangle$, both being binary—and a natural number n, let $G^n(\langle S_1,R_1\rangle, \langle S_2,R_2\rangle)$ be the following two-person game: Each player has n moves, a move being the choice of either an element or of a subset of one of the sets S_i ($i = 1, 2$); player I and II alternate, player II choosing in such a way that in two successive moves of I, II either two elements of S_1, S_2 or two subsets of S_1, S_2 are chosen. After a play of the game is over there are given two sequences

$$\langle \sigma_1^1, \ldots, \sigma_n^1 \rangle, \quad \langle \sigma_1^2, \ldots, \sigma_n^2 \rangle$$

such that for all j ($j = 1, \ldots, n$): Either σ_j^1 is an element of S_1 and σ_j^2 an element of S_2 or σ_j^1 is a subset of S_1 and σ_j^2 a subset of S_2.

Player II has won the play resulting in such sequences iff they are isomorphic, i.e., iff for all j, k the following conditions are satisfied:

1. If σ_i^1, σ_j^1 are elements then

$$\sigma_i^1 = \sigma_j^1 \leftrightarrow \sigma_i^2 = \sigma_j^2.$$

$$R_1(\sigma_i^1, \sigma_j^1) \leftrightarrow R_2(\sigma_i^2, \sigma_j^2).$$

2. If σ_i^1 is an element, σ_j^1 is a set then

$$\sigma_i^1 \in \sigma_j^1 \leftrightarrow \sigma_i^2 \in \sigma_j^2.$$

A strategy for player I is a function τ' associating to an initial segment

$$\langle \sigma_1^1, \ldots, \sigma_{k-1}^1 \rangle, \quad \langle \sigma_1^2, \ldots, \sigma_{k-1}^2 \rangle$$

a next move, i.e. an object σ_k^i ($i = 1$ or $i = 2$); a strategy τ'' for player II is defined on initial segments

$$\langle \sigma_1^1, \ldots, \sigma_{k-1}^1 \rangle, \quad \langle \sigma_1^2, \ldots, \sigma_k^2 \rangle$$

$$\langle \sigma_1^1, \ldots, \sigma_k^1 \rangle, \quad \langle \sigma_1^2, \ldots, \sigma_{k-1}^2 \rangle.$$

A strategy τ' (τ'') is a winning strategy for player I (II) iff each play

$$\langle \sigma_1^1, \ldots, \sigma_n^1 \rangle, \quad \langle \sigma_1^2, \ldots, \sigma_n^2 \rangle$$

where the k-th move of I (II) corresponds to the function τ' (τ'') is won by I (II).

LEMMA 4.3 (G1) In a game $G^n(\langle S_1, R_1 \rangle, \langle S_2, R_2 \rangle)$ exactly one of the two players has a winning strategy. ($G^n(\langle S_1, R_1 \rangle, \langle S_2, R_2 \rangle)$) is a game of "perfect information"; see, for example, [10]). ∎

For every n, $n \in N$, an equivalence relation $\underset{n}{\equiv}$ in the class of binary structures is defined as follows: $\langle S_1, R_1 \rangle \underset{n}{\equiv} \langle S_2, R_2 \rangle$ iff player II has a winning strategy in the game $G^n(\langle S_1, R_1 \rangle, \langle S_2, R_2 \rangle)$. We then have

LEMMA 4.4   (G2)   For a sentence φ of monadic second order logic there is an integer n such that $\langle S_1, R_1 \rangle \equiv_n \langle S_2, R_2 \rangle$ implies that φ holds in $\langle S_1, R_1 \rangle$ iff φ holds in $\langle S_2, R_2 \rangle$. ∎

LEMMA 4.5   (G3)   The relation $\equiv_n$ has (for every n) finitely many equivalence classes. ∎

(For proofs of Lemma 4.4 (G2), 4.5 (G3) cf. [4], [6].)

LEMMA 4.6   (G4)   If C is a class of binary structures and if the structures $\underline{E}_i = \langle S_i, R_i \rangle$ $(i = 1, 2)$ satisfy $\underline{E}_1 \equiv_n \underline{E}_2$ then for every structure $\underline{S}$ the substitutes $\underline{S}(x | \underline{E}_i)$ also satisfy

$$\underline{S}(x | \underline{E}_1) \equiv_n \underline{S}(x | \underline{E}_2).$$ ∎

We give an informal proof; a more detailed proof is given in [3]. Because of $\underline{E}_1 \equiv_n \underline{E}_2$, there is a winning strategy τ for player II in the corresponding game $G^n(\underline{E}_1, \underline{E}_2)$. We have to describe a winning strategy for II in the game $G^n(\underline{S}(x | \underline{E}_1), \underline{S}(x | \underline{E}_2))$. The choices of II in a play are determined by the following rules:

1. If I has chosen an element in $\underline{S}$—different from x—II chooses the same element.
2. If I has chosen an element of—say—$\underline{E}_1$, II chooses the element in $\underline{E}_2$ according to the strategy τ.
3. If I has chosen a subset T in the structure—say—$\underline{S}(x | \underline{E}_1)$, the choice of II is determined as follows: Let T' be the intersection of T with $\underline{S}$, T'' the intersection of T with $\underline{E}_1$; therefore: $T = T' \cup T''$. Let T^* be the subset of the structure $\underline{E}_2$ corresponding to T'' on the basis of the strategy τ in the game $G^n(\underline{E}_1, \underline{E}_2)$. II then chooses—in the game $G^n(\underline{S}(x | \underline{E}_1), \underline{S}(x | \underline{E}_2))$—the set $T' \cup T^*$.

It is not difficult to show that the strategy defined in this way is a winning strategy for II.

On the basis of these lemmas we are now ready to prove the theorem.

Let the class C be defined by the sentence φ of monadic second order logic and choose n according to Lemma 4.4 (G2). The equivalence relation $\equiv_n$ has (Lemma 4.5 (G3)) finitely many classes; we show

$$\langle E_1, R_1 \rangle \equiv_n \langle E_2, R_2 \rangle \rightarrow \langle E_1, R_1 \rangle \, \rho_C \, \langle E_2, R_2 \rangle$$

which implies that ρ_C has finitely many classes. Let $\langle S, R \rangle$ be a structure and let $\underline{S}_i$ $(i = 1, 2)$ be the structure obtained by substituting $\langle E_i, R_i \rangle$ for an element x in S. By Lemma 4.6 (G4), we have $\underline{S}_1 \equiv_n \underline{S}_2$ and by the choice of n according to Lemma 4.4 (G2): φ holds in $\underline{S}_1$ iff it holds in $\underline{S}_2$. We, therefore, have $\underline{E}_1 \; \rho_C \; \underline{E}_2$ and the theorem is proved.

4.5 MODULAR COUNTING

THEOREM 4.3 (RC) If C is a class of (binary) structures closed under isomorphism and of finite character then the function f^C satisfies a linear recurrence relation mod m: There is an integer d, $1 \leq d$, and integers a_i, $i = 1,\ldots,d$, such that for all n, $d < n$:

$$f^C(n) \equiv \sum_{i=1}^{d} a_i f^C(n-i) \mod m. \qquad \blacksquare$$

In what follows we assume that the class C is a class of structures with just one binary relation R; the general case (many binary relations) has the same proof. In order to be able to carry out an inductive proof, Theorem 4.3 (RC) has to be generalized.

Let C be a class of R-structures. Assume furthermore that A is a finite (possibly empty) set, G a group of permutations of A, and $\underline{A}$ a set of binary relations on A which is invariant under G.

We consider structures on the set $S := A \; \dot{\cup} \; \{1,2,\ldots,n\}$ (i.e., A and $\{1,2,\ldots,n\}$ are treated as disjoint). The group G of permutations on A is extended to a permutation group on S by putting: $g(i) = i, i = 1,\ldots,n$.

We then define

$$U(A,G,\underline{A};n)$$

to be the set of R-structures on S such that

1. $R \in C$
2. $R/A^2 \in \underline{A}$
   (R/A^2: restriction of R to A)
3. $^g R \neq R$ for $g \in G^*$ ($= G \backslash \{\text{Id}\}$)

THEOREM 4.4 (RC)$'$ If C is of finite character then the function $n \to \# U(A,G,\underline{A};n)$ satisfies a linear recurrence relation mod $(\#G)\cdot m$ ($m \in N^+$).

$\blacksquare$

Theorem 4.3 (RC) is a special case of (RC)$'$; one simply puts $A = \wedge, G = \{\text{Id}\}$. Theorem 4.4 (RC)$'$ is proved by induction on m (or: number of prime divisors of m). Assume $m = 1$; define two structures given by R_1,R_2 on $A \; \dot{\cup} \{1,2,\ldots,n\}$ to be equivalent iff for some g in G: $^g R_1 = R_2$.

The number of structures in an equivalence class is, therefore, equal to the order of G and we have

$$\#U(.\,.\,.\,;n) \equiv 0 \mod \#G;$$

the function satisfies a trivial recurrence relation. For the inductive step, a stronger theorem is proved. Let C, A, $\underline{A}$ and G be as above and kept fixed.

We enumerate, furthermore, the pairs of unary relations on the set A:

$$(R_i', R_i''), \quad i = 1, \ldots, r.$$

There are $2^{\#A}$ unary relations on A and $4^{\#A}$ pairs, i.e. we have $r = 4^{\#A}$. Let $\vec{B} = (B_1, \ldots, B_r)$ be an r-tuple of sets, assumed to be disjoint and put

$$B = \bigcup_{i=1}^{r} B_i.$$

The class C of structures is of finite character; there exists, therefore, a set $\underline{B}$ (a "basis") of structures such that every structure is ρ_C-equivalent to some structure of $\underline{B}$. We assume that the one-element structure belongs to $\underline{B}$. Furthermore let $\vec{E}$ be a map assigning to an element b of B a structure $\vec{E}(b)$ of $\underline{B}$. If $\underline{S}$ is a structure defined on a set S containing B as subset, $\underline{S}(\vec{E}|B)$ is the structure obtained from $\underline{S}$ by substituting $\vec{E}(b)$ for every b, i.e. $\underline{S}(\vec{E}|B)$ is

$$\underline{S}(b_1|\vec{E}(b_1))(b_2|\vec{E}(b_2)), \ldots, (b_j|\vec{E}(b_j)).$$

(The order has no effect on the result.) The binary relation defining $\underline{S}(\vec{E}|B)$ will be denoted by $R(\vec{E}|B)$.

Let $V(\vec{B}, \vec{E}; n)$ be the set of R-structures on

$$A \cup B \cup \{1, 2, \ldots, n\}$$

such that

1. $R(\vec{E}|B) \in C$
2. $R/A^2 \in \underline{A}$
3. $R(a,b) = R_i'(a)$ for $a \in A$, $b \in B_i$
   $R(b,a) = R_i''(a)$ for $a \in A$, $b \in B_i$

4. $^gR \neq R$ for $g \in G^*$.

$v(\vec{B}, \vec{E})$ is the function whose value for n—$v(\vec{B}, \vec{E}; n)$—is the number of elements of $V(\vec{B}, \vec{E}; n)$.

Let $F = F(C, A, \underline{A}, G)$ be the set of these functions, i.e. $g \in F$ iff there is $\vec{B}$ and $\vec{E}$ such that

$$g = v(\vec{B}, \vec{E}).$$

Assume m given and let p be a prime divisor of m. We define F_0 to be the subset of F defined by the following condition: $g \in F_0$ iff there exist $\vec{B}$ and $\vec{E}$ such that

$$\#B_i \le (p-1)\,\#\underline{B} \quad \text{and}$$

$$g = v(\vec{B}, \vec{E})$$

F_0 is finite; $F_0 = \{v_1, \ldots, v_s\}$.

LEMMA 4.7 (RC_1) For w, $w \in F$, there are integers a_j $(j = 1, \ldots, s)$ and a function q, $q: N \Rightarrow N$, satisfying a linear recurrence relation mod $(\#G) \cdot m$ such that

$$w \equiv \sum_{j=1}^{s} a_j v_j + q \mod (\#G) \cdot m. \qquad \blacksquare$$

We first deduce Theorem 4.4 $(RC)'$ from Lemma 4.7 (RC_1).

Consider a structure of $V(\vec{B}, \vec{E}; n)$. The element n—as an element of the set $A \cup B \cup \{1, 2, \ldots, n\}$—is in relation to the elements of A according to some i: $R(a, n) = R_i'(a)$, $R(n, a) = R_i''(a)$ (for all a in A).

If we insert n into B_i and define $\vec{E}^i(n)$ as the one-element structure, we have defined in a unique way an element of $V(\vec{B}^i, \vec{E}^i; n-1)$ ($\vec{B}^i = (B_1, \ldots, B_i \cup \{n\}, \ldots, B_r)$). Every element of $V(\vec{B}^i, \vec{E}^i; n-1)$ is obtained in this way and the sets $V(\vec{B}, \vec{E}; n)$ and $\bigcup_{i=1}^{r} V(\vec{B}^i, \vec{E}^i; n-1)$ have the same number of elements. For v in F, there exist, therefore, w_i $(i = 1, \ldots, r)$ in F such that

$$v(n) = \sum_{i=1}^{r} w_i(n-1).$$

Assume v to be an element v_k of F_0 $(k = 1, \ldots, s)$. We have

$$v_k(n) = \sum_{i=1}^{r} w_i^{(k)}(n-1).$$

By Lemma 4.7 (RC_1):

$$w_i^{(k)}(n-1) \equiv \sum_{j=1}^{s} a_{ij}^k v_j(n-1) + p_i^k(n-1)$$

$$\sum_{i=1}^{r} w_i^{(k)}(n-1) \equiv \sum_{j=1}^{s} b_{kj} v_j(n-1) + q_k(n-1)$$

$$v_k(n) \equiv \sum_{j=1}^{s} b_{kj} v_j(n-1) + q_k(n-1).$$

($\equiv$ mod $(\#G)\cdot m$, q_k satisfying a linear recurrence relation mod $(\#G)\cdot m$.)

The function associating $\#U(A,G,\underline{A};n)$ to n is one of the function $v_1,\ldots,v_s$. We show that these functions satisfy a linear recurrence relation mod $(\#G)\cdot m$. Let the relation for q_k be

$$q_k(n-1) \equiv \sum_{h=2}^{d} c_{kh} q_k(n-h). \qquad (4.2)$$

(d may be assumed independent of k.)

Substituting

$$q_k(n-h) \equiv v_k(n-h+1) - \sum_{j=1}^{s} b_{kj} v_j(n-h) \quad (k = 1,\ldots,s)$$

into Equation (4.2) we have

$$v_k(n) - \sum_{j=1}^{s} b_{kj} v_j(n-1) \equiv \sum_{h=2}^{d} c_{kh} v_k(n-h+1) - \sum_{h,j} c_{kh} b_{kj} v_j(n-h)$$

$$v_k(n) \equiv \sum_{h=1}^{d} \sum_{j=1}^{s} a_{hj} v_j(n-h).$$

Let $\bar{a}$ be the residue of a in Z mod $(\#G)\cdot m$. The functions $\overline{v_k}$ then map N to a finite set and there exist n_1, n_2 such that $d < n_1 < n_2$ and $\overline{v}_j(n_1 - h) = \overline{v}_j(n_2 - h)$ for all j,h ($1 \leq h \leq d$, $1 \leq j \leq s$).

We then have

$$v_j(n_1 + \ell) = v_j(n_2 + \ell)$$

for all j and ℓ in N. The functions $\overline{v}_j$ are periodic—period $(n_2 - n_1)$—for large arguments and, hence, satisfy a linear recurrence relation.

Lemma 4.7 (RC_1) is an immediate consequence of Lemma 4.8 (RC_2) (C, A, $\underline{A}$, G, $(B_1, \ldots, B_r)$, $\underline{B}$, m and p as before):

LEMMA 4.8 (RC_2) If

$$\#B_1 > (p-1)\,\#\underline{B}$$

then there exist $B^*, B^* = (B_1^*,\ldots,B_r^*)$, an integer t, maps F^k ($k = 1,\ldots,t$) and q ($q\colon N \Rightarrow N$, satisfying a linear recurrence relation mod $(\#G)\cdot m$) such that

$$\#B_1^* = \#B_1 - (p-1); \quad B_i^* = B_i \quad (i = 2,\ldots,r)$$

$$v(\vec{B},\vec{E};n) \equiv \sum_{k=1}^{t} v(\vec{B^*},\vec{F}^k;n) + q(n) \bmod (\#G)\cdot m. \qquad \blacksquare$$

Lemma 4.7 (RC_1) follows from Lemma 4.8 (RC_2) by reducing the sets B_i as long as they are big; we end up with sets of cardinality at most $(p-1) \# \underline{B}$, i.e., with functions belonging to F_0.

Proof of Lemma 4.8 (RC_2)   Assuming $\#B_1 > (p-1) \# \underline{B}$, there is an element of $\underline{B}$ which is the $\vec{E}$-image of (at least) p elements $b_0, \ldots, b_{p-1}$ of B_1. We put $B_1' := \{b_0, \ldots, b_{p-1}\}$ and $B_1'' := B_1 \setminus B_1'$, $\vec{E}(b_i) =: E_0$ $(i = 0, \ldots, p-1)$; let h_0 be a permutation which permutes B_1' cyclically.

The group G (defined on A) and h_0 (on B_1') generate a group H of permutations on

$$A \cup B \cup \{1, 2, \ldots, n\}$$

of order $\#G \cdot p$.

The set $V(\vec{B}, \vec{E}; n)$ of structures on this set splits into V_1, V_2 according to whether $^{h_0}R \neq R$ (in V_1) or $^{h_0}R = R$ (in V_2). We first look at the set V_1.

Because of $^gR \neq R$ for $g \in G^*$ and $^{h_0}R \neq R$, we have for all h in H^* ($= H \setminus \{\mathrm{Id}\}$): $^hR \neq R$. We define A' to be

$$A \cup \bigcup_{b \in B} \vec{E}(b).$$

The set $\underline{A}'$ of R-structures on A' is defined in such a way that we have

$$V_1(\vec{B}, \vec{E}; n) = U(A', H, \underline{A}'; n).$$

Because of our inductive hypothesis, the function

$$n \rightarrow \# U(A', H, \underline{A}'; n)$$

satisfies a linear recurrence relation mod $(\#H) \cdot \dfrac{m}{p}$. We have $(\#H) \cdot \dfrac{m}{p} = (\#G) \cdot m$ and q defined by

$$q(n) = \# V_1(\vec{B}, \vec{E}; n)$$

satisfies a linear recurrence relation mod $(\#G) \cdot m$.

We now study the set $V_2(\vec{B}, \vec{E}; n)$; the structures of this set are invariant under h_0.

We had

$$B_1 = \{b_0, \ldots, b_{p-1}\} \cup B_1''.$$

We put

$$B_1^* = \{b_0\} \cup B_1'', \quad B_i^* = B_i \ (i = 2, \ldots, r)$$

$$\vec{B}^* = (B_1^*, \ldots, B_r^*).$$

Let $W(\vec{B};n)$ be the set of R-structures on

$$A \cup B \cup \{1, \ldots, n\}$$

satisfying the following conditions

1. $R/A^2 \in \underline{A}$
2. $R(a,b) = R_i'(a)$ for $a \in A$, $b \in B_i$
   $R(b,a) = R_i''(a)$ for $a \in A$, $b \in B_i$
3. $^gR \neq R$ for $g \in G^*$.

Let W_2 be the subset of W defined by $^{h_0}R = R$. Furthermore, let $\underline{W}$ be the set of R-structures on $B_1' = \{b_0, \ldots, b_{p-1}\}$ invariant under h_0:

$$\underline{W} = \{\sigma_1, \ldots, \sigma_t\}; \quad \text{so} \quad t = \#\underline{W}.$$

We define maps α_1, α_2 on the set of structures W_2; $\alpha_1(R)$ is the restriction of R—defined on

$$A \cup B_1' \cup B_2'' \cup \overset{r}{\underset{i=2}{\bigcup}} B_i \cup \{1, 2, \ldots, n\} -$$

to the set

$$A \cup \{b_0\} \cup B_1'' \cup \overset{r}{\underset{i=2}{\bigcup}} B_i \cup \{1, \ldots, n\}$$

(i.e., to $A \cup B^* \cup \{1, 2, \ldots, n\}$); $\alpha_2(R)$ is the restriction of R to B_1' $(= \{b_0, \ldots, b_{p-1}\})$.

The pair (α_1, α_2) maps W_2 bijectively onto $W(\vec{B}^*;n) \times \underline{W}$. For $k = 1, \ldots, t$ we define $\vec{E}^k$ on B^* as follows:

$$\vec{E}^k(b) = \vec{E}(b) \quad \text{for} \quad b \neq b_0;$$

$$\vec{E}^k(b_0) = \sigma_k(b_0|E_0, \ldots, b_{p-1}|E_0)$$

(E_0 is equal to $\vec{E}(b_i)$, $i = 0, \ldots, p-1$.)

The structure $\sigma_k(b_0|E_0, b_1|E_0, \ldots, b_{p-1}|E_0)$ is ρ_C-equivalent to a structure F_0^k of $\underline{B}$. Putting

$$\vec{F}^k(b) = \begin{cases} \vec{E}(b) & (b \neq b_0) \\ F_0^k & (b = b_0) \end{cases}$$

we have

$$\# V_2(\vec{B}, \vec{E}; n) = \sum_{k=1}^{t} \# V(\vec{B}^*, \vec{F}^k; n). \tag{4.3}$$

For an R-structure $\underline{S}$ of $W_2(\vec{B};n)$ $\underline{S}$ belongs to V_2 iff

$$R(\vec{E}|B) \in C.$$

Consider $\alpha_1(R), \alpha_2(R)$ and assume $\alpha_2(R)$ to define the structure σ_k. Then

$$R(\vec{E}|B) \text{ is isomorphic to } \alpha_1(R)(\vec{E}^k|B^*).$$

The structure $\alpha_1(R)(\vec{E}^k|B^*)$ belongs to C iff $\alpha_1(R)(\vec{F}^k|B^*)$ belongs to C which in turn holds iff $\alpha_1(R) \in V(\vec{B}^*, \vec{F}^k; n)$. Equation 4.3 is, therefore, established, Lemma 4.8 (RC$_2$) proved.

REFERENCES

1. Blatter, Chr. and Specker, E., "Le nombre de structures finies d'une théorie à caractère fini," *Sciences Mathématiques*, Fonds National de la Recherche Scientifique, Bruxelles 1981, 41–44.

2. Blatter, Chr. and Specker, E., "Modular periodicity of combinatorial sequences," *Abstracts Am. Math. Soc.* 4 (1983), 313.

3. Blatter, Chr. and Specker, E., "Recurrence relations for the number of labeled structures on a finite set," *Logic and Machines, Lecture Notes in Computer Science*, 171 (1984), 43–61.

4. Ehrenfeucht, A., "Application of games to some problem of mathematical logic," *Bull. Acad. Pol.*, Cl. III, 5 (1957), 35–37.

5. Evans, J. W., Harary, F. and Lynn, M. S., "On the computer enumeration of finite topologies," *Communications of the ACM* 10 (1967), 295–297.

6. Fraïssé, R., "Sur quelques classifications des systèmes de relations," *Publ. Sci. Univ. Alger Ser.* A, 1 (1954), 35–182.

7. Gessel, I. M., "Combinatorial proofs of congruences," preprint.

8. Goulden, I. P., Jackson, D. M. and Reilly, J. W., "The Hammond series of a symmetric function and its application to P-recursiveness," *SIAM J. Alg. Disc. Meth.* 4 (1983), 179–193.

9. Motzkin, T. S., "Sorting numbers for cylinders and other classification numbers," *Proc. of Symposia in Pure Mathematics* 19 (1971), 167–176.

10. von Neumann, J. and Morgenstern, O., *Theory of Games and Economic Behavior*, 2nd ed., Princeton University Press, Princeton, N.J., 1947.

11. Shafaat, A., "On the number of topologies definable for a finite set," *J. Australian Math. Soc.* 8 (1968), 194–198.

12. Stanley, R. P., "Differentiably finite power series," *Europ. J. Combinatorics* 1 (1980), 175–188.

13. Touchard, J., "Propriétés arithmétiques de certains nombres récurrents," *Ann. Soc. Sci. Bruxelles* 53A (1933), 21–31.

Part II
Database Theory

Chapter 5

Fundamentals of Dependency Theory

MOSHE Y. VARDI*

5.1 INTRODUCTION

A *database management system* (DBMS) is essentially a computer system containing a large permanent store of data, with special routines and procedures for handling that data. As such systems evolved over the years, certain ideas emerged as the key features of DBMS's: *integration*, *views*, and *data independence*.

Integration means that a DBMS enables many applications to share data in common, thus sharing costs and eliminating redundancy. Integration does not mean that all applications have to adopt the same *view* of the data. Rather, every application can have its own view, thus "seeing" only the data that is relevant to it. Finally, *data independence* means that the application programs are shielded from the details of the physical organization of the data, and they need not be affected by a physical reorganization of the data.

The main problem with DBMS's that were developed in the 1960s was that they did not quite achieve data independence. While application programs did not have to deal with details of physical storage, they were still dependent on the ordering in which data was stored, on the way in which it was indexed, and on the access paths that were *a priori* chosen by the database designer.

The *relational model* was introduced by Codd (18) with the goal of achieving a greater degree of data independence. It is based on two fundamental ideas:

1. All information in a relational database is represented as data values in relations (tables).

2. No information is represented by the ordering among columns or tuples (rows) in the relations.

---

* Address: IBM Almaden Research Center K53-802, 650 Harry Rd., San Jose, CA 95120-6099, USA.

Thus, one can say that the relational model of data is almost devoid of semantics. A tuple in a relation represents a relationship between certain values, but it does not represent any information about the nature of this relationship, such as whether it is a one-to-one or a one-to-many relationship.

One approach to remedy this deficiency is to devise means to specify the missing semantics. These semantic specifications are called *semantic* or *integrity constraints*, since they specify which databases are meaningful for the application and which are meaningless. Of particular interest are the constraints called *data dependencies*, or dependencies for short.

Dependency theory, the theory of data dependencies in the relational model, has been an active area of research in the last decade. This article is meant to serve as an introduction to this area. Rather than describe the historical development of the theory, we shall describe it with the wisdom of hindsight. More comprehensive surveys can be found in the books (43, 56) and in (29).

5.2 BASIC DEFINITIONS

5.2.1 The Relational Model

We now describe the mathematical model that aims at capturing our intuition about tables where both columns and tuples are essentially unordered. The first thing that we model is the fact that columns in a table have names; these are the column headings. In dependency theory they are called *attributes*. We assume that attributes are symbols taken from a given finite set $U = \{A_1, \ldots, A_n\}$. Following customary notation in dependency theory, we use the letters A, B, C, $\ldots$, H to denote attributes, and we use R, S, $\ldots$, X, Y, Z to denote attribute sets. We usually do not distinguish between the attribute A and the attribute set $\{A\}$. The union of X and Y is denoted by XY. Thus, ABD denotes the set $\{A,B,D\}$. The complement of X in U is denoted by $\overline{X}$.

Underlying each column in a table there is a domain of values, out of which the entries in that column are taken. Thus, with each attribute A we associate a set $DOM(A)$, called the *domain* of A. For simplicity we assume that $DOM(A)$ is an infinite set. (This assumption is not always realistic. Consider, for example, the attribute *SEX*.) We denote by *Dom* the set $\bigcup_{A \in U} DOM(A)$.

A tuple spanning a set of columns is essentially an assignment of an entry to each column, where the entries are taken from the corresponding domains. Thus, a *tuple* on an attribute set X is a mapping $u:X \rightarrow Dom$, such that $u(A) \in DOM(A)$ for all $A \in X$. A *relation* on X is a set of tuples on X. (We do not yet require that this set be finite, even though this seems to be a very reasonable requirement, but we allow it to be either finite or infinite. We shall come back to this point later.) If I is a relation on X, then X is called the *scheme* of I.

Here are some more conventions. We denote tuples by the letters u, v, . . . , and we denote relations by the letters I, J, ... Unless explicitly stated otherwise, a tuple is a tuple on U and a relation is a relation on U.

Example 5.1

Consider the following table:

EMP	DEPT	MGR
Hilbert	Math	Gauss
Pythagoras	Math	Gauss
Turing	Computer Science	von Neumann

This is a relation on the attribute set {EMP, DEPT, MGR}. The domain of EMP is the set of employees, the domain of DEPT is the set of departments, and the domain of MGR is the set of managers. The relation consists of three tuples, each one being a mapping from the set of attributes to their associated domains. For example, the first tuple is a mapping u such that $u(\text{EMP})$ = Hilbert, $u(\text{DEPT})$ = Math, and $u(\text{MGR})$ = Gauss. ∎

5.2.2 Operations on Relations

We now describe two operations of Codd's *relational algebra* (20). The *projection* operation is a unary operations on relations whereby a subset of the columns is selected. That is, if I is a relation on X and Y is a subset of X, then the projection of I on Y, denoted $\pi_Y(I)$, is obtained by deleting the columns corresponding to attributes in $Y - X$ and eliminating duplicate tuples in the result.

We now give a formal definition. For a tuple w on X and $Y \subseteq X$, we denote by $w[Y]$ the restriction of w to Y. Thus, $w[Y]$ is a tuple on Y. (Note that for tuple w on X and an attribute $A \in X$, $w[A]$ is a tuple on A, while $w(A)$ is an element in $DOM(A)$. We will not distinguish, however, between the two.) Let I be a relation on X and $Y \subseteq X$. Then $\pi_Y(I) = \{w[Y] : w \in I\}$. Thus $\pi_Y(I)$ is a relation on Y.

Example 5.2

Let I be the relation in Example 5.1. $\pi_{\{DEPT, MGR\}}(I)$ is the relation:

DEPT	MGR
Math	Gauss
Computer Science	von Neumann

$\pi_{\{EMP,DEPT\}}(I)$ is the relation:

EMP	DEPT
Hilbert	Math
Pythagoras	Math
Turing	Computer Science

The *join* operation can be viewed as the dual of the projection operation. It combines together tuples from several relations when these tuples agree on the columns that they have in common. Formally, if $I_1, \ldots, I_k$ are relations on $X_1, \ldots, X_k$, respectively, then their join, denoted $I_1 * \cdots * I_k$ (or $\overset{k}{\underset{j=1}{*}} I_j$), is a relation on $X = \overset{k}{\underset{j=1}{\cup}} X_j$ defined by

$$\overset{k}{\underset{j=1}{*}} I_j = \{w \text{ is a tuple on } X : w[X_j] \in I_j, \text{ for } 1 \leq j \leq k\}.$$

Note that the join is commutative and associative.

Example 5.3

Consider the two relations of Example 5.2. Their join is the relation of Example 5.1.

The reader may wonder whether the projection and the join are inverse to each other. The following examples show that this is not the case.

Example 5.4

Let I be the relation

A	B	C
0	0	0
1	0	1

Then $\pi_{AB}(I) * \pi_{BC}(I)$ is the relation

A	B	C
0	0	0
1	0	1
0	0	1
1	0	0

Example 5.5

Let I be the relation

A	B
0	0
0	1

Let J be the relation

B	C
0	0
0	1

Then $\pi_{AB}(I * J)$ is the relation

A	B
0	0

and $\pi_{BC}(I * J)$ is the relation

B	C
0	0
0	1

■

The following lemma asserts that the above examples are typical.

LEMMA 5.1

1. Let I be a relation on X, and let $X_1, \ldots, X_m$ be attribute sets such that $X = \bigcup_{j=1}^{m} X_j$. Then $I \subseteq \mathop{*}\limits_{j=1}^{m} \pi_{X_j}(I)$.

2. Let $I_1, \ldots, I_m$ be relations on $X_1, \ldots, X_m$, respectively. Then $\pi_{X_j}(\mathop{*}\limits_{k=1}^{k} I_k) \subseteq I_j$. ■

The simultaneous projection of I on $X_1, \ldots, X_m$ (as in Lemma 5.1(1)) is called a *decomposition*. If we are lucky to have that $I = \mathop{*}\limits_{j=1}^{m} \pi_{X_j}(I)$, then we say that the decomposition of I to $\pi_{X_1}(I), \ldots, \pi_{X_m}(I)$ is *lossless*, since these relations can be joined to recover the original relation with no loss of information. If $I \subset$

$\overset{m}{\underset{j=1}{*}} \pi_{X_j}(I),$ then we say that the decomposition is *lossy* (we use $\subseteq$ to denote containment, and we use $\subset$ to denote *proper* containment).

5.3 FUNCTIONAL DEPENDENCIES

5.3.1 Motivation

When designing a relational database, we are often faced with a choice between alternative sets of relation scheme. Some choices are better than others for various reasons. Consider, for example, the database in Example 5.1. This database suffers from several problems, called *anomalies* by Codd (19):

1. *Redundancy*. The information that Gauss is the manager of the Mathematics Department is repeated more than once.
2. *Possible inconsistency*. Suppose now that we are asked to change Hilbert's manager from Gauss to von Neuman. Then we are faced with the situation that the Mathematics Department has two managers. It is doubtful whether that was the intention of the change.

Indeed, it seems that a better database design would be to store the data in relations as in Example 5.2, which does not suffer from the above anomalies.

A close look at the problem suggests that the source of the problem is that the first design ignores certain dependencies in the data, e.g., the fact that (as we suppose) every department has a unique manager. In other words, there is a *functional dependency* between DEPT and MGR. We start now with the study of functional dependencies, and shall come back later to the issue of database design.

5.3.2 Functional Dependencies

A *functional dependency* (abbr. fd) is a statement that describes a semantic constraint on data (19). Formally, an fd is an expression of the form $X \rightarrow Y$, read *X functionally determines Y*, where X and Y are attribute sets. $X \rightarrow Y$ is *over* an attribute set R if $XY \subseteq R$. $X \rightarrow Y$ is *satisfied* by a relation I on R if $X \rightarrow Y$ is over R and for all tuples $u, v \in I$, if $u[X] = v[X]$, then $u[Y] = v[Y]$. Intuitively, I satisfies $X \rightarrow Y$ if $I[XY]$ can be viewed as a function from tuples on X to tuples on Y. I satisfies a set Σ of fd's if I satisfies all fd's in Σ. A set Σ of fd's is said to be *over* an attribute set R if all fd's in Σ are over R, e.g., the set $\{A \rightarrow B, BC \rightarrow D\}$ is over the set $ABCDE$.

Example 5.6

Consider again the relation:

EMP	DEPT	MGR
Hilbert	Math	Gauss
Pythagoras	Math	Gauss
Turing	Computer Science	Von Neumann

It is easy to verify that this relation satisfies the fd's EMP→DEPT, DEPT→MGR, and MGR→DEPT. It does not, however, satisfy the fd DEPT→EMP. ∎

A set of fd's can be viewed as a semantic specification for the database. That is, if we are given a set Σ of fd's, then only relations that satisfy all fd's in Σ are considered "meaningful." Relations that do not satisfy some fd in Σ cannot be actual representation of the data for the application in mind. In order to allow for symbolic manipulation of semantic specification, it stands to reason that we should be able to test mechanically for *equivalence* and *redundancy*. Two sets Δ and Σ of fd's are *equivalent* if they are satisfied by the same relations, i.e., if I satisfies Δ if and only if I satisfies Σ, for all relations I. In that case we also say that Δ is a *cover* for Σ. A set Σ of fd's is *redundant* if there is a proper subset Δ of Σ, i.e., $\Delta \subset \Sigma$, such that Δ and Σ are equivalent.

It is easy to see that both equivalence and redundancy reduce to a more basic notion, that of *implication*. A set Σ of fd's *implies* an fd σ, denoted $\Sigma \models \sigma$, if I satisfies σ whenever I satisfies Σ, for all relations I. Clearly, Σ is redundant if and only if there is some fd $\sigma \in \Sigma$ such that $\Sigma - \{\sigma\} \models \sigma$. Also, Δ and Σ are equivalent if and only if $\Delta \models \sigma$ for all $\sigma \in \Sigma$ and $\Sigma \models \delta$ for all $\delta \in \Delta$.

The relevance of implication to database theory became apparent in Bernstein's work on database design (8, 9), and was confirmed in later works, e.g., (13, 49). Today, implication is considered to be perhaps the most fundamental notion in dependency theory.

So far we have allowed both finite and infinite relations. We can try to be more realistic and consider only finite relations. Thus, we say that Σ *finitely implies* σ, denoted $\Sigma \models_f \sigma$, if I satisfies σ whenever I satisfies Σ for all *finite* relations I. Clearly, if $\Sigma \models \sigma$, then also $\Sigma \models_f \sigma$, but the reverse entailment does not seem to hold *a priori*. That is, it is conceivable that $\Sigma \models_f \sigma$, but there is some *infinite* relation I such that $I \models \Sigma$ and $I \not\models \sigma$.

As we said, we are interested in automatic manipulation of fd's. So we would like to solve the following decision problems. The *implication problem* is to decide, given a set Σ of fd's and an fd σ, whether $\Sigma \models \sigma$. The *finite implication problem* is to decide, given a set Σ, of fd's and an fd σ, whether $\Sigma \models_f \sigma$. Note that these are two independent decision problems. That is, a solution to any one of them does not solve the other one.

The reader may ask why we bother to deal with unrestricted implication at all, since finite implication seems to be the more interesting notion. The answer is that the relationship between implication and finite implication is a very significant one, as we shall see later.

5.3.3 Functional Dependencies and First-Order Logic

It is not hard to see that, as was observed by Nicolas (47), fd's can be represented as sentences in first-order logic. There is a minor difficulty, since our definition of relations is different from the way relations are usually defined. For the sake of this translation we assume that the attributes are ordered. Thus, if $R = \{A_1, \ldots, A_k\}$, then rather than view a relation on R as a set of mappings from R to *Dom*, we can view it as a subset of $DOM(A_1) \times \cdots \times DOM(A_k)$. For example, if $R = ABCD$, then we can assume that the attributes A, B, C, and D label the first, second, third, and fourth columns, correspondingly.

Consider now the fd $AB \rightarrow C$. We can express it by the first-order sentence

$$(\forall abc_1c_2d_1d_2)((\mathbf{R}abc_1d_1 \wedge \mathbf{R}abc_2d_2) \supset c_1 = c_2)).$$

Here $(\forall abc_1c_2d_1d_2)$ is shorthand for $(\forall a\forall b\forall c_1\forall c_2\forall d_1\forall d_2)$, i.e., all variables are universally quantified. $\mathbf{R}$ is the predicate symbol referring to the relevant relation. (Note that we have used here individual variables as in (15, 28) rather than tuple variables as in (47).) It is easy to see that we can express arbitrary fd's in this manner.

Since fd's are first-order sentences, we can apply certain operations to them. For example, if σ and τ are fd's, then we can consider $\sigma \wedge \tau$. Now $\sigma \wedge \tau$ is not an fd, but it is a perfectly legitimate first-order sentence. Similarly, we can consider $\neg\sigma$. That means that the implication and the finite implication problems can be reduced to classical decision problems for first-order logic. Let $\Sigma = \{\sigma_1, \ldots, \sigma_k\}$. Then $\Sigma \models \sigma$ if and only if $\sigma_1 \wedge \cdots \wedge \sigma_k \wedge \neg\sigma$ is *unsatisfiable*, and $\Sigma \models_f \sigma$ if and only if $\sigma_1 \wedge \cdots \wedge \sigma_k \wedge \neg\sigma$ is *finitely unsatisfiable*. (A sentence is (finitely) satisfiable if it has a (finite) model. It is (finitely) unsatisfiable if it has no (finite) model.)

By Godel's Completeness Theorem, unsatisfiability is *partially decidable*. That is, there is a procedure $\mathbf{P}_1$ with the following property. When given an unsatisfiable sentence τ, $\mathbf{P}_1$ will terminate and tell us that τ is unsatisfiable. When given a satisfiable sentence, τ, $\mathbf{P}_1$ will either terminate and tell us that τ is satisfiable or it will not terminate. Since implication reduces to unsatisfiability, it follows that the implication problem is partially decidable.

On the other hand, it is easy to see that finite satisfiability and, therefore, finite *nonimplication* are also partially decidable. To find out whether τ is finitely satisfiable we just have to enumerate all finite structures and check whether they happen to be models of τ. Since the collection of finite models (up to isomorphism) is clearly enumerable, if τ is finitely satisfiable, then our procedure will terminate and will tell us that τ is finitely satisfiable. If τ is not finitely satisfiable, then our procedure will not terminate. Let us call this procedure $\mathbf{P}_2$.

Suppose now that satisfiability and finite satisfiability coincide, that is, whenever there is a model, then there is also a finite model. Then both satisfiability and nonsatisfiability are partially decidable. But then it follows that they are actually decidable (51). Given a sentence τ, we simply run both $\mathbf{P}_1$ and $\mathbf{P}_2$ in parallel. Now, one of these procedures is guaranteed to terminate with an answer, and of course we can never get contradictory answers. So we have a decision procedure for satisfiability. We know very well, however, that satisfiability of first-order logic is undecidable, which means that satisfiability and finite satisfiability do not coincide. But for many classes of first-order sentences satisfiability and finite satisfiability do coincide, and for such classes satisfiability is decidable. Indeed, the standard technique for proving decidability for classes of first-order sentences is by proving that satisfiability and finite satisfiability coincide (23). Similarly, if we could prove that implication and finite implication coincided for fd's, then it would follow that the implication problem is decidable (and of course so also would be the finite implication problem, since it would be equivalent to the implication problem).

Let us see now what kind of first-order sentences we get when we reduce (finite) implications of fd's to first-order (finite) unsatisfiability. As we saw before, fd's are essentially universal sentences. When we reduce (finite) implication to (finite) unsatisfiability, we take the conjunction of several fd's with the negation of an fd. The resulting sentence $\sigma_1 \wedge \cdots \wedge \sigma_k \wedge \neg\sigma$ can be written as an $\forall^*\exists^*$ sentence, that is, a sentence in prenex normal form whose quantifier prefix consists of a string of universal quantifiers followed by a string of existential quantifiers. The class of such sentences is known as the *initially extended Bernayes-Schonfinkel class*. We abbreviate this long name and call this class the BS class. The BS class has been studied by logicians in the 1920s, and they have shown that satisfiability and finite satisfiability for this class coincide (23). Thus, we have proven the following theorem.

THEOREM 5.1   For fd's, implication and finite implication coincide, and the corresponding decision problems (which also coincide) are decidable.   ■

This was the good news. The bad news is that though the decision problem for the BS class is decidable, it is highly intractable; even nondeterministic algorithms for this problem require exponential time (39). Thus, reducing implication of fd's to unsatisfiability of BS sentences does not give us a *practical* algorithm. Since the sentences that arise from the reduction of implication to unsatisfiability form a proper subclass of the BS class, we still can hope to find a better algorithm for the implication problem for fd's. To develop such an algorithm we have to study the properties of fd's in more detail.

5.3.4 Formal System for Functional Dependencies

We now try to gain better understanding of fd implication by studying *formal systems*. Formal systems consist of *axiom schemes* and *inference rules* (axiom schemes can be viewed as inference rules with no premises). Given a formal system **F**, a *derivation* of a dependency σ from a set Σ of fd's is a sequence $\sigma_1, \ldots, \sigma_n$, where σ_n is σ and each σ_i is either an instance of an axiom scheme or follows from preceding dependencies in the sequence by one of the inference rules. $\Sigma \vdash \sigma$ denotes that there is a derivation of σ from Σ. We say that **F** is *sound* if $\Sigma \vdash \sigma$ entails $\Sigma \models \sigma$, and it is *complete* if $\Sigma \models \sigma$ entails $\Sigma \vdash \sigma$. (Note that we are now talking solely about unrestricted implication, since we know that implication and finite implication coincide for fd's.)

Since fd's can be expressed as first-order sentences, it might be argued that there is no need to develop formal systems for fd's, because any formal system for first-order logic will do. However, fd's are just a fragment of first-order logic, a fragment that seems to be suitable to expressing integrity constraints of databases. As we are trying here to gain better understanding into implication of fd's, we would like to have a formal system which would enable us to infer only fd's and not general first-order sentences, unlike a formal system for first-order logic.

Formal systems for implication of fd's were first studied by Armstrong (2), even though the importance of implication was not yet realized when his paper appeared in 1974. We present here a formal system **FD** that is somewhat different from Armstrong's system. **FD** consists of one axiom scheme and two inference rules:

> **FD**0 (reflexivity axiom): $\vdash X \rightarrow \varnothing$.
> **FD**1 (transitivity): $X \rightarrow Y,\ Y \rightarrow Z \vdash X \rightarrow Z$.
> **FD**2 (augmentation): $X \rightarrow Y \vdash XZ \rightarrow YZ$.

Note that the above axiom and rules are schemes; any attribute set can be substituted for X, Y, and Z.

Example 5.7

Let $U = ABCDE$, let Σ consists of the fd's $A \rightarrow B$, $A \rightarrow C$, and $BC \rightarrow DE$, and let σ be $A \rightarrow E$. We show that $\Sigma \vdash \sigma$. By **FD**2, we have $A \rightarrow B \vdash A \rightarrow AB$ and

$A{\rightarrow}C \vdash AB{\rightarrow}BC$. By **FD1**, we have $A{\rightarrow}AB$, $AB{\rightarrow}BC \vdash A{\rightarrow}BC$, and $A{\rightarrow}BC$, $BC{\rightarrow}DE \vdash A{\rightarrow}DE$. Now, by **FD0** and **FD2**, we have $\vdash DE{\rightarrow}E$, so by another application of **FD1**, we get $\Sigma \vdash A{\rightarrow}E$. ∎

Before proving soundness and completeness, we need a technical lemma.

LEMMA 5.2 $X{\rightarrow}Y, X{\rightarrow}Z \vdash X{\rightarrow}YZ$.

Proof By **FD2**, $X{\rightarrow}Y \vdash X{\rightarrow}XY$, and $X{\rightarrow}Z \vdash XY{\rightarrow}YZ$. The claim follows by **FD1**. ∎

THEOREM 5.2 The system **FD** is sound and complete.

Proof

Soundness: To prove soundness it suffices to show that the axiom and the inference rules are sound. **FD0** is vacuously sound. Let I be a relation, and let $u, v \in I$. Suppose that I satisfies $X{\rightarrow}Y$ and $Y{\rightarrow}Z$. If $u[X] = v[X]$, then $u[Y] = v[Y]$, so $u[Z] = v[Z]$. Thus, I satisfies $X{\rightarrow}Z$, and **FD1** is sound. Finally, suppose that I satisfies $X{\rightarrow}Y$. If $u[XZ] = v[XZ]$, then $u[X] = v[X]$, so $u[Y] = v[Y]$, and therefore $u[YZ] = v[YZ]$. Thus, I satisfies $XZ{\rightarrow}YZ$, and **FD2** is sound.

Completeness: We have to show that if $\Sigma \models \sigma$, then $\Sigma \vdash \sigma$. We prove the contrapositive: if $\Sigma \nvdash \sigma$, then $\Sigma \nvDash \sigma$.

Let σ be $X{\rightarrow}Y$. Define an attribute set $X^{+} = \{A : \Sigma \vdash X{\rightarrow}A\}$. By **FD0** and **FD2**, we have that $\vdash X{\rightarrow}A$, for $A \in X$, so $X \subseteq X^{+}$. By Lemma 5.2, we have that $\Sigma \vdash X{\rightarrow}X^{+}$. We claim that Y is not a subset of X^{+}. Suppose it is. Then by **FD0** and **FD2**, $\Sigma \vdash X^{+}{\rightarrow}Y$, and since we know that $\Sigma \vdash X{\rightarrow}X^{+}$, it follows, by **FD1**, that $\Sigma \vdash X{\rightarrow}Y$—a contradiction. Thus, there must be some attribute B that is a member of Y but not a member of X^{+}.

We construct a relation I as follows. I consists of two tuples u and v, such that u and v agree precisely on X^{+}. For example, $u[A] = 0$ for each attribute A, $v[A] = 0$ for each attribute $A \in X^{+}$, and $v[A] = 1$ for each attribute $A \in U - X^{+}$. Clearly , $u[A] = v[X]$ but $u[Y] \neq v[Y]$. So I does not satisfy $X{\rightarrow}Y$.

We now claim that I satisifes Σ. Let $S{\rightarrow}T$ be an fd in Σ. Suppose that $u[S] = v[S]$. But then we must have that $S \subseteq X^{+}$. Thus, by **FD0**, **FD1**, and **FD2**, we have that $S{\rightarrow}T \vdash X^{+}{\rightarrow}T$. Now, by **FD0** and **FD2**, we have that $\vdash T{\rightarrow}A$ for $A \in T$. Therefore, by **FD1**, we have that $\Sigma \vdash X^{+}{\rightarrow}A$, for all attributes $A \in T$. But then $T \subseteq X^{+}$ and $u[T] = v[T]$.

Thus, I satisfies Σ and it does not satisfy σ, so $\Sigma \nvDash \sigma$. ∎

Note that the above proof is also a direct proof that for fd's implication and finite implication coincide, since the *counterexample* relation that we have constructed is finite (a counterexample relation for an implication $\Sigma \models \sigma$ is a relation that satisfies Σ but not σ).

5.3.5 Functional Dependencies and Propositional Logic

What is perhaps the most important fact about implication of fd's is buried in the proof of the completeness of the system **FD**. Before stating it, we need some definitions. A *two-tuple relation* is a relation that contains at most two tuples. To make things simpler we assume that a two-tuple relation consists of precisely two, possibly identical, tuples. We say that a set Σ of fd's *implies* an fd σ *with respect to two-tuple relations*, denoted $\Sigma \models_2 \sigma$, if I satisfies σ whenever I satisfies Σ, for all two-tuple relations I. Clearly, if $\Sigma \models_f \sigma$, then also $\Sigma \models_2 \sigma$. The proof of Theorem 5.2 shows that the reverse entailment also holds.

THEOREM 5.3 Let Σ be a set of fd's, and σ be an fd. Then $\Sigma \models \sigma$ if and only if $\Sigma \models_f \sigma$ if and only if $\Sigma \models_2 \sigma$. ∎

The reader may wonder why the sudden interest in two-tuple relations. After all, most real databases usually contain more than just two tuples. Before explaining the importance of Theorem 5.3, we define a new notion of implication, seemingly unrelated to our previous definition. This definition is based on viewing fd's as formulas in propositional logic. According to this view, each attribute can be viewed as a propositional symbol that can be assigned truth values. Thus, we define a *relational truth assignment* ψ as a mapping $\psi: U \rightarrow \{0,1\}$. We extend ψ to give truth assignment to attribute sets by defining $\psi(X) = \prod_{A \in X} \psi(A)$. That is, ψ assigns the value 1 to X if and only if it assigns the value 1 to all attributes in X. We can now extend relational truth assignments to assign truth values to fd's in the following manner: ψ assigns the value 1 to $X \rightarrow Y$ if only if whenever $\psi(X) = 1$, then also $\psi(Y) = 1$. For example if $\psi(A) = 1$, $\psi(B) = 1$, and $\psi(C) = 0$, then $\psi(A \rightarrow B) = 1$ and $\psi(AB \rightarrow C) = 0$. We can also extend ψ to sets of fd's by defining $\psi(\Sigma) = \prod_{\sigma \in \Sigma} \psi(\sigma)$. That is, ψ assigns the value 1 to the set Σ if and only if it assigns the value 1 to all fd's in Σ. We say that a set Σ of fd's *propositionally implies* an fd σ, denoted $\Sigma \models_p \sigma$, if $\psi(\Sigma) = 1$ entails $\psi(\sigma) = 1$ for any relational truth assignment ψ. This notion of implication for dependencies may seem to be quite unmotivated. Surprisingly enough, propositional implication turns out to coincide with implication.

THEOREM 5.4 (26) Let Σ be a set of fd's, and σ be an fd. Then $\Sigma \models \sigma$ if and only if $\Sigma \models_p \sigma$.

Proof By Theorem 5.3, it suffices to show that $\Sigma \models_2 \sigma$ iff $\Sigma \models_p \sigma$. The basis for this equivalence is a simple correspondence between relational truth assignments and two-tuple relations.

Let ψ be a relational truth assignment. Then $I_\psi = \{u, v\}$ is a two tuple relation such that $u[A] = v[A]$ iff $\psi(A) = 1$. Let $I = \{u, v\}$ be a two-tuple relation. Then ψ_I is a relational truth assignment such that $\psi(A) = 1$ iff $u[A] = v[A]$. Let τ be any fd. The reader can verify that $\psi(\tau) = 1$ iff I_ψ satisfies τ, and I satisfies τ iff $\psi_I(\tau) = 1$. Similar correspondence holds for sets of fd's. Suppose now that $\Sigma \models_2 \sigma$. We want to show that $\Sigma \models_p \sigma$. Let ψ be a relational truth assignment such that $\psi(\Sigma) = 1$. Then I_ψ satisfies Σ, and since $\Sigma \models_2 \sigma$, it must be the case that I_ψ satisfies σ. But then $\psi(\sigma) = 1$. We have shown that $\psi(\Sigma) = 1$ entails $\psi(\sigma) = 1$ for any relational truth assignment σ, so $\Sigma \models_p \sigma$. An analogous argument shows that if $\Sigma \models_p \sigma$, then also $\Sigma \models_2 \sigma$. ∎

The significance of Theorem 5.4 is that it enables us to view fd's as formulas in propositional logic. Namely, the fd $A_1 \cdots A_k \to B_1 \cdots B_l$ can be viewed as the formula $A_1 \wedge \cdots \wedge A_k \supset B_1 \wedge \cdots \wedge B_l$, where the A's and the B's are viewed as propositional symbols. Furthermore, such a formula is equivalent to a set of *Horn* formulas, and so is its negation. (Horn formulas are formulas in one of the following forms: $A_1 \wedge \cdots \wedge A_k \to B$, B, or $\neg A_1 \vee \cdots \vee \neg A_k$, where the A's and B are propositional symbols.) For example, the formula $A \supset BC$ is equivalent to the set $\{A \supset B, A \supset C\}$, and the formula $\neg(A \supset BC)$ is equivalent to the set $\{A, \neg B \vee \neg C\}$. Thus, the conjunction $\sigma_1 \wedge \cdots \wedge \sigma_k \wedge \neg \sigma$ is equivalent to a set of Horn formulas. While no polynomial algorithm is known for satisfiability of propositional logic, for Horn formulas satisfiability can be tested in polynomial time. So, as a consequence of Theorem 5.4, we obtain a polynomial time algorithm for the implication problem for fd's.

Interestingly, a polynomial time algorithm for fd implication was discovered by Beeri and Bernstein (3) independently of the discovery of the correspondence between fd's and propositional logic. Their algorithm is based on a fast construction of *closure* sets with respect to a given set of fd's. Formally, the *closure* of an attribute set X with respect to a set Σ of fd's, denoted $cl_\Sigma(X)$, is the set $\{A : \Sigma \models X \to A\}$ (so the set X^+ in the proof of Theorem 5.2 is exactly $cl_\Sigma(X)$). Note that $X \subseteq cl_\Sigma(X)$. The proof of the following lemma is easy and is left to the reader.

LEMMA 5.3 $\Sigma \models X \to Y$ if and only if $Y \subseteq cl_\Sigma(X)$. ∎

Thus, to test implication of $X \to Y$ by Σ it suffices to construct $cl_\Sigma(X)$ and then to test whether $Y \subseteq cl_\Sigma(X)$.

Algorithm 5.1

Input:　A set Σ of fd's and an attribute set X.
Output:　$cl_\Sigma(X)$.
　CLOSURE(Σ, X)
　begin
　　$Y := X$;
　　while there exists an fd $S \rightarrow T$ in Σ such that $S \subseteq Y$ and $T \not\subseteq Y$ **do**
　　　$Y := YT$
　　end while
　return(Y)
　end.

We have to show that CLOSURE(Σ, X) terminates and indeed returns $cl_\Sigma(X)$.

LEMMA 5.4　CLOSURE(Σ, X) terminates and returns $cl_\Sigma(X)$.

Proof　The algorithm clearly terminates. Let Z be the set constructed by the algorithm. We show first that $Z \subseteq cl_\Sigma(X)$ by induction on the steps of the algorithm. That is, we show that $Y \subseteq cl_\Sigma(X)$ at all stages of the algorithm. Originally, the claim is true, since $Y = X$. Suppose now that the claim is true for Y, and that there is an fd $S \rightarrow T$ in Σ such that $S \subseteq Y$. It is easy to see that in this case $\Sigma \models X \rightarrow A$ for all $A \in YT$ (use the formal system **FD**). Thus, $YT \subseteq cl_\Sigma(X)$.

It remains to show that it is impossible that Z is a proper subset of $cl_\Sigma(X)$. Suppose it is, and let $B \in cl_\Sigma(X) - Z$. Since $B \in cl_\Sigma(X)$, it means that $\Sigma \models X \rightarrow B$. Let $I = \{u, v\}$ be a two-tuple relation such that $u[A] = v[A]$ iff $A \in Z$. Clearly, I does not satisfy $X \rightarrow B$. We claim now that I satisfies Σ. Suppose it does not. Then there must be some fd $S \rightarrow T$ in Σ such that $S \subseteq Z$ but $T \not\subseteq Z$. But in this case the algorithm could not have terminated. Thus, I satisfies Σ, but it does not satisfy $X \rightarrow B$, so $\Sigma \not\models X \rightarrow B$—a contradiction. It follows that $Z = cl_\Sigma(X)$.　　　　■

The alert reader may have noticed the similarity in the proofs of Theorem 5.2 and Lemma 5.4. Indeed, one can view an execution of the algorithm as an organized derivation in the formal system **FD**.

Example 5.8

Let $U = ABCDEF$, and let Σ consists of the fd's $A \rightarrow B$, $A \rightarrow C$, and $BC \rightarrow DE$. Let us calculate $cl_\Sigma(A)$. Initially $Y = A$. We then apply the fd $A \rightarrow B$, since $A \subseteq Y$, and set $Y = AB$. We then apply the fd $A \rightarrow C$ and set $Y = ABC$. Finally, we apply the fd $BC \rightarrow DE$ and set $Y = ABCDE$. So $cl_\Sigma(A) = ABCDE$.　　　　■

It is not hard to implement CLOSURE to run in polynomial time. Beeri and Bernstein showed how to implement it to run in *linear* time.

THEOREM 5.5   (3) The implication problem for fd's can be solved in time that is linear in the length of the input.   ∎

5.3.6   Covers

Now that we can test implication efficiently, we can also test equivalence and redundancy efficiently. In particular, we can find efficiently *nonredundant covers*. (Recall the Δ is a cover for Σ if Δ and Σ are equivalent.)

Algorithm 5.2

> Input: A set Σ of fd's.
> Output: A nonredundant cover of Σ.
>   NONREDUN(Σ)
>   **begin**
> $\Delta := \Sigma$;
>   **for** each fd σ in Δ **do**
>   **if** $\Delta - \{\sigma\} \models \sigma$ **then** $\Delta := \Delta - \{\sigma\}$
>   **end for**
>   **return**(Δ)
>   **end**.

Example 5.9

Let $U = ABC$, and let Σ consist of the fd's $A{\rightarrow}B$, $B{\rightarrow}A$, $B{\rightarrow}C$, and $A{\rightarrow}C$. Then NONREDUN(Σ) returns the set $\{A{\rightarrow}B, B{\rightarrow}A, A{\rightarrow}C\}$. Note that the set returned by the algorithm depends on the order in which Σ is presented. If Σ is presented in the order $\{A{\rightarrow}B, A{\rightarrow}C, B{\rightarrow}A, B{\rightarrow}C\}$, then NONREDUN($\Sigma$) returns the set $\{A{\rightarrow}B, B{\rightarrow}A, B{\rightarrow}C\}$. Note that $\{A{\rightarrow}B, B{\rightarrow}A, AB{\rightarrow}C\}$ is also a nonredundant cover of Σ.   ∎

The above example shows that a given set of fd's can have many nonredundant covers, some of which may not be a subset of the given set. For economical reasons it is desirable to find the cover with the smallest number of fd's. Formally, Δ is a *minimum cover* of Σ if Δ is a cover of Σ and whenever Γ is also a cover of Σ then $|\Delta| \leq |\Gamma|$. Algorithm 5.2 supplies us with nonredundant covers, but these are not necessarily minimum covers.

THEOREM 5.6   (42) There is an algorithm for finding minimum covers in time that is quadratic in the length of the input.   ∎

At this point the reader may suspect that everything we care to know about fd's can be found in polynomial time. Unfortunately, this does not seem to be the case, as is demonstrated by a slight variant of the minimum cover problem, which is to find a *minimum contained cover of* Σ. A cover Δ of Σ is a *contained cover* if $\Delta \subseteq \Sigma$. Δ is a minimum contained cover of Σ if it is a contained cover of Σ, and there is no smaller contained cover of Σ. Formally, the minimum contained cover problem is: given a set Σ of fd's and an integer k, is there a contained cover Δ of Σ such that $|\Delta| \leq k$?

THEOREM 5.7   (8) The minimum contained cover problem is NP-complete.

∎

NP-complete problems are problems that can be solved in polynomial time using "guesses" (in the minimum cover problem we can guess a subset of Σ and check that it is a cover of Σ and has at most k fd's), but probably cannot be solved in polynomial time by any deterministic algorithm. We assume familiarity with the theory of NP-completeness. A good textbook in the subject is (31).

Notice that if we could actually find minimum contained covers in polynomial time, then we could clearly solve the minimum contained cover problem in polynomial time. Thus, Theorem 5.7 can be viewed as strong evidence to the intractability of finding minimum contained covers.

5.4   DATABASE SCHEMA DESIGN

5.4.1   Normal Forms

We have argued in Section 5.3.1 that certain ways of storing the data might be better than other ways. In the example studied, it is better to store the data in two relations, one on {EMP, DEPT} and one on {DEPT, MGR}, rather than store it in one relation on {EMP, DEPT, MGR}. The decisions on the organization of the data are taken during the *database design* process. We concentrate here on one aspect of that process, which is the design of the *database schema*. The database schema specifies a list of relation schemes and a set of relations that are meaningful for each relation scheme. The latter is specified by means of dependencies. Formally, a *relation schema* is a pair (R, Σ) where R is a relation scheme, i.e., a set of attributes, and Σ is a set of fd's over R. (Note that we distinguish between a relation *scheme*, which is just an attribute set, and a relation *schema*, which consists also of a set of fd's.) A *database schema* is a collection $\mathbf{D} = ((R_1, \Sigma_1), \ldots , (R_k, \Sigma_k))$ of relation schemas, where $\bigcup_{i=1}^{k} R_i = U$. A database $\mathbf{B}$ over $\mathbf{D}$ is an assignment of a relation to each relation schema in $\mathbf{D}$, that is, each relation schema (R_i, Σ_i) in $\mathbf{D}$ is assigned a relation on R_i that satisfies Σ_i.

Example 5.10

A database schema for the database of Example 5.1 is

$$((\{EMP, DEPT, MGR\}, \{EMP \rightarrow DEPT, DEPT \rightarrow MGR\})).$$

A database schema for the database of Example 5.2 is

$$((\{EMP, DEPT\}, \{EMP \rightarrow DEPT\}),$$

$$(\{DEPT, MGR\}, \{DEPT \rightarrow MGR\})). \qquad \blacksquare$$

The problems described in Section 5.3.1 follow from the fact that an fd is more than just a semantic constraint; it is also a description of a basic piece of data. The fd DEPT→MGR says that every department has a unique manager, and it also intuitively says that the relationship between departments and managers is an independent semantic relationship. Without this functional dependency, the relationship between department and managers would have been merely a projection of the relationship between employees, departments, and managers, and there would be no anomalies. Thus, the source of the problem is the embedding of an independent semantic relationship in a bigger context. Note, however, that the mere presence of an fd does not necessarily cause a problem.

Example 5.11

Consider the database schema $((\{EMP, DEPT, SAL\}, \{EMP \rightarrow DEPT, EMP \rightarrow SAL\}))$, with the database:

EMP	DEPT	SAL
Hilbert	Math	$20000
Pythagoras	Math	$25000
Turing	Computer Science	$40000

For this database there is no problem of redundancy and possible inconsistency, even though the relationship between, say, employees and their departments is embedded in a bigger context, that of {EMP, DEPT, SAL}. The difference between this example and the problematic one is that here the bigger relationship, that of {EMP, DEPT, SAL}, is not independent from the smaller one, that of {EMP, DEPT}, since EMP functionally determines both DEPT and SAL. $\quad \blacksquare$

The above observation on the problem led Codd to the definition of the several *normal forms* (19, 21). We jump immediately to the strongest of them, the so-called *Boyce-Codd Normal Form* (BCNF). We first need a few definitions. Let $\mathbf{D} = ((R_1, \Sigma_1), \ldots, (R_k, \Sigma_k))$ be a database schema, and let $\Sigma = \bigcup_{i=1}^{k} \Sigma_i$. We say that an attribute set X is a *determinant* of R_i if $X \subseteq R_i$ and there is an attribute $A \in R_i - X$ such that $\Sigma \models X \rightarrow A$. X is a *superkey* of R_i if $X \subseteq R_i$ and $\Sigma \models X \rightarrow R_i$. We say that **D** is in BCNF if whenever X is a determinant of R_i, then X is a superkey of R_i. The intuition behind this definition is that if X is a determinant of R_i but not a superkey of R_i, then we have a semantic relationship embedded within a bigger independent context.

Example 5.12

The database schema

$$((\{EMP, DEPT, MGR\}, \{EMP \rightarrow DEPT, DEPT \rightarrow MGR\}))$$

is not in BCNF, since DEPT is a determinant but not a superkey. The database schema

$$((\{EMP, DEPT\}, \{EMP \rightarrow DEPT\}),$$

$$(\{DEPT, MGR\}, \{DEPT \rightarrow MGR\}))$$

is in BCNF.   ∎

5.4.2   Normalization through Decomposition

The solution suggested in Section 5.3.1 to the problem of anomalies was to change the database schema from

$$((\{EMP, DEPT, MGR\}, \{EMP \rightarrow DEPT, DEPT \rightarrow MGR\}))$$

to

$$((\{EMP, DEPT\}, \{EMP \rightarrow DEPT\}),$$

$$(\{DEPT, MGR\}, \{DEPT \rightarrow MGR\})),$$

and at the same time replace the relation on {EMP, DEPT, MGR} by its projections on {EMP, DEPT} and {DEPT, MGR}.

We noted before, however, that a decomposition of a relation into its projection can be lossy. Fortunately, the presence of fd's can guarantee the losslessness of the decomposition.

THEOREM 5.8   (34) Let I be a relation on R, and let X, Y, and Z be attribute sets such that $XYZ = R$. If I satisfies $X \rightarrow Y$, then the decomposition of I into $\pi_{XY}(I)$ and $\pi_{XZ}(I)$ is lossless.

Proof Let $J = \pi_{XY}(I) * \pi_{XZ}(I)$. We know that $I \subseteq J$, so we have to show that $J \subseteq I$. Let $u \in J$. Then $u[XY] \in \pi_{XY}(I)$ and $u[XZ] \in \pi_{XZ}(I)$. Thus, there are tuples $v, w \in I$ such that $u[XY] = v[XY]$ and $u[XZ] = w[XZ]$. Consequently, $v[X] = w[X]$, and since I satisfies $X \to Y$, it follows that $w[XY] = v[XY] = u[XY]$. Thus $w[XYZ] = u[XYZ]$, so $w = u$, since $XYZ = R$. $\blacksquare$

This suggests the process of *normalization* through *decomposition*. We need first some notation. Let Σ be a set of fd's, and let X be an attribute set. Then $\pi_X(\Sigma) = \{S \to T : S \to T \in \Sigma \text{ and } ST \subseteq X\}$. Let $\mathbf{D} = ((R_1, \Sigma_1), \ldots, (R_k, \Sigma_k))$ be database schema that is not in BCNF. Then there is a relation schema (R_i, Σ_i) and an attribute set X such that X is a determinant of R_i but is not a superkey of R_i. That is, there is an attribute $A \in R_i - X$ such that $\Sigma \models X \to A$, where $\Sigma = \bigcup_{i=1}^{k} \Sigma_i$. We then replace (R_i, Σ_i) by two relation schemas (R_i^1, Σ_i^1) and (R_i^2, Σ_i^2), where $R_i^1 = XA$, $R_i^2 = R_i - \{A\}$, and $\Sigma_i^j = \pi_{R_i^j}(\Sigma_i)$.

Corresponding to the decomposition of the relation schema (R_i, Σ_i) there is the decomposition of the relation on R_i into relations on R_i^1 and R_i^2. This decomposition is justified because of Theorem 5.8.

Since the process of normalization through decomposition produces smaller and smaller relation schemes it is clear that it must terminate producing a database schema in BCNF.

Example 5.13 (56)

Let $U = CTHRSG$, where C stands for "Course," T stands for "Teacher," H stands for "Hour," R stands for "Room," S stands for "Student," and G stands for "Grade." Σ consists of the following fd's:

$C \to T$	each course has one one teacher,
$HR \to C$	only one course can meet in a room at one time,
$HT \to R$	a teacher can be only in one room at one time,
$CS \to G$	each student has only one grade in each course, and
$HS \to R$	a student can be in only one room at one time.

We start with the database schema (U, Σ). This schema is not in BCNF, since CS is not a superkey of U, but $CS \to G$ is in Σ. Thus, we decompose U into CSG and $CTHRS$. The resulting database schema is $(CSG, \Sigma_1), (CTHRS, \Sigma_2))$, where $\Sigma_1 = \pi_{CSG}(\Sigma) = \{CS \to G\}$, and $\Sigma_2 = \pi_{CTHRS}(\Sigma) = \{C \to T, HR \to C, HT \to R, HS \to R\}$.

This schema is still not in BCNF, since C is not a superkey of $CTHRS$, but $C \to T$ is in Σ_2. So we decompose $CTHRS$ into CT and $CHRS$. The resulting database schema is $((CSG, \Sigma_1), (CT, \Sigma_3), (CHRS, \Sigma_4))$, where $\Sigma_3 = \pi_{CT}(\Sigma_2) = \{C \to T\}$, and $\Sigma_4 = \pi_{CHRS}(\Sigma_2) = \{HR \to C, HS \to R\}$.

This schema is still not in BCNF, since *HR* is not a superkey of *CHRS*, but $HR{\rightarrow}C$ is in Σ_4. So we decompose *CHRS* into *HRC* and *HRS*. The resulting database schema is

$$((CSG, \{CS{\rightarrow}G\}),$$
$$(CT, \{C{\rightarrow}T\}),$$
$$(HRC, \{HR{\rightarrow}C\})$$
$$(HRS, \{HS{\rightarrow}R\}))$$

The four relation schemas of this database schema tabulate respectively:

1. grades for students in courses,
2. the teacher of each course,
3. the hours and rooms where each course meet, and
4. the rooms in which students can be found at given hours.

This design is not a very good one. Rather than keep information about the rooms in which students can be found at given hours, it would make more sense to keep the information about the courses that students take at given hours. If we added to Σ the fd $CH{\rightarrow}R$ (which is redundant, since it follows from the other fd's), then we could have decomposed *CHRS* into *HRC* and *HSC*, yielding a more intuitive database schema. ∎

5.4.3 Problems with BCNF

In order to do normalization through decompositions we have to be able to check for violation of BCNF. Unfortunately, checking violations of BCNF is probably an intractable problem.

THEOREM 5.9 (3) The following problem is NP-complete: determine for a given database schema **D** whether **D** is not in BCNF.

Proof To prove that the problem is NP-complete we first have to show that it is in NP, and then we have to show that it is NP-hard, i.e., we have to reduce a known NP-complete problem to it.

We first show that the problem is in NP, i.e., can be solved in polynomial time using "guesses." Let $\mathbf{D} = ((R_1, \Sigma_i), \ldots, (R_k, \Sigma_k))$, and let $\Sigma = \bigcup_{i=1}^{k} \Sigma_i$. If **D** is not in BCNF, then there is some relation scheme R_i, an attribute set $X \subseteq R_i$, and an attribute $A \in R_i - X$ such that $\Sigma \models X{\rightarrow}A$ but $\Sigma \not\models X{\rightarrow}R_i$. To check that **D** is not in BCNF we guess R_i, X, and A, and check that the above conditions are satisfied. Clearly, this can be done in polynomial time.

To show that the problem is NP-hard we reduce it to the *hitting set problem*, which was shown to be NP-complete in (31). The hitting set problem is formulated as follows. Given a family $B_1, \ldots, B_m$ of subsets of a set $T = \{A_1, \ldots, A_n\}$, one has to decide if there exists a set $W \subseteq T$ such that for each i, $1 \le i \le m$, W and B_i have precisely one element in common. Such a W is called a *hitting set*. We now show a polynomial time algorithm that maps each instance the hitting set problem to a database schema, such that there exists a hitting set if and only if the produced schema is not in BCNF.

We take the set U of attributes to be $\{A_1, \ldots, A_n, B_1, \ldots, B_n, C, D\}$. The database schema consists of the following relation schemas. For each A_i and B_j such that $A_i \in B_j$, we have a relation schema $(A_iB_j, \{A_i{\to}B_j\})$. We also have a relation schema $(B_1 \cdots B_mC, \{B_1 \cdots B_m{\to}C\})$. Finally, we also have a relation schema

$$(A_1 \cdots A_nCD, \{CD{\to}A_1 \cdots A_n\} \cup \{A_iA_j{\to}CD : i \ne j$$

$$\text{and there is some } B_k \text{ such that } A_i \in B_k \text{ and } A_j \in B_k\}).$$

Clearly, we can generate this schema in polynomial time. Let Σ consists of all the fd's in the relation schemas.

Let $W \subseteq T$ be a hitting set. Then for each B_j there is some A_i such that $A_i \in W \cap B_j$. Therefore, $\Sigma \models W{\to}B_j$. It follows that $\Sigma \models W{\to}C$. That is, W is a determinant of $A_1 \cdots A_nCD$. We claim that $cl_\Sigma(W) = WB_1 \cdots B_mC$, so W is not a superkey of this relation schema. To prove this we have to show that for every fd τ in Σ either the left-hand side of τ is not a subset of $cl_\Sigma(W)$ or the right-hand side of τ is a subset of $cl_\Sigma(W)$. This can be shown by a case analysis.

Conversely, suppose that **D** is not in BCNF. A case analysis shows that the violation can be only in the last relation scheme. Suppose that $W \subseteq A_1 \cdots A_nCD$ is a determinant but not a key. This can happen only if W has precisely one element in common with each of the B_i's. So $W \cap T$ is a hitting set. ∎

Theorem 5.9 indicates one problem with normalization through decomposition. There is another problem with normalization, which goes beyond the issue of computational tractability. The basic idea underlying normalization is that of replacing a problematic database schema with a nonproblematic one. But this would clearly be meaningless unless the new schema in some sense represents the old one. This issue, the relationship between database schemas, is a significant issue in database theory, and we shall not go into it here ((4) is a good introduction to that subject). Rather we consider here normalization of database schemas of the form (U, Σ) (i.e., with a single relation schema). Such schemas are called *universal* schemas.

Let $\mathbf{D} = (U, \Sigma)$ be a universal schema, and let $\mathbf{D}' = ((R_1, \Sigma_1), \ldots, (R_k, \Sigma_k))$ be a database schema. We want to find conditions under which it makes sense to say that $\mathbf{D}'$ *represents* $\mathbf{D}$. We have already implicitly referred to one condition: that there is no loss of information in storing the data as a database over $\mathbf{D}'$ rather than a database over $\mathbf{D}$. There is, however, another natural condition: that all the Σ_i's be implied by Σ and that the Σ_i's together imply all the dependencies in Σ. To see why this is necessary, consider the following example.

Example 5.14

Let $U = CAZ$, where C stands for "City," A stands for "Address," and Z stands for "Zipcode." Σ consists of the following dependencies:

$CA \rightarrow Z$ city and address together determine the zipcode, and

$Z \rightarrow C$ the zipcode determines the city.

Let $\mathbf{D} = (U, \Sigma)$, and let $\mathbf{D}' = ((ZC, \{Z \rightarrow C\}), (ZA, \varnothing)\}$. Consider the following database $\mathbf{B}$ on $\mathbf{D}'$:

Z	C
10017	New York
10018	New York

Z	A
10017	33 1st Ave.
10018	33 1st Ave.

Does this database make sense? We claim it does not. Let us see why.

Consider the tuples of the relation on ZA in $\mathbf{B}$. This tuples represent data about addresses and their zipcodes. But this data make sense only if with each pair (address, zipcode) we can associate a city. Let c_1 and c_2 be the associated cities. That is, with (10017, 33 1st Ave.) we associate the city c_1, and with (10018, 33 1st Ave.) we associate the city c_2. But we know that the zipcode determines the city, so from the data in the relation on ZC it follows that both c_1 and c_2 must be "New York." But then we get that there are two zipcodes associated with the same address in New York, which violates the fd $CA \rightarrow Z$.

The problem with $\mathbf{D}'$ is that it represents the fd $Z \rightarrow C$, but it does not represent the fd $CA \rightarrow Z$. ■

Thus, in order for a database schema $\mathbf{D}'$ to represent a universal schema, the decomposition associated with $\mathbf{D}'$ should be lossless, and $\mathbf{D}'$ should *preserve* all dependencies in the universal schema. We now formalize these conditions. Let $\mathbf{D} = (U, \Sigma)$ be a universal schema, and let $\mathbf{D}' = ((R_1, \Sigma_1), \ldots, (R_k, \Sigma_k))$

be a database schema. We say that $\mathbf{D}'$ *represents* $\mathbf{D}$ if the following conditions hold:

1. For every relation I on U that satisfies Σ, the decomposition of I into $\pi_{R_1}(I), \ldots, \pi_{R_k}(I)$ is lossless.

2. $\Sigma \models \Sigma'$ and $\Sigma' \models \Sigma$, where $\Sigma' = \bigcup_{i=1}^{k} \Sigma_i$.

Looking again at the decomposition process we see that starting with a database schema $\mathbf{D} = (U, \Sigma)$ it produces a database schema $\mathbf{D}'$ such that condition (1) and half of condition (2) above are satisfied and $\mathbf{D}'$ is in BCNF. What we would like is to strengthen that to get a database schema that represents $\mathbf{D}$ and is in BCNF. Unfortunately, this is impossible.

THEOREM 5.10   Let $U = CAZ$, and let $\Sigma = \{CA{\rightarrow}Z, Z{\rightarrow}C\}$. There is no database schema in BCNF that represents $\mathbf{D} = (U, \Sigma)$.

Proof   We have seen in Example 5.14 that the schema $((ZC, \{Z{\rightarrow}C\}), (ZA, \varnothing))$ does not represent $\mathbf{D}$. An exhaustive analysis shows that no database schema in BCNF represents $\mathbf{D}$. ∎

Since not every universal database schema can be represented by a database schema in BCNF, this raises a natural decision problem: given a universal database schema (U, Σ), decide if there exists a database schema in BCNF that represents $\mathbf{D}$. We call this the *BCNF normalizability problem*.

THEOREM 5.11   (3)   The BCNF normalizability problem is NP-hard. ∎

5.4.4   Third Normal Form and Normalization via Synthesis

We saw in the previous section that BCNF is too stringent. Given a database schema $\mathbf{D} = (U, \Sigma)$ it is not always possible to get a database schema in BCNF that represents $\mathbf{D}$, and even when it is possible, it might be computationally intractable. One solution to the problem is to consider a somewhat weaker normal form that would be easier to use even though it may not solve all the anomalies. The *Third Normal Form* (3NF) is such a normal form (19). (Historically, 3NF came before BCNF.)

We need a few definitions. Let $\mathbf{D} = ((R_1, \Sigma_1), \ldots, (R_k, \Sigma_k))$ be a database schema, and let $\Sigma = \bigcup_{i=1}^{k} \Sigma_i$. We say that X is a *key* of R_i if X is a superkey of R_i and no proper subset of X is a superkey of R_i. An attribute $A \in R_i$ is *prime* in R_i if there is some key X of R_i such that $A \in X$. X is a *strong determinant* of R_i if $X \subseteq R_i$ and there is a nonprime attribute $A \in R_i - X$ such that $\Sigma \models X{\rightarrow}A$.

We say that **D** is in 3NF if whenever X is a strong determinant of R_i, then X is a superkey of R_i.

Example 5.15

Consider the universal schema $(ABCD, \{AB{\rightarrow}C\})$. $ABCD$ is a superkey but is not a key. ABD is a key. A, B, and D are prime attributes. AB is a strong determinant but is not a key, so this schema is not in 3NF. Consider now the schema $((ABC, \{AB{\rightarrow}C\}), (ABD, \varnothing))$. This schema is in 3NF and it represents the previous schema. ∎

Example 5.16

Consider the universal schema $(CAZ, \{CA{\rightarrow}Z, Z{\rightarrow}C\})$. CA is a key, so C is a prime attribute. Z is a determinant, but it is not a strong determinant. This schema is in 3NF but is not in BCNF. Consider the following database over this schema.

C	A	Z
New York	33 1st Ave.	10017
New York	34 1st Ave.	10017
New York	33 5th Ave.	10100

This database still suffers from the anomalies described in Section 5.3.1. ∎

3NF is a relaxation of BCNF that is designed to make decomposition work. When we have an fd $X{\rightarrow}A$ in a relation scheme R_i, we want to decompose R_i into XA and $R_i - A$. If, however, A is prime, then there some key $Y \subseteq R_i$ such that $A \in Y$. When be decompose R_i as suggested, the fd $Y{\rightarrow}R_i$ (since Y is a key) is lost, so the resulting schema does not represent the original one. If A is not prime, no such problem arises. Thus, 3NF does not solve all the anomalies, but, as we shall soon see, it has the property that every universal schema can be represented by a schema in 3NF. In fact, we even have a polynomial time algorithm that produces such a schema. The algorithm (9) works by "synthesizing" the relation schemas rather than refine the universal schema by successive decompositions. Thus, the method is called *normalization through synthesis*.

Before describing the synthesis approach, we show that normalization through decomposition is not a practical approach even when we try to achieve 3NF.

THEOREM 5.12   (7)   The following problem is NP-hard: determine for a given database scheme **D** whether **D** is not in 3NF.

Proof   To show that the problem is NP-hard we reduce it to the *prime attribute problem*, which was shown to be NP-complete in (41). The prime attribute problem is to determine for a universal schema $\mathbf{D} = (U, \Sigma)$ and an attribute $A \in U$ whether A is prime in U. Let $\mathbf{D} = (U, \Sigma)$ be a universal schema, and let $A \in U$. Let F be a new attribute. We define a universal schema $\mathbf{D}' = (U', \Sigma')$, where $U' = UF$, and $\Sigma' = \Sigma \cup \{U \rightarrow F\} \cup \{BF \rightarrow U : B \neq A\} \cup \{F \rightarrow A\}$. We claim that A is prime in U if and only if $\mathbf{D}'$ is in 3NF.

The argument is as follows. Because of the fd $U \rightarrow F$, every key of U is also a key of U'. In addition, BF is a key of U' for every $B \neq A$. Thus, A is prime in U' if and only if it is prime in U. Furthermore, all other attributes are prime in U'. Thus, F is a strong determinant of U' if and only if A is not prime in U. Since F is not a superkey of U', $\mathbf{D}'$ is in 3NF if and only if A is prime in U.

∎

To describe the synthesis algorithm we need some technical machinery.

LEMMA 5.5 $X \rightarrow A_1 \cdots A_k \models X \rightarrow A_i$, $1 \leq i \leq k$, and $\{X \rightarrow A_i : 1 \leq i \leq k\} \models X \rightarrow A_1 \cdots A_k$. ∎

As a consequence of the above lemma, we can always convert our fd's to fd's have a single attribute on the right-hand side. Such fd's are said to be in *canonical form*. For a set Σ of fd's, let CANONICAL(Σ) a *canonical cover* of Σ, i.e., a cover of Σ where all fd's are in canonical form.

Let Σ be a set of fd's and let $X \rightarrow Y$ be an fd in Σ. We say that $X \rightarrow Y$ is *reduced* in Σ if there is no proper subset Z of X such that $\Sigma \models Z \rightarrow Y$. Clearly, if $X \rightarrow Y$ is not reduced, then we can replace it by an fd with a smaller left-hand side. Σ is reduced if all fd's in Σ are reduced. The following algorithm uses our efficient test for implication of fd's to construct a reduced cover of Σ.

Algorithm 5.3

Input: A set Σ of fd's.
Output: A reduced cover of Σ.
   REDUCE(Σ)
   begin
      $\Delta := \Sigma$;
     for each fd $X \rightarrow Y$ in Δ **do**
       for each attribute A in X **do**
        if $\Delta \models X - A \rightarrow Y$ **then**
         remove A **from** X **in** $X \rightarrow Y$ **in** Δ
       end for
     end for
    return(Δ)
   end.

LEMMA 5.6   Let Σ be a nonredundant set of fd's in canonical form. Then REDUCED(Σ) is a reduced nonredundant canonical cover of Σ.

Proof   Clearly all fd's stay in canonical form, and it is easy to see that the algorithm does not introduce any redundancy.   ■

Let Σ be a set of fd's, and let R be a relation scheme. A *key* of R with respect to Σ is an attribute set X such that $\Sigma \models X{\rightarrow}R$ and for no proper subset Y of X we have that $\Sigma \models Y{\rightarrow}R$. The following algorithm construct keys.

Algorithm 5.4

> Input: A set Σ of fd's and a relation scheme R.
> Output: A key of R with respect to Σ
>   KEY(R,Σ)
>   **begin**
> $X:= R$;
>   **for** each attribute A in R **do**
>   **if** $\Sigma \models X - A{\rightarrow}R$ **then** $X:= X - A$
>   **end for**
>   **return**(X)
>   **end**.

We can now describe the synthesis algorithm.

Algorithm 5.5

> Input: A universal schema (U,Σ).
> Output: A database scheme **D** in 3NF that represents (U,Σ).
>   3NF(U,Σ)
>   **begin**
> $\Delta:=$ REDUCED(NONREDUN(CANONICAL(Σ)))
> $X:=$ KEY(U,Δ)
> $\mathbf{D}:= \varnothing$
>   **for** each fd $Y{\rightarrow}A$ in Δ **do**
> $\mathbf{D}:= \mathbf{D} \cup (YA, \pi_{YA}(\Delta))$
>   **end for**
> $\mathbf{D}:= \mathbf{D} \cup (X, \varnothing)$
>   **return**
>   **end**.

Informally, the algorithm starts by finding a reduced nonredundant canonical cover of Σ. Then for every fd in that cover a relation schema is created. Finally, a key for U is added as another relation scheme. It is clear that the algorithm terminates in polynomial time. We now prove its correctness.

THEOREM 5.13 (56) Let (U, Σ) be a universal schema. Then $3NF(U, \Sigma)$ is in 3NF and it represents (U, Σ).

Proof Let $3NF(U, \Sigma) = ((R_1, \Sigma_1), \ldots, (R_k, \Sigma_k))$, where (R_k, Σ_k) is the last relation schema to be added, i.e., R_k is a key of U with respect to Σ and $\Sigma_k = \emptyset$. We first show that $3NF(U, \Sigma)$ is a database schema, i.e., $\bigcup_{i=1}^{k} R_i = U$. We know that $\Delta \models R_k \rightarrow U$, so $cl_\Delta(R_k) = U$. Therefore, for every attribute $A \in U - R_k$, there must be some fd $Y \rightarrow A$ in Δ, so $A \in R_i$ for some i, $1 \leq i \leq k - 1$. Let Δ be the reduced nonredundant canonical cover of Σ. Let (R_i, Σ_i) be a relation schema of $3NF(U, \Sigma)$.

We now show that $3NF(U, \Sigma)$ is in 3NF. There are two cases: either $1 \leq i \leq k - 1$ and R_i came from an fd $Y \rightarrow A$ in Δ, or $i = k$ and R_k is a key of U with respect to Σ. Consider the first case, where $R_i = YA$. We claim that Y is a key of R_i. Suppose it is not. Then there is a proper subset Z of Y such that $\Sigma \models Z \rightarrow YA$. But that means that $Y \rightarrow A$ is not reduced in Δ—contradiction. Thus, the only attribute in R_i that is possibly not prime is A. If there is a violation of 3NF in YA, then that means that there is a proper subset Z of Y such that $\Sigma \models Z \rightarrow A$. But that means that $Y \rightarrow A$ is not reduced in Δ—contradiction. Consider now the second case. If there is a violation of 3NF in R_k, then that means that there is a proper subset Z of R_k and an attribute $A \in R_k - Z$ such that $\Sigma \models Z \rightarrow A$. But then $\Sigma \models R_k - A \rightarrow U$, so R_k is not a key of U with respect to Σ—contradiction.

We now show that $3NF(U, \Sigma)$ represents (U, Σ). We first have to show that the decomposition associated with this schema is lossless, that is, for every relation I on U that satisfies Σ, the decomposition of I into $\pi_{R_1}(I), \ldots, \pi_{R_k}(I)$ is lossless. The proof of this claim is out of the scope of this article. The reader is referred to (5, 59). It remains to show that $3NF(U, \Sigma)$ preserves the dependencies in Σ. But this is obvious, since $\bigcup_{i=1}^{k} \Sigma_i = \Delta$, and Δ is a cover of Σ. ∎

The synthesis algorithm presented above is actually a simplified version of the algorithm in (5) (which is an improvement of the algorithm in (9)). The algorithm there has the property that it synthesize a database schema with a minimal number of relation schema, namely, given a universal schema (U, Σ), the algorithm synthesizes a database schema **D** that is in 3NF and represents

(U, Σ), such that no database schema $\mathbf{D}'$ that is in 3NF and represents (U, Σ) has fewer relation schemas than $\mathbf{D}$.

5.5 MULTIVALUED DEPENDENCIES

5.5.1 Motivation

We have seen in the previous sections that the presence of certain functional dependencies in a database schema can cause certain problems, called *anomalies*. We show now that anomalies can also occur in the absence of fd's.

Example 5.17

Consider the following relation:

EMP	CHILD	SKILL
Hilbert	Hilda	Math
Hilbert	Hilda	Physics
Pythagoras	Peter	Math
Pythagoras	Paul	Math
Pythagoras	Peter	Philosophy
Pythagoras	Paul	Philosophy
Turing	Peter	Computer Science

This relation does not obey any fd besides trivial ones such as EMP→EMP. Nevertheless, it still suffers from the anomalies:

1. *Redundancy.* Several pieces of information, e.g., the information that Pythagoras is skillful in Mathematics, is repeated more than once.
2. *Possible inconsistency.* Suppose now that we are asked to delete the tuple ⟨Pythagoras, Peter, Math⟩. Since there seems to be no connection between employees' children and employees' skills, it is not clear whether the absence of this tuple is consistent with the rest of the tuples, as Pythagoras is still skillful in mathematics and Peter is still his son. ∎

A close look in the above example suggest that even though we have no fd's here, there is nevertheless some dependency among the data, since every employee determines a *set* of children and a *set* of skills. Such dependency is called a *multivalued dependency*.

5.5.2 Multivalued Dependencies

A *multivalued dependency* (abbr. mvd) is a statement that describes a semantic constraints on data (25, 61). Formally, an mvd is an expression of the form $X \twoheadrightarrow Y$, read X *multi-determines* Y, where X and Y are attribute sets. $X \twoheadrightarrow Y$ is *over* an attribute set R if $XY \subseteq R$. $X \twoheadrightarrow Y$ is *satisfied* by a relation I on R if $X \twoheadrightarrow Y$ is over R for all tuples $u, v \in I$, if $u[X] = v[X]$, then there exists a tuple $w \in I$ such that $w[X] = u[X] = v[X]$, $w[Y] = u[Y]$, and $w[R - XY] = v[R - XY]$. (Of course, if I satisfies $X \twoheadrightarrow Y$, then there must also exist a tuple $w' \in I$ such that $w'[X] = u[X] = v[X]$, $w'[Y] = v[Y]$, and $w'[R - XY] = u[R - XY]$.) Intuitively, the mvd $X \twoheadrightarrow Y$ says that every "X-value" determines a set of "Y-values," independently of the entries in the attributes of $R - XY$. For most of this section, we deal only with relations on U, so the term "$R - XY$" in the above definition can be replaced by "$\overline{XY}$."

Example 5.18

The relation in Example 5.17 satisfies the mvd's EMP$\twoheadrightarrow$CHILD and EMP$\twoheadrightarrow$SKILL. It does not satisfy the mvd CHILD$\twoheadrightarrow$EMP. Intuitively, every employee has a set of children and a set of skills, and these two sets are independent of each other. ∎

Several notions that have been defined for fd's can be analogously defined for mvd's. The reader is asked to go through the definitions of Sections 5.3.2, 5.3.3, and 5.3.4, substituting "mvd" for "fd" in the definitions.

Mvd's, like fd's, can be expressed in first-order logic. For example, suppose that $U = ABCD$ and that the attributes A, B, C, and D label the first, second, third, and fourth columns, correspondingly. Then the mvd $AB \twoheadrightarrow C$ can be expressed by the first-order sentence

$$(\forall abc_1 c_2 d_1 d_2)((\mathbf{R}abc_1 d_1 \wedge \mathbf{R}abc_2 d_2) \supset \mathbf{R}abc_1 d_2)).$$

This makes the discussion of Section 5.3.3 relevant to mvd's. In particular, (finite) implication of mvd's is reducible to (finite) unsatisfiability of the BS class. Thus, we get:

THEOREM 5.14   For mvd's, implication and finite implication coincide, and the corresponding decision problems (which also coincide) are decidable. ∎

As with fd's, this does not give us a practical algorithm for testing implication. In the next section, we study formal systems for mvd's in order to get such an algorithm.

5.5.3   Formal System for Multivalued Dependencies

A formal system for mvd's was studied in (10) and proven to be sound and complete. Several systems have been investigated in (11, 12, 24, and 45). The system **MVD** that we present here is somewhat different from the systems studied in those articles. **MVD** consists of one axiom scheme and two inference rules:

MVD0 (complementation axiom): $\vdash X \twoheadrightarrow \overline{X}$.

MVD1 (augmentation): $X \twoheadrightarrow Y \vdash XZ \twoheadrightarrow YZ$.

MVD2 (difference): $X \twoheadrightarrow Y,\ S \twoheadrightarrow T \vdash X \twoheadrightarrow Y - T$, if $S \cap Y = \varnothing$.

Example 5.19

Let $U = ABCD$, and let Σ consists of the mvd's $A \twoheadrightarrow BC$ and $D \twoheadrightarrow B$, and let τ be $AB \twoheadrightarrow BD$. We show that $\Sigma \vdash \tau$. By **MVD2**, we have $A \twoheadrightarrow BC$, $D \to B \vdash A \twoheadrightarrow C$. By **MVD0**, we have $\vdash A \twoheadrightarrow BCD$. By **MVD2**, we have $A \twoheadrightarrow BCD,\ A \twoheadrightarrow C \vdash A \twoheadrightarrow BD$. By **MVD1**, we have $A \twoheadrightarrow BD \vdash AB \twoheadrightarrow BD$.

∎

Before proving soundness and completeness we need two lemmas.

LEMMA 5.7

1. $\vdash X \twoheadrightarrow U$.
2. $\vdash X \twoheadrightarrow X$.
3. $X \twoheadrightarrow Y \vdash X \twoheadrightarrow \overline{Y}$.
4. $X \twoheadrightarrow Y,\ S \twoheadrightarrow T \vdash X \twoheadrightarrow Y \cap T$, if $Y \cap S = \varnothing$.
5. $X \twoheadrightarrow Y,\ X \twoheadrightarrow Z \vdash X \twoheadrightarrow Y \cap Z$.
6. $\vdash X \twoheadrightarrow A$, if $A \in X$.

Proof

1. By **MVD0**, we have $\vdash \varnothing \twoheadrightarrow U$. By **MVD1**, we have $\varnothing \twoheadrightarrow U \vdash X \twoheadrightarrow U$.
2. By **MVD0**, we have $\vdash \varnothing \twoheadrightarrow U$. By **MVD2**, we have $\varnothing \twoheadrightarrow U$, $\varnothing \twoheadrightarrow U \vdash \varnothing \twoheadrightarrow \varnothing$. By **MVD1**, we have $\varnothing \twoheadrightarrow \varnothing \vdash X \twoheadrightarrow X$.
3. By **MVD0**, $\vdash X \twoheadrightarrow \overline{X}$. By **MVD2**, $X \twoheadrightarrow \overline{X}$, $X \twoheadrightarrow Y \vdash X \twoheadrightarrow \overline{X} - Y$. By **MVD1**, $X \twoheadrightarrow \overline{X} - Y \vdash X \twoheadrightarrow \overline{Y}$.
4. By (3), $S \twoheadrightarrow T \vdash S \twoheadrightarrow \overline{T}$. By **MVD2**, $X \twoheadrightarrow Y$, $S \twoheadrightarrow \overline{T} \vdash X \twoheadrightarrow Y - \overline{T}$. But $Y - \overline{T} = Y \cap T$.
5. By **MVD0**, $\vdash X \twoheadrightarrow \overline{X}$. By (4), $X \twoheadrightarrow \overline{X}$, $X \twoheadrightarrow Y \vdash X \twoheadrightarrow \overline{X} \cap Y$. By (4), $X \twoheadrightarrow \overline{X} \cap Y$, $X \twoheadrightarrow Z \vdash X \twoheadrightarrow \overline{X} \cap Y \cap Z$. By **MVD1**, $X \twoheadrightarrow \overline{X} \cap Y \cap Z \vdash X \twoheadrightarrow Y \cap Z$.

6. By **MVD0**, $\vdash X \twoheadrightarrow \overline{X}$. By **MVD1**, $X \twoheadrightarrow \overline{X} \vdash X \twoheadrightarrow \overline{X}A$. By (2), $\vdash X \twoheadrightarrow X$. By (5), $X \twoheadrightarrow X, X \twoheadrightarrow \overline{X}A \vdash X \twoheadrightarrow A$. ■

LEMMA 5.8   Let W be an attribute set, and let I be a two tuple relation $\{u, v\}$ such that u and v agree precisely on $\overline{W}$, i.e., $u[\overline{W}] = v[\overline{W}]$ and $u[A] \neq v[A]$ for all $A \in W$. Then I satisfies the mvd $S \twoheadrightarrow T$ if and only if either $S \cap W \neq \emptyset$, $W \subseteq T$, or $W \cap T = \emptyset$.

Proof   Suppose first that $S \cap W \neq \emptyset$. Then $u[S] \neq v[S]$, and I satisfies $S \twoheadrightarrow T$ vacuously. Suppose now that $S \cap W = \emptyset$. Then $u[S] = v[S]$, so there should be a tuple $w \in I$ such that $w[S] = u[S] = v[S]$, $w[T] = u[T]$, and $w[\overline{ST}] = v[\overline{ST}]$. If $W \subseteq T$, then take w to be u, and if $W \cap T = \emptyset$, then take w to be v. Conversely, suppose that I satisifes $S \twoheadrightarrow T$. Then, either $u[S] \neq v[S]$, in which case $S \cap W \neq \emptyset$, or there is a tuple $w \in I$ such that $w[S] = u[S] = v[S]$, $w[T] = u[T]$, and $w[\overline{ST}] = v[\overline{ST}]$. But w must be either u, in which case $W \subseteq T$, or it must be v, in which case $W \cap T = \emptyset$. ■

We can now prove soundness and completeness.

THEOREM 5.15   The system **MVD** is sound and complete.

Proof Soundness: We show that the axiom and the inference rules are sound. Let I be a relation on U, and let $u, v \in I$. Suppose that $u[X] = v[X]$. To show that **MVD0** is sound, we need a tuple $w \in I$ such that $w[X] = u[X] = v[X]$, $w[\overline{X}] = u[\overline{X}]$, and $w[\emptyset] = v[\emptyset]$ (since $\overline{X\overline{X}} = \emptyset$). Clearly, u is the desired tuple.

Suppose now that I satisfies $X \twoheadrightarrow Y$ and that $u[XZ] = v[XZ]$. Then $u[X] = v[X]$, so there is a tuple $w \in I$ such that $w[X] = u[X] = v[X]$, $w[Y] = u[Y]$, and $w[\overline{XY}] = v[\overline{XY}]$. Since $u[XZ] = v[XZ]$, it follows that $w[XZ] = u[XZ] = v[XZ]$ and $w[YZ] = u[YZ]$. Now $\overline{XYZ} \subseteq \overline{XY}$, so $w[\overline{XYZ}] = v[\overline{XYZ}]$. Thus, **MVD1** is sound.

Finally, suppose that I satisfies $X \twoheadrightarrow Y$ and $S \twoheadrightarrow T$, and that $u[X] = v[X]$. Then there is a tuple w such that $w[X] = u[X] = v[X]$, $w[Y] = u[Y]$, and $w[Z] = v[Z]$, where $Z = \overline{XY}$. Thus, $w[XZ] = v[XZ]$. Since $Y \cap S = \emptyset$, we have that $S \subseteq XZ$, so $w[S] = v[S]$. Therefore, there is a tuple $p \in I$ such that $p[S] = v[S] = w[S]$, $p[T] = v[T]$, and $p[\overline{ST}] = w[\overline{ST}]$. Since $u[x] = v[X] = w[X]$, clearly $p[X] = v[X] = w[X]$. Since $S \cap Y = \emptyset$, we have that $Y - T \subseteq \overline{ST}$, so $p[Y - T] = w[Y - T] = u[Y - T]$. Finally, $\overline{X(Y - T)} = Z \cup (T - X)$, so $p[\overline{X(Y - T)}] = v[\overline{X(Y - T)}]$, since $p[T] = v[T]$ and $p[Z] = v[Z]$. Thus, **MVD2** is sound.

Completeness: We have to show that if $\Sigma \models \sigma$, then $\Sigma \vdash \sigma$. We prove the contrapositive: if $\Sigma \nvdash \sigma$, then $\Sigma \nvDash \sigma$.

Let σ be $X \twoheadrightarrow Y$. Suppose that $\Sigma \vdash X \twoheadrightarrow Y - X$. Then, by **MVD2**, $\Sigma \vdash X \twoheadrightarrow Y$. Thus, we can assume without loss of generality that X and Y are disjoint. Consider the collection of sets that are provably multidetermined by X:

$$rhs_\Sigma(X) = \{Z : \Sigma \vdash X \twoheadrightarrow Z\}.$$

By Lemma 5.7, $rhs_\Sigma(X)$ is a Boolean algebra, since it contains a maximal element and is closed under complement and intersection. An *atom* in a Boolean algebra is a minimal nonzero element. Since $rhs_\Sigma(X)$ is a field of finite sets, it is clear that every nonempty set in $rhs_\Sigma(X)$ includes an atom. That is, $rhs_\Sigma(X)$ is an *atomic* Boolean algebra. In an atomic Boolean algebra every element is the union of the atoms that it contains. The collection of these atoms is called the *dependency basis* of X with respect to Σ, denoted $dep_\Sigma(X)$. Thus,

$$dep_\Sigma(X) = \{Z : Z \neq \varnothing, \Sigma \vdash X \twoheadrightarrow Z, \text{ and if } \Sigma \vdash X \twoheadrightarrow R, R \subseteq Z,$$

$$\text{and } R \neq \varnothing, \text{ then } R = Z\}.$$

Note that the sets in $dep_\Sigma(X)$ form a partition of U, by Lemma 5.7.

Since $\Sigma \nvdash X \twoheadrightarrow Y$, it follows that Y is not in $rhs\,\Sigma_\Sigma(X)$. Thus, Y is not a union of sets in $dep_\Sigma(X)$. Consequently, there is a set W in $dep_\Sigma(X)$, such that W *intersects Y nontrivially*, i.e., $W \nsubseteq Y$ and $W \cap Y \neq \varnothing$. Since $W \in rhs_\Sigma(X)$, we have $\Sigma \vdash X \twoheadrightarrow W$. We claim that $W \cap X = \varnothing$. Suppose not, and let $A \in W \cap X$. By Lemma 5.7, $A \in dep_\Sigma(X)$, so we must have that $W = A$. But then W cannot intersect Y nontrivially.

We construct a relation I as follows. I consists of two tuples u and v, such that u and v agree precisely on $\overline{W}$. For example, $u[A] = 0$ for each attribute A, $v[A] = 0$ for each attribute $A \in \overline{W}$, and $v[A] = 1$ for each attribute $A \in W$.

By Lemma 5.8, I satisfies an mvd $S \twoheadrightarrow T$ if and only if either $S \cap W \neq \varnothing$, or $W \subseteq T$, or $W \cap T = \varnothing$. Since X is disjoint from W and W intersects Y nontrivially, it follows that I does not satisfy $X \twoheadrightarrow Y$.

We now claim that I satisfies Σ. Let $S \twoheadrightarrow T$ be an mvd in Σ. If I does not satisfy $S \twoheadrightarrow T$, then $S \cap W = \varnothing$, $W \nsubseteq T$, and $W \cap T \neq \varnothing$, by Lemma 5.8. But then, by Lemma 5.7, $X \twoheadrightarrow W, S \twoheadrightarrow T \vdash X \twoheadrightarrow W \cap T$, so $W \cap T$ should be in $dep_\Sigma(X)$. But $W \cap T \subset W$, so we cannot have both W and $W \cap T$ in $dep_\Sigma(X)$. It follows that I satisfies $S \twoheadrightarrow T$.

Thus, I satisfies Σ and it does not satisfy σ, so $\Sigma \nvDash \sigma$. ∎

As with fd's, the completeness proof is also a direct proof that for mvd's implication and finite implication coincide, since the *counterexample* relation that we have constructed is finite.

5.5.4 Testing Implication of Multivalued Dependencies

As with fd's, the most important fact about implication of mvd's is buried in the proof of the completeness of the system **MVD**. We recall the definition of the *dependency basis*, where now, by the completeness of **MVD**, we can replace $\vdash$ by $\models$:

$$dep_\Sigma(X) = \{Z : Z \neq \varnothing, \Sigma \models X \twoheadrightarrow Z, \text{ and if } \Sigma \models X \twoheadrightarrow R, R \subseteq Z,$$

$$\text{and } R \neq \varnothing, \text{ then } R = Z\}.$$

The following properties of the dependency basis follow from the proof of Theorem 5.15.

LEMMA 5.9   (10)

1. $dep_\Sigma(X)$ is a partition of U,
2. for each $A \in X$, we have $A \in dep_\Sigma(X)$, and
3. $\Sigma \models X \twoheadrightarrow Y$ if and only if Y is a union of sets in $dep_\Sigma(X)$.   ∎

It follows from Lemma 5.9 that if we can efficiently construct dependency bases, then we can efficiently test implication of mvd's. Beeri (6) was the first to describe a polynomial time algorithm for the construction of the dependency basis. We describe here a better algorithm, Hagihara et al. (35).

Algorithm 5.6

Input: The set U of all attribute, an attribute set X, and a set Σ of mvd's.
Output: The dependency basis of X with respect to Σ.

```
DEP(U, X, Σ)
begin
  DEP = {X̄}
  for each attribute A in X do DEP:= DEP ∪ {A}
  end for
  while there is some W in DEP and some S⟶⟶T in Σ such that
      S ∩ W = ∅ and T ∩ W ≠ ∅ and W ⊈ T do
        DEP:= DEP ∪ {W ∩T, W − T} − {W}
  end while
  return(DEP)
end.
```

We have to show that $DEP(U, X, \Sigma)$ terminates and indeed returns the dependency basis of X with respect to Σ.

LEMMA 5.10 $DEP(U,X,\Sigma)$ terminates and returns $dep_\Sigma(X)$.

Proof   The algorithm starts by constructing a partition of U and then goes on to refine that partition. Thus, it must terminate. We now show that the algorithm returns the dependency basis of X.

We first show that if at any stage of the algorithm W is a set in DEP, then $\Sigma \models X \twoheadrightarrow W$. Before the main loop of the algorithm, DEP gets the value $\{A : A \in X\} \cup \{\overline{X}\}$. By Lemma 5.7, for each W in this partition we have $\Sigma \models X \twoheadrightarrow W$. In the main loop of the algorithm we replace a set W in DEP by $W \cap T$ and $W - T$, provided there is an mvd $S \twoheadrightarrow T$ in Σ such that S is disjoint from W and W intersects T nontrivially. But in that case, by **MVD2** and Lemma 5.7, $\Sigma \models X \twoheadrightarrow W - T$ and $\Sigma \models X \twoheadrightarrow W \cap T$.

Suppose now that $DEP(U,X,\Sigma)$ is not the dependency basis of X. Then there is a set Y in $DEP(U,X,\Sigma)$ and a set W in $dep_\Sigma(X)$ such that W is a proper subset of Y. We claim that $Y \cap X = \varnothing$. Suppose not, and assume $A \in Y \cap X$. But since A is in $DEP(U,X\Sigma)$, it must be the case that $Y = A$. But then W cannot be a proper subset of Y.

We construct a relation I as follows. I consists of two tuples u and v, such that u and v agree precisely on $\overline{Y}$. By Lemma 5.8, I satisfies an mvd $S \twoheadrightarrow T$ if and only if either $S \cap Y \neq \varnothing$, or $Y \subseteq T$, or $Y \cap T = \varnothing$. Since X is disjoint from Y and W is a proper subset of Y, it follows that I does not satisfy $X \twoheadrightarrow W$.

We now claim that I satisfies Σ. Let $S \twoheadrightarrow T$ be an mvd in Σ. If I does not satisfy $S \twoheadrightarrow T$, then $S \cap Y = \varnothing$, $Y \not\subseteq T$, and $Y \cap T \neq \varnothing$, by Lemma 5.8. But then Y should be replaced in DEP by $Y \cap T$ and $Y - T$. It follows that I satisfies $S \twoheadrightarrow T$. Thus, I satisfies Σ and it does not satisfy $X \twoheadrightarrow W$. But we have shown that $\Sigma \models X \twoheadrightarrow W$—a contradiction. It follows that $DEP(U,X,\Sigma)$ must be $dep_\Sigma(X)$.   ∎

The alert reader may have noticed the similarity in the proofs of Theorem 5.15 and Lemma 5.10. Indeed, one can view an execution of the algorithm as an organized derivation in the formal system **MVD**.

Example 5.20

Let $U = ABCD$, and let Σ consists of the mvd's $A \twoheadrightarrow BC$ and $D \twoheadrightarrow B$. Let us calculate $dep_\Sigma(AB)$. Initially DEP is assigned the partition $\{A,B,CD\}$. We then apply the mvd $A \twoheadrightarrow BC$ and replace CD by C and D. So $dep_\Sigma(AB) = \{A,B,C,D\}$.   ∎

It is not hard to implement DEP to run in polynomial time. Galil (30) has shown how to implement it to run in almost linear time.

THEOREM 5.16   (30) The implication problem for mvd's can be solved in time $O(n\log n)$, where n is the length of the input.   ■

5.5.5 Multivalued Dependencies and Propositional Logic

Looking again in the proofs of Theorem 5.15 and Lemma 5.10, we see that the counterexample relation constructed there is a two-tuple relation.

THEOREM 5.17   Let Σ be a set of mvd's, and σ be an mvd. Then $\Sigma \models \sigma$ if and only if $\Sigma \models_f \sigma$ if and only if $\Sigma \models_2 \sigma$.   ■

As in Section 5.3.5, this suggests a correspondence between mvd's and propositional logic. With fd's the correspondence shed some light on fd's. Here, surprisingly, the correspondence sheds some light on propositional logic. In order to define propositional implication for mvd's, we have to extend relational truth assignments to assign truth values to mvd's: ψ assigns the value 1 to $X \twoheadrightarrow Y$ if and only if whenever $\psi(X) = 1$, then $\psi(Y) = 1$ or $\psi(\overline{XY}) = 1$.

THEOREM 5.18   (52) Let Σ be a set of mvd's, and σ be an mvd. Then $\Sigma \models \sigma$ if and only if $\Sigma \models_p \sigma$.

Proof   By Theorem 5.17, it suffices to show that $\Sigma \models_2 \sigma$ iff $\Sigma \models_p \sigma$. The basis for this equivalence is a simple correspondence between relational truth assignments and two-tuple relations.

Let ψ be a relational truth assignment. Then $I_\psi = \{u, v\}$ is a two-tuple relation such that $u[A] = v[A]$ iff $\psi(A) = 1$. Let $I = \{u, v\}$ be a two-tuple relation. Then ψ_I is a relational trugh assignment such that $\psi(A) = 1$ iff $u[A] = v[A]$. Let τ be an mvd $X \twoheadrightarrow Y$. We claim that $\psi(\tau) = 1$ iff I_ψ satisfies τ, and I satisfies τ iff $\psi_I(\tau) = 1$.

Suppose first that $\psi(\tau) = 1$. Let $R = \{A : \psi(A) = 1\}$. If $\psi(X) = 0$, then $X \not\subseteq R$, so $u[X] \neq v[X]$ and I_ψ satisfies τ. Suppose now that $\psi(X) = 1$. Then $X \subseteq R$, so $u[X] = v[X]$. For I_ψ to satisfy τ there should be a tuple $w \in I_\psi$ such that $w[X] = u[X] = v[X]$, $w[Y] = u[Y]$, and $w[\overline{XY}] = v[\overline{XY}]$. If $\psi(Y) = 1$, then $Y \subseteq R$, so we can take w to be v. If $\psi(\overline{XY}) = 1$, then $\overline{XY} \subseteq R$, so we can take w to be u. So I_ψ satisfies τ.

Suppose now that I satisfies τ. Let $R = \{A : u[A] = v[A]\}$. If $u[X] \neq v[X]$, then $X \not\subseteq R$, so $\psi_I(X) = 0$, and $\psi_I(X \twoheadrightarrow Y) = 1$. If $u[X] = v[X]$, then there should be a tuple $w \in I$ such that $w[X] = u[X] = v[X]$, $w[Y] = u[Y]$, and $w[\overline{XY}] = v[\overline{XY}]$. If w is u, then $u[\overline{XY}] = v[\overline{XY}]$, so $\overline{XY} \subseteq R$ and $\psi_I(\overline{XY}) = 1$. If w is v, then $u[Y] = v[Y]$, so $Y \subseteq R$ and $\psi_I(R) = 1$. At any case $\psi_I(X \twoheadrightarrow Y) = 1$.

A similar correspondence between ψ and I_ψ and between I and ψ_I holds for sets of mvd's. Suppose now that $\Sigma \models_2 \sigma$. We want to show that $\Sigma \models_p \sigma$. Let ψ be a relational truth assignement such that $\psi(\Sigma) = 1$. then I_ψ satisfies Σ, and since $\Sigma \models_2 \sigma$, it must be the case that I_ψ satisfies σ. But then $\psi(\sigma) = 1$. We have shown that $\psi(\Sigma) = 1$ entails $\psi(\sigma) = 1$ for any relational truth assignment σ, so $\Sigma \models_p \sigma$. An analogous argument shows that if $\Sigma \models_p \sigma$, then also $\Sigma \models_2 \sigma$. $\blacksquare$

Theorem 5.18 enables us to view mvd's as formulas in propositional logic. Let $X = A_1 \cdots A_k$, $Y = B_1 \cdots B_l$, and $\overline{XY} = C_1 \ldots C_m$. Then the mvd $X \twoheadrightarrow Y$ can be viewed as the formula

$$A_1 \wedge \cdots \wedge A_k \supset (B_1 \wedge \cdots \wedge B_k) \vee (C_1 \wedge \cdots \wedge C_k).$$

For example, if $U = ABC$, then the mvd $A \twoheadrightarrow B$ can be viewed as the formula $A \supset B \vee C$. This formula is not equivalent to a set of Horn formulas. Thus, the results of Section 5.5.4 together with the correspondence between mvd's and propositional logic yield a polynomial time algorithm for a subclass of propositional logic.

5.5.6 Functional and Multivalued Dependencies

So far we have considered functional and multivalued dependencies separately. Since both types of dependencies express natural semantic constraints, their interaction is also of importance. As for fd's alone and mvd's alone, the (finite) implication problem for fd's and mvd's is reducible to the (finite) unsatisfiability problem for the BS class. Thus, the problems coincide and they are decidable. As before, we resort to formal systems in order to gain a better understanding.

The interaction of fd's and mvd's was first studied in (10). We present here a formal system **FD − MVD** that is somewhat different from the system in (10). The system consists of the system **MVD**, an axiom and an inference rules for fd's, and two rules that describe the interaction between fd's and mvd's.

FD3 (reflexivity): $\vdash X \rightarrow A$, if $A \in X$.

FD4 (union): $X \rightarrow Y$, $X \rightarrow Z \vdash X \rightarrow YZ$.

FD5 (decomposition): $X \rightarrow Y \vdash X \rightarrow A$, if $A \in Y$.

FD − MVD0 (translation): $X \rightarrow Y \vdash X \twoheadrightarrow Y$.

FD − MVD1 (intersection): $X \twoheadrightarrow Y$, $S \rightarrow T \vdash X \rightarrow Y \cap T$, if $S \cap Y = \varnothing$.

MVD0 (complementation axiom): $\vdash X \twoheadrightarrow \overline{X}$.

MVD1 (augmentation): $X \twoheadrightarrow Y \vdash XZ \twoheadrightarrow YZ$.

MVD2 (difference): $X \twoheadrightarrow Y$, $S \twoheadrightarrow T \vdash X \twoheadrightarrow Y - T$, if $S \cap Y = \varnothing$.

Example 5.21

Let $U = ABCD$. We show that $A{\to}B, B{\to}C \vdash A{\to}C$. (This derivation is done by one step using **FD**1 in the system **FD**, but this rule does not belong to the system **FD** − **MVD**.) By **FD** − **MVD**0, $A{\to}B \vdash A{\to\to}B$. By Lemma 5.7, $A{\to\to}B \vdash A{\to\to}CD$ (since the system **MVD** is a subset of the system **FD** − **MVD**). By **FD** − **MVD**1, $A{\to\to}CD, B{\to}C \vdash A{\to}C$. ∎

THEOREM 5.19   The system **FD** − **MVD** is sound and complete.

Proof

Soundness: We leave it to the reader to prove that the rules **FD**3 and **FD**4 are sound. Consider the rule **FD** − **MVD**0. Let I be a relation that satisfies $X{\to}Y$. Let $u, v \in I$ such that $u[X] = v[X]$. Then there should be a tuple $w \in I$ such that $w[X] = u[X] = v[X], w[Y] = v[Y]$, and $w[\overline{XY}] = v[\overline{XY}]$. But $u[Y] = v[Y]$, since I satisfies $X{\to}Y$, so take w to be v. Consider now the rule **FD** − **MVD**1. Let I be a relation that satisfies $X{\to\to}Y$ and $S{\to}T$, where $S \cap Y = \varnothing$. Let $u, v \in I$ such that $u[X] = v[X]$. There is a tuple $w \in I$ such that $w[X] = u[X] = v[X], w[Y] = v[Y]$, and $w[\overline{XY}] = v[\overline{XY}]$. Since $S \cap Y = \varnothing, w[S] = v[S]$, so $w[T] = v[T]$. Since $w[Y] = u[Y]$, we have that $u[Y \cap T] = v[Y \cap T]$, as desired.

Completeness: Again we prove that if $\Sigma \nvdash \sigma$, then $\Sigma \nvDash \sigma$. Consider first the case that σ is an mvd $X{\to\to}Y$. As in the proof of Theorem 5.15, we define the dependency basis of X with respect to Σ (which now contains both fd's and mvd's).

$$dep_{\Sigma}(X) = \{Z : Z \neq \varnothing, \Sigma \vdash X{\to\to}Z, \text{ and if } \Sigma \vdash X{\to\to}R, R \subseteq Z,$$

$$\text{and } R \neq \varnothing, \text{ then } R = Z\}$$

As in the proof of Theorem 5.15, since $\Sigma \nvdash X{\to\to}Y$, there is a set W in $dep_{\Sigma}(X)$, such that W intersects Y nontrivially, $\Sigma \vdash X{\to\to}W$, and $W \cap X = \varnothing$. We construct a relation I with two tuples u and v, such that u and v agree precisely on $\overline{W}$.

By Lemma 5.8, I satisfies an mvd $S{\to\to}T$ if and only if either $S \cap W \neq \varnothing, W \subseteq T$, or $W \cap T = \varnothing$. Consequently I does not satisfy $X{\to\to}Y$ and I satisfies all mvd's in Σ. It remains to show that I satisfies all fd's in Σ.

Let $S{\to}T$ be an fd in Σ. If $u[S] = v[S]$, then $S \cap W = \varnothing$. If $T \cap W = \varnothing$, then $u[T] = v[T]$, so assume that $T \cap W \neq \varnothing$. Let $A \in T \cap W$. By **FD**5, $S{\to}T \vdash S{\to}A$; by **FD** − **MVD**1, $X{\to\to}W, S{\to}A \vdash X{\to}A$; and by **FD** − **MVD**0, $X{\to}A \vdash X{\to\to}A$. Thus, $A \in dep_{\Sigma}(X)$. But since $A \in W$, it follows that $W = A$, contradicting the fact that W nontrivially intersects Y. Thus, I satisfies Σ and it does not satisfy σ, so $\Sigma \not\models \sigma$.

We now consider the case that σ is an fd $X \to Y$. If $\Sigma \not\vdash X \to Y$, then there is some attribute $B \in Y$ such that $\Sigma \not\vdash X \to B$ (by **FD4** and **FD5**). Again let $X^+ = \{A : \Sigma \vdash X \to A\}$. Since $\Sigma \not\vdash X \to B$, we have that $B \notin X^+$. Let W be the set in $dep_\Sigma(X)$ such that $A \in W$ (since, as we observed in the proof of Theorem 5.15, $dep_\Sigma(X)$ is a partition of U). As before, we construct a relation I with two tuples u and v that agree precisely on W.

We claim that $X \cap W = \varnothing$. Suppose not, and let $A \in X \cap W$. By Lemma 5.7, $A \in dep_\Sigma(X)$, so we must have $W = A$. But then $A = B$, and $\vdash X \to B$ by **FD3**. It follows that $u[X] = v[X]$ and $u[B] \neq v[B]$, so I does not satisfy σ. It remain to show that I satisfy Σ. This is done as in the case that σ is an mvd. Thus, I satisfies Σ and it does not satisfy σ, so $\Sigma \not\models \sigma$. ∎

As with fd's alone and mvd's alone, the ideas in the completeness proof can be used to devise an efficient algorithm for testing implication of fd's and mvd's.

THEOREM 5.20   (30) The implication problem for fd's and mvd's can be solved in time $O(n \log n)$, where n is the length of the input. ∎

5.5.7   Database Schema Design and Embedded Mvd's

In Section 5.5.1 we saw that multivalued dependencies cause certain anomalies. Again, *decomposition* seems to be the solution.

Example 5.22

The solution to the problems describe in Example 5.17 is to decompose the relation into the following relations:

EMP	CHILD
Hilbert	Hilda
Pythagoras	Peter
Pythagoras	Paul
Turing	Peter

EMP	SKILL
Hilbert	Math
Hilbert	Phisics
Pythagoras	Math
Pythagoras	Philosophy
Turing	Computer Science

Intuitively, this decomposition seems to be lossless. ■

Our intuition in decomposing a relation that has multivalued dependencies is justified by the following theorem.

THEOREM 5.21 (25) Let I be a relation on R, let $X \twoheadrightarrow Y$ be an mvd, and let $Z = R - XY$. If I satisfies $X \twoheadrightarrow Y$, then the decomposition of I into $\pi_{XY}(I)$ and $\pi_{XZ}(I)$ is lossless.

Proof Let $J = \pi_{XY}(I) * \pi_{XZ}(I)$. We know that $I \subseteq J$, so we have to show that $J \subseteq I$. Let $w \in J$. Then $w[XY] \in \pi_{XY}(I)$ and $w[XZ] \in \pi_{XZ}(I)$. Thus, there are tuples $u, v \in I$ such that $w[XY] = u[XY]$ and $w[XZ] = v[XZ]$. In particular, $u[X] = v[X]$. But then there is a tuple $w' \in I$ such that $w'[X] = u[X] = v[X]$, $w'[Y] = u[Y]$, and $w'[Z] = v[Z]$. Consequently, $w'[XYZ] = w[XYZ]$, so $w = w'$. ■

Based on the above ideas a schema design theory was developed for mvd's (e.g., (22, 25, 40, 62)). This theory, however, suffers from a basic difficulty that did not arise with fd's. This difficulty stems from an essential difference between fd's and mvd's. An fd $X \to Y$ is "context independent," that is, its satisfaction in a relation depends only on the entries for the attributes in XY. More formally:

THEOREM 5.22 Let I be a relation on R, and let $X \to Y$ be an fd such that $XY \subseteq R$. Then I satisfies $X \to Y$ if and only if $\pi_{XY}(I)$ satisfies $X \to Y$. ■

Mvd's, in contrast are "context dependent," since satisfaction of an mvd $X \twoheadrightarrow Y$ in a relation on R depends also on the entries for the attributes in $R - XY$. (In fact the relation on XY always satisfies $X \twoheadrightarrow Y$.) Thus, while with fd's we could mix together fd's that come from different relation schemas, we cannot do the same with mvd's, since these mvd's may have different "contexts." The solution to this difficulty is to change the notation for mvd's, so as to make them "context independent." Such mvd's are called *embedded mvd's* (25), since their "context" can be properly embedded in the global "context" (we shall see in a minute what these contexts are).

An *embedded mvd* (abbr. emvd) is an expression of the form $X \twoheadrightarrow Y | Z$, where X, Y, and Z are attribute sets. $X \twoheadrightarrow Y | Z$ is *over* an attribute set R if $XYZ \subseteq R$. $X \twoheadrightarrow Y | Z$ is *satisfied* by a relation I on R if $X \twoheadrightarrow Y | Z$ is over R and for all tuples $u, v \in I$, if $u[X] = v[X]$, then there exists a tuple $w \in I$ such that $w[X] = u[X] = v[X]$, $w[Y] = u[Y]$, and $w[Z] = v[Z]$. Intuitively, the mvd $X \twoheadrightarrow Y | Z$ says that every "X-value" determines a set of "Y-values" and a set of "Z-values" and these two sets are independent of each other. Here the "global context'' is the relation scheme R, and the ''context'' of $X \twoheadrightarrow Y|Z$ is XYZ. Since XYZ can be a proper subset of R, $X \twoheadrightarrow Y|Z$ is said to be embedded.

Example 5.23

Consider the following relation:

EMP	CHILD	BIRTHDATE	SKILL
Hilbert	Hilda	June 1, 1899	Math
Hilbert	Hilda	June 1, 1899	Physics
Pythagoras	Peter	July 4, 320BC	Math
Pythagoras	Paul	July 4, 322BC	Math
Pythagoras	Peter	July 4, 320BC	Philosophy
Pythagoras	Paul	July 4, 322BC	Philosophy
Turing	Peter	Feb. 28, 1937	Computer Science

This relation does not satisfy the mvd EMP$\twoheadrightarrow$CHILD. It does, however, satisfy the emvd EMP$\twoheadrightarrow$CHILD$|$SKILL. (It also satisfies the mvd EMP$\twoheadrightarrow$SKILL.) ∎

The following theorem formalizes the ''context independence'' of emvd's.

THEOREM 5.23   Let I be a relation on R, and let $X \twoheadrightarrow Y|Z$ be an emvd over R. Then I satisfies $X \twoheadrightarrow Y|Z$ if and only if $\pi_{XYZ}(I)$ satisfies $X \twoheadrightarrow Y|Z$. ∎

At this point the reader probably expects us to present a sound and complete formal system for emvd's, to get an efficient algorithm for testing implication, and to develop schema design theory. Unfortunately, none of this has been done. The (finite) implication problem for emvd's has stayed open since emvd's were defined in 1977. This is one of the major open problems in dependency theory.

To see why emvd's differ from mvd's in such a radical way, consider the way emvd's are expressed in first-order logic. For example, suppose that $U = ABCD$ and that the attributes A, B, C, and D label the first, second, third, and fourth columns, correspondingly. Then the mvd $A \twoheadrightarrow B|C$ can be expressed by the first-order sentence:

$$(\forall abc_1c_2d_1d_2)(\exists e)((\mathbf{R}ab_1c_1d_1 \wedge \mathbf{R}ab_2c_2d_2) \supset \mathbf{R}ab_1c_2e)).$$

The difference between this sentence and the sentences that express fd's and mvd's is that this sentence has an existential quantifier that follows the universal quantifiers. This existential quantifier makes a big difference. In particular, the sentence $\sigma_1 \wedge \cdots \wedge \sigma_k \wedge \neg\sigma$, where the σ_i's are emvd's, is not in the BS class any more.

While several inference rules for emvd's have been investigated (e.g., (36)), no complete formal system is known. The following theorem says that for emvd's solving the implication problem and finding a complete formal system are equivalent.

THEOREM 5.24   (16) The implication problem for emvd's is solvable if and only if there is a sound and complete formal system for emvd's.

Proof

Only if: Suppose that the implication problem for emvd's is solvable, and consider the formal system consisting of one inference rule:

$$\sigma_1, \ldots, \sigma_k \vdash \sigma, \quad \text{if } \{\sigma_1, \ldots, \sigma_k\} \models \sigma.$$

Clearly, this formal system is sound and complete for emvd's.

If: Suppose that **EMVD** is a sound and complete formal system for emvd's. Let Σ be a set of emvd's, and let σ be an emvd. To decide whether $\Sigma \models \sigma$ we list every possible sequence (without repetitions) of emvd's over the attributes that occur in Σ and σ and check whether the sequence is a derivation of σ from Σ by **EMVD**. Since there is a finite number of such sequences, this process must terminate. Hence, the implication problem for emvd's is solvable.　　　■

In Theorem 5.24 we implicitly assume that a formal system has to be effective, that is, it can be effectively checked whether a given sequence of dependencies is a derivation in the system. The formal systems **FD**, **MVD**, and **FD $-$ MVD** are, of course, effective. In (48, 55) another way in which formal systems can be restricted is considered. A formal system is said to be *k-ary* if all inference rules in the system are of the form $\sigma_1, \ldots, \sigma_n \vdash \sigma$, where $n \leq k$. For example, the formal systems **FD**, **MVD**, and **FD $-$ MVD** are all 2-ary.

THEOREM 5.25   (48, 55) For all $k > 0$, there is no sound and complete k-ary formal system (possibly noneffective) for implication and finite implication of emvd's.　　　■

5.6   MORE DATA DEPENDENCIES

5.6.1   Motivation

So far we have introduced fd's, mvd's, and emvd's. Do we need any more? Indeed we do, for several reasons.

The first reason is that life is not simple. There are semantic constraints that cannot be described by any of the dependencies introduced so far. We mention two examples.

Example 5.24

1. Consider a database with two relations: the relation ES(Employee, Salary) and the relation DM(Department, Manager). Each manager, however, is also an employee. So we would like to express the constraint that every manager entry in the DM relation appears as an employee entry in the ES relation. Such a constraint is called an *inclusion dependency* (27), and is written $DM[M] \subseteq ES[E]$.

2. Let I be a relation on X, and let $X_1, \ldots, X_m$ be attribute sets such that $X = \bigcup_{j=1}^{m} X_j$. We have observed in Section 5.2.2 that the decomposition of I to $\pi_{X_1}(I), \ldots, \pi_{X_m}(I)$ could be lossy. We can impose on I the constraint that the above decomposition be lossless. Such a constraint is called a *join dependency* (1, 50), and is written $*[X_1, \ldots, X_m]$. ∎

Another reason to introduce more dependencies is in the hope of solving the (finite) implication problem for emvd's. It is conceivable that for a larger class of dependencies a decision procedure would be apparent, while the specialization of the algorithm for emvd's is too murky to be visible. Also, a larger class of dependencies may have an elegant formal system that the narrower class of emvd's lacks. Even if one only cares about fd's, there is a technical reason to introduce more general dependencies, since fd's do not have enough expressive power when dealing with projections of relations. We now make the latter comment more precise.

We have mentioned that we view the language of dependencies as a semantic specification language. From this point of view, dependencies are means to specify classes of "semantically meaningful" relations. Given a set Σ of dependencies over an attribute set R, let $SAT_R(\Sigma)$ be the class of all relations on R that satisfy Σ. Thus, $SAT_R(\Sigma)$ is the class of all "semantically meaningful" relations on R with respect to Σ. A set Ψ of relations on R is an *fd-class* if there is a set Σ of fd's such that $\Psi = SAT_R(\Sigma)$. The definition of an *mvd-class* is analogous. Given a set Ψ of relations on R, and an attribute set $S \subseteq R$, let $\pi_S(\Psi)$ be the projection on S of the relations in Ψ, i.e., $\pi_S(\Psi) = \{\pi_S(I) : I \in \Psi\}$. Such a class of relations is called a *projective class*.

Projective classes arise very naturally in the context of *user views*. Very often certain users are not allowed to see the whole database but only a portion of it, a portion that may be defined by projection. For example, very often most users would not be allowed to see the salary data in a personnel database. If the class of "meaningful" relations in the database is $SAT(\Sigma)$, the class of "meaningful" relations for these users might be $\pi_S(SAT_R(\Sigma))$, for an appropriate attribute set S. One would like our specification language to be able to specify also projective classes, i.e., one would like the projection of an fd-class to be an fd-class and the projection of an mvd-class to be an mvd-class. Unfortunately, this is not the case.

THEOREM 5.26 (28, 33) There is a projection of an fd-class that is not an fd-class.

Proof Let Σ be a set of fd's over R, let $\Sigma^+ = \{\sigma : \Sigma \models \sigma\}$, let $\Psi = SAT_R(\Sigma)$, and let $\Omega = \pi_S(\Psi)$. We claim that Ω is an fd-class if and only if $\Omega = SAT_S(\pi_S(\Sigma^+))$. Clearly the latter is a sufficient condition, so we prove that it is also necessary.

Suppose that $\Omega = SAT_S(\Delta)$ for some set Δ of fd's over S. Let I be a relation on S. If I satisfies Δ, then $I \in \Omega$, so $I = \pi_S(J)$ for some $J \in \Psi$. But then J satisfies Σ^+, so I satisfies $\pi_S(\Sigma^+)$. Consequently, $\Delta \models \pi_S(\Sigma^+)$. Suppose that $\pi_S(\Sigma^+) \not\models \Delta$. That is, there is an fd $X{\rightarrow}Y$ in Δ such that $\pi_S(\Sigma^+) \not\models X{\rightarrow}Y$. If $\Sigma \models X{\rightarrow}Y$, then $X{\rightarrow}Y \in \pi_S(\Sigma^+)$, since $XY \subseteq S$—a contradiction. Thus, $\Sigma \not\models \Delta$, which means that there is a relation I that satisfies Σ but not Δ. But then $\pi_S(I) \in \Omega$ and $\pi_S(I)$ does not satisfy Δ—contradiction. Therefore, $\Omega = SAT_S(\Delta) = SAT(\pi_S(\Sigma^+))$.

Let $R = ABCDE$, let $S = ABCD$, and let Σ consists of the fd's $A{\rightarrow}E$, $B{\rightarrow}E$, and $CE{\rightarrow}D$. It can be verified that $\Delta = \pi_S(\Sigma^+) = \{AC{\rightarrow}D, BC{\rightarrow}D\}$. We claim that $SAT_S(\Delta) \neq \pi_S(SAT_R(\Sigma))$.

Consider the relation I on S:

	A	B	C	D
u_1	1	3	5	7
u_2	2	4	5	8
u_3	1	4	6	8

Clearly, I satisfies Δ. Nevertheless, I is not in $\pi_S(SAT_R(\Sigma))$. Suppose it is, that is $I = \pi_S(J)$, where J satisfies Σ. Then there are tuples $v_1, v_2, v_3 \in J$ such that $u_1[S] = v_1[S]$, $u_2[S] = v_2[S]$, and $u_3[S] = v_3[S]$. Since J satisfies $A{\rightarrow}E$, and $v_1[A] = u_1[A] = u_3[A] = v_3[A]$, we must have $v_1[E] = v_3[E]$. Similarly, since J satisfies $B{\rightarrow}E$, and $v_2[B] = u_2[B] = u_3[B] = v_3[B]$, we must have $v_2[E] = v_3[E]$. Also $v_1[C] = u_1[C] = u_2[C] = v_2[C]$. But then $v_1[CE] = v_2[CE]$, and, since J satisfies $CE{\rightarrow}D$, we must have $v_1[D] = v_2[D]$. But then $u_1[D] = u_2[D]$—which is not the case. $\blacksquare$

In the next section, we define a class of dependencies that generalizes the classes that we have seen so far.

5.6.2 Dependencies

Studying the dependencies that we have defined so far (fd's, mvd's, emvd's, and, informally, inclusion dependencies), we see that they all have a common structure: they say "if you see a certain pattern of tuples in the database, then you must also see this." In the case of fd's, "this" refers to the equality of certain entries, while for the other dependencies, "this" is another tuple that must also be in the database. For example, if $U = ABC$, then the fd $A \rightarrow B$ says that if you see two tuples that agree on A, then they must also agree on B. The mvd $A \rightarrow\!\!\!\rightarrow B$ says that if you see two tuples that agree on A, then there should be a tuple that agrees with these tuples on A, agree with the first tuple on B, and agree with the second tuple on C. Thus, fd's can be called *equality-generating dependencies*, while mvd's can be called *tuple-generating dependencies*.

We now generalize these ideas and define a general class of semantic constraints, which we simply call *dependencies*. We choose to describe dependencies as first-order sentences as in (15, 28), rather than use the equivalent formalisms of (16) and (60). To use first-order logic, we assume that the attributes are ordered, so we do not have to refer to them explicitly. We start by allowing databases with many relations. The atomic formulas are those that are either of the form $\mathbf{P}x_1 \cdots x_d$, where $\mathbf{P}$ is the name of a d-ary relation and the x_i's are individual variables, or of the form $x = y$, where x and y are individual variables. Formulas of the former type are called *relational formulas* (because they say that a certain tuple exists in the relation), and formulas of the latter type are called *equalities*. A *dependency* is a first-order sentence

$$(\forall y_1 \cdots y_k)(\exists x_1 \cdots x_l)(A_1 \wedge \cdots \wedge A_p \supset B_1 \wedge \cdots \wedge B_q)$$

where the A_i's and B_i's are atomic formulas. To capture our intuition about what this sentences should say, we put more syntactic restrictions. First, we want the dependency to say "if you see a certain pattern of tuple then . . . ," so we require all the A_i's to be relational formulas in the variables $y_1, \ldots, y_k$, that all the y_j's occur in the A_i's, and that $p \geq 1$ and $k \geq 1$. We want the B_i's to talk about existence of tuples or about equalities among entries of tuples, so we require that $q \geq 1$. We do not require that $l \geq 1$; if $l = 0$, then there are no existential variables.

Example 5.25

The dependency

$$(\forall yy_1y_2y_3y_4)(\exists xx_1x_2)(\mathbf{R}yy_1y_2 \wedge \mathbf{R}yy_3y_4 \supset$$

$$\mathbf{R}xx_1x_2 \wedge x = y \wedge x_1 = y_2 \wedge x_2 = y_4 \wedge y_1 = y_2),$$

says that if there are two tuples that agree on the first argument, then there should be a tuple that agrees with these tuples on the first argument, agrees with the first tuple on the second argument, and agrees with the second tuple on the third argument. Note that this dependency can also be written as

$$(\forall yy_1y_2y_3y_4)(\mathbf{R}yy_1y_2 \wedge \mathbf{R}yy_3y_4 \supset \mathbf{R}yy_1y_4 \wedge y_1 = y_2). \qquad \blacksquare$$

Example 5.26

The dependency

$$(\forall y_1 y_2)(\exists x_1)(\mathbf{P}y_1 y_2 \supset \mathbf{R}y_2 x_1)$$

says that if a value occurs as an entry in the second argument of a tuple in the **P** relation, then that value occurs also as the first argument of a tuple in the **R** relation. We have termed such dependencies as *inclusion dependencies*.   ∎

We now consider classification of dependencies to several subclasses. If the dependency talks about more than one relation, e.g., the dependency in Example 5.26 talks about the relation **P** and the relation **R**, then it is an *interrelational* dependency. If it talks only about one relation, e.g., the dependency in Example 5.25 talks only about the relation **R**, then it is an *intrarelational* or *unirelational* dependency. For simplicity we deal from now on only with unirelational dependencies.

The second classification has to do with the pattern of occurrence of variables in the dependencies. Suppose that the dependency talks about the relation **R**. If no variable occurs in two different argument positions of **R** and we have an equality $y_1 = y_2$ only if y_1 and y_2 occur in the same argument position of **R**, then the dependency is *typed*, otherwise it is *untyped*. The intuition behind this classification is that in a typed relation the domains that underly distinct columns are disjoint and constitute distinct *types*. Thus, a typed dependency does not require any interaction between values in different columns.

Example 5.27

The dependency

$$(\forall y y_1 y_2 y_3 y_4)(\mathbf{R}y y_1 y_2 \wedge \mathbf{R}y y_3 y_4 \supset \mathbf{R}y y_1 y_4),$$

is typed. The dependency

$$(\forall y_1 y_2)(\exists x_1)(\mathbf{R}y_1 y_2 \supset \mathbf{R}y_2 x_1)$$

is untyped. Thus, fd's, mvd's, emvd's, and join dependencies are all typed dependencies, while inclusion dependencies are untyped dependencies.   ∎

The following classification has to do with the structure of the dependencies. If $l = 0$, i.e., there are no existential quantifiers, then the dependency is *full* otherwise it is *embedded* (the term "embedded" is not quite appropriate here, but it is borrowed from emvd's). If all the B_i's are equalities, then the dependency is an *equality-generating dependency* (egd). If all the B_i's are relational formula, then the dependency is a *tuple-generating dependency* (tgd). For example, an fd is a full egd, an emvd is a tgd, and an mvd is a full tgd.

The above forms can be viewed as certain syntactical normal forms.

THEOREM 5.27

1. A (typed) dependency is logically equivalent to a set of (typed) egd's and tgd's.
2. A (typed) full dependency is logically equivalent to a set of (typed) full egd's and tgd's. ∎

Thus, from now on, we use the term "dependencies" to refer to egd's and tgd's.

We conclude this section by observing that egd's have the expressive power that fd's lack. We define egd-class analogously to fd-class. That is, a class Ψ of relations is an egd-class if there is a set Σ of egd's such that $\Psi = SAT(\Sigma)$.

THEOREM 5.28   (28)   The projection of an egd-class is an egd-class. ∎

Note that since every fd-class is an egd-class, it follows from the theorem that the projection of an fd-class is an egd-class.

5.6.3   The Implication Problem

We can now recast the discussion of Section 5.3.3 in more general terms: for full dependencies the (finite) implication problem reduces to the (finite) unsatisfiability problem of the BS class.

THEOREM 5.29   For full dependencies, implication and finite implication coincide, and the corresponding decision problems are decidable. ∎

Following our standard course, we should now come up with a formal system for full dependencies, and then with an efficient implication testing algorithm. A formal system was indeed developed in (16), but unlike the case with fd's and mvd's, that formal system does not lead to an efficient decision procedure. The best decision procedure for testing implication of full dependencies runs in exponential time. Surprisingly, this bound is the best possible.

THEOREM 5.30   (17)   The implication problem for typed full dependencies is EXPTIME-complete. ∎

A problem is EXPTIME-complete if it can be solved in exponential time and it is also as hard as any problem that can be solved in exponential time. Since it is known that there are problems that can be solved in exponential time and do require exponential time, it follows that EXPTIME-complete problems require exponential time. Thus, an EXPTIME-completeness is a proof that the problem is intractable. In contrast, NP-completeness is a strong suggestion rather than a proof that the problem is intractable, since it proves intractability only under the assumption that there are problems that can be solved in nondeterministic polynomial time but not in deterministic polynomial time.

The reduction of (finite) implication to (finite) unsatisfiability of the BS class depends crucially on the fact that full dependencies are universal sentences, and therefore, the reduction does not hold for embedded dependencies.

THEOREM 5.31 (15) For embedded dependencies, implication and finite implication differ.

Proof Let $\mathbf{R}$ be a binary relation name. Let Σ consists of the dependency σ_1:

$$\forall y_1 y_2 \exists x (\mathbf{R} y_1 y_2 \supset \mathbf{R} y_2 x)$$

and σ_2:

$$\forall y_1 y_2 y_3 (\mathbf{R} y_1 y_2 \wedge \mathbf{R} y_2 y_3 \supset \mathbf{R} y_1 y_3).$$

σ_1 says that $\mathbf{R}$ is *serial*, i.e., every node has an outgoing edge. σ_2 says that $\mathbf{R}$ is a *transitive* relation. Let σ be the dependency

$$\forall y_1 y_2 \exists x (\mathbf{R} y_1 y_2 \supset \mathbf{R} xx).$$

σ says that if $\mathbf{R}$ is nonempty, then it must be *reflexive* on some node.

We claim that $\Sigma \not\models \sigma$ but $\Sigma \models_f \sigma$. We first show that $\Sigma \not\models \sigma$. Let $\mathbf{R}$ be interpreted by the binary relation $I = \{(i, j) : i \leq j\}$. It is easy to check that I satisfies Σ but not σ. Suppose, however, that $\mathbf{R}$ is interpreted by a finite nonempty binary relation I and that I that satisfies Σ. Because of σ_1, the relation I must contain a cycle, i.e., a sequence of nodes $a_1, \ldots, a_n$ such that $(a_i, a_{i+1}) \in I$, for $1 \leq i \leq n - 1$, and also $(a_n, a_1) \in I$. But because of σ_2, we must have $(a_1, a_1) \in I$, so I satisfies σ. ∎

Theorem 5.31 suggests that the (finite) implication problem for dependencies might be undecidable, which is indeed the case. (Note, however, that there are classes of dependencies for which implication and finite implication differ, but both the implication problem and the finite implication problem are decidable (38).

THEOREM 5.32 (15, 17) The implication and the finite implication problems for dependencies are undecidable. ∎

Well, so much for our hope to prove decidability for emvd's by extending the class of dependencies. But all may not be lost yet. It is still conceivable that we can find a decidable class of dependencies that that contains the class of emvd's. Let us look more closely at the first-order syntax of emvd's (see Section 8.5.7). Emvd's have the following four properties:

1. they are typed,
2. they are tgd's,
3. they have a single relational formula on the right-hand side of the implication, and
4. they have at most two formulas on the left-hand side of the implication.

Dependencies that satisfy properties (1)–(3) are called *template dependencies* (54). The class of template dependencies seems to be quite a natural class; in fact, it is the smallest class of dependencies that contains the class of emvd's and is known to have a sound and complete formal system (16, 54). Thus, one might hope that this class is decidable. Unfortunately, this is not the case.

THEOREM 5.33   (32, 58) The implication and finite implication problems for template dependencies are undecidable.   ∎

In fact, Vardi (58) proved undecidability for even a smaller class of dependencies, the class of *projected join dependencies*. Nevertheless, the implication problem for emvd's remains tantalizingly open.

5.6.4 Global Decision Problems

So far we have concentrated almost exclusively on the implication problem. Our interest in the implication problem was originally, however, rather secondary. Our primary interest was in properties of sets of dependencies, such as equivalence and redundancy, which happen to reduce to implication. Now that we know that the implication problem is undecidable, we have to reconsider equivalence and redundancy. For simplicity we consider here only finite relations. Recall that two sets Δ and Σ of dependencies are *equivalent* if they are satisfied by the same relations, and a set Σ of dependencies is *redundant* if there is a proper subset Δ of Σ such that Δ and Σ are equivalent. The *redundancy problem* is to determine whether a given finite set of dependencies is redundant (we concentrate on redundancy, since undecidability of equivalence follows easily from undecidability of implication).

More generally, we would like to be able to check other properties of sets of dependencies. This gives rise to decision problems that we call *global*, to contrast it with the implication problem, which we view as a *local* decision problem. (This terminology is borrowed from the theory of finitely presented groups (14). The problem of whether two words in a finitely presented group are equal is a local problem, while the problem whether a finitely presented group is, say, simple is global.) Our interest in global decision problem comes from the fact that we view a set of dependencies as a semantic specification for a database. The ability to recognize properties of such specification seems to be essential to the task of verifying their consistency and correctness. We now describe several global properties of interest. We assume that the language contains a relation name $\mathbf{R}$ of some unspecified arity, and that $\mathbf{R}$ will be interpreted by a relation I.

A relation I is *trivial* if $I = \{(a, a, \ldots, a)\}$ for some element a, that is, I consists of a single tuple with the same entries in all columns. It is easy to verify that a trivial relation satisfies all dependencies. A set Σ is *inconsistent* if a relation I satisfies Σ only if I is trivial. If Σ is inconsistent, then it is probably not a meaningful semantic specification. (In general, inconsistency means having no model. But, since every set of dependencies is satisfiable by the trivial relation, we define inconsistency as having no nontrivial models.)

Let $\Sigma^+ = \{\sigma : \Sigma \models_f \sigma\}$, i.e., Σ^+ is the set of dependencies implied by Σ. Σ is *complete* if $\Sigma \cup \{\sigma\}$ is inconsistent for all $\sigma \not\in \Sigma^+$. If Σ is complete, then there is no point in trying to extend it, since every dependency σ is either a consequence of Σ, or yields an inconsistent specification if added to Σ.

For any relation I, let $DEP(I)$ be the set of all dependencies satisfied by I, i.e., $DEP(I) = \{\sigma : I \text{ satisfies } \sigma\}$. I is an *Armstrong relation* for a set Σ of dependencies, if $DEP(I) = \Sigma^+$. Σ is *Armstrong* if it has an Armstrong relation. (This terminology, (28, 44), is suggested by the approach in (2).) The motivation for this property is as follows. Suppose that I satisfies Σ. In general, I satisfies not only Σ^+, but also other dependencies as well. These dependencies are satisfied "accidentally." If, on the other hand, I is an Armstrong relation for Σ, then it does not satisfy any "accidental" dependencies. Thus, I can be viewed as a representative instance for the collection of databases specified by Σ, namely $SAT(\Sigma)$. Such representative instances seems to be useful in the process of database design (46, 53).

The last property that we consider is *decidability*. Undecidability of the implication problem means that the set $\{(\Sigma, \sigma) : \Sigma \models_f \sigma\}$ is not recursive. It is possible, however, that for a particular set Σ of dependencies, the set Σ^+ is recursive. This means that for this particular Σ the implication problem is decidable, i.e., we can check whether $\Sigma \models_f \sigma$ for any given σ. In this case we say that Σ is *decidable*, clearly, a desirable property.

A property P *implies* a property Q, if P is a subset of Q, i.e., if a set Σ of dependencies is P, then it is also Q. The relationship between the above defined properties is as follows.

THEOREM 5.34   Inconsistency implies completeness, which implies Armstrongness, which implies decidability.

Proof

1. Suppose that Σ is inconsistent. Then it has only trivial models. But the trivial relation satisfies all dependencies, so Σ^+ is the set of all dependencies. Thus, the condition of completeness is satisfied vacuously.

2. Suppose that Σ is complete. We have to consider two cases. First, Σ might be inconsistent. In that case, Σ^+ is the set of all dependencies, so any trivial relation is an Armstrong relation for Σ. If Σ is not inconsistent, then it has a nontrivial model, i.e., there is a nontrivial relation I such that I satisfies Σ. We claim that I is an Armstrong relation for Σ. Indeed, suppose that I satisfies σ, but σ is not in Σ^+. Since I is nontrivial and it satisfies $\Sigma \cup \{\sigma\}$, it follows that $\Sigma \cup \{\sigma\}$ is consistent, which contradicts the completeness of Σ.

3. Suppose that Σ is Armstrong. Then there is a relation I such that $DEP(I) = \Sigma^+$. Thus, σ is in Σ^+ if and only if I satisfies σ. Since it is decidable whether I satisfies σ, it follows that Σ^+ is recursive.   ■

In general, a *property* P is a set of finite sets of dependencies. We usually say that a set Σ *is* P instead of saying that it is *in* P. For example, the property of completeness is the set of all complete finite sets of dependencies. Of course, we would like our properties to be *decidable*, i.e., recursive. We are going to state a general negative result about decidability of properties, but we need first some definitions.

A property P is *trivial* if either all finite sets of dependencies are P or none is. Clearly, only nontrivial properties are of interest. The following definition is inspired by Theorem 5.34. We say that a property P is *well-behaved* if it contains the property of inconsistency, i.e., if every inconsistent set is P. For example, decidability, Armstrongness, completeness, and, of course, inconsistency are all well-behaved properties.

To define the next notion we need to redefine the operation of *projection* in accordance with our current convention of ordered columns. Let I be an n-ary relation, and let $i_1, \ldots, i_k$ be a sequence such that $1 \leq i_1 < \cdots < i_k \leq n$. The *projection* of I on the arguments $i_1, \ldots, i_k$ is

$$\pi_{\langle i_1, \ldots, i_k \rangle}(I) = \{(a_{i_1}, \ldots, a_{i_k}) : (a_1, \ldots, a_n) \in I\}.$$

Let Σ be a set of dependencies on an n-ary relation $\mathbf{R}$, and let Δ be a set of dependencies on a k-ary relation $\mathbf{P}$. We say that Δ is a *projection* of Σ if there is a sequence $1 \leq i_1 < \cdots < i_k \leq n$ such that $SAT(\Delta) = \pi_{\langle i_1, \ldots, i_k \rangle}SAT(\Sigma)$. In other words, Δ is a projection of Σ if it is the specification of the projections of the relations specified by Σ. We say that a property P is *hereditary* if it is inherited by projections, that is, if Σ is P and Δ is a projection of Σ, then Δ is also P.

We can now state the general result.

THEOREM 5.35 (57) Let P be a nontrivial, well-behaved, and hereditary property. Then P is undecidable. In particular, inconsistency, completeness, Armstrongness, and decidability are undecidable. ∎

Looking back at the properties studied here, we see that redundancy is different from, say, completeness. Completeness is a semantic property; that is, if Σ is complete and Δ is equivalent to Σ, then Δ is also complete. This is not the case with redundancy, which is a syntactic property. In particular, redundancy is not an hereditary property, so it is not covered by Theorem 5.35. Nevertheless, the reader should not get too hopeful.

THEOREM 5.36 (57) Redundancy is undecidable. ∎

5.7 CONCLUDING REMARKS

We have gone through a whole span of dependency theory, from the "meek" functional dependencies, for which most decision problems are efficiently solvable, to the general "mean" family of dependencies, for which almost nothing of interest seems to be solvable. Our voyage have been motivated by the desire to automate the process of database design. So what is the moral?

Perhaps it would be instructive to draw an analogy with another discipline. Twenty years ago it was widely believed that a powerful and efficient proof procedure that can create logical demonstrations would be a major step in getting a machine to behave intelligently. Years passed, the desired proof procedure continued to elude researchers, and this approach was rendered naive and simplistic. Current research in artificial intelligence is detailed and nitty-gritty rather than vague and general.

We believe that the hope of fully automating the process of database design is similarly naive and simplistic. Modelling the real world is an immensely complicated task for which perhaps no elegant algorithm exists. One should view the theoretical foundations that have been laid as a basis on which to develop heuristics and practical methodologies.

5.8 ACKNOWLEDGMENTS

I am grateful to Ron Fagin, Kari-Jouko Raiha, and Pierre Wolper for many valuable comments on previous drafts of this article.

5.9 REFERENCES

1. Aho, A.V., Beeri, C., Ullman, J.D., "The theory of joins in relational databases," *ACM Trans. on Database Systems* 4(1979), pp. 297–314.

2. Armstrong, W.W., "Dependency structure in data base relationships," *Proc. IFIP 74*, North-Holland, 1974, pp. 580–583.

3. Beeri, C., Bernstein, P.A., "Computational problems related to the design of normal form relational schemas," *ACM Trans. on Database Systems* 4(1979), pp. 30–59.

4. Beeri, C., Bernstein, P.A., Goodman, N., "A sophisticate's introduction to database normalization theory," *Proc. 4th Int'l Conf. on Very Large Data Bases*, Berlin, 1978, pp. 113–124.

5. Biskup, J., Dayal, U., Bernstein, P.A., "Synthesizing independent database schemas," *Proc. ACM-SIGMOD Int'l Conf. on Management of Data*, 1979, pp. 143–152.

6. Beeri, C., "On the membership problem for multivalued dependencies," *ACM Trans. on Database Systems* 5(1980), pp. 241–259.

7. Beeri, C., Private communication.

8. Bernstein, P.A., "Normalization and functional dependencies in the relational model," Ph.D. Dissertation, Tech. Rep. CSRG-60, University of Toronto, 1975.

9. Bernstein, P.A., "Synthesizing third normal form relations from functional dependencies," *ACM Trans. on Database Systems* 1(1976), pp. 277–298.

10. Beeri, C., Fagin, R., Howard, J.H., "A complete axiomatization for functional and multivalued dependencies in database relations," *Proc. ACM-SIGMOD Int'l Conf. on Management of Data*, Toronto, 1977, pp. 47–61.

11. Biskup, J., "On the complementation rule for multivalued dependencies in data base relations," *Acta Informatica* 10(1978), pp. 297–305.

12. Biskup, J., "Inferences of multivalued dependencies in fixed and undetermined universe," *Theoretical Computer Science* 10(1980), pp. 93–105.

13. Beeri, C., Mendelzon, A.O., Sagiv, Y., Ullman, J.D., "Equivalence of relational database schemes," *SIAM J. Comput.* 10(1981), pp. 647–656.

14. Boone, W.W., "Decision problems about logical systems as a whole and recursively enumerable degrees of unsolvability," In *Contributions to Mathematical Logic* (H.A. Schmidt, K. Schutte, and H.J. Thiele, eds.), North-Holland, 1968, pp. 13–33.

15. Beeri, C., Vardi, M.Y., "The implication problem for data dependencies," *Proc. 8th Int'l Colloq. on Automata, Language, and Programming*, Acre, Israel, 1981, Lecture Notes in Computer Science 115, Springer-Verlag, 1981, pp. 73–85.

16. Beeri, C., Vardi, M.Y., "Formal system for tuple and equality generating dependencies," *SIAM J. Computing* 13(1984), pp. 76–98.

17. Chandra, A.K., Lewis, H.R., Makowsky, J.A., "Embedded implicational dependencies and their inference problem," *Proc. 13th ACM Ann. Symp. on Theory of Computing*, 1981, pp. 342–354.

18. Codd, E.F., "A relational model of data for large shared data banks," *Comm. ACM* 13(1970), pp. 377–387.

19. Codd, E.F., "Further normalization of the data base relational model," in *Data Base Systems* (R. Rustin, ed.), Prentice-Hall, N.J., 1971, pp. 33–64.

20. Codd, E.F., "Relational completeness of database sublanguages," in *Data Base Systems* (R. Rustin, ed.), Prentice-Hall, N.J., 1972, pp. 65–98.

21. Codd, E.F., "Recent investigations in relational database systems," *Proc. IFIP 74*, North-Holland, 1974, pp. 1017–1021.

22. Delobel, C., "Semantics of relations and the decomposition process in the relational data model," *ACM Trans. on Database Systems* 3(1978), pp. 201–222.

23. Dreben, B.S., Goldfarb, W.D., *"The decision problem—solvable classes of quantificational formulas,"* Addison Wesley, 1979.

24. Fagin, R., *"Multivalued dependencies and a new normal form for relational databases,"* IBM Research Report RJ1812, IBM Research Laboratory, San Jose, 1976.

25. Fagin, R.. "Multivalued dependencies and a new normal form for relational databases," *ACM Trans. on Database Systems* 2(1977), pp. 262–278.

26. Fagin, R., "Functional dependencies in a relational database and propositional logic," *IBM J. Research and Development* 21(1977), pp. 534–544.

27. Fagin, R., "A normal form for relational databases that is based on domains and keys," *ACM Trans. on Database Systems* 6(1981), pp. 387–415.

28. Fagin, R., "Horn clauses and database dependencies," *J. ACM* 29(1982), pp. 952–985.

29. Fagin, R., Vardi, M.Y., "The theory of data dependencies—a survey," in *Mathematics of Information Processing*, Proc. Symp. in Applied Mathematics 34, American Mathematical Society, 1986, pp. 19–72.

30. Galil, Z., "An almost linear-time algorithm for computing a dependency basis in a relational database," *J. ACM* 29(1982), pp. 96–102.

31. Garey, M.R., Johnson, D.S., *"Computers and intractability—a guide to the theory of NP-completeness,"* Freeman, San Francisco, 1979.

32. Gurevich, Y., Lewis, H.R., "The inference problem for template dependencies," *Proc. ACM Symp. on Principles of Database Systems*, Los Angeles, 1982, pp. 221–229.

33. Ginsburg, S., Zaiddan, S.M., "Properties of functional-dependency families," *J. ACM* 29(1982), pp. 678–698.

34. Heath, I.J., "Unacceptable file operations in a relational database," *Proc. ACM-SIGFIDET Workshop on Data Description, Access, and Control*, San Diego, 1971.

35. Hagihara, K., Ito, M., Taiguchi, K., Kasami, T., "Decision problems for multi-valued dependencies in relational databases," *SIAM J. on Computing* 8 (1979), pp. 247–264.

36. Ito, M., Taniguchi, K., Kasami, T., "Membership problem for embedded multi-valued dependencies under some restricted conditions," *Theoretical Computer Science* 23(1983), pp. 175–194.

37. Karp, R.M., "Reducibility among combinatorial problems," in *Complexity of Computer Computations*, Plenum Press, New York, 1972, pp. 85–104.

38. Kannelakis, P.C., Cosmadakis, S.S., Vardi, M.Y., "Unary inclusion dependencies have polynomial-time inference problems," *Proc. 15th ACM Symp. on Theory of Computing*, Boston, 1983, pp. 264–277.

39. Lewis, H.R., "Complexity results for classes of quantificational formulas," *J. Computer and System Sciences* 21(1980), pp. 317–353.

40. Lien, Y.E., "Hierarchical schemata for relational databases," *ACM Trans. on Database Systems* 6(1981), pp. 48–69.

41. Lucchesi, C.L., Osborn, S.L., "Candidate keys for relations," *J. Computer and System Sciences* 17(1978), pp. 270–279.

42. Maier, D., "Minimum covers in the relational database model," *J. ACM* 27(1980), pp. 664–674.

43. Maier, D., "*The theory of relational databases*," Computer Science Press, Rockville, 1983.

44. Makowsky, J.A., "Characterizing database dependencies," *Proc. 8th Int'l Colloq. on Automata, Language, and Programming*, Acre, Israel, 1981, Lecture Notes in Computer Science 115, Springer-Verlag, 1981, pp. 86–97.

45. Mendelzon, A.O., "On axiomatizing multivalued dependencies in relational databases," *J. ACM* 26(1979), pp. 37–44.

46. Mannila, H., Raiha, K.J., "Small Armstrong relations for database design," *Proc. 4th ACM Symp. on Principles of Database Systems*, Portland, 1985, pp. 245–250.

47. Nicolas, J.M., "First order logic formalizations for functional, multivalued and mutual dependencies," *Proc. ACM-SIGMOD Int'l Conf. on Management of Data*, 1978, pp. 40–46.

48. Parker, D.S., Parsaye-Ghomi, K., "Inference involving embedded multivalued dependencies and transitive dependencies," *Proc. ACM-SIGMOD Int'l Conf. on Management of Data*, 1980, pp. 52–57.

49. Rissanen, J., "Independent components of relations," *ACM Trans. on Database Systems* 2(1977), pp. 317–325.

50. Rissanen, J., "Theory of relations for databases—a tutorial survey," *Proc. 7th Symp. on Math. Found. of Computer Science*, Portland, 1978, Lecture Notes in Computer Science 64, Springer-Verlag, pp. 537–551.

51. Rogers, H., "*Theory of recursive functions and effective computability*," McGraw-Hill, 1967.

52. Sagiv, Y., Delobel, C., Parker, D.S., Fagin, R., "An equivalence between relational database dependencies and a subclass of propositional calculus," *J. ACM* 28(1981), pp. 435–453.

53. Silva, A.M., Melkanoff, M.A., "A method for helping discover the dependencies of a relation," in *Advances in Database Theory* (H. Gallaire, J. Minker, and J.M. Nicolas, eds.), Plenum Press, 1981, pp. 115–133.

54. Sadri, F., Ullman, J.D., "A complete axiomatization for a large class of dependencies in relational databases," *J. ACM* 29(1982), pp. 363–372.

55. Sagiv, Y., Walecka, S., "Subset dependencies as an alternative to embedded multivalued dependencies," *J. ACM* 29(1982), pp. 103–117.

56. Ullman, J.D., "*Principles of database systems*," Computer Science Press, Rockville, 1982.

57. Vardi, M.Y., "Global decision problems for relational databases," *Proc. 22nd IEEE Symp. on Foundations of Computer Science*, Nashville, 1981, pp. 198–202.

58. Vardi, M.Y., "The implication and the finite implication problems for typed template dependencies," *J. Computer and System Sciences* 28(1984), pp. 3–28.

59. Vardi, M.Y., "A note on lossless database decomposition," *Information Processing Letters* 18(1984), pp. 257–260.

60. Yannakakis, M., Papadimitriou, C., "Algebraic dependencies," *J. Computer and System Sciences* 21(1982), pp. 2–41.

61. Zaniolo, C., "*Analysis and design of relational schemata for database systems*," Technical Report UCLA-ENG-7769, Department of Computer Science, UCLA, July 1976.

62. Zaniolo, C., Melkanoff, M.A., "On the design of relational database schemata," *ACM Trans. on Database Systems* 6(1981), pp. 1–47.

Part III
Analysis of Algorithms

Chapter 6

Mathematical Methods in the Analysis of Algorithms and Data Structures*

PHILIPPE FLAJOLET[†]

Abstract—This presentation is intended both as a tutorial and a partial review of advanced mathematical methods in the *average case analysis* of algorithms and data structures. An analysis usually decomposes into several combinatorial enumeration problems (of words, trees, permutations, distributions . . .) whose outcome is then subjected to asymptotic analysis in order to obtain results in a form that is easy to interpret.

The main technique to solve combinatorial enumeration problems is via the use of generating functions. The approach presented here is called the *symbolic operator method*: a large set of combinatorial constructions have direct translations as operators on counting generating functions, so that functional equations over generating functions can be obtained rather directly for many combinatorial structures of interest.

The main technique for asymptotic analysis in this context relies on *complex analysis*: analytic function theory and uses of Cauchy's residue theorem. In most cases the asymptotic behavior of coefficients of a generating function can be recovered directly from the generating function itself with a proper choice of integration contour (singularity analysis, saddle point methods . . .).

These methods are briefly illustrated with several examples relating to: (1) tree manipulation algorithms in compiling and symbolic manipulation systems; (2) sorting and searching techniques based on comparisons between keys; and (3) digital search algorithms.

---

*Lecture Notes for *A Graduate Course on Computation Theory*, Udine (Italy), September–October 1984.

†INRIA, Rocquencourt, 78150 - Le Chesnay, France.

6.1   AN INTRODUCTION TO THE ANALYSIS OF ALGORITHMS

This section describes, informally, the basic problems involved in the average case analysis of algorithms using Knuth's example of the *max-finding* procedure that determines the maximum value of an array. We use this leading example to introduce generating function techniques and to discuss the relevance of asymptotic analysis. We conclude this section with a brief overview of the main methods used in the analysis of algorithms.

The task of *analyzing* an algorithm consists of predicting the resources that the algorithm will consume when it receives as input, data of some fixed size n. Several *complexity measures* corresponding to various notions of resource consumption may be defined:

1. Time complexity measure (τ): this is the time the algorithm takes to process a particular data on a given machine model; it may be expressed either in terms of machine cycles or time units (microseconds for instance); Knuth (1, 2) has defined an abstract machine model MIX, typical of many existing machines, in which all the algorithms presented are programmed, time being measured by the number of machine cycles.

2. *Storage complexity measure* (σ): this may be measured by the number of bits, bytes, words, or more abstractly, records that the algorithm consumes.

Simplified measures may be considered for particular algorithms. For a sorting algorithm, one often restricts attention to the number of comparisons performed or to the number of records moved (these are simplified time-complexity measures). For algorithms operating on some external storage device, like a disk, a critical determinant of efficiency is usually the number of disk accesses (again a simplified time-complexity measure) or the number of disk pages used (a simplified storage complexity measure).

Let A be an algorithm that operates on a set of inputs $\mathbf{E}$; the size of an element ω of $\mathbf{E}$ is denoted by $|\omega|$ (usually the size of a word is its length, the size of an array is its dimension, the size of a graph is the number of its nodes, the size of a file the number of elements it comprises, etc. . . . .). Three quantities can be defined to characterize the behavior of algorithm A over the set $\mathbf{E}_n$ of inputs of size n under a given complexity measure μ. With $\mu a[\omega]$ denoting the complexity w.r.t. measure μ of algorithm A on input $\omega \in \mathbf{E}$, we introduce:

1. the *best-case complexity*:

$$\mu a_n^{BEST} = \min\{\mu a[\omega]/\omega \in \mathbf{E}_n\} \qquad (6.1)$$

2. the *worst-case complexity*:

$$\mu a_n^{WORST} = \max\{\mu a[\omega]/\omega \in \mathbf{E}_n\} \qquad (6.2)$$

3. the *average-case complexity*:

$$\mu a_n^{AVERGE} \equiv \overline{\mu a}_n = \mathbf{E}\{\mu a[\omega]/\omega \in \mathbf{E}_n\}. \tag{6.3}$$

Quantities (6.1) and (6.2) give indications concerning extremal bounds on the complexity of A when applied to data of size n. Their determination usually requires the construction of particular combinatorial configurations that force extremal behaviors of the algorithm. Our main interest here is in the average complexity of some of the classical algorithms and data structures. Notice that in (6.3), we have used the notation $\mathbf{E}\{X\}$ denoting the *expectation* of the random variable X. The determination of the average-case complexity of an algorithm, therefore, requires introduction of a *probabilistic model* in order for this expectation to be properly defined.

Each class of algorithmic problem usually carries one or a few natural probabilistic models. If $\mathbf{E}_n$ is finite, the *empirical model* will consist of considering all elements of $\mathbf{E}_n$ to be equally likely. Such models are often considered when analyzing algorithms that operate on words, term trees, or expression trees in compiling or in symbolic manipulation systems. For comparison-based sorting algorithms, a simple model consists of assuming that elements to be sorted are drawn independently from some continuous distribution; this *independence model* is equivalent to assuming that the algorithm is applied to the reduced set $\mathbf{E}_n^*$ of all permutations of $[1 . . n]$, with each permutation being equally likely (having probability $1/n!$). For hashing algorithms, one will usually assume hashed values to be independent and uniformly distributed over the address space $[1 . . m]$; there, this *uniform model* is again equivalent to assuming each of the m^n address sequences to be equally likely.

The preceding discussion indicates that many probabilistic models for analysis are equivalent to a model in which elements of either $\mathbf{E}_n$ or of a finite subset $\mathbf{E}_n^*$ of $\mathbf{E}_n$ are equally likely, having each probability $1/(\mathrm{card}\,\mathbf{E}_n)$ or $1/(\mathrm{card}\,\mathbf{E}_n^*)$. In that case, the average-case complexity of algorithm A can be reexpressed (identifying here $\mathbf{E}_n$ and $\mathbf{E}_n^*$) as:

$$\overline{\mu a}^n = \frac{1}{\mathrm{card}\,\mathbf{E}_n} \sum_k k \cdot \sigma_{n,k} \tag{6.4a}$$

where

$$\sigma_{n,k} = \mathrm{card}\{\omega \in \mathbf{E}_n/\mu a[\omega] = k\} \tag{6.4b}$$

Formula (6.4a) is nothing but the standard form of expectations $\mathbf{E}\{X\} = \sum_k k\, \Pr(X = k)$, since the probability $\Pr(X = k)$ is equal to $\sigma_{n,k}/(\mathrm{card}\,\mathbf{E}_n)$.

This brief discussion shows that the problem of analyzing algorithms reduces to *counting* various *classes of combinatorial structures* (words, trees, permutations, distributions, graphs, ...) according to their sizes and the values of some parameters related to the algorithm under consideration.

6.1.1   An Example: The Max-Finding Algorithm

Let $X[1..n]$ be an array of positive real numbers. The following sequence of Pascal instructions returns in *max* the value of the largest element in $X[1..n]$

```
max: = -1;
for i: = 1 to n do
  if max<X[i] then max: = X[i];
```

Apart from its data $X[1..n]$, this simple program uses two auxiliary variables (*max* and *i*) so that its storage complexity is 2 (we do not count the input) or $n+2$ (we count it), the unit being the storage required to keep one integer or real number. A more interesting question is the time complexity of that program. Knuth analyzes it by translating it into some fixed machine language (*MIX*) which in Pascal notation, is equivalent to using only a very reduced set of Pascal instructions, like:

```
max: = -1;
i: = 0;
1 : i: = i+1;
if i>n then goto 2;
if max ≥ X[i] then goto 1;
max: = X[i];
goto 1;
2 : . . .
```

This form is also equivalent to a flowchart (graph) like that of Figure 6.1. Thus, on almost any classical (nonparallel) computer, a compiled form of the program will execute:

1. a fixed number of assignments to initialize *max* and *i*;
2. $(n+1)$ comparisons of the form $i>n$?
3. $(n+1)$ incrementations of index *i*
4. n comparisons of the form $max \geq X[i]$?
5. a variable number (between 1 and n) of assignments $max: = X[i]$.

In summary, the time complexity of max finding (*maxf*) on almost any conceivable machine is going to be of the form:

$$\tau maxf[X] = C_0 + C_1 n + C_2 EXCH[X] \qquad (6.5)$$

where $EXCH[X]$, for X an array, is the number of times the instruction $max: = X[i]$ is executed (the number of "exchanges" or updates of *max*). Quantities C_0, C_1, C_2 are so-called *implementation constants* that reflect the execution time of elementary instructions for the machine on which the program is executed.

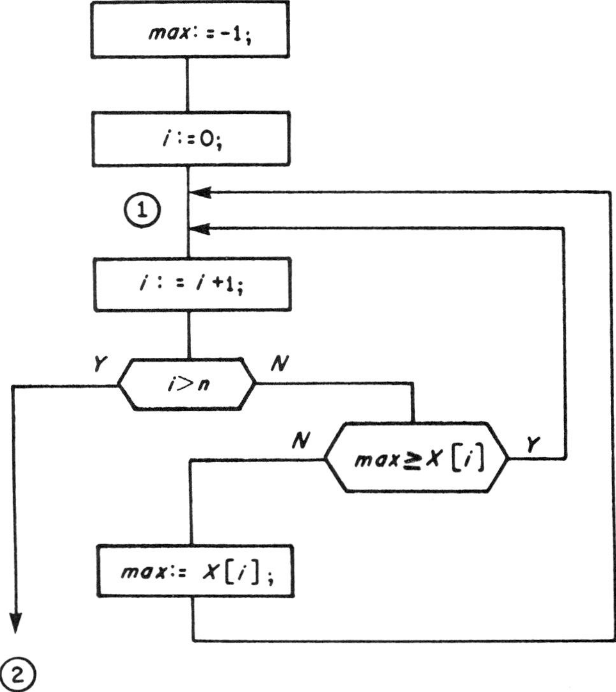

Figure 6.1 The flowchart corresponding to a low-level implementation of the max-finding procedure.

The above sketch shows that the analysis of an algorithm starts with a *flow analysis* where one determines the number of times each instruction is executed; taking advantage of the structure of the program considered reduces the number of independent parameters to a minimum (using the "Kirchhoff's laws," see 1, pp 95, 167–168). With some experience, a program can be analyzed directly at the level of the Pascal source program, and we shall do so in the rest of this paper. (One could also formally specify costs associated to Pascal constructs for a given machine and a given compiler.)

Formula (6.5) is our starting point for analysis. Notice that $EXCH[X]$ is equal to the number of left-to-right maxima of vector X, i.e. the number of elements (indices $j \in [1..n]$) such that for all $i < j$: $X[i] < X[j]$. Thus, $EXCH[X]$ is equal to 1 iff $X[1]$ is the largest element of the array $X[1..n]$ and $EXCH[X]$ is equal to n iff $X[1..n]$ is already sorted in increasing order: $X[1] < X[2] < X[3]$ .... These are obviously the extremal configurations, whence

PROPOSITION 6.1   The max finding procedure has extremal complexities described by:

$$\tau maxf_n^{BEST} = (C_0 + C_2) + C_1 n$$

$$\tau maxf_n^{WORST} = C_0 + (C_1 + C_2)n,$$

where C_0, C_1, C_2, are implementation dependent constants.

To obtain more information on the algorithm when used repeatedly, we proceed to study it under the following probabilistic model:

MODEL 6.1   (Uniform-Independent Model)   The n elements of array X are assumed to be independently drawn from a uniform $[0,1]$ distribution.

Let J denote the unit interval $[0,1]$. For X a random variable (vector) over J^n, we are interested in the probabilities

$$p_{n,k} = \Pr(EXCH[X] = k).$$

These probabilities can be evaluated by computing multiple integrals. When $n = 2$, for instance, one has:

$$p_{2,1} = \Pr(X[1] \geq X[2]) = \iint_{x_1 \geq x_2} dx_1\,dx_2$$

$$p_{2,2} = \Pr(X[1] < X[2]) = \iint_{x_1 < x_2} dx_1\,dx_2$$

so that

$$p_{2,1} = \frac{1}{2}; \quad p_{2,2} = \frac{1}{2},$$

and the expected value of $EXCH$ is

$$\overline{exch_2} = \frac{1}{2} \cdot 1 + \frac{1}{2} \cdot 2 = \frac{3}{2}.$$

To avoid computation of multiple integrals, one introduces an alternative model:

MODEL 6.2   (The permutation model)   The array X is a permutation of $[1 . . n]$, each permutation being taken with equal probability $(1/n!)$.

One has the important:

LEMMA 6.1   For the analysis of the max-finding procedure, the Uniform-Independent Model and the Permutation Model are equivalent.

Proof Associate to each array $X[1. .n]$ consisting of n distinct elements its *order type* $\tau = \tau_1, \tau_2, \ldots, \tau_n$ defined by

- $\tau_1, \tau_2, \ldots, \tau_n$ is a permutation of $[1. .n]$
- for all i,j: $\tau_i < \tau_j$ iff $X[i] < X[j]$.

The order type is a reduced presentation of the order properties of elements of array X. For instance, if

$$X = (3.14, 2.71, 0.55, 1.41, 1.73)$$

then

$$\tau = (5, 4, 1, 2, 3).$$

(Write a 1 under the smallest element of X, a 2 under the second smallest, etc. . . . .) Obviously, if $\tau(X)$ is the order type of vector X, $EXCH[X] = EXCH[\tau(X)]$.

The first observation is now that under Model 1, the probability that two array elements coincide is 0, so that the order type of a random array (under model 6.1.1.) is defined with probability 1. The main observation is that each order type is equally likely, by simple symmetry considerations. For instance, if $n = 3$,

$$\int_{\substack{x_1<x_2>x_3 \\ x_1>x_3}} dx_1\, dx_2\, dx_3 = \int_{x_1>x_2>x_3} dx_1\, dx_2\, dx_3.$$

Thus, each order type under Model 1 has probability $1/n!$. Since the cost of the algorithm depends only on the underlying order type of the input, the lemma is established. ∎

Observations: (1) The equivalence result will hold true for any model where array elements are taken independently from some continuous distribution (i.e. no point has a nonzero mass) like Gaussian, exponential, etc. . . . , so that the permutation model is really equivalent to a general independence model. (2) The same equivalence will apply to all algorithms that are only sensitive to the relative order of their input "keys." Thus, comparison-based algorithms (bubble sort, heapsort, quicksort . . .) are always analyzed under the permutation model. ∎

The interest of the permutation model is that the analysis reduces to a counting problem. Let $s_{n,k}$ denote the number of permutations of $[1. .n]$ such that $EXCH(\sigma) = k$; from Lemma 6.1, we have:

$$p_{n,k} = \frac{s_{n,k}}{n!}$$

$$\overline{exch}_n = \frac{1}{n!} \sum_k k\, s_{n,k}$$

We now proceed to prove:

THEOREM 6.1　The max-finding procedure has average cost (under the permutation model) given by

$$\tau maxf_n = C_0 + C_1 n + C_2 H_n$$

where H_n denotes the n-th harmonic number:

$$H_n = 1 + \frac{1}{2} + \frac{1}{3} + \cdots + \frac{1}{n}.$$

Proof　Consider the set of all permutations σ of $[1. \, .n]$ whose parameter *EXCH* has value k (there are $s_{n,k}$ of these). Two cases can occur: (i) the last element σ_n is equal to n so that $\sigma_1 \sigma_2 \cdots \sigma_{n-1}$ has $(k-1)$ as value of *EXCH* (this can happen in $s_{n-1,k-1}$ ways); (ii) the last element has one of the values $1, 2, \ldots ,$ $n-1$; thus $\sigma_1 \sigma_2 \cdots \sigma_{n-1}$ already contains value n and has k as value of *EXCH* (this can happen in $(n-1) \times s_{n-1,k-1}$ ways). Whence, the *recurrence*:

$$s_{n,k} = s_{n-1,k-1} + (n-1)s_{n-1,k}. \tag{6.6}$$

Equation (6.6) is similar to the recurrence defining elements of the Pascal triangle. It makes it possible to determine inductively all the $s_{n,k}$.

In order to derive information from Equation (6.6), we introduce generating functions. We define for each n, the quantity

$$s_n(x) = \sum_{k=1}^{n} s_{n,k} x^k.$$

Multiplying both sides of equality (6.6) by x^k and summing over k, we get:

$$s_n(x) = x s_{n-1}(x) + (n-1)s_{n-1}(x) = (x + (n-1))s_{n-1}(x).$$

Now from initial values $s_0(x) = 1$; $s_1(x) = x$; $s_2(x) = x(x+1) \cdots$ and the above recurrence, we find the explicit form for $s_n(x)$:

$$s_n(x) = \prod_{j=0}^{n-1} (x + j). \tag{6.7}$$

From there we can easily conclude since

$$\overline{exch_n} = \frac{1}{n!} \sum k s_{n,k} = \frac{s_n'(1)}{s_n(1)} \tag{6.8}$$

where the logarithmic derivative of (6.7) permits to determine the value of (6.8) since:

$$\frac{s_n'(x)}{s_n(x)} = \frac{1}{x} + \frac{1}{x+1} + \cdots + \frac{1}{x+n-1}. \qquad \blacksquare$$

6.1.2 Generating Functions and Combinatorial Enumerations: A Preliminary Discussion

The previous approach is important. To count a class of structures of size n, we decompose it into simpler (smaller) classes. This *decomposition* is reflected by a main *recurrence* relation (recurrence (6.6) on the example of max-finding). The recurrence relation is then attacked by the use of *generating functions*, on our example only a technical trick, leading to an explicit form (expression (6.7) on the example). We shall see later that, for essential reasons, generating functions are a tool of considerable generality.

We first set:

DEFINITION 6.1 Let $\{a_k\}_{k\geq 0}$ be a sequence of complex numbers. The *ordinary generating function* (o.g.f.) of sequence $\{a_k\}$ is defined as

$$a(z) = \sum_k a_k z_k. \tag{6.9}$$

The *exponential generating function* (e.g.f.) of sequence $\{a_k\}$ is defined as

$$\hat{a}(z) = \sum_k a_k \frac{z^k}{k!}. \tag{6.10}$$

Notations: We let $[z^n]f(z)$ denote the coefficient of z^n in $f(z)$ in the Taylor expansion of f around $z = 0$. Thus,

$$f(z) = \sum_{n\geq 0} f_n z^n \Rightarrow [z^n]f(z) = f_n.$$

We extend that notation by setting:

$$\left[\frac{z^n}{n!}\right] f(z) = n! [z^n] f(z).$$

Those notations read as "coefficient of z^n" $\left(\text{resp. coefficient of } \dfrac{z^n}{n!}\right)$ in $f(z)$.

Equations (6.9), (6.10) associate power series to sequences of numbers. In the most general case, (6.9) and (6.10) are to be taken as defining *formal power series* on which the arsenal of classical algebra can be applied. In most cases of interest, however, the series defined by (6.9) and (more often) (6.10) are convergent, so that methods of classical analysis can further be applied to them.

The advantage of generating functions (series) over sequences satisfying recurrence relations is that they are endowed with a more visible algebraic structure (a field structure essentially). Table 6.1 summarizes the correspondence between some important operations on sequences and generating functions (we have omitted there obvious boundary conditions).

Table 6.1

The translation of operations on sequences into operators on generating functions: sum (1); Cauchy (convolution) product (2); binomial Cauchy (convolution) product (3); backward and forward shifts (4–5); differentiation and integration (6–7).

Sequences	o.g.f.	e.g.f.
1. $c_n = a_n \pm b_n$	$c(z) = a(z) \pm b(z)$	$\hat{c}(z) = \hat{a}(z) \pm \hat{b}(z)$
2. $c_n = \sum_{k=0}^{n} a_k b_{n-k}$	$c(z) = a(z) \times b(z)$	——
3. $c_n = \sum_{k=0}^{n} \binom{n}{k} a_k b_{n-k}$	——	$\hat{c}(z) = \hat{a}(z) \times \hat{b}(z)$
4. $c_n = a_{n-1}$	$c(z) = za(z)$	$\hat{c}(z) = \int_0^z \hat{a}(z)\,dz$
5. $c_n = a_{n+1}$	$c(z) = (a(z) - a(0))/z$	$\hat{c}(z) = \dfrac{d}{dz}\hat{a}(z)$
6. $c_n = na_n$	$c(z) = z\dfrac{d}{dz}a(z)$	$\hat{c}(z) = z\dfrac{d}{dz}\hat{a}(z)$
7. $c_n = \dfrac{a_n}{n}$	$c(z) = \int_0^z [a(t) - a(0)]\dfrac{dt}{t}$	$\hat{c}(z) = \int_0^z [\hat{a}(t) - \hat{a}(0)]\dfrac{dt}{t}$

From this table results that a large number of nonlinear recurrences—those that obtain by combinations of 1–7 in Table 6.1—over number sequences correspond to *functional equations* over generating functions that may often be solved using the classical tools of algebra and analysis.

Examples

1. If $c_n = \sum_{k=0}^{n} a_k$, then $c_n = \sum_{k=0}^{n} a_k U_{n-k}$ where $U_j \equiv 1$, so that $c(z) = a(z)(1-z)^{-1}$; thus $a(z) = c(z)(1-z)$ whence $a_n = c_n - c_{n-1}$. This is the simplest case of an *inversion* relation. (In this case it could of course have been derived by elementary algebra.)

2. If $c_n = \sum_{k=0}^{n} \binom{n}{k} a_k$, then $\hat{c}(z) = e^z \hat{a}(z)$; thus $\hat{a}(z) = e^{-z}\hat{c}(z)$ and $a_n = \sum_{k=0}^{n} (-1)^k \binom{n}{k} c_{n-k}$, yet another inversion relation.

3. The implicit relation ($n \geq 0$)

$$4^n = \sum_{k=0}^{n} a_k a_{n-k}$$

with the initial condition $a_0 = 1$ is equivalent to a non-linear recurrence defining the a_n inductively:

$$a_n = \frac{1}{2}\left(4^n - \sum_{k=1}^{n-1} a_k a_{n-k}\right).$$

Introducing generating functions for the original relation, we find:

$$(a(z))^2 = \frac{1}{1 - 4z}$$

whence,

$$a(z) = \frac{1}{\sqrt{1 - 4z}},$$

and the solution to the original recurrence is found, by standard Newton expansion of $(1 - 4z)^{-1/2}$, to be:

$$a_n = \binom{2n}{n}.$$

4. The relation between generating functions $c(x) = a(x + x^2)$ corresponds (as can be checked by expanding) to the recurrence relation:

$$c_n = \sum_k a_{n-k}\binom{n-k}{k}. \qquad \blacksquare$$

Other operations on sequences have translations into generating functions; sometimes, however, analycity of intervening power series in some domain may be required. A most notable formula is for the Hadamard product: if $c_n = a_n b_n$ then

$$c(z) = \frac{1}{2i\pi}\int a(t)b\left(\frac{z}{t}\right)\frac{dt}{t}$$

for a suitable contour encircling the origin in the t-plane (this, therefore, assumes that the generating functions have a nonzero radius of convergence). Also, there is a simple relation between ordinary and exponential generating functions, via the *Laplace-Borel* transform (a mere notational variant of the classical Laplace transform):

$$a(z) = \int_0^\infty \hat{a}(zt)e^{-t}\,dt.$$

6.1.3   Asymptotic Methods: A Preliminary Discussion

Once an exact expression for the analysis of an algorithm (like that of Theorem 6.1) has been obtained, it is natural to establish approximations that may be of a more interpretable form. To that purpose, one determines asymptotic expansions of expressions under consideration with respect to the parameter n, as n gets large. In most cases, the expressions so obtained are quite accurate (typically within a few percents of the exact values) as soon as n exceeds 20–50. These asymptotic forms make comparison between algorithms much simpler.

   Elementary problems usually require only simple asymptotic methods based on *real approximations*. In the case of the max-finding procedure, we have:

THEOREM 6.2   The max-finding procedure has average cost given by:

$$\tau maxf_n = C_1 n + C_2 \log n + O(1).$$

Proof From the standard comparison between a decreasing function and an integral results that[1]

$$\frac{1}{k+1} < \int_k^{k+1} \frac{dt}{t} < \frac{1}{k}$$

so that, by summation:

$$H_{n+1} - 1 < \log(n+1) < H_n$$

and

$$H_n = \log n + O(1). \qquad \blacksquare$$

Notice that a better approximation for H_n is available, and one has the stronger form

$$H_n = \log n + \gamma + \frac{1}{2n} + O\!\left(\frac{1}{n^2}\right).$$

and the expansion can be pushed to any degree of accuracy.

---

[1] We let log denote the natural logarithm $\log = \log_e$ and occasionally make use of the notation $lg = \log_2$.

In the above approximation, we have made use of some of the classical notations of Landau, which we now recall:

Notations: (1) $f(n) = O(g(n))$ iff for some constant c and for all n larger than some fixed n_0:

$$|f(n)| < c\,g(n).$$

(2) $f(n) = o(g(n))$ iff for all c there exists an n_0 such that for all n larger than n_0:

$$|f(n)| < c\,g(n).$$

In most applications, only a few terms of asymptotic expansion will suffice to give precise information on the behaviors of algorithms. For instance, if $C_0 = C_1 = C_2 = 1$, the ratio between the approximation of Theorem 6.2 and the exact value of Theorem 6.1, namely:

$$q_n = \frac{C_0 n + C_2 \log n}{C_0 + C_1 n + C_2 H_n}$$

satisfies: $q_{10} = 0.882$, $q_{20} = 0.934$, $q_{50} = 0.971$.

Amongst real analysis methods for obtaining asymptotic expansions, one may mention:

1. The approximation of finite sums of continuous functions by integrals. For instance, to approximate

$$S_n = \sum_{k=1}^{n-1} \sqrt{k(n-k)}$$

consider

$$\frac{S_n}{n^2} = \sum_{k=1}^{n-1} \sqrt{\frac{k}{n}\left(1 - \frac{k}{n}\right)} \cdot \frac{1}{n}$$

which is a Riemann sum relative to the function $\sqrt{x(1-x)}$. Thus as $n \to \infty$:

$$\frac{S_n}{n^2} \sim \int_0^1 \sqrt{x(1-x)}\,dx$$

so that

$$S_n = \frac{\pi n^2}{8} + o(n^2)$$

2. More general expansions are obtained by the use of the *Euler Maclaurin summation formula*. That formula covers the case of H_n above and it provides

full asymptotic expansions for the error introduced when approximating discrete sums by integrals. Assume the interval $[a, b]$ is subdivided into sub-intervals of length $h = \dfrac{b-a}{n}$, then we have:

$$\sum_{k=1}^{n} f(a+kh) \sim \frac{1}{h} \int_{a}^{b} f(x)\,dx + \sum_{k \geq 1} \frac{B_k}{k!} h^{k-1} [f^{(k-1)}(x)]_a^b,$$

where $[g(x)]_a^b = g(b) - g(a)$ and B_k is the k-th Bernoulli number defined as:

$$B_k = \left[\frac{x^k}{k!}\right] \frac{x}{e^x - 1},$$

$$B_0 = 1, B_1 = -\frac{1}{2}, B_2 = \frac{1}{6}, B_3 = 0, B_4 = -\frac{1}{30} \cdots.$$

Apart from the purpose of simplifying expressions, equally important reasons for performing asymptotic approximations are that often functional equations over generating functions are available but: (1) either these equations lead to functions too complicated to be expanded, or (2) they only define the functions implicitly and no closed-form expression is available. Nonetheless, in many such cases one can still obtain asymptotic expansions for the coefficients using complex analysis.

For instance, Polya in 1937, has obtained the asymptotic expansion of coefficients of a function satisfying a functional equation of the form

$$f(z) = \frac{1}{1 - zf(z^2)}$$

for which little is known beyond the continued fraction expansion:

$$f(z) = -\cfrac{1}{1 - \cfrac{z}{1 - \cfrac{z^2}{1 - \cfrac{z^4}{\cdots}}}}.$$

This function occurs in the enumeration of structurally different isomeres of alcohols of the form $C_nH_{2n+1}OH$. Similarly, the counting of balanced 2–3 trees leads to the functional equation:

$$f(z) = z + f(z^2 + z^3)$$

from which Odlyzko (41) has shown that

$$f_n \sim \frac{\varphi^n}{n} w(\log n)$$

for some continuous periodic function w, with φ being the golden ratio $(1 + \sqrt{5})/2$.

The major tool in obtaining these asymptotic estimates is the *Cauchy integral formula* that relates the values of a generating function in a *complex domain* to its coefficients:

$$[z^n]f(z) \;=\; \frac{1}{2i\pi} \int_\Gamma f(z)\,\frac{dz}{z^{n+1}} \, ,$$

for a suitable contour of integration Γ.

6.1.4   Overview of Methods for the Analysis of Algorithms

The main paths to be taken when analyzing algorithms and data structures are depicted in Figure 6.2. Main steps are:

1. Extracting basic combinatorial parameters, the original problem is transformed in this way into a combinatorial enumeration problem of a more or less classical type.
2. Obtaining exact (explicit) expressions for the average cost of the algorithm under consideration when applied to an input of size n, if at all possible.
3. Obtaining asymptotic values of these average costs for large n (this phase may or may not be carried out from the previous one).

The main methods are as follows

1. Flow analysis (*FLOW*): the use of various conservation laws (Kirchhoff's laws) possibly in relation with combinatorial properties of objects (e.g., a binary tree with n binary modes has $(n + 1)$ external nodes) leads to a minimal set of parameters (random variables) whose expectation/distribution under the probabilistic model of use is sought.
2. Symbolic operator method (*OPER*): this is the method of choice for obtaining generating functions of average values and enumeration quantities. It uses a set of mapping lemmas with which a working kit of combinatorial constructions can be mapped directly into operators over generating functions. In this way rather complicated generating function expressions are obtained often at relatively small cost.
3. Complex analysis methods (*COMPLEX*): for going from functional equations over generating functions to asymptotics of their coefficients. One uses local analysis of generating functions (it is sufficient that these be defined implicitly; an explicit form is not required) around singularities, saddle points. . . . The main tool is Cauchy's integral formula. Another important tool is the Mellin integral transform.

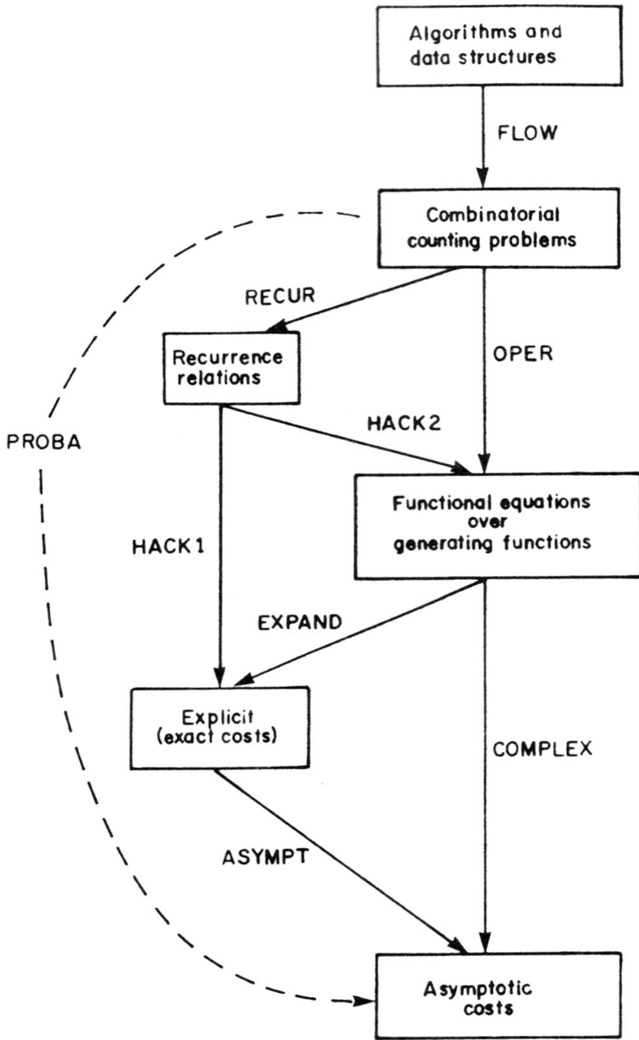

Figure 6.2   Main paths for the analysis of algorithms.

Other classical and important routes are:

4. Recurrences based on decompositions (*RECUR*): by looking at the way structures together with associated parameters decompose into simpler structures, one is often lead to recurrences. In happy cases, the recurrences obtained in this way can be solved explicitly by elementary methods (*HACK$_1$*). In other cases forming generating functions leads to functional equations after some calculations (*HACK$_2$*); however, in almost all cases where the chain *RECUR + HACK$_1$* or *RECUR + HACK$_2$* succeeds, it can be bypassed by the simpler symbolic operator method.

5. Taylor expansions (*EXPAND*): this applies essentially to cases where exact forms for generating functions exist. One then uses the classical tools of algebra and analysis to extract coefficients of generating functions. The direct asymptotic analysis of these explicit forms (*ASYMPT*) relies then largely on real analysis techniques—like the Euler Maclaurin summation formula—and sometimes on complex analysis methods (Mellin transform techniques, most notably).

6. Direct probabilistic methods (*PROBA*): in many cases—mostly graph algorithms and combinatorial optimization problems—one can replace the analysis of a complicated parameter by that of a much simpler one which may be asymptotically equal, equal with high probability etc. . . . This way of approaching problems has been well illustrated by works of Erdos, Renyi, and other Hungarian mathematicians, whence, the name of Hungarian methods sometimes given to them.

6.2 COMBINATORIAL ENUMERATION METHODS— THE SYMBOLIC OPERATOR APPROACH

Many set theoretical constructs of interest in combinatorial enumerations (Cartesian product, power-set and "sequence-of" constructions . . .), translate directly into operators over generating functions. Unlabelled constructions translate over *ordinary generating functions* while labelled constructions translate over *exponential generating functions*. A large portion of classical exact enumeration results can be derived simply within that framework, which is also very well suited to solving counting problems arising in the analysis of algorithms and data structures.

6.2.1 The Symbolic Operator Method

We define here a *class of combinatorial structures* as a pair of a finite or denumerable set $\mathbf{C}$ and a function $w: \mathbf{C} \rightarrow N$ called the *size* or *weight* function, such that for all n, $w^{-1}(n)$ is finite. We let $\mathbf{C}_n$ denote the set of all structures in C that have size n. The *counting problem* for C is to determine the integer sequence $\{c_n\}_{n \geq 0}$ defined by

$$c_n = |w^{-1}(n)| = \operatorname{card} C_n$$

that is, to determine for each n how many elements in C have size n. The size function is often alternatively denoted by $|\cdot|$ or $|\cdot|_C$ if the dependence on C is to be emphasized.

The *ordinary generating function* (o.g.f.) of C (with respect to weight w) is the formal power series

$$c(z) = \sum_{n \geq 0} c_n z^n. \tag{6.11}$$

The *exponential generating function* (e.g.f.) of C (with respect to w) is the formal power series

$$\hat{c}(z) = \sum_{n \geq 0} c_n \frac{z^n}{n!} \tag{6.12}$$

It is useful to notice that $c(z)$ and $\hat{c}(z)$ can be expressed alternatively as

$$c(z) = \sum_{\sigma \in C} z^{w(\sigma)} ; \quad \hat{c}(z) = \sum_{\sigma \in C} \frac{z^{w(\sigma)}}{w(\sigma)!}. \tag{6.13}$$

To see it, observe that the term z^n in (6.13) appears as many times as there are structures of size n in C.

The main approach which we explore here for the counting problem of C is via the generating functions $c(z)$ or $\hat{c}(z)$.

A *combinatorial construction* Φ of degree k is an operation, in the usual set-theoretic sense, that associates to k classes of structures $C_1, C_2, \ldots, C_k$ a class $A = \Phi(C_1, C_2, \ldots, C_k)$. Its specification thus needs describing how the sizes of the result relates to the size of the operands.

DEFINITION 6.2   A combinatorial construction $A = \Phi(C_1, C_2, \ldots, C_k)$ is *admissible* iff the counting sequence $\{a_n\}$ of A depends only on the counting sequence $\{c_{1,n}\}, \{c_{2,n}\} \cdots$ of $C_1, C_2 \cdots$.

Thus, in the case of an admissible construct, no further internal structural information on $C_1, C_2 \ldots$ is required to solve the counting problem for A.

If Φ is an admissible construction, there exists an operator Ψ over formal power series such that

$$A = \Phi(C_1, C_2, \ldots, C_k) \Rightarrow a(z) = \Psi(c_1(z), c_2(z), \ldots, c_k(z))$$

($a(z), c_1(z) \cdots$ are the o.g.f. of classes $A, C_1, \cdots$).

Similarly, Φ defines an operator $\hat{\Psi}$ on exponential generating functions:

$$\mathbf{A} = \Phi\,(\mathbf{C}_1, \mathbf{C}_2, \ldots, \mathbf{C}_k)\ \Phi \Rightarrow \hat{a}(z) = \hat{\Psi}(\hat{c}_1(z), \hat{c}_2(z), \ldots, \hat{c}_k(z))$$

($\hat{a}(z)$, $\hat{c}_1(z)$ $\cdots$ being the e.g.f. of classes $\mathbf{A}$, $\mathbf{C}_1$, $\cdots$).

Usually, a given construct Φ will translate in a simpler manner into either ordinary or exponential generating functions.

Notations: In the sequel, we adhere, unless otherwise stated, to the notational convention of representing a class ($\mathbf{C}$), the counting sequence ($\{c_n\}$ or $\{C_n\}$) and the corresponding generating functions ($c(z)$ or $C(z)$; $\hat{C}(z)$ or $\hat{c}(z)$) by the same group of letters.

The remainder of this section is devoted to the presentation of a number of admissible constructions. Admissibility lemmas thus map these combinatorial constructions into operators over generating functions. The counting problem for a class $\mathbf{C}$, therefore, reduces to finding a suitable construction of $\mathbf{C}$ in terms of simpler structures (and possibly $\mathbf{C}$ itself if the construction is recursive) by means of admissible constructions: if the construction is nonrecursive, then the generating function for $\mathbf{C}$ will obtain as a functional on simpler functions. If the definition is recursive, then one obtains a *functional equation* defining $c(z)$ (or $\hat{c}(z)$) implicitly. We call this approach the *symbolic operator method* for counting problems.

Notice that while the classical enumeration approach based on producing recurrences from suitable decompositions is very sensitive to small variations on the formulation of the problem considered, the operator approach is usually far more flexible. Before presenting admissible constructions for ordinary generating functions (Section 6.2.2) and for exponential generating functions (Section 6.2.3), we illustrate this method formally by an example taken from the counting of permutations.

Note: The example that follows—the counting of permutations according to properties of their cycles—is only meant to demonstrate the "physics" of the translation mechanism and the necessary concepts and lemmas introduced in Section 6.2.2 and 6.2.3.

Example: Let $\mathbf{P} = \cup \mathbf{P}_n$ by the class of all permutation, with $\mathbf{P}_n$ the set of permutations of size n, i.e. permutation over $[1\,..\,n]$. A direct reasoning (value

1 can appear in any of n positions, value 2 in any of the remaining $(n-1)$ positions . . .) shows that

$$p_n = \operatorname{card} \mathbf{P}_n \equiv n!, \qquad (6.14)$$

and the e.g.f. of the class of all permutations is

$$\hat{p}(z) = \sum_{n \geq 0} n! \frac{z^n}{n!} = \frac{1}{1-z}. \qquad (6.15)$$

Equations (6.14) and (6.15) being clearly equivalent.

One way to arrive at (6.15) by the symbolic operator method is to construct permutations at *"sets-of"* *cyclic permutations* (each permutation has a unique cycle decomposition). If $\mathbf{C}$ is the class of cyclic permutations, $c_n = (n-1)!$ so that the e.g.f. of $\mathbf{C}$ is

$$\hat{c}(z) = \sum (n-1)! \frac{z^n}{n!} = \sum \frac{z^n}{n}.$$

Thus, one has:

$$\hat{c}(z) = \log(1-z)^{-1} \qquad (6.16)$$

Now the set-of construction in this context is known, in the operator approach to correspond to a left composition with an exponential (see Section 6.2.3 for precise statements); here this gives $\hat{p}(z) = \exp(\hat{c}(z))$ or:

$$\hat{p}(z) = \exp\{\log(1-z)^{-1}\}. \qquad (6.17)$$

Equation (6.17) is also clearly equivalent to (6.16) whence to (6.15).

This seemingly useless complicated detour is important since the method behind the derivation of (6.17) allows for a large number of variations leading to much less trivial counting results.

1. Restrictions on the number of cycles. Let $\mathbf{P}^\Gamma$ be the set of permutations whose number of cycles is in some fixed set $\Gamma \subset \mathbf{N}$; the corresponding exponential generating function is obtained by left composition with $\gamma(u) = \sum_{j \in \Gamma} \frac{u^j}{j!}$ (so that $\Gamma = \mathbf{N}$ gives back the exponential) of the e.g.f. of cyclic permutations. For instance, the e.g.f. of permutations having an even number of cycles is

$$\hat{q}(z) = \cosh(\log(1-z)^{-1}) = \frac{1}{2}\left(\frac{1}{1-z} + 1 - z\right)$$

so that there $q_n = \dfrac{n!}{2}$ for $n \geq 2$.

2. Restrictions on cycle length: let $^\Lambda\mathbf{P}$ be the set of permutations whose cycles all have length in a fixed set $\Lambda \subset \mathbf{N}$. The corresponding exponential generating function is obtained by replacing in (6.17) the function $\log(1-z)^{-1}$ by the function $\lambda(z) = \sum_{j \in \Lambda} \dfrac{z^j}{j}$, (so that $\Lambda = \mathbf{N}$ gives back Equation (6.17)). For instance, to obtain the e.g.f. the permutations without cycles of length 1, replace $\log(1-z)^{-1}$ by $\log(1-z)^{-1} - z$ so that this function is

$$\hat{r}(z) = \frac{e^{-z}}{1-z}.$$

From there follows the (19th century) results that the number of derangements (permutations without fixed points) is

$$r_n = \sum_{j=0}^{n} \frac{(-1)^j}{j!}.$$

3. Joint restrictions of the two previous types can be combined defining the class $^\Lambda\mathbf{P}^\Gamma$ whose e.g.f. is $\gamma(\lambda(z))$. For instance, to obtain the e.g.f. $\hat{s}(z)$ of permutations having an odd number of cycles each of an odd length, take

$$\gamma(u) = \frac{1}{2}(e^u - e^{-u})$$

$$\lambda(z) = \frac{1}{2}(\log(1+z) - \log(1-z)) = \log\sqrt{\frac{1+z}{1-z}}$$

so that

$$\hat{s}(z) = \frac{z}{\sqrt{1-z^2}},$$

whence by expanding

$$s_{2n+1} = \frac{(2n)!(2n+1)!}{2^{2n}(n!)^2}.$$

This example illustrates the flexibility of the operator approach, i.e. its *insensitivity* to a large number of changes in definitions of combinatorial structures.

6.2.2 Admissible Constructions for Ordinary Generating Functions

A kit of admissible constructions for o.g.f.'s is displayed on Table 6.2, together with the corresponding operators over generating functions. Definitions and mapping lemmas follow.

Table 6.2
Admissible constructions for ordinary generating functions (o.g.f.)

Construction		Operator
Disj. union	$\mathbf{C} = \mathbf{A} + \mathbf{B}$	$c(z) = a(z) + b(z)$
Cart. product	$\mathbf{C} = \mathbf{A} \times \mathbf{B}$	$c(z) = a(z) \cdot b(z)$
Diagonal	$\mathbf{C} = \Delta(\mathbf{A} \times \mathbf{A})$	$c(z) = a(z^2)$
Sequence-of	$\mathbf{C} = \mathbf{A}^*$	$c(z) = (1 - a(z))^{-1}$
Marking	$\mathbf{C} = \mu\mathbf{A}$	$c(z) = z\dfrac{d}{dz}a(z)$
Substitution	$\mathbf{C} = \mathbf{A}[\mathbf{B}]$	$c(z) = a(b(z))$
Set-of	$\mathbf{C} = 2^{\mathbf{A}}$	$c(z) = \exp\left(a(z) - \dfrac{1}{2}a(z^2) + \dfrac{1}{3}a(z^3) \cdots\right)$
Multiset-of	$\mathbf{C} = M\{\mathbf{A}\}$	$c(z) = \exp\left(a(z) + \dfrac{1}{2}a(z^2) + \dfrac{1}{3}a(z^3) \cdots\right)$

DEFINITION 6.3 A class $\mathbf{C}$ is the *union* (*sum*) of two classes $\mathbf{A}$ and $\mathbf{B}$ which we denote by $\mathbf{C} = \mathbf{A} + \mathbf{B}$ iff:

1. in the set-theoretic sense $\mathbf{C} = \mathbf{A} \cup \mathbf{B}$;
2. sizes $|\cdot|_{\mathbf{A}}$ and $|\cdot|_{\mathbf{B}}$ are compatible over $\mathbf{A} \cap \mathbf{B}$ and $|x|_{\mathbf{C}} =$ if $x \in \mathbf{A}$ then $|x|_{\mathbf{A}}$ else $|x|_{\mathbf{B}}$.

DEFINITION 6.4 A class $\mathbf{C}$ is the *cartesian product* of classes $\mathbf{A}$ and $\mathbf{B}$, denoted by $\mathbf{C} = \mathbf{A} \times \mathbf{B}$, iff

1. in the set-theoretic sense $\mathbf{C} = \mathbf{A} \times \mathbf{B}$;
2. $|(\alpha, \beta)|_{\mathbf{C}} = |\alpha|_{\mathbf{A}} + |\beta|_{\mathbf{B}}$.

DEFINITION 6.5 A class $\mathbf{C}$ is the *sequence* class of class $\mathbf{A}$ iff with ε a structure of size 0 (called the empty structure):

$$\mathbf{C} = \{\varepsilon\} + \mathbf{A} + \mathbf{A} \times \mathbf{A} + \mathbf{A} \times \mathbf{A} \times \mathbf{A} + \cdots$$

with size being defined consistently with unions and cartesian products.

DEFINITION 6.6 A class $\mathbf{C}$ is the *diagonal* of $\mathbf{A} \times \mathbf{A}$ denoted by $\mathbf{C} = \Delta(\mathbf{A} \times \mathbf{A})$ iff $\mathbf{C}$ consists of all elements (α, α), $\alpha \in \mathbf{A}$, with

$$|(\alpha, \alpha)|_{\mathbf{C}} = 2|\alpha|_{\mathbf{A}}.$$

DEFINITION 6.7   A class $\mathbf{C}$ is the *marking* of class $\mathbf{A}$ denoted by $\mathbf{C} = \mu\mathbf{A}$ iff

$$\mathbf{C} = \sum_{n=0}^{\infty} A_n \times [1..n]$$

with $|(\alpha, v)|_{\mathbf{C}} = |\alpha|_{\mathbf{A}}$.

DEFINITION 6.8   A class $\mathbf{C}$ is the *composition* of class $\mathbf{A}$ and $\mathbf{B}$, denoted by $\mathbf{C} = \mathbf{A}[\mathbf{B}]$, iff

$$\mathbf{C} = \sum_{n=0}^{\infty} \mathbf{A}_n \times \mathbf{B} \times \mathbf{B} \times \cdots \times \mathbf{B},$$

the number of factors in the general term being equal to n, with $|(\alpha, \beta_1, \beta_2, \ldots, \beta_n)|_{\mathbf{C}} = |\beta_1|_{\mathbf{B}} + |\beta_2|_{\mathbf{B}} + \cdots + |\beta_n|_{\mathbf{B}}$.

DEFINITION 6.9   A class $\mathbf{C}$ is the *powerset class* of class $\mathbf{A}$ denoted $\mathbf{C} = 2^{\mathbf{A}}$ iff, in the set theoretic sense, $\mathbf{C}$ is the class *finite* of subsets of $\mathbf{A}$:

$$|\{\alpha_1, \alpha_2, \ldots, \alpha_k\}|_{\mathbf{C}} = |\alpha_1|_{\mathbf{A}} + |\alpha_2|_{\mathbf{A}} + \cdots + |\alpha_k|_{\mathbf{A}}.$$

DEFINITION 6.10   A class $\mathbf{C}$ is the *multiset class* of class $\mathbf{A}$ denoted $\mathbf{C} = M\{\mathbf{A}\}$ iff $\mathbf{C}$ consists of finite multisets of elements of $\mathbf{A}$ of the form $\{\alpha_1^{j_1}, \alpha_2^{j_2}, \ldots, \alpha_k^{j_k}\}$ (α^j means α repeated j times) and

$$|\{\alpha_1^{j_1}, \alpha_2^{j_2}, \cdots, \alpha_k^{j_k}\}|_{\mathbf{C}} = j_1|\alpha_1|_{\mathbf{A}} + j_2|\alpha_2|_{\mathbf{A}} + \cdots + j_k|\alpha_k|_{\mathbf{A}}.$$

A few words of explanation are in order. We say that $\mathbf{C}$ is the *disjoint union* of $\mathbf{A}$ and $\mathbf{B}$ if the intersection $\mathbf{A} \cap \mathbf{B}$ is empty. The notion of a cartesian product of classes (and of diagonals) is the standard one with the size of a couple being the sum of the sizes of its components; the notion extends trivially to the product of any number of factors. The notion of a power class also corresponds to the standard power set construction. The power multiset class of $\mathbf{A}$, $M\{\mathbf{A}\}$ is the class of sets of elements of $\mathbf{A}$ with repetitions allowed; it again corresponds to the standard multiset construction.

Composition and marking are useful when dealing with objects like trees, graphs, and words consisting of *atomic elements* (nodes, edges, positions, etc. . .) where the size of a structure is the number of elements it comprises. A marked structure from $\mu\mathbf{A}$ in this context is then a structure of $\mathbf{A}$ augmented by distinguishing one of its elements. Similarly, the substitution operation $\mathbf{A}[\mathbf{B}]$ is equivalent to constructing all structures obtained from some $\alpha \in \mathbf{A}$ by substituting to all atomic elements of α objects from β still retaining the structural properties of α (this is really a sort of "marked" substitution).

Notice also that, in order for the sequence construction $\mathbf{A}^*$, substitution construction $\mathbf{B}[\mathbf{A}]$ and multiset-of construction $M\{\mathbf{A}\}$, to be defined (i.e., to result in sets that are classes of structures satisfying the finiteness condition of $|\ |^{-1}$), one has to impose for infinite classes the condition that $\mathbf{A}$ contains no structure of size 0. We shall also impose a similar restriction on the set-of construction. Accordingly, these conditions ensure that the operators given in Table 6.2 are well-defined operators over formal power series.

We have

THEOREM 6.3   The constructions of disjoint union, cartesian product, diagonal, sequence-of, marking, substitution, set-of (powerset), and multiset are admissible.

The corresponding operators are given in Table 6.2. The proof of this theorem proceeds through a chain of easy lemmas.

LEMMA 6.2   If $\mathbf{A} \cap \mathbf{B} = \phi$ and $\mathbf{C} = \mathbf{A} + \mathbf{B}$, then $c(z) = a(z) + b(z)$.

Proof $c_n = a_n + b_n$.   ∎

LEMMA 6.3   If $\mathbf{C} = \mathbf{A} \times \mathbf{B}$ then $c(z) = a(z) \cdot b(z)$.

Proof

$$c(z) = \sum_{(\alpha,\beta)\in\mathbf{C}} z^{|(\alpha,\beta)|}$$

$$= \sum_{\alpha\in\mathbf{A}}\sum_{\beta\in\mathbf{B}} z^{|\alpha|+|\beta|} = \sum_{\alpha\in\mathbf{A}} z^{|\alpha|} \cdot \sum_{\beta\in\mathbf{B}} z^{|\beta|}. \qquad ∎$$

LEMMA 6.4   If $\mathbf{C} = \Delta(\mathbf{A} \times \mathbf{A})$ then $c(z) = a(z^2)$.

Proof $c_{2n} = a_n; c_{2n+1} = 0$.   ∎

LEMMA 6.5   If $\mathbf{C} = \mathbf{A}^*$, then $c(z) = (1-a(z))^{-1}$.

Proof $c(z) = \sum_{k\geq 0} (a(z))^k$.   ∎

LEMMA 6.6   If $\mathbf{C} = \mu\mathbf{A}$, then $c(z) = z\dfrac{d}{dz}a(z)$.

Proof $c_n = na_n$.   ∎

LEMMA 6.7   If $\mathbf{C} = \mathbf{A}[\mathbf{B}]$, then $c(z) = a(b(z))$.

Proof   From the union and cartesian product mapping lemmas, one has

$$c(z) = \sum_k b_k c(z)^k.$$ ∎

LEMMA 6.8   If $\mathbf{C} = 2^{\mathbf{A}}$, then

$$c(z) = \exp\left\{ \sum_{j=1}^{\infty} \frac{(-1)^{j-1}}{j} a(z^j) \right\}$$

Proof   Class $\mathbf{C}$ is isomorphic to the finite size elements of the (infinite) cartesian product

$$\mathbf{C} = \prod_{\alpha \in \mathbf{A}} \{\{\varepsilon\} + \{\alpha\}\}$$

(ε a null structure of size 0) so that translating to generating functions

$$c(z) = \prod_{\alpha \in A} (1 + z^{|\alpha|})$$

and grouping terms:

$$= \prod_{n=1}^{\infty} (1 + z^n)^{a_n}.$$

Computing $\log c(z)$, we find:

$$\log c(z) = \sum_{n=1}^{\infty} a_n \log(1 + z^n)$$

$$= \sum_{n=1}^{\infty} a_n \sum_{j=1}^{\infty} \frac{(-1)^{j-1}}{j} z^{nj}$$

$$= \sum_{j=1}^{\infty} \frac{(-1)^{j-1}}{j} \sum_{n=1}^{\infty} a_n z^{nj}$$

$$= \sum_{j=1}^{\infty} \frac{(-1)^{j-1}}{j} a(z^j).$$ ∎

LEMMA 6.9   If $\mathbf{C} = M\{\mathbf{A}\}$, then

$$c(z) = \exp\left\{ \sum_{j=1}^{\infty} \frac{1}{j} a(z^j) \right\}.$$

Proof   The class **C** is isomorphic to the finite size elements of the (infinite) cartesian product

$$\mathbf{C} = \prod_{\alpha \in \mathbf{A}} \{\alpha\}^*$$

so that by the mapping lemma for the sequence construction

$$c(z) = \prod_{\alpha \in A} (1 - z^{|\alpha|})^{-1}$$

$$= \prod_{n=1}^{\infty} (1 - z^n)^{-a_n}$$

and the calculation develops as in the previous case.   ∎

6.2.3   Admissible Constructions for Exponential Generation Functions

We consider in the whole of this section particular classes of combinatorial structures consisting of *labelled objects*. Corresponding constructions have natural interpretation in terms of exponential generating functions.

We shall first motivate our constructions over labelled structures by an example, namely determining the number of connected graph over a set of n distinguished vertices. Let $\mathbf{G} = \bigcup_n \mathbf{G}_n$ be the class of *labelled graphs* where $\mathbf{G}_n$ is the set of all undirected graphs over the set of vertices $[1 . . n]$. Let $\mathbf{K}$ be the subclass of $\mathbf{G}$ consisting of all graphs of $\mathbf{G}$ that are connected. One interesting question is the relation between the quantities $k_n = \mathrm{card}(\mathbf{K}_n)$ and $g_n = \mathrm{card}(\mathbf{G}_n)$. Notice first that one has directly

$$g_n = 2^{\frac{n(n-1)}{2}} = 2^{\binom{n}{2}} \tag{6.18}$$

since a graph over n vertices is obtained by selecting a subset of the set of the $\binom{n}{2}$ possible edges. The graphs corresponding to $n = 3$ are depicted in Figure 6.3.

To approach the determination of $\{k_n\}_{n \geq 0}$, we define $\mathbf{G}_n^{(c)}$ as the class of graphs consisting of c connected components so that $\mathbf{G}_n^{(1)} = \mathbf{K}_n$, and we start by relating $g_n^{(c)} = \mathrm{card}\,\mathbf{G}_n^{(c)}$ to k_n. Let us take first $c = 2$.

The cartesian product $\mathbf{K} \times \mathbf{K}$ generates couples of connected graphs. But one has $\mathbf{G}^{(2)} \neq \mathbf{K} \times \mathbf{K}$ for the following two reasons:

1. Connected components of graphs in $\mathbf{G}^{(2)}$ are not ordered, while components of elements of $\mathbf{K} \times \mathbf{K}$ are, by definition of the cartesian product.

2. Elements of $\mathbf{K} \times \mathbf{K}$ are *not* well labelled in the sense that structures of size n do not have elements (nodes) labelled with distinct integers from $[1 . . n]$.

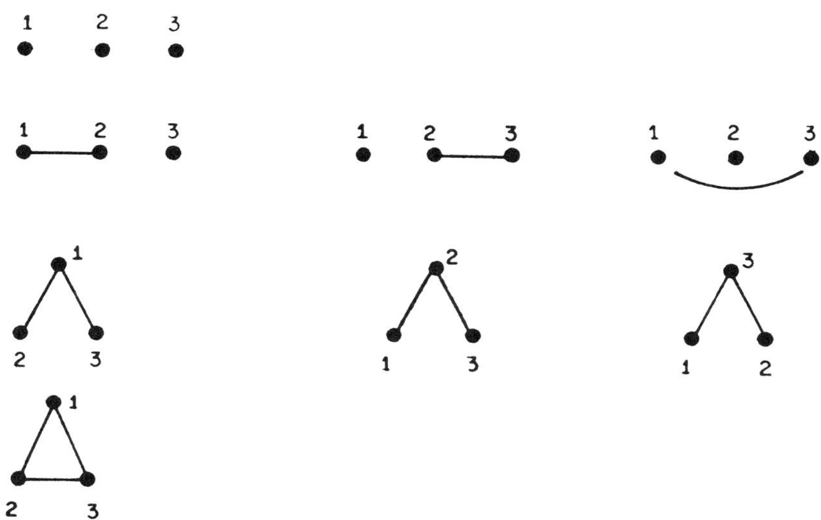

Figure 6.3 The labelled graphs over the set of vertices $\{1,2,3\}$. From this table results that $g_3 = 8$ and $k_3 = 4$.

To take care of problem 2, one must *relabel* objects from $\mathbf{K} \times \mathbf{K}$ to make them well-labelled objects.

DEFINITION 6.11   A *bipartition* Π of $[1. \, .n]$ is a pair $\Pi = (\alpha, \beta)$ of subsets of $[1. \, .n]$ such that $\alpha \cup \beta = [1. \, .n]$, $\alpha \cap \beta = \varnothing$. The *type* of the bipartition is the integer pair $(|\alpha|, |\beta|)$.

Let $c = (u, v)$ be a pair of labelled structures, so that u is labelled by elements from $[1. \, .l]$ and v is labelled by elements of $[1. \, .m]$. The *action* of a bipartition $\Pi = (\alpha, \beta)$ of type (l, m) on $c = (u, v)$ is defined as the pair $\bar{c} = (\bar{u}, \bar{v})$ where $\bar{u}$ is obtained from u by replacing labels $1, 2, \ldots l$ by $\alpha_1, \alpha_2, \ldots \alpha_l$ and $\bar{v}$ is similarly obtained from v by replacing labels $1, 2, \ldots, m$ by $\beta_1, \beta_2, \ldots, \beta_m$ where

$$\alpha_1 < \alpha_2 < \cdots < \alpha_m; \quad \beta_1 < \beta_2 < \cdots < \beta_m$$

are the elements taken in increasing order of α and β. The action of Π on u and v is denoted by $\Pi\langle(u, v)\rangle$.

Example

Let $c = (u, v)$ be defined by

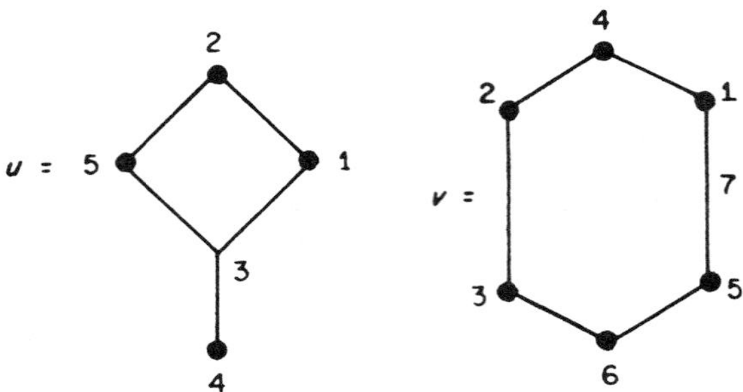

Consider the bipartition $\Pi = (\{3,5,6,9,12\}, \{1,2,4,7,8,10,11\})$; its type is $(5,7)$ so that its action on (u, v) is defined. The result is the couple:

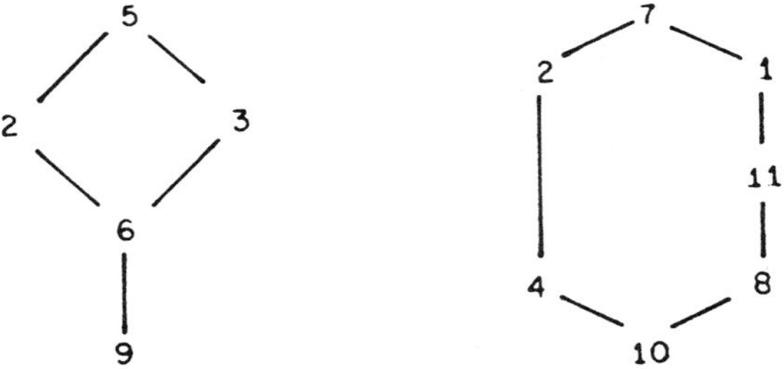

which is a well-labelled structure over $[1. \,.12]$. ■

DEFINITION 6.12   The *partitional product* of two labelled structures $\bar{u}$ and $\bar{v}$ denoted by $u * v$ is defined as the set

$$u * v = \left\{ \Pi\langle (u, v) \rangle \mid \Pi \; \textit{of type} \; (|u|, |v|) \right\}$$

The *partitional product* of two classes of (labelled) structures $\mathbf{A}$ and $\mathbf{B}$ is defined as

$$\mathbf{A} * \mathbf{B} = \bigcup_{\substack{u \in \mathbf{A} \\ v \in \mathbf{B}}} (u * v).$$

(The *size* of any element of $(u * v)$ is $|u| + |v|$).

Returning to our original problem concerning the enumeration of labelled graphs, we thus see that the partitional product $\mathbf{K} * \mathbf{K}$ generates all well-labelled couples of connected graph. Each graph of $\mathbf{G}^{(2)}$ formed with two connected components K_1, K_2 thus appears in $\mathbf{K} * \mathbf{K}$ twice: once as (K_1, K_2) and once as (K_2, K_1). We can, therefore, write the symbolic equations:

$$2\mathbf{G}^{(2)} = \mathbf{K} * \mathbf{K} \qquad (6.19a)$$

$$\mathbf{G}^{(2)} = \frac{1}{2}(\mathbf{K} * \mathbf{K}) \qquad (6.19b)$$

The main interest of the partitional product for enumerations is the following:

LEMMA 6.10   If classes $\mathbf{A}$ and $\mathbf{B}$ have exponential generating functions $\hat{a}(z)$ and $\hat{b}(z)$, then the exponential generating function $\hat{c}(z)$ of class $\mathbf{C} = \mathbf{A} * \mathbf{B}$ satisfies:

$$\hat{c}(z) = \hat{a}(z) \cdot \hat{b}(z).$$

Proof   If u and v are structures of $\mathbf{A}$ and $\mathbf{B}$ of respective size l and m, then the number of bipartitions of type (l, m) is the binomial coefficient

$$\binom{l + m}{l}.$$

Thus, the cardinality C_n of $\mathbf{C}_n$ satisfies the recurrences:

$$c_n = \sum_{l+m=m} \binom{l + m}{l} a_l b_m,$$

$$c_n = \sum_{l=0}^{n} \binom{n}{l} a_l b_{n-l},$$

$$\frac{c_n}{n!} = \sum_{l=0}^{n} \frac{a_l}{l!} \frac{b_{n-l}}{(n-l)!}.$$

From the last equality, the lemma follows.   ■

We have, thus, found for $\hat{g}^{(2)}(z)$ the relation

$$\hat{g}^{(2)}(z) = \frac{1}{2}(\hat{k}(z))^2.$$

A straightforward generalization shows that more generally

$$\hat{g}^{(c)}(z) = \frac{1}{c!}(\hat{k}(z))^c. \qquad (6.20)$$

Since $G = \sum\limits_{c=0}^{\infty} G^{(c)}$, we find from (6.20) the relation

$$\hat{g}(z) = 1 + \hat{k}(z) + \frac{1}{2!}(\hat{k}(z))^2 + \frac{1}{3!}(\hat{k}(z))^3 + \cdots$$

($\mathbf{G}^{(0)}$ consists of the empty graph on 0 vertices), or:

$$\hat{g}(z) = \exp(\hat{k}(z)). \tag{6.21}$$

Using (6.18) and inverting (6.21), we have thus found:

PROPOSITION 6.3   The exponential generating function of the class of labelled graphs satisfies

$$\hat{k}(z) = \log\left(1 + \sum_{n \geq 1} 2^{n(n-1)/2} \frac{z^n}{n!}\right). \qquad\blacksquare$$

Notice that the above series is *divergent*; however $\hat{k}(z)$ is defined as a formal power series that can be evaluated by $\log(1+u) = u - \dfrac{u^2}{2} + \dfrac{u^3}{3} \cdots$. Taking coefficients, we find:

$$k_n = \sum_{j \geq 1} \frac{(-1)^{j-1}}{j} \sum_{n_1 + n_2 + \cdots + n_j = n\,;\, n_j \geq 1} \binom{n}{n_1, n_2, \ldots, n_j} 2^{\binom{n_1}{2} + \binom{n_2}{2} + \cdots + \binom{n_j}{2}},$$

from which one can conclude for instance:

PROPOSITION 6.4   As n tends to infinity the ratio k_n/g_n tends to 1. $\blacksquare$

Thus, almost all graphs of size n are connected for large n.

DEFINITION 6.13   The k-th *partitional power* ($k \geq 1$) of class $\mathbf{A}$ is defined by

$$\mathbf{A}^{\langle k \rangle} = \mathbf{A} * \mathbf{A} * \cdots * \mathbf{A}$$

where the number of factors is equal to k. When $k = 0$, $a^{\langle 0 \rangle}$ is defined as a class consisting of a unique structure of size 0 (called the empty structure or null structure and usually denoted by ε).

The partitional complex $\mathbf{A}^{\langle * \rangle}$ of $\mathbf{A}$ is defined as the disjoint union (sum):

$$\mathbf{A}^{\langle * \rangle} = \sum_{k=0}^{\infty} \mathbf{A}^{\langle k \rangle}.$$

DEFINITION 6.14   The k-th Abelian partitional power of class $\mathbf{A}$ is defined as

$$\mathbf{A}^{[k]} = \{\{w_1, w_2, \ldots, w_k\} \mid (w_1, w_2, \ldots, w_k) \in \mathbf{A}^{\langle k \rangle}\}$$

The abelian partitional complex $a^{[*]}$ of a is defined as the sum

$$a^{[*]} = \sum_{k=0}^{\infty} a^{[k]}.$$

Notice that the partitional complex construct is for labelled objects the analogue of the sequence construct (order of elements in k-tuples count); the abelian partitional is an analogue of the power-set construct (orders of elements are *not* taken into account). We then have:

LEMMA 6.11   Assume that $\mathbf{C} = \mathbf{A}^{\langle * \rangle}$, then

$$\hat{c}(z) = \frac{1}{1 - \hat{a}(z)}.$$
■

LEMMA 6.12   Assume that $\mathbf{C} = \mathbf{A}^{[*]}$, then

$$\hat{c}(z) = \exp(\hat{a}(z)).$$
■

Proofs are direct extensions of the previous ones. For the partitional complex, one has:

$$\hat{c}(z) = \sum_{k \geq 0} (\hat{a}(z))^k = \frac{1}{1 - \hat{a}(z)}.$$

For the Abelian partitional complex, each element of $\mathbf{A}^{[k]}$ corresponds to $k!$ elements of $\mathbf{A}^{\langle k \rangle}$. In symbols

$$\mathbf{A}^{\langle k \rangle} \equiv k! \, \mathbf{A}^{[k]},$$

so that, there

$$\hat{c}(z) = \sum_{k \geq 0} \frac{1}{k!} (\hat{a}(z))^k = \exp(\hat{a}(z)).$$

In summary, we get:

THEOREM 6.4   The constructions: disjoint union, partitional product, partitional complex, abelian partitional complex and marking are e.g.f. admissible.

The corresponding operators are given in Table 6.3. Other operations (min-rooting, labelled substitution) could also be shown to be e.g.f. admissible.

Table 6.3
Admissible constructions for exponential generating functions (e.g.f.)

Construction		Operator
Disj. union	$\mathbf{C} = \mathbf{A} + \mathbf{B}$	$\hat{c}(z) = \hat{a}(z) + \hat{b}(z)$
Partit. prod.	$\mathbf{C} = \mathbf{A} * \mathbf{B}$	$\hat{c}(z) = \hat{a}(z) \cdot \hat{b}(z)$
Partit. complex	$\mathbf{C} = \mathbf{A}^{\langle * \rangle}$	$\hat{c}(z) = (1 - \hat{a}(z))^{-1}$
Abel. part. complex	$\mathbf{C} = \mathbf{A}^{[*]}$	$\hat{c}(z) = \exp(\hat{a}(z))$
Marking	$\mathbf{C} = \mu\mathbf{A}$	$\hat{c}(z) = z\dfrac{d}{dz}\hat{a}(z)$
Labelled subst.	$\mathbf{C} = \mathbf{A}[\mathbf{B}]$	$\hat{c}(z) = \hat{a}(\hat{b}(z))$
Min-rooting	$\mathbf{C} = \rho\mathbf{A}$	$\hat{c}(z) = \displaystyle\int_0^z \hat{a}(z)\,dz$

6.2.4 Sample Applications

We give here some brief indications on how to derive a collection of classical combinatorial enumeration results within the framework of the symbolic operator method. (For a thorough treatment, see the book by Goulden and Jackson (7) or Stanley's survey (9).) From our previous discussions, the problem reduces to finding proper constructions (decompositions) for classes of combinatorial structures in terms of admissible set-theoretic constructs.[2]

1. Combinations: Let $\mathbf{C}$ be the power set of $[1 . . m]$, where m is a fixed integer; an element of $\mathbf{C}$ is sometimes called a *combination* of elements of $[1 . . m]$. Then:

$$\mathbf{C} \approx \prod_{\xi=1}^{m} (\{\varepsilon\} + \{\xi\})$$

with ε the null structure (of size 0). Thus, translating to o.g.f.:

$$C(z) = (1 + z)^m$$

and the number of n-combinations of a set of m elements is:

$$[z^n](1 + z)^m = \binom{m}{n}.$$

---

[2]We use the notation $\mathbf{C} \approx \mathbf{D}$ to indicate that there exists a weight/size preserving bijection (isomorphism) between $\mathbf{C}$ and $\mathbf{D}$, so that the counting problems for $\mathbf{C}$ and $\mathbf{D}$ are equivalent.

2. Combinations with repetitions. Let $\mathbf{M}$ be the multiset class of $[1\,.\,.m]$. An element of $\mathbf{M}$ is sometimes called a *combination with repetitions* of elements of $[1\,.\,.m]$. Thus:

$$\mathbf{M} \approx \prod_{\xi=1}^{m} \{\xi\}^{*}$$

$$M(z) = (1 - z)^{-m}$$

so that the number of n-combinations with repetitions of a set with m elements is found to be:

$$[z^n](1 - z)^{-m} = \binom{n + m - 1}{m - 1}$$

3. Arrangements. An *arrangement* of n elements of $[1\,.\,.m]$ is an injective map from $[1\,.\,.n]$ to $[1\,.\,.m]$. The set $\mathbf{A}$ of all arrangements with m fixed has the presentation:

$$\mathbf{A} \approx (\{\varepsilon\} + \{\underline{1}\})^{<m>}$$

where $\underline{1}$ represents a labelled structure of size 1. Thus, the e.g.f. of $\mathbf{A}$ is:

$$\hat{A}(z) = (1 + z)^{m}$$

and the number of n-arrangements from a set with m elements is:

$$\left[\frac{z^n}{n!}\right](1 + z)^{m} = n(n - 1)(n - 2) \cdots (n - m + 1).$$

4. Set partitions. A *partition* of a set $\mathbf{S}$ is a family of sets $b = \{\beta_1, \cdots, \beta_k\}$ such that the β_j—called blocks—are pairwise disjoint and cover $\mathbf{S}$. Let $\mathbf{B}$ be the family of all partitions of an initial segment of $\mathbf{N} = \{1, 2, 3, \cdots\}$. Then:

$$\mathbf{B} \approx \{\{\underline{1}\} + \{\underline{1}\,\underline{2}\} + \{\underline{1}\,\underline{2}\,\underline{3}\} + \cdots\}^{[*]}.$$

thus

$$\hat{B}(z) = \exp(e^z - 1).$$

From that last equation results that the number of partitions of a set with n elements is the n-th Bell number

$$B_n = \left[\frac{z^n}{n!}\right]\exp(e^z - 1)$$

$$= \frac{1}{e}\sum_{k\geq 0}\frac{k^n}{n!}.$$

A similar reasoning shows that the number of partitions of a set of cardinality n comprising k blocks is:

$$S_{n,k} = \left[\frac{z^n}{n!}\right]\frac{(e^z - 1)^k}{k!}$$

$$= \frac{1}{k!}\sum_{0 \le j \le k}\binom{k}{j}(-1)^j(k - j)^n,$$

a Stirling number of the second kind.

5. Permutations. We have already examined the decomposition of *permutations* into cycles. If **C** is the class of all cyclic permutations and **P** the class of all permutations, then $\mathbf{P} \approx \mathbf{C}^{[*]}$. In particular, the class of permutations with k cycles, $\mathbf{C}^{[k]}$, has for e.g.f.:

$$\hat{C}^{[k]}(z) = (-\log(1 - z))^k.$$

Let $s_{n,k}$ be the number of permutations of $[1..n]$ with k cycles; $s_{n,k}$ is a Stirling number of the first kind and $s_{n,k} = [z^n/n!]\hat{C}^{[k]}(z)$. Using bivariate generating functions, we easily find:

$$\sum_k \hat{C}^{[k]}(z) \equiv \sum_{n,k} s_{n,k}u^k\frac{z^n}{n!} = (1 - z)^{-u}$$

whence by expanding the identity:

$$\sum_k s_{n,k}u^k = u(u + 1)(u + 2) \cdots (u + n - 1)$$

Thus, these numbers coincide with those appearing in the analysis of the max-finding procedure:

$$s_{n,k} = [u^k]u(u + 1)(u + 2) \cdots (u + n - 1).$$

6. Integer compositions. A *composition* of the integer n is a sequence $(\pi_1, \cdots, \pi_k)$ such that each π_j is an integer larger than 0, and the π_j add up to n. The set **CO** of all compositions satisfies:

$$\mathbf{CO} \approx \mathbf{I}^*$$

where **I** is the set of integers ≥ 1, and the weight of integer $k \in \mathbf{I}$ is $w(k) = k$. We thus have:

$$CO(z) = \frac{1}{1 - I(z)} \quad \text{where } I(z) = z + z^2 + z^3 + \cdots$$

so that the number of compositions of an integer n is:

$$[z^n]\frac{1 - z}{1 - 2z} = 2^{n-1} \quad (n \ge 1).$$

7. Integer partitions. A *partition* of integer n is defined like a composition, except that one imposes the further restriction that the π_j form a nondecreasing sequence. Let **IP** be the class of all integer partitions. One can see that:

$$\mathbf{IP} \approx \{1\}^* \{2\}^* \{3\}^* \cdots$$

where again the weight of integer k is equal to k itself. From there one obtains the generating function expression:

$$IP(z) = \prod_{k \geq 1} (1 - z^k)^{-1}.$$

As was pointed out in the introduction, a large number of enumeration results follow from these combinatorial constructions. For instance, the number of (set) partitions of a set of n elements where each block has size at most h is:

$$\left[\frac{z^n}{n!} \right] \exp(e_h(z) - 1),$$

where e_h is the truncated exponential series:

$$e_h(z) = \sum_{j=0}^{h} \frac{z^j}{j!}.$$

Compositions or (integer) partitions into bounded summands can be dealt with in a similar fashion.

6.3 ASYMPTOTIC METHODS FROM COMPLEX ANALYSIS

Asymptotic counting of combinatorial structures can in most cases be obtained directly from generating functions. The method relies on basic analytic function theory (contour integrals). The main techniques are singularity analysis and saddle point methods. Also, the Mellin transform has turned out to be an important tool in the study of many combinatorial sums arising in the analysis of algorithms.

The problem examined in this section is an *inversion problem*. Given some information about a generating function $f(z)$—at best an *explicit form*, at worst only a *functional equation* defining the function *implicitly*—how to recover some asymptotic information on the n-th Taylor coefficient f_n of $f(z)$.

One way is to obtain explicit forms for the coefficients f_n, if at all possible. For instance, assume we are interested in the probability that a random permutation of $[1 . . n]$ has no fixed point (i.e. no cycle of length 1). From the preceding chapter, this probability is:

$$\pi_n^{\langle 1 \rangle} = [z^n] \frac{e^{-z}}{1 - z}$$

from which follows the explicit form:

$$\pi_n^{\langle 1 \rangle} = \sum_{k=0}^{n} \frac{(-1)^k}{k!}.$$

Observing that $\pi_n^{\langle 1 \rangle}$ is a partial sum of the expansion of $\exp(-1)$, we find:

$$\pi_n^{\langle 1 \rangle} = e^{-1} + O\left(\frac{1}{(n+1)!}\right).$$

However, if we need the probability that a permutation has no cycles of length 1 or 2, we find

$$\pi_n^{\langle 2 \rangle} = [z^n]\frac{e^{-z-z^2/2}}{1-z}$$

and expanding leads to a double sum, whose approximation, though feasible, requires some work. The problem gets worse if cycle lengths of the form 1, 2, ..., k are prohibited.

In general, the complexity of that method increases drastically as the size of the defining equation grows. With techniques we are going to examine in this section, one can reason as follows:

The function $f(z) = \exp(-z - z^2/2)/(1 - z)$ has a unique *singularity* (a pole) at $z = 1$). Around that pole, one has:

$$f(z) \sim \frac{e^{-3/2}}{1-z},$$

therefore:

$$[z^n]f(z) \sim [z^n]\frac{e^{-3/2}}{1-z}$$

and the quantity on the r.h.s. is equal to $e^{-3/2}$, independently of n, so that:

$$f_n \sim e^{-3/2} \quad (n \to \infty).$$

The basic inversion theorem to be used to justify that reasoning is *Cauchy's residue theorem*, or equivalently *Cauchy's integral formula* for coefficients of analytic functions, namely:

$$[z^n]f(z) = \frac{1}{2i\pi} \int_\Gamma f(z)\, dz \tag{6.22}$$

for Γ a simple closed contour around the origin.

The choice of the integration contour Γ in Equation (6.22) is guided by several principles detailed below. In many cases, that formula makes it possible to extract useful asymptotic information about $f_n = [z^n]f(z)$.

1. If $f(z)$ is *meromorphic* in the complex plane $\mathbf{C}$, extend Γ to a circle of large radius, taking residues of the integrand of (6.22) into account.

2. If $f(z)$ has *nonpolar singularities* on its circle of convergence, take for Γ a contour that comes close to the singularity in order to extract information from the singular behavior of the function. If the function is small around its singularity, take a contour that extends beyond the circle of convergence; if it is "moderately" large, take a contour that partly coincides with the circle of convergence; if it is "very" large, take a contour properly contained in the disk of convergence and use saddle point methods like in (3) below.

3. If $f(z)$ is *entire*, take Γ to be a circle that crosses the *saddle point(s)* of $f(z)$.

Notice that these methods do not always require $f(z)$ to be explicitly determined: it is often sufficient that some *local* properties of $f(z)$ be obtained from defining equations.

Finally, a number of combinatorial sums can be studied asymptotically by means of the *Mellin (integral) transform* that associates to a real function $f(x)$ a transformed function $f^*(s)$ of the complex variable s defined by:

$$f^*(s) = \int_0^\infty f(x)x^{s-1}\, dx.$$

Mellin transform techniques apply well to the asymptotic analysis of *harmonic sums* that are of the form:

$$F(x) = \sum_k \alpha_k g(\beta_k x),$$

and they also rely on the use of a complex inversion theorem.

For this chapter, the main references are (12) and (10).

6.3.1 The Exponential Order Formula for Coefficients of Analytic Functions

We start by recalling a few basic definitions:

DEFINITION 6.15　A function $f(z)$ of the complex variable z is said to be *analytic* at $z = a$ if it has a power series expansion, also called *Taylor expansion*, convergent in a neighborhood of a:

$$f(z) = \sum_{n \geq 0} c_n(z - a)^n. \tag{6.23}$$

A function $f(z)$ of the complex variable z is said to be *meromorphic* at $z = a$ if in a neighborhood of a it has for $z \neq a$ a convergent expansion (called a *Laurent expansion*) of the form:

$$f(z) = \sum_{n \geq -M} c_n(z - a)^n. \tag{6.24}$$

If $c_{-M} \neq 0$, then $f(z)$ has a *pole* of order M at $z = a$.

A function is analytic (meromorphic) in a domain iff it is analytic (meromorphic) at every point of the domain. A point at which an analytic function ceases to be analytic is called a *singularity* of the function. We let $\mathrm{Sing}(f)$ denote the set of singularities of function f.

DEFINITION 6.16   If $f(z)$ has a pole of order $M \geq 1$ at $z = a$, the coefficient c_{-1} of its Laurent expansion at $z = a$ is called the *residue* of f at $z = a$ and is denoted by:

$$\mathrm{Res}(f(z); z = a).$$

With a slight extension of our previous notations, we could write:

$$\mathrm{Res}(f(z); z = a) = \left[\frac{1}{z - a}\right] f(z).$$

Examples

1. $f(z) = \exp\left(z + \dfrac{z^2}{2}\right)$ has no singularity in the whole of the complex plane
   C; it is an *entire* function.
2. $f(z) = e^{-z - z^2/2}/(1 - z)^2$ has a double pole at $z = 1$, where local expansions reveal that

$$f(z) = \frac{e^{-3/2}}{(z - 1)^2} - \frac{2e^{-3/2}}{(z - 1)} + O(1)$$

   so that $\mathrm{Res}(f(z); z = 1) = -2e^{-3/2}$.
3. $f(z) = e^{-z/2 - z^2/4}/\sqrt{1 - z}$ is analytic in $|z| \leq 1$ except for a nonpolar singularity at $z = 1$.

We can now state the celebrated Cauchy residue theorem:

THEOREM 6.5   [Cauchy's residue theorem]   Let Γ be a simple closed curve oriented positively, and assume that f is meromorphic in a domain D containing Γ in its interior, and has no poles on Γ. Then:

$$\frac{1}{2i\pi} \int_{\Gamma} f(z)\,dz = \sum_{s} \mathrm{Res}(f(z); z = s) \tag{6.25}$$

where the sum is over the set of all poles s of $f(z)$ in the interior of Γ.   ∎

In particular the integral of an analytic function along a closed contour is equal to 0. An immediate consequence of Theorem 6.5 is:

THEOREM 6.6 [Cauchy's integral coefficient formula]   Let Γ be a simple closed contour, oriented positively, with the origin in its interior, that is contained inside the domain of analyticity of $f(z)$. Then:

$$f_n \equiv [z^n] f(z) = \frac{1}{2i\pi} \int_\Gamma f(z) \frac{dz}{z^{n+1}}. \tag{6.26}$$

Proof   By Cauchy's residue theorem, the integral is equal to $\mathrm{Res}(f(z)/z^{n+1}; z = 0)$ which is exactly f_n. ∎

An important property of analytic functions is that the radius of convergence of the Taylor expansion of f at a denoted $R(f; a)$ satisfies

$$R(f; a) = \min\{|s - a| \mid s \in \mathrm{Sing}(f)\}.$$

In other words an analytic function always has a singularity on its circle of convergence.

We can now state a theorem relating the *exponential order* of coefficients of an analytic function to the *location of its singularities*.

THEOREM 6.7   [The exponential coefficient bound]   If $f(z) = \Sigma f_n z^n$ is such that:

$$R = \min_{s \in \mathrm{Sing}(f)} |s|$$

then for any $\varepsilon > 0$:

$$R^{-n}(1 - \varepsilon)^n \underset{i.o.}{<} |f_n| \underset{a.e.}{<} R^{-n}(1 + \varepsilon)^n. \tag{6.27}$$

The notation $a_n \underset{i.o.}{<} b_n$ means that a_n is smaller than b_n *infinitely often* (for infinitely many values of n) while $a_n \underset{a.e.}{<} b_n$ means that $a_n < b_n$ *almost everywhere* (except for at most a finite number of values of n).

Proof   If the lower bound was not satisfied, then $f(z)$ would be analytic in a larger domain. The upper bound follows from Cauchy's integral formula taking as integration contour a circle of radius $R(1 - \eta)$ where $(1 - \eta)^{-1} \equiv (1 + \varepsilon)$. ∎

Applications

1. For the exponential generating function of *surjections*[3] $f(z) = \dfrac{1}{2 - e^z}$, we have:

$$\mathrm{Sing}(f) = \{\log 2 + 2ik\pi \mid k \in \mathbf{Z}\}$$

so that $R = \log 2$ and for any ε:

$$\left(\frac{1}{\log 2}\right)^n (1 - \varepsilon)^n \underset{i.o.}{<} f_n \underset{a.e.}{<} \left(\frac{1}{\log 2}\right)^n (1 + \varepsilon)^n.$$

2. With $f(z) = e^{-z/2 - z^2/4}/\sqrt{1 - z}$, the singularity nearest to the origin is $z = 1$, so that:

$$(1 - \varepsilon)^n \underset{i.o.}{<} f_n \underset{a.e.}{<} (1 + \varepsilon)^n$$

3. Consider the functional equation $f(z) = z + f(z^2 + z^3)$ defining $f(z)$ implicitly. Iterating the equation, we find:

$$f(z) = \sum_{k \geq 0} \sigma^{(k)}(z) \tag{6.28}$$

where $\sigma(z) = z^2 + z^3$, and $\sigma^{(k)}(z)$ denotes the k-th iterate of $\sigma(z)$. The fixed points of σ are:

$$z_0 = 0; \quad z_1 = \frac{-1 - \sqrt{5}}{2}; \quad z_2 = \frac{-1 + \sqrt{5}}{2}.$$

One can observe that z_0 is an attractive fixed point of σ so that the sum (6.28) converges fast in a neighborhood of the origin. On the other hand, the sum (6.28) becomes infinite when $z = z_2$. (There it becomes a sum of infinitely many identical terms that are nonzero.) A slightly more refined analysis reveals that z_2 is the singularity of f nearest to the origin. Since $1/z_2$ is the well-known *golden ratio* $\varphi = \dfrac{1 + \sqrt{5}}{2}$, we have the bounds:

$$\varphi^n(1 - \varepsilon)^n \underset{i.o.}{<} f_n \underset{a.e.}{<} (1 + \varepsilon)^n. \qquad \blacksquare$$

As a final conclusion to this section, if R is the distance of the origin to the nearest singularity of f, we have:

$$f_n = \vartheta(n)R^{-n} \tag{6.29}$$

---

[3] The coefficient of $z^n/n!$ in $f(z)$ is the number of surjections from $[1 . . n]$ onto an initial segment of $\mathbf{N}$.

where ϑ grows *i.o.* faster than any decreasing exponential α^n, $\alpha < 1$ and grows *a.e.* slower than any increasing exponential β^n, $\beta > 1$. It is the purpose of the next sections to indicate methods by which the growth of the *subexponential factor* $\vartheta(n)$ can be precisely quantified. One has for instance for the above examples:

1. $f_n = O\left(\left(\dfrac{1}{\log 2}\right)^n\right)$;

2. $f_n = O(n^{-1/2})$;

3. $f_n = O\left(\dfrac{\varphi^n}{n}\right)$;

and fuller asymptotic expansions can be obtained in all cases.

6.3.2 Rational Fractions and Meromorphic Functions

We have seen in the last section that the *location of singularities* of a function determines the *exponential growth* of its coefficients. In this, and the next section, we refine on that observation showing that the *nature of the singularities* is related to the growth of the *subexponential factor* $\vartheta(n)$ that appears in the formula:

$$f_n \sim \vartheta(n) R^{-n}.$$

We start with the simplest class of functions, namely the *rational fractions*. These are of the form

$$f(z) = \frac{N(z)}{D(z)} \tag{6.30}$$

for two (relatively prime) polynomials $N(z)$ and $D(z)$. If $f(z)$ is to be analytic at 0, one should further assume that $D(0) \neq 0$. Since $N(z) \equiv D(z)f(z)$, the coefficients of a rational fraction (6.30) satisfy a *linear recurrence relation*

$$\sum_k f_{n-k} D_k = 0$$

with initial conditions determined by $N(z)$. Conversely any linear recurrence relation leads to a generating function that is a rational function.

The asymptotics of coefficients of rational fractions is easy enough. Let $\alpha_1, \alpha_2, \ldots$ be the (finite) set of zeros of $D(z)$. Then the *partial fraction decomposition* of $f(z)$ is:

$$f(z) = \sum_{j,k} \frac{c_{j,k}}{(z - \alpha_j)^k}$$

$$= \sum_{j,k} \frac{\gamma_{j,k}}{(1 - z/\alpha_j)^k}. \tag{6.31}$$

The sum in (6.31) is finite and all coefficients $\gamma_{i,k}$ such that k is larger than the order of the root α_j of $D(z)$ are equal to zero.

From (6.31), taking coefficients, we get:

$$f_n = \sum_{j,k} \gamma_{j,k} \alpha_j^{-n} \binom{n+k-1}{k-1}, \tag{6.32}$$

and since the binomial coefficient is a polynomial of degree $(k-1)$ in n:

THEOREM 6.8   If $f(z) = \dfrac{N(z)}{D(z)}$ is a rational fraction that is analytic at the origin, then the n-th Taylor coefficient of f has the exact expression:

$$f_n = \sum_j \alpha_j^{-n} \Pi_j(n) \tag{6.33}$$

where the α_j are the poles of f and each Π_j is a polynomial whose degree is equal to the multiplicity of the pole of f at α_j minus 1.

Notice that if the α_j are arranged in order of increasing modulus, then (6.33) has the character of an asymptotic expansion in which each term is *exponentially smaller* than the previous one. Notice also that nonreal α's will correspond to *fluctuating terms* since, if $\alpha = \rho e^{i\varphi}$:

$$\alpha^{-n} = \rho^{-n}(\cos(n\varphi) - i\sin(n\varphi)).$$

A result very similar to Theorem 6.8 holds much more generally for *meromorphic* functions. One has:

THEOREM 6.9   Let $f(z)$ be meromorphic for $|z| \le R$ and analytic for $|z| = R$. Let $\alpha_1, \alpha_2, \ldots,$ be the (finite) set of poles of $f(z)$ with modulus less than R. Then there exist polynomials $\Pi_1, \Pi_2, \ldots,$ such that

$$f_n = \sum_j \alpha_j^{-n} \Pi_j(n) + O(R^{-n}). \tag{6.34}$$

The degree of Π_j is equal to the order of the pole α_j minus 1.

Notice that the remainder term is exponentially smaller than any of the terms in the sum (6.34). We present two proofs of Theorem 6.9.

Proof 1   [Method of subtracted singularities]

If $f(z)$ has a pole of order δ_j at α_j, then for some function h_j analytic at α_j:

$$f(z) = \frac{h_j(z)}{(z - \alpha_j)^{\delta_j}}.$$

Expanding h_j around α_j up to terms of order δ_j, we find a polynomial Q_j, namely

$$Q_j = \sum_{r \le \delta_j} \frac{1}{r!} \frac{d}{dz^r} h_j(z) \bigg|_{z = \alpha_j} (z - \alpha_j)^r$$

such that:

$$f(z) - \frac{Q_j(z)}{(z - \alpha_j)^{\delta_j}}$$

is analytic at $z = \alpha_j$. Thus, the rational fraction obtained by collecting singular contributions from poles:

$$Q(z) = \sum_j \frac{Q_j(z)}{(z - \alpha_j)^{\delta_j}}$$

is such that $f(z) - Q(z)$ is analytic for $|z| \le R$. Writing

$$[z^n]f(z) = [z^n]Q(z) + [z^n](f(z) - Q(z))$$

and applying Theorem 6.8 to the first term, the Cauchy exponential bound to the second term concludes the proof of the theorem.

Proof 2   [Contour integration method]

Let φ be a number $0 \le \varphi < 2\pi$ be such that the half-ray $\mathrm{Argt}(z) = \varphi$ crosses no pole of $f(z)$ with modulus less than R. Let ρ be smaller than the radius of convergence of f at 0. Consider the contour (see Figure 6.4):

$$\Gamma = \Gamma_1 + \Gamma_2 + \Gamma_3 + \Gamma_4$$

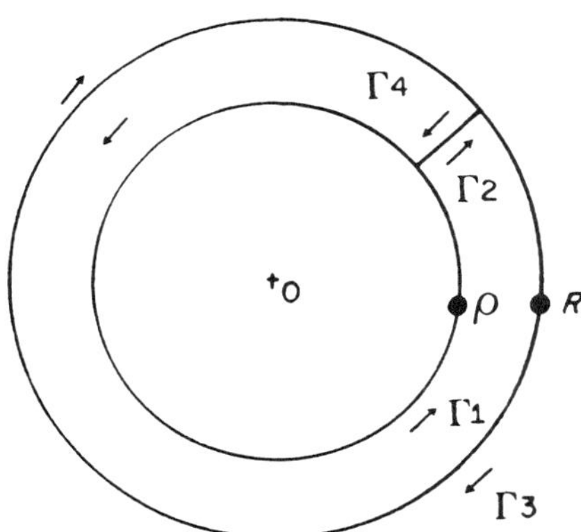

Figure 6.4   The integration contour used to extract coefficients of meromorphic functions.

where

$$\Gamma_1 = \{z \mid |z| = \rho\}$$

$$\Gamma_2 = \{z \mid \rho \le |z| \le R;\ \mathrm{Argt}(z) = \varphi\}$$

$$\Gamma_3 = \{z \mid |z| = R\}$$

$$\Gamma_4 = -\Gamma_2.$$

Γ_1 is oriented positively (anticlockwise), Γ_3 negatively (clockwise); Γ_2 is traversed in the direction from Γ_1 to Γ_3, and Γ_4 is the same as Γ_2 except that the orientation is reversed.

The contour Γ encircles all the poles of $f(z)$ with modulus less than R in a clockwise direction. Therefore, by the residue theorem.

$$\frac{1}{2i\pi} \int_\Gamma f(z) \frac{dz}{z^{n+1}} = -\sum_j \mathrm{Res}(f(z)z^{-n-1};\ z = \alpha_j) \qquad (6.35)$$

(Notice the minus sign due to the orientation of Γ.) Now the integral decomposes into

$$\frac{1}{2i\pi} \int_\Gamma = \frac{1}{2i\pi} \int_{\Gamma_1} + \frac{1}{2i\pi} \int_{\Gamma_2} + \frac{1}{2i\pi} \int_{\Gamma_3} + \frac{1}{2i\pi} \int_{\Gamma_4}.$$

Contributions relative to Γ_2 and Γ_4 cancel each other. The contribution relative to Γ_4 is $O(R^{-n})$ by trivial majorization. Finally $\dfrac{1}{2i\pi} \int_{\Gamma_1}$ is equal to f_n. Thus the proof is completed once we check that each of the residues in (6.35) is of the form $\alpha_j^{-n} \Pi_j(n)$. ∎

Examples

1. Let **R** be the set of 0–1 strings without 2-*runs* (i.e., no two consecutive *ones* may appear in these strings). One has the description:

$$\mathbf{R} = (\varepsilon + 1)(0(\varepsilon + 1))^*$$

so that:

$$r(z) = (1 + z)\frac{1}{1 - z(1 + z)}$$

$$= \frac{1 + z}{1 - z - z^2}.$$

From the partial fraction decomposition of $r(z)$, we get:

$$r_n = \frac{1 + \sqrt{5}}{2\sqrt{5}}\left(\frac{1 + \sqrt{5}}{2}\right)^n - \frac{1 - \sqrt{5}}{2\sqrt{5}}\left(\frac{1 - \sqrt{5}}{2}\right)^n.$$

2. Let $f(z) = 1/(2 - e^z)$ whose set of singularities has been already determined. The residue at $a = \log 2$ of f is $-\dfrac{1}{2}$. By periodicity of the exponential, this is also equal to the residue of f at any other pole. The sum of residues in Theorem 6.9 appears to be convergent, so that one can write the *exact* formula:

$$[z^n]\frac{1}{2 - e^z} = \frac{1}{2}\left(\frac{1}{\log 2}\right)^{n+1} \sum_{k\in\mathbf{Z}} \chi_k^{-n-1},$$

where:

$$\chi_k = 1 + \frac{2ik\pi}{\log 2}.$$

3. The probability that a random permutation of $[1..n]$ has no cycle of length $\leq k$ is:

$$\pi_n^{\langle k\rangle} = [z^n]\frac{e^{-z - \frac{z^2}{2} - \frac{z^3}{3} \cdots - \frac{z^k}{k}}}{1 - z},$$

so that for any positive real R:

$$\pi_n^{\langle k\rangle} = e^{-H_k} + o(1)$$

with $H_k = 1 + \dfrac{1}{2} + \dfrac{1}{3} + \cdots + \dfrac{1}{k}.$ ∎

Notice finally that these expansions are usually quite good owing to the fast decrease of terms. For instance,

$$[z^{10}]\frac{1}{2 - e^z} = \frac{34082521}{1209600} = 28.1766873346$$

while the *first* term of the asymptotic expansion yields:

$$\frac{1}{2}\left(\frac{1}{\log 2}\right)^{11} = 28.1766873361 \ !$$

6.3.3 Nonpolar Singularities

Assume that a function $f(z)$ has a unique singularity of smallest modulus α. Results from the last section entail that, when f is meromorphic, we can *translate* an asymptotic relation for the function:

$$f(z) \sim g(z) \quad z \to \alpha, \tag{6.36}$$

where α is the singularity nearest to the origin, into the corresponding relation for coefficients:

$$[z^n]f(z) \sim [z^n]g(z) \quad n \to \infty. \tag{6.37}$$

We propose here to describe general conditions under which the transition from (6.36) to (6.37) can be effected, relaxing the conditions that functions be meromorphic or singularities be of a polar type.

Developments in this section assume that asymptotic information is available for the function in some area of the complex plane around its singularity. They make it possible to translate $O(\cdot)$ estimates for functions into $O(\cdot)$ estimates for coefficients, whence the name of *transfer* or *translation* lemmas given to them.

One of the main uses of transfer lemmas is as follows. Assume we have an asymptotic expansion for f around α in the form:

$$f(z) = \sigma_1(z) + \sigma_2(z) + \cdots + \sigma_k(z) + O(g(z)), \tag{6.38}$$

for some elementary functions $\sigma_1 \ldots$ belonging to an asymptotic scale. Then, if proper conditions are satisfied, (6.38) translates into

$$f_n = \sigma_{1,n} + \sigma_{2,n} + \cdots + \sigma_{k,n} + O(g_n). \tag{6.39}$$

Application of this method, therefore, calls for two types of results:

1. Building up a *catalogue* of coefficients of standard singular functions appearing in asymptotic expansions, in exact or asymptotic form, using real or complex analysis.
2. Establishing conditions under which transfer lemmas hold true.

Notice also that these methods can be trivially extended when a function has a finite number of singularities on its circle of convergence. Just add up the contributions to the coefficients coming from each singularity.

Table 6.4 provides a simplified catalog of the asymptotic form of coefficients of some standard functions. Such a catalog can be built from direct expressions available for coefficients or from contour integration techniques. For instance:

$$[z^n] - \log(1 - z) = \frac{1}{n}$$

$$[z^n](1 - z)^{-s} = \frac{s(s + 1)(s + 2) \cdots (s + n - 1)}{n!} = \binom{s + n - 1}{s - 1}.$$

As to transfer lemmas, they are summarized in Table 6.5. (Notice, in passing, the analogy between Tables 6.4 and 6.5.) We shall prove here:

Table 6.4
A simplified catalogue of the asymptotic form of coefficients of some standard singular functions.

Function	Coeff.	
$\log(1 - z)^{-1}$	$\dfrac{1}{n}$	
$(1 - z)^r$	$\dfrac{n^{-r-1}}{\Gamma(-r)}$	$r \neq 0, 1, 2, \cdots$
$(1 - z)^r \log^s(1 - z)^{-1}$	$\dfrac{n^{-r-1}}{\Gamma(-r)} \log^s n$	$r \neq 0, 1, 2, \cdots$
$(1 - z)^r \log^s(1 - z)^{-1}$	$r! n^{-r-1}$	$r = 0, 1, 2, \cdots$

THEOREM 6.10

1. Assume that $g(z)$ is analytic in the domain

$$D = \{z \mid |z| \leq 1, z \neq 1\}$$

and that as z tends to 1 inside D, one has:

$$g(z) = O(|1 - z|^{-s})$$

with $s > 1$. Then:

$$[z^n] g(z) = O(n^{s-1}).$$

2. Assume that $g(z)$ is analytic in the indented disk:

$$D = \{z \mid |z| \leq 1 + \delta, \vartheta < |\text{Argt}(z - 1)| < 2\pi\}$$

Table 6.5
A simplified set of transfer results (see Theorem 6.10 for validity conditions).

Function	Coeff.	Cond.
$O(\log(1 - z))$	$O\left(\dfrac{\log n}{n}\right)$	
$O((1 - z)^{-s})$	$O(n^{s-1})$	$s \geq 1$
$O((1 - z)^r)$	$O(n^{-r-1})$	$r \geq 0$

where δ, ϑ are such that $\delta > 0$, $0 < \vartheta < \dfrac{\pi}{2}$. Assume that, as z tends to 1 inside D:

$$g(z) = O(|1 - z|^r)$$

with $r > 0$. Then:

$$[z^n]\, g(z) = O(n^{-r-1}).$$

Proof   (Sketch)

(i)   Use the Cauchy formula with a contour Γ that consists of the circle $|z| = 1$ except for a small notch at distance $1/n$ of $z = 1$: $\Gamma = \Gamma_0 + \Gamma_1$ where

$$\Gamma_0 = \left\{ z \mid |z| \le 1,\ |z - 1| = \frac{1}{n} \right\}$$

$$\Gamma_2 = \left\{ z \mid |z| = 1,\ |z - 1| \ge \frac{1}{n} \right\}.$$

Next, evaluate each integral using trivial bounds. One has:

$$\int_{\Gamma_0} f(z)\frac{dz}{z^{n+1}} = O\left(\frac{1}{n}\left(\frac{1}{n} \right)^{-s} \right)$$

$$\int_{\Gamma_1} f(z)\frac{dz}{z^{n+1}} = O\left(\int_{\vartheta_0}^{\pi} |1 - e^{i\vartheta}|^{-s} d\vartheta \right).$$

there ϑ_0 is the argument of the intersection of Γ_0 and Γ_1 in the upper half plane.

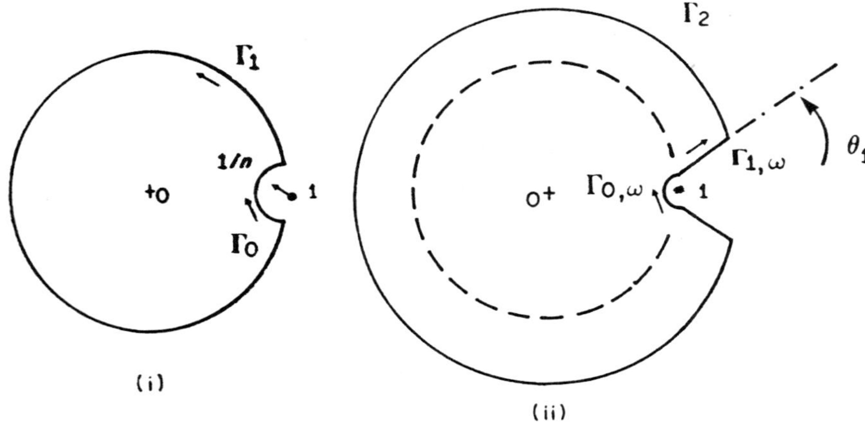

Figure 6.5   The contours used in order to establish Theorem 6.10.

(ii) Use likewise the Cauchy integral formula with a contour

$$\Gamma = \Gamma_{0,\omega} + \Gamma_{1,\omega} + \Gamma_2$$

where

$$\Gamma_{0,\omega} = \{z \mid |z - 1| = \omega, |\mathrm{Argt}(z - \rho)| > \vartheta_1\}$$

$$\Gamma_{1,\omega} = \{z \mid |z - 1| \geq \omega, |z| < r_1, \mathrm{Argt}(z - \rho) = \vartheta_1\}$$

$$\Gamma_2 = \{z \mid |z| = r_1, |\mathrm{Argt}(z - \rho)| \geq \vartheta_1\}$$

for some r_1: $1 < r_1 < 1 + \delta$ ($\delta > 0$) and ϑ_1: $\vartheta < \vartheta_1 < \dfrac{\pi}{2}$, letting ω shrink to 0. ∎

A full discussion of the proof is given in papers by Odlyzko (41) and Flajolet-Odlyzko (23).

Notes

1. Many more results are available using these techniques. The underlying idea is to take a contour of integration that comes close to the singularity. If the function is *small* (i.e., tends to 0) as the argument approaches the singularity then one tries to extend the contour of integration outside the disk of convergence in a manner similar to what was done for polar singularities. If the function is *large* then the contour can stay within the disk of convergence of the function.

2. The fact that the singularity of the function was assumed to be at $z = 1$ is of course not restrictive (otherwise, normalize the function). Also, the case where the function has a *finite* number of singularities on its circle of convergence can be dealt with using composite contours. The outcome is that contributions from each of the singularities cumulate.

3. The classical *Darboux-Polya* method is in the same spirit. It, however, assumes *smoothness conditions* while here our conditions concern *orders of growth* only. The present approach lends itself nicely to generalizations; also in some cases, only order-of-magnitude informations are available and it appears to be well-suited to combinatorial enumeration problems.

4. *Tauberian theorems* assume much weaker conditions on the function g: basically all that is required is some information on the function as $z \to 1^{-}$ along the *real axis*. However, in the context of combinatorial enumerations, they do not seem to provide information for the same variety of singular behaviors while they require some so-called Tauberian side conditions that may be hard to establish. ∎

Examples

1. When counting certain combinatorial configurations (''clouds''), one encounters the generating function:

$$f(z) = \frac{e^{-z/1 - z^2/4}}{\sqrt{1 - z}}$$

$$= \frac{e^{-3/4}}{\sqrt{1 - z}} + O(|1 - z|^{1/2}).$$

   Thus, by the transfer lemma (Theorem 6.10(1)):

$$[z^n]f(z) = [z^n]\frac{e^{-3/4}}{\sqrt{1 - z}} + O(n^{-3/2})$$

$$= \frac{e^{-3/4}}{\sqrt{\pi n}} + O(n^{-3/2}).$$

2. Let $f(z)$ be the solution analytic at the origin of equation:

$$f = z(1 + f + f^2).$$

   that is:

$$f(z) = \frac{1 - z - \sqrt{1 - 2z - 3z^2}}{2z}.$$

   Function f is the o.g.f. of unary binary trees, in which each node has degree 0, 1, or 2. The dominant singularity of $f(z)$ is at $z = 1/3$ (the other one is at $z = -1$), where locally f admits an expansion of the form:

$$f(z) = A\sqrt{1 - 3z} + O(|1 - 3z|^{3/2})$$

   from which one finds:

$$[z^n]f(z) = \frac{3^{n+1}}{2\sqrt{\pi n^3}} + O(3^n n^{-5/2}). \qquad \blacksquare$$

6.3.4 Saddle Point Bounds

We only give here a brief introduction to the subject of *saddle point methods*, which allow derivation of asymptotic expansions for integrals of analytic functions depending on a (large) parameter. In the context of extracting coefficients of analytic functions, one way of conceiving these methods is as a refinement of trivial bounds on the Cauchy integral formula.

Assume throughout this section that $f(z)$ is an analytic function that is *entire* and has *positive coefficients*. By Cauchy's integral formula, one has:

$$f_n \equiv [z^n]f(z) = \frac{1}{2i\pi} \int_\Gamma f(z) \frac{dz}{z^{n+1}}. \tag{6.40}$$

Take as contour of integration Γ a circle of radius R. Since $f(z)$ has positive coefficients, we have for any z such that $|z| = R$: $|f(z)| \leq f(R)$, and thus, from trivial majorizations of (6.40):

$$\begin{aligned} f_n &\leq \frac{1}{2\pi} \frac{f(R)}{R^{n+1}} 2\pi R \\ &\leq \frac{f(R)}{R^n}. \end{aligned} \tag{6.41}$$

The bound (6.41) is valid for *any* positive R. Notice that $f(R)/R^n$, which is infinite at $R = 0$ and $R = \infty$ is unimodal over $\mathbf{R}^+$. Thus, there is a real number $\rho: 0 < \rho < \infty$ that minimizes $f(R)/R^{n+1}$. That number is a root of equation:

$$\frac{d}{dR} \frac{f(R)}{R^n} = 0$$

so that it satisfies:

$$\rho f'(\rho) - nf(\rho) = 0. \tag{6.42}$$

In other words:

THEOREM 6.11   Let f be entire and have positive coefficients. Define the function $w(u)$ by:

$$w(u) = \frac{uf'(u)}{f(u)}.$$

Then the n-th Taylor coefficient of $f(z)$ satisfies the bound:

$$f_n \leq \frac{f(w^{\langle -1\rangle}(n))}{(w^{\langle -1\rangle}(n))^n}, \tag{6.43}$$

where $w^{\langle -1\rangle}(\cdot)$ denotes the functional inverse of $w(\cdot)$.

Example

Take $f(z) = \exp(z)$. Then $[z^n]f(z) \equiv 1/n!$. We have trivially: $w(u) = u$ so that $w^{\langle -1\rangle}(n) \equiv n$, whence by Theorem 6.11 the (expected) bound:

$$\frac{1}{n!} \leq \frac{e^n}{n^n},$$

a weak form of Stirling's formula.   ∎

Note: Since the bound (2) is valid for any R, the function $w(\cdot)$ need not be inverted exactly and may be solved only asymptotically or *approximately*. Of course, the better the approximation, the better the bound.

Example

Let f_n be the number of involutions in the set of permutations of $[1. \, . n]$. Involutions are characterized by the fact that they have only cycles of length 1 and 2. Thus, their e.g.f. is:

$$\hat{f}(z) \equiv \sum_n f_n \frac{z^n}{n!} = \exp\left(z + \frac{z^2}{2} \right).$$

In that case, $w(u) = \dfrac{u + u^2}{2}$, so that an approximation to $w^{\langle -1\rangle}(n)$ is $\sqrt{n}$, whence:

$$f_n \leq n! \, n^{-n/2} e^{\sqrt{n} + n/2}. \qquad \blacksquare$$

The estimates we have just seen can be refined. In many cases of interest, only a *small fraction of the contour* contributes significantly to the integral. There, local approximations can be performed and an asymptotic estimate of the integral (instead of just an upper bound) can be obtained.

The saddle point method applies to integrals of the form:

$$I = \frac{1}{2i\pi} \int_\Gamma e^{h(z)} \, dz, \qquad (6.44)$$

where $h(z) = h_n(z)$ depends on a large parameter n. The case of Cauchy's formula (6.40) corresponds to the particular form:

$$h(z) \equiv h_n(z) = \log f(z) - (n + 1)\log z.$$

The method proceeds as follows:

1. Determine $R = R_n$ such that:

$$\left. \frac{d}{dz} h(z) \right|_{z=R} = 0. \qquad (6.45)$$

Quantity R is called a *saddle point* of the integrand resulting from the local topography of the surface defined by $|h(z)|$ and $|e^{h(z)}|$. Notice that with the notations of Theorem 6.11, one has $R_n = w^{\langle -1\rangle}(n+1)$ which is expected to be close to the quantity $w^{\langle -1\rangle}(n)$ appearing in Theorem 6.11. The idea is to evaluate integral (6.44) using as contour Γ a circle of radius R satisfying (6.45).

2. Select an adequate angle $\vartheta = \vartheta_n$ (usually ϑ will be small), satisfying the two (conflicting) requirements:

$$\int_{\Gamma/\Gamma[\vartheta]} e^{h(z)}\,dz \ll \int_{\Gamma} e^{h(z)}\,dz. \tag{C1}$$

$$e^{h(z)} \approx e^{h(R) + \frac{1}{2}h''(R)(z-R)^2} \qquad z \in \Gamma[\vartheta] \tag{C2}$$

There $\Gamma[\vartheta]$ denotes the part of the circle $|z| = R$ consisting of points z such that $|\mathrm{Argt}(z)| \leq \vartheta$. Condition (C1) requires ϑ to be large enough so that the dominant part of the integral comes from $\Gamma[\vartheta]$ while condition (C2) requires ϑ to be small enough that local expansions be valid.

3. If (C1) and (C2) are satisfied, then one has:

$$I \approx \frac{1}{2i\pi} \int_{\Gamma(\vartheta)} e^{h(R) + \frac{1}{2}h''(R)(z-R)^2}\,dz.$$

The last step is now to *complete* the integral; setting $z = R + it$ then completing the integral:

$$I \approx \frac{1}{2\pi} \int_{-\infty}^{+\infty} e^{-\frac{t^2}{2}h''(R)}\,dt, \tag{C3}$$

a Gaussian integral that can be evaluated, leading to:

$$I \approx \frac{e^{h(R)}}{\sqrt{2\pi h''(R)}}.$$

What we have seen above is general enough to apply to a wide class of integrals depending on a (large) parameter. Restricting ourselves to the special form of integral (6.40), we can state:

THEOREM 6.12   Assuming approximations (C1), (C2), (C3) to be valid, one has:

$$[z^n]f(z) \sim \frac{e^{h(R_n)}}{\sqrt{2\pi h''(R_n)}}, \tag{6.46}$$

where:

$$h(z) = \log f(z) - (n+1)\log z$$

$$R_n = w^{\langle -1\rangle}(n+1)$$

$$w(u) = \frac{uf'(u)}{f(u)},$$

and $w^{\langle -1\rangle}(\cdot)$ is the functional inverse of $w(\cdot)$.

Applications

1. Stirling's formula:

$$[z^n]e^z \sim \frac{e^n n^{-n}}{\sqrt{2\pi n}}.$$

2. The number of involutions:

$$\left[\frac{z^n}{n!}\right] e^{z+z^2/2} \sim \frac{1}{\sqrt{2}} n^{n/2} e^{-n/2+\sqrt{n}-1/4}$$

3. The number of set partitions (10, p. 108):

$$\left[\frac{z^n}{n!}\right] \exp(e^z - 1) \approx \left(\frac{n}{e \log n}\right)^n. \qquad\blacksquare$$

6.3.5 Mellin Transform Techniques

The *Mellin transform* associates to a real function $f(x)$ defined over $[0; +\infty]$ a complex function $f^*(s)$ written $\mathbf{M}[f(x); s]$ or $\mathbf{M}[f(\cdot)]$, and given by:

$$f^*(s) = \int_0^\infty f(x) x^{s-1}\, dx. \qquad (6.47)$$

If f is continuous and satisfies:

$$f(x) = O(x^\alpha) \quad x \to 0$$

$$f(x) = O(x^\beta) \quad x \to \infty$$

then, it is easy to see that the transform (6.47) is defined in the strip, called the *fundamental strip*, $-\alpha < \mathrm{Re}(s) < -\beta$. Let $\delta(x)$ be the function whose value is 1 for $0 \le x \le 1$ and 0 for $1 < x$; it is easy to see that:

$$\mathbf{M}[\delta(x) x^\alpha] = \frac{1}{s + \alpha}$$

and, thus, the Mellin transform associates to a (particular) function that is $O(x^\alpha)$ at 0 a transformed function with a pole at $s = -\alpha$. From this observation, proceeding by linearity, it is easy to see that more generally, the transform of a function with an *asymptotic expansion* around 0 of the form:

$$f(z) \sim \sum_j c_j x^{\alpha^j}$$

is a function meromorphic in a left half plane that has a pole of residue c_j at $s = -\alpha_j$. Smaller terms in that expansion correspond to poles that are farther to the left. A similar reasoning applies to asymptotic expansions towards ∞ (poles farther to the right correspond to smaller contributions). In other words:

1. The asymptotic expansions of a function at 0 (or ∞) are reflected by the poles of its Mellin transform in a left half-plane (a right half plane respectively).

The converse of that property is also (mildly conditionally) true. To prove this, one starts with the *inversion formula*, that corresponds to the classical Fourier inversion:

$$f(x) = \frac{1}{2i\pi} \int_{c-i\infty}^{c+i\infty} f^*(s) x^{-s}\, ds \tag{6.48}$$

where c is in the fundamental strip of f. (Notice the analogy with (6.47).) If $f^*(s)$ is meromorphic, one can evaluate the integral in (6.48) by residues: take as contour of integration the vertical line $\mathrm{Re}(s) = c$ completed by a large contour in the left half-plane. Under (often satisfied) suitable conditions, one can apply Cauchy's residue theorem to that integral and get:

$$f(x) \sim \sum_a Res[f^*(s) x^{-s}; \, s = \alpha] \tag{6.49}$$

where the sum is extended to all poles α of $f^*(s)$ to the right of the vertical line $\mathrm{Re}(s) = c$. Notice that if f^* has only simple poles, then (6.49) can be rewritten as:

$$f(x) \sim \sum_\alpha \mathrm{Res}[f^*(s); \, s = \alpha] x^{-\alpha} \tag{6.50}$$

where the asymptotic nature of expansion (6.50) is obvious. If $f^*(s)$ has multiple poles, then generalized expansions with powers of $\log x$ appear. In summary:

2. The poles of a Mellin transform in a left half-plane (right half plane) translate (under certain smallness conditions of $f^*(s)$ towards $i\infty$) into terms of an asymptotic expansion of $f(x)$ at 0 (resp. $+\infty$).

Thus, the correspondence between asymptotic properties of f and singularities of f^* fares both ways. This justifies the importance of that transform for asymptotic analysis.

The usefulness of the Mellin transform is also due to a very elementary functional property, namely:

$$\mathbf{M}[f(ax); \, s] = a^{-s} f^*(s) \quad a \geq 0,$$

which using linearity (assuming summations and integrations may be interchanged) extends to:

$$\sum_k \lambda_k f(a_k x) \xrightarrow{\;\mathbf{M}\;} \left(\sum_k \lambda_k a_k^{-s} \right) f^*(s). \tag{6.51}$$

Sums on the left-hand side of (6.51) are called *harmonic sums*. Equation (6.51) shows that:

3. Harmonic sums are transformed by the Mellin transform into the product of a generalized Dirichlet series and the transform of the basis function.

We shall only illustrate some of these points by means of a few elementary examples.

Examples

1. Let $f(x) = e^{-x}$. The transform of f is the classical Gamma function:

$$\Gamma(s) = \int_0^\infty \exp(-x)x^{s-1}\, dx.$$

with $\langle 0; +\infty \rangle$ as fundamental strip. To the term $(-1)^k \dfrac{x^k}{k}$ in the expansion of f around 0, there corresponds (Point A above) a simple pole of $\Gamma(s)$ at $s = -k$ with:

$$\Gamma(s) \sim \frac{(-1)^k}{k!}\frac{1}{s+k} \qquad s \to -k$$

In other words, the expansion:

$$e^{-x} \sim \sum_{k \geq 0} \frac{(-1)^k}{k!} x^k$$

translates into the *meromorphic* expansion:

$$\Gamma(s) \approx \sum_{k \geq 0} \frac{(-1)^k}{k!}\frac{1}{s+k},$$

and in that case both expansions are actually convergent.

2. The following sum appears in relation to the analysis of the expected height of a planar tree with n nodes:

$$S(x) = \sum_{k \geq 1} d(k)e^{-k^2 x^2} \tag{6.52}$$

where $d(k)$ is the number of *divisors* of k. Sum (6.52) is typically a harmonic sum whose transform is ($\zeta(s)$ is the Riemann zeta function);

$$S^*(s) = \frac{1}{2}\zeta^2(s)\Gamma\left(\frac{s}{2}\right), \tag{6.53}$$

where the fundamental strip of (6.53) is $\langle 1; +\infty \rangle$. Function S^* has a double pole at $s = 1$ and a simple pole at $s = 0$. Hence, the meromorphic expansion:

$$S*(s) \approx \frac{1}{2}\Gamma\left(\frac{1}{2}\right)\frac{1}{(s-1)^2} + \frac{C_1}{s-2} + \frac{1}{4s},$$

whence:

$$S(x) \sim -\sqrt{\pi}\frac{\log x}{x} + \frac{C_1}{x} + \frac{1}{4} + O(x^M) \quad x \to 0,$$

for any positive M.

The Mellin transform has a host of applications to: (1) situations where number-theoretic functions appear (like above the divisor function); (2) nonstandard asymptotic expansions corresponding to periodicities. Examples are: height of trees, carry propagation, digital trees or tries. . . .

6.4 APPLICATIONS

Algebraic and analytic methods of previous chapters can be used to analyze fundamental parameters of such diverse structures as: permutations (sorting), paths (merging), distributions (occupancy statistics and hashing), words (string manipulation algorithms). . . .

Trees of various sorts, as they have simple recursive specifications, demonstrate in a simple manner how a coherent set of algebraic and analytic methods is attached to a given data structure.

It is our purpose here to offer a brief guide to some of the literature on the subject of analysis of algorithms and data structures, putting enumeration and asymptotic methods in perspective. Since we cannot afford the space necessary to discuss the vast existing literature, we shall restrict ourselves to examining a few *data structures*, closely related to trees, and corresponding algorithmic processes.

6.4.1 Trees and Tree Manipulation Algorithms

This section discusses *uniform* statistics on trees of various compositions. It corresponds to what was called in Section 6.1, the empirical model and is relevant to algorithms operating on trees or symbolic expressions as occurs in compilers, symbolic manipulation systems, and theorem proving. The trees we consider are thus *term trees* in some algebraic structure.

Consider first the family **B** of (planar) *binary trees*, it is a (data) structure recursively defined by:

$$\mathbf{B} = \blacksquare + \langle \circ, \mathbf{B}, \mathbf{B}\rangle \tag{6.54}$$

where "$\blacksquare$" denotes an empty tree (nullary node), and "$\circ$" denotes an internal (binary) node. (We have used an obvious linearized notation for trees.) Define the size of a binary tree to be the number of internal nodes it comprises. Equation (6.54) translates into the fixed point equation for the corresponding generating function $B(z)$:

$$B(z) = 1 + zB^2(z), \tag{6.55}$$

a quadratic equation that has the solution:

$$B(z) = \frac{1 - \sqrt{1 - 4z}}{2z} \tag{6.56}$$

Whence, the explicit result:

$$B_n = \frac{1}{n + 1}\binom{2n}{n}, \tag{6.57}$$

and from Stirling's formula:

$$B_n \sim \frac{4^n}{\sqrt{\pi n^3}}. \tag{6.58}$$

The transition from (6.54) to (6.55) is general enough. Let Ω be a subset of the nonnegative integers. Consider the family $\mathbf{T} \equiv \mathbf{T}[\Omega]$ of trees such that (out)degrees of nodes are restricted to be in the set Ω (binary trees correspond to $\Omega = \{0, 2\}$). Such a family is called, after Meir and Moon (40) the *simple family of trees* associated to degree constraints Ω. Define ω_k to be equal to 1 if $k \in \Omega$ and 0 otherwise. One can write for $\mathbf{T}$ the symbolic equation:

$$\mathbf{T} = \sum_k \omega_k \langle \circ, \mathbf{T}, \mathbf{T}, \cdots, \mathbf{T} \rangle. \tag{6.59}$$

where the number of occurrences of $\mathbf{T}$ in the general term of the sum is equal to k. With the size of a tree now defined as the total number of nodes that tree comprises, Equation (6.59) translates into:

$$T(z) = z\omega(T(z)) \tag{6.60}$$

where $\omega(u) = \sum_k \omega_k x^k$.

The Taylor coefficients of the solution $T(z)$ of (6.60) can be obtained exactly using the *Lagrange Inversion Theorem* (12) that relates the coefficients of the multiplicative powers of a function $(\omega(\cdot))$ to those of its functional inverse (related to T) Equation (6.60) is a prototype application of that theorem that gives:

THEOREM 6.13   The number of trees of size (total number of nodes) n in the family defined by degree constraints Ω is:

$$T_n \equiv \frac{1}{n}[u^{n-1}]\omega(u)^n. \tag{6.61}$$

Notice that in Formula (6.61), the ω_k need not be 0–1 parameters. Allowing for general integral ω_k will make it possible to count term trees, that is, trees whose nodes are labelled with operators; in that case ω_k represents the number of operators of degree (arity) k.

If $\omega(u)$ is simple enough, then Theorem 6.13 will provide useful counting results. We mention here:

1. The number of general trees ($\omega_k \equiv 1$ for all k, i.e. $\omega(u) = (1 - u)^{-1}$) of size n is:

$$\frac{1}{n}\binom{2n - 2}{n - 1}.$$

2. The number of t-ary trees ($t \geq 2$), i.e. $\omega(u) = 1 + u^t$ with a total of $tn + 1$ nodes (and thus with n t-ary internal nodes) is:

$$\frac{1}{tn + 1}\binom{tn + 1}{n}.$$

In case $\omega(u)$ has a more complex form, one has to resort to asymptotic analysis, and indeed (40) have shown that Formula (6.58) obtained here by elementary methods nicely generalizes.

Function $T(z)$ in Equation (6.60) is the solution (in y) of:

$$F(z, y) = 0, \quad F(z, y) \equiv y - z\omega(y). \tag{6.62}$$

Thus (6.62) defines y implicitly as a function of z. From the *implicit function theorem*, we know that a solution y with value y_0 at a point z_0 ($F(z_0, y_0) = 0$) is analytically continuable provided:

$$\left.\frac{\partial}{\partial y}F(z, y)\right|_{(z_0, y_0)} \neq 0.$$

From there can be seen that the singularity (-ies) of y closest to the origin is (are) the quantity (-ies) of smallest modulus ρ such that (ρ, τ) are a set of solutions of the system:

$$F(\rho, \tau) = 0; \quad \left.\frac{\partial}{\partial y}F(z, y)\right|_{(\rho, \tau)} = 0.$$

Hence, here:

$$\rho = \frac{\tau}{\omega(\tau)} \tag{6.63}$$

where τ is one of the roots of equation:

$$\omega(\tau) - \tau\omega'(\tau) = 0. \tag{6.64}$$

Assume for simplicity that there is a unique τ of smallest modulus satisfying (6.64). Then, around (ρ, τ) the dependency between y and z is locally of the form:

$$(\tau - y)^2 - A(z - \rho) = 0, \tag{6.65}$$

as can be checked using the expansion of F. From (6.65), one can establish formally that y has the form:

$$y(z) = h_1(z) + h_2(z)\sqrt{1 - \frac{z}{\rho}} \tag{6.66}$$

where h_1 and h_2 are analytic at $z = \rho$. That form lends itself nicely to a singularity analysis (of a ''square-root'' type) and one gets the very general result of (40) which we state in the little restrictive case where $T(z)$ has a unique singularity on its circle of convergence (the same assumption is made in the rest of this section):

THEOREM 6.14   (40)   If $T(z)$ has a unique singularity on its circle of convergence, the number of trees in $\mathbf{T}[\Omega]$ with size n satisfies asymptotically:

$$T_n \equiv T_n[\Omega] \sim C\rho^{-n}n^{-3/2}$$

where the constants C and ρ are given explicitly by $\rho = \tau/\varphi(\tau)$ and $C = (\varphi(\tau)/(2\pi\varphi''(\tau)))^{1/2}$ with τ the smallest positive root of the equation $\varphi(\tau) - \tau\varphi'(\tau) = 0$.

The main methods for estimating tree parameters are as follows:

1. The symbolic operator approach is a convenient tool for writing symbolic equations in the style of (6.54), (6.60). One may have though to extend it to equations over *multisets* (elements are taken with multiplicities corresponding to values of the parameter to be analyzed (15, 49, 28)).
2. Most generating functions have expressions in terms of the implicitly defined function $T(z)$. Thus, the Lagrange inversion theorem is an important tool that often leads to exact counting results otherwise difficult to attain.
3. Singularity analysis of intervening generating functions is also of constant use in this context. Since function $T(z)$ has algebraic singularities, the methods of Section 6.3 often apply here. Other important techniques are saddle point methods and Mellin transform techniques in those cases where, in summations, there appear coefficients of an arithmetical nature.

Some examples follow. We only sketch the main steps of derivations.

The simplest of all tree algorithms is certainly *recursive tree traversal*: to traverse a tree in preorder, visit its root, then recursively traverse all its root subtrees in left-to-right order. The time complexity of that procedure is clearly linear in the size of the tree, while its storage complexity is equal to the maximum size of the recursion stack, a quantity that coincides with the *height* of the tree.

The first result on the expected height of planar trees has been obtained by De Bruijn et al.

THEOREM 6.15 (18) The expected height of a general planar tree (all node degrees allowed) with n nodes satisfies:

$$\overline{H}_n = \sqrt{\pi n} + O(1).$$

Proof Let **G** be the family of general trees:

$$\mathbf{G} = \circ + \langle \circ, \mathbf{G} \rangle + \langle \circ, \mathbf{G}, \mathbf{G} \rangle + \langle \circ, \mathbf{G}, \mathbf{G}, \mathbf{G} \rangle \cdots \tag{6.67}$$

An equation similar to (6.67) describes the family $\mathbf{G}^{[h]}$ of trees with height at most h:

$$\mathbf{G}^{[h+1]} = \circ + \langle \circ, \mathbf{G}^{[h]} \rangle + \langle \circ, \mathbf{G}^{[h]}, \mathbf{G}^{[h]} \rangle$$
$$+ \langle \circ, \mathbf{G}^{[h]}, \mathbf{G}^{[h]}, \mathbf{G}^{[h]} \rangle \cdots \tag{6.68}$$

whence the equations:

$$g(z) = \frac{z}{1 - g(z)}; \quad g^{[h+1]}(z) = \frac{z}{1 - g^{[h]}(z)} \tag{6.69}$$

from which follows that:

$$g(z) = \frac{1 - \sqrt{1 - 4z}}{2}; \quad g^{[h]}(z) = z\frac{F_{h+1}(z)}{F_{h+2}(z)} \tag{6.70}$$

where the F's satisfy the linear recurrence relation:

$$F_{h+2}(z) = F_{h+1}(z) - zF_h(z).$$

The F's can be expressed as functions of $g(z)$ itself and using Lagrange inversion, one gets:

$$g_{n+1} - g_{n+1}^{[h]} = \sum_j \binom{2n}{n+1 - j(h+2)} - 2\binom{2n}{n - j(h+2)} \tag{6.71}$$
$$+ \binom{2n}{n-1 - j(h+2)}$$

and:

$$\overline{H}_{n+1} = \sum_k d(k)\left[\binom{2n}{n+1 - k} - 2\binom{2n}{n - k} + \binom{2n}{n-1 - k}\right]. \tag{6.72}$$

The asymptotic evaluation of (6.72) calls for evaluations of sums of the form:

$$S_n = \sum_k d(k) \frac{\binom{2n}{n-k}}{\binom{2n}{n}}. \tag{6.73}$$

Using the Gaussian approximation of binomial coefficients, (6.73) is approximated by $T(1/\sqrt{n})$ where:

$$T(x) = \sum_k d(k) e^{-k^2 x^2}. \tag{6.74}$$

The problem is thus to evaluate asymptotically $T(x)$ given by (6.74) when x tends to 0. The Mellin transform of $T(x)$ is readily determined to be

$$T^*(s) = \frac{1}{2} \zeta^2(s) \Gamma\left(\frac{s}{2}\right) \tag{6.75}$$

It has a double pole at $s = 1$, a simple pole at 0 whence the asymptotic expansion

$$T(x) = \frac{1}{x}(\text{Co} \log x + C_1) + C_2 + O(x^m), \tag{6.76}$$

as $x \to 0$, for any $m > 0$. A combination of expansions of the form (6.76) leads to the statement of the theorem. ∎

That result has been generalized by Flajolet and Odlyzko who proved:

THEOREM 6.16   (23)   The expected height of a tree of size n in a simple family of trees satisfies:

$$\overline{H}_n \sim A\sqrt{n}$$

where the explicitly computable constant A is $A = (2\pi/(\varphi(\tau)\varphi''(\tau)))^{1/2}\varphi'(\tau)$.

Returning to the notations of equations (6.59), (6.60), we see that the generating function of trees of height at most h, $T^{[h]}$, is defined by the recurrence:

$$T^{[h+1]}(z) = z\omega(T^{[h]}(z)) \tag{6.77}$$

with $T^{[0]}(z) = z$, and the generating function of height of trees is:

$$H(z) = \sum_h [T(z) - T^{[h]}(z)]. \tag{6.78}$$

The scheme (6.78) is nothing but an iterative approximation scheme to the fixed point equation (6.60) determining T. A singularity analysis of (6.77) leads to the result. This necessitates determining the behavior of the iterative scheme

(6.77) near $z = \rho$, which is a *singular iteration problem*, from which one can prove that:

$$H(z) \sim \frac{K}{1 - \dfrac{z}{\rho}} \log \frac{1}{1 - \dfrac{z}{\rho}} .$$

and the result of Theorem 6.15 follows directly.

Methods similar to those employed in the proof of Theorem (6.16) had been introduced in an earlier analysis of Odlyzko (41), where he counted the number of balanced 2–3 trees of size n.

THEOREM 6.17 (41) The number of balanced 2–3 trees with n external nodes satisfies:

$$E_n \sim \frac{\varphi^n}{n} W(\log n)$$

where φ is the golden ratio $\dfrac{1 + \sqrt{5}}{2}$ and $W(\cdot)$ is a continuous and periodic function.

Odlyzko's result actually includes the counting of a variety of balanced trees. Such trees occur in the management of "dictionaries" and they allow insertions, deletions, and queries to be performed in guaranteed $O(\log n)$ time. The occurrence of the golden ratio in Theorem 6.17 is to be expected after the discussion in Section 6.3 of the equation $f(z) = z + f(z^2 + z^3)$ that is satisfied by the o.g.f. of the E_n.

The next algorithm to be examined is *pattern matching* on trees. The problem is to detect occurrences of a given pattern tree in a larger text tree. For instance, in symbolic manipulation systems, one may look for cases of application of a rewrite rule of the form:

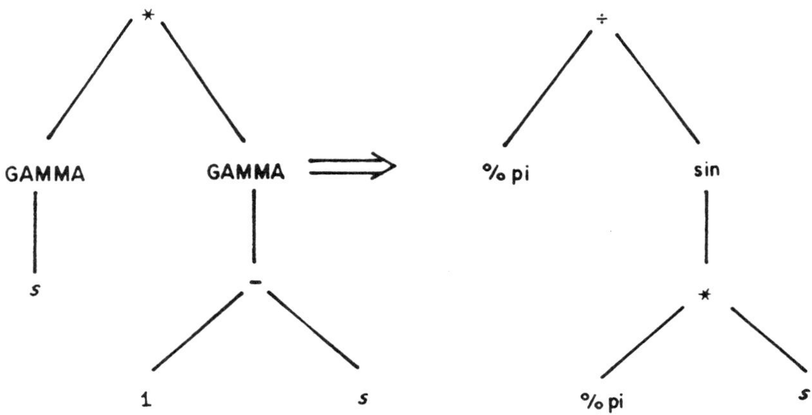

and recognizing cases where the pattern on the l.h.s. appears calls for a pattern-matching algorithm.

Contrary to what happens in the case of strings where efficient worst case linear time algorithms are known, it is conjectured here that no linear time algorithm may exist for tree-matching. The *sequential tree matching algorithm* corresponds to a simple backtracking search. It operates as follows:

1. For each node of the text tree, examine the subtree rooted at that node to see if it matches the pattern, using the comparison procedure below.

2. To compare a subtree against a pattern, traverse simultaneously the pattern tree and the text's subtree in preorder and abort that traversal as soon as a mismatch is detected.

The sequential matching algorithm clearly has a quadratic worst case complexity of the form $O(n^2)$. However, one can prove in contrast that the expected case is linear, namely:

THEOREM 6.18   (49)   The sequential tree matching algorithm, when applied to a fixed pattern P and all trees of size n, has expected cost given by:

$$\overline{\tau\,match_n} \sim w(P)n$$

where $w(P)$ is a function of the structure of pattern P that is uniformly bounded by an absolute constant: $w(P) \le W$.

The proof of the theorem depends on the following lemma (49):

LEMMA 6.13   For a simple family of trees and a fixed pattern P with i internal nodes and e external nodes, the asymptotic probability of occurrence of P at a random node of a large random tree of size n satisfies:

$$occ_n^{\langle P \rangle} \sim \tau^{e-1}\rho^i.$$

Proof: The algebraic part of the proof is a direct application of the symbolic operator method applied to multisets of trees. Generating functions for the number of tree occurrences have simple expressions in terms of the function $T(z)$ and a singularity analysis yields the statement of the lemma.   ∎

The same type of analysis can be applied to a large variety of tree algorithms. In (28), the authors set up a general framework within which a number of algorithms on trees can be (semi-) automatically analyzed. As an illustration, we cite:

THEOREM 6.19   The symbolic differentiation algorithm has, for any set Ω of operators and any set Δ of differentiation rules with at least one ''expanding'' rule, the average case complexity:

$$\tau \overline{diff}_n \;=\; C(\Omega, \Delta) n^{3/2} \;+\; O(n).$$

A less standard singular behavior occurs in the problem known as the *common subexpression problem* or *tree compaction* where a tree is compacted into a *dag* by avoiding duplication of identical substructures. The singularity in that case is of the form (29)

$$\frac{1}{\sqrt{(1 - z)} \log(1 - z)^{-1}}$$

and one finds:

THEOREM 6.20 (29) The expected size of the (maximally compacted) dag representation of a random tree of size n in a simple family of trees satisfies:

$$\overline{K}_n \;=\; \gamma \frac{n}{\sqrt{\log n}} \;+\; O\!\left(\frac{n}{\log n}\right). \qquad\blacksquare$$

Thus, the gain to be expected when compacting trees into dags should be expected to approach 100 percent as the trees get large, although convergence may be quite slow.

Finally, *register allocation* in compiling is the subject of (27, 36). The optimal register allocation strategy for expressions involving binary operators has been determined by Ershov as early as 1958. We have:

THEOREM 6.21 (27, 36) The expected number of registers to evaluate a binary tree of size n using Ershov's optimal algorithm satisfies:

$$\overline{R}_n \;=\; \log_4 n \;+\; P(\log_4 n) \;+\; o(1).$$

where $P(u)$ is a periodic function of its argument that has period 1 and small amplitude.

Proof: In the analysis, there appears the combinatorial sum:

$$V_n \;=\; \sum_{k \geq 1} v_2(k) \binom{2n}{n - k}$$

in which $v_2(k)$ is the exponent of 2 in the prime number decomposition of k. Exponential approximations lead to analogous sums with the binomial coefficient replaced by an exponential (*vide* Eqns. (6.73)–(6.74)). The Mellin transform of the approximation is:

$$\frac{1}{2} \frac{\zeta(s)}{2^s - 1} \Gamma\!\left(\frac{s}{2}\right)$$

and its line of regularly spaced poles $s = \dfrac{2ik\pi}{\log 2}$ corresponds to periodic fluctuations in the form of a Fourier series. $\blacksquare$

Notice on this example the first occurrence of periodicity phenomena of a nontrivial nature.

6.4.2   Digital Searching and Sorting Algorithms

Let S be a finite set of distinct binary strings (or *keys*), each of some fixed length $l \le +\infty$. To the set S is canonically associated a special type of tree, called a *trie* and denoted by *trie*(S), that is defined recursively as follows:

1. If card$(S) = 0$ then *trie*(S) is the empty tree
2. If card$(S) = 1$ then *trie*(S) consists of a unique node (leaf) labelled with the unique element of S
3. If card$(S) \ge 2$ let S_0 and S_1 be the subsets of S formed by elements beginning with a 0 and a 1, respectively; let S_j^* $(j = 0, 1)$ denote the set of elements of S_j stripped of their initial bit; then *trie*(S) is defined as:

$$trie(S) = \langle \circ,\ trie(S_0^*),\ trie(S_1^*) \rangle.$$

If leftmost edges in a tree are labelled with zeros and rightmost edges are labelled with ones, then the set of all labellings from the root of the tree to the leaves is a minimal prefix set of S. For this reason, tries are also known in coding theory as *prefix trees*.

Tries as a data structure have been discovered by Fredkin (see (2)) and they support *insertions, deletions,* and *queries*: to retrieve a key from a trie, for instance, follow a path from the root of the tree that is guided by the successive bits of the key to be found, branching left on 0's and right on 1's. By construction, if l is finite, the worst case cost of these operations is $O(l)$ which represents a logarithmic cost if $l \approx \log_2 n$. If $l = \infty$ (the results will basically apply for finite l as soon as $l \gg \log_2 n$) then, under the assumption that bits of keys are uniform and independent, the expected cost of any of the above operations is $\log_2 n + O(1)$ as we propose to show.

The probability that a trie formed with n random keys has a leftmost trie of size k and a rightmost trie of size $n - k$ as the *Bernoulli probability*:

$$p_{n,k} = \frac{1}{2^n}\binom{n}{k}. \tag{6.79}$$

Let $v[t]$, $w[t]$, $\cdots$ denote parameters of tries, like path length, number of nodes. $\ldots$ Let v_n, w_n, $\cdots$ be the expectations of $v[t]$, $w[t]$, $\cdots$ when the tries t are built from a set of n random keys, and let, finally, $v(z)$, $w(z)$, $\cdots$ denote the corresponding exponential generating functions. From the form (6.79) of splitting probabilities, we find the following relations between structural definitions of parameters and *exponential generating functions* of expected values:

$$v[t] = w[t] + x[t] \Rightarrow v(z) = w(z) + x(z) \tag{6.80}$$

$$v[t] = w[t_0] \times x[t_1] \Rightarrow v(z) = w\left(\frac{z}{2}\right) \times x\left(\frac{z}{2}\right) \tag{6.81}$$

where t_0 and t_1 denote the left and right subtrees of t. There (6.80) is nothing but the additive property of expectations and generating functions while (6.81) comes from the equalities

$$v_n = \sum_{k=0}^{n} p_{n,k} w_k \cdot x_{n-k} \tag{6.82}$$

or equivalently,

$$\frac{v_n}{n!} = \frac{1}{2^n} \sum_{k=0}^{n} \frac{w_k}{k!} \cdot \frac{x_{n-k}}{n-k'}.$$

Let us first analyze the storage occupation of tries. The number of internal nodes of a trie t, denoted by $s[t]$, satisfies the recursive definition:

$$s[t] = s[t_0], U[t_1] + U[t_0]s[t_1] + 1, \tag{6.83}$$

where U is the constant *unit valuation* $U[t] \equiv 1$, and (6.83) holds as soon as the number of keys in t exceeds 1. Thus using the general scheme (6.80)–(6.81) in (6.83), observing that $U(z) = e^z$ and taking care of initial conditions, we find for the corresponding e.g.f. $s(z)$ the equation:

$$s(z) = 2e^{z/2}s\left(\frac{z}{2}\right) + e^z - 1 - z \tag{6.84}$$

since the e.g.f. of $U[\cdot]$ is $U(z) = e^z$. Equation (6.84) can be solved by iteration, and we get the explicit form:

$$s(z) = \sum_{k \geq 0} 2^k \left[e^z - \left(1 + \frac{z}{2^k}\right) e^{\left(1 - \frac{1}{2^k}\right)z} \right] \tag{6.85}$$

so that taking coefficients in (6.84):

$$s_n = \sum_{k \geq 0} 2^k \left[1 - \left(1 - \frac{1}{2^k}\right)^n - \frac{n}{2^k}\left(1 - \frac{1}{2^k}\right)^{n-1} \right]. \tag{6.86}$$

The next step in the derivation is to use Mellin transforms. To that purpose, the simplest way consists of introducing the function:

$$S(x) = \sum_{k \geq 0} 2^k \left[1 - e^{-x/2^k}\left(1 + \frac{x}{2^k}\right) \right] \tag{6.87}$$

which derives from (6.86) when we use the exponential approximation:

$$(1 - a)^n \approx e^{-an}$$

and substitute x for n. One can justify that approximation here and show that s_n = $S(n) + O(n^{1/2})$ (see (2), p.131).

The interest of the form (6.87) is that it is a harmonic sum. Its Mellin transform is defined for $-2 < \mathrm{Re}(s) < -1$ and from the preceding chapter we find that it is

$$S^*(s) = -\frac{(s + 1)\Gamma(s)}{1 - 2^{s+1}}. \tag{6.88}$$

Poles to the right of the fundamental strip of S^* determine the asymptotic behavior of $S(x)$ as x gets large. There is a simple pole $s = 0$ that is due to $\Gamma(s)$ and poles at points $\chi_k = -1 + \dfrac{2ik\pi}{\log 2}$ for $k \in \mathbf{Z}$ due to the denominator of (6.88). Computing residues, we find the following theorem of Knuth (using suggestions by De Bruijn, see [(2), pp. 131ff]):

THEOREM 6.22   (2)   The expected storage occupation (measured by the number of internal nodes) of a trie built on n uniform and independent keys is:

$$s_n = \sum_{k \geq 0} 2^k \left[1 - \left(1 - \frac{1}{2^k} \right)^n - \frac{n}{2^k} \left(1 - \frac{1}{2^k} \right)^{n-1} \right],$$

a quantity that is asymptotic to:

$$\frac{n}{\log 2}(1 + Q(\log_2 n)) + O(\sqrt{n})$$

where $Q(u)$ is a periodic function with period 1, mean value 0 and Fourier expansion given by:

$$Q(u) = \sum_{k \in \mathbf{Z}/\{0\}} q_k e^{-2ik\pi u}; \quad q_k = \frac{1}{\log 2}(1 + \chi_k)\Gamma(\chi_k)$$

with $\chi_k = -1 + \dfrac{2ik\pi}{\log 2}$.

The expected cost of a positive search in a trie is p_n/n where p_n is the expected path length when n keys are present in the trie. Path length $p[t]$ is defined inductively by:

$$p[t] = p[t_0]U[t_1] + U[t_0]p[t_1] + |t| \tag{6.89}$$

which, as before leads to

$$p(z) = 2e^{z/2}p\left(\frac{z}{2}\right) + z(e^z - 1)$$

whence the exact expression:

$$p_n = n\sum_{k\geq 0}\left[1 - \left(1 - \frac{1}{2^k}\right)^{n-1}\right]$$

One has $p_n \sim nP(n)$ where:

$$P(x) = \sum_{k\geq 0}(1 - e^{-x/2^k})$$

whose Mellin transform is given by:

$$P(x) = -\frac{\Gamma(s)}{1 - 2^s}$$

Thus, a residue calculation shows that:

THEOREM 6.23 (2) Under the uniform model, the expected cost of a positive search in a trie of size n is:

$$\sum_{k\geq 0}\left[1 - \left(1 - \frac{1}{2^k}\right)^{n-1}\right]$$

a quantity that is asymptotic to:

$$\log_2 n + \frac{\gamma}{\log 2} + \frac{1}{2} + R(\log_2 n) + O\left(\frac{1}{\sqrt{n}}\right)$$

where $R(u)$ is a periodic function with period 1, mean value 0 and Fourier expansion given by:

$$R(u) = \sum_{k\in\mathbf{Z}/\{0\}} r_k e^{-2ik\pi u}; \quad r_k = \frac{1}{\log 2}\Gamma(\chi_k)$$

with $\chi_k = \dfrac{2ik\pi}{\log 2}$.

An important use of tries is as an access method for large files stored on disk. A *b-trie* with leaf capacity equal to b ($b \geq 1$) is obtained by modifying the initial definition of tries in such a way that the recursive splitting is stopped as soon as a subset of size b or less is encountered. Leaves can, thus, contain up to b elements and can be stored in pages on disk. *Dynamic Hashing* is obtained in that way when the trie is built on hashed values of records instead of records themselves (thus ensuring uniformity of pseudo-keys on which the trie is built). The previous methods easily generalize, and one finds (2, 39, 22) for Dynamic Hashing and the closely related *Extendible Hashing* scheme.

THEOREM 6.24   (2, 39, 20)   Under the uniform model, the number of pages necessary to store the file using a Dynamic or Extendible Hashing scheme with page capacity b is:

$$\frac{n}{b \log 2}(1 + Q_1(\log_2 n)) + O(\sqrt{n}),$$

where Q_1 is a periodic function with mean value 0.   ∎

Thus, under both schemes, pages tend to be about 70 percent full ($\log 2 = 0.69 \ldots$).

Extendible hashing relies on a further paging of the internal nodes of the trie. The corresponding analysis have been given by Flajolet (21) and Regnier (under a Poisson model) (43). The analysis is closely related to the analysis of height in tries. Letting $\pi_{n,h}$ denote the probability that a trie with n keys has height $\leq h$, one finds with $e_b(z)$ denoting the truncated exponential:

$$\pi_{n,h} = \left[\frac{z^n}{n!}\right] e_b\left(\frac{z}{2^h}\right)^{2^h}. \tag{6.90}$$

From there, limiting distributions can be determined using saddle point methods. In this way, one obtains:

THEOREM 6.25   (21, 43)   Under the uniform model, the expected size of the paged directory in the Extendible Hashing scheme is asymptotic to:

$$n^{1 + 1/b} Q_2(\log n)$$

where Q_2 is a periodic function with mean value close to $4/b$.

Many more results follow using these techniques. The underlying splitting process with the Bernoulli splitting probabilities of (6.79) appears as a model of some *polynomial factorization* algorithms, of *communication protocols* and more classically of *radix exchange sort*. We can cite here [(2), pp. 131ff]:

THEOREM 6.26   (2)   Radix-exchange sort of n keys when applied to infinitely long strings uses an average of $n \log_2 n + O(n)$ comparisons.

A systematic discussion of algebraic methods involved in all these analyses is given in (25). The corresponding asymptotic methods are discussed in (26). A detailed analysis of Dynamic and Extendible Hashing is given in Regnier's thesis (43).

6.4.3 Comparison-Based Searching and Sorting

Binary search trees are also amongst the oldest known data structures. Let S be a sequence of distinct real numbers (or of any totally ordered set): $S = (s_1, s_2, \cdots, s_n)$. The *binary search tree* built on S is denoted by $bst(S)$ and is defined recursively as follows:

1. Make the first element s_1 of S the root of the tree.
2. Separate the remaining elements $(s_2, s_3, \cdots, s_n)$ into two subsequences $S_<$ and $S_>$, where $S_<$ ($S_>$) is the subsequence consisting of elements smaller (larger) than s_1. Then:

$$bst(s) = \langle s_1, bst(S_<), bst(S_>) \rangle. \tag{6.91}$$

Observe that once a binary search tree has been built, the sequence is almost sorted since a preorder traversal, that takes only linear time, will list the elements in increasing sorted order.

Binary search trees support insertions, deletions, and queries (2) as we shall now see in expected $O(\log n)$ time under the uniform-independence model (or equivalently under the permutation model, where S is taken to be a random permutation of $[1 . . n]$).

The basic principle is that a tree of size n is formed of two similar subtrees of size K and $n - 1 - K$ where K is a random variable between 0 and $n - 1$ with probability distribution:

$$\Pr(K = k) = \frac{1}{n} \tag{6.92}$$

independently of n. Equation (6.92) reflects the fact that the first element of a random permutation can take any of the possible values with equal probability $(1/n)$. As in the preceding section, it is easy to set up schemes that associate to parameters of trees generating functions of expected values.

Let $v[t], w[t], \cdots$ be functions of trees; let $v_n, w_n, \cdots$ be their corresponding average values and let $v(z), w(z), \cdots$ be the corresponding *ordinary generating functions*. With t_0 and t_1 denoting the left and right subtrees of tree t, one has (compare with (6.80), (6.81)):

$$v[t] = w[t] + x[t] \Rightarrow v(z) = w(z) + x(z) \tag{6.93}$$

$$v[t] = w[t_0] \times x[t_1] \Rightarrow v(z) = \int_0^z w(t)x(t)\, dt. \tag{6.94}$$

Thus, again any additive-multiplicative valuation over binary search trees can be analyzed, and in general one will have a set of *integral equations* that reduce to a *differential system* for associated generating functions.

As a first example, consider the problem of determining the expected path length of binary search trees. Path length is here defined inductively by:

$$p[t] = p[t_0] + p[t_1] + |t| \tag{6.95}$$

From (6.93), (6.94), we find:

$$p(z) = 2\int_0^z p(t)\frac{dt}{1-t} + \frac{z}{(1-z)^2} \tag{6.96}$$

which differentiates into:

$$p'(z) - 2\frac{p(z)}{1-z} - \frac{1+z}{(1-z)^3} = 0. \tag{6.97}$$

Equation (6.97) can be solved by the *variation-of-constant* method, and we find:

$$p(z) = 2\frac{\log(1-z)^{-1} - z}{(1-z)^2}$$

$$= 2H'(z) - \frac{2+z}{(1-z)^2}$$

where $H(z) \equiv \sum_n H_n z^n$ is the generating function of the harmonic numbers. Hence, expanding and performing simple asymptotics:

THEOREM 6.27   The expected number of comparisons to sort a sequence of n elements building a binary search tree is under the uniform-independent permutation model

$$p_n = 2(n+1)H_{n+1} - 3n - 2$$

and asymptotically:

$$p_n = 2n \log n + (2\gamma - 3)n + O(\log n) \qquad \blacksquare$$

As an immediate corollary to Theorem 6.27, we derive that the expected cost of a positive search in a b.s.t. of size n is $2 \log_2 n + O(1)$.

Height of binary search trees leads to interesting equations over generating functions. Let h_n denote the expected height of a binary search tree with n nodes. Then, using (6.92), one finds:

$$h(z) = \sum_{h \geq 0} [y(z) - y_h(z)] \tag{6.98}$$

where $y_0(z) = 1$ and

$$y_{h+1}(z) = 1 + \int_0^z y_h^2(t)\, dt \tag{6.99}$$

and $y(z) \equiv y_\infty(z) = (1-z)^{-1}$.

Thus, the y_h form a sequence of *Picard approximants* to y_∞. Although it is natural to conjecture that:

$$h(z) \sim \frac{c}{1-z} \log \frac{1}{1-z} \tag{6.100}$$

for some constant c, the singular expansion (6.100) appears to be amazingly difficult to establish. Devroye (19), using the theory of certain types of branching processes, has determined directly the asymptotic form of h_n:

THEOREM 6.28 (19) The expected height of a binary search tree with n nodes satisfies:

$$h_n \sim c \log n$$

where $c = 4.311070\cdots$ is the root of $(2e/c)^c = e$ that is >2. ∎

Returning to the scheme (6.93), (6.94), we see that it will apply to any additive-multiplicative function of a splitting process whose probabilities satisfy (6.92). There are at least three instances where the splitting probabilities have this specific form:

1. *Quicksort.* A way of sorting that resembles closely the recursive definition (6.91) of binary search trees. Essentially quicksort is characterized by an *in place* partitioning of S into $S_<$ and $S_>$. (Also, these two sets are replaced by their mirror images.)
2. *Heap-ordered trees* or nonbalanced heaps. Trees canonically associated to sequences of distinct elements. Let S be such a sequence, then it can be decomposed into:

$$\langle S_{left}, \min(S), S_{right} \rangle \tag{6.101}$$

with S_{left} (S_{right}) being the factor of S formed with elements to the left (right) of $\min(S)$. Using decomposition (6.101) recursively, a tree is canonically related to a sequence; it is characterized by the fact that labels increase along any branch starting at the root, and so constitutes a heap-ordered tree. Since in a random permutation, the minimum value occurs at any place with equal probability, (6.92) is satisfied, so that again the scheme (6.93)–(6.94) can be used.
3. *Multidimensional search trees* or k–d-trees. They serve to represent sets of multidimensional records consisting of several fields: a search tree is formed by using successive fields cyclically as discriminators as one proceeds along a branch from the root.

We shall only cite here a few results along those lines:

THEOREM 6.29 The expected number of comparisons to sort n elements using Quicksort is:

$$\overline{C}_n = 2(n+1)\left(H_{n+1} - \frac{4}{3}\right) \sim 2n\log n + 2n\left(\gamma - \frac{4}{3}\right) + O(\log n).$$

The reader is referred to (2) and Sedgewick's papers (44), (45), (47), for a complete discussion of the complexity of Quicksort.

THEOREM 6.30 The expected number of comparisons required to perform extraction of the minimum in a heap-ordered tree of size n is:

$$\overline{C}_n = O(\log n).$$

Heap-ordered trees serve to implement mergeable priority queues. An efficient representation is in the form of *pagodas* (30).

THEOREM 6.31 (24) The expected number of elementary field comparisons required to perform a partial match query in a k–d-tree of size n when records have dimension k and s fields are specified in the query satisfies asymptotically:

$$\overline{C}_n^{[s/k]} \sim K n^{1 - s/k + \vartheta(s/k)}$$

where $\vartheta(u)$ is the root in $[0;1]$ of equation:

$$(\vartheta + 3 - u)^u(\vartheta + 2 - u)^{1-u} - 2 = 0.$$

Proof: The proof of Theorem 6.31 proceeds by first setting a system of integral equations for generating functions of costs using (6.93)–(6.94). That system reduces to a differential system of order $2k - s$. It cannot be solved explicitly in terms of standard transcendental functions. However, using the classical theory of regular singular points of differential systems, a singularity analysis can be performed and Theorem 6.31 follows. ∎

A result akin to Theorem 6.31 has recently been established for *quad-trees* (22). See also Puech's work (42) for related applications.

We should finally mention that decomposition (6.101) which corresponds to the symbolic equation:

$$\mathbf{P} \approx \varepsilon + \{\min\} \times (\mathbf{P} * \mathbf{P})$$

for the set $\mathbf{P}$ of all permutations is an important starting point for obtaining many statistics over permutations (runs, left-to-right minima . . .).

6.4.4 Conclusions

We have tried to demonstrate in a few cases, the role of generating functions as a crucial tool in the analysis of algorithms and data structures. The general pattern behind these analyses can be described as follows:

Each class of simple data structures carries with it a natural class of generating functions with a particular algebraic structure and a set of analytic properties that can be used both for exact and asymptotic analysis.

Table 6.6 illustrates the algebraic translation mechanisms for multiplicative valuations of trees in each of the three cases considered previously: planar binary trees with the uniform statistics, digital tries, and binary search trees.

The set of resolution techniques, as we have seen, are for each case:

1. Lagrange inversion and singularity analysis of functions with algebraic singularities.
2. Difference equations: iteration and Mellin transform techniques.
3. Differential equations: exact solution methods (operators, variation-of-constant) and the theory of regular singular points.

Amongst the many areas in the analysis of algorithms that are natural applications of these methods and that we have not had time to discuss, we would like to mention:

1. The cycle structure of permutations and the problem of *in situ* permutation (1, 3, 5).
2. Inversion tables for permutations and sorting algorithms: bubble sort, insertion sort (2), and shellsort (50).
3. 2-sorted permutations, lattice path, and merging algorithms (2), (46).
4. Distributions, occupancy statistics, and hashing algorighms (2), (31), (37), (32).
5. String statistics (32).
6. Random graphs and set-merging ("Union-Find") algorithms (38).

Table 6.6

For each class of trees, description of the splitting sizes and probabilities; translation over generating functions of a multiplicative valuation on subtrees: (1) for o.g.f. of cumulated values; (2) for e.g.f. of expected values; (3) for o.g.f. of expected values.

Trees	Splitting of n	Splitting Pb.	$v[t] = w[t_0], x[t_1]$
1. Planar Bin.	$\langle k, n-1-k \rangle$	$\dfrac{B_k B_{n-k-1}}{B_n}$	$v(z) = zw(z)x(z)$
2. Tries	$\langle k, n-k \rangle$	$\dfrac{1}{2^n}\binom{n}{k}$	$v(z) = w(z/2)x(z/2)$
3. Bin. Search	$\langle k, n-1-k \rangle$	$\dfrac{1}{n}$	$v(z) = \displaystyle\int_0^z w(t)x(t)\,dt$

Problems in the area of the exact analysis of algorithms may be of several types:

1. *Finding proper decompositions* of combinatorial problems in a way that lends itself to treatment by generating functions. If that approach succeeds, it usually has a high yield since, as we have tried to demonstrate, a large number of analyses will be amenable to a uniform treatment.
2. *Finding approximate models* that fall into category (1) if the combinatorial structure of the original problem is too intricate to lead to an exact analytic model.
3. *Finding exact or asymptotic solutions for functional equations* over generating functions, for models arising from (1) or (2).

To the category of (1), or most probably (2), there belongs the analysis of AVL trees, 2–3 trees and other *balanced structures* under the permutation model. See (34) for an analysis of a data structure that does not have a randomness preservation property and (48) for an analysis of heapsort.

A simple example of (3) is provided by the problem of the distribution of the number of comparisons in Quicksort. The bivariate generating function satisfies:

$$\frac{\partial}{\partial z} C(z, q) = qC(qz, q)^2$$

and the problem there is to determine the asymptotic behavior of the coefficients of polynomials $[z^n] C(z, q)$. Related limiting distribution results have been obtained by Louchard and Jacquet and Regnier (35). However, despite the practical importance of Quicksort (there are several hundred thousand implementations running since Quicksort is part of the standard sort available on the Unix system) the form of the limiting distribution is yet unknown.

6.5   REFERENCES

Instead of giving here a complete bibliography, we shall restrict ourselves to indicating general references for the subject covered in Sections 6.1–6.3 together with brief historical and bibliographical comments and citing the set of papers whose results are mentioned in Section 6.4.

6.5.1   General References

The subject of analyzing algorithms is as old as algorithms, and thus predates the advent of computers. For instance, in his discussion of the analytical engine, Babbage evaluates the complexity of his (mechanical) integer multiplication method in terms of the number of "turns of the handle" (a measure certainly very relevant to his application). After computers became used for nonnumerical data processing, it became obvious that some algorithms performed in a greatly varying manner depending on the specific configuration of the input data, a fact not so frequent with numerical algorithms. Average case analysis naturally emerged as a simple way of obtaining global information on the effectiveness of an algorithm, when it is used repeatedly. It is the merit of Knuth, in Volume 1 of *The Art of Computer Programming* (first published in 1968) to have shown that a large number of classical algorithms could be exactly analyzed, even at the very detailed level of assembly language programs. Knuth also demonstrated the importance of combinatorial enumeration techniques and asymptotic analysis in that context. For the subjects covered here, the basic references are thus:

1. D. E. Knuth. *The Art of Computer Programming, Volume 1: Fundamental Algorithms*, Addison-Wesley, Reading, Mass., (1968).
2. D. E. Knuth. *The Art of Computer Programming, Volume 3: Sorting and Searching*, Addison-Wesley, Reading, Mass., (1973).

For a presentation of many algorithms of interest in computer science, one may refer to:

3. R. Sedgewick. *Algorithms*, Addison-Wesley (1983).
4. G. Gonnet. *Handbook of Algorithms and Data Structures*, Addison-Wesley (1984).

The goals and methods of average case analysis of algorithms are discussed in Knuth's invited lecture at the 1971 IFIP Congress. An interesting recent survey is given by Sedgewick in:

5. R. Sedgewick. "Mathematical Analysis of Combinatorial Algorithms," in *Probability Theory and Computer Science*, Louchard and Latouche Editors, Academic Press (1983).

The following booklet, corresponding to lecture notes from the course on analysis of algorithms at Stanford University, discusses in greater detail some of the points studied here (most notably saddle point methods).

6. D. Greene and D. E. Knuth. *Mathematics for the Analysis of Algorithms*, Birkhaeuser Verlag (1981).

Two other books on that subject are:

R. Kemp. *Fundamentals of the Average-Case Analysis of Particular Algorithms*, Wiley-teubner Series in Computer Science, J. Wiley, New York (1984).

and for an elementary introduction:

P. Purdom, C. Brown. *The Analysis of Algorithms*, Holt, Rinehart and Winston (1985).

Concerning the combinatorial enumeration problems, the 19th century technique was almost invariably the set-up of recurrences. In a book (*Combinatory Analysis*) published in 1915, Major Percy MacMahon was the first one to systematically depart from the recurrence approach. MacMahon developed a very personal algebraic view of the field of combinatorial analysis. That approach was revived in the sixties through works by Rota, Foata, and Schutzenberger. The symbolic operator approach is exposed systematically in the reference book of Jackson and Goulden:

7. I. Goulden and D. Jackson. *Combinatorial Enumerations*, J. Wiley, New York (1983).

The reading of that book may be complemented by the encyclopedic (and generating function oriented) book of Comtet:

8. L. Comtet. *Advanced Combinatorics*, D. Reidel, Dordrecht (1974).

A short survey of the domain of combinatorial enumerations appears in:

9. R. Stanley. Generating Functions, in *Studies in Combinatorics*, M.A.A. Monographs, G-C. Rota Ed., pp. 100–141 (1978).

The field of asymptotic analysis is much closer to classical (pure and applied) mathematics, so that many standard references exist. We shall only mention two very useful problem solving oriented books:

10. N. G. De Bruijn. *Asymptotic Methods in Analysis*, reprinted by Dover (1984).
11. C. Bender and S. Orszag. *Advanced Mathematical Methods for Scientists and Engineers*, McGraw-Hill (1978).

and the necessary background from complex analysis can be found in:

12. P. Henrici. *Applied Computational and Complex Analysis*, J. Wiley, New York, 2 Vol. (1974, 1977).

A concise survey of asymptotic counting techniques is given by:

13. E. Bender. "Asymptotic Methods in Enumerations," *SIAM Review* **16**, pp. 485–515 (1974).

and the book of Sachkov provides a complete exposition of probabilistic and asymptotic methods in combinatorial analysis:

14. V. N. Sachkov. *Verojatnostnie Metody v Kombinatornom Analize*, Nauka, Moscow (1978).

Finally, for further applications of the symbolic operator method to the analysis of algorithms, one may refer to the following works:

15. P. Flajolet. *Analyse d'algorithmes de manipulation d'arbres et de fichiers*, Cahiers du B.U.R.O. **34–35**, Paris (1981), 209p.
16. D. Greene. "Labelled Formal Languages and Their Uses" (Thesis), Stanford University Rep. STAN-CS-83-982 (1983), 148p.
17. J-M. Steyaert. *Complexité et Structure des Algorithmes*, Thesis, University of Paris VII (1984), 215p.

Additional references are to be found in the list that follows.

6.5.2 Specialized References

18. N. G. De Bruijn, D. E. Knuth and S. O. Rice: The Average Height of Planted Plane Trees, in *Graph Theory and Computing*, R. C. Read Ed. (1972), pp. 15–22.

19. L. Devroye: "The Average Height of Binary Search-Trees, *manuscript* (1985).

20. R. Fagin, J. Nievergelt, N. Pippenger, R. Strong: Extendible Hashing—A Fast Access Method for Dynamic Files, *ACM Trans. on Database Systems* **4**(1979), pp. 315–344.

21. P. Flajolet: On the Performance Evaluation of Extendible Hashing and Trie Searching, *Acta Informatica* **20** (1983), pp. 345–369.

22. P. Flajolet, G. Gonnet, C. Puech, M. Robson: Variations on Quad-trees, *in prep.* (1985).

23. P. Flajolet, A. Odlyzko: The Average Height of Binary Trees and Other Simple Trees, *J. of Comp. and System Sc.* **25** (1982), pp. 171–213.

24. P. Flajolet, C. Puech: Partial Match Retrieval of Multidimensional Data, *J.A.C.M.* **33** (1986), pp. 371–407.

25. P. Flajolet, M. Regnier, D. Sotteau: Algebraic Methods for Trie Statistics, *Annals of Discr. Math.* **25**, pp. 145–188 (1985).

26. P. Flajolet, M. Regnier, R. Sedgewick: Some Uses of the Mellin Integral Transform in the Analysis of Algorithms, in *Combinatorial Algorithms on Words*, A. Apostolico and Z. Galil Eds., Springer NATO ASI Series F, **18**, pp. 241–254 (1985).

27. P. Flajolet, J-C. Raoult, J. Vuillemin: The Number of Registers Required to Evaluate Arithmetic Expressions, *Theoret. Comp. Sc.* **9**, (1979), pp. 99–125.

28. P. Flajolet, J-M. Steyaert: A Complexity Calculus for Classes of Recursive Search Programs over Tree Structures, in *Proc. 22nd IEE Symp. on Found. of Comp. Sci. (F.O.C.S.)*, Nashville (1982), pp. 386–393.

29. P. Flajolet, P. Sipala, J-M. Steyaert: Compacted Representations of Trees, *in prep.* (1985).

30. J. Francon, G. Viennot, J. Vuillemin: Pagodas (1978).

31. G. Gonnet, I. Munro: The Analysis of Linear Probing Sort by the Use of a New Mathematical Transform, *J. of Alg.* (1985).

32. G. Gonnet: Expected Length of the Longest Probe Sequence in Hashing, *J.A.C.M.* **28**(1981), pp. 289–304.

33. L. Guibas, A. Odlyzko: Strings Overlaps, Pattern Matching and Non-transitive Games, *J. Comb. Theory (A)* **30** (1981), pp. 183–208.

34. A. Jonassen, D. E. Knuth: "A Trivial Algorithm Whose Analysis Isn't," *Journal of Computer and System Sciences* **16**, pp. 301–322 (1978).

35. P. Jacquet, M. Regnier: Limiting Distributions for Trie Parameters, *in prep.* (1985).

36. R. Kemp: The Average Number of Registers Needed to Evaluate a Binary Tree Optimally, *Acta Informatica* **11** (1979), pp. 363–372.

37. A. G. Konheim, B. Weiss: An Occupancy Discipline and Applications, *S.I.A.M. J. Applied Math.* **14** (1966), pp. 1266–1274.

38. D. E. Knuth, A. Schonage: The Expected Linearity of a Simple Equivalence Algorithm, *Theoretical Comp. Sc.* **6** (1978).

39. P. A. Larson: Dynamic Hashing, *BIT* **18** (1978), pp. 184–201.

40. A. Meir, J. W. Moon: On the Altitude of Nodes in Random Trees, *Canad. J. Math* **30** (1978), pp. 997–1015.

41. A. Odlyzko: Periodic Oscillations of Coefficients of Power Series that Satisfy Functional Equations, *Adv. in Math.* **44** (1982), pp. 180–205.

42. C. Puech: *Methodes d'Analyse de Structures de Donnees Dynamiques*, Thesis, Univ. of Orsay (1984).

43. M. Regnier: *Evaluation des Performances du Hachage Dynamique*, Thesis, Univ. of Orsay (1983).

44. R. Sedgewick: The Analysis of Quicksort Programs, *Acta Informatica* **7** (1977), pp. 327–355.

45. R. Sedgewick: Quicksort with Equal Keys, *S.I.A.M. J. Computing* **6** (1977).

46. R. Sedgewick: Data Movement in Odd-Even Merging, *S.I.A.M. J. on Computing* **7** (1978).

47. R. Sedgewick: *Quicksort*, Garland Pub. Co., New York (1980).

48. R. Sedgewick: "The Asymptotic Behaviour of Heapsort," *in prep*.

49. J-M. Steyaert, P. Flajolet: Patterns and Pattern-Matching in Trees: An Analysis, *Inf. and Control* **58** (1983), pp. 19–58.

50. A. C. Yao: Analysis of (h,k,l)-Shellsort, *J. of Alg.* **1** (1980).

Acknowledgments

This work has benefited from numerous discussions with participants of the Algorithms Seminar at INRIA especially C. Puech, J-M. Steyaert and M. Regnier, as well as notable influences from A. Odlyzko, R. Sedgewick, H. Prodinger, G. Gonnet and from the lecture notes of the Course of Analysis of Algorithms taught at Stanford University by D. E. Knuth and A. C. Yao.

Part IV
Concurrency and Distributed Algorithms

Chapter 7

Proving Correctness of Concurrent Programs: A Quick Introduction

KRZYSZTOF R. APT*

Abstract—A systematic presentation of the assertional method of proving correctness of concurrent programs is provided. Various proof systems for nondeterministic programs, disjoint parallel programs, parallel programs with shared variables and synchronization constructs are studied. Special emphasis is put on the issue of fairness.

7.1 INTRODUCTION

The aim of this paper is to explain a particular approach to correctness of concurrent programs. Design of concurrent programs is a difficult art and construction of correctness proofs of concurrent programs is an equally nontrivial task. To better understand the issues at stake, let us study a very simple example program.

7.1.1 An Example of a Concurrent Program

Consider the following simple problem:

Problem.   Write a program that finds a zero of a function f from integers into integers.

---

*Current address: C.W.I., Kruislaan 413 1098 SJ Amsterdam, The Netherlands. This paper was written during author's stay at IBM Thomas J. Watson Research Center, P.O. Box 218, Yorktown Heights, NY 10598.

We wish to explore the fact that a search for positive and nonpositive zeroes can be done in parallel.

Solution 1

Consider the following program S_1:

$$S_1 \equiv \text{found:} = \textbf{false}; \ x: = 0;$$
$$\quad \textbf{while} \ \neg \ \text{found} \ \textbf{do} \ x: = x + 1;$$
$$\qquad \text{found:} = f(x) = 0$$
$$\textbf{od}.$$

Then S_1 stops when a positive zero of f is found. Similarly, the following program S_2 stops when a nonpositive zero of f is found:

$$S_2 \equiv \text{found:} = \textbf{false}; \ y: = 1;$$
$$\quad \textbf{while} \ \neg \ \text{found} \ \textbf{do} \ y: = y - 1;$$
$$\qquad \text{found:} = f(y) = 0$$
$$\textbf{od}.$$

Thus, the program $[S_1 \| S_2]$, the parallel composition of S_1 and S_2, stops when a zero of f is found and is a solution to the problem.

Unfortunately, this is not always the case. Imagine the following scenario. Let f have only one zero, a positive one. Consider now an execution of $[S_1 \| S_2]$ in which initially only its first component is activated until it terminates once the zero of f is found. At this moment the second component is activated, *found* is reset to **false** and since no other zeroes of f exist, *found* will never be reset to true. In other words, the execution of $[S_1 \| S_2]$ will never terminate.

Obviously, our mistake consisted of initializing found to **false** twice—once in each component. A straightforward fix-up consists of initializing *found* only once, outside the parallel composition. This brings us to the following solution.

Solution 2

Let

$$S_1 \equiv x: = 0;$$
$$\quad \textbf{while} \ \neg \ \text{found} \ \textbf{do} \ x: = x + 1;$$
$$\qquad \text{found:} = f(x) = 0$$
$$\textbf{od}$$

and

$$S_2 \equiv y: = 1;$$
$$\quad \textbf{while} \ \neg \ \text{found} \ \textbf{do} \ y: = y - 1;$$
$$\qquad \text{found:} = f(y) = 0$$
$$\textbf{od}.$$

Then

$$S \equiv \textbf{found: } = \textbf{false}; [S_1 \| S_2]$$

is a solution to the problem.

But is it actually? Suppose once again that f has exactly one zero, a positive one, and consider an execution of S in which initially the second component is activated until the control reaches the assignment $found := f(y) = 0$. Then only its first component is activated until $found$ is set to **true** upon finding the zero of f. Suppose that at this moment the second component is activated again and so $found$ is reset to false. Now, since no other zeroes of f exist, $found$ will never be reset to **true** and this execution of S will never terminate. Thus, the above solution is incorrect.

What went wrong here? A close inspection of the scenario just presented reveals that the problem arose because of the fact that $found$ could be reset to **false** once it was already **true**. In this way the information that a zero of f was found got lost.

One way of correcting this mistake is by ensuring that found is never reset to **false** inside of the parallel composition. To this purpose it is sufficient to replace the unconditional assignment

$$\text{found: } = f(x) = 0$$

by the conditional one:

$$\text{if } f(x) = 0 \textbf{ then } \text{ found: } = \textbf{true fi}$$

and similarly with the other assignment to *found*.

In such a way we obtain the following solution.

Solution 3

Let

$$\begin{aligned}
S_1 \equiv\ & x: = 0; \\
& \textbf{while } \neg \text{ found do } x: = x + 1; \\
& \quad \text{if } f(x) = 0 \textbf{ then } \text{ found: } = \textbf{true fi} \\
& \textbf{od}
\end{aligned}$$

and

$$\begin{aligned}
S_2 \equiv\ & y: = 1; \\
& \textbf{while } \neg \text{ found do } y: = y - 1; \\
& \quad \textbf{if } f(y) = 0 \textbf{ then } \text{ found: } = \textbf{true fi} \\
& \textbf{od}.
\end{aligned}$$

Then

$$S \equiv \textbf{found: } = \textbf{false}; [S_1 \| S_2]$$

is a solution to the problem.

But is it really? Suppose that f has only positive zeroes and consider an execution of S in which the first component S_1 of the parallel program $[S_1 \| S_2]$ is never activated. Then this execution will never terminate even though f has a zero.

The above scenario is a debatable one. One might object that an execution sequence in which one component of a parallel program is never activated is not a legal one. After all, the main reason for writing parallel programs is that the components can and will be executed in parallel. In more technical terms, we should decide whether we adopt the hypothesis of *fairness* which here means that every component of a parallel program is eventually activated. If we adopt it, then the last solution is a correct one and the just exhibited execution sequence of S is illegal. If we reject it then the last solution is incorrect as the exhibited execution sequence of S is legal.

We shall now present a solution which is appropriate when the fairness hypothesis is not adopted. Surprisingly, as it will turn out in Section 7.3.5, the proof of correctness of the above solution under the assumption of fairness will amount to the proof of correctness of Solution 5 under no assumption of fairness.

The solution consists of building into the above program S an abstract *scheduler* which will ensure that each component of the parallel program is eventually executed. To this purpose we need a new programming construct—**await B then R end** allowing to temporarily suspend an execution of a component. Informally, a component of a parallel program executes an **await**-statement if the Boolean expression B evaluates to **true**. The statement R is then executed as an indivisible action, i.e. an action which cannot be interrupted by an activation of another component.

With each parallel component we associate a *priority* variable which is used by the scheduler. The scheduler activates the component with the lowest priority and updates the priorities of all the components. A component with the higher priority is suspended until its priority becomes the lowest.

Summarizing, this solution has the following form:

Solution 4

Let

$$S_1 \equiv x: = 0;$$
$$\textbf{while} \ \neg \ \text{found} \ \textbf{do}$$

> **await** $z_1 \leq z_2$ **then**
> $z_1: = \ ?; \ z_2: = z_2 - 1$
> **end**;

$$x: = x + 1;$$
$$\textbf{if} \ f(x) = 0 \ \textbf{then} \ \text{found} : = \textbf{true fi}$$
$$\textbf{od}$$

and

$$S_2 \equiv y: = 1;$$

while $\neg$ found **do**

> **await** $z_2 \leq z_1$ **then**
> $z_2: = ?;\ z_1: = z_1 - 1$
> **end**;

$y: = y - 1;$
if $f(y) = 0$ **then** found $: =$ **true fi**
od.

Then

$$S \equiv z_1: = ?;\ z_2: = ?;\ \text{found}: = \textbf{false}; [S_1 \| S_2]$$

is a solution to the problem when the fairness hypothesis is not adopted.

$z: = ?$ stands here for a *random assignment* which denotes an assignment of an arbitrary nonnegative integer to the variable z. (If you feel uncomfortable about this instruction, you can replace it in the above program by an assignment to a fixed nonnegative integer, say 0.) The scheduling parts are framed. Note that they are activated only once per a loop round. An infinite execution sequence in which only one parallel component is activated is now impossible because of the continuous decrease of the priority variable of the other component and the continuous resetting of the component priority variable to a nonnegative value.

But is S really a solution to the problem? Consider an execution sequence of S in which a zero is found by the first component at the moment when $z_1 \leq z_2$ holds and the second component is suspended in front of the **await**-statement. Then the first component will terminate and the second component will remain suspended forever. Thus, this execution sequence will terminate but in an improper way. This might be still considered as unharmful because, after all, the program eventually stops as desired when a zero is found. However, such a solution is unacceptable in the context in which the above program is to be followed by another one and thus activated upon *proper* termination of the first one.

In other words, we are interested here in solutions free from *deadlock*—a situation in which no progress is possible even though not all parallel components have properly terminated.

A deadlock free solution in our problem can be obtained by an appropriate modification of the last solution. To this purpose it is enough to build into the program a *signaling scheme* that will release one component in case of the (proper) termination of the other one. We, thus, introduce two new variables, called end_1 and end_2, which will indicate whether the first, respectively, the second component, has terminated. A suspended component will always be released when the other component has terminated because of an additional disjunct in the **await**-condition.

Summarizing, this solution has the following form:

Solution 5

Let

$$S_1 \equiv x: = 0;$$
    while $\neg$ found do
    await $z_1 \leq z_2$ $\boxed{\vee \text{ end}_2}$ **then**
    $z_1: = ?; \quad z_2: = z_2 - 1$
    end;
    $x: = x + 1;$
    if $f(x) = 0$ **then** found $: =$ **true fi**
    od;
    $\boxed{\text{end}_1: = \textbf{true}}$

and

$$S_2 \equiv y: = 1;$$
    while $\neg$ found **do**
    await $z_2 \leq z_1$ $\boxed{\vee \text{ end}_1}$ **then**
    $z_2: = ?; \quad z_1: = z_1 - 1$
    end;
    $y: = y - 1;$
    if $f(y) = 0$ **then** found $: =$ **true fi**
    od;
    $\boxed{\text{end}_2: = \textbf{true}.}$

Then

$$S \equiv z_1: = ?; \quad z_2: = ?; \quad \text{end}_1: = \textbf{false}; \quad \text{end}_2: = \textbf{false}; \quad \text{found}: = \textbf{false}; \quad [S_1 \| S_2]$$

is a deadlock-free solution to the problem when the fairness hypothesis is not adopted.

The signaling scheme built into the previous solution is framed.

We assure the reader that the above solution is correct. It is by no means an efficient solution—for example, the assignments to the priority variables can be performed outside the **await**-statements. On the other hand, the last two transformations are special cases of the transformations we study in this paper and the above discussion should facilitate their understanding.

7.1.2 The Correctness Problem

We hope to have convinced the reader that the design and correctness of concurrent programs is not a simple issue. The problem we discussed in the previous subsection seemed to be completely trivial and yet several, sometimes subtle errors crept in. It should be clear that an informal justification of the correctness of concurrent programs is not sufficient. After all, we produced in the previous subsection at least two incorrect correctness proofs.

There have been a number of formal approaches to correctness of concurrent programs. Before we briefly discuss them, we should perhaps first agree what program properties we actually wish to prove.

In the case of sequential programs, i.e. those in which a control resides at each moment in only one control point, these usually are:

(1) Delivering correct results.
    For example a sorting program should indeed sort the input.
(2) Termination.
    For example a sorting program should always terminate.
(3) Lack of failures.
    For example there should be no division by zero, no overflow, etc.

In the case of concurrent programs, i.e. those in which a control can reside at the same time in several control points, as observed before we are additionally interested in establishing:

(4) Deadlock freedom.
(5) Correctness under the fairness assumption.

It should be stressed that this list is by no means exhaustive. In fact, there is an important class of *continuously operating* concurrent programs (i.e. those which never terminate), that is not taken into consideration in this paper. Mutual exclusion algorithms belong to this class of programs. For this type of program, properties other than termination are relevant.

There have been a number of formal approaches to program correctness which were proposed and used in the literature. The most common of them is that based on an *operational reasoning*. It consists of an analysis in terms of the execution sequences of the given program. To this purpose an informal understanding of the program semantics is used. While this analysis is usually successful in the case of sequential programs, it is much less so in the case of concurrent programs. The number of possible execution sequences is then most often forbiddingly large and it is very easy to overlook a possible execution sequence.

A different approach is that based on an *axiomatic reasoning*. According to this approach, in order to prove that a program S satisfies a property P we should find a proof system T with a language $L(T)$ such that

(1) T is sound for the program S, i.e. any theorem of T is true for S,
(2) the property of P can be expressed in $L(T)$ by a formula φ,
(3) φ can be proved in T.

(Strictly speaking, the operational reasoning is a special, degenerate case of the axiomatic reasoning in which the property P constitutes the only axiom of the proof system. Then properties (2) and (3) are trivial and the whole burden of the proof lies on property (1).)

This approach started with the seminal paper of Hoare (24), where an axiomatic proof method based on the use of assertions was proposed to prove correctness of simple **while**-programs. His approach, often called Hoare's logic, has received a great deal of attention since then. An interested reader may wish to consult Apt (11) for a survey of various Hoare-style proof systems proposed for several programming constructs used in the imperative programming languages. In 1976 this approach was extended to the case of concurrent programs by Owicki and Gries (36, 37) and Lamport (27). The aim of this paper is to provide a systematic exposition of this method applied to various types of concurrent programs.

It should be stressed here that there are other approaches to the correctness of concurrent programs. They are not discussed in this paper. Perhaps the most important among them is the one started by Pnueli (38) and further developed by Manna and Pnueli (30, 31, 32), which is based on *temporal logic*. This approach allows one to study more complicated properties than those listed above and is particularly useful when dealing with continuously operating concurrent programs.

7.1.3 Preliminaries

Throughout the paper we fix an arbitrary assertion language containing two Boolean constants **true** and **false**. Its formulas are called *assertions* and denoted by the letters p, q, r. Quantifier free formulas are called *Boolean expressions* and are denoted by the letter B.

We assume that the variables are of the type **integer** or **Boolean**. Variables are denoted by the letters x, y, z, u, a, b. Their type is fixed by the context in which they are used. Expressions are denoted by the letters s, t. $p[t/u]$ stands for a *substitution* of t for all free occurrences of u in p. By a *correctness formula* we mean a construct of the form $\{p\}S\{q\}$ where p, q are assertions and S is a program. The classes of programs considered will be defined in the subsequent sections.

The programs are executed over a domain consisting of all integers and $\{\textbf{true},\ \textbf{false}\}$ with the usual operations available. By a (proper) *state* we mean a function assigning to all variables a value from the domain. States are denoted by the letters σ, τ. The notions of a value of an expression t in a state σ (written as $\sigma(t)$), truth of an assertion p in a state σ (written as $\models p(\sigma)$) and truth of an assertion are defined as usual. By $\sigma[d/x]$, where d is a value from the domain, we mean the state obtained from σ by assigning to x the value d and retaining the values of other variables.

We allow three special states: $\perp$ reporting divergence of a program, **fail** reporting a failure in an execution of a program, and $\triangle$ reporting deadlock in an execution of a program. We have by definition $\not\models p(\perp)$, $\not\models p(\textbf{fail})$ and $\not\models p(\triangle)$ for all formulas p. We define $[p]$ to be the set of all states σ which satisfy p, i.e., such that $\models p(\sigma)$ holds.

We say that $\{p\}S\{q\}$ is true in the sense of *partial correctness* (and write $\models \{p\}S\{q\}$) if all properly terminating computations of S starting in a state satisfying p terminate in a state satisfying q. We say that $\{p\}S\{q\}$ is true in the sense of *total correctness* (and write $\models_{\text{tot}}\{p\}S\{q\}$) if it is true in the sense of partial correctness and moreover, all computations of S starting in a state satisfying p properly terminate. We shall consider in this paper various other notions of program correctness.

A program semantics $\mathcal{M}_n[[S]]$ of a program S is a mapping from the set Σ of proper states into the subsets of $\Sigma \cup \{\perp, \textbf{fail}, \triangle\}$. Each program semantics $\mathcal{M}_n[[\cdot]]$ fixes a notion of program correctness defined by

$$\models_n\{p\}S\{q\} \quad \textit{iff} \quad \mathcal{M}_n[[S]]([p]) \subseteq [q]$$

where

$$\mathcal{M}_n[[S]]([p]) = \bigcup_{\sigma \in [p]} \mathcal{M}_n[[S]](\sigma).$$

We shall consider here various semantics, among others partial correctness semantics $\mathcal{M}[[\cdot]]$ and total correctness semantics $\mathcal{M}_{\text{tot}}[[\cdot]]$ related to the notions of partial and total correctness, respectively.

All proof systems discussed in this paper are geared towards proving correctness formulas in various senses. All considered proof systems are *sound* in the sense that every provable correctness formula is true in an appropriate sense. Soundness proofs of the discussed proof systems are omitted but relevant lemmas are often exhibited.

7.2 NONDETERMINISTIC PROGRAMS

To make this paper self-contained, we review, in this section, the correctness of nondeterministic programs in the style of Dijkstra (13, 14). We concentrate here on the issue of fairness as the results concerning it will be of relevance in the following section. More extensive treatment of the subject can be found in (4).

We allow as atomic actions the skip statement and assignment statement. Programs are built using the composition operator ``;'' and allowing

—the *alternative command*

$$[\,\square_{i=1}^{m} B_i \rightarrow S_i\,]$$

and

—the *repetitive command*

$$*[\underset{i=1}{\overset{m}{\square}} \, B_i \rightarrow S_i]$$

where B_i are Boolean expressions (called *guards*) and S_i are programs.

Nondeterministic programs form a good starting point to study parallel programs. This is due to the fact that every parallel program $[S_1 \| \ldots \| S_n]$ is equivalent in an appropriate sense to the nondeterministic program

$$*[\underset{i=1}{\overset{n}{\square}} \, \text{enabled } (S_i) \rightarrow \text{execute } S_i \text{ one step}]$$

where the definition of executing S_i one step depends on the way the atomic actions are defined in the context of parallel composition.

The nondeterministic programs in which only the alternative commands of the form $[B \rightarrow S_1 \, \square \, \neg B \rightarrow S_2]$ and repetitive commands of the form $*[B \rightarrow S]$ are used, are called *deterministic* programs or **while**-programs. Note that the above commands correspond to the customary commands **if** B **then** S_1 **else** S_2 **fi** and **while** B **do** S **od**, respectively. **while**-programs are deterministic in the sense that they produce at most one final state.

We shall also use other constructs which can be straightforwardly defined in terms of the alternative and repetitive commands.

7.2.1 Semantics

We recall here simple semantics of nondeterministic programs due to Hennessy and Plotkin (23). The semantics is based on the consideration of a transition relation '$\rightarrow$' between pairs $\langle S, \sigma \rangle$ consisting of a program S and a state σ. The intuitive meaning of the relation

$$\langle S_1, \sigma \rangle \rightarrow \langle S_2, \tau \rangle$$

is the following: executing S_1 one step in a state σ can lead (nondeterministically) to a state τ with S_2 being remainder of S_1 still to be executed. It is convenient to assume the empty program E. Then S_2 is E if the considered step of S_1 leads to state τ with S_1 properly or improperly terminated. We assume that, for any S, we have $E; S = S; E = S$.

We define the above relation by the following clauses where $\sigma \neq \perp$, fail, $\triangle$:

(1) $\langle \text{skip}, \sigma \rangle \rightarrow \langle E, \sigma \rangle$,

(2) $\langle x := t, \sigma \rangle \rightarrow \langle E, \sigma[\sigma(t)/x] \rangle$,

(3) $\langle [\underset{i=1}{\overset{m}{\square}} \, B_i \rightarrow S_i], \sigma \rangle \rightarrow \langle S_i, \sigma \rangle$ if $\models B_i(\sigma)$,

(4) $\langle [\overset{m}{\underset{i=1}{\square}} B_i \to S_i], \sigma \rangle \to \langle E, \textbf{fail} \rangle$ if $\models \overset{m}{\underset{i=1}{\bigwedge}} \neg B_i(\sigma)$,

(5) $\langle *[\overset{m}{\underset{i=1}{\square}} B_i \to S_i], \sigma \rangle \to \langle S_i; *[\overset{m}{\underset{i=1}{\square}} B_i \to S_i], \sigma \rangle$ if $\models B_i(\sigma)$,

(6) $\langle *[\overset{m}{\underset{i=1}{\square}} B_i \to S_i], \sigma \rangle \to \langle E, \sigma \rangle$ if $\models \overset{m}{\underset{i=1}{\bigwedge}} \neg B_i(\sigma)$,

(7) if $\langle S_1, \sigma \rangle \to \langle S_2, \tau \rangle$ then $\langle S_1; S, \sigma \rangle \to \langle S_2; S, \tau \rangle$.

Let $\to^*$ stand for the transitive, reflexive closure of $\to$.

We now introduce the following definitions.

DEFINITION 7.1

(1) We say that S can *diverge from* σ if there exists an infinite sequence $\langle S_i, \sigma_i \rangle$ $(i = 0, 1, \ldots)$ such that

$$\langle S, \sigma \rangle = \langle S_0, \sigma_0 \rangle \to \langle S_1, \sigma_1 \rangle \to \ldots .$$

(2) We say that S can *fail from* σ if for some S_1

$$\langle S, \sigma \rangle \to^* \langle S_1, \textbf{fail} \rangle.$$

(3) A finite or infinite sequence $\langle S_i, \sigma_i \rangle$ $(i = 0, 1, \ldots)$ such that

$$\langle S, \sigma \rangle = \langle S_0, \sigma_0 \rangle \to \langle S_1, \sigma_1 \rangle \to \ldots$$

which cannot be extended is called a *computation of S starting in* σ.

We now define two types of semantics for the nondeterministic programs by putting

$$\mathcal{M}[[S]](\sigma) = \{\tau : \langle S, \sigma \rangle \to^* \langle E, \tau \rangle\}$$

and

$$\mathcal{M}_{\text{tot}}[[S]](\sigma) = \mathcal{M}[[S]](\sigma) \cup \{\bot : S \text{ can diverge from } \sigma\}$$
$$\cup \{\textbf{fail} : S \text{ can fail from } \sigma\}.$$

Next, we provide four different proof systems to prove different types of correctness of nondeterministic programs.

7.2.2 Partial Correctness

The following proof system allows us to prove partial correctness of the nondeterministic programs:

AXIOM 1:   SKIP AXIOM

$\{p\}$ skip $\{p\}$

AXIOM 2:   ASSIGNMENT AXIOM

$$\{p[t/x]\}\ x := t\{p\}$$

RULE 3:   COMPOSITION RULE

$$\frac{\{p\}\ S_1\ \{r\},\ \{r\}\ S_2\ \{q\}}{\{p\}\ S_1\ ;\ S_2\ \{q\}}$$

RULE 4:   ALTERNATIVE COMMAND RULE

$$\frac{\{p \wedge B_i\}\ S_i\ \{q\},\ i = 1, \ldots, m}{\{p\}\ [\ \underset{i=1}{\overset{m}{\square}}\ B_i \to S_i]\ \{q\}}$$

RULE 5:   REPETITIVE COMMAND RULE

$$\frac{\{p \wedge B_i\}\ S_i\ \{q\},\ i = 1, \ldots, m}{\{p\}\ *[\ \underset{i=1}{\overset{m}{\square}}\ B_i \to S_i]\ \{p \wedge \underset{i=1}{\overset{m}{\bigwedge}}\ \neg B_i\}}$$

RULE 6:   CONSEQUENCE RULE

$$\frac{p \to p_1,\ \{p_1\}\ S\ \{q_1\},\ q_1 \to q}{\{p\}\ S\ \{q\}}$$

We call this proof system PC and write $\vdash_{PC} \varphi$ to denote the fact that the correctness formula φ can be proved in PC using for the consequence rule all true assertions as axioms. We use an analogous notation for the other proof systems.

7.2.3   Total Correctness

Nondeterministic programs can fail to terminate properly because of *failures*. According to (14) a failure arises if at the moment of starting an execution of an alternative command all its guards evaluate to false. Obviously the rule of alternative command does not exclude such a possibility. The following modification of this rule ensures the desired property.

RULE 7:   ALTERNATIVE COMMAND RULE II

$$\frac{p \to \underset{i=1}{\overset{m}{\vee}}\ B_i,\ \{p \wedge B_i\}\ S_i\ \{q\},\ i = 1, \ldots, m}{\{p\}\ [\ \underset{i=1}{\overset{m}{\square}}\ B_i \to S_i]\ \{q\}}$$

The first premise guarantees that at the moment an alternative command is to be executed at least one of its guards evaluates to true.

Next, we have to take care of termination of repetitive commands. The current version of the rule of repetitive commands is clearly insufficient for this purpose. We follow here the approach of (9) and modify rule 5 as follows.

RULE 8:   REPETITIVE COMMAND RULE II

$$\frac{\{p(n) \wedge B_i\}\, S_i\, \{\exists\, l < n\; p(l)\},\ i = 1, \ldots, m}{\{\exists\, n\; p(n)\}\, *[\,\overset{m}{\underset{i=1}{\Box}}\, B_i \to S_i]\, \{\exists\, n\; p(n) \wedge \overset{m}{\underset{i=1}{\bigwedge}} \neg B_i\}}$$

Here $p(n)$ is an assertion with a free variable n which does not appear in $*[\,\overset{m}{\underset{i=1}{\Box}}\, B_i \to S_i]$ and ranges over natural numbers. We call n a *parameter variable*.

We call the resulting proof system TC.

7.2.4   Weak Fairness

We observed in the introduction that fairness is a natural assumption concerning parallel programs. The modeling of parallel programs by the nondeterministic ones given at the beginning of this section is appropriate only if the assumption of fairness is adopted for nondeterministic programs, as well. The exact form of this assumption depends on the type of parallel programs we wish to simulate.

There are at least two natural fairness assumptions which can be adopted in the case of nondeterministic programs. The first of them is *weak fairness*.

DEFINITION 7.2   Let a computation ξ of a nondeterministic program S be given.

(1) We say that a guard B of S is *enabled* if it evaluates to true at the moment the control in the program is just before it.

(2) We say that ξ is *weakly unfair* if it is infinite and there exists a guard B of S which from a certain moment on is continuously enabled and never selected for execution.

(3) We say that ξ is *weakly fair* if it is not weakly unfair.

For example, the only infinite computation of the program

$b := $ **true**;
$*[b \to $ skip $\Box\; \neg b \to b := $ **false**$]$

is weakly unfair, i.e., it is not weakly fair. On the other hand the infinite computation of the program

$$a:= \textbf{true};$$
$$*[a \rightarrow b:= \neg b \ \square \ b \rightarrow a:= \textbf{false}]$$

in which only the first guard is selected is weakly fair since the second guard is not continuously enabled in it.

We now define the weakly fair semantics of nondeterministic programs by putting

$$\mathcal{M}_{\text{wfair}}[[S](\sigma) =$$
$$\mathcal{M}[[S]](\sigma) \cup \{\bot : S \text{ can diverge from } \sigma \text{ by a weakly fair computation}\}$$
$$\cup \{\textbf{fail} : S \text{ can fail from } \sigma\}.$$

We say that $\{p\}\ S\ \{q\}$ *holds under the assumption of weak fairness* ($\models_{\text{wfair}} \{p\}\ S\ \{q\}$ in short) if every weakly fair computation of S starting in a state satisfying p properly terminates in a state satisfying q.

We now present a proof system appropriate for proving correctness of non-deterministic programs under the assumption of weak fairness. We follow here the approach of Apt and Olderog (8) and of Apt, Pnueli and Stavi (9).

Let S be a given nondeterministic program. We proceed by the following steps:

Step 1.   Transform S into a program $T_{\text{wfair}}(S)$ that generates exactly all weakly fair computations of S.

By Step 1, $\models_{\text{wfair}} \{p\}\ S\ \{q\}$ iff $\models_{\text{tot}} \{p\}\ T_{\text{wfair}}(S)\ \{q\}$ (under certain restrictions).

Step 2.   Find a proof system allowing to prove total correctness of the programs of the form $T_{\text{wfair}}(S)$.

Step 3.   Transform the proof system from Step 2 into a proof system allowing to prove $\models_{\text{wfair}} \{p\}\ S\ \{q\}$ directly without reference to $T_{\text{wfair}}(S)$.

ad Step 1

Consider the following program

$$x:= 0;\ b:= \textbf{true};$$
$$*[b \rightarrow x:= x + 1 \ \square\ b \rightarrow b:= \textbf{false}].$$

Under the assumption of weak fairness, this program always terminates but any nonnegative integer can be the final value of x. It is known (see essentially Dijkstra (14)) that this effect cannot be achieved by the nondeterministic programs studied here.

To control this unbounded nondeterminism we allow in $T_{\text{wfair}}(S)$ the *random assignment*

$$x:= \ ?$$

which sets x to an arbitrary nonnegative integer and thus has the following semantics:

$$\langle x := ?, \sigma \rangle \rightarrow \langle E, \sigma[d/x] \rangle \text{ for every } 0 \le d.$$

Observe that under the assumption of weak fairness the above program is equivalent to

$x := ?; b := \textbf{false}.$

To make the approach easier to follow, consider first a special case.

Case 1. S is of the form $*[\overset{m}{\underset{i=1}{\square}} B_i \rightarrow S_i]$ where each S_i is deterministic. Following Apt and Olderog (8) we define $T'_{\text{wfair}}(S)$ as follows:

$T'\text{wfair}(S) \equiv z_1 := ?; \ldots ; z_m := ?;$

$\quad *[\overset{m}{\underset{i=1}{\square}} B_i \wedge \text{turn} = i \rightarrow S_i; z_i := ?;$

$\quad\quad \textbf{for } j \ne i \textbf{ do}$
$\quad\quad [B_j \rightarrow z_j := z_j - 1 \square \neg B_j \rightarrow z_j := ?]$
$\quad\quad \textbf{od}$
$\quad]$

where $\text{turn} = i \equiv i = \min\{j | z_j = \min\{z_k | B_k\}_{k=1,\ldots,m}\}$ and the variables z_1, $\ldots$, z_m do not occur in S.

The variables $z_1, \ldots, z_m$ can be interpreted as *priorities* assigned to the subprograms $S_1, \ldots, S_m$, respectively. The addition of the conjuncts turn $= i$ to the guards B_i make the guards deterministic (i.e., mutually exclusive). At each moment when the control is at the main loop entry a guard with the smallest priority is selected for execution. After the execution of the corresponding subprogram S_i the priorities are recomputed.

The exact relation between S and $T'_{\text{wfair}}(S)$ is expressed by the following lemma where $Z = \{z_1 \ldots, z_m\}$.

LEMMA 7.1   For all states σ $\mathcal{M}_{\text{wfair}}[[S]](\sigma) = \mathcal{M}_{\text{tot}}[[T'_{\text{wfair}}(S)]](\sigma) \mod Z$. $\quad\square$
The notation "mod Z" suggests that the states produced by the programs agree on all variables except those in Z.

COROLLARY 7.1   For all assertions p and q which do not contain $z_1, \ldots, z_m$ as free variables

$$\models_{\text{wfair}} \{p\} S \{q\} \text{ iff } \models_{\text{tot}} \{p\} T'_{\text{wfair}}(S) \{q\}. \quad\square$$

Consider now the general case.

Case 2. S is an arbitrary nondeterministic program.

We proceed by the following successive steps (see Apt, Pnueli and Stavi (9)):

(1) Replace each subprogram $*[\overset{m}{\underset{i=1}{\square}} B_i \rightarrow S_i]$ of S by

$$*[\overset{m}{\underset{i=1}{\bigvee}} B_i \rightarrow [\overset{m}{\underset{i=1}{\square}} B_i \rightarrow S_i]]$$

(2) Replace each subprogram $[\overset{m}{\underset{i=1}{\square}} B_i \rightarrow S_i]$ of S by the following subprogram:

$\quad$ **for** $j := 1$ **to** m **do** $[B_j \rightarrow z_j := z_j - 1 \ \square \ \neg B_j \rightarrow z_j := ?]$ **od**;
$\quad [\overset{m}{\underset{i=1}{\square}} B_i \wedge \bar{z} \geq 0 \rightarrow z_i := ?; S_i].$

$\quad$ where $\bar{z} \geq 0$ stands for $z_1 \geq 0 \wedge \ldots \wedge z_m \geq 0$.

(3) Rename all variables $z_1, \ldots, z_m$ appropriately so that each alternative command has its "own" set of these variables.

Call the resulting program $T_{\text{wfair}}(S)$.

This transformation is not a straightforward generalization of the first transformation. First, the guards in the transformed program are not deterministic. Secondly, this transformation introduces failures which will result once a priority variable is decreased below zero. More formally the following holds. Here the subscript "wtot" refers to weak total correctness—a notion obtained by disregarding possible failures in the definition of total correctness.

LEMMA 7.2   For all states σ

$$\mathcal{M}_{\text{wtot}}[[T_{\text{wfair}}(S)]](\sigma) = \mathcal{M}_{\text{wfair}}[[S]](\sigma) - \{\textbf{fail}\} \bmod Z. \quad \square$$

The presence of failures allows us only to conclude the following.

COROLLARY 7.2   For all assertions p and q which do not contain $z_1, \ldots, z_m$ as free variables and all programs S

$\models_{\text{wfair}} \{p\} S \{q\}$ iff $\models_{\text{wtot}} \{p\} T_{\text{wfair}}(S) \{q\}$
and $\forall \sigma \ [\models p(\sigma) \Rightarrow S$ does not fail from $\sigma]$. $\quad \square$

ad Step 2.

To prove weak total correctness of the programs of the form $T_{\text{wfair}}(S)$ we have to take care of the random assignments. To this purpose we introduce the following axiom.

AXIOM 9:   RANDOM ASSIGNMENT AXIOM

$$\{\forall x \geq 0 \ p\} \ x := ? \ \{p\}.$$

However, it is not sufficient to add the above axiom to the proof system defined in Section 2.3. The reason is that in the presence of random assignments some programs always terminate but the actual number of steps does not depend on the initial state and is unbounded. An example of such a program is

$$S \equiv *[b \wedge 0 < y \rightarrow$$
$$[b \rightarrow y := ?; \quad b := \textbf{false}$$
$$\square \neg b \rightarrow y := y - 1$$
$$]$$
$$]$$

To prove total correctness of such programs the repetitive command rule II (rule 8) is not sufficient. An appropriate modification is obtained by allowing the parameter variable to range over ordinals instead of natural numbers. We thus adopt the following rule instead of rule 8:

RULE 10:   REPETITIVE COMMAND RULE III

$$\frac{\{p(\alpha) \wedge B_i\} \, S_i \, \{\exists \beta < \alpha \, p(\beta)\}, \ i = 1, \ldots, m}{\{\exists \alpha \, p(\alpha)\} \, *[\overset{m}{\underset{i=1}{\square}} \, B_i \rightarrow S_i]\{\exists \alpha \, p(\alpha) \wedge \overset{m}{\underset{i=1}{\bigwedge}} \neg B_i]}$$

where $p(\alpha)$ is an assertion with a free variable α which does not appear in the programs and ranges over ordinals.

ad Step 3

Corollary 2 states that in order to prove total correctness of a nondeterministic program S under the assumption of weak fairness it essentially suffices to prove weak total correctness of $T_{\text{wfair}}(S)$. But instead of proving the correctness of $T_{\text{wfair}}(S)$ directly we rather transform the proof into a direct proof of S by "absorbing" the transformation into the assertions of existing rules. Finally, we take care of the problem of failures in the same way as in Section 7.2.3, i.e., by adding a new premise to the hypotheses of the (new) alternative command rule.

This procedure leads to the following new proof rules for alternative and repetitive commands.

RULE 11:   WFAIR ALTERNATIVE COMMAND RULE

$$p \rightarrow \overset{m}{\underset{i=1}{\bigvee}} B_i,$$

$$\{\exists \bar{z}_1, \ldots, \bar{z}_m \exists z_i p \, [\textbf{if } B_j \textbf{ then } z_j + 1 \textbf{ else } \bar{z}_j \textbf{ fi}/z_j]_{j \neq i} \wedge B_i \wedge \bar{z} \geq 0\}$$
$$S_i$$
$$\{q\}, \ i = 1, \ldots, m$$

$$\{p\} \ [\overset{m}{\underset{i=1}{\square}} \ B_i \rightarrow S_i] \ \{q\}$$

RULE 12:   WFAIR REPETITIVE COMMAND RULE

$$\{\exists \bar{z}_1, \ldots, \bar{z}_n \exists z_i \ p(\alpha) \ [\textbf{if } B_j \textbf{ then } z_j + 1 \textbf{ else } \bar{z}_j \textbf{ fi}/z_j]_{j \neq i} \wedge B_i \wedge \bar{z} \geq 0\}$$
$$S_i$$
$$\{\exists \beta < \alpha \ p(\beta)\}, \ i = 1, \ldots, m$$

$$\{\exists \alpha \ p(\alpha)\} \ *[\overset{m}{\underset{i=1}{\square}} \ B_i \rightarrow S_i] \ \{\exists \alpha \ p(\alpha) \wedge \overset{m}{\underset{i=1}{\bigwedge}} \neg B_i\}$$

where $p(\alpha)$ is as in rule 10.

Summarizing, the proof system appropriate for proving total correctness of nondeterministic programs under the weak fairness hypothesis consists of axioms 1 and 2 and rules 3, 11, 12, and 6. The random assignment axiom is not needed— it was only used to derive the final form of the above two rules.

7.2.5 Strong Fairness

Another natural fairness assumption is that of strong fairness.

DEFINITION 7.3   Let ξ be a computation of a nondeterministic program S.

(1) We say that ξ is *strongly unfair* if it is infinite and there exists a guard B of S which from a certain moment on is infinitely often enabled and never selected for execution.

(2) We say that ξ is *strongly fair* if it is not strongly unfair.

Now, the hypothesis of strong fairness can be treated in an analogous way as that of weak fairness. To obtain a transformation realizing strong fairness we simply replace in the corresponding transformations, from Step 1 in the previous section, the updating of priority variables $[B_j \rightarrow z_j := z_j - 1 \ \square \neg B_j \rightarrow z_j := \ ?]$ by

$$[B_j \rightarrow z_j: = z_j - 1 \ \square \neg B_j \rightarrow \text{skip}]$$

The remaining steps in the development of the proof system for strong fairness are the same as before and omitted.

7.3 PARALLEL PROGRAMS

We now consider parallel programs. These are programs of the form

$$S \equiv S_0; [S_1\|.\ .\ .\|S_n]$$

where S_0, called an *initial part*, consists of a (possibly empty) sequence of assignments and $S_1, \ldots, S_n$—called the *components of the parallel program*—are deterministic programs. For a moment we disallow synchronization constructs in the component programs.

7.3.1 Semantics

Their semantics is obtained by augmenting the list of clauses given in Section 7.2.1 by the following one handling the parallel composition.

(8) if $\langle R_i, \sigma \rangle \rightarrow \langle R_i', \tau \rangle$ then

$$\langle [R_1\|.\ .\ .\|R_n], \sigma \rangle \rightarrow \langle [R_1\|.\ .\ .\|R_{i-1}\|R_i'\|R_{i+1}\|.\ .\ .\|R_n], \tau \rangle$$

This leads to two types of semantics of parallel programs—$\mathcal{M}$ and $\mathcal{M}_{\text{tot}}$ defined similarly as before but this time with $\langle \underbrace{[E\|.\ .\ .\|E]}_{n \text{ times}}, \tau \rangle$ as the final configuration.

We shall also consider a third semantics taking into account the fairness assumption. To this purpose we introduce the following notions.

DEFINITION 7.4   Let ξ be a computation of a parallel program $S \equiv S_0; [S_1\|.\ .\ .\|S_n]$.

(1) We say that the component S_i $(1 \leq i \leq n)$ *has terminated in* ξ if for some $R_1, \ldots, R_n$ and τ where $R_i \equiv E$, $\langle [R_1\|.\ .\ .\|R_n], \tau \rangle$ is an element of ξ.

(2) We say that the component S_i is *active* in the step

$$\langle [R_1\|.\ .\ .\|R_n], \sigma \rangle \rightarrow \langle [R_1'\|.\ .\ .\|R_n'], \tau \rangle$$

of ξ if $\langle R_i, \sigma \rangle \rightarrow \langle R_i', \tau \rangle$.

(3) We say that ξ is *unjust* if some component S_i did not terminate in ξ and is only finitely many times active in ξ.

(4) We say that ξ is *just* if it is not unjust.

We now define the just semantics of parallel programs by putting

$$\mathcal{M}\text{just } [[S]] (\sigma) = \mathcal{M} [[S]] (\sigma)$$
$$\cup \{\perp: S \text{ can diverge from } \sigma \text{ by a just computation}\}$$
$$\cup \{\textbf{fail}: S \text{ can fail from } \sigma\}$$

This semantics takes care of the fairness assumption mentioned in the introduction. Thus, Solution 3 from the introduction is a correct solution to the zero finding problem in the case when the above semantics is adopted.

It should be observed that all three semantics introduced here handle parallelism by reducing it to an arbitrary interleaving of the executions of the components program—at each step only one component of the program is active. Whether this is a realistic approximation of a truly parallel execution of a parallel program depends on how *atomic actions* of parallel programs are defined. By an atomic action we mean a statement within a component whose execution cannot be interrupted by the activation of another component.

The usual requirement concerning the parallel execution is that *concurrent reading and writing* is disallowed, i.e., an execution of an assignment to a variable x cannot interrupt or be interrupted by any other action referring to x. This requirement is satisfied if assignments and evaluations of the guards are considered as atomic actions.

The granularity of interleaving can be increased here by decreasing the size of atomic actions. This can be achieved by allowing only very simple types of assignments and Boolean expressions whose execution blocks other components for a more negligible amount of time.

7.3.2 Disjoint Parallelism

The main difficulty in studying parallel programs lies in the use of *shared variables*. A variable is called *shared* if it can be modified within one component of a parallel program and moreover is referred to within another. Then the behavior of the latter component can depend on the behavior of the first one. This can result in a nondeterministic behavior of a parallel program with deterministic components. To see this, consider, for example, the program $x := 0$; $[x := 1 \parallel y := x]$ in which the final value of y is either 0 or 1.

Because of these difficulties it is natural to study first parallel programs without shared variables. Such programs are called *disjoint parallel programs* and were originally studied in Hoare (25).

More formally, let free (S) stand for the set of all variables which occur in S and let change (S) stand for the set of all variables of S which can be modified by it, i.e., which appear on the left-hand side of an assignment.

Then $S \equiv S_0; [S_1 \parallel \ldots \parallel S_n]$ is called a *disjoint parallel program* if

$$\text{free } (S_i) \cap \text{change } (S_j) = \phi \text{ for } i \neq j.$$

Thus the program $[x := z \parallel y := z]$ is a disjoint parallel program but $[x := z \parallel y := x]$ or $[x := z \parallel x := y]$ is not.

The following proof rule dealing with disjoint parallel programs was proposed by Hoare in (25):

RULE 13:   RULE OF DISJOINT PARALLEL COMPOSITION

$$\frac{\{p_i\}\ S_i\ \{q_i\},\ i = 1, \ldots, n}{\{\bigwedge_{i=1}^{n} p_i\}\ [S_1\|\ldots\|S_n]\ \{\bigwedge_{i=1}^{n} q_i\}}$$

provided free $(p_i, q_i) \cap$ change $(S_j) = \emptyset$ for $i \neq j$.

Observe that the proviso of the rule is indeed needed. For example, the true premises $\{y = 1\}\ x\!:= 0\ \{y = 1\}$ and $\{\textbf{true}\}\ y\!:= 0\ \{\textbf{true}\}$ should not lead to the conclusion $\{y = 1\}\ [x\!:= 0 \| y\!:= 0]\ \{y = 1\}$.

Note the natural connection between the condition imposed on the programs S_i and the condition of the rule.

The above rule is a useful one but it does not suffice to prove all properties of disjoint parallel programs. It is not difficult to prove that the correctness formula $\{x = y\}\ [x\!:= x + 1 \| y\!:= y + 1]\ \{x = y\}$ cannot be proved in the proof system PC from Section 2.2 augmented by the above rule. Let us see where a possible proof actually breaks down.

We clearly have

$$\{x = z\}\ x\!:= x + 1\ \{x = z + 1\}$$

and

$$\{y = z\}\ y\!:= y + 1\ \{y = z + 1\}$$

so by the rule of disjoint parallel composition

$$\{x = z \wedge y = z\}\ [x\!:= x + 1 \| y\!:= y + 1]\ \{x = z + 1 \wedge y = z + 1\}.$$

Now by the rule of consequence

$$\{x = z \wedge y = z\}\ [x\!:= x + 1 \| y\!:= y + 1]\ \{x = y\}.$$

However, we cannot replace the pre-assertion $x = z \wedge y = z$ by $x = y$ since clearly the latter does not imply the former. On the other hand, we have

$$\{x = y\}\ z\!:= x\ \{x = z \wedge y = z\}$$

so by the composition rule

$$\{x = y\}\ z\!:= x;\ [x\!:= x + 1 \| y\!:= y + 1]\ \{x = y\}.$$

We can now obtain the desired formula by dropping the assignment $z\!:= x$. Formally this requires use of a new rule allowing to delete assignments to the so-called auxiliary variables. This brings us to the following definition.

DEFINITION 7.4   Let A be a set of variables of a program S. We call A the set of *auxiliary variables* of S if

(1) All variables of A appear in S only in assignments,

(2) No variable of S from outside A depends on the variable from A. In other words there does not exist an assignment $x := t$ within S such that $x \notin A$ and free $(t) \cap A \neq \phi$.

For example, $\{z\}$ is a set of auxiliary variables of the program $z := x; [x := x + 1 \| y := y + 1]$ but $\{x\}$ is not as z depends on x.

Informally, (1) states that the auxiliary variables do not affect the control flow of the program and (2) states that they do not affect the data flow of the program.

The following rule was first introduced by Owicki and Gries in (36) for the case of arbitrary parallel programs.

RULE 14:   RULE OF AUXILIARY VARIABLES

Let A be a set of auxiliary variables of a program S and let S' be obtained from S by deleting all assignments to the variables in A. Then

$$\frac{\{p\}\, S\, \{q\}}{\{p\}\, S'\, \{q\}}$$

provided free $(q) \cap A = \phi$.

Now, using the above rule we can complete the proof of the correctness formula $\{x = y\} [x := x + 1 \| y := y + 1] \{x = y\}$ by dropping the assignment to z.

Adding the last two rules to the proof systems for partial, respectively total correctness, we obtain proof systems appropriate for proving partial, respectively total correctness of disjoint parallel programs.

Consider now the problem of justice. It may come out as a surprise that this is not a real issue for disjoint parallel programs. This follows from the following simple lemma.

LEMMA 7.3   For all disjoint parallel programs S

$$\mathcal{M}_{\mathrm{tot}}[[S]] = \mathcal{M}_{\mathrm{just}}[[S]]$$

holds.

Proof   For any given state σ and a parallel program S we have $\mathcal{M}_{\mathrm{just}}[[S]](\sigma) \subseteq \mathcal{M}_{\mathrm{tot}}[[S]](\sigma)$. Consider now the converse implication. The only possible difference can lie in the existence of an infinite computation. So suppose that $\perp \in \mathcal{M}_{\mathrm{tot}}[[S]](\sigma)$ and let ξ be an infinite computation of S starting in σ.

Because of disjointness of the components, ξ is infinite because of a looping within a single component. Now, if ξ is not just, then it can easily be transformed into a just computation by simply activating sufficiently often the components of S which did not terminate in ξ. Insertion of these steps does not affect the behavior of other components because of their disjointness. The resulting computation is an infinite just computation of S starting in ξ. So $\perp \in \mathcal{M}_{\text{just}}[[S]](\sigma)$. $\quad\Box$

This lemma implies that there is no difference in proving total correctness of disjoint parallel programs with or without the assumption of justice.

7.3.3 Parallel Programs with Shared Variables

Consider now the general case. Then, rule 13 is still sound. However, this time it is completely inadequate. Take, for example, the program $S \equiv [x := x + 1 \,\|\, x := x + 1]$. Then $\{x = 0\}\ S\ \{x = 2\}$ is true. However, because of the restriction of the rule in the case of S, x cannot be referred to in the assertions. A possible use of the rule of auxiliary variables cannot remedy this problem and consequently the correctness formula $\{x = 0\}\ S\ \{x = 2\}$ cannot be proved in the proof system studied in the previous section.

Partial Correctness

To overcome this difficulty we have to find a proof rule for parallel composition which allows references in assertions to the shared variables. We follow here the approach of Owicki and Gries (36).

First, we introduce the notion of a proof outline. Consider the following proof of (partial) correctness of the gcd program:

$$
\begin{aligned}
&\{x = a \wedge y = b \wedge a > 0 \wedge b > 0\} \\
&\quad \{p\} \\
&*[x > y \rightarrow \{p \wedge x > y\} \\
&\qquad x := x - y \\
&\qquad \{p\} \\
&\quad \Box\ x < y \rightarrow \{p \wedge x < y\} \\
&\qquad\quad y := y - x \\
&\qquad\quad \{p\} \\
&\quad] \\
&\{x = y \wedge p\} \\
&\{x = y = \text{gcd}\,(a,b)\}
\end{aligned}
$$

where

$$
p \equiv \text{gcd}(x,y) = \text{gcd}(a,b).
$$

The proof is presented here in a special form, called a *proof outline*. A proof outline consists of a program interspersed with assertions. Each subprogram R is preceded and succeeded by an assertion called pre(R) and post(R), respectively. These assertions satisfy certain natural conditions (see below) which make the application of the appropriate rules justified. Observe that we refer here to the proofs of partial correctness.

The following lemma due to Owicki (34) clarifies the notion of a proof outline.

LEMMA 7.4   Let S be a deterministic program and let $S_1, \ldots, S_k$ be the list of all subprograms of S. Then $\vdash_{\mathrm{PC}} \{p\}\, S\, \{q\}$ iff there exist assertions $\mathrm{pre}(S_i)$ and $\mathrm{post}(S_i)$ for $i = 1, \ldots, k$ such that

(i) $p \to \mathrm{pre}(S)$, $\mathrm{post}(S) \to q$,

(ii) $\mathrm{pre}(S_i) \to \mathrm{post}(S_i)[t/x]$ if S_i is $x := t$,

(iii) $\mathrm{pre}(S_i) \to \mathrm{pre}(S_j)$, $\mathrm{post}(S_j) \to \mathrm{pre}(S_l)$, $\mathrm{post}(S_l) \to \mathrm{post}(S_i)$ if S_i is $S_j; S_l$,

(iv) $\mathrm{pre}(S_i) \wedge B \to \mathrm{pre}(S_j)$, $\mathrm{pre}(S_i) \wedge \neg B \to \mathrm{pre}(S_l)$, $\mathrm{post}(S_j) \to \mathrm{post}(S_i)$, $\mathrm{post}(S_l) \to \mathrm{post}(S_i)$ if S_i is **if** B **then** S_j **else** S_l **fi**,

(v) $\mathrm{pre}(S_i) \to \mathrm{post}(S_i)$, $\mathrm{post}(S_j) \wedge B \to \mathrm{pre}(S_j)$, $\mathrm{post}(S_j) \wedge \neg B \to \mathrm{post}(S_i)$ if S_i is **while** B **do** S_j **od**.

Proof   See (essentially) Owicki (34). $\square$

The proof outlines satisfy the following easy to prove lemma.

LEMMA 7.5   (Strong soundness for deterministic programs)

Suppose that a proof outline of $\{p\}\, S\, \{q\}$ is given. Then for every computation of S which starts in a state σ satisfying p if

$$\langle S, \sigma \rangle \to^* \langle R; R_1, \sigma_0 \rangle \to^* \langle R_1, \sigma_1 \rangle$$

for a subprogram R of S and some R_1, σ and σ_0, then

$$\models \mathrm{pre}(R)(\sigma_0) \quad \text{and} \quad \models \mathrm{post}(R)(\sigma_1). \quad \square$$

Informally, the conclusion of this lemma states that for every computation of S starting in a state satisfying p and every substatement R of S if the control is in front of R then $\mathrm{pre}(R)$ holds and if the control is just after R then $\mathrm{post}(R)$ holds. In other words, the pre- and post-assertions hold at the appropriate moments.

This lemma is a generalization of the usual soundness theorem concerning the proof system PC.

Now observe that the above lemma does not hold any more when we consider proof outlines of the components of a parallel program simultaneously. Indeed, consider the proof outlines

$$\{x = 0\}\, x := x + 1\, \{x = 1\}$$

and

$$\{x = 0\}\, x := 0\, \{x = 0\}$$

and a computation of the program $[x := x + 1 \parallel x := 0]$ starting in a state in which $x = 0$ holds. Then it is not true that whenever the control is after $x := x + 1$, $x = 1$ holds. The reason is that the above proof outlines do not take into account a possible interaction of the other components. This brings us to the following definitions.

DEFINITION 7.5   Given a proof outline of $\{p\}\ S\ \{q\}$ and a statement R with a pre-assertion $\text{pre}(R)$, we say that R *does not interfere with* the proof outline of $\{p\}\ S\ \{q\}$ if the following two conditions hold

(1) for all subprograms T of S:

$$\{\text{pre}(T) \wedge \text{pre}(R)\}\ R\ \{\text{pre}(T)\}$$

(R preserves all pre-assertions)

(2) $$\{q \wedge \text{pre}(R)\}\ R\ \{q\}$$

(R preserves the final post-assertion).

DEFINITION 7.6   The proof outlines of $\{p_1\}\ S_1\ \{q_1\}, \ldots, \{p_n\}\ S_n\ \{q_n\}$ are *interference-free* if no assignment from one component interferes with the proof outline of another component.

We now introduce the following proof rule

RULE 15:   RULE OF PARALLEL COMPOSITION

$$\frac{\text{proof outlines of } \{p_i\}\ S_i\ \{q_i\},\ i = 1, \ldots, n \quad \text{are interference-free}}{\{\bigwedge_{i=1}^{n} p_i\}\ [S_1 \parallel \ldots \parallel S_n]\ \{\bigwedge_{i=1}^{n} q_i\}}\ .$$

The following lemma constitutes a counterpart of Lemma 7.5 and justifies the above rule.

LEMMA 7.6   (Strong soundness for parallel programs)

Suppose that interference-free proof outlines of $\{p_1\}\ S_1\ \{q_1\}, \ldots, \{p_n\}\ S_n\ \{q_n\}$ are given. Then for every computation of $[S_1 \parallel \ldots \parallel S_n]$ which starts in a state σ satisfying $\bigwedge_{i=1}^{n} p_i$ if

$$\langle [S_1 \parallel \ldots \parallel S_n], \sigma \rangle \to^* \langle [R_1 \parallel \ldots \parallel R_n], \sigma_0 \rangle \to^* \langle [T_1 \parallel \ldots \parallel T_n], \sigma_1 \rangle$$

for a subprogram R of S_i such that $R_i \equiv R; T_i$, then

$$\models \text{pre}(R)(\sigma_0) \quad \text{and} \quad \models \text{post}(R)(\sigma_1).$$

In particular, if

$$\langle [S_1 \,\|\ldots\| \, S_n], \sigma \rangle \rightarrow^* \langle [E \,\|\ldots\| \, E], \sigma_1 \rangle$$

then $\models \bigwedge_{i=1}^{n} q_i(\sigma_1)$.

Proof Straightforward by induction on the length of the computation. $\Box$

To see the use of this rule consider the correctness formula $\{x = 0\}\, [x:= 0 \,\|\, x:= x + 1]\, \{x = 0 \vee x = 1\}$ with the following proof presented in the form of proof outlines:

$$\{x = 0\}$$
$$[\{x = 0 \vee x = 1\}\, x:= 0\, \{x = 0 \vee x = 1\}$$
$$\|\, \{x = 0\}\, x:= x + 1\, \{x = 0 \vee x = 1\}$$
$$]$$
$$\{x = 0 \vee x = 1\}$$

Note that the proof outlines are indeed interference-free.

Unfortunately, as in the case of disjoint parallelism the above proof rule is not sufficient for proving all properties of parallel programs.

It is easy to see that this rule does not suffice to prove the correctness formula $\{x = 0\}\, [x:= x + 1 \,\|\, x:= x + 1]\, \{x = 2\}$. Indeed, suppose by contradiction that for interference-free proof outlines

$$\{x = 0\}$$
$$[\{p_1\}\, x:= x + 1\, \{q_1\}$$
$$\|\, \{p_2\}\, x:= x + 1\, \{q_2\}$$
$$]$$
$$\{x = 2\}$$

holds.

Then also

$$\{x = 0\}$$
$$[\{p\}\, x:= x + 1\, \{q\}$$
$$\|\, \{p\}\, x:= x + 1\, \{q\}$$
$$]$$
$$\{x = 2\}$$

is a valid proof where $p \equiv p_1 \wedge p_2$ and $q \equiv q_1 \wedge q_2$. We thus have

(1) $x = 0 \rightarrow p$,

(2) $\{p\}\, x:= x + 1\, \{p\}$ by interference freedom, i.e., for all x
$$p(x) \rightarrow p(x + 1).$$

Then by induction $\forall x \geq 0 \; p(x)$ and since $\{p\} \; x := x + 1 \; \{q\}$ holds, $\forall x \geq 1$ $q(x)$ is true. But then q cannot imply $x = 2$. Contradiction.

As in the case of disjoint parallelism we strengthen the proof system by supplementing it with the rule of auxiliary variables. This time, however, we also need an additional construct allowing to turn a deterministic program R into an indivisible action: $\langle R \rangle$. To better understand its function in conjunction with the rule of auxiliary variables consider the following correctness proof.

The proof outlines

$$\{x = z\} \; x := x + 1 \; \{x = x + 1\}$$

and

$$\{z = 0\} \; \langle x := x + 1; z := 1 \rangle \; \{z = 1\}$$

are interference-free. Using the parallel composition rule and the composition rule we obtain $\{x = 0\} \; z := 0; \; [x := x + 1 \; \| \; \langle x := x + 1; z := 1 \rangle] \; \{x = z + 1 \wedge z = 1\}$, so by the consequence rule

$$\{x = 0\} \; z := 0; \; [x := x + 1 \; \| \; \langle x := x + 1; z := 1 \rangle] \; \{x = 2\}.$$

Now by the rule of auxiliary variables

$$\{x = 0\} \; [x := x + 1 \; \| \; \langle x := x + 1 \rangle] \; \{x = 2\}.$$

But the assignments are by assumption indivisible actions so we can drop the brackets around $x := x + 1$ and obtain the correctness formula discussed here.

To justify the above proof we need to modify the notions of a proof outline and of interference freedom.

In the definition of a proof outline we simply do not put any assertion within a subprogram of the form $\langle R \rangle$. On the other hand, we require that $\{pre(R)\} \; R$ $\{post(R)\}$ be provable in the proof system PC. In the definition of interference freedom we now require that no assignment *and* no subprogram of the form $\langle R \rangle$ of one component interferes with the proof outline of another component.

Finally, we need the following natural rule.

RULE 16: REDUCTION RULE

Let S' be obtained from S by replacing each subprogram of S of the form $\langle R \rangle$, where R is an assignment, by R. Then

$$\frac{\{p\} \; S \; \{q\}}{\{p\} \; S' \; \{q\}}.$$

This completes the presentation of the proof system. Observe that the above proof system is appropriate for proofs of partial correctness only as the proof outlines referred to the proof system PC.

Total Correctness

In order to prove total correctness of parallel programs, we first introduce a notion of a proof outline appropriate for total correctness. As before, a proof outline consists of a program interspersed with assertions. They now satisfy the same conditions as before with the exception of the following ones for the case of **while**-subprograms:

$$(v') \quad r(n) \wedge B \rightarrow \mathrm{pre}(S_j), \; \mathrm{post}(S_j) \rightarrow \exists m < n \; r(m), \; \mathrm{pre}(S_i) \rightarrow \exists n \; r(n),$$

$\exists n \; r(n) \wedge \neg B \rightarrow \mathrm{post}(S_i)$ if S_i is **while** B **do** S_j **od**, where $r(n)$ is an assertion with a free variable n which does not appear in S_i and ranges over natural numbers.

The following lemma justifies this new definition of a proof outline.

LEMMA 7.7   Let S be a deterministic program and let $S_1, \ldots, S_n$ be the list of all subprograms of S. Then $\vdash_{\mathrm{TC}} \{p\} \, S \, \{q\}$ iff there exist assertions $\mathrm{pre}(S_i)$ and $\mathrm{post}(S_i)$ for $i = 1, \ldots, k$ such that the conditions (i)–(iv) of Lemma 7.4 and (v') listed above are satisfied.

Proof   The proof proceeds by induction on the structure of the program S. We consider here only the case of **while**-programs. The proofs of other cases are the same as in Lemma 7.4.

Let S be of the form **while** B **do** S_0 **od**.

If part

Suppose that $\vdash_{\mathrm{TC}} \{p\} \, S \, \{q\}$ holds for some assertions p and q. The last steps of the proof must have consisted of an application of rule 8 (the rule of repetitive command II) followed by a possibly empty number of applications of the consequence rule which can be combined into exactly one application. We thus have $p \rightarrow \exists n \; r(n)$, $\exists n \; r(n) \wedge \neg B \rightarrow q$ and

$$\vdash_{\mathrm{TC}} \{r(n) \wedge B\} \, S_0 \, \{\exists m < n \; r(m)\} \tag{7.1}$$

for some assertion $r(n)$ with a free variable n which does not occur in S and ranges over natural numbers.

We now define the pre- and post-assertions for S and S_0 putting $\mathrm{pre}(S) \equiv p$, $\mathrm{post}(S) \equiv q$, $\mathrm{pre}(S_0) \equiv r(n) \wedge B$, $\mathrm{post}(S_0) \equiv \exists m < n \; r(m)$.

Note that the relevant conditions listed in (i) and (v') of Lemma 7.4 are obviously satisfied.

Since (7.1) holds, by the induction hypothesis there exist appropriate pre- and post-assertions for all subprograms of S_0 which satisfy the conditions listed in the lemma. Disregard the new definitions of $\mathrm{pre}(S_0)$ and $\mathrm{post}(S_0)$ which satisfy the condition (i) w.r.t. (7.1). All other pre- and post-assertions together with those defined above satisfy the conditions of the lemma w.r.t. $\{p\} \, S \, \{q\}$.

Only if part

Suppose that the appropriate assertions satisfying the conditions of the Lemma 7.4 for $\{p\}\, S\, \{q\}$ exist. Delete now from this list the assertions $\mathrm{pre}(S) \to \exists n\, r(n)$ and $\exists n\, r(n) \wedge \neg B \to \mathrm{post}(S)$ concerning the program S and listed in (v'). In such a way, we obtain appropriate assertions which satisfy the conditions of the lemma in the case of the correctness formula $\{r(n) \wedge B\}\, S_0\, \{\exists m < n\, r(m)\}$.

By the induction hypothesis $\vdash_{\mathrm{TC}} \{r(n) \wedge B\}\, S_0\, \{\exists m < n\, r(m)\}$. By the assumption the assertions $p \to \mathrm{pre}(S)$, $\mathrm{pre}(S) \to \exists n\, r(n)$, $\exists n\, r(n) \wedge \neg B \to \mathrm{post}(S)$ and $\mathrm{post}(S) \to q$ hold, so by the consequence rule $\vdash_{\mathrm{TC}} \{p\}\, S\, \{q\}$ holds as desired. $\square$

To prove total correctness of parallel programs it is sufficient to use the same proof rules as before but now using the proof outlines for total correctness.

As an example consider the program $S \equiv [\textbf{while } x > 0 \textbf{ do } x := x - 1 \textbf{ od } \|\ x := 0]$. We now prove $\{\textbf{true}\}\, S\, \{x = 0 \vee x = -1\}$ in the sense of total correctness. We present the proof in the form of proof outlines together with an appropriate commentary.

$$
\begin{aligned}
&\{\textbf{true}\}\\
&\quad z := 0\ ;\\
&\quad \{z = 0\}\\
&[\ \{\exists n\, p(n)\}\\
&\qquad \textbf{while } x > 0 \textbf{ do } \{n \ge x + 1 \wedge \textbf{if } z = 1 \textbf{ then } x = 0 \textbf{ else } x > 0 \textbf{ fi}\}\\
&\qquad\quad x := x - 1\\
&\qquad\quad \{\exists m < n(m \ge x + 1) \wedge \textbf{if } z = 1 \textbf{ then } x = 0 \vee x = -1 \textbf{ else}\\
&\qquad\quad x \ge 0 \textbf{ fi}\}\\
&\qquad \textbf{od}\\
&\quad \{\exists n\, p(n) \wedge x \le 0\}\\
&\|\ \{z = 0\}\\
&\qquad \langle x := 0\ ;\ z := 1\rangle\\
&\quad \{z = 1\}\\
&]\\
&\quad \{\exists n\, p(n) \wedge x \le 0 \wedge z = 1\}\\
&\quad \{x = 0 \vee x = -1\}
\end{aligned}
$$

where $p(n) \equiv n \ge x + 1 \wedge \textbf{if } z = 1 \textbf{ then } x = 0 \vee x = -1 \textbf{ else } x > 0 \textbf{ fi}$.

Consecutive occurrences of assertions indicate an application of the consequence rule.

First, observe that we indeed deal with proof outlines. The assertions to verify are

$$p(n) \wedge x > 0 \to n \ge x + 1 \wedge \textbf{if } z = 1 \textbf{ then } x = 0 \textbf{ else } x > 0 \textbf{ fi}$$

and

$$\exists m < n(m \geq x + 1) \wedge \textbf{if } z = 1 \textbf{ then } x = 0 \vee x = -1 \textbf{ else } x \geq 0 \textbf{ fi} \rightarrow$$
$$\exists m < n \; p(m).$$

They are clearly satisfied. Next we prove the interference freedom. The variable x is not mentioned in the second proof outline. Thus, the assignment $x := x - 1$ does not interfere with the second proof outline. Consider now the statement $\langle x := 0; z := 1 \rangle$ and the first proof outline.

We clearly have

$$\{\exists n \; p(n) \wedge z = 0\} \; \langle x := 0 \; ; \; z := 1 \rangle \; \{\exists n \; p(n)\}.$$

The other two cases are equally straightforward to verify. The desired result now follows by the parallel composition rule, rule of auxiliary variables, and the reduction rule.

There still remains an issue of total correctness of parallel programs with shared variables under the assumption of justice. We shall handle this problem after discussing the synchronization constructs.

7.3.4   General Parallel Programs

In a realistic situation parallel programs are executed in the presence of some synchronization constraints. These constraints cannot be expressed using the syntax discussed so far. Following Owicki and Gries (36) we now additionally allow within the context of parallel composition of programs the construct of the form **await B then R end** where R is a deterministic program. Informally, a component program executes an **await**-statement iff with its turn to execute the Boolean expression B evaluates to true. R is then executed as an indivisible action.

The await-construct is of course too powerful to be implemented efficiently but it allows to model various other more realistic synchronization constructs. For the purpose of correctness proofs of the parallel programs using the latter constructs such a modeling, however inefficient, suffices.

The above programs are subsequently called *general parallel programs* (GP programs, in short).

We now define the semantics of GP programs by adding the following clause to the list considered up until now:

(9) $\langle \textbf{await } B \textbf{ then } R \textbf{ end}, \sigma \rangle \rightarrow \langle E, \tau \rangle$
       if $\models B(\sigma)$ and $\langle R, \sigma \rangle \rightarrow^* \langle E, \tau \rangle$.

Introduction of the **await**-statements leads to a new possibility of abnormal termination of a program—that of a deadlock.

DEFINITION 7.7

(1) A configuration $\langle [S_1 \| . \ . \ .\| S_n], \sigma \rangle$ is called *deadlocked* if for some i $S_i \not\equiv E$ and moreover $\langle [S_1 \| . \ . \ .\| S_n], \sigma \rangle$ has no successor w.r.t. the relation "$\rightarrow$".

(2) We say that a GP program S *can deadlock from* σ if for some deadlocked configuration $\langle S', \tau \rangle$, $\langle S, \sigma \rangle \rightarrow^* \langle S', \tau \rangle$.

We now define a new $\mathcal{M}_{tot}$ semantics of GP programs taking into account the possibility of deadlocks:

$$\mathcal{M}_{tot}[[S]](\sigma) = \mathcal{M}[[S]](\sigma) \cup \{\perp: S \text{ can diverge from } \sigma\}$$
$$\cup \{\triangle: S \text{ can deadlock from } \sigma\}$$

where fail is not mentioned because by the syntax restrictions no failure can now arise.

Two different semantics of GP programs taking into account the fairness or justice assumption will be defined and discussed later.

To prove correctness of GP programs, we have to in the first place provide a proof rule concerning the **await**-statement. The following rule was proposed in (36):

RULE 17:   AWAIT RULE

$$\frac{\{p \wedge B\} \, R \, \{q\}}{\{p\} \textbf{ await } B \textbf{ then } R \textbf{ end } \{q\}}$$

Using this rule in conjunction with the proof system PC or TC we can prove partial or total correctness of the components of GP programs. However, in order to deal adequately with the semantics of the **await**-statements we adopt the following refined definitions of proof outlines. By a *normal* subprogram of a GP program we mean a subprogram which is not a proper subprogram of an **await**-statement. Then a proof outline of $\{p\} \, S \, \{q\}$, where S is a component program, is the program S together with the assertions p, q and $\mathrm{pre}(S_i)$, $\mathrm{post}(S_i)$ for all normal subsets S_i of S which satisfy the following conditions:

a) for partial correctness

    $1°.$ $\vdash_{PC} \{\mathrm{pre}(S_i) \wedge B\} \, R \, \{\mathrm{post}(S_i)\}$
            if S_i is **await** B **then** R **end**,
    $2°.$ conditions (i)–(v) of Lemma 7.4;

b) for total correctness

    $3°.$ $\vdash_{TC} \{\mathrm{pre}(S_i) \wedge B\} \, R \, \{\mathrm{post}(S_i)\}$
            if S_i is **await** B **then** R **end**,
    $4°.$ conditions (i)–(iv) of Lemma 7.4,
    $5°.$ conditions (v') concerning total correctness.

Similarly as before it is easy to prove the following lemma:

LEMMA 7.8   Let S be a component of a GP program. Then,

(1) $\vdash_{\text{PC}\,+\;\text{rule 16}} \{p\}\, S\, \{q\}$ iff there exists a proof outline for partial correctness of $\{p\}\, S\, \{q\}$.

(2) $\vdash_{\text{TC}\,+\;\text{rule 16}} \{p\}\, S\, \{q\}$ iff there exists a proof outline for total correctness of $\{p\}\, S\, \{q\}$. $\square$

Also, in the same way as before, we accommodate the definition of proof outlines to cater for the case of subprograms of the form $\langle R \rangle$. We intend to use rule 15 to prove correctness of GP programs. To this purpose we have to modify appropriately the definition of interference freedom. We now say that proof outlines for components of a GP program are *interference-free* if no assignment or an **await**-statement or a subprogram of the form $\langle R \rangle$ of one component interferes with the proof outline of another component.

Using now rules 14–16 we can prove partial correctness of GP programs. However, to prove total correctness of GP programs, it is not sufficient to use proof outlines for total correctness for the component programs—in presence of the await-statements we still have to handle the problem of *deadlock freedom*.

We follow here the approach of (36). Let $S \equiv [S_1 \|. \,. \,.\| S_n]$ be a GP program. An n-tuple of programs $\langle R_1, \ldots, R_n \rangle$ is called a *blocked tuple* if

(1) each R_i is either an **await**-statement being a subprogram of S_i or E,

(2) $\exists\, i\; R_i \not\equiv E$.

Suppose that interference-free proof outlines for partial correctness of $\{p_1\}\, S_1\, \{q_1\}$, $\ldots$, $\{p_n\}\, S_n\, \{q_n\}$ are given. With each blocked tuple $\langle R_1, \ldots, R_n \rangle$ of S we associate an n-tuple $\langle r_1, \ldots, r_n \rangle$ of assertions defined as follows:

if $R_i \equiv$ **await** B **then** R **end** then $r_i \equiv \text{pre}(R_i) \wedge \neg B$,
if $R_i \equiv E$ then $r_i \equiv q_i$.

Suppose now that interference-free proof outlines for total correctness of $\{p_1\}\, S_1\, \{q_1\}, \ldots, \{p_n\}\, S_n\, \{q_n\}$ are given. We then associate with each blocked tuple $\langle R_1, \ldots, R_n \rangle$ of S the corresponding n-tuple of assertions as before but we prefix each assertion with $\exists n_1 \ldots \exists n_k$ where $n_1, \ldots, n_k$ are parameter variables occurring in it.

The following can be proved for proof outlines for both partial and total correctness. If S is executed in an initial state satisfying the assertions $p_1, \ldots, p_n$ and deadlocks then the corresponding assertions $r_1, \ldots, r_n$ associated with the reached blocked tuple are satisfied.

We say that S is *deadlock-free relative to the assertion p* if in the computations of S starting in a state satisfying p deadlock cannot arise. The following lemma is a direct consequence of the above.

LEMMA 7.9 Suppose that interference-free proof outlines of $\{p_1\}\ S_1\ \{q_1\}, \ldots,$
$\{p_n\}\ S_n\ \{q_n\}$ are given. Then $S \equiv [S_1 \parallel \ldots \parallel S_n]$ is deadlock-free relative to
$\bigwedge_{i=1}^{n} p_i$ if for all blocked tuples $\langle R_1, \ldots, R_n \rangle$, $\neg \bigwedge_{i=1}^{n} r_i$ holds for the corresponding tuple of assertions $\langle r_1, \ldots, r_n \rangle$. $\square$

This lemma allows us to handle the proofs of deadlock-freedom. Thus, to
prove total correctness of a GP program it is enough to find appropriate proof
outlines for total correctness which satisfy the conditions of the above lemma.
Then the conclusion of rule 15 holds in the sense of total correctness.

7.3.5 Justice and Fairness

Justice

Consider the program

$$b: = \textbf{true};\ [\textbf{while}\ b\ \textbf{do skip od} \parallel b: = \textbf{false}].$$

Under the assumption of justice this program always terminates and without this
assumption termination is not guaranteed. Thus, in the presence of shared variables, there is a difference between total correctness of parallel programs under
and without the assumption of justice. To prove total correctness of parallel
programs under the assumption of justice we follow the approach of Olderog
and Apt (33) and as in the case of nondeterministic programs we use program
transformations.

Let $S \equiv S_0;\ [S_1 \parallel \ldots \parallel S_n]$ be a parallel program with shared variables. We
define $T_{\text{just}}(S)$ as the program obtained from S by the following steps:

(1) prefix S with an initialization part

$$\text{INIT} \equiv z_1: = ?;\ \ldots;\ z_n: = ?;\ \text{end}_1: = \textbf{false};\ \ldots;\ \text{end}_n: = \textbf{false},$$

(2) replace every loop **while** B **do** R **od** of a component S_i by

```
while B do
   await z̄ ≥ 1 then z_i: = ?;
      for j ≠ i do
      [¬ end_j → z_j: = z_j − 1 □ end_j → skip]
            od;
   end;
   R
od,
```

(3) suffix every component S_i by

$$\text{END}_i \equiv \text{end}_i: = \textbf{true}.$$

We assume that none of the variables in the set $Z = \{z_1, \ldots, z_n, \text{end}_1, \ldots, \text{end}_n\}$ occurs in the original program S.

The following lemma clarifies the relation between the programs S and $T_{\text{just}}(S)$:

LEMMA 7.10   For every parallel program S and a state σ

$$\mathcal{M}_{\text{just}}[[S]](\sigma) = \mathcal{M}_{\text{tot}}[[T_{\text{just}}(S)]](\sigma) - \{\triangle\} \bmod Z. \quad \square$$

A proof can be found in (33). The following corollary is immediate.

COROLLARY 7.3   For all assertions p and q without free variables from the set Z

$$\models_{\text{just}} \{p\}S\{q\} \text{ iff } \models_{\text{tot-}\triangle} \{p\}T_{\text{just}}(S)\{q\}. \quad \square$$

Here the subscript "tot-$\triangle$" refers to total correctness modulo deadlocks—a notion obtained by disregarding possible deadlocks in the definition of total correctness.

Now, to prove total correctness modulo deadlocks of $T_{\text{just}}(S)$, we first have to take care of random assignments. To this purpose it is necessary to refine the notion of a proof outline for total correctness in the presence of random assignments. While proving total correctness of the component programs we shall now use repetitive command rule III instead of repetitive command rule II. This requires replacement of the conditions concerning the **while**-subprograms ((v$'$) of the subsection on total correctness) of Section 7.3.3 by the following ones:

(v$''$) $r(\alpha) \wedge B \rightarrow \text{pre}(S_j)$, $\text{post}(S_j) \rightarrow \exists \beta < \alpha r(\beta)$, $\text{pre}(S_i) \rightarrow \exists \alpha r(\alpha)$, $\exists \alpha r(\alpha)$
$\wedge \neg B \rightarrow \text{post}(S_i)$
if S_i is **while** B **do** S_j **od**, where $r(\alpha)$ is an assertion with a free variable α which does not appear in S_i and ranges over ordinals,

and add the following concerning random assignments:

(vi) $\text{pre}(x: = ?) \rightarrow \forall x \geq 0 \, \text{post}(x: = ?)$.

Thus, to prove total correctness of a parallel program S under the assumption of justice it is enough to:

(1) Find proof outlines for the total correctness of the component programs of $T_{\text{just}}(S)$. They are to satisfy the conditions listed under b) in Section 7.3.4 but with (v$'$) replaced by (v$''$), and (vi) added.

(2) Prove that they are interference free.

(3) Apply the rule of parallel composition (rule 15) and possibly the composition rule, the rule of auxiliary variables, reduction rule, and consequence rule.

(4) Apply the following rule.

RULE 18: JUSTICE RULE

$$\frac{\{p\}\ T_{\text{just}}(S)\ \{q\}}{\{p\}\ S\ \{q\}}$$

Observe that in contrast to the case of nondeterministic programs we did not "absorb" the transformation $T_{\text{just}}(S)$ into the assertions of existing rules. For parallel programs the idea of absorption does not work properly. This is due to the interference freedom test which has to deal with the assignments to the auxiliary variables from the set Z and perhaps some other ones. Even if assignments to these variables were absorbed into the assertions of the proof outlines for the components of S, they would reappear in the final test of interference freedom. Therefore, we rather propose to apply the transformations as a part of the correctness proofs.

Weak Fairness

In the presence of the **await**-statements the assumption of justice is not any more an appropriate one. To see this consider the program

$$S \equiv [\textbf{while true do}\ \text{skip}\ \textbf{od}\ \|\ \textbf{await false then}\ \text{skip}\ \textbf{end}].$$

Then for any state σ

$$\mathcal{M}_{\text{just}}[[S]](\sigma) = \phi$$

i.e. the program S neither diverges nor converges! Intuitively, the program S should diverge as there is no way to activate its second component and the first one diverges.

An appropriate notion of fairness is obtained by replacing in the definition of justice the notion of termination of a component by the notion of *enabledness*.

DEFINITION 7.8 Let $S \equiv S_0; [S_1 \|. . .\| S_n]$ be a GP program and let ξ be a computation of S.

(1) We say that the i-th component is *enabled* in the configuration $\langle [T_1 \|. . .\| T_n], \sigma \rangle$ if T_i is not terminated, i.e. $T_i \not\equiv E$ and whenever T_i is of the form **await** B **then** R **end**; T_i' then $\models B(\sigma)$ holds.

(2) We say that ξ is *weakly unfair* if it is infinite and some component is from a certain moment on continuously enabled, but is only finitely many times active in ξ.

(3) We say that ξ is *weakly fair* if it is not weakly unfair.

Note the close correspondence between the notion of weak fairness for non-determinisitc and general parallel programs. We now define a weakly fair semantics of GP programs by putting

$$\mathcal{M}_{\text{wfair}}[[S]](\sigma) = \mathcal{M}[[S]](\sigma)$$
$$\cup \{\perp: S \text{ can diverge from } \sigma \text{ by}$$
$$\text{a weakly fair computation}\}$$
$$\cup \{\triangle: S \text{ can deadlock from } \sigma\}.$$

Observe that under the assumption of weak fairness the program S considered above diverges, i.e.

$$\mathcal{M}_{\text{wfair}}[[S]](\sigma) = \{\perp\}.$$

To prove total correctness of GP programs under the assumption of weak fairness similarly as before we first exhibit an appropriate program transformation provided in (33).

Let $S \equiv S_0; [S_1 \|. . .\| S_n]$ be a GP program. We first need to formalize the notion of enabledness. To this purpose we introduce new auxiliary variables pc_1, $\ldots$, pc_n which will be used as a restricted form of program counters indicating when the component S_i is in front of an **await**-statement, and if so in front of which one. To this end, we assign to every occurrence of an **await**-statement in S_i a unique number $\ell \geq 1$ as a label. Let L_i denote the set of all these labels for S_i and let B_ℓ denote the Boolean guard of the **await**-statement labeled by ℓ. We assume that $0 \notin L_i$. We now put

$$\text{enabled}_i \equiv \neg\text{end}_i \wedge \bigwedge_{\ell \in L_i} (pc_i = \ell \rightarrow B_\ell).$$

In contrast to the case of justice we have to check here the enabledness of a component in front of every **while**-statement or an atomic statement (33). More precisely, we need the following notion.

DEFINITION 7.9   By an *immediate atomic statement* of a loop **while** B **do** R **od** we mean an atomic statement, an **await**-statement or a **while**-statement which is a subprogram of R but which lies outside any while-statements within R.

For example in the program

$$\textbf{while } B \textbf{ do while } C \textbf{ do } x: = 1 \textbf{ od od}$$

the assignment $x: = 1$ is an immediate atomic statement of the inner loop and **while** C **do** $x: = 1$ **od** is the only immediate atomic statement of the outer loop.

The program $T_{\text{wfair}}(S)$ is now obtained from S by

(1) prefixing S with an initialization part

$$\text{INIT} \equiv z_1: = ? \quad ; . . . ; z_n: = ?;$$
$$\text{end}_1: = ? ; . . . ; \text{end}_n: = ?;$$
$$pc_1: = 0 \quad ; . . . ; pc_n: = 0,$$

(2) replacing every substatement ℓ: **await** B_ℓ **then** R **end** of S_i by

$$pc_i := \ell; \text{ await } B_\ell \text{ then } R; pc_i := 0 \text{ end},$$

(3) inserting in every loop **while** B **do** R **od** of a component S_i
   a. in front of the first immediate atomic statement of R:

$$\text{TEST}_i \equiv \textbf{await } \bar{z} \geq 1 \textbf{ then } z_i := ?;$$
$$\textbf{for } j \neq i \textbf{ do}$$
$$[\text{enabled}_j \rightarrow z_j := z_j - 1 \ \Box \ \neg \text{ enabled} \rightarrow z_j := ?]$$
$$\textbf{od}$$
$$\textbf{end},$$

   b. in front of every other immediate atomic statement of R:

$$\text{RESET}_i \equiv \textbf{await true then}$$
$$\textbf{for } j \neq i \textbf{ do}$$
$$[\text{enabled}_j \rightarrow \text{skip} \ \Box \ \neg \text{ enabled}_j \rightarrow z_j := ?]$$
$$\textbf{od}$$
$$\textbf{end}$$

(4) suffixing every component S_i of S with $\text{END}_i \equiv \text{end}_i := \textbf{true}$.

We assume that none of the variables in the set $z = \{z_1, \ldots, z_n, \text{end}_1, \ldots, \text{end}_n, pc_1, \ldots, pc_n\}$ occurs in the original program S.

The following lemma whose proof can be found in (33) relates the programs S and $T_{\text{wfair}}(S)$:

LEMMA 7.11   For every GP program S and a state σ

$$\mathcal{M}_{\text{wfair}}[[S]](\sigma) - \{\triangle\} = \mathcal{M}[[T_{\text{wfair}}(S)]](\sigma) - \{\triangle\} \bmod Z. \quad \Box$$

COROLLARY 7.4   For all assertions p and q without free variables from the set Z

$$\models_{\text{wfair-}\triangle} \{p\}S\{q\} \text{ iff } \models_{\text{tot-}\triangle} \{p\}T_{\text{wfair}}(S)\{q\}. \quad \Box$$

Here the subscript "wfair-$\triangle$" refers to total correctness under the assumption of weak fairness but modulo deadlocks.

This corollary shows that in order to prove total correctness of a GP program under the assumption of weak fairness it is enough to

(1) Prove total correctness modulo deadlocks of T_{wfair} in the same way as in the case of justice.

(2) Prove deadlock freedom of S using Lemma 7.9 from Section 7.3.4.

Strong Fairness

Analogously to the case of nondeterministic programs there is another natural fairness assumption concerning GP programs—that of strong fairness. According to this hypothesis a component of a GP program will be activated if it is infinitely often enabled. This is a stronger requirement than that of weak fairness which guarantees activation of a component only if it is continuously enabled. More precisely we adopt the following definition.

DEFINITION 7.10   Let $S \equiv S_0; [S_1 \| . . . \| S_n]$ be a GP program and let ξ be a computation of S.

(1) We say that ξ is *strongly unfair* if it is infinite and some component is infinitely often enabled but is only finitely many times active in ξ.

(2) We say that ξ is *strongly fair* if it is not strongly unfair.

The strongly fair semantics $\mathcal{M}_{\text{sfair}}$ is defined in an analogous manner as the $\mathcal{M}_{\text{wfair}}$ semantics. To prove total correctness of GP programs under the strong fairness assumption we proceed through the same steps as in the case of weak fairness. The corresponding transformation $T_{\text{sfair}}(S)$ is defined by applying steps 1, 2, and 4 of $T_{\text{wfair}}(S)$ but with the following new step 3.

(3) Insert in front of every immediate atomic statement of every **while**-loop of S_i

$$\text{TEST}_i \equiv \textbf{await } \bar{z} \geq 1 \textbf{ then } z_i: = ?;$$
$$\textbf{for } j \neq i \textbf{ do}$$
$$[\text{enabled}_j \rightarrow z_j: = z_j - 1 \quad \square \; \neg\text{enabled} \rightarrow \text{skip}]$$
$$\textbf{od}$$
$$\textbf{end}.$$

As in the case of weak fairness the following lemma relates the program S and $T_{\text{sfair}}(S)$ (see (33)):

LEMMA 7.12   For every GP program S and a state σ

$$\mathcal{M}_{\text{sfair}}[[S]](\sigma) - \{\triangle\} = \mathcal{M}[[T_{\text{sfair}}(S)]](\sigma) - \{\triangle\} \bmod Z.$$

where Z is defined as in the previous subsection. $\square$

The remaining steps in proving total correctness under the strong fairness are exactly the same as in the previous section and are omitted.

FURTHER READING

The approach to program correctness studied in this paper has been applied to several other classes of concurrent programs. For the benefit of the reader we now provide a number of pointers to the literature.

The **await**-statement considered in Sections 7.3.4 and 7.3.5 is a very inefficient synchronization construct. A more efficient synchronization statement—the *conditional critical region* statement coupled with the use of resources, originally suggested in Hoare (25), is studied from the point of view of program correctness in Owicki and Gries (37). Clarke (12) discusses the issue of systematic construction of resource invariants for the programs written in the above language.

The correctness of programs written in CSP, *Communicating Sequential Processes*, a language introduced in Hoare (26), has been studied in several papers. A proof system motivated by the proof system from Section 7.3.4 for the GP programs is introduced in Levin and Gries (29). A proof system motivated by the proof system of (37) for the language using resources, is presented in Apt, Francez, and De Roever (7). Apt (5) provides a simpler and structured exposition of the latter system and lists other entries to the literature on the subject of correctness of CSP programs.

The correctness of programs written in DP, *Distributed Processes*, a language introduced in Brinch Hansen (11), has been studied in Gerth, De Roever, and Roncken (19).

The correctness of a fragment of ADA involving tasks has been most extensively studied in Gerth and De Roever (18). Alternative proof systems were presented in Barringer and Mearns (10) and Schlichting and Schneider (40). In the last paper also, proof rules for asynchronous message passing are introduced.

In Francez, Hailpern, and Taubenfeld (16) a communication abstraction mechanism called Script is introduced and proof rules for programs using it are presented. Finally, De Roever (39) provides an overview of the proof systems introduced in Apt, Francez, and De Roever (7), Gerth, De Roever, and Roncken (19) and Gerth and De Roever (18).

The issue of fairness has not been considered in any of the above papers. Correctness of CSP programs under the assumption of fairness is studied in Grumberg, Francez, and Katz (22).

Correctness proofs of nontrivial concurrent programs using the above methods have been given in various papers. We only mention here correctness proofs of a parallel garbage collector given in Gries (21), of a distributed algorithm maintaining message—routing tables in a network given in Lamport (28) of the "Dutch National Torus," a program written in DP, given in (20), and of a solution to the distributed termination problem of Francez (15) given in Apt (5).

Finally, the issue of soundness and completeness of the above systems has been studied—for the language studied in Section 7.3.4 in Apt (2), for the language using critical section statement in Owicki (34), for CSP in Apt (3) and for a fragment of ADA in Gerth (17).

ACKNOWLEDGMENTS

E. Börger talked me into writing this paper. The exposition owes much to the joint work done with E.-R. Olderog and profited from the discussions with A. Pnueli. N. Francez commented on the previous version.

REFERENCES

1. Apt, K.R., "Ten years of Hoare's logic, a survey—part I," *ACM TOPLAS* 3(4), pp. 431–483, 1981.
2. Apt, K.R., "Recursive assertions and parallel programs," *Acta Information* 15, pp. 219–232, 1984.
3. Apt, K.R., "Formal justification of a proof system for Communicating Sequential Processes," *Journal ACM* 30(1), pp. 197–216, 1983.
4. Apt, K.R., "Ten years of Hoare's logic, a survey—nondeterminism, part II," *Theoretical Computer Science* 28, pp. 83–109, 1984.
5. Apt, K.R., "Proving correctness of CSP programs—a tutorial," in: Proc. International Summer School "Control Flow and Data Flow: Concepts of Distributed Programming," Marktoberdorf, Springer-Verlag, to appear.
6. Apt, K.R., "Correctness proofs of distributed termination algorithms," *ACM TOPLAS* 8(3), pp. 388–405, 1986.
7. Apt, K.R., Francez, N. and de Roever, W.P., "A proof system for Communicating Sequential Processes," *ACM TOPLAS* 2(3), pp. 359–385, 1980.
8. Apt, K.R. and Olderog, E.-R., "Proof rules and transformations dealing with fairness," *Science of Computer Programming* 3, pp. 65–100, 1983.
9. Apt, K.R., Pnueli, A. and Stavi, J., "Fair termination revisited—with delay," *Theoretical Computer Science* 33, pp. 65–84, 1984.
10. Barringer, H. and Mearns, I., "Axioms and proof rules for Ada tasks," *IEEE Proc.* 129, Part E, 2, pp. 38–48, 1982.
11. Brinch, Hansen P., "Distributed process: a concurrent programming concept," *Communications ACM* 21(11), pp. 934–941, 1978.
12. Clarke, E.M., Jr., "Synthesis of resource invariants for concurrent programs," *ACM TOPLAS* 2(3), pp. 338–358, 1980.
13. Dijkstra, E.W., "Guarded commands, nondeterminacy and formal derivation of programs," *Communications ACM* 18(8), pp. 453–457, 1975.
14. Dijkstra, E.W., "A Discipline of Programming," Prentice Hall, Englewood Cliffs, 1976.
15. Francez, N., "Distributed termination," *ACM TOPLAS* 2(1), pp. 42–55, 1980.
16. Francez, N., Hailpern, B., and Taubenfeld, G., "Script: A communication mechanism and its verification," *Science of Computer Programming* 6(1), pp. 35–89, 1986.
17. Gerth, R., "A sound and complete Hoare axiomatization of the Ada-rendezvous," in: *Proc. ICALP* 82, Lecture Notes in Computer Science, vol. 140, Springer-Verlag, pp. 252–264, 1982.
18. Gerth, R., and De Roever, W.P., "A proof system for concurrent ADA programs," *Science of Computer Programming*, 4(2), pp. 159–205, 1984.
19. Gerth, R., De Roever, W.P., and Roncken, M., "Procedures and concurrency: a study in proof," in: Proc. 5th International Symposium on Programming, Lecture Notes in Computer Science, vol. 137, Springer-Verlag, pp. 132–163, 1982.
20. Gerth, R., De Roever, W.P., and Roncken, M., "A study in Distributed Systems and Dutch Patriotism," in: *Proc. 2nd Conference FCT and TCS*, Bangalore, 1982.
21. Gries, D., "An exercise in proving parallel programs correct," *Communications ACM* 20(12), pp. 921–930, 1977.

22. Grumberg, O., Francez, N. and Katz, S., "Fair termination of Communicating Process," in: *Proc. 3rd Annual Symposium on Principles of Distributed Computing*, Vancouver, Canada, pp. 254–265, 1984.

23. Hennessy, M.C.B. and Plotkin, G.D., "Abstraction for a simple programming language," in: *Proc. 8th Symposium on Mathematical Foundations of Computer Science, Lecture Notes in Computer Science*, vol. 74, Springer-Verlag, pp. 108–120, 1979.

24. Hoare, C.A.R., "An axiomatic basis for computer programming," *Communications ACM* 12(10), pp. 576–580, 583, 1969.

25. Hoare, C.A.R., "Towards a theory of parallel programming," in: *Operating Systems Techniques*, pp. 61–71, (C.A.R. Hoare, R.H. Ferrat, eds.), Academic Press, 1972.

26. Hoare, C.A.R., "Communicating Sequential Processes," *Communications ACM* 21(8), pp. 666–677, 1978.

27. Lamport, L., "Proving the correctness of multiprocessor programs," *IEEE Transactions on Software Engineering*, vol. SE-3(2), pp. 125–143, 1977.

28. Lamport, L., "An assertional correctness proof of a distributed algorithm," *Science of Computer Programming* 2(3), pp. 175–206, 1982.

29. Levin, G. and Gries, D., "A proof technique for Communicating Sequential Processes," *Acta Informatica* 15(3), pp. 281–302, 1981.

30. Manna, Z. and Pnueli, A., "Verification of concurrent programs: the temporal framework," in: *The Correctness Problem in Computer Science*, pp. 215–273, (R.S. Boyer and J.S. Moore, eds.), Academic Press, 1982.

31. Manna, Z. and Pnueli, A., "Verification of concurrent programs: temporal proof principles," in: *Proc. Workshop on Logic of Programs, Lecture Notes in Computer Science*, vol. 131, Springer-Verlag, pp. 200–252, 1982.

32. Manna, Z. and Pnueli, A., "Proving precedence properties: temporal way," in: *Proc. ICALP '83, Lecture Notes in Computer Science*, vol. 154, Springer-Verlag, pp. 491–512, 1983.

33. Olderog, E.-R. and Apt, K.R., "Fairness in parallel programs: the transformational approach," *Institut für Inform. und Prakt. Math.*, Christian-Albrechts-Universität Kiel, Tech. Report 8402, 1984.

34. Owicki, S., "Axiomatic proof techniques for parallel programs," Computer Science Dept., Cornell University, PhD thesis, 1975.

35. Owicki, S., "A consistent and complete deductive system for verification of parallel programs," in: *Proc. 8th Annual Symposium on Theory of Computing*, pp. 73–86, 1976.

36. Owicki, S. and Gries, D., "An axiomatic proof technique for parallel programs I," *Acta Informatica* 6, pp. 319–340, 1976.

37. Owicki, S. and Gries, D., "Verifying properties of parallel programs: an axiomatic approach," *Communications ACM* 19(5), pp. 279–285, 1976.

38. Pnueli, A., "The temporal logic of programs," in: *Proc. 18th Annual Symposium on Foundations of Computer Science*, pp. 46–57, 1977.

39. De Roever, W.P., "The cooperation test: a syntax directed verification method," in: *Proc. Advanced Course on Logics and Models for Verification and Specification of Concurrent Systems*, La Colle-sur-Loup, Springer-Verlag, 1985.

40. Schlichting, R.D. and Schneider, F.B., "Using message passing for distributed programming: proof rules and disciplines," *ACM TOPLAS* 6(3), pp. 402–431, 1984.

Chapter 8

Distributed Network Algorithms*

ELI SHAMIR[†]

8.1 INTRODUCTION AND SCOPE

Distributed computing takes place on distributed multiprocessor systems. One way to classify such systems is by the strength of coupling: In loosely coupled networks, the processors do not share memory, do not share a clock and the only communication is along links in an asynchronous mode. Highly coupled systems are synchronized, have swift communication mechanisms, even via shared memory. If the shared memory is of random access type, then perhaps a border is crossed into the realm of parallel random access machines, which are usually considered outside the scope of distributed systems.

Another way to classify distributed systems and computing is by the strength of cooperation. Minimal cooperation takes the form of operating system services which provide monitoring required to avoid collisions, deadlocks, and starvations. More positive cooperation can set as a goal the rational utilization of common resources. A high degree of cooperation means running joint tasks that are beyond the power of one processor. Again, at this extreme end, we cross into the domain of parallel computation.

Distributed computing is a wide and rapidly growing field. Under natural interpretation, it encompasses topics of concurrency, synchronization, communication design and protocols for local area networks and extended networks, programming languages, and systems like CSP (Communicating Sequential Processes), heavy semantic issues such as verification, program specification and

* Supported in part by the U.S.-ISRAEL Binational Science Foundation Grant 3432/83.
† Leibniz Center for Research in Computer Science, Institute of Mathematics and Computer Science, Hebrew University, Jerusalem.

development, knowledge dissemination in systems, reliability, and fault tolerance. Some of these topics are dealt with in other chapters of this volume.

We delineate the scope of distributed network algorithms studied in this chapter. A network is a system of processor nodes and communication links. Nodes and links can be labelled or unlabelled. The various models and assumptions, which constitute the rules of the game for distributed network algorithm are outlined in Section 8.2. From a very general point of view, a distributed algorithm is designed to accomplish a task that depends on inputs distributed at n various nodes. Succinctly, one can say a global function is computed from a diffused, distributed data. However, the emphasis is definitely not on the difficulty of the functional relation once all the relevant input data is assembled, but on the coordination, communication, judgment, and reasoning involved in assembling the relevant input or partial results from the various nodes to the right places at the right times where computation can be made and output should emerge. Therefore, network algorithms are often useful subroutines of other distributed algorithms (and of each other). The typical tasks, which are dealt with in network algorithms, involve various structure informations about the network. The problems of traversal, input collection, and leader election play a key role. They come up naturally, even if one chooses to carry parts of the computations in a centralized fashion, using a chosen leader to do the task. Algorithms are also developed for some other tasks of general use, like load-sharing, routing, matching, disjoint paths, and selection by rank.

At this point, it is also a good idea to read the conclusion section of this chapter where the main themes which recur in the presentation are summarized.

Another issue of fundamental importance in distributed computing is reliability and fault tolerance, under random faults or possibly malicious coordinated action of bad processors and bad links (colloquially known as Byzantine Generals). The basic coordination, agreement, and input-collection must be reconsidered from this point of view, not only because, in practice, malfunction and faults arise, but also because it reveals more deeply how knowledge spreads in distributed systems. We have to be content in giving reference to a few fundamental articles on these topics.

8.2 MODELS OF DISTRIBUTED SYSTEMS, MODES OF COMPUTING, AND COSTS

In constructing models we take some rules and constraints involved in the notions of distributed system, come up with various frameworks and then endeavor to design and analyze algorithms in these frameworks. Centralized sequential systems were also studied on such a basis, and even after decades of systematic activity, there are still gaps between algorithms and actual computing. The gaps are currently much wider for distributed systems, because of the novelty and inherent complexity of the issues. Still, the profound importance of formulating models and carrying out a theoretic study of algorithms, in parallel with implementation activity, is well established and amply justified.

A distributed system consists of a set of processors **P**, individual processes are situated at nodes of a graph, and some pairs of nodes are connected by *links*. A link is a triplet (port of P, communication channel, port of Q). The graph spanned by the nodes and links (we also use vertices and edges) is also referred to as the *topology* of the network. Unless otherwise specified, the node-processors are not restricted in their computing power or storage.

The following assumptions (with possible variations listed below) sound like "firmware constraints," but the dividing line between them and "software constraint" is vague:

1. *Labels:* Nodes are labelled by distinct labels (identifier, id), but we also consider anonymous networks.

2. *Port direction:* Port serves for input and output to a node. Communication links are bidirectional (separating input from output and unidirectional links is possible).

3. *Port id:* Within each node, each port has a unique port id. Messages arriving through that part are stamped by the port id. But processors do not know the id of the other end of the links.

4. *Sequencing:* Messages arrive at a node one at a time. In synchronous computation, this assumption may be changed.

5. *Finite delay:* The links are reliable, each message sent arrives intact after a finite but *unpredictable* delay.

6. *Fifo (First in first out):* Messages sent over a link in a certain direction arrive at the target node in the order sent.

7. *Topology knowledge:* In each case, we specify what is known to each processor—nothing, or the type of the network, or its size (number of nodes) etc.

We proceed to describe modes of algorithms:

1. *State-machines:* An algorithm **A** specifies the behavior of each processor P, modeled as a state machine. A state transition occurs only when P receives a message. The new state and message sent out (what and where to) is a function of the state and the message received.

2. *Break-in (wake up pattern):* A node starts executing **A** in an initial state. Some arbitrary nonempty set of nodes *initiate* **A** (wake up and start without receiving a message—spontaneous wake up).

3. *Termination:* Termination for a node occurs when a node reaches a terminal state, outputs a value and *halts*. Standard global termination occurs when all processors are in their terminal states.

4. *Task computations:* General tasks are specified by an I/O relation. An input [resp. output] configuration for a distributed system is a map

$$\alpha : \mathbf{P} \Rightarrow IN \quad [resp. \ \omega : \mathbf{P} \Rightarrow OUT]$$

where *IN* and *OUT* are prescribed domains of values. An algorithm **A** realizes (or is correct for) a given I/O relation R if any *run* of **A**, *starting* with input configuration α, *terminates* with output configuration ω, and $(\alpha, \omega) \in R$.

We make a few comments about distributed algorithm and task computations:

1. **Nondeterminism:** A distributed Algorithm **A** is *non-deterministic*, because of arbitrary break-in patterns and delays in message arrival.

2. **Termination** (versus **Eventual Termination**): In standard termination all processors know that the system terminated. A relaxed concept is *eventual termination*: Some processors did not reach their terminal state, but in fact, looking from outside, one can argue that a specific state configuration (representing a correct output) is reached and no further messages will arrive at any P (without some P knowing it). We shall see examples of eventual termination. Many studies were done on *distributed termination*, which usually signifies an appended procedure that converts an eventual termination into standard termination. Several network algorithms and ideas arise in connection with distributed termination (e.g., a *leader* can affect distributed termination).

3. **Forever programs:** Operating system algorithms, which monitor systems that have to live and function forever, are not well captured by specifying I/O relations.

4. **Partial correctness:** This refers to a well-known distinction, where termination is not promised, but if it occurs then $(\alpha, \omega) \in R$.

5. **Relaxed correctness:** Given R, another relation R' is defined and (α, ω) is required to be in R'. Usually R' extends R hence relaxation. In particular for a distributed algorithm computing a function f, the normal mode requires that $\omega = (f(\alpha), \ldots , f(\alpha))$. A relaxed notion requires that $f(\alpha)$ will appear at some nodes, and the other nodes output a ''don't care'' value X. We suggest ''spot-correctness'' as an appropriate name.

After correctness, one is most interested in complexity measures, and the costs of the computation.

8.2.1 Primary Cost: Number of Messages

There is a real danger of flooding a network with messages. Thus, the primary cost available in general for a distributed algorithm **A** is the number of messages or number of message-bits which are sent over the links during runs of **A**. Usually one takes the worst case, i.e., maximum with respect to all inputs and all possible runs of the (nondeterminatic) algorithm **A**. If there is an upper bound on message arrival time and break-in time of processors, then the worst case elapsed *time* from the first start to termination makes sense as another (secondary) cost (for synchronous systems, see below).

8.2.2 The Synchronous Mode

This is the crucial shibboleth of distributed algorithms, separating the tame from the shrew. It does not affect the computing power, but makes a big difference in cost, efficiency, design, and verification convenience. In the synchronous mode, there is a global clock, which marks cycles to all the processors that run their programs in parallel, i.e., at each cycle beat, each processor decides according to its state, on which links to send messages and what messages to send. Each node then receives any message sent to it and uses the received messages and its state to decide on its next state. Some variations are possible, e.g., sending and receiving one message at a cycle.

If we assume also simultaneous start (break-in) by all processors, then clearly the algorithm becomes deterministic—this model is called *SYN-SYM*. Without simultaneous start—just *SYN*, and asynchronous is *ASYN*. For a *SYN-SYM* algorithm **A**, the number of cycles from start to termination is an important cost measure. Again, the worst case over all inputs is understood, unless otherwise stated.

8.2.3 Mutual Simulation of *SYN* and *ASYN*

Clearly a synchronized system can simulate any run of an asynchronized one (and so compute its I/O relation). Conversely an asynchronous network can simulate a synchronous algorithm, e.g., by keeping and comparing local clocks. Each node has a local clock counting mod 3. It proceeds to the next step only if its clock differs from all the neighboring clocks by ≤ 1 up or down. This is verified by sending and receiving synchronization messages (for each cycle). This clearly guarantees that the execution is done in unison, but the cost in terms of messages and cycles may be high.

8.2.4   Uniformity of Programs

When the processors are labelled, the execution of the program at each P depends on $id(P)$. A standard assumption for distributed algorithm **A** is that **A** depends uniformly on $id(P)$. One way to understand this (which we follow) is to consider the label as an input, otherwise the programs are identical at all the nodes. Other ways are possible, and there are further constraints. One may require that labels enter only in commands which compare their order (see Sec. 8.3.4.3).

8.2.5   Anonymous Networks

There are no labels, and the programs at each node are indistinguishable. In this case symmetry of the highest degree is achieved. Its detection and breaking is a key issue. We shall see also randomized procedure to break symmetry (Sec. 8.5.4).

Whenever programs are written for a family of networks and some parameter (e.g., network size) is used, we strive to have programs, say $\mathbf{A}(n)$, uniform in the parameter n, in a sense (adopted from parallel circuits) that a Turing machine with very small memory can output the description of $\mathbf{A}(n)$ given n as an input.

8.2.6   Upper and Lower Bounds

Upper bounds for tasks are established by giving a correct algorithm of a desired model which computes the task. Lower bound on costs of a problem are obtained by a logical mathematical analysis of the model constraints using information theoretic tools, adversary arguments and other means. Algorithms become more specialized and structured as we go from

$$ASYN \quad \text{to} \quad SYN \quad \text{to} \quad SYN\text{-}SYM$$

So the message cost of an algorithm does not decrease as we move to a more structured model, but we strive to improve the algorithm and get better, more economic upper bounds. As for lower bound, an intuitive rule is that if we prove a lower bound for a model **M** that is relatively more deterministic than **M'** then the lower bound holds for **M'**. In some cases **M** is easier to study (Sec. 8.4.2). But if $\mathbf{M'} = ASYN$, $\mathbf{M} = SYN$ we have a completely different ball game, and getting precise lower bounds is quite difficult.

8.3   DISTRIBUTED COMPUTING ON A RING

In practice and in theory the ring topology has a unique attraction. Its simple, perfectly uniform structure and known symmetries make it ideal for complete analysis. Yet most of the fundamental issues in distributed computing do emerge but are relatively easy to understand and to settle. Our long discussion here reflects the amount of research devoted to distributed rings.

8.3.1 Anonymous Rings—Basic Results

The system consists of n processors arranged on a bidirectional ring. Every processor P is linked to its direct neighbors called $left(P)$ and $right(P)$, by distinguished ports. The ring is *oriented* if for every P, $left(right(P)) = P$. For anonymous rings, the processors and their programs carry no labels, they are indistinguishable, names and labels are used only for reference in discussing them. We study tasks and functions with Boolean or numerical domains, first for *ASYN*, then for the *SYN* model with some variations, but first some general results about computability.

THEOREM 8.1

1. A numerical **SUM** algorithm **A** cannot be correct for rings of size n, n', $n \neq n'$.
2. A Boolean **XOR** algorithm cannot be correct for even and odd size rings.
3. If f is non-constant, no **A** works correctly for f on infinitely many ring sizes.

Proof It is assumed processors receive no knowledge of the ring size. For (1), consider an all one input configuration, $\alpha(\cdot) \equiv 1$. Every procesor on both-sized rings receives the same sequence of messages, so the same output should emerge. The proof of (2) is similar, (3) is left to the reader.

From now on we assume that the size parameter n (hence the entire topology) is known to each processor. It is also convenient to consider the local orientation (of $left(P)$ and $right(P)$) as part of the input to P, specified in messages by one bit, say 0 for left 1 for right.

Any map $\sigma : \mathbf{P} \Rightarrow \mathbf{P}$ induces a map on ring functions f by $\sigma f(P) = f(\sigma P)$. We are especially interested in symmetry maps.

THEOREM 8.2 A necessary and sufficient condition for a relation (task) R to be computable on a ring of size n is the invariance under each symmetry σ, i.e.,

$$(\alpha, \omega) \in R \Rightarrow (\sigma\alpha, \sigma\omega) \in R \tag{*}$$

The symmetries of odd size rings and of even rings of a fixed orientation are the cyclic shifts. For unoriented even size ring, they are the cyclic shifts and the reflections (elements of the dyadic group).

Proof The necessity of the condition (*) is clear, the sufficiency follows from the input collection algorithm below.

Example—Orienting a Ring

The task of orienting a ring means computing, upon no input except for the local orientation of each P, an output configuration of zeros and ones such that if processors which output zero reverse their port names then the ring is (consistently) oriented. There is no orientation algorithm for even-size rings because there are input configurations that are symmetric under (mirror) reflection, e.g., the two half-rings oriented in the opposite way. Odd rings can be oriented by majority (input collection algorithm below).

In a pioneering work, Angluin shows impossibility of choosing a leader in anonymous networks with symmetries by the same argument: If P is chosen by an algorithm **A**, then σP must also be chosen, the contention cannot be resolved because of symmetry.

Collecting the entire input configuration (including local orientation) at any node P, represented as a string of n symbols where P's input serves as a point of reference, is clearly the most general task.

ASYN Input Collection Algorithm

Each P *starts* by sending a message $(\alpha(P), b(P))$ to both neighbors. Here $\alpha(\cdot)$ is the input, $b(\cdot)$ is an orientation *bit*, 0 to *left*(P), 1 to *right*(P). Next, P receives and forwards $\dfrac{n}{2} - 1$ messages from *left*(P) to *right*(P), and $\dfrac{n}{2} - 1$ messages from *right*(P) to *left*(P), then P *halts*. Each P knows n, so by simple counting it can construct from the sequence of messages received a string representing correctly the entire input configuration. (This may fail for networks with a more complex topology.)

Now each P can locally compute any task. If that task is computable, i.e., invariant under the symmetries, then the output is consistent. The cost of the input collection is $n(n - 1)$ messages (also for even n, under a minor modification) of the form $(\alpha(\cdot), b(\cdot))$.

Clearly, the input collection can also run on unidirectional-oriented rings.

THEOREM 8.3 *ASYN* **A** computing the Boolean **AND** costs $\Omega(n^2)$ messages.

Proof To estimate the worst case cost of an algorithm **A**, we imagine an adversary scheduler that manipulates the delays of messages to make life hard for **A**. The tactic of the adversary is to achieve a maximum symmetry. It schedules all messages at discrete cycle times, and all messages issued in one cycle arrive in the next cycle. Now compare the computations of **A**, which are now synchronized, on two input configuration: α is all one, α' is also all one except for $\alpha'(1)$. Consider the computation of **A**, which is scheduled in cycles as described, on a symmetric, all-one input α. If, at some cycle, some node P did not receive a message, then no node received a message and the computation halts. So if T is the termination cycle, the computation costs $T \cdot (n-1)$ messages.

Now consider **A** on input α' which is the same as α (all-one) except at one node, say $P = 1$, where $\alpha(1)$ is zero. The node $Q = \dfrac{n+1}{2}$, opposite to P on the ring, must receive the same sequence of messages in both computations for the first $\dfrac{n}{2}$ cycles until a message from node 1 can arrive. But

$$\mathbf{AND}(\alpha) = 1, \quad \mathbf{AND}(\alpha') = 0 \quad \text{so } T \geq \frac{n}{2}, \quad \text{and the cost } T \cdot (n-1) \geq \Omega(n^2).$$

Clearly, the same lower bound is valid for the **OR** function, which computes the maximum of n Boolean inputs.

COROLLARY 8.1   When the inputs are not necessarily distinct, **MAX** may cost $\Omega(n^2)$ messages for *ASYN* **A**. The **MAX** of distinct inputs is discussed in the next section.

Functions with linear or less than quadratic cost can be described, but they are rare. Almost all functions have quadratic complexity.

THEOREM 8.4   On *ASYN* ring, the probability that a random Boolean function of n variables costs less than $\dfrac{n^2}{4}$ messages is less than $2^{-2^{n/2}}$.

Proof   Let α be the all-one input, β an input with a block of $\dfrac{n}{2}$ contiguous ones. If $f(\alpha) \neq f(\beta)$, the argument of Theorem 2.1.6 shows that the cost of any **A** on α or β is at least $\dfrac{n^2}{4}$. Thus, if the cost is less than $\dfrac{n^2}{4}$, $f(\alpha) = f(\beta)$. There are at least $2^{\frac{n}{2}}$ strings β, so the probability that a random f satisfies $f(\alpha) = f(\beta)$ is less than $2^{-2^{n/2}}$. Being shift-invariant has probability $\geq 2^{-n}$. So a fraction of at most $2^{-(2^{n/2}-n)}$ of the computable functions on a ring can be computed in less than $\dfrac{n^2}{4}$ messages.

Distributed computing on a ring can be made messagewise more efficient in case (i) distinct input values around the ring or (ii) a synchronized ring. We shall do both cases. The contention among processors for leadership plays a key role in both cases.

8.3.2 Leader Election—Distinct Labels

Assume there is leader in the ring. Then the input collection is facilitated. Leader initiates a message in one direction. Each node P that receives this message appends its own $(\alpha(P), b(P))$ [the orientation bit $b(\cdot)$ is relative to the message direction] and forwards the augmented message from one side to the other side. When the leader receives his message back, it can figure out the entire input configuration. It computes the output (the required task) and propagates it around. This costs $O(n)$ messages, but the messages are strings of size $O(n)$. [Indeed, using information-theoretic arguments lower bound $\Omega(n^2)$ on bit messages was established.]

A situation where a leader is efficiently elected is described in the following theorem.

THEOREM 8.5 Assume the processors around the *ASYN* ring of size n have distinct labels, or equivalently they obtain distinct input values, taken from an ordered domain. Then the processor holding the maximum value is elected as a leader by a distributed algorithm using $O(n \cdot \log n)$ messages. This holds also for unidirectional ring. Moreover, $\Omega(n \cdot \log n)$ messages is the *ASYN* lower bound for the task of electing a ring leader.

Proof The algorithm **A** is actually a competition protocol of $O(\log n)$ rounds. Each winner P at round k (if $k = 0$, every P is a winner) enters round $k + 1$. In this round, P sends its value to both directions. Then each winner Q compares its value with the values received from the nearest winners at its left side and right side. If Q holds a local maximum of the three distinct values, it *wins*. Else, Q becomes a loser and drops out of the competition, but as a good sport it keeps forwarding messages in the ensuing rounds.

Claim In any arrangement of r distinct values around a ring, the number of local maxima is at most $\dfrac{r}{2}$.

Thus, the number of rounds until a single winner remains is $\leq \log_2 n$. At each round each P (whether a winner or loser) sends out (and receives) two messages. Hence, the message complexity of **A** is bounded by $2n \cdot \log_2 n$.

The description of **A** was worded as if there is a global separation between rounds. Surely, this global separation is not temporal—since we did not assume synchronization—but logical. During a round each P sends a pair and receives a pair of messages. Since messages arrive in the order sent, the separation into rounds is sharply defined at each P and this is logically sufficient for the correctness and the complexity analysis of **A**. For a unidirectional ring, one more trick is needed. Each comparison of values of three neighboring competitors to determine a local maximum is done by proxy, at a place to which the three has access. At the start of a given round, the winners (like P, Q, R depicted in Figure 8.1) hold distinct winning values $m(\cdot)$. Here $m(P)$ is not $val(P)$ but $val(S)$ for some S to the left of P. During a round, P receiving from Q (at his left) (i) the value $m(Q)$, (ii) the value $\max(m(Q), m(R))$ and compares them with $m(P)$. It can now determine whether $m(Q)$ is a local maximum of the three, in which case P (not Q) is the winner and updates its value to $m(Q)$, otherwise P is a loser. Clearly the analysis for correctness and message complexity up to the point where one winner remains with $m(P) = \max_{Q} val(Q)$ is the same as for the bidirectional ring. One more pass around the ring locates the ''true'' winner S whose input value is the maximum.

Figure 8.1 Unidirectional election.

$$\searrow \quad R \quad \nearrow \max(\,,\,) \quad \searrow \quad Q \quad \nearrow \max(m(Q), m(R)) \quad \searrow \quad P \quad \nearrow$$
$$\nearrow \quad \searrow \quad m(R) \quad \nearrow \quad \searrow \quad m(Q) \quad \nearrow \quad \searrow$$

A lower bound $\Omega(n \cdot \log n)$ for leader election in *ASYN* labelled ring with distinct labels is known. Related results for the *SYN* model are discussed below.

8.3.3 Synchronized Ring Algorithms

The computable tasks remain the same for *SYN* rings, but message complexity decreases. The quadratic lower bound for *ASYN* rings depends strongly on standard termination—all processors reach the terminating state. Consider, however, the following algorithm for computing **AND**. Each P with input 0 sends a message in both directions and enters state 0 (terminating). Each P with input 1 is initially at state 1, and if it receives a message, it forwards it and enters state 0. Eventually, either each P is in state 0, in case **AND** = 0, or each P remain in state 1, in case **AND** = 1, i.e., an all-1 input configuration. Thus, if eventual termination is allowed, this **AND** algorithm requires $O(n)$ messages. The catch is that a processor in state 1 does not know *when* the computation is over. But in the *SYN-SYM* model, P simply counts $\left\lfloor \dfrac{n}{2} \right\rfloor$ cycles from the start, if by that time it did not receive a message it deduced correctly that **AND** = 1. In fact, an upper bound on message delays and break in delays suffices for P to compute a timeout interval I. Having accepted no message during I, P deduced a symmetric ring configuration in which no message is ever initiated.

In fact, all of the *SYN-SYM* algorithms described in this section can be adopted to *ASYN* with eventual termination, using the same *number* of messages (but not number of bits, this may have to be $\Omega(n^2)$).

The key algorithm is input collection. Now for the *SYN-SYM* model, instead of assembling the input at each P, the plan is to assemble it at a leader—or several leaders, in case of ties. Thus input collection is intertwined with the competition to elect a leader as two co-routines. The algorithm $\mathbf{C}$ proceeds in rounds. Any winning processor P at round k manages to assemble a string $w(P)$ (relative to P) encoding the input configuration along an arc which P controls. The strings $w(P)$ serve as labels for the competition in round $(k+1)$. These labels need not be distinct. The extreme cases when the competition at a round is globally tied correspond to symmetries in input configurations (periodic repetitions of β or β^R segments). The timeout principle is employed to break the symmetry, deduce the form of the configuration and proceed.

8.3.3.1 The Input Collection Algorithm C

This algorithm runs $O(\log n)$ rounds. Each round costs $O(n)$ messages. At a start of round k each winner P holds as a value a string $w(P)$. This w encodes the input configuration (including orientations of processors) along an arc $\alpha(P)$ which P controls and P's location is marked in w. The arc-collection $\{\alpha(P)|P$ *winner*$\}$ forms a partition of the ring. At $k = 1$ each P is a winner, $\alpha(P) = \{P\}$.

If a single winner P controls the whole ring, it has encoded the entire ring configuration, and (if necessary) it can be circulated around the ring.

After an intermediate round $k - 1$, several processors together control the ring. These are the winners entering round k. Losers will simply forward messages. For a winner P a round consists of several *phases*:

1. It sends/receives strings to/from the closest winners on both sides.

2. It compares its own string $w(P)$ with the two received from neighbors, using lexicographic order on strings. P is a *local maximum* (*LM*) if $w(P)$ is not smaller than the other two, and strictly larger than one of them. [Notice: at most 2/3 of values situated around a ring can be *LM*.]

3. [If no P is *LM*, see (1') below.] If P is *LM*, it sends a message in both directions to establish control over an extended arc. A P that is not *LM* will forward the first message M it receives—it will belong to the extended arc to be controlled by M's initiator. A P which receives a second message M', or the first message M in case P is a *LM*, is the end point of the extended arc α of M's initiator.

4. The processors P within an extended arc annexed by Q which is *LM*, forward their values $w(P)$ to Q as follows: A null message is initiated at both ends of $\alpha(Q)$, and sent traveling toward Q, when this message passes P, it concatenates an encoding of $w(P)$ to the traveling message. The encoding is

$w(P)$ itself if P forwards the message from its left to its right, and $w(P)^R$ (reversed) in the other case.

If some LM is found in phase (2) of a round, then each P receives a message during phase (3). The LM processors (at most two-thirds of the winners in round k) proceed as winners to round $(k+1)$. The others become losers.

If no LM was found in phase (2), then nobody initiated, nobody received a message in phase (3). In this case, after a timeout of $\dfrac{n}{2}$ cycles, all processors start phase (1') below. Note that now strings compared in phase (2) result in a tie, hence all the input-segments they encode must be w or w^R for some fixed w. Phases (1')–(4') constitute another competition, based on comparing local orientations. For two neighboring participants, we say that P points at Q if Q is the first contender to the right of P. Now P is a LM if it is pointed by both neighboring contenders. At most, one half of the contenders around the ring are LM.

PHASE (1'): Each P sends a message to its right direction.

PHASE (2'): P is LM if it receives two messages.

PHASE (3') and (4') are the same as (3) and (4) above.

If again no LM is found in PHASE (2') then it is easy to see that the local orientation among contenders around the ring has a period of 1 or 2, the input configuration must have been w^k or $(ww^R)^k$ for a suitable w. Both the period and w are available to the processors, which proceed to distribute them in the arc they control.

This concludes the description of the algorithm $\mathbf{C}$, which clearly costs $O(log\ n)$ rounds, each round $O(n)$ cycles, $O(n)$ messages.

8.3.3.2 *Remark: Orientation*

If the ring is consistently oriented, algorithm $\mathbf{C}$ can be simplified, and it can be made to use unidirectional messages only. As presented here, it collects local orientation bits and these can be used to compute global orientation by majority vote. In fact, the orientation competition phases of $\mathbf{C}$ suffice for that.

8.3.3.3 *Break-in Synchronization*

The algorithm $\mathbf{C}$ is of *SYN-SYM* type. One can modify it to the *SYN* model, but a more satisfying alternative is to prepene it (or any other *SYN-SYM* algorithm) by a specially designed algorithm $\mathbf{S} \in SYN$, which will do the task of break-in synchronization in $O(n \log n)$ messages. $\mathbf{S}$ will awake processors and synchronize their local clocks counts to the count of the earliest starting processor(s) (which awoke spontaneously). As the reader expects, **S** runs a competition based on the number of cycles lapsed from break-in, i.e. on the clock value *count(P)*. At most, two-thirds of the winning processors survive after each round, and their count is adopted on the arcs they control. If a single processor survives, or if a

```
    {Initially all processors have count = -1
    and status = loser}
if wakes up spontaneously
    then begin
    count: = 0;
    status: = winner;
    message_count: = 0;
    send count to left (P) and to right (P)
    end;
repeat forever
    begin
    count: = count + 1:
    if count = 2kn (for some k>0).
        then if no message was received in last 2n cycles
            then halt
    else
        if status = winner
            then send count to left (P) and to right (P);
    if count ≠ 2kn
        then if received message M
            then if status = loser
                then begin
                forward M + 1;
                count: = max(M + 1, count)
                end
    else {status = winners}
            then begin
            message-count: = message-count + 1;
            count: = max(M + 1, count);
            if message-count = 2
                then if not local maximum
                    then status: = loser
                    else message-count: = 0
                end
end
```

Figure 8.2   Break-in Synchronization Algorithm **S**.

round is everywhere tied, then all processors are in fact synchronized. Some additional features were introduced in **S**, which is formally described in Figure 8.2: When P forwards a time-count M it received in the previous cycle, it increases it to $M + 1$ (since unfortunately time advances inexorably). Winners start round k only at count $2kn$. This guarantees a clear separation between rounds, since each message reaches destination in less than n cycles and since

$$|count(P) - count(Q)| \leq \frac{n}{2}$$

for every P, Q.

REMARK 8.1 *Bit complexity.* For *SYN* algorithms, it is always possible to encode message values (up to some known bound) by *bit messages plus delay*, e.g., value k is encoded by a bit in sub-cycle k. This may affect time complexity by a sizeable factor. In some cases, a clever encoding may result in small change (say a constant factor in message and time complexity). This is true for the break-in synchronization algorithm (left to the reader to verify). The tradeoff between messages (size or even number) and time in the *SYN* model make the proofs of lower bounds much harder, especially for labelled rings.

8.3.4 Synchronized Rings—Lower Bounds

Lower-bound proofs are quite subtle for *SYN* rings, as we just observed. We have seen $\Omega(n^2)$ messages lower-bounds for *ASYN*, we aim at $\Omega(n \cdot \log n)$ bounds for *SYN-SYM* algorithms. These rely on combinatorial results about iterated string homomorphism which we state without proofs. The framework for the lower-bound arguments consists of:

1. An algorithm **A** computing a function (or a task) f;
2. Two input configurations of length n, I_1, I_2, $1 = f(I_1) \neq f(I_2) = 0$;
3. R_1, R_2, the runs of **A** on I_1, I_2, respectively. Cycle k is active if either R_1 or R_2 send message on cycle k.

Observation: The state of processor P after r active cycles depends only on the $(2r + 1)$ long input segment centered at P (that is, the r-neighborhood of P).

We need the following combinatorial property:

Fooling pair: I_1, I_2 is *a fooling pair* for f of size n (with parameters $\alpha, \beta > 0$) if:

(**F**). For every string w, $|w| \leq \alpha n$ if w occurs in I_1 or I_2, then w occurs in each of I_1 and I_2, at least $\frac{\beta n}{|w|}$ times.

THEOREM 8.6   If f has a fooling pair then an algorithm **A** computing f runs $T \geq \dfrac{\alpha n}{2}$ active cycles and uses $M \geq \dfrac{1}{2}\beta n L(\alpha \cdot n)$ messages, where $L(m) = \left[\displaystyle\sum_{1}^{m} \frac{1}{k}\right] = (\approx \log m)$.

Proof   If $T < \dfrac{\alpha n}{2}$ and, say, processor P outputs 1 on cycle T in the run R_1 on I_1, then $(2T+1) \leq \alpha n$ and the $(2T+1)$ input segment centered at P occurs also in I_2, centered around Q. So Q must 1 in the run R_2 on I_2, but $f(I_2) \neq 1$, a contradiction. Now let $r < \alpha \dfrac{n}{2}$. In R_1 or R_2, a processor P sends a message in round r. The $2r+1$-input segment centered at P occurs $\beta r/(2r+1)$ times in I_1 and I_2, so that many processors must send a message on round r in R_1 and R_2. The total number of messages is at least:

$$\sum_{k=0}^{(T-1)} \frac{\beta \cdot n}{(2r+1)} \geq \frac{\beta n}{2} \sum_{0}^{2T} \frac{1}{k} = \frac{\beta n}{2} L(\alpha n).$$

REMARK 8.2   The formulation of the fooling pair assumption is actually too strong. One can either relax it and derive the same lower bound, or leave it and strengthen the conclusion by using a relaxed notion of correctness, as mentioned in Section 8.1.

The construction of fooling pairs is based on iterated string homomorphism, i.e., maps $h : \Sigma \Rightarrow \Sigma^*$ that are extended to $h : \Sigma^* \Rightarrow \Sigma^*$ by $h(xa) = h(x) \cdot h(a)$. Say $\Sigma = \{0, 1\}$ and assume

Uniformity: $|h(o)| = |h(o)| = d$. Then

$$(z_k, y_k) = (h^k(0), h^k(1))$$

will be a fooling pair for f with suitable parameters provided $f(x_k) \neq f(y_k)$ and provided every word of length 2 occurs in both in $h^c(o)$ and $H^c(1)$, for some c.

This construction covers a sparse set of n-values, $n = d^k$. It is possible to prove that even without uniformity, iterations of a mixing homomorphism applied to fixed arguments can have a dense set of lengths and exhibit the required occurrence property needed for fooling.

THEOREM 8.7   *SYN* algorithms for

    (i)   XOR   (iii) BREAK-IN SYNCHRONIZATION
    (ii) ORIENTATION   (iv) RANDOM BOOLEAN FUNCTION

require $\Omega(n \log n)$ messages.

Proof sketch   The same homomorphism $h(0) = 011$, $h(1) = 100$ is used to construct fooling pair for all cases. Case (i) is very easy to verify. For (ii), we have to interpret 0 and 1 in the input configuration as opposite orientations.

For (iii) let 0 [resp. 1] in place i of the input configuration signify that P_i breaks-in one after [resp. before] P_{i-1}. The details of showing that a pair is fooling (should give distinct outputs by the task definition) are left as an exercise to the reader. In case (iv) one shows by counting that the probability is small that a random function f satisfies $f(x_k) = f(y_k)$ for all fooling pair candidates (x_k, y_k).

REMARK 8.3   The lower bound argument based on fooling pairs can be pushed to labelled ring *SYN* algorithms, provided the labels effect the moves only via label comparisons, i.e. the order relation between them. The fooling pair requirement will be that order-equivalent segments of the input configurations will recur many times.

8.4   COMPLETE NETWORKS

Trees and rings are connected networks with minimal number of links. In a complete network there is a link between any two nodes. If this is economically feasible, then many computations become simpler, and broadcasting methods, sending the same message over all (or part of the) issuing links, become attractive. Still it is important not to flood the network with messages. From this point of view, we discuss the leader election problem for labeled complete network under the *SYN* model.

8.4.1   Leader Election

The simplest solution is: Let each initiator broadcast its *id* to all neighbors. Then all initiators elect the highest *id* among them as a leader. This takes one broadcast cycle and $O(n^2)$ messages, which is achieved if $\Omega(n)$ nodes are initiators.

By a controlled spread, gradually increasing the number of broadcast links, we can bring the communication complexity down to $n \cdot \log n$ which is, in turn, optimal, at the cost of increasing time to $O(\log n)$ cycles which is optimal for that many messages.

The election algorithm **E** which we now present runs competition rounds, ranking competitors by lexicographic order of the values (*level*, *id*) they hold, where *level*(Q) is the seniority of Q in the algorithm, the number of rounds (double cycles) lapsed since Q broke in. Whenever Q drops out of the competition, it adopts the values of its unique conquerer. The general form of round k is:

PHASE 1 communicates to PHASE 2;
PHASE 2 communicates to PHASE 3.

8.4.1.1   Round k of the Election Algorithm E

PHASE 1

> (P winner). If P has all its links traversed, then P is elected. Else, P sends its current value ($level(P)$, $id(P)$) over K untraversed links (which thereby become traversed), where $K = \min(2^k, |untraversed|)$ (this is the controlled spread).

PHASE 2

> (any P). Receives all messages of PHASE 1, sets
>
> ($level(P)$, $id(P)$) : $= \max\{(l, id) \mid$ *over all received values including its own.*
>
> sends an acknowledgement to the single node Q which communicated the max value. Finally it increases *level* by 1.

PHASE 3

> (P winner). If P received acknowledgments to all K message sent out in PHASE 1 (then it captures all K nodes), it proceeds as a winner to round $(k + 1)$.

The analysis of **E** is simple. At round k, the sets of captured nodes are disjoint. So unless k is the last round, at most $n/2^k$ winners proceed to the next round so **E** terminates at round $log\, n + 1$, and the number of messages is $\leq(2^{(k+1)} \cdot n/2^k) + n = 3n$ (n bit messages $+2n$ messages of $log\, n$ bits). The total number is $\leq 3n \cdot log\, n$ for all rounds.

REMARK 8.4   The controlled spread can be tuned to any desired value. By issuing c^k messages, the algorithm runs in $2\, \log_c n$ rounds, $2cn \cdot \log_c n$ messages, c can be a function of n. A full range of complexity pairs are obtained, from $n \log n$ up n^2 messages, from $log\, n$ down to one rounds.

REMARK 8.5   *ASYN* election in $O(n \cdot log\, n)$ messages can be designed along similar lines, using controlled spread. It is more complicated and quite wasteful in *ASYN* time, i.e. there is a sequence of about n messages which follow each other in linear order.

8.4.2   Synchronous Lower Bound

Consider any algorithm **E** that performs a *SYN* election in the complete labeled network. To estimate its communication complexity, we use an adversary argument. The adversary will schedule the nondeterministic choices inherent in cycles of **E**. These are of two kinds:

1. *P* choice to wake-up (break-in)

2. *P* choice of a subset of links, among the previously unused ones, to convey messages in the current cycle. It is crucial for lower bound that the unused links are in indistinguishable.

Given a run of **E**, we focus on those "link-opening" messages described in (ii), with specified source and destination, and call them *events*. Also we define for this run of **E**:

R_i = set of all events at cycle i; $X = (R_0, R_1, \ldots)$ is an *execution*;

X_k = prefix up to k of the execution X;

G_k = the graph spanned by the edges used in X_k;

C_k = a connectivity component of G_k, also called an X_k cluster.

All of these definitions will be applied also to generalized runs of **E**, which are called *stopping runs* (and stopping executions) because they are allowed to stop local clocks under suitable conditions. The definition of a stopped run of **E** is by induction on the cycles: If a X_{j-1}-cluster does not receive any message in (the next) cycle j of a normal run of **E**, then C is stopped from any action at cycle j, i.e., the local clocks at C remain at $j - 1$.

An equivalent effect to such stopping is to shift all messages that occurred before cycle j and involved nodes in C one cycle forward. All these messages are internal to C, since C is a cluster in X_{j-1}. The net effect is that nodes in C wake-up and break-in one cycle later. Thus, by a simple induction argument we see that any stopping run (and stopping execution) of **E** has an equivalent normal run. In the stopping model it is more convenient to formulate the adversary tactics. The algorithm **E** must arrive at G_j being connected (i.e. containing a spanning tree) or else a universally agreed election is impossible. The adversary tries, by stopping, to delay the formation of large clusters and delay the inter-cluster messages as long as possible.

Given a run of **E**, we describe inductively the construction of a stopping execution, intertwined with the decisions of the adversary which clusters to stop and where to channel outgoing messages. W.l.o.g. assume $n = 2^q$. First let $\mathbf{P}_0$, $\ldots$, $\mathbf{P}_q$ be a sequence of partitions of the node-set; $\mathbf{P}_j$ partitions it into disjoint classes of size 2^j. Let $\mathbf{P}_o$ consist of singletons, and each class of $\mathbf{P}_j$ is the union of two classes of $\mathbf{P}_{j-1}$.

Now we construct a consistent sequence $X_{i(o)}, \ldots, X_{i(q)}$ of stopped execution prefixes (each is a prefix of the next one). $X_{i(0)}$ does not contain any event but each node is awakened. Assume $X_{i(j)}$ was constructed so that each cluster of $X_{i(j)}$ is fully contained in one class of $\mathbf{P}_j$. The adversary can (and will) stop a full class of $\mathbf{P}_{(j+1)}$ *unless* for every node Q in the class, its degree in $G_{i(j)}$ *plus* (the number of outgoing links carrying events of the next cycle in the run) *is less than* 2^{j+1}. With this size condition for nonstopping, the adversary can channel the outgoing events to destinations within the class. The clusters in classes of $\mathbf{P}_{j+1}$ can be stopped because they do not receive messages from the outside. Once all the classes of $\mathbf{P}_{j+1}$ are stopped, we have constructed $X_{i(j+1)}$. Clearly its clusters are contained in $\mathbf{P}_{j+1}$.

After $X_{i(q)}$ is constructed, we run $\mathbf{E}$ with no stopping to its conclusion, where the network must be one cluster. Clearly at the end, there are at least $n/2^j$ nodes of degree $\geq 2^j$, for $j = 0, \ldots, q-1$. Thus, the total number of events is at least $(n/2) \cdot \log n$. (Recall $n = 2^q$.)

REMARK 8.6   By a similar argument, it is possible to show that election which terminates in $\leq 1/2 \log_c n$ cycles must have executions with at least $n \log n \cdot (c-1)/(2 \log c)$ events. In particular a message-optimal algorithm, that requires $n \log n$ messages, must run $\Omega(\log n)$ cycles.

8.5   GENERAL NETWORK ALGORITHMS

The task of leader election was discussed in great detail for rings and complete networks. A leader serves (as leaders should) to facilitate the basic network functions of input-collections, computation (centralized), and information spread. The paths from a leader to each node are evident for those special topologies.

For networks of a general topology, the basic task comprises of finding a leader *and* paths to the nodes, i.e., the distributed creation of a rooted spanning tree. Initiating distributed depth first search with suitable collision handling will do the job.

Having a spanning tree, on a subset of m nodes, many basic tasks can be accomplished in $O(m)$ messages by a standard routine:

Tree Broadcast Routine   The root can broadcast to all nodes, each node relays the message to its sons, until it hits a leaf. In the opposite direction, leaves can answer (or initiate) messages by relaying to the father. Any father node can *filter* information by selecting to transmit one message (say with a maximum value) from its subtree.

8.5.1   Minimum-Weight Spanning Tree

We present here an ambitious *ASYN* algorithm for the creation of a *minimum-weight* spanning tree (**MST**) in a connected graph with given edge weights, the weight of a tree being the sum of its edge weights. This 10-year-old algorithm had a considerable impact on the area of distributed algorithms, especially the ideas used to economize on messages, down to $O(n \log n + |E|)$, which is also the lower bound.

We present a high-level description of the distributed **MST** algorithm. As often happens, it evolves from a suitably chosen sequential algorithm **S**:

Repeat

1. Select an arbitrary vertex v of the current (contracted) graph H. Designate its minimum-weight incident link (v, x).
2. Contract v and x to a single node

until the contracted graph consists of a single vertex.

A maximal set of nodes in the original network, which contracted to a single vertex in an intermediary stage graph is called a **Fragment**.

The basic invariant assertion which **S** preserves is: The subnetwork consisting of the original nodes and links designated up to a certain stage is a forest, which induces a *min-weight spanning tree* on each fragment. Moreover, the newly designated link in (1) joins two fragments.

In the distributed elaboration of **S**, each fragment is coordinated by one of its nodes, called the core. The progress can be viewed as a succession of conceptual rounds, doing P1–P2:

P1. Fragment synchronization.

P2. Selection of a min-outgoing link.

In P1, the core of F broadcasts along the spanning tree to all nodes the unique id of F. In P2, each node of F picks up from its unused links the minimum link *which is going outside the fragment*. The global minimum is then filtered up from the leaves. The node which has this min-outgoing link e becomes the new core and sends along e a *request to merge*.

How does one ascertain that a link $e = uv$ is indeed outgoing from a fragment? To this end u sends an *inquiry* containing its fragment id to v crossing out the link if the reply shows equality. This inquiries consume up to $O(|E|)$ messages. With this difficulty overcome, it is not hard to come up with an *ASYN* distributed implementation of the whole **MST**, with complexity $O(n^2)$. This bound cannot be lowered. In some runs, fragments may grow by just one element and actually go through $\frac{n}{2}$ rounds of P1–P2. We shall describe now the clever controls used to bring the complexity of messages down to $0(n \log n + |E|)$. These ideas were found very useful in optimizing other distributed algorithms.

The id of a fragment is augmented by a *level* variable, which imposes a dynamic hierarchy on fragments, when F with name (*level, id*) merges with F'

with name ($level'$, id') the name of F prevails if $level = level'$, a new name ($level + 1$, $id*$), is created for the merge. If $level$ is set to 0 for $|F| = 1$ then clearly $|F| \geq 2^{level(F)}$. So $level$ is globally bounded by $\log n$. Moreover, if it is possible to arrange that each node goes through P1–P2 at most one per level value, then the communication cost of the controlled **MST** comes down to $0(n \log n + |E|)$.

The purpose of the control is to ascertain that

$$\# \text{ Request to merge goes from } F \text{ to } F' \text{ only if}$$

$$l = level(F) \leq l' = level(F')$$

The actual control is imposed on replies to inquiry messages. A low level F holds back its reply to an inquiry from higher level F' until $level(F)$ becomes $\geq level$ in the inquiry (as a result of merges).

If request to merge goes from F to F' (*see* #) *and* $l < l'$, then the search for min-link in F, if needed at all, becomes part of (extension of) the search in F', and its cost is charged to the level of F'.

Yet another control is needed if F sends a request to merge to F' of the same level, because a name change is involved in such a merge. Indeed F' may wish to merge with F'' at the same level, F'' with F''', etc. This may create some chaos in updating names (and levels). However, such a sequence of length k of same level inquiries to join must terminate with F_k sending along a link e a request to merge F_{k+1} and F_{k+1} is of a higher level (a resolved case) or F_{k+1} has the same level and also came to the conclusion to send a request to merge to F_k along the reverse of the link e. When this happens, both ends release the control and the merge is effected (with a level increase). Thus, we augment # by stipulating: A request to merge from F to F' of the same level along e is put on hold until F' requests to merge F along e or until F' increases the level as a result of other merges.

This concludes the high level description of the rather involved **MST** algorithm. Its authors claim to have tested it on a variety of inputs.

8.5.2 Directed Networks

Only a brief indication of the basic problems is given. The main issue here is distributed traversal—the process of scanning all of the nodes. Election of a leader is reducible to traversal as follows: Each initiator starts a traversal. Whenever two traversal processes meet, the one with the lower id is killed. The worst case communication complexity is like n traversals. This factor of n can be reduced to $\log n$, or even to $O(1)$, i.e., get down to $O[n|E| + n^2 \log n]$ for election, by an algorithm based on the following sequential version

1. Select one outgoing link from every node. Such a set of directed nodes contain a set of disjoint cycles.
2. The subgraph obtained by contracting any of the cycles (to a single vertex) is still strongly connected.
3. Repeated application of 1 and 2 contracts the network to a single node.

Coming back to traversal, why is it harder for directed networks? For the undirected case, depth-first search is the preferred traversal method, serving as a template for many data-structure and network problems. Its efficient fast implementation on parallel machine is also highly important and only recently solved. But depth-first traveral employs backtracking, retreat paths from a fully backtracked node (with all descendants scanned). Such backtracking paths would traverse directed links in the wrong direction.

Thus, an additional computation is needed to secure backtracking paths, on the fly with depth first search. The additional structure involved is called an *in-tree* or *in-forest*, a subnetwork containing the required backtracking paths.

8.5.3 Load Sharing in Network

We discuss a task which, like garbage collection, is a distributed operating system service. How to match loaded processors with idle ones, so that the load can be shared. The solution we propose involves a novel technique. Packets do random walk in the network (e.g., the "cosmic cube" described in the next section), sampling, and collecting load statistics needed for the matching and sharing. This kind of "system routine" provides a reasonably and adaptive solution.

Let n be the number of processor nodes, I the set of idle processors, $|I| = i$. When a node becomes *idle* (this can be tuned), it creates a packet with its label and C empty slots. The packet is sent to perform a random walk in the network, sampling the nodes until it meets (another) idle node, whereupon it is sent back directly to its origin. The packet carries in its slots the addresses and loads of the C most-loaded processor it has visited. When the originator node receives back its packet K, it sends a request to match message directly to the most loaded v_1 sampled in the slots of K. If v_1 is matched, the request is sent to v_2, the next-most loaded one, etc. If all the C samples in K are matched nodes, (and if the originator is still idle) the packet is reissued into the network.

The number of packets in the system is always $|I|$, the number of idle nodes. We consider the stochastic process of match-making, driven by the packets random walk. The main (nontrivial) argument is that the process continues to evolve independently of the pairs matched in the past. For this argument, it is convenient to assume first that the number of slots in a packet is unlimited. So the expected length of a search of a packet is $\dfrac{n}{|I|}$, and the number of messages

by all packets until say $\dfrac{|I_o|}{2}$ idle ones are matched is $O(n)$.

To remove the assumption of unlimited number of slots, we obseve that a packet has an even chance (1/2) to hit one of the $|I|$ top-loaded nodes before it hits I again. So $\log_2 n$ slots would suffice but even a buffer of three slots is good if we settle for a fixed chance > 0 of hitting top-loaded before hitting I. Thus, even for matching with $\dfrac{|I|}{2}$ top-loaded nodes $O(n)$ messages suffice.

We sketched the analysis for the most basic routine. It can be tuned and refined, and yields fast parallel time in the *SYN* model.

8.5.4   Essential Uses of Randomization

The routine of load-sharing uses random steps in the random walk of the packets. We discuss now two essential uses of random steps in distributed systems: To break deadlocks caused by symmetry, and to reduce congestion in routing messages through networks.

For the ring topology, we argued in detail why symmetry obstructions render some tasks *uncomputable*. In brief, initial configuration (or data) invariant under symmetry must evolve into symmetric configuration by identical programs at the various nodes. This argument stops being valid if the programs contain random instructions (typically random choice from a given set) because the *outcomes* of this random step is likely to be different at different nodes. The success of random steps in solving control and coordination tasks in distributed systems—and at a low cost—is really spectacular. One of the best known examples is the "dining philosophers" problem.

The ring of K processors is materialized by K philosophers sitting each before his plate of spaghetti at a round table. Between each pair of plates there is one fork (so K forks altogether). A philosopher, whose preoccupation is *THINK*, becomes hungry from time to time. But to switch to *EAT* state, he needs the two forks, at the left side and the right side of his plate. The problem is: Design a (fork-sharing) protocol **F** such that, if each philosopher follows **F** then whenever P_i (some philosopher) becomes hungry at t, he will eventually hold two forks at $t' > t$ and start to *EAT*, no matter how the processors are scheduled in their *THINK*, Hungry, *EAT* cycles.

There are symmetric schedules which must lead to deadlock if the protocol F is deterministic, e.g., everybody becomes hungry at the same time, everybody lifts his left fork, everybody puts it down, etc. However, if before lifting a fork (when he holds none), P tosses a fair coin, and if HEAD [TAIL] is up he lifts his left [right] fork, then such suitably specified *randomized* protocol solves the problem with probability 1, i.e., it can be proved (which is reasonable but not easy) that for the vast majority of runs of the algorithm *on any specified schedule*, no deadlock or starvation arises.

Feasible architectures of multi-processor computers that are truly parallel must have a multitude of modules or units, and allow swift massive communication of data, partial results, etc. between the modules. The communication subnetwork (which may be the whole one) and the routing methods should avoid congestion and bottlenecks, even though the underlying graph of nodes and links is sparse, because of technological limitations. The use of randomization and distributed routing (with or without synchronization) is very useful in avoiding congestion.

Many designs were proposed and studied. Here we consider one, the n-dimensional unit cube ("cosmic cube") which is actually implemented these days. The nodes are all $N = 2^n$ binary vectors of length n. Two nodes are connected by a link if their vectors agree on all but one coordinate (i.e., they differ only in the i'th dimension, $1 \le i \le n$, their Hamming distance is 1). Each node is incident on n links, the diameter of the network is also n.

Suppose each node sends some messages addressed to other nodes. This can be decomposed into a union of a few partial permutations $v \Rightarrow \phi(v)$ where $v \neq v'$ implies $\phi(v) \neq \phi(v')$. If the decomposition is not into few permutations, then broadcasting and memory sharing methods should be employed but the routing of a permutation is the crucial issue.

The proposed randomized routing is basically: First route v to a random node $\pi(v)$ then route $\pi(v)$ to $\phi(v)$, with few extra conventions. The routes are uniquely determined by the address tickets attached to the messages (packets) and the nodes easily determine locally along which link to forward a packet. The only problem is that some "bad" permutation ϕ might under deterministic routing, create long queues of packets at nodes, causing coongestion and delays. However:

THEOREM 8.8   Given $\epsilon > 0$ there exist $K = K(\epsilon)$ such that the randomized algorithm routes any permutation in parallel time $K \cdot n$ with probability $1 - \epsilon$.

Thus, the vast majority of runs will finish within constant times the network diameter. The parallel time in the claim is convenient, but not essential. The "static" claim is that (with high probability) no more than $K \cdot n$ packets routes share a link with a given route. Similar more sophisticated and stronger results of the same kind were proved for other regular network architecture (butterflies, d-way shuffles, etc.) Even when formal proofs are hard to obtain, the principle that randomization in routing avoids congestion seems a pretty good heuristic. Other remarkable uses were found recently for coordination in unreliable distributed systems.

8.6 FROM SEQUENTIAL TO DISTRIBUTED ALGORITHMS

It became clear that, for many problems, an important start for a distributed algorithm is a suitable sequential one which is amenable to distributed implementation. Modifications, sometimes major, are needed for improved or optimal complexity. Still, some general principles of transformation would be very useful. We take up the issue on some basic programs of greedy type, some search methods with limited backtrack and some recursive programs, in an effort to exhibit and explicate principles of transformation from sequential to distributed algorithms.

8.6.1 Greedy Algorithms—Coloring Graphs

A *coloring* is a map $\phi : V \Rightarrow [1, \ldots, u]$ that assigns a "color" $\phi(x)$ to each node $x \in V$, such that if (i, j) is a link then $\phi(i) \neq \phi(i)$. The aim is to have u, the number of colors, as small as possible. Typical applications of coloring are found in scheduling problems. Each node represents a task. A link (edge) between nodes i, j is a constraint stipulating that the tasks P_i, P_j cannot be scheduled at the same time (or same space) slot, e.g., because they use a resource which can serve only one at a time. Coloring gives a schedule of the task within u slots. A monochromatic set of nodes (scheduled in the same slot) is an independent set of nodes of the graph: No link joins two nodes of the set.

Straightforward algorithms which construct a maximal independent set or a coloring are typically of *greedy* character: The nodes are scanned in some fixed sequential order, and the best current decision is made about this node: put it in the independent set if possible, or give it the minimal consistent color. For coloring, the greedy algorithm assigns.

$$\# \qquad\qquad \phi(i) = MEX\ \{\phi(j) \mid j < i, (j, i)\ is\ a\ link\},$$

Where *MEX* of a set of natural number is the minimal one excluded from the set.

The transformation to distributed algorithm is clear. Node i can and will color itself, according to $\#$, once it received the colors of all nodes $j < i$ that we linked to i. Then it broadcasts its name and color to all (remaining) neighbors.

Clearly the number of messages is $O(|E|)$. More interesting is an estimate on the parallel time, or what is the longest chain of messages? In "bad" graphs (e.g., nodes order on a line or around a ring), the chain is $O(n)$. But for random graphs it is easy to show that almost surely the longest chain is bounded by $O\{MIN[\log n, d]\}$ when $d(n)$ is the expected degree of a node.

8.6.2 Search Algorithms: Perfect Matching, Disjoint Paths

A matching M in a graph $G = (V, E)$ is a subset of edges no two of which meet at a node. For *perfect matching* (or 1-factor), it is required also that all of the nodes are covered by the edges of the matching. In a bipartite graph $G = (U, W, E)$ where $E \subseteq U \times W$, a perfect matching amounts to a 1–1 onto map M from U to W where $M \subseteq E$.

The theory and the construction of matchings is of fundamental importance in graph theory and numerous applications. Its algebraic ramifications and algorithmic theory are also quite intriguing. Only recently fast parallel (randomized) algorithms for constructing perfect matchings were found.

Greedy methods can construct a *maximal* matching (which is an independent set in the line-graph of G) but not a perfect-matching (or a *maximum cardinality* matching). For this, *search methods* are adopted, which allow replacement of edges by other edges to facilitate the *augmentation* of a matching M. Consider the following *alternating path*:

$$w \text{ -------- } v \text{ ——— } w \text{ -------- } \qquad \text{ -------- } y$$
$$e_1 \qquad e_2 \qquad e_3 \qquad e_{2k+1}$$

the free (unmatched) node x tries to match v along the edge e_1. But v is matched to w in M by the edge e_2 so w tries e_3 and so on. Even-indexed (solid) edges are in M, odd-indexed (broken) edges are in $E - M$. If e_{2k+1} hits y which is free, then an *augmenting* path is obtained. The even edges are thrown out of M. The odd edges replace them. The new matching contains one extra matched pair (both x and y are now covered).

A perfect matching (or a maximum cardinality one) can always be obtained from a matching M by an *alternate-augment* sequence. Many sequential algorithms are based on this. Actually, most max-flow algorithms in networks are elaborations of the augmenting path technique.

An alternating *tree* rooted at X is one where all tree-paths from root to leaves are alternating paths, and if a leaf y is free, then the tree contains an augmenting path (*a success!*).

Growing alternating *trees* is the main feature of transforming the alternate-augment method into an efficient distributed form (and is good for other purposes). In some round of the algorithm, free nodes grow alternating trees. If a tree is a *success* (which is likely since it has many paths to the leaves), a backtrack is avoided. Standard tree braodcasting is applied to extract one augmenting path and effect the augmentation in a distributed fashion. Roots that did not have success with their trees enter the next phase and start anew. This is the only form of backtrack. If the number of rounds can be made small ($O(\log n)$ is the goal), a highly efficient algorithm is obtained. Several controls and assumptions are useful here:

1. *Keep the trees disjoint during a round.* This is a considerable simplification, which is easily achieved. A node receives requests to join from several trees, picks one of them, and thereafter turns down all other requests (a highly recommended ethics in the sociology of matchings).

2. *Controlled growth of the trees.* A node sends at most two requests to join along two (unused) graph edges, thus leaving edges for future phases. The resulting tree is at most binary, some nodes may have just one or no sons because the requests were turned down (all trees compete on the same population).

3. *Synchronization.* All trees grow level-by-level in a Synchronized Fashion, and are forced to stop after (about) $\log_2 n$ levels. In this case, a nice branching-process analysis applies to the performance of the algorithm on random graphs: If $k(\geq log\, n)$ free nodes start a round, each has a probability $\alpha > 0$ (independent of n and k) to grow to size $O\left(\dfrac{n}{k}\right)$ and have a success, so that αk augmentations result by the end of a round. This is a geometric sequence decrease for k, and it is not hard to show then that $O(log\, n)$ rounds suffices for getting a perfect matching (almost surely in suitable random graph spaces).

Disjoint Paths.   Growing disjoint trees performs well for the hard problem of finding many node-disjoint paths in a graph between given pairs $(x_1, y_1), \ldots ,$ (x_k, y_k). Here both the x's and y's grow the trees. In the synchronized mode and for random graphs, there is a positive chance that a given pair (x_i, y_i) grows trees to size $O\left(\dfrac{n}{k}\right)$ (for $k \leq \sqrt{n}$) successfully, i.e., these trees meet and a path between x_i and y_i is found. Hence, on one round $\alpha \cdot k$ disjoint paths are constructed in parallel, $\alpha > 0$ independent of n and k.

8.6.3   Median Selection by Distributed Recursion

In transforming recursive programs to distributed form it is necessary to maintain, conceptually or physically, the centralized regime of exit from one copy, enter a new copy of the recursive routine. A processor, on its own, may lack the information determining when to recurse. A rather painless but useful resolution of recursive call synchronization is to have a leader at the root of a spanning tree collect information and issue instructions to all processors to enter a new copy, and also control the exits.

Consider a simple example. A bag B of N elements is divided among a network P of processors, k is given and the task is to select the kth largest element. This is the *rank selection problem* (sometimes referred to as the *median* or k-selection).

A simple recursive algorithm performing rank selection on input (B, k) is:

1. **If** B contains one element; **return** that element.
2. Choose element m from B at random;
3. Partition B into three subbags *BL*, *BE*, *BS*, which consist of the elements of B that are larger than m, equal to m, and smaller than m, respectively;

4. Let

$$(B', k') = \begin{cases} (BL, k) & \text{if } k < |BL| \\ (BE, m) & \text{if } |BL| < k \le |BL| + |BE| \\ (BS, k - |BL| - |BE|) & \text{if } |BL| + |BE| < k \end{cases}$$

5. **return** the element produced by applying rank selection to (B', k').

To transform this program, consider first the nonrecursive parts. A spanning tree is constructed and used throughout. Using standard tree-broadcast technique, the local counts of each processor can be added up to give global counts of subbags. Now, random selection of an element m (step 2) can be carried out distributively if each node P imposed some order relation on its local bag and on the links leading to its tree-sons, and if it knows how many elements each son has in its bag. Having m, each node does the comparisons and the local partition, the sizes of BL, BE, BS, and the parameters (B', k') for the recursive call are computed at the root.

The *recursion coordination* is also done at the root. It counts the number of elements still alive (belonging to the current version of B). If several elements are alive, a recursion instruction is issued, if only one element is left alive, it is summoned to the root. At this point each node can exit from its recursion— this is because the recursion is a simple tail recursion. In more complex programs, exit coordination may be necessary.

The communication complexity of the distributed implementation is easily estimated. The expected number of recursive calls is $O(\log N)$, the worst case is $O(N)$. For each call, $O(|P|)$ messages (the size of the tree) suffice. There is an initial investment in constructing the spanning tree.

8.7 CONCLUSION

The essence of distributed network algorithms is to convey information, by messages only, between the processor nodes about their status, values they hold and the topology of the network (the way they figure it). This is needed for tasks ranging from minimal coordination (like load-sharing) to more ambitious joint computations like minimum spanning tree, median selection (involving recursion), or perfect matching.

There is a real danger in flooding the network with messages. Hence, the keen interest in reducing message complexity—and parallel time. Various clever controls and methods are applied to get economical, even optimal algorithms.

Symmetries in the network and input configurations pose major obstacles to tasks computations. This is no surprise because symmetries lead to deadlocks, the horror of distributed systems. We have treated this issue in great detail for anonymous rings. In a similar vein, local symmetries or repetitions of subconfigurations many times yield lower bounds on message complexity.

An extreme form of symmetry breaking is a leader election which, with the help of a spanning tree to exert its leadership, facilitates all kinds of tasks in the network. Naturally, leader election, traversal and spanning tree play a very prominent role in distributed algorithms for various network topologies.

It is remarkable that the natural steps involved in leader election can be partly followed and elaborated to break some symmetries and perform input collection without leader election.

A different attack on symmetry and deadlock breaking comes from the use of randomized steps, as seen in the dining philosophers problem. Randomization is highly useful for many other situations such as reducing congestion while routing many messages in sparse networks.

The more subtle algorithms we presented usually consist of a sequence of rounds, each round being essentially parallel. The round division is conceptual or actual—if synchronization is imposed. The rounds structure usually originates from a suitable sequential algorithm. We also discussed principles of transforming sequential to distributed form even for recursive programs.

Even though the *ASYN* and *SYN* models are equivalent in computing power, message and time complexity, along with difficulty of design and verification, they decrease significantly when synchronization is imposed, because the degree of nondeterminism is reduced or eliminated. For loose cooperation, distributed operating system tasks, it is too much to require synchronization. For high degree of cooperation, it is much "safer" and practical to employ the *SYN* model.

The reliability issue in sequential programming is mainly concerned with bugs in the programs. For distributed processing failure, random or malicious malfunction is a severe problem. We reiterate the statement in the last paragraph of the introduction, to the effect that the studies of partly reliable, Byzantine-like distributed system developed deep understanding of the processes of distributed computation, but this is beyond the scope of this chapter.

8.8 BIBLIOGRAPHIC REMARKS AND REFERENCES

Principles of Distributed Computing (PODC) is the name of an annual ACM Symposium (in Canada), which started in 1982. Its proceedings provide an excellent source and account for much of the current work in the area. Also several new journals devoted mainly to distributed computing started recently.

We made an extensive use of two recent works, parts of which were reported in *PODC* 85. Most of Section 8.3 is based on a work of C. Attiya, M. Snir, and M. Warmuth (7). Much of Section 8.4, on complete network, is based on a 1985 UCLA thesis of Y. Afek (1, 2). I thank the authors for allowing me to include material here from their partly unpublished works.

Several authors published leader election algorithms for distinct-labels rings (9, 18). Burns' thesis (8) gives also a lower bound and has an extensive bibliography up to 1981.

The minimum-weight spanning tree algorithm dated from 1977, but the final form appeared in (15). Our presentation followed (14). Results about directed network traversal and election are found in (1, 2).

The verification of the randomized protocol for the Dining Philosophers is given in (17). Randomized routings in networks are analysed in (25, 24, 3).

In Sections 8.5 and 8.6, Load-Sharing, Graph-Coloring, Perfect Matchings, and Disjoint Paths algorithms are given in (21, 20, 19, 22), respectively. Rank Selection recursive algorithms are discussed in (23). (11) is a good survey on the consensus problems in unreliable distributed systems. (10) gives a survey and the most recent randomized solutions to such problems. (12) presents the lower bounds for the basic consensus problems in an unreliable distributed network in a very elegant manner, utilizing some ideas from Angluin pioneering work (4).

8.9 REFERENCES

1. Afek, Y., *"Distributed Algorithms for Election in Unidirectional and Complete Networks," Ph.D Thesis*, UCLA 1985.
2. Afek, Y., and Gafni, E., "Time and message bounds for election in synchronous and asynchronous complete networks," *PODC 85*, 175–185.
3. Aleliunas, R., "Randomized parallel communication," *PODC 82*, 60–72.
4. Angluin, D., "Local and global properties in networks of processors," *Proceedings 12 ACM Symp. on Theory of Computing*, 1980, 82–93.
5. Awerbuch, B., "Communication time trade-offs in network synchronization," *PODC 85*, 272–276.
6. Attiya, C., Snir, M., and Warmuth, M., *Computing on an Anonymous Ring*, Research Report 85-2, CS dept. Hebrew University, 1985.
7. Attiya, C., Snir, M., and Warmuth, M., "Computing on an anonymous ring," *PODC 85*, 196–203.
8. Burns, J.E., *Complexity of Communication Among Asynchronous Processes*, Tech. Report, Georgia Inst. of Tech. GIT-ICS 81-101.
9. Dolev, D., Klawe, M., and Rodeh, M., "Unidirectional algorithms for extrema finding in a circle," *J. of Algorithms 3* (1982), 245–260.
10. Feldman, P., and Micali, S., "Byzantine agreement in constant expected time," *Proceeding 26 Symp. on Foundations of Computer Science* (1985), 263–275.
11. Fischer, M.J., *The Consensus Problem in Unreliable Distributed System, (a Brief Survey)*, YALE/DCS/RR-273, 1983.

12. Fischer, M.J., Lynch, N.A., and Merritt, M., "Easy impossibility proofs for distributed consensus problems," *PODC 85*, 59–70.

13. Fredrickson, G., and Lynch, N., *A General Lower Bound for Election of a Leader in a Ring*, CSD-TR-512, Perdue University, 1985.

14. Gafni, E., "Improvements in time complexity of two message-optimal algorithms," *PODC 85*, 175–185.

15. Gallager, R.G., Humblet, P.A., and Spira, P.A., "A distributed algorithms for minimum-weight spanning trees," *Tran on Program. Lang. Syst. 5* (1983), 66–67.

16. Korach, E., Moran, S., and Zaks, S., "Tight lower bounds on some distributed algorithms for a complete network of processors," *PODC 84*, 199–207.

17. Lehmann, D., and Rabin, M., "On the advantage of free choice: A symmetric and full distributed solution of the dining philosophers problem," *Proceedings 8th ACM Symp. on Principles of Programming Languages*, 133–148.

18. Peterson, G.L., "An $O(n \log n)$ unidirectional Algorithms for the Circular Extreme Problem," ACM *Trans Program. Lang. Syst. 4* (1982), 758–762.

19. Shamir, E., and Upfal, E., "N-processors graphs distributively achieve perfect matchings in $O(\log^2 N)$ Beats," *PODC 82*, 238–241.

20. Shamir, E., and Upfal, E., "Sequential and distributed graph coloring algorithms with performance analysis in random graph spaces," *J. of Algorithms 5* (1984), 488–501.

21. Shamir, E., and Upfal, E., "*Load sharing in distributed systems*," Report RJ 5315, IBM Almaden Research Center, 1986.

22. Shamir, E., and Upfal, E., "A fast parallel construction of disjoint paths in networks," *Annals of Disc. Math. 24* (1985), 141–154.

23. Shrira, L., Francez, N., and Rodeh, M., "Distributed k-selection from a sequential to a distributed algorithm," *PODC 83*, 143–153.

24. Upfal, E., "An efficient scheme for parallel communication," *JACM 31* (1984), 507–517.

25. Valiant, L., "A scheme for fast parallel communication," *SIAM J. on Computing 11* (1982), 350–361.

Index